Introduction to Collective Behavior and Collective Action

Introduction to Collective Behavior and Collective Action

SECOND EDITION

David L. Miller
Western Illinois University

WAVELAND
PRESS, INC.

Prospect Heights, Illinois

DEDICATION

To my teachers,
Carl Couch, Clark McPhail, Robert Stewart, and Charles Tucker,
with great fondness and gratitude

For information about this book, write or call:
Waveland Press, Inc.
P.O. Box 400
Prospect Heights, Illinois 60070
(847) 634-0081
www.waveland.com

Contents

PART III
COLLECTIVE BEHAVIOR AND COLLECTIVE ACTION: THREATS TO THE SOCIAL ORDER

Foreword

David Miller's excellent second edition is a fascinating read about a wide spectrum of collective human phenomena. Through the comparative lens of both collective behavior and collective action perspectives he ingeniously examines his subject matter and simultaneously introduces readers to the theoretical and methodological strengths and weaknesses of those perspectives.

In my judgment the traditional collective behavior perspective had two weaknesses and one strength. First, most scholars who worked in that tradition assumed a cognitively crippled individual whose perceptions and actions were impaired by "the crowd mind" or social structural strain. Second, there was no research methodology telling other scholars what was important to look for or listen to in the field nor how to record and analyze those observations. Evidence for collective behaviorists' theoretical claims tended to be of the armchair variety: long on apocryphal accounts and superficial observations, and short on direct observation reports. The strength of this perspective was an intellectual curiosity about a wide spectrum of collective phenomena that human beings pursue with and in relation to one another. Ironically, the scholar who coined the term collective behavior—Robert Park—viewed elementary political collective behavior as the source of change in existing social institutions and occasionally the source of new ones.

The collective action perspective has two strengths and at least one weakness. First, collective action scholars initially embraced a model of the rational actor posited by economic theorists. Many of those scholars have now abandoned the "rational calculus" actor, although not rationality, because the mini-max calculus is a principle that alone cannot explain the range of cognitive processes and purposive actions that must be addressed. Second, collective actionists boldly employed research methods—surveys, archival document analysis, and direct observation—that had served in other areas of the social sciences and began to apply, adapt, and improve them to study the phenomena with which they were concerned. While they have investigated different units of analysis, and at different levels, they have nonetheless accumulated a large body of knowledge. The glaring weakness of this perspective in my judgment is that, with few exceptions, inquiry has been limited to political phenomena. One of Miller's contributions is to challenge more students to think about and proceed with the examination of a wider range of collective phenomena—religious, sport, economic and cultural gatherings, and the individual and collective actions of performers and spectators therein—from the collective action perspective.

All social life at micro, meso, and macro levels of analysis depends upon generic communication processes. It is difficult to distinguish rumor from those processes. Thus, Miller usefully emphasizes the continuities across rather than the differences between communication processes in unfamiliar or extraordinary circumstances and those in familiar and ordinary situations. The fact that we do not yet have a comprehensive and generally agreed-upon explanation for how communication works everywhere is no reason to ignore its importance or to shrink from the challenge of developing such an explanation.

Miller takes up some topics that are neither politically correct nor even acknowledged as legitimate objects of research by many collective action scholars. Readers are well served by Miller's intellectual curiosity about and his scholarly treatment of those topics. His chapter on mass hysteria is the best overview I've read, particularly his excellent recasting of the "War of the Worlds" story and his own research on the Enfield monster. Incapacitating fear and mindless emotional displays are rare phenomena. Panic and hysteria are fuzzy concepts that neither describe nor explain and should be abandoned. They cloud the path for future clear-headed and systematic examinations of important phenomena those concepts have obscured; for example, the development of collective nausea, dizziness, and fainting within gatherings, and what Kathleen Tierney (1994) calls the "collective preoccupation" of people in advance of forecasted disasters and other extraordinary phenomena.

Miller's evenhanded discussion of UFOs neither dismisses nor debunks all the reported sightings nor, to his credit, does he advance a brief for such sightings. Like reports of Marian apparitions, these sightings are legitimate and important perceptual phenomena that should be investigated and can be explained. His treatment of UFOs as residual cultural icons is original and intriguing.

My hope is that Miller's fine treatment of sporting events will engage students to pursue research on collective action in other conventional gatherings, including religious services, symphony concerts, opera, and the theatre. We have just scratched the surface of all that is of sociological significance in these areas.

Migration due to natural disaster, religious, political, or ethnic persecution at point of origin, or the prospect of freedom from persecution at some destination is an important phenomenon for investigation in many areas of sociology. Miller is to be commended for addressing the sources, processes, and consequences of collective migration, including the formation, structure, and function of temporary communities in the refugee camps established en route or at journey's end.

Miller's descriptions of disasters are excellent and his summaries of disaster research are well done. Much of that research was spawned by the Disaster Research Center, founded by Henry Quarantelli and Russell Dynes at Ohio State University in the early 1970s and relocated to the University of Delaware in the mid-1980s. The DRC has generated an enormous body of knowledge about the actions of individuals and organizations in natural and human-made disasters around the world. Human beings may be at their best amidst the chaos of disaster impact and aftermath, engaging in purposive and selfless individual and collective action in the most difficult circumstances. This may be the most damning evidence against traditional collective behaviorist claims about the crippled cognition of individuals in stressful and problematic situations.

If migration, disasters, and riots are threats to social order, then protest events and social movements should be viewed as sources of social reordering, as constructive negative feedback on the failures of societies to live up to their own national constitutions or to the even higher standards of the Universal Declaration of Human Rights.

Miller's treatment of protest events is a welcome introduction to what is a huge and growing body of scholarship in sociology and political science in the United States and Europe. I applaud his recognition of the different methodological approaches to protest, ranging from experimental studies of protest (Gamson et al.), to the use of archival data to examine protest over longer periods in time (Tilly, McAdam, Tarrow), to my own efforts to systematically observe and record collective action during protest events in progress.

Last but not least, Miller provides excellent summaries of Turner and Killian's emergent-norm theory and Smelser's value-added theory of social movements. His introduction to Zald and McCarthy's resource mobilization theory is an excellent if general overview. Those interested in political process theory and analysis may wish to consult McAdam's (1981) work regarding the twentieth-century Civil Rights movement and Tilly's (1995, 1996) analysis of the origins of social movements in nineteenth-century Great Britain.

Overall, this is a superior introductory text notwithstanding the few quibbles some readers may have over what was omitted, abbreviated, or not quite "spot on." The book is ingeniously organized, well written, and filled with textual and graphic illustrations that will challenge the imagination and expand the intellectual horizons of instructor and student alike. Read and enjoy!

Clark McPhail

Preface

In 1985 I published *Introduction to Collective Behavior*, and it has remained in print and been used in classes until this writing. Now, a second edition with a new title, *Introduction to Collective Behavior and Collective Action*, has been written to take its place. I have tried to remain faithful to my 1985 intentions of producing a genuine teaching text, written with both the student and the teacher in mind.

For the student, I have tried to create an intuitive feel for the subject matter by using numerous descriptive narratives. Although some narratives have been retained from *Introduction to Collective Behavior*, many new narratives have been written especially for this book.

For the teacher, *Introduction to Collective Behavior and Collective Action* not only updates coverage of the field of collective behavior, but it also provides the first systematic overview of collective action theory and research written for an introductory text. This volume is also the first to provide a side-by-side presentation and comparison of these two perspectives. The text contains the following useful features:

Each chapter is divided into separate collective behavior and collective action sections. This provides clarity of presentation and aids in the comparison and discussion of the two perspectives. A large number of topics are covered, ranging from rumor to social movements. Narratives and descriptive accounts introduce each topic, reducing the need for extensive outside readings.

Individual topics are examined from the standpoint of both collective behavior and collective action perspectives. Collective behavior perspectives include the mass hysteria, emergent-norm, and value-added theories. Collective action theories include the social behavioral interactionist model, the resource mobilization perspective, and political process theory.

Over the last half century, the field of collective behavior and collective action has generated some of the most innovative research methods in sociology. Chapter 3 provides an overview of these methods. In this chapter students gain an appreciation of the problems involved in studying unanticipated events, and the use of historical material and field experiments. New to this edition are a discussion of techniques used in observing gatherings and computer modeling of collective behavior and collective action. Methodological discussions are found in other chapters, as well.

Introduction to Collective Behavior and Collective Action offers a number of alternatives for course design. The text covers traditional collective behavior topics, such as rumor, mass hysteria, UFOs, fads, migrations, disasters, and riots, from which one can design a course that focuses on popular culture. An entirely new chapter on sports has been added. The increasing influence of the Internet and the media is discussed throughout the text.

This text is also suitable for teaching a course that focuses on social movements. For instance, chapters 1 through 4, and chapters 12 through 16 provide a sound social movement sequence. The first four chapters introduce students to the traditional collective behavior theories and theories of collective action, as well as research methods and communication processes. Chapters 12 through 16 cover riots, protest, and social movement politics. These chapters focus on the origins, dynamics and policing of protest, and the characterizations and explanations of social movements from the standpoints of collective behavior and collective action. Chapters on protest and social movements include discussion of the policing of protest and Public Order Management Systems.

Acknowledgements

I would first like to acknowledge those who were very instrumental in the production of this book. Neil Rowe and Gayle Zawilla of Waveland Press are to be thanked for their long-term interest in this project. Without their gentle prodding, patience and support, and Gayle's editing, this book probably would not have been written. I must also thank Ms. Carol Skiles for her hours of excellent typing and sharp-eyed proofreading. Her skills and cheerful manner made all of our jobs easier.

I would like to thank Clark McPhail for the excellent discussion on collective action and perception control theory that appears as the Appendix to the text.

I first met Todd Bernhardt, Adell Newman, and Nicole Timko when they were graduate students in our sociology program at Western Illinois University. I enjoyed having them in my classes and seminars. They each contributed work that is contained or cited in this book. I also hold the abilities of Ethelyn O. Brewster, Charles Clark, and Bill Lovecamp in very high regard. When they were graduate students, I asked them to review my work in progress. Their suggestions were very helpful and greatly appreciated.

I must also thank Eric Dunning, Patrick Murphy, and John Williams of the Sir Norman Chester Centre for Football Research at the University of Leicester, England. They made available to me, without reserve, their knowledge and the resources of the Centre during my 1987–88 sabbatical. Their work on the sociology of sport and football hooliganism opened a whole new area of sociological interest for me. Beyond this, they offered friendship and support to my family while we were in England. Their efforts helped make this year in England one of our family's fondest memories.

I am indeed fortunate to have met with Ron Wohlstein, Dan Miller, Mike Katovich and Stan Saxton at nearly every Midwest Sociological Society meeting for the past 25 years. Sometimes we only had time for a few words between paper sessions; sometimes we talked long into the night. We will all sadly miss our dear friend and colleague, Stan Saxton, who left us in 1999.

I want to thank former and present members of our department for providing me with intellectual insights and generous portions of encouragement while I worked on this book. These colleagues are John Wozniak, Richard Mathers, Rick Schaefer, Ken Mietus, Polly Radosh, Brendan Maguire, Bill Faulkner, Diane Sandage, Don Cambell, and Mike Fimmen.

I want especially to thank my sister, Laurie Johnson, and her husband, Larry Johnson, who so generously opened their home to my colleagues and me when we did research in the Washington, D.C. area. Their support contributed especially to my work at the National Fire Academy and my 1997 participation in the Collective Action Project observation team.

Finally, while writing this book, my best friend and wife, Kitty Miller, has helped me appreciate and enjoy the many blessings bestowed upon us by our children, our grandchildren, and my mother. More than anyone, Kitty's daily help and encouragement have made the completion of this book possible.

PART
I

INTRODUCTION
THEORY AND RESEARCH

CHAPTER 1

COLLECTIVE EVENTS AND SOCIAL LIFE

I was confused at first, wondering why all these people were just standing around with so much shooting going on. Then this column of Yankees marched right by 'em, and you know, those people hooted and booed and the Yanks didn't do anything about it at all . . . not like any Yankees I ever saw. I started looking to join the fight myself and worked my way around to figure where the safest place would be to get in . . . when I'll be damned if I didn't get a good view of what the Southern army looked like. Land sakes kid, there must have been 500 of 'em with at least 20 guns and 40 or 50 mounted boys. And that pitiful little column of Yanks didn't have a hundred men . . . there was one little mountain howitzer blazing back at all that Southern artillery and it didn't look like the fight would last more than five minutes . . . fact is, I couldn't figure why the Yanks would stand and fight against such odds. (Duke, 1997)

The narrator above is not describing a Civil War battle of 1864 but rather a Civil War reenactment that took place in 1997. The reenactment of Civil War battles in the United States has grown in popularity since the 1980s. On any weekend, companies, regiments and corps of both Union and Confederate reenactors stage battles portraying not only soldiers but battlefield doctors and nurses, war correspondents, wives, merchants and other historically accurate roles that figured in the great conflict. These events are often planned months in advance, may raise money for charities, and often draw thousands of reenactors and spectators to the battle sites.

Reenacting Civil War battles is one of the fantastic number and variety of collective events that make up our social lives. Collective events occur when people come together and carry out activities together. Collective events may be small and simple, such as a yard sale, or large and complex, such as the 1996 Million Man March in Washington, DC. Collective events may regularly celebrate important religious and national holidays and decide the year's world sports championships. Collective events may be an occasion for the dedication of parks, highways and buildings, the launching of sales campaigns, or the commemoration of heroes. Pastime activities such as sports, hobbies, and clubs are the basis for many collective events. Some collective events may be responses to unexpected happenings such as natural disasters, terrorist attacks, the outbreak of war, the extreme popularity of a movie such as *Titanic*, or a new consumer item such as the Beanie Babies of the 1990s. Today's social life is a patchwork of collective events, from craft shows and flea markets to national celebrations and large-scale social movements.

We experience collective events with our family, friends, neighbors, and coworkers as well as strangers. People attend sporting events and concerts in the company of family members and friends. Every year people in the United States heft sandbags against rising floodwaters and clean up after tornadoes and hurricanes with their families, friends, and neighbors as well as with volunteers from outside their communities.

We also experience collective events vicariously, through books, magazines, newspapers, cable and satellite television, and the Internet. Most Americans experienced the Los Angeles riot of 1992 vicariously, through a collage of news bites of burning buildings, violent attacks, armed citizens, and police shooting tear gas and chasing looters. The more shocking and exciting of these images were shown repeatedly. Late-night radio talk shows give us impressions of current political discontent and public concerns. People increasingly obtain their views of alternative lifestyles, cults, and groups that make up social movements from "reality-based" programming that presently saturates the cable channels. Websites, lists, and chat rooms on the Internet give us access to interest groups of all persuasions, from crafts and hobbies to political action. Even though images of collective events from these sources are quite compelling, we are seldom in a position to fully judge their accuracy.

COLLECTIVE BEHAVIOR AND COLLECTIVE ACTION

Sociologists have studied many types of collective events—celebrations, ceremonies, riots, fads, disasters, demonstrations and social movements—from the perspective of collective behavior and, more recently, from the standpoint of collective action.

The term *collective behavior* came into use in the 1920s when Samuel Henry Prince (1920) discussed "collective behavior" in his study of disasters. The first introductory sociology text ever published, Park and Burgess's *Introduction to the Science of Sociology* (1921), also included a chapter on collective behavior. It is interesting to note that one of the earliest books written about crowds, Charles Mackay's *Memoirs of Extraordinary Popular Delusions and the Madness of Crowds* ([1852] 1980), never used the term "collective behavior." Likewise, Gustave LeBon ([1895]1960), who is often credited as the "father of collective behavior," never used the term when he wrote about the crowd. The early work of Mackay and LeBon focused on crowd excitement and included discussions of moral epidemics, popular delusions, manias, and follies, as well as the fickleness, sentimentality, irrationality, and amorality of crowds. These views came to dominate nearly a century of sociological writing about the crowd and collective behavior.

Carl Couch (1968) challenged these views as stereotypes when he suggested that crowds are no more or no less bizarre than other social systems. Evidence to support this view was soon forthcoming. Researchers working through the newly established Disaster Research Center at Ohio State University regularly began to find that survivors of disaster were capable of caring for themselves and others and restoring order to their communities rather quickly—that they did not stampede from danger or become helpless because of emotional shock, as earlier stereotypes suggested. In the 1970s Clark McPhail began systematic observation of crowds at demonstrations, sporting events, and shopping malls. After about ten years of observation, he concluded that much of what previously had been written about crowds and *collective behavior* was inaccurate. To distinguish his work from this earlier tradition, he began to refer to crowds as gatherings and to write about *collective action* within gatherings. By the 1980s, sociologists began to use the term "collective action" to reflect the purposive nature of the civil rights and anti-war movements of the 1960s.

The perspectives of collective behavior and collective action present very different explanations of the collective events that are part of our daily lives. At present each view has its advocates and supporters among sociologists. This book is intended to give you an understanding and appreciation of both approaches to collective events.

How did collective behavior and collective action come to be the focus of sociological study? To answer this question we must look at some Western history and the "new science" of sociology, as it was set forth by the early writers.

The Idea of Collective Behavior

Two tremendous forces of social change were unleashed during the eighteenth century: the first was the *industrial revolution,* which was well underway in England by the late 1700s, and the second was the rise of *popular democracy* that culminated in the American and French revolutions. By 1850, the two great revolutions of industrialization and democracy had swept away the old order of Europe.

For hundreds of years prior to the eighteenth century, the old order had rested on the rigid social distinctions between the nobility, clergy, peasant, and serf. Each had a clear and traditionally defined role in society, and few people questioned or seriously challenged this arrangement. The old order also had a decidedly rural character. Land ownership was the surest—and nearly the only—source of wealth, power, and respectability. The nobility and the Church, of course, owned most of the land. Everyday life followed the relaxed rhythm of the seasons. Nearly everyone worked from sunup to sundown, planting in the spring, harvesting in the fall, and spending long winters isolated in small hamlets and villages scattered across Europe.

Well into the 1600s, much commerce in Europe was highly seasonal and carried out through the tradition of the fair. In the late spring and early winter, merchants, craftsmen, and entertainers would pay stall fees to the town or church for the privilege of using the "fair grounds" outside the towns and abbeys. People of the region would gather here for a fortnight (two weeks) of trading. The fair also served as an opportunity for people to renew social contacts with others and as an occasion for worship, matchmaking, exchanging of information, celebration and merrymaking. The amount of commerce and other forms of social contact peaked during the local fairs and declined greatly at other times of the year (Gies, 1969:1–22; 211–23).

The industrial revolution changed all of this in a surprisingly short time. With the invention of the steam engine came factories, the ownership of which soon challenged ownership of land as a source of wealth. A new social class, composed of industrialists and the merchants who sold the products of their factories, began to rival the power and prestige of the nobility. Factories also changed the character and rhythm of social life. Peasants and serfs left the land and crowded into the cities to be near the factories. Ways of life suited to small communities quickly eroded under the fierce competition for jobs, food, and shelter in the cities. The pace of work was now set not by the seasons but by the erratic fluctuations of the marketplace. New factories also destroyed the influence of centuries-old guilds or protective associations for skilled workers. In the factories and mines, people adjusted as best they could to the nearly inhumane work pace and sixteen- to eighteen-hour workdays.

In the old order, most opposition to the nobility took the form of localized banditry, such as described in the legend of Robin Hood. Many of these primitive rebels did indeed seek to rob the rich and give to the poor, although the majority probably robbed the rich and poor alike. Disputes, when they arose, were usually local affairs and centered on such things as poaching, lost or stolen livestock, and family problems.

The nature of social conflict changed fundamentally as the industrial revolution put an end to the isolation and provincialism of rural life. Conflict over the necessities of everyday life began to be eclipsed by conflict over ideas. The masses began to hold political views, and these views began to count for something in the affairs of nations. Terms such as *radicalism*, *liberalism*, and *conservatism* arose to describe the development of conflicting political views.

In many respects, the American and French revolutions were the first to be fought in the name of clearly political ideals. Chief among these ideals was that of democracy. As conceived in these revolutions, democracy was more than simply the right to vote; it also included ideas such as the age of majority and the age of consent, which shattered the tyranny of the eldest male in family life. Democracy also embodied the ideal of public education. Education would now be enjoyed not only by the elite but by the masses as well. Further, public education was conceived as a practical education, suited to making people into productive workers, good soldiers, and intelligent voters. In England, France, and America, most of these changes occurred within a sixty- or seventy-year period, or about one generation. The Western social order that had for centuries repelled repeated invasions of hordes of barbarians had quickly crumbled before the onslaught of the factory and the idea of democracy. This new social order had indeed arrived with shocking suddenness and finality.

The great revolutions of industrialization and democracy produced a wave of intellectual activity in Western society. Advances occurred on all fronts in the physical and biological sciences. A new science of sociology was established that, from its beginning, sought to explain the causes and effects of the great revolutions. In the process, nearly all of the central concepts of modern sociology were set down—concepts such as society, community, social change, norms, anomie, class, status, party, property, power, prestige, formal organizations, authority, and alienation. These concepts were made part of sociology and modern thought by such writers as Comte, Marx, Durkheim, Weber, Michels, Pareto, Veblin, and Spencer. These writers usually discussed the origins and consequences of the great revolutions in deliberately cold and analytical terms. Their style of writing was often heavy and unattractive, and their lines of analysis frequently took them far from the immediately obvious. It is not surprising, then, that the writers' new scientific objectivity was taken as a lack of concern for the blood and fire of real-life conflicts by many readers who had witnessed them firsthand.

For at least one critic, this omission represented a fundamental error. Gustave LeBon dismissed the sociological classics as "ill-observed fact" and "pure imagination" ([1895] 1960:48). For LeBon, the key to understanding the origins and consequences of the great revolutions was their *emotional component*. It was the intense emotions of widespread and mindless expectations, hero worship, hatred, and fear that eliminated the possibility of orderly social change and made precipitous and bloody revolution inevitable. This intense emotional atmosphere was created in the crowds that were a daily occurrence in the streets of the rapidly growing industrial centers of Europe and America. Change would remain unpredictable, disorderly, and bloody until the crowd was brought into check.

Fortunately, LeBon's work succeeded in sensitizing readers to the role of crowds and emotions in social change rather than convincing them to abandon sociology altogether. In 1912, William H. Prince, an Anglican priest from Canada, transmitted news stories from the U.S.S. *Montmagny* describing the rescue of survivors from the *Titanic*. Five years later, Prince helped with the rescue and recovery work following the 1917 Halifax Munitions explosion. Each of these disasters killed more than 1,500 people. Then, in 1920, Prince outlined a primitive theory of what he called "collective behavior" in his Ph.D. thesis, *Catastrophe and Social Change* (Scanlon, 1988). Prince argued that large-scale disasters such as those he had experienced create "fluidity" in otherwise rigid social structures, which then allows "collective behavior" to create progressive social change. Thus, the sinking of the *Titanic* served as the stimulus for modern safety standards for ship construction and operation. Likewise, city planning, zoning ordinances, and building codes were created in the aftermath of major urban conflagrations such as the Chicago Fire of 1871 or the Halifax explosion. More recently, because their early-warning systems failed, the National Weather Service made major changes in their severe-weather tracking procedures and policies following the deadly Plainfield, Illinois tornado of 1990.

In the first American introductory sociology text, *Introduction to the Science of Sociology*, Ernest Burgess (1921) included a chapter entitled "collective behavior" in which crowds, publics, sects, mass movements, propaganda, and fashion were discussed. In this book, collective behavior was defined as the behavior of people under the influence of a collective impulse. The collective impulse, manifested as social unrest and social contagion, was fundamentally different from the impulses that guide normal behavior. The collective impulse was defined as a type of rapport or hypnosis that produced a loss of self-control and increased people's suggestibility.

For many years thereafter, the field served as a kind of dumping ground for a wide variety of social phenomena that at first glance seemed to reflect the operation of the collective impulse. Such phenomena displayed characteristics different from those expected of socialized individuals, formal organizations, and institutions. According to this thinking, socialized individuals are normally law abiding; therefore, lynch mobs and riots must be part of collective behavior. Formal organizations such as the military instill discipline in members; therefore, mutinies must be part of collective behavior. Institutions such as the male-dominated family meet fundamental human needs; therefore, women's suffrage and other feminist movements must be collective behavior.

Those who suggested that lynch mobs, mutinies, and the suffrage movement belonged in the field of collective behavior usually had little interest in studying these topics. Collective behavior was also seen as a sub-area within which fads, crazes, hysterias, and other odd events could be discussed and studied without imparting a sensationalistic and nonsensical taint to general sociology.

The field of collective behavior is unusually diverse in terms of the kinds of events studied and the competing theories developed to explain these events. In general, however, the field has been defined in three ways: collective behavior as aroused emotion; collective behavior as an adaptive response; and collective behavior as a response to social strain.

Collective Behavior as Aroused Emotion Clearly, there is a long-standing tradition which defines collective behavior as spontaneous social behavior directed by aroused and extreme emotion that distorts people's normal critical abilities and exaggerates their normal likes, dislikes, and loyalties (LeBon [1895], 1960; Park and Burgess, 1921; Blumer, 1939; Brown, 1954; Klapp, 1972; Lofland, 1981). This definition is most easily applied to people's behavior within crowds.

It is often said that people do things in crowds that they would not do, either as individuals or in the company of their family and friends, and it is certainly not difficult to illustrate this line of reasoning. Some crowds seem to distort people's critical abilities. We witness political rallies at which people cheer approvingly as politicians rattle off one cliché after another. In some crowds, people seem to lose their usual inhibitions and caution. During Pentecostal revivals, for example, normally modest people quiver, shake, and speak loudly in tongues. Crowds also appear to intensify hatreds. In the spring of 1992, viewers across the country were shocked to witness a mob's brutal assault of a Los Angeles truck driver during the rioting that followed the acquittal of police who were on trial for the beating of Rodney King (McPhail, 1994).

Finally, crowds appear to intensify people's attraction to certain objects and activities. Peak phases of fads and crazes usually involve crowds. Each decade of the twentieth century has been characterized by some type of popular crowd revelry. In the 1920s, for instance, there were goldfish swallowing and dancing the Charleston. There were the dance marathons of the 1930s. In the 1950s, fraternities and residence halls competed to see who could stuff the most people into phone booths or small autos. In the 1970s, crowds of naked people ran or "streaked" across college campuses, stadiums, and shopping malls. Styles of "wild" concert behavior such as crowd surfing and mosh pits developed around rock groups of the 1980s and 1990s such as Nine Inch Nails and Pearl Jam. To the uninitiated, people in these crowds appeared out of control as they thrashed about violently. In 1996, stadium crowds at baseball, football, and basketball games competed to break the record for the largest macarena dance.

Defining collective behavior in terms of aroused emotion is intended to set collective behavior apart from social action that occurs within institutionalized relationships, such as the family, or formal organizations, such as established political parties or corporate hierarchies. Defining collective behavior in terms of aroused emotion, however, also calls our attention away from the seemingly instrumental and adaptive aspects of people's behavior. Among the initiated, for instance, there are "appropriate" ways to crowd surf and "proper" attire and actions for the mosh pit. As we shall see in later chapters, in spite of fright, grief, and shock, sur-

Crowd surfing is a popular pastime at rock concerts. Both the crowd surfer and the people in the audience who carry her are participants in this form of collective activity. © Neal Preston/ CORBIS.

vivors of disasters are usually able to mount effective rescue and recovery efforts within minutes after disaster strikes. They gather information, discuss alternative lines of action, evaluate possible outcomes, and form definite plans and strategies.

Collective Behavior as Adaptive Response A definition encompassing adaptive phenomena conceptualizes collective behavior as emergent and transitory social behavior that is an adaptive response to new or ambiguous situations (Turner and Killian, 1957; Lang and Lang, 1961). This definition calls attention to collective response to situations for which no preexisting rules or expectations (norms) apply. In this sense, collective behavior is adaptive and problem-solving behavior in which people identify problems, clarify expectations for appropriate conduct, make plans, and enter new social relationships.

The conspicuous and rapid adoption of new products and activities is part of fads and crazes. Europe's seventeenth century was made more turbulent by successive waves of large-scale speculation in tulips, tobacco, corn, chocolate, and other products introduced through new trade routes. South Sea island societies were disrupted by the unannounced and rapid introduction of modern technology by way of invading armies during World War II. Types of social movements referred to as cargo cults were formed throughout the South Pacific as a response to this exposure to new objects, ideas, and people. Cargo cults actually date from the 1800s as a response to early European exploration but expanded greatly after World War II. These groups of indigenous island people believed spirits would bring cargoes of modern goods to them if they carried out the correct magic rituals (which often mimicked activities of military forces, such as marching and calisthenic drills). These cults sometimes built their own nonfunctional versions of airplane landing strips and radio towers in hopes that the cargoes would come.

What we now know as the Internet originally was a system used to connect mainframe computers at a few universities in the late 1960s, and fewer than a thousand Internet hosts existed in 1983 when the personal computer began to appear in our homes. Thereafter, the growth of the Internet was phenomenal, with the number of hosts often doubling and sometimes tripling every 24 months. By 1997, the number of hosts had exceeded 16 million (Zakon, 1997). Recent localized efforts by parents to censor or otherwise restrict pornography, hate groups, and other objectionable sites on the Internet is an adaptive response to a new and invasive technology that is attractively packaged and available to children.

Even when collective behavior is a response to new or ambiguous situations, people may adopt traditional forms of association and propose traditional solutions. For example, whites volunteered by the hundreds to assist African Americans throughout the "Freedom Summer" of 1963. Many of these volunteers were not content with the role of civil rights worker. African Americans began to complain that these volunteers tended to seek out, sometimes in an abrasive manner, the traditional white roles of boss, planner, or strategist. This difficulty eventually led to the expulsion of many white volunteers from civil rights groups. Similarly, although the hippie communes of the 1960s and 1970s were considered by many to be a new departure from the middle-class lifestyle of the 1950s, this break was not complete. In many communes women continued to fill the traditional roles of cook and housekeeper and remained sexually and emotionally subservient to men. As another example, the Christian Coalition's 1996 proposal to turn their fundamentalist doctrine into government policy to solve current social ills is a theme that has been heard periodically in the United States since the 1700s.

In the instances discussed above, collective behavior is an active but transitory phase of larger processes of social change. The citizens band radio fad of the 1970s, the video game fad of the 1980s, and the explosive growth of the Internet in the 1990s were temporary phases in the rapid introduction of products that later became permanent features of our material culture.

Collective Behavior as Response to Social Strain While many aspects of collective behavior represent responses to new or ambiguous situations in which few guidelines for conduct exist, it must also be noted that people sometimes confront situations for which they have quite clear definitions and objectives. Breakdowns in the social structure such as disasters, deteriorating economic conditions, and value conflicts quite logically seem to increase individual and, in turn, collective levels of anxiety, hostility, and desires to "set things right." The term *social strain* is often used by sociologists (and others) to refer to these breakdowns in social structure and resulting emotions. Collective behavior has been defined as uninstitutionalized responses to social strain (Blumer, 1939; Smelser, 1962; Perry and Pugh, 1978; Rose, 1982). Collective behavior—be it panic, fads, wild celebrations, riots, religious revivals, or revolutionary social movements—represents mobilization in order to eliminate or otherwise cope with social strain.

Consider the events that occurred during April of 1963, when African Americans began a series of marches in Birmingham, Alabama, to demand the desegregation of public facilities, equal voting rights, and fair employment opportunities. There was little new or ambiguous about the conditions they were protesting or the demands they were presenting. The white response to these marches was violent. Birmingham police used dogs, fire hoses, and mass arrests to halt the marches. Four black children died in church bombings, protest leader Medgar Evers was assassinated, and both black and white civil rights workers were harassed, beaten and, in some instances, killed. This violent response sparked hundreds of other civil rights demonstrations throughout the nation and voter registration drives throughout the South.

These instances of collective behavior represent responses to old and recurring problems and clearly defined opportunities, threats, groups, or objects. The paradigm that social strain produces collective behavior is intuitively quite appealing, and this view guided initial sociological thinking about the urban disorders that swept U.S. cities between 1965 and 1973. Numerous studies sought to show the relationship between empirical measures of social strain and participation in these riots and social movements.

If social strain produces collective behavior as this view suggests, the relationship is probably not straightforward or direct. For instance, protest, social movements, and revolutions may, in the long run, improve the economic well-being and increase the liberties of participants. In the short run, however, they generally produce the opposite results. Gary Marx (1980) points out that strikes, boycotts, and civil disobedience may be the cause of social breakdown rather than the reverse. When the strike is finally settled or the hostilities of revolution cease, conditions of social breakdown are likely to be greater than when the strike or revolution began. Wages have been lost, factories and crops may have been destroyed, repressive laws may have been enacted, and domestic and international markets and sources of credit may have been lost. The relationship between social strain and the incidence of collective behavior is an unresolved question.

Types of Collective Behavior

Recall that collective behavior initially served as a dumping ground for any and all social phenomena that at first glance seemed to reflect impulses different from those expected of socialized individuals, formal organizations, and institutions. Because of this, it may well be that there is no characteristic or set of characteristics common to all the phenomena that were "dumped" into the field of collective behavior.

In order to comprehend the diversity of the field, Gary Marx (1980) cataloged the phenomena that have been studied by people who contributed to the field. Marx also considered what the field should encompass, given the existing although incomplete definitions of collective behavior. His survey of the literature led him to conclude that the field of collective behavior embodies six traditional and interrelated topics.

Problems within Social Systems First, there is an interest in social systems that are in a pronounced state of breakdown, strain, maladaption, crisis, or disruption. Much of the disaster and crisis research falls within this area. Quite clearly, this area also includes the study of protest, political violence, rebellions and revolutions, most migrations, and many social movements.

Undifferentiated Groups Second, there is an interest in newly emerged or undifferentiated groups, referred to as the masses and the public (Blumer, 1939).

Here the concern is with such issues as the methods and effects of mass advertising and the nature and operation of public opinion. Newly emerged groups include celebrating throngs, crowds of rioters, spectator crowds at the scenes of accidents and fires, people standing in line to purchase concert tickets, and some disaster response groups.

Communication Processes Third, there is the interest in the processes involved in the development and communication of collective images. This includes a concern for the development of symbols and ideologies of social movements and generalized or widespread images and beliefs of fear, dissatisfaction, exploitation, scapegoats, and hostility. Many of these concerns are reflected in the study of rumor.

Since the 1980s the growth of cable and satellite television, the Internet, and the use of cellular phones has greatly altered and expanded the ways in which people can form groups to pursue their aims. The advent of continuous and often on-the-scene coverage of news events has altered our perception of our social world.

Social Influence and Interaction Fourth, there is an interest in direct, immediate, visual, and highly involving social influence and interaction. This includes the concern with audience reactions to speakers and decision making within the crowd. Concern with the relative effects of face-to-face versus mediated recruitment into groups of various sorts also falls within this area.

Group Emotion Fifth, there is an interest in highly emotional states collectively experienced by groups. This includes panics, hysterias, collective visions, and extreme instances of suggestibility.

Behavior Outside of Traditional Culture Throughout the collective behavior literature, there is an interest in behavior outside of or in special relationship to traditional culture. This category includes an interest in novel behavior, such as fads, or innovative behavior during disasters. Also standing outside traditional culture are collective and criminal acts such as looting, outbursts of vandalism, smuggling, and trading in illegal goods and services. Finally, there is behavior directed toward institutionalizing alternate forms of action. This includes the social movement to establish the juvenile justice system in the United States during the 1880s as well as the desegregation and civil rights movements of the 1960s, and, since 1973, the sustained efforts by many groups to overturn the *Roe v. Wade* Supreme Court decision.

This sixth category is very broad in terms of the range of events it encompasses. In addition, behavior outside of traditional culture also includes elements of the other five categories. That is, interest in social systems in a pronounced state of breakdown (first category) can include events outside a system's traditional culture, such as the emergence of new religions. Other events, such as reform movements, are in keeping with that culture and may even seek to reinforce dominant cultural themes. Figure 1.1 illustrates the relationship of these six categories to each other and to traditional culture.

COLLECTIVE ACTION: A NEW OUTLOOK

Ever since the general idea of collective behavior emerged in the 1800s with the work of Mackay and LeBon, scholars and researchers have speculated about how

FIGURE 1.1: The Field of Collective Behavior

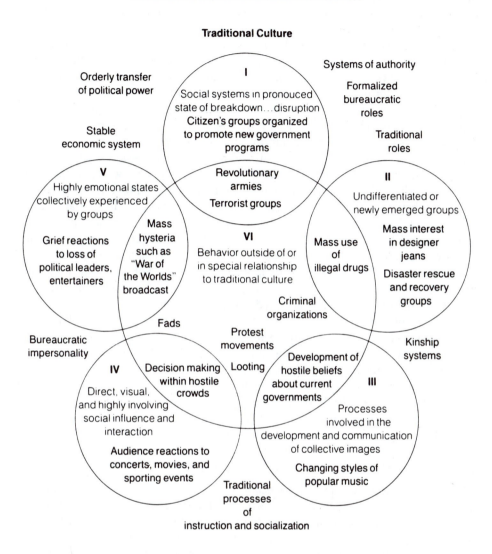

collective behavior differs from "normal" social behavior. The most popular and enduring views, of course, are outlined above—collective behavior as aroused emotion, collective behavior as a response to new and ambiguous conditions, or collective behavior as a response to social strain. It is important to note, however, that some sociologists sought to identify similarities between collective behavior and routine social behavior. For instance, Prince (1920) cast collective behavior as an adaptive and socially useful response. Other early scholars, notably Park and Blumer, suggested that there might be no real difference between collective behavior and other forms of social behavior. Park (1924:42), for example, once defined sociology as the "science of collective behavior." Blumer (1957) noted that in a broad sense collective behavior refers to the behavior of two or more people who are acting together. Recall that Carl Couch (1968) characterized the crowd and collective behavior as no more or no less pathological and bizarre than other social systems. Milgram and Toch (1969:509) define the crowd simply as "people in sufficiently close proximity that the fact of aggregation comes to influence behavior" and made no mention of aroused emotions.

In the 1980s, some sociologists began to use the term "collective action" instead of "collective behavior" when referring to politically oriented social movements, such as the civil rights movement of the 1950s and 1960s (Tilly, 1975; Simon, 1982). The use of the term collective action began as a way of underscoring the many important aspects of these movements that were clearly purposive and directed toward reasonable ends. Also, social movements were often based on traditional forms of association, such as the family, church, neighborhood, or work association. Social movements adopted traditional modes of expression, such as processions or marches. By using the term collective action rather than collective behavior, writers sought to avoid the implication that social movements were non-purposive behavior based on mass excitement and hysterical or irrational beliefs.

McPhail (1996) now uses the term *gathering* to refer to two or more people in a common location because the term *crowd* has acquired such diverse meanings and inaccurate connotations. He also uses the term *collective action* to refer to social movements and the behavior of people in gatherings. For McPhail, given our present knowledge of what people do in gatherings, social movements, and other collective phenomena, the terms crowd and collective behavior are obsolete.

The concept of collective action encourages more unified conceptual and analytical approaches across sociology's subject matter. It also encourages efforts to discover commonalties among phenomena seen as quite separate, such as the actions of corporate executives in response to the latest move of a competitor or a protest group responding to a court order. The collective action approach gives new insights into seemingly bizarre events such as hysterias, panics, and fads. It lessens the need to call upon novel explanations such as "crowd mentality" to account for collective phenomena (Marx, 1980).

Collective Behavior or Collective Action?

The increasing use of the term collective action by researchers does *not* mean that the field of collective behavior has been abandoned or that theories of collective behavior are irrelevant. Nearly all fields of study within sociology consist of both "old" and "new" theories. Sometimes, "old" theories are rejuvenated with new methodologies. It is usually important that we understand the old theories in order to appreciate the direction taken by the new theories and the research they engender.

Old theories still retain considerable historical interest, and obsolete theories may be our only link to phenomena that are ignored by new theories and their proponents. For instance, there are recent mass sightings of UFOs that are more extensive than anything reported back in the 1950s and 1960s. There are popular UFO websites and chat groups on the Internet. Presently, you can find some type of UFO show or story on cable television every day of the week. Communities are still disrupted by alleged monster sightings, and wild rumors and other stories circulate throughout neighborhoods and on the Internet. While "mass hysterias" are a major part of the collective behavior tradition, collective action theory has not led us to investigate such phenomena. Indeed, because the collective action approach emphasizes purposive action, the approach may trivialize or direct investigative efforts away from such apparently "irrational" activities.

Specialists within a field may abandon the old theories, while the majority of sociologists outside the field continue to perceive the field in terms of the older, more familiar theories. In fact, few if any introductory sociology texts today use the term collective action and retain "collective behavior" theories and terminology (Wohlstein, 1992). Recent sociology journals, on the other hand, are more likely to contain articles about collective action.

While it is tempting to use the terms "collective behavior" and "collective action" interchangeably, the precise usage of these terms will be maintained throughout this book. The collective behavior perspective still retains theoretical and empirical utility, and the collective action perspective gives name to a fundamental paradigm shift that has reoriented theoretical frames and methodological strategies in recent years.

PLAN OF THE BOOK

In Part I of this book we will cover basic theories and research. Theories of both collective behavior and collective action will be presented in the next chapter. We will begin with the first theory of collective behavior ever to be articulated, namely, mass hysteria theory. This theory defines the field in terms of aroused emotion and began with the writings of Gustave LeBon. In *The Crowd* ([1895] 1960), LeBon presented a very negative assessment of the mental unity of crowds and the role of crowds, popular democracy, and revolutions in national events. He laid the groundwork for a theoretical tradition that endured almost unchallenged for nearly 50 years. One must understand mass hysteria theory in order to appreciate the direction of most early work within the field.

Next, the emergent norm theory developed by Ralph Turner and Lewis Killian will be outlined. This theory casts collective behavior as an adaptive response to novel or unique social conditions. This approach emphasizes the impact of norms, collective definitions, and social roles in the development of collective behavior and de-emphasizes the role of aroused emotion.

Finally, Neil Smelser's value-added theory of collective behavior will be considered. The value-added model is the most comprehensive of the approaches that view collective behavior as a response to stressful societal conditions. The value-added theory divides the field into collective episodes of crazes, panics, hostile outbursts, and value- and norm-oriented social movements.

We will then consider theories of collective action, giving particular attention to the work of Clark McPhail. Many new and traditional concerns are examined from the standpoint of processes of crowd formation, behavior within gatherings, and their dispersal. Taken together, these processes provide insight into how celebrations, civil disorders, disaster responses, and other collective events develop. On a larger scale, these processes tell us a great deal about rallies, marches, and confrontations, which are important components of migrations, protests, social movements, and revolutions.

The resource mobilization perspective, first articulated by John D. McCarthy and Mayer N. Zald, will also be presented. This perspective extends the focus of collective action from gatherings to detailed case studies of social movements and social movement organizations. From this standpoint, the success of social movements requires that social movement organizations mobilize social networks and material resources. Political process theory will also be presented. This perspective focuses on the dynamics of protest and includes the work of Doug McAdam, William Gamson, and Michael Lipsky. The political process perspective offers to explain how people articulate their grievances and the possibilities of successfully redressing them. This is a necessary condition for initiating a program of resistance. The political process perspective also includes consideration of tactics of protest that can be used to press the demands of relatively powerless groups.

The theories of collective behavior and collective action that will be presented in chapter 2 will be our guides throughout the remainder of the text. In later chapters we will also consider several theories that address a narrower range of concerns than the general theories. These "midrange" theories are more readily understood when introduced with specific subject matter. Davies' (1969) J-curve theory of revolution, for example, will be considered in chapters dealing with revolutionary social movements and political violence. Davies' theory is an alternative to Smelser's view of structural strain and represents an early movement in the direction of collective action theory.

In chapter 3 we present the problems and methods of collective behavior/collective action research. Three major problems have greatly influenced the character of this research and set it apart from research conducted in other areas of sociology. First, there is the problem of studying unanticipated events, such as reactions to disasters or the development of riots. Second, there is the problem of studying the crowd. Directly studying crowds is not an easy task, and before the 1970s discussions of crowd behavior were based on informed speculation rather than systematic observation. Only in the past fifteen years have researchers attempted to systematically observe, record, and otherwise analyze what people do in crowds. Finally, there is the problem of studying collective behavior under controlled conditions. Various moral, legal, and practical considerations limit the kinds of events that can be produced and manipulated for the purpose of studying collective behavior under controlled conditions. Simply put, one cannot yell "Fire!" in a crowded theater to study panic. In chapter 3, we also consider how the basic research methods of sociology have been adapted and applied to the study of collective behavior and collective action. We will consider methods such as the analysis and use of historical material, simple and participant observation, survey research, experiments and computer simulation.

In Part Two we will consider topics that have been largely or exclusively studied as collective behavior—as Gary Marx (1980) has observed, topics reflecting a concern for what has been studied and what should be studied, given the existing definitions of the field.

Chapters 4 through 8 concern events that most of us have encountered firsthand. In chapter 4 we examine rumor and communication. We will look briefly at the origin and character of the Internet and its effect on rumor and communication. We will see how the information contained in rumors fits into our daily lives.

In chapters 5 and 6 we will explore the sometimes related matters of mass hysterias and UFOs. Among the mass hysterias discussed are the aftermath of the "War of the Worlds" radio broadcast of 1938, epidemics of mysterious rashes and fainting, and the periodic sighting of monsters such as Bigfoot. Nearly every week, people in the United States report seeing mysterious objects like flying saucers. To many people, mass hysterias and UFOs represent collective delusions and silliness. Still, a closer examination of these events reveals a great deal about what we take for granted in our social life.

In chapter 7 we examine fads and fashion, to which nearly every aspect of social life is subject. To some, fads and fashion represent people's mindless and often quite costly preoccupation with superficialities. To others, fads and fashion are fundamental ingredients in community life and social change. In chapter 8 we will examine sports as part of our collective life. The largest crowds we may ever encounter accompany sporting events. Sports may constitute social movements and even threats to the social order.

In Part Three we will consider threats to the social order. Most of these topics have been studied from the collective action standpoint during the last decade. In chapter 9 we examine migrations that result from natural catastrophes such as drought, as well as broken economies, racial and ethnic hatred, and war. Throughout the world today, millions of people are homeless because of these conditions. Much recent research has been done on the support of refugee camps. Chapters 10 and 11 concern disaster. In chapter 10 we will see how individuals cope with disaster. We will consider people's nonadaptive or "panic" responses, adaptive responses, and altruistic responses to disaster. In chapter 11 we look at disaster from the standpoint of the many groups and organizations that work together to carry out rescue and recovery efforts. In chapters 12 and 13 we examine riots. Chapter 12 addresses the question of who participates in riots. In chapter 13 we will look at how police riot training and tactics have changed during the past fifty years. In chapter 14 we consider protest—the means through which people with limited financial and organizational resources can influence the political process. Finally, we discuss social movements in chapters 15 and 16. The conditions under which different types of social movements arise will be discussed in chapter 15. In chapter 16 we examine how demonstrations and marches are organized as central features of social movements.

The subject matter of collective behavior and collective action spans a wide range of topics, from the silliness of fads to the deadly serious business of revolutions. Throughout this text, we provide examples that give an intuitive feel for collective behavior and collective action. Considerable attention has been given to the who, what, when, and where of the events in question. Though we present both early work (collective behavior) and current work (collective action) in the field, each student should keep in mind that there is always room for additional insights, more studies, and new theories.

PERSPECTIVES ON COLLECTIVE BEHAVIOR AND COLLECTIVE ACTION

MARSEILLE, France (AP)—For the second consecutive day, tear gas drifted through the streets of this port city. The World Cup that Marseille hoped to celebrate with parades, concerts and bicycle races on the beach has not gone according to plan.

French riot police had to intervene again on Monday to stop fighting between fans of England's and Tunisia's soccer teams. As of 9 P.M., 16 more people had been arrested and 22 treated at local hospitals, according to a spokesperson for the regional prefecture. On Sunday night, 35 people were hospitalized . . . during rioting in the old port of Marseille. . . .

The first incident on Monday occurred outside the gates of the Stade-Velodrome approximately two hours before the start of the England and Tunisia game in Group G. As fans emerged from the metro and made their way toward the stadium, groups of Tunisian and English supporters began hurling bottles and cans at each other and exchanging blows. According to police, 10 English fans were arrested.

Three hours later, there would be more altercations, injuries and arrests at the Prado beach . . . . shortly after striker Alan Shearer gave England a 1–0 lead in the forty-third minute of the match that England would end up winning, 2–0.

"Until then, it was calm," said Maxime Dray, 30, of Marseille who was sitting in the temporary stands. "Before the match, there were English and Tunisian fans playing soccer together on the grass. When the game started, the Tunisian fans went into the stands, and the English stayed on the grass. But after Shearer scored, some of the English fans turned around and started taunting the Tunisian supporters."

According to Dray and Hilde Smet, a Belgian, someone threw a bottle in the direction of the English fans, who quickly retaliated. The opposing fans began throwing bottles, cans, rocks and plastic seats at each other. Dray said thousands of bystanders, including elderly people and parents with young children, were forced to flee. "A group of English fans charged toward the stands, and there was general panic," Dray said. . . .

The prefecture's spokesperson said 18 people were treated at local hospitals because of injuries suffered at Prado beach. . . ."It's war," said one French teen-ager of North African descent, as he limped away from the beach.

"It was the hooligans against us," said Ramzi Hizi, an 18-year-old French youth whose parents are Tunisian immigrants as he pointed to a large bruise on his wrist he said was caused by a rock. "I don't know why people are surprised. When the English fans come to town, it is always like this." (*New York Times*, 1998)

PERSPECTIVES ON COLLECTIVE BEHAVIOR

Our social life is composed of a wide variety of collective events, some of which are characterized by the expression of intense emotions like the confrontations between English and Tunisian soccer fans described above. Early writers such as Mackay found such crowd "madness" to be of great interest. LeBon was struck by the even more spectacular, emotion-laden events that were part of revolutions and uprisings against authority. The concern for collectively experienced and expressed emotion is the basis of the earliest general theory in the field of collective behavior.

Mass Hysteria Theory

On May 27, 1871, the heart of Paris was in flames. Thousands had already died in the six days of bloody, hand-to-hand fighting that had continued without pause through the districts, streets, and across the barricades of the city. These were the final hours of what Karl Marx came to describe as "the first modern revolution"—the Paris Commune of 1871. Parisians were not in revolt against an oppressive hereditary monarchy, as was the case in 1793. Rather, they were in revolt against the government of the National Assembly that had been popularly elected four months earlier. The National Assembly turned out to be composed primarily of conservatives and anarchists who, just three weeks after their election, began to vote measures that directly threatened the economic survival of the almost destitute Parisian working class. On March 10, 1871, the National Assembly transferred the seat of government from Paris to Versailles. On March 26, the Commune of Paris was established. The Paris Commune of 1871 was a self-proclaimed governing body of men and women who declared Paris to be a free, politically self-determined city. Similar communes were established in the French cities of Lyons, Marseilles, Toulouse, LeCreusot, Saint-Etienne, and Narbonne.

Prominent among the Paris communards were socialists, anarchists, pacifists, humanitarians, and a few Marxists—the red banner of socialism hung over Paris. During the next ten weeks, the men and women of the Paris Commune of 1871 voted for a moratorium on payment of commercial bills and an agreement to transfer the operation and ownership of abandoned factories to workers; they also voted to lower salaries of public officials. The commune approved a law forbidding employers the right to deduct penalties from the wages of workers and declared a strict separation of church and state. During this time the commune also directed the construction of barricades throughout the streets of Paris.

On the afternoon of May 21, National Assembly armies entered Paris. This was the start of Bloody Week, in which fighting was house by house, barricade by barricade. During the fighting, communards burned many memorials of former governments, including the Royal Palace, the Tuileries Palace, the Hôtel de Ville, and the home of the president of the National Assembly. These buildings were architectural and historical treasures that contained countless art objects. Buildings housing important government and financial records were also destroyed. Hundreds of other buildings were set ablaze by the incendiary weapons used by the troops of the National Assembly. Communards executed at least one hundred prisoners, including the archbishop of Paris. Forces of the National Assembly, in turn, shot more than twenty thousand communards and Parisians. By the end of May, much of the beauty of Paris was destroyed, corpses still lay in the streets, and crowds of mourners gathered at mass graves.

Throughout this episode, there was an underlying sense that large-scale events were unfolding at an unusually rapid and dangerous pace. Within weeks after the hasty election of the National Assembly and its transfer of government from Paris to Versailles, at least seven cities broke from the National Assembly and established themselves as independent communes. The common denominator in all these events was the crowd. Before it had fully assessed and consolidated its base of power, the National Assembly—in brief, noisy, and crowdlike deliberation—began to pass edicts having tremendous economic and political impact. The communes were led by men and women who usually had large followings in the crowds of urban workers but little political experience. The communes arrived at edicts by noisy debate and vote but little formal procedure.

During this period there occurred a devastating amount of fighting and destruction. A year earlier, French men and women would have died to protect their national treasures from harm; now, these treasures were put to the torch because they were symbols of the old order. Discipline broke down among troops of the National Assembly as they used incendiaries against the barricades, seemingly mindless of the carnage and unnecessary property damage they might cause. Bands of soldiers brutally executed their compatriots in large numbers. Afterward, troops stripped and mutilated many of the corpses. It was as if a civilized people had, for a time, slipped back into the barbarism of a distant past.

Gustave LeBon: **The Crowd** One eyewitness to these terrible days in Paris was the French scientist, physician, philosopher, militarist, writer, and world traveler Gustave LeBon (1841–1931). For LeBon these events were more than a national tragedy—they also demanded an explanation. Throughout the rest of his writing career, LeBon probed the workings of crowds, representative forms of government, and social movements. The ideas LeBon set forth, and their subsequent interpretation by others, came to constitute the social contagion or *mass hysteria theory* within the field of collective behavior. It should be noted here that the terms "social contagion" and "mass hysteria" have been used interchangeably by sociologists. The term "mass hysteria" is used more frequently in the media and is probably more familiar to most readers and, therefore, will be used throughout this book.

LeBon's most influential and widely acclaimed book was *The Crowd*, published in 1895. In very bold terms, LeBon states that all crowds exert a profound and inherently negative influence on people. He describes this influence as contagious or rapidly transmitted mental unity that emerges whenever people interact in a group—be it the National Assembly of 1871, a parliament, or a revolutionary crowd. For LeBon, contagious mental unity was the root cause of the horrors he witnessed in 1871. Those who followed in the tradition established by LeBon argue, however, that contagious mental unity emerges only in some crowds and under certain conditions. Nonetheless, throughout the mass hysteria literature, contagious mental unity is considered to be a powerful and mischievous force.

Effect on Individuals By the end of the nineteenth century, terminology used by Darwin in his essays on biological evolution had been popularized into jargon embellishing most discussions of economics, politics, and society. LeBon uses this terminology throughout *The Crowd.* He states that the contagious mental unity of crowds reduces the mental capacity of enlightened and cultured people to the level of "those inferior forms of evolution" such as "women, savages, and children" (see the boxed material on mass hysteria and women).

LeBon's discussion of the effects of the crowd on individuals concludes that the crowd transforms rational, law-abiding people into violent, irrational enemies of the state. According to LeBon, this transformation begins with intensified emotion and behavior: people lose their sense of reserve and inhibitions to act; the tempo of their behavior is rapid. Accompanying this state of arousal is a shared willingness to follow suggestions, which LeBon describes as similar to the hypnotic trance. The crowd is unable to sustain focus and moves rapidly from one object or idea to another, but it does sustain a fearful degree of unanimity of mood and action. This contagious mental unity overcomes the individual's rational capabilities. People in the crowd do not reflect on outcomes of their action; perceptions are distorted, and feelings of power emerge that become the basis of attack on authorities. Without critical ability and powers of reflection, people within crowds are incapable of respect for social standards, conventions, and institutions. LeBon's crowd is amoral.

Effect on Society LeBon stated that Western society was entering an age of crowds. Henceforth, through the action of crowds, the masses would figure ominously in the destinies of nations. When LeBon wrote *The Crowd,* explosive population increases and massive rural-to-urban migrations had transformed the very character of social life within Western society. Prior to the eighteenth century, the hamlets and villages of the British Isles and the European continent seldom contained more than one hundred residents. The population of Rome at the birth of Christ was approximately 350,000, making it at that time the largest city in human history. Rome's population had declined dramatically in the third century A.D., and until 1700 no city in Europe had a population greater than 80,000—most populations were below 30,000. In 1801, London was probably the largest city in the world, with a population of 100,000. Judged by later standards, social life had been carried out for centuries in very small social groupings.

Prior to the eighteenth century, most inland hamlets and villages were totally isolated for weeks and months because of seasonal deterioration of roads and trails. Snow or mud made commercial overland travel impossible; casual travel was exhausting, usually dangerous, and infrequent. At the height of the Roman Empire, an official could travel from Rome to the British Isles in thirteen days. Seventeen hundred years later, this journey still took thirteen days for British officials of state who traveled "post haste, sparing no expense."

These conditions changed dramatically following Telford and McAdam's development of techniques for building relatively inexpensive, all-season roads in the 1730s. Telford and McAdam produced the first major innovations in road-building technology since the Egyptian roads of 2000 B.C. During the last half of the eighteenth century, at least three times as many miles of roads were built in Europe and Britain as had been built during the Roman Empire. By the 1840s, railroads began to connect rapidly growing European population centers,

Mass Hysteria Theory and Women: A Century of Progress?

LeBon stated that the contagious mental unity of crowds reduced the mental functioning of enlightened and cultured people to the level of "those inferior forms of evolution" such as "women, savages, and children." Perhaps it is inaccurate to attribute the sexual bias of later social contagion/mass hysteria studies entirely to LeBon; however, throughout the mass hysteria literature, it is assumed that women are very susceptible to hysterical outbursts:

—1895—

It will be remarked that among the special characteristics of crowds there are several—such as impulsiveness, irritability, incapacity to reason, the absence of judgment, and of the critical spirit, the exaggeration of the sentiments, and others besides—which are almost always observed in beings belonging to inferior forms of evolution—in women, savages, and children, for instance. (LeBon [1895], 1960:36)

—1945—

Naturally the more suggestible people accepted the story at face value. Of these only a small percentage reported physical symptoms from "gassing," presumably because of some personal motivation toward, or gratification from, such symptoms. It might be predicted from psychological and psychiatric literature, those who succumbed to the "mental epidemic" were mostly women and were, on the average, below the general population in educational and economic level. This supports the above analysis and puts the "phantom anesthetist" of Mattoon, in some aspects at least, into a familiar psychological pattern. (Johnson, 1945:234–35)

—1965—

The incident under study occurred in a southern clothing manufacturing plant. . . . Within about one week in the summer of 1962 sixty-two persons suffered what was purported to be insect bites and received some kind of medical treatment. . . . Almost all (54) of the victims were women. . . . A physician and entomologist from the Communicable Disease Center in Atlanta visited the plant but could find no toxic element capable of causing these symptoms. . . . The only reasonable conclusion seemed to be that this was a phenomenon that was "almost exclusively psychogenic in nature.". . . We interviewed only women. (Kerckhoff, Back, and Miller, 1965:388–92)

—1972—

A typical example of human milling leading to a stampede would be a fire in an auditorium. Perhaps a woman in the audience whispers audibly to her companion, "Do you smell smoke?" Her companion answers, "No. Do you think there is a fire?" The lady on the other side hears the word fire and looks alarmed, asking, "Is there a fire?" The first two ladies now see her scared look and, being alarmed by it, look scared themselves. This frightens the third lady even more, and now all their scared looks are being observed by others in the audience. A little smoke or some triggering stimulus such as a raised voice can bring on a condition in which many people are scared, frightening each other by their own behavior more than by the signs of the external situation. Running could precipitate a stampede. (Klapp, 1972:44)

—1991—

Rates of illness were higher and more severe symptoms were present in certain groups and subgroups of students. The illness preferentially struck chorus members from one of the middle schools, particularly girls in the soprano section. These students were in close proximity to one another so that symptom transmission through sight and sound would be facilitated, accounting for part of this pattern. . . . Our investigation of the Santa Monica epidemics identified the characteristic features of mass hysteria described in other epidemics. (Small, et al., 1991) and by the 1850s, the telegraph had connected England to the European continent. Within a hundred years, a degree of geographic mobility and interpersonal communication had been achieved that was unprecedented in human history. LeBon was correct in his claims that mass society had arrived. Because of increased geographic mobility and the capacity to communicate among themselves, larger portions of the rapidly growing populations of Europe were able to intrude on the political processes that once had been carried out only by elites.

For LeBon, the great civilizations of the past had been created by small intellectual aristocracies—the "rivalries of sovereigns" and "councils of princes" determined the courses of empires and nations. Decisions were made and policies established in the quiet halls, chapels, libraries, and gardens of nobles and high officials. The institutions and laws of these civilizations were the embodiment of the cumulative wisdom derived from the calm deliberations of intelligent and cultured men.

In contrast, the age of crowds would be a new Dark Ages, an era of barbarism wherein the crowd would assume the prerogatives and power of earlier sovereign classes. Central to this transition were criminal juries, electoral bodies, and parliamentary assemblies, which LeBon characterizes as special types of crowds. Criminal juries had become part of the judicial operations that once had been the sole domain of magistrates appointed by the king. Unlike a magistrate as judge, the jury displayed "suggestibility" and had only a "slight capacity for reasoning." Intellectuals or tradesmen—it made no difference—were each likely to deliver faulty verdicts. Electoral crowds, invested with the power of electing people to office, had a pronounced absence of critical spirit and aptitude for reasoning. Voters responded best to flattery and fantastic promises. For LeBon, universal suffrage brought society's "inferior elements" into the political process. The work of parliaments was always inferior to that of isolated statesmen and specialists. The parliamentary assemblies of different nations produced strikingly similar debates, votes, and ill-conceived decisions. All parliaments had an unavoidable tendency to produce financial waste and to destroy individual liberty. For LeBon, juries, electorates, and parliaments had the power of tyrants and the wisdom of fools.

LeBon stated that the workings of modern institutions could not be accounted for in terms of economic or political theory. He characterizes the theories of Durkheim, Marx, Weber, and others as mixtures of "ill-observed fact" and "pure imagination" that could easily be transformed into the rallying cries of revolutionaries. Elaborate theories were unnecessary for LeBon, because the massive upheavals of the eighteenth and nineteenth centuries obviously resulted from distortions in people's judgment and action caused by contagious mental unity. In this sense, LeBon presents a single-factor explanation of Western history.

Although LeBon is quite definite in his descriptions of the effects of contagious mental unity, he remains quite vague when explaining how this mental unity emerged in crowds. For this reason, Robert K. Merton (1960) characterizes LeBon as a problem finder rather than a problem solver.

Sigmund Freud, a contemporary and critic of LeBon, attempted to explain contagious mental unity as the result of crowd members' unconscious love of the crowd leader. This psychoanalytic explanation, set forth in *Group Psychology and the Analysis of the Ego* (Freud, [1921] 1945), has had relatively little impact within the field of collective behavior, but other attempts to account for contagious mental unity are part of mass hysteria theory.

Herbert Blumer: Circular Reaction In 1934, thirty-nine years after publication of *The Crowd*, Herbert Blumer wrote an essay called "Outline of Collective Behavior" ([1934] 1969). Blumer's "Outline" is much less value-laden than LeBon's *The Crowd*. For example, contagious mental unity is not described as similar to the mental processes of "inferior forms of evolution." Unlike *The Crowd*, Blumer's "Outline" is a more objective classification and analysis of crowd-related phenomena. More so than LeBon, Blumer attempts to describe a social-psychological mechanism through which mental unity develops. He suggests that remarkable events create tensions that dispose people to behave like a crowd. Once underlying tensions are created, people move about in an aimless and random fashion, which Blumer calls *milling*.

According to Blumer, the milling process can transform human interaction in a fundamental way. He states that there is ordinarily a largely covert, interpretive phase to human interaction; that is, one person responds to another by interpreting the other's gestures and remarks, rehearsing or visualizing a possible response, and then conveying a response. This phase of interaction acts as a buffer that lengthens the time between stimulus and response, thus allowing people to differentiate themselves from others by composing responses rather than mirroring, in a simple stimulus-response fashion, the other's action. Finally, it is within the interpretive phase of interaction that rationality resides, where outcomes of action are envisioned, and where alternative lines of action are compared.

Under conditions of intense milling, the interpretive phase of the act is disrupted; in some situations, it may become so noisy that people cannot hear themselves think. As the interpretive phase of interaction deteriorates, the buffer effect is lost and behavior becomes intense and rapid, differentiation becomes more difficult, and people act alike—unanimity in mood and action prevails. Finally, with the interpretive phase of interaction gone, people become suggestible and irrational. Blumer describes this state as *circular reaction*, which he calls the natural mechanism of collective behavior.

Blumer presents a classification of crowds based on focus and internal cohesiveness. Acting crowds develop a sense of goal (focus) and a plan of action to achieve the goal (cohesiveness). An example of the acting crowd is a throng of townspeople who assemble a brass band and hastily build a speaker's platform in anticipation of an impromptu visit from their governor. An expressive crowd lacks a goal and is primarily just a setting for tension release, often through rhythmical action such as applause, dancing, or singing. An expressive crowd, for example, is an audience offering a standing ovation at the end of a concert.

Blumer states that aggregates of people dispersed over large geographic areas can, under conditions of social unrest, assume some of the characteristics of compact acting and expressive crowds. The public is an aggregate of people, often from the same social class, who are concerned with a specific issue. The public discusses ways to meet the issue, such as a community deciding on a school bond referendum. The mass is composed of anonymous individuals from many social strata; it is loosely organized, does not engage in discussion, and behaves in terms of each individual seeking to answer his or her own needs. Blumer cites the California gold rush of 1849 and other human migrations as examples of mass behavior. The widespread adoption of computer games and the Internet by all economic strata of American society would also fit within Blumer's definition of the mass.

While LeBon places great emphasis on the destructive effects of crowds,

Blumer considers the manner in which collective behavior evolves into new forms of group and institutional conduct to be the greater concern. Within crowds, publics, and the mass appear new expectations, values, conceptions of rights and obligations, tastes, and moods upon which new social systems are founded. For LeBon, crowds marked the end of civilization; for Blumer, crowds played an important part in the development of new forms of social life.

Orrin E. Klapp: Tensions and Social Definitions When protest of the Vietnam War was at its peak in 1972, Orin E. Klapp published *Currents of Unrest: An Introduction to Collective Behavior* and in the book advocated that a national tension measurement and management agency be established. The goal of this agency would be the prediction of disruptive or politically threatening outbursts of unrest, such as riots and protest. For Klapp, such outbursts of unrest are mass hysterias fueled by national tensions. For Americans, these tensions arise from cultural values of work and achievement, and the trauma of adjusting to rapid and continuous change. Using a domino metaphor, Klapp argues that people became involved in mass hysterias when sufficiently sensitized or "tilted" by tensions. Mass hysterias start when the weakest people buckle under tension, which in turn may trigger mass hysteria among substantial portions of the "respectable rank and file" and finally lead to the bandwagon stage, in which almost everyone participates. Such episodes may act as "safety valves," because after the hysteria has run its course, tensions are lower and people are much less responsive to the mood of other people.

According to Klapp, the content of mass hysterias depends on the defining process—only after meanings and beliefs are built up can contagion develop. He cites the early organizational efforts and slogans of ecology groups as a "belief-building" prelude to mass hysteria. For Klapp, stark images and simple beliefs, often skillfully manipulated by leaders, exert hypnotic control over people's behavior during mass hysterias. Klapp suggested that government policies should encourage religion and sports in order to allow for more constructive expression of these national tensions.

The preconceptions and questions many students bring to their first course in collective behavior derive largely from mass hysteria theory. The text they used in their introductory sociology course probably presented collective behavior from the standpoint of mass hysteria theory. This theory has fostered many familiar phrases used to describe crowds. These phrases often compare the behavior of humans to that of animals: crowds can be led like "a flock of sheep"; crowds are likely to "stampede" in emergencies; crowds "roar" their approval or disapproval. Further, terms such as social *contagion, mob* psychology and crowd *mentality* are used to describe the decisions and actions of groups with whom we disagree. Let us now turn to other theories of collective behavior.

Emergent-Norm Theory

One of the largest rallies against the Vietnam war occurred in Washington, DC, on the last weekend of October, 1967. It was billed as the rally that would end the war. It didn't. However, for the nearly 250,000 people who attended, it was a memorable event.

During those three days, one was impressed by the pervasive concern of the protesters that this be a nonviolent protest. On Friday evening a clean-cut young man approached a group of less well-groomed young people camped in the backyard of a Georgetown residence. He announced that he had a large supply of cherry bombs and said he would give them to the protesters if they would throw them at police and soldiers during Saturday's rally at the Lincoln Memorial. His proposal was initially greeted with derisive laughter and then with outright hostility. One protester pointed out how stupidly dangerous it would be to discharge fireworks around nervous and perhaps trigger-happy soldiers. The fellow with the cherry bombs left shortly after a young woman offered a rather vulgar plan for disposing of his explosives. Later, someone suggested that the cherry bombs were probably supplied by the FBI in an effort to discredit the protest.

Saturday's rally consisted of antiwar speeches throughout the morning, as protesters assembled around the reflecting pool between the Lincoln Memorial and the Washington Monument. At about 1:00 P.M., the march to the Pentagon started. By early evening large groups of protesters were "sitting in" on the steps and parking malls of the Pentagon. Thousands of others were camped on the surrounding grounds. Sandwiches, coffee, milk, and soft drinks were being passed hand to hand throughout the crowd. This welcome food and drink seemingly appeared from nowhere and added to the relaxed and festive atmosphere.

Troops made their first serious efforts to remove the crowds from the steps of the Pentagon at about 9:00 P.M. There was shouting, shoving, kicking, and the use of nightsticks and gun butts as troops moved into the crowd sitting before them. This clamor ceased abruptly each time the television floodlights came on. At one point, protesters standing in the rear of the crowd began to throw fruit, pop cans, and other trash at the soldiers. Protesters sitting at the feet of the soldiers turned back and shouted for the barrage to cease. One particularly loud voice shouted, "If you want action, come up here and sit in the first row. Otherwise, knock it off!" This comment was cheered by protesters, and the chant "Peace now" went up. Nothing more was thrown at the soldiers. Throughout this rally, there were alterations in people's moods; diverse activities and behavior occurred; people offered definitions of appropriate conduct to one another. These features of the event are important from the standpoint of emergent-norm theory.

Ralph H. Turner and Lewis M. Killian The first edition of Ralph H. Turner and Lewis M. Killian's *Collective Behavior* was published in 1957. These authors present a view of collective behavior that departs greatly from mass hysteria theory. The *emergent norm* approach is based on the view that the impact of groups on individuals resembles *normative constraint* rather than contagious mental unity. Turner and Killian argue that total uniformity of mood and behavior within the crowd is seldom observed. Within crowds various motives for participation exist, diverse feelings are in evidence, and many types of behavior can be observed. Those gathered at a protest rally, such as the 1967 antiwar rally described above, have a variety of motives for being there in addition to protest. Some may be seeking excitement, sex, or drugs. Police and protest leaders are concerned with maintaining order while FBI agents are concerned with national security, and those selling protest buttons, with making money. Seldom will all these people express the same feelings or act in unison. Turner and Killian refer to these features of the crowd as *differential expression*.

Behavior within the crowd is guided by "norming acts," such as nonvocal gestures and verbal statements, that establish parameters or norms for conduct. In the previous example, protesters taunted and occasionally verbally abused soldiers and police, but this abuse was not extended to throwing cherry bombs or trash. Under a norm, people experience implicit and explicit social pressure to conform overtly to a particular line of behavior. Compliance with a norm is not a function of heightened suggestibility or emotional arousal. Unlike the emotion-charged settings described in mass hysteria theory, Turner and Killian argue that compliance with norms occurs in quiet settings, such as funerals, as well as settings characterized by excitement and arousal. They also state that most crowd behavior is guided by traditional norms.

Frequently, however, crowds confront novel or ambiguous situations, and hence the norms that guide behavior are emergent, new, and untried. When people join together to rescue friends and neighbors after a community disaster, for instance, an ephemeral or temporary division of labor emerges. The emergent patterns of authority and lines of communication may be quite different from those extant prior to the disaster. Heavy equipment operators, for example, may find themselves in positions of authority, giving orders to bankers and city officials. Teenagers may become rescue workers and couriers of important information, performing tasks that involve greater responsibility than usual. To the casual observer, these arrangements may seem chaotic; however, Turner and Killian argue that they are an effective, normatively guided collective response to urgent situations.

Classification of Crowd Participants For Turner and Killian, collective behavior is basically social behavior, guided by both traditional and emergent norms. Even in crowded settings where excitement is high, people retain critical ability and a sense of personal identity, and they behave in terms of personal motives. Turner and Killian use individual motives as a basis for a five-category classification of crowd participants. The classification categories reflect a decreasing level of personal identification with the events and issues that are part of any specific episode of collective behavior.

The first type of participant is the person who feels a strong personal commitment, or ego involvement, with the situation at hand. Consequently, the ego-involved participant is likely to demand or incite immediate action. In a disaster-struck community, ego involvement characterizes those whose family and property are in jeopardy. They are the first to initiate rescue efforts and may be the most active in organizing and directing rescue teams.

The second type of participant is motivated by feelings of generalized concern and is typified by outsiders who converge on disaster-struck communities to assist in rescue and cleanup operations. Their families are safe—the concerned are simply being good neighbors. The concerned participant is unlikely to take the initiative but very likely to follow the lead of others and comply with emerging norms.

The third type of participant is the insecure. People may participate in collective action because doing so offers a sense of direction and identity. Adolescents, who are casting off the identity of the child and striving to achieve adult status, find temporary security in associating with other youths at rock concerts or within religious fellowships, cults, or protest groups. In the case of disasters, young people may derive a sense of importance to the community as they carry messages, clear rubble, or heft sandbags.

Curiosity is the fourth type of individual motivation considered by Turner and Killian. Rescue and reconstruction efforts are often hindered when large numbers of people converge on the disaster scene and survey the wreckage. Protesters are often outnumbered by spectators to the confrontation. Curiosity can be easily transformed. Spectators may cheer or jeer protesters and become involved in battles between police and demonstrators. Spectators at disasters may aid in rescue efforts or, perhaps, turn to looting.

The final category of motivation is ego detachment, often characterized by an attitude of exploitation. Those who loot at disaster scenes do so because they can emotionally divorce themselves from the plight of others. Profiteers who sell fresh water and gasoline at exorbitant prices are ego detached. But ego detachment need not entail an exploitive attitude. For example, professional rescue, medical, and media workers must be able to face the threat of personal injury or confront scenes of horrendous suffering while maintaining a degree of emotional detachment in order to efficiently perform their jobs.

Individual Tendencies For Turner and Killian, people retain a clear sense of personal motivation when participating in collective behavior. Some researchers have used people's statements of their attitudes and beliefs as measures of "individual tendencies" to participate in collective behavior. These measures of individual tendencies have been examined to determine whether, for example, people expressing negative attitudes toward police are more likely than others to riot. Ascribed statuses, such as sex and ethnicity, and achieved statuses, such as level of education and occupation, have been examined. Do workers of low occupational prestige, for example, engage in wildcat strikes and protest more often than workers in higher status occupations?

In 1971 Clark McPhail reviewed the volumes of riot participation studies conducted between 1965 and 1970. McPhail pointed out that at least 215 separate individual tendency variables had been examined in efforts to account for individuals' participation in riots. These variables included "attitude statements" regarding race relations and the political process in the United States. Other variables included "socioeconomic attributes," such as occupation and level of education, and "demographic attributes," such as age, sex, and length of residence in the city where the riot occurred. We will consider McPhail's review of the riot participation studies in later chapters; here it is sufficient to note that these studies constitute one of the largest bodies of research in the collective behavior literature. Few of the riot participation studies explicitly acknowledge the emergent norm theory and the point of view that the influence of the crowd does not supersede people's personal motives for action. Still, these studies proceed on the assumption that an examination of people's motives, attitudes, frustrations, and fears is the key to understanding riot participation.

Turner and Killian's approach to collective behavior is a clear departure from the mass hysteria approach. They utilize conventional sociological views regarding the effects of social norms and individual behavioral predispositions and contend that these influences continue to operate within the crowd and in social movements.

Value-Added Theory

For Neil Smelser, collective behavior is an effort to change society, or *the uninstitutionalized restructuring of values, norms, organization of motivation, and situational facilities within society.* The values, norms, organization of motivation, and situational facilities are the *components of social action* that provide the basis of all social behavior in society. That is to say, all social behavior is based on or contains components of values, norms, motives, and knowledge. For Smelser, there are five types of collective behavior: (1) the panic, (2) the craze, (3) the hostile outburst, (4) the norm-oriented social movement, and (5) the value-oriented social movement. These phenomena occur as *collective episodes.* Collective episodes are readily identified, relatively large-scale events that cluster in time and within certain parts of the social structure. Respective examples might include the stock market crash of 1929 (a panic) and the widespread interest in and phenomenal sales of Beanie Babies in the 1990s (a craze). Hostile outbursts include the waves of killing between Hutu and Tutsi tribes of Rwanda and Zaire that have intensified since 1994. Norm-oriented social movements aim at enacting specific reforms in society, such as local and national movements to regulate Internet content. Value-oriented movements seek to establish a whole new social order based on alternate values. For example, during the 1980s and 1990s Islamic fundamentalist groups sought to overthrow secular governments throughout the world and replace them with theocratic systems.

Components of Social Action The components of social action to which Smelser referred are the elemental forces other than individual personalities that order, regulate, and direct behavior within a society. The components of social action are concepts fundamental to the structure-functionalist theory in sociology, originally formulated by Talcott Parsons (1951).

The most general component of social action within a society is the set of *social values,* or shared beliefs identifying the goals toward which the members of the society should strive. Sociologists often identify personal achievement, activity and hard work, affluence, efficiency and usefulness, progress, democracy, free enterprise, and belief in God as the dominant social values in the United States. Almost everything people do in the United States is judged in relation to these values. In many societies, those who wander the streets without jobs or money are ignored by authorities, but in the United States it is generally viewed as fitting and proper that such people be arrested for vagrancy. The polluters of most industrial nations, including the United States, can quite convincingly justify their refusal to reduce pollution in terms of efficiency and cost-effectiveness. Prayer in schools is held dearly in the hearts of many people in America. Many Christian groups work to bring frequent and open prayer back into the public schools. Since 1962, when the United States Supreme Court removed prayer, these groups have envisioned the return of prayer as a way of countering many other social ills, including the reduction of violence and drug use in the schools.

Societal norms are the second component of social action and are the explicit and implicit rules that govern the pursuit of values. Much of civil and criminal law in the United States directly and indirectly regulates the manner in which the value of personal achievement is pursued. Parents devote a great deal of time, effort, tears, and money to keep their children actively involved in school, sports, and the arts. Much conflict between generations is the result of young people subscribing to norms of personal achievement that differ widely from those of their parents.

The third component of social action is *organization of motivation,* which refers to the specific, implicit, and explicit requirements accompanying statuses, roles, groups, and organizations that constitute the social structure of a society. Much of what people do in society depends on the socially derived expectations for the ascribed statuses of men and women. In particular, societies set forth rather clear expectations of what work shall rightfully be carried out by men and what work shall rightfully be carried out by women. Social action within families is directed in large part by the expectations accompanying the roles of spouse, parent, and child. Finally, much social action is directed toward and judged in terms of fulfilling the demands accompanying group membership—e.g., being a good Shriner—and occupational role—e.g., being a good IBM executive.

The final and most immediate component of social action is the situational facilities—tools, skills, and knowledge of the environment—that people have at their disposal. Occupants of statuses and roles, and members of groups and organizations, have different amounts of physical resources and knowledge that determine how easily and adequately they can meet the requirements of these positions. Some people have little difficulty in meeting parental role requirements because they have great situational facilities at their disposal: healthy children, adequate income, and relatively large amounts of unencumbered time to devote to children. Parents of physically or emotionally disabled children, parents with inadequate income, parents whose careers involve long absences from the home, parents with limited or inaccurate knowledge of child development, and many single parents have fewer situational facilities with which to meet parental role requirements. Consequently, they have greater difficulty with, and derive less satisfaction from, their parental roles.

Restructuring the Social Action Components Institutionalized means are used in all societies to restructure the components of social action. Many groups interested in promoting public health, such as the American Lung Association, create images and social values that would discourage smoking among teenagers and the general population. Institutionalized means are used to change organization of motivation, or social structure. Governments use taxes, tax credits, and transfer payments to promote or discourage the growth of groups and organizations. The Equal Rights Amendment (ERA) was an effort to restructure the legal and social expectations that accompany the status of women. Finally, situational facilities can be altered through institutionalized means. Some employers have made efforts to integrate the situational facilities of work with those of their employees' families. This includes such innovations as variable or "flex-time" work schedules, paternity leaves, child daycare programs, and family vacation programs. On a larger scale, the minimum wage, free public education, public libraries, and welfare programs are designed to expand the situational facilities available in society.

The components of social action can also be restructured through uninstitutionalized means. That is, the restructuring occurs apart from, and at times counter to, traditional channels of authority and decision making, communication, and sources of political and economic power.

Different collective episodes involve different components of social action. In panics and crazes, people's immediate concern is with situational facilities. In a panic, people are concerned with getting to and through the nearest exit or selling their stock before prices hit rock bottom. In the case of a craze people are concerned with acquiring the current hot consumer item or exploiting the rapidly rising price of a particular stock. Panics and the collapse of crazes are often preludes to hostile outbursts. Concern shifts to identifying and punishing the individuals, groups, and organizations responsible for the damage done earlier. Angry crowds may demand removal of public officials. Minority groups become scapegoats and often are attacked and sometimes expelled from the country. In the case of rebellions and revolutions, hostile outbursts may involve attempts to overthrow or totally restructure the government. In these cases, hostile outbursts may become part of larger-scale norm- and value-oriented social movements, as people begin to question the norms that govern relationships between groups in society and the values these norms reflect.

In summary, Smelser employs the functionalist model of social action to explain collective behavior. Social behavior within society is determined by the components of social action: social values, societal norms, organization of motivation, and situational facilities. In society, institutionalized means exist for altering the components for social action. Even so, there are times when people use uninstitutionalized means to alter the components of social action. This is collective behavior: collective episodes of uninstitutionalized efforts to alter the values, norms, organizations, groups, statuses, roles and distribution of resources in the society. We now turn to Smelser's value-added explanation of why people depart from institutionalized means of change and take up uninstitutionalized means.

COLLECTIVE BEHAVIOR HAS MANY CAUSES

Collective behavior episodes such as the financial panic that accompanied the stock market crash of 1929 are often described as "spontaneous," which usually indicates that the collective behavior event was unexpected by authorities, spectators, and even the participants themselves. Often, such episodes seem to be triggered by an everyday, routine happening, such as a normal fluctuation in trading volume and stock prices. Many urban civil disorders, for example, are described as having been sparked by a routine arrest. The most exact meaning of the term *spontaneous* is occurring without external cause. Applying this definition to collective behavior is somewhat problematic. It usually is taken to mean that spontaneous collective behavior is caused solely by the *internal mental states* of participants: their individual attitudes, perceptions, and fears.

Closer examination of collective behavior events, however, invariably suggests causes other than the mental states of participants. For instance, many urban civil disorders started on weekends and during the late afternoon and evening, when people were relatively free from the competing demands of school and work. Arrests that precipitated initial phases of disorder were not as routine as often assumed. These arrests involved breakdowns in police communication procedure, lengthy delays in removing arrested persons from the scene, and unusually large numbers of spectators (See chapters 12–13).

All of this suggests that collective behavior episodes, even seemingly spontaneous ones, can be viewed as the result of a *combination of causal factors*. No single factor by itself is sufficient to produce the event in question. However, several factors occurring together and in combination can produce a collective behavior episode. Neil J. Smelser's *Theory of Collective Behavior* (1962) presents a "several-factors-occurring-together" approach—what Smelser refers to as a *value-added* explanation of collective behavior.

An Example of the Value-Added Explanation

In *Theory of Collective Behavior*, Smelser used the stock market crash of 1929 as an example of a collective episode of panic. While the stock market could have taken several months to gradually adjust to worsening economic conditions, instead it "crashed," losing over a third of its value in just a few days. His analysis of the crash also illustrates the working of the value-added process and how several factors worked together to produce the crash.

On Thursday, October 24, 1929, trading on the New York Stock Exchange began what promised to be another glorious day of profit making. During the previous five years, the trend in the market had been almost invariably upward. For those Americans with money to invest, "playing the market" had become an almost irresistible opportunity to amplify one's wealth. Stock dividends were of secondary concern—the rate of increase in the selling value of stock was the major attraction. What one bought today could be sold at a handsome profit three weeks from now. Blue-chip stocks, as well as newly formed and imaginatively financed issues in "investment trusts," were traded and retraded at ever increasing values. For the past few years, the market had perked along, trading 2 to 5 million shares a day, with only occasional and brief pauses in the upward trend in prices.

Thursday was to be different. Trading began heavily, and by 10:00 A.M. the ticker had dropped behind, unable to record the fast pace of trading. As the ticker fell behind, prices began to sag. More and more people began to sell, uncertain as to what was happening to prices other than that they were falling. There was also another concern—stop-loss orders. For their own protection, most brokers had standing orders calling for the sale of stock whenever a specified price was reached. As prices fell, they would cross increasing numbers of stop-loss orders, automatically dumping even more securities on the falling market. By 11:00 A.M. people were panic selling, and the floor of the Exchange resembled bedlam. The sound of this distress could be heard on the streets outside the Exchange; a crowd gathered, and police were sent out to keep order. The stock market crash of 1929 was underway. At the end of the day, stock averages had dropped by twelve points. Almost 13 million shares had been traded, exceeding the previous all-time high by more than 5 million.

Friday and Saturday the stock market was indecisive. In Sunday's papers and sermons, many stock analysts, politicians, and clergy expressed the view that the worst was over. In fact, it had just begun. On Monday, more than nine million shares were traded, and stock averages dropped forty-nine points. Tuesday, the ticker ran almost three hours behind as nearly seventeen million shares were traded, and averages fell forty-three points. In less than a week, the stock market panic of 1929 had erased almost two years of gain. Investment trust stocks that survived had lost about two-thirds their value of a week earlier. Even blue chips such as Westinghouse were selling at half their previous value. Stocks would continue to slide lower for another three years and would not recover their early 1929 values for another decade. The most rapid and dramatic adjustments, however, already had occurred.

Contrasting the crash of 1929 with more recent stock market dynamics is informative. On the worst day of the crash the market dropped forty-nine points on a volume of nine million shares. In October of 1987 and again in October of 1997, the Dow Jones Industrials took 500-point plunges on volumes of 300 to 600 million shares. Unlike the 1929 crash, the losses sustained in the 1987 and 1997 crashes were regained within a few months. Almost seventy years after the 1929 crash, on March 29, 1999, the Dow Jones Industrials surged nearly 200 points and closed above 10,000 for the first time in history.

Structural Conduciveness The market-driven economy and U.S. ideas of the profit motive and free enterprise are not found in all societies. Throughout history, societies have used barter systems instead of monetary systems, exchanging chickens for pigs, bananas for potatoes, and horses for wives. Rates of exchange, such as ten chickens for one pig, were not established so much by immediate supply and demand as by centuries of tradition or religious practice. For the Catholic Church of the Middle Ages, charging interest on borrowed goods or money was viewed as the sin of usury, an offense against God's law. In some societies, trading could only be carried out on certain days or times of the year, only between certain people within the society, and only after the proper ceremonial rites had been observed. Within such societies, precipitous and large-scale transfer of property from one group to another was rare. Likewise the total collapse of the worth of some barter item was unlikely. In terms of the value-added theory, the conditions of structural conduciveness in small, traditional barter economies do not permit, or clearly work against, financial panic.

In contrast, by 1929 conditions of structural conduciveness on the floor of the New York Stock Exchange made large-scale transfers of wealth from one person or group to another commonplace. The stock ticker, in use for nearly thirty years, conveyed moment-by-moment results of stock transactions to branch exchanges and corporate boardrooms across the country. Hundreds of large investors had standing orders to sell all their stock if prices dipped below a certain level. Individually, these stop-loss orders offered some protection to the investor. Taken collectively, these orders would assure that as stock prices fell, more and more stocks would be placed on the market, further depressing prices.

Structural Strain A variety of conditions within society can produce strain, which, according to value-added theory, is the driving force behind all collective episodes. The uninstitutionalized activity of the collective episode is directed toward reducing structural strain and restoring equilibrium within the social system. In the case of the stock market crash of 1929, a number of sources of structural strain increased the likelihood of a massive and potentially violent reorganization of the stock market.

Societal values are quite enduring, and we can assume that personal achievement and hard work were societal values, even in 1929. These values could have been a source of strain in the few years preceding the crash. The sense of a prudent and closely watched investment had given way to a feeling of easily acquired riches. The speculative profit of the last months prior to the stock market crash was not in keeping with the ideals of personal achievement and hard work. People with money to invest were, in a sense, taking advantage of a system that temporarily offered the chance for profit without the traditional responsibilities of ownership. This clearly was the case for those entering the market through the investment trusts, who indirectly owned stock in actual businesses. This era has often been described as a period of needless speculation, although most investors must have occasionally reflected on the old axioms that "what goes up must come down" and "all good things must come to an end."

The ease with which they made money in the stock market may have caused occasional twinges of guilt and anxiety among people who normally placed a high value on personal achievement and hard work. But the most important source of structural strain lay in the economic conditions this speculation produced. Briefly stated, speculation pushed the market value of stock far above what was reasonable, given the current corporate earnings and the general business climate.

In the final three months before the crash, there had been a broad downturn in most economic indicators. Steel production had declined by about 10 percent. Most factory output had declined, inventories were growing, and workers were being laid off across the country. Home building, which had been declining all year, went into a dramatic June-September slump. Normally, the stock market makes fairly rapid downward adjustments to such developments, but this was not the case in the final months before the crash, as the stock market registered almost daily gains of at least five points. It was inevitable that business conditions would force an adjustment in stock prices.

Generalized Belief In the fall of 1929, economic conditions clearly indicated that a large-scale adjustment in stock prices was in the offing. Nothing, however, indicated that the adjustment would take the form of a rapid and almost total collapse of the market. For such a violent reaction, a third value-added component was necessary—a generalized *hysterical* belief. Smelser identifies the generalized hysterical belief as a belief that assigns the power to destroy to ambiguous elements in the environment. This belief restricts people's attention to only one concern—escape. In this case, people's financial assets were endangered, not their physical safety.

Many first-time investors entered the market in the two years preceding the crash. To these people, investment in the market was just a simple matter of putting money into the market and watching it grow. When the real threat of total financial ruin presented itself on Thursday, October 24, the entire workings of the stock market suddenly represented an "ambiguous situation" to the novices. Escape, in the form of immediately dumping one's investments, seemed the only means of coping with the situation.

For more seasoned investors, there were other fears and ambiguities. They knew that stock prices were out of line with current business conditions and that a downward adjustment was overdue, but the investment trusts were an unknown entity. Their stock had led the upward trend in the market in the past months. It was feared they might also lead the downward trend. Finally, they knew that the stop-loss orders could trigger a massive price slide.

After Thursday's drop in stock prices, many declared that the worst was over. Even the analysts of *The New York Times*, who had predicted disaster for more than a year, felt that the market had finally reached a realistic plateau. However, there were many rumors that major investors would soon be selling out. Perhaps such conflicting information only added to the novices' fear that they really knew little about the workings of the market. In any event, the many assurances of the weekend were insufficient to overcome the widespread concern of investors. Thursday had ruined some investors and reduced the wealth of many others by half. The fears of this latter group may have led to the initial wave of heavy selling on Monday's market.

Mobilization for Action On Thursday, October 24, three of the five value-added determinants were in place; the next was mobilization for action. In the case of panic, this is the event (or events) that poses an immediate threat and gives shape to generalized anxieties. The most immediate factor in the mobilization for action was the stock ticker failing to keep pace with transactions. This had happened several times before, but in those instances the ticker had fallen behind in a rising market. Then, the only anxiety generated was that of waiting to find out how much richer one had become. Only once before, about eight months earlier, had the ticker fallen behind in a sagging market. It, too, had been a terrible day.

It is nerve-wracking to know that your stocks are failing but not by how much: you think that when the ticker catches up with transactions, your stock will be worthless. Smelser draws an analogy between this situation and trying to get to a partially blocked exit in a burning theater. If you move in an orderly fashion with the other patrons, the exit may be blocked before you reach it; if you dash ahead, you may escape. The rush to sell one's stock is the financial equivalent of dashing for the exit. In both situations, the mad rush adds to the confusion and may ultimately lead to large-scale tragedy. During the three worst days of the stock market crash, the ticker fell behind within forty-five minutes of the opening of trading, and final prices were not available for at least two hours after the close of trading. During those awful hours, people were literally "selling blind."

The "models" available for action are another factor in mobilization for action during panic. Many accounts of those three days mention the behavior of influential and well-known bankers, brokers, and members of the stock exchange while they were on the trading floor. These prominent and influential people appeared nervous and worried. Their sell orders were given in a conspicuous manner. A flurry of rumors occurred each time these people left the trading floor to attend hastily called conferences. The apparent fear and indecision of major figures in the financial community prompted others to sell stock.

Action of Social Control The final value-added determinant is action of social control, which in this case refers to the actions of leaders and authorities to prevent or control panic. This can be done by *modifying other value-added determinants.* That is, leaders may provide information that can counter generalized beliefs and take actions that can alter structural conduciveness, reduce structural strain, or prevent mobilization. Throughout his discussion of action of social control, Smelser points out that a failure to act usually contributes to the scope and severity of the collective episode. The inaction of leaders has been frequently noted as an aggravating factor in the stock market crash. On Friday, a group of bankers asked President Hoover to urge Americans to buy up the new "bargains" the market had just created, but Hoover did not heed this plea.

During the weekend, the newspapers were full of advertisements urging calm and declaring that the worst was over. On the floor of the Exchange, however, actions had spoken louder than words. On Thursday at half past one, Richard Whitney, the acting president of the Exchange and floor trader for National City Bank, made large and conspicuous purchases of industrial stocks. The market immediately began a recovery that held Thursday's losses to only twelve points. Many accounts suggest that this purchase was calculated to give confidence to investors, but in any event, nothing of this sort was attempted on Monday and Tuesday. The market was left to fend for itself.

Finally, directors of the Exchange considered the idea of closing or shortening the hours of the Exchange to allow some sense of orderliness to develop. It has also been suggested that events on Wall Street began to be affected by loss of sleep. Weary traders had begun to confuse, forget, and lose their clients' sell-orders. The first short day of trading did not come until Thursday. Wednesday's market had stabilized, however, and the "Crash of '29'" was over.

Economic historians generally agree that by fall of 1929, the stage was set for a large adjustment in stock prices. There is much less agreement regarding why the adjustment was so damaging. Smelser's value-added analysis of collective behavior offers an explanation of why the adjustment took the form of a sudden, widespread, and financially disastrous selling of stock.

The elements of Smelser's model—the components of social action, the value-added determinants, and the five types of collective episodes—are presented in Figure 2.1. The relationships among these elements are also illustrated. In later chapters, we will consider Smelser's value-added explanation of civil disorders and social movements.

FIGURE 2.1: Smelser's Value-Added Model of Collective Behavior

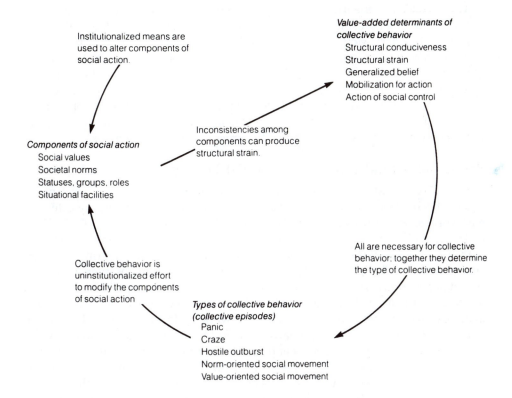

The mass hysteria, emergent-norm and value-added theories of collective behavior attempt to distinguish collective behavior from the "normal" social behavior that transpires within families, organizations, communities, and the political sphere. These theories seek to identify the emotional disturbances, ambiguous social stimuli, or social stresses that cause people to depart from normal behavior and to engage in "collective behavior." These theories were developed out of a long-term fascination with the crowd and crowd-related events but not necessarily out of careful, detailed, and systematic study of these phenomena.

PERSPECTIVES ON COLLECTIVE ACTION

Collective action theories represent a substantial departure for the collective behavior tradition. Theories of collective action make no sharp and fundamental distinction between collective action and other forms of social behavior. The collective action theory was developed in the course of observing demonstrations and marches (McPhail, 1991) and making detailed historical case studies of social movements and protest cycles such as the U.S. Civil Rights Movement (McAdam, 1982). As such, collective action theories are more empirically grounded than theories of collective behavior. As McPhail stated in *The Myth of the Madding Crowd*, "It is misguided to debate the pros and cons of competing explanations before the phenomena to be explained have first been examined, specified, and described" (1991:xxiii).

Three collective theories will be presented below. First, there is the social behavioral interactionist (SBI) theory that has been developed and articulated, in large part, by Clark McPhail. The SBI theory offers an explanation of the formation and dispersal of gatherings and the identification and explanation of frequently observed patterns of behavior within gatherings. The resource mobilization theory of McCarthy and Zald and the political process theory of McAdam, Gamson, and Lipsky will also be presented. These theories offer us an explanation of the origins of social movements and social movement organizations. These theories also focus on the dynamics of protest campaigns.

Social Behavioral Interactionist (SBI) Theory

In 1968, Clark McPhail took a team of six first-semester graduate students to observe the behavior of passengers at airline ticket counters and boarding gates in a medium-size air terminal. Nearly thirty years later, on October 4, 1997, McPhail took a team of over sixty trained observers to the very large Stand In the Gap rally of the Promise Keepers on the National Mall in Washington, DC. During the intervening years, McPhail, his colleagues and many other teams of observers used pencil and paper, film, and videotape to record people's activities at political, sport, and religious events, as well as in crowds found in everyday locations such as shopping malls and workplaces. The progress of this work is documented by McPhail in numerous papers and is also summarized in *The Myth of the Madding Crowd* (1991).

Those studying political protest and social movements were the first to suggest that collective action was purposive. Tilly (1978), for example, noted that people participating in protest actions and social movements set goals for themselves, even though some of these goals may appear to be trivial, contradictory, or unrealistic to others. These writers were also the first to use the concept of "collective action" to refer to social movements and protest campaigns.

As he accumulated information, McPhail concluded that crowds are not antisocial as earlier theories of collective behavior claimed. In fact, crowds are seldom disorderly, let alone the source of violence against persons or property. Breaking away from these earlier theoretical views, McPhail began to use the term "gathering" rather than "crowd" to refer to a collection of two or more persons in a common location.

In the course of his work, McPhail also concluded that the evidence clearly indicates that people's behavior in gatherings is purposive and consists of sequences of contextual, goal-oriented actions. These sequences can be simple and of short duration, such as a ripple of applause at a high school basketball game, or intricate and sustained, such as congregational singing during a religious service. Following the lead of Tilly, McAdam, and others, McPhail (McPhail and Tucker, 1990; McPhail, 1996) extended the term collective action to refer to people acting together in gatherings. Collective action, whether cheering a touchdown or planning a political protest, encompasses a wide range of purposive activities.

Explaining Collective Action In order to remain consistent with the view that collective action is purposive, researchers such as Berk (1974) applied familiar economic-choice models such as "game theory" and "the mini-max principle" of human behavior to the analysis of political protest. These economic-choice models suggest that people make collective action choices that lead to "winning" (game theory) or which minimize costs and maximize gains (mini-max principle). Applied to collective action, economic-choice models frame theory and research in terms of explaining and studying how decisions are made in the crowd or how protest groups select protest strategies.

In *The Myth of the Madding Crowd*, McPhail argued that economic-choice or rational calculus models of behavior, while very popular during most of the twentieth century, do not provide adequate explanations for collective action. That is, mini-max instructions only tell people *why* they should engage in one behavior rather than another. While this is certainly important, people do not accomplish what they do only by making choices based on anticipated rewards and costs. Game or mini-max choices do not tell people how to put a selected solution or plan of action into operation. Finally, economic-choice theories cannot account for the moment-by-moment, sometimes dramatic, sometimes mundane, and sometimes unanticipated variation in purposive individual and collective action that is readily observed in gatherings.

Interestingly, McPhail has adapted a variant of *control systems theory* to account for purposive and variable individual and collective action. Control systems call to mind devices such as home thermostats, cruise controls on automobiles, industrial robots, and computer guidance systems for rockets. McPhail does not suggest that our brains are computers or that human beings are robots. However, control systems theory, the theory of how things such as these operate, includes concepts such as *input function, comparator* (or *comparison*) *function*, and *output function* that can be adapted to the analysis and explanation of human action systems. People receive sensory *input* from others as they attend to their surroundings. McPhail notes that people *compare* their present actions and the actions of others with previous actions and outcomes. On the basis of such comparisons, they adjust their behavioral *outputs*. For instance, patrons in a busy supper club may smell smoke and hear announcements to leave the building. Immediately, people note their own location in the dining area with respect to the location and the movements of others toward exits. People then make frequent adjustments to their movements as they leave the building. People attempt to locate and leave with the family or friends that accompanied them. People try to accommodate their movements to the prevailing flow of movement and to avoid hard physical contact with other people and objects. Perception control systems can be disrupted—dense smoke, the failure of emergency lighting systems, and high levels of background noise can degrade sensory input and make it difficult to compare one's own actions with those of others. The movement of others and the number and density of others present make it impossible to move independently.

◆*Perception Control Theory* Control systems theory was first applied to human action in the 1970s by William T. Powers, a systems theorist. He used the term *perception control theory* to refer to his application of control systems theory to human behavior (Powers, 1973).

Soon after he became acquainted with Powers's work, McPhail concluded that it was a viable explanation that explicitly connects purposive human beings' goals, their experiences or perceptions, and their actions. It is a very powerful theory in both the scope of its application and the empirical evidence for its application to purposive individual action and collective action (McPhail, 1994, 1991; McPhail and Tucker, 1990; McPhail, Powers and Tucker, 1992; Schweingruber, 1995; Tucker, Schweingruber and McPhail, 1999).

Perception control theory is based on the social behavioral interactionist view first stated by George Herbert Mead (1938) that people in a given language community possess comparable repertoires of cues, gestures, words and other significant symbols which, because they are comparable, constitute a vocabulary of shared meaning. It is this underlying presence of significant symbols and shared meaning that provides the basis of social behavior in gatherings and all other occasions. It is from the shared repertoire that instructions for behavior are drawn. Some instructions for behavior are cues to conduct that identify social objects with respect to which people can orient and adjust their behavior. Such instructions name, locate and denote whether objects are good, bad, dangerous, and so on. These instructions may be verbal statements such as "The picket signs are in the blue van," or gestures such as smiles, salutes, and "flipping the bird." The face of Mickey Mouse, McDonald's golden arches, the letters "IBM" and the Nike swoosh, for instance, are recognized the world over. These graphic identifiers serve as instructions that can establish and orient people with respect to social objects, individual goals and shared objectives.

Other instructions for behavior specify action with respect to social objects. Some instructions specify movement toward or away from objects and include statements like "Let's go to the U2 concert next week," or the pointing and directing gestures used by police as they control traffic at the scene of an accident. These instructions also tell people when activities are to begin, at what rate they are to be carried out, and when they are to end. This category of instructions includes statements like "Let's run up to the stage when they play 'Sunday Bloody Sunday,'" written schedules that tell people when religious services begin or trains depart, and hurry-up or slow-down gestures. Instructions for behavior precede collective responses by a portion of people in the gathering, be it the momentary bowing of heads or an extended march to petition city officials.

From the standpoint of perception control theory, people must monitor and interpret one another's behavior in order for collective action to occur—that is, people can, through sight, sound and touch, monitor the behavior of others and adjust their own behavior accordingly. Perception control theory assumes that individuals adjust their own behavior on the basis of its perceived discrepancy in direction, speed, tempo, and substantive content from the activity of others. It is by way of perceiving glances, movements, gestures, or hearing instructions, cheers and chants that we come to identify objectives within gatherings, and even come to make inferences about the intentions of others with respect to these objectives. It is by way of observing the direction, speed, and tempo of the movement of others that we can adjust our own behavior with respect to a particular objective.

In large public demonstrations the dense, spatial arrangement of people, intrusive noise, and obscuring barriers usually interfere with monitoring. It is then necessary to have large numbers of demonstration marshals, often equipped with bullhorns, cellular phones, and two-way radios to monitor and direct marches, prayers, chants and other organized activities involving all or a portion of the gathering. Similarly, emergency evacuations of nightclubs and hotels may be greatly hindered by obtrusive noise and dense smoke. Only a portion of people in the gathering can initiate movement toward the exits; orderly movement, if initiated, will break down as sensory conditions deteriorate.

McPhail (1991; 1994) identifies three sources of perception control input: independent instruction, interdependent instruction, and organizational instruction. Elementary collective action such as chants and applause, or collective action occurring among small numbers of people, can occur by way of independent instructions. Independent instructions are "self-instructions" that come from within a person's repertoire of behaviors. People confronted with similar circumstances generate similar independent instructions. Independent instruction can occur with a minimum of social interaction, such as a nod of the head, a shrug, or a glance.

More complex forms of collective action by larger numbers of people require more extensive, interdependent instruction. When a group of people are confronted with the mutual problem of what to do or where to begin, they interact and improvise solutions that draw upon their social repertoires. This interdependent instruction can include proposals, counterproposals, and compromises that yield a collective action sequence that no one individual might have independently considered, proposed, or pursued.

The most complex forms of collective action require advance interaction of some of the participants to organize instructions and plans for the remaining participants. This organizational instruction includes planning, rehearsing, mobilizing, cueing and monitoring. For instance, leaders of participating contingents meet in advance of large demonstrations to formulate plans for such things as points of assembly, routes for feeder marches and the main march, and times at which the demonstration is to begin and end. Later, organizers meet with some of the participants to train and rehearse demonstration marshals. Finally, at the demonstration, organizers cue marshals and participants to implement the complex sequences of collective action that have been formulated in advance.

Collective action exists across a continuum ranging from very simple and brief chants, cheers, and applause within gatherings to waves and cycles of demonstrations and protests that may last for years. Across this broad continuum, the sources of objectives and instructions may vary, from two or more individuals independently confronting a similar situation, to people interacting to improvise the resolution of a shared problem, to people carrying out the plans formulated by their group or organization.

These sources of instruction may be co-present in large gatherings. The more complex the behavior to be accomplished, the more social interaction and social organization are needed to establish a common objective and provide the related instructions for who is to do what, with whom, when, where and how. (For a more detailed treatment of perception control theory, see the Appendix.)

Collective Action Defined As previously noted, McPhail defines collective action as the behavior of two or more people. This sets collective action apart from that of the isolated individual and calls our attention to the fact that most human behavior is carried out in the presence of others. The behavior of two or more people has incredible variety, but some of the behaviors most often observed in gatherings are *locomotion*, such as walking, running, or dancing; *orientation*, such as clustering and spectating; *vocalization* and *verbalization*, such as cheering, booing, singing, or reciting prayers. Other frequently observed behaviors are *gesticulation*, such as saluting, waving the arms above the head, or raising a fist; and *manipulation*, such as applauding, synchro-clapping, or throwing objects. While humans are constantly active, collective action exists when behaviors such as those identified are judged as common or convergent in terms of direction, velocity, tempo, and substantive content. In large gatherings it is rare that *all* members act together; if they do, it is in the form of relatively simple activities such as cheering or applause, and unanimous activity is of short duration.

Gatherings The gathering together of people is a fundamental feature of social behavior. Many collective action events are preceded by and involve gatherings. For example, Wednesday, August 11, 1965, was a hot and humid day in Los Angeles. In the Watts section of the city hundreds of people were sitting on their front porches, and children were playing on the sidewalks and in the street. A few people noticed a police car, with flashing lights, parked in the street. People began to walk toward the police cruiser and saw that two officers were in the process of arresting a young man for a traffic violation. The arrest entailed some shouting and shoving. Coincidentally, the young man's mother arrived on the scene and became quite upset.

As more and more people stood around the arrest scene, this gathering became increasingly conspicuous. Additional police cruisers and motorcycles began to arrive at the scene, with lights flashing and sirens on. This event could now be seen and heard for several blocks up and down the street, and people began to converge from even greater distances. Because of the large number of civilians and the snarl of police vehicles, police were no longer able to complete the arrest and leave the scene in an orderly manner. Before police made their way out of the congested area, citizens were injured and police vehicles damaged. Crowd activity continued through the Watts area until midnight. Late Friday afternoon, arsonists set several fires that again provided gathering points for crowds; and one of the largest racial disorders in our nation's history, the Watts riot of 1965, was underway.

Like collective action, routine social events are preceded by the gathering together of people. It is interesting to watch from one's office window as students trudge along sidewalks and between university buildings as morning classes begin. One can see faculty members hastily maneuvering their cars into parking spaces. Some faculty members arrive in the departmental office breathlessly clutching their lecture notes. They quickly check their mailboxes, exchange greetings, grab a quick cup of coffee, and then rush off to their classrooms. Students arrive in various stages of alertness, and typically, just after the lecture begins, a few stragglers wade over the other students to unoccupied seats. Another day of classes has begun!

McPhail (1989; 1991) classifies gatherings according to their behavioral composition. The most inclusive category is that of *prosaic gatherings*, where the behavioral composition is relatively simple, including shoppers at malls, people waiting in lines for rides at amusement parks, gatherings at store openings, and spectators at fires and arrests. In these commonplace gatherings, the main activity is hanging out, waiting, browsing, and spectating. Less common are *demonstration gatherings*, where the modal behaviors are the protest or promotion of some principle, person, collectivity, or condition—for example, political demonstrations, sports rallies, and worship services. Collective action in demonstrations includes chanting, singing, marching and picketing in addition to those behaviors found in prosaic gatherings. Even less common but perhaps the most elaborate are state *ceremonial gatherings*, such as inaugurations, royal weddings and state funerals, where the modal behaviors celebrate or mourn status passages. In addition to behaviors found in prosaic and demonstration gatherings, state ceremonies often include choreographed marching and manipulation of rifles and flags, oaths of allegiance, and arranged seating for spectators and participants.

McPhail also classifies gatherings according to their interpersonal composition. Many prosaic gatherings are what McPhail identifies as "periodic assemblages," or recurrent gatherings that contain a majority of the same participants each time they recur. Periodic assemblages often routinely recur at the same location, on a fixed schedule. Periodic assemblages include work groups, classes, and weekly or nightly gatherings at local churches and taverns.

Large gatherings are usually "nonperiodic assemblages," in which the majority of people in them have not assembled before and are not likely to assemble again. Nonperiodic assemblages include spectators at accidents and fires; shoppers in large, urban malls; and participants and spectators in large demonstrations and state ceremonial gatherings.

The Assembling Process Gatherings are intermittent events. Assembling processes, through which gatherings occur, are a form of convergent behavior. During the assembling process, people move to a common location. People may initially be dispersed over small or large areas. Some assembling movements may be entirely on foot, but assembling is often supplemented with the use of vehicles.

Using a questionnaire methodology, McPhail and Miller (1973) studied a medium-range assembling process that resulted in a late evening airport gathering of about four thousand students and townspeople prior to the arrival of a victorious basketball team. This assembling process began shortly after the radio broadcast of the game (about 8:30 P.M.) and culminated about midnight, when the team arrived. The distance from the center of campus to the airport was about ten miles. A few arrests were made, and newspapers carried descriptions of littering, theft, and minor vandalism at the airport. Clark McPhail and Jane Bailey (1979; Bailey and McPhail, 1979) replicated this study with a gathering of about three hundred students and townspeople at the scene of an apartment-house fire. Assembling began about 9:00 P.M. and occurred over a ten-block area.

Finally, this author has studied periodic assembling—the daily movements of students to an 8:00 A.M., first-period class taught by one of my colleagues. Using a questionnaire administered each day of class for three weeks, I obtained the names of people each student encountered prior to class and a description of the activities in which they engaged. Students who missed class filled out a similar questionnaire, detailing whom they were with and what they were doing in lieu of attending class.

The SBI Explanation of Assembling

Social behavioral interactionist (SBI) theory begins with the fundamental point that collective action is purposive activity. Much of McPhail's work during the past thirty years has been devoted to identifying and describing the forms of collective action that occur most frequently in gatherings. In *The Myth of the Madding Crowd* (1991), McPhail uses perception control theory to explain the moment-by-moment, sometimes dramatic, sometimes mundane variation in purposive individual and collective action in gatherings.

Studies of the assembling process such as those outlined above suggest that the most essential event in the production and completion of such processes is that people receive equivalent assembling instructions that establish a location and time for an event and specify movement to that location. The sights and sounds accompanying many events are sufficient to establish short-range assembling processes among people who are close enough to see, hear, and walk to the location of the event. Flashing lights, sirens, use of loudspeakers, and formations of uniformed police are among the many cues to establish that "something is happening," thereby creating a focal point for movement. The convergent gaze of onlookers provides cues to the direction of the event. Convergent locomotion, such as walking, running, or marching, provides cues to the direction and rate of movement toward the event. The size of the assembly itself has an effect on the assembling process; the larger the gathering, the more visible and noisy it is.

For medium-range assembling, word-of-mouth assembling instructions are important. These instructions can establish event locations outside people's immediate surroundings and at future times and dates; for example, "Let's go to the circus tonight!" Medium-range assembling entails an amount of lead-time between the receipt of first assembling instructions and the pending gathering. It is therefore possible that people who have previously engaged in activities relevant to the gathering can be targeted for assembling instructions by others. For example, prior to the airport gathering, band members, student reporters, and perhaps alumni were sought out by others and given instructions to be at the airport when the victorious team arrived.

While the receipt of assembling instructions seems to be necessary for the initiation of assembling movements, not everyone completes movement to gatherings. Completion of assembling movements depends on access to the event location. For medium-range assembling, walking or running to the location may be impossible or take too much time. Access to bicycles, motorcycles, or autos becomes essential and may also target vehicle owners for assembling instructions. Many students reported, for example, that they first learned of the airport event when others asked them to provide rides.

Competing instructions and demands are important factors in determining who completes assembling movements. Many people who started for the airport were deflected en route. For example, some students wanted, or were asked by others, to stop at bars, restaurants, or apartments along the way. While at these places, radio and TV announcements as well as people en route provided additional assembling instructions that occasioned further movement toward the airport. Some students, however, received no further assembling instructions and did not resume their trip to the airport. Competing demands such as work schedules, deadlines for class assignments, dormitory hours, and prior appointments encumbered the free time of some students and resulted in their absence from the airport event. Students who missed first-period class almost always reported being engaged in activities with other students who did not have a first-period class. Students with free periods frequently implicated fellow students in lines of activity, such as drinking coffee and conversing in the union, which resulted in absence from class.

In summary, for people to initiate and complete assembling movements, they must receive assembling instructions and have access to transportation and an amount of relatively free or negotiable time during which movement can occur. Given this, the completion of assembling movements also entails either an absence of competing instructions or recurring assembling instructions that keep people on the path, or trajectory, toward the assembly site.

FIGURE 2.2: Assembling Process

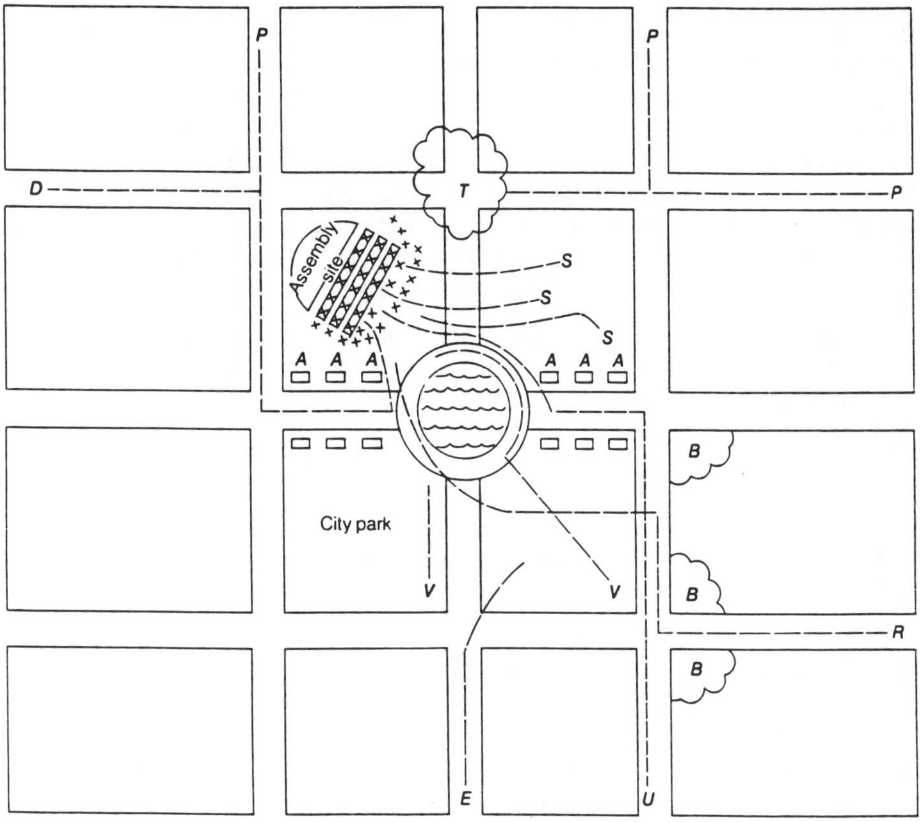

Assembling Movements

Long-range assembling

D	Antinuclear demonstrators
P	Police
U	Counterdemonstrators (unemployed construction workers from Sammy's Bar)
R	Television news crew
E	Street theater people

Short-range assembling

S	Picnickers who notice crowd move closer
A	Traditional bench sitters (elderly, winos, pigeon feeders)
B	Pedestrian shoppers who gather and watch crowd
T	Traffic jam—spectators and irate motorists
V	Hot dog vendors

Collective Action within Gatherings

At first glance it often appears that there is great uniformity of behavior within crowds. For instance, it may appear that everyone in a crowd is staring in rapt attention at a speaker or that basketball fans are all cheering wildly while looking toward the play under the basket. Further analysis of such events often reveals something quite different. For instance, photos may show several small clusters of people throughout the crowd looking at one another instead of at the speaker or the court. Film and video records of these crowds reveal an even greater diversity of behavior, and many of the "other" activities within the crowd are of short duration. Only rarely do all or nearly all of the members of the crowd do the same thing, and these activities are also of short duration.

Convergence Clusters The most elementary, and perhaps common, form of collective action is the convergence of small clusters of two to five people within gatherings. McPhail (1991; 1996) suggests that convergence clusters are usually composed of family members, friends, or acquaintances who travel together to the event or meet at the gathering. In the study of the airport crowd, for example, 83 percent of the respondents indicated that they traveled to the airport with at least one other friend or acquaintance. Most of these groups remained together at the rally and returned together (75 percent and 87 percent, respectively). Findings like this run counter to the assumption that crowds are composed primarily of elementary and transitory social relationships that contribute to crowd "instability." The influence of family members, friends, and organizational ties and demands must play a part in the conceptualization, description, and analysis of gatherings.

Convergent Orientation Another form of collective action discussed by McPhail is convergent orientation. The "natural" form of the spectator crowd in an unobstructed area is the ring, with the object of focus in the center of the ring (Milgram and Toch, 1969). Stages, risers, ropes, and other barriers may alter the form of the spectator ring to that of the arc. Among spectators, the portion of the gathering facing or spectating in the same direction can vary but is seldom complete, and, if complete, then of momentary duration. Convergent orientation in marching bands and drill team performances, however, is more complete, uniform, and of longer duration.

Collective Vocalization We are all familiar with the collective oohs, aahs, yeas, whistling, and hissing that are part of spectator behavior at athletic events. Occasionally, such vocalizations occur at religious and political events. These collective vocalizations occur less frequently in prosaic and state ceremonial gatherings. Laughter can be observed among clusters of people in nearly all gatherings, while crying is comparatively rare.

Collective Verbalization Chanting, singing, praying, reciting, and pledging are all forms of collective verbalization that regularly accompany demonstrations and ceremonial gatherings. The rowdy songs and chants of the British football (soccer) hooligan contrast sharply with the devout canticle used in church services, but both represent the same form of collective verbalization—people simultaneously engaged in the same substantive speech or song.

Collective Gesticulation Fingers, hands, arms, and other body parts can be positioned or moved to form significant symbols. Hitler's fascist salute, even

Objects like this Atlanta Braves fan's tomahawk are manufactured specifically for collective manipulation by fans at sports events. © Kevin Fleming/CORBIS.

today, brings forth images of Nazi Germany and World War II. Clenched fists, various finger extensions, and the raising and waiving of arms signify expressions of power, solidarity, resistance, defiance, preeminence, victory, and peace, to name a few. The significance of these gestures varies from time to time and from place to place. The "peace sign," for instance, made by extending and separating the index and middle fingers is, if made improperly, an obscene gesture in England. Collective gesticulation is frequently accompanied by collective vocalization and verbalization in demonstrations and state ceremonial gatherings.

Collective Manipulation The most common form of collective manipulation is applause. Less common variants of applause are synchro-clapping (applause in tempo) and finger snapping. Objects of all sorts are collectively manipulated in gatherings. Sports fans wave hankies, scarves, hats, and even objects manufactured for that specific purpose when their teams score; they ignite cigarette lighters at rock concerts as a tribute to performers. Hymnals, rosaries, and candles are used collectively in religious services. Collective manipulation can take the form of throwing objects in a common direction. British soccer hooligans throw seats, pub darts, and stones at opposing fans, while at the opera and ballet, flowers are traditionally thrown onto the stage. More complex forms of collective manipulation include card stunts, sometimes collectively carried out by thousands of people as part of the pageantry of athletic contests and political rallies. Another complex form of collective manipulation is the pushing/carrying of objects. This collective action includes rocking and overturning buses and cars during civil disorders as well as carrying banners, floats, and effigies in parades.

Collective Locomotion Human locomotion includes walking, running, skipping, standing, sitting, and dancing. Collective locomotion is an important feature of people's behavior in gatherings—for example, the up-and-down movements of people as they sit, stand, bow, and kneel in unison during religious services. Elsewhere, members of gatherings at rock concerts and athletic events can be seen jumping in unison with the music, or when teams score. The "wave" (synchronized standing and sitting), first seen at athletic events in the mid-1980s, is still a common part of our sporting events. McPhail refers to such movements as collective vertical locomotion

Collective horizontal locomotion, which includes the movements of small clusters of shoppers about a shopping mall or clusters of travelers entering and exiting waiting areas, may also take the form of queues, or waiting lines. We routinely encounter queues in fast-food restaurants, outside auditoriums, and in banks and grocery stores—that is, whenever people await service, entry, or exit. Amusement parks such as Disney World illustrate the ways in which the location of counters and guardrails, the synchronization of rides, and the use of public address systems and signs can be combined to efficiently accommodate very high volumes of queuing and "through movement."

Inconvenience and even tragedy can result when little attention is given to the regulation of high-volume queuing movement. On December 10, 1979, eleven people suffocated and others were injured in a crowd waiting outside Cincinnati's Riverfront Coliseum prior to a concert by a rock group, the Who. Some accounts noted that many in the crowd had been intoxicated and rowdy. It is also clear, however, that the relatively unregulated "first-come, best-seated" festival seating arrangements, the unusually long wait, the use of only one entrance, and the lack of security personnel contributed to the size and density of the gathering. Neither promoters nor coliseum personnel attempted to establish orderly queuing when people began to arrive more than six hours prior to the concert. As the crowd increased in size, at the rate of about twenty-five people per minute, the opportunity to reposition people into queues soon faded. In the final minutes before the coliseum doors were opened, people were packed so tightly in the waiting area that police were unable to get to those who were being injured and suffocated.

Collective horizontal locomotion within gatherings also includes surges, or the more or less simultaneous movement of adjacent persons over short distances when approaching or leaving the gathering, or toward some object or event developing within the gathering. Surges contributed to the deaths prior to the Who concert, as well as the ninety-six deaths in the Hillsborough stadium during the April, 1989 Liverpool vs. Nottingham Forest semifinal soccer match.

Finally, an elaborate form of collective horizontal locomotion is marching. At one end of the continuum are the loosely parallel movements and irregular marching speed and tempo of demonstration marches. At the other end of the marching continuum are the symmetrical alignment, address and cadence and complex routines of military drill teams during state ceremonial gatherings, or precision high school marching bands during halftime shows.

McPhail notes that the history of collective action and social movements is the history of people marching from place to place. Certainly, the organization and use of marches has been a major component of protest, rebellion, and revolution throughout history. From the Hebrews' march out of Pharaoh's Egypt to the 1995 Million Man March in Washington, people have used marches to present and

Cubs win! Cubs win! Thirty-four thousand people leave Chicago's Wrigley Field. The dispersals of crowds following sporting events are among the largest routine dispersal processes found in human social behavior. These and other large-scale dispersals usually occur without incident, but occasionally people are injured when dispersal processes break down. (Photo by Grant Bogue.)

press their claims on rights and resources. Revolutions often begin with the violent dispersal of marches. Joseph Stalin noted how the Cossack's whip and saber "rendered a great service" by infuriating marching street crowds and onlookers in pre-Revolutionary Russia. McPhail identifies the march as a fundamental form of collective action. Consideration of how marches are organized and carried out, as well as the response of authorities to them, can give us a "nuts and bolts" understanding of protest, rebellion, and revolution.

Diaspora: The Process of Dispersal McPhail uses the term *diaspora*, which derives from the Greek term meaning "scattering," to refer to the dispersal of gatherings. The dispersal of gatherings usually occurs routinely in response to instructions for dispersal or movement to different locations. Dispersal instructions and dispersal are occasioned by the termination time of events, most of which are known in advance. We know, for example, the time at which university classes end or the time at which a movie lets out. We can only approximate the termination time of athletic events such as football games, which terminate when two full halves have been played. The end of most events is an occasion for instruction specifying movement of small groups and individuals to other places, such as classrooms, dormitories, libraries, homes, bars, or restaurants. In these instances, dispersal is the result of people initiating movement to new locations and pending events.

The termination time for some gatherings, such as those at the scene of fires or beer parties, is quite indefinite or open-ended. Often one can observe these gatherings decrease in size as the starting times for other activities approach. For example, the author observed a gathering of approximately 150 people at the scene of a fire that started at 3:30 one warm and pleasant fall afternoon. About 4:45, the size of the crowd began to dwindle noticeably, even though firefighters were still battling the blaze. The next day I discussed the fire with students who had been at the scene, and they said that they had watched the fire until it was time to return to their dormitories and apartments for dinner.

The dispersal of gatherings usually occurs without incident. For example, I have delivered almost five thousand lectures to classes ranging in size from 10 to 280 students. In none of these instances did a class fail to disperse at the conclusion of my lecture, nor has anyone ever been injured leaving the classroom. Though we seldom read about such events in the newspapers, even large numbers of people can usually evacuate theaters, restaurants, stores, auditoriums, and nightclubs under emergency conditions without injuring themselves and others. McPhail suggests that when people are confronted with emergency evacuations, they provide "quite rational instructions for dispersal" in the direction of the exits known to them. This is in sharp contrast to the mass hysteria or panic image of emergency evacuations, which suggests that people are likely to become irrational and "stampede" at the first hint of danger.

Rather than accounting for the development of stampedes, perception control theory casts the problem as one of accounting for the deterioration and breakdown of initially sensible and rather orderly dispersal processes. At the outset, people leaving nightclubs and hotels may form orderly, continuously moving queues and assist one another to exits. When smoke and noise make it impossible for people to monitor one another's behavior or to see exits and barriers to movement, the movement of queues may become sporadic or deteriorate into surging. Even controlled dispersal will not allow all occupants to escape under extreme circumstances. Overcrowding, exceeding twice to three times the legal occupancy limit, may virtually insure casualties when flames spread rapidly or toxic fumes accumulate. Narrow doors, hallways, and stairwells constrict movement and increase crowd density. It is at such places of "crowd extrusion" that people are crushed. These conditions are common to almost all stampedes cited in the panic literature. Under such "death trap" circumstances, it is questionable whether the alleged panic had any substantial effect on the tragic outcome.

Beyond Gatherings

Gatherings, such as spectators at the scene of a fire or fans at a pep rally, seldom last more than a few hours. Even gatherings of hundreds of thousands of people seldom cover more area than a large city park or square. Collective action encompasses phenomena that extend well beyond these temporal and spatial boundaries.

The Event McPhail (1989; 1991) uses the term *event* to refer to a related sequence of two or more gatherings spread across a time frame of up to twenty-four hours. The 1968 March on the Pentagon, for instance, was organized by a coalition of antiwar groups and was the single largest anti-Vietnam war demonstration of the era. While there were numerous preliminary rallies in the proceeding days, the "main event" consisted of a large morning rally at the Lincoln Memorial, a midday march to the Pentagon, and a late afternoon/early evening rally at the Pentagon. The rally-march-rally sequence frequently is the form of a demonstration event. The term "event" can also be applied to the interrelated gatherings during day-long celebrations, festivals, and vigils, such as The Million Man March of 1995.

The Campaign Many collective action events and gatherings are, in a sense, a continuation or extension of the previous day's activities. The events and gatherings may occur at the same location and time and may involve many of the same or related substantive issues, organizers, participants, or spectators. McPhail uses the term "campaign" to refer to such a recurring sequence of events and gatherings within a single geographical-political community, across several days, weeks, or even months. The term is widely used to refer to the series of events and gatherings used by politicians to get elected and by evangelists to save souls. While we first associate the term "campaign" with the efforts of political and religious groups, it can also be applied to the events and gatherings that are part of extended celebrations, festivals, and vigils.

The Wave The spread or repetition of similar campaigns, events, and gatherings across different geopolitical states, communities, or locations within a time frame of weeks or months is referred to as a "wave." Within weeks of the February 1, 1960 lunch counter sit-in at Greensboro, North Carolina, sit-ins had occurred in dozens of cities and most of the Southern states. These sit-ins were organized at the local level, although participants clearly were aware that similar groups were using the same strategy elsewhere. The term "wave" can be applied to the dissemination of less serious events, such as gatherings of "streakers" during the streaking fad of March 1974. Streaking had been reported worldwide within a month. Perhaps streaking was the first "world fad." More recently, the wave of protests at hundreds of abortion clinics across the United States represent the efforts of both national, state, and local Right-to-Life organizations.

The Trend The term "trend" is often used to describe periods of economic growth and decline. Similarly, McPhail uses the term "trend" to refer to the rise and fall in the frequency of waves, campaigns, and events that occur across geopolitical states or communities during a time frame of several years. Often-noted trends include the rise and decline in the use of particular kinds of protest activity, such as the sit-in giving way to the boycott, or civil rights protest subsiding in the 1970s as the environmental movement expanded.

COLLECTIVE ACTION AND SOCIAL MOVEMENTS

In addition to prosaic, religious, sports, and political gatherings, the collective action orientation focuses on social movements and the political processes involved in protest. The resource mobilization theory focuses on social movements and the growth of social movement organizations. This theory also focuses on the interaction among social movement organizations. The political process theory (discussed in the next section) encompasses the strategic process that leads to the success or failure of social movement organizations.

Resource Mobilization Theory

Meyer Zald and Roberta Ash (1964) set forth a new approach to social movements. Their work, and that of others who followed their lead, has come to be known as the resource mobilization (RM) approach to social movements. The RM approach assumes that there will almost always be sufficient strain or breakdown in society to produce social movement activity. The central concern in the resource mobilization approach is gaining an understanding of how social movements accumulate resources, how they acquire members, and how they maintain member commitment.

The RM theory defines a *social movement* as the opinions and beliefs that indicate preferences for changing statuses, roles, and relationships among groups within a society. Opinions and beliefs may also indicate preferences for changing the distribution of rewards within the society (McCarthy and Zald, 1973). Identified in this fashion, social movements represent little more than noticeable and articulated shifts in people's views about their society.

Social Movement Organizations Shifts of view, or social movements, become consequential in society largely through social movement organizations. A *social movement organization* (SMO) is a complex and often formal organization that attempts to implement the goals of the social movement. As such, the SMO represents the outward organizational manifestation of a social movement. An example of a social movement organization would be the Student Nonviolent Coordinating Committee (SNCC), which was organized in the 1960s to implement the goal of increased civil rights for African Americans. Other examples include the militia organizations that were organized in the 1990s and currently flourish on the Internet.

The RM definitions of social movements and social movement organizations represent a clear distinction that is not made in other discussions of social movements. In Smelser's value-added model, beliefs are essential in differentiating value-oriented from norm-oriented social movements. The RM approach generally keeps the "belief" components separate from and secondary to the organizational components of social movements. According to the RM theory, the important differences and similarities among such diverse groups as civil rights organizations, paramilitary units, and environmental protest groups are their organizational goals, structures, and tactics rather than their ideologies, beliefs, and values.

Social Movement Industries A social movement may foster a number of movement organizations that pursue nearly the same goals and use similar tactics. These groups compete for a limited amount of material resources and the same pool of potential members. In some instances, these SMOs may cooperate to mount large-scale demonstrations, boycotts, or lobbying campaigns. A cluster of similarly oriented and interrelated SMOs is referred to as a *social movement industry* (SMI). One example of an SMI consisted of the Southern Christian Leadership Conference (SCLC), the Congress of Racial Equality (CORE), and the Student Nonviolent Coordinating Committee. These civil rights organizations pursued similar goals and employed similar tactics during the 1960s. Further, they competed for donations and membership among segments of the population sympathetic to the cause of civil rights. Today, we see similar SMIs in the areas of environmental concern and religious fundamentalism.

The Social Movement Sector The largest unit of analysis in the RM framework is the *social movement sector* (SMS), which refers to the large conglomeration of all social movement organizations within the society. In the United States, this includes all the diverse groups promoting causes ranging from environmentalism to religious revival. It includes groups favoring or opposing abortion, gun control, legalized marijuana, school prayer, and censoring the Internet. According to the RM theory, some societies can support larger social movement sectors than others. The size of the SMS is dependent on the amount of discretionary income and time available within the society. Societies in which people have discretionary income and free time to devote to their favorite causes will have larger social movement sectors than societies in which people have less of these resources. Also, the SMS competes with other sectors of the economy. While people may donate money to save the rain forests and spend the summer as an eco-tourist, they may also use their money and time to buy airline tickets and take a summer vacation to Disney World.

Competition among Movement Organizations It would seem that organizations within a movement industry would cooperate with one another because they seek similar goals. Also, cooperation is likely among organizations that have overlapping membership and leadership. This type of cooperation was observed among the SNCC, CORE, and SCLC civil rights groups in the 1960s.

According to the RM theory, cooperation can occur for various other reasons as well. For instance, cooperation is likely when external threats confront a number of SMOs in an industry. Government and corporate broadsides against "environmental fanatics" are likely to bring forth a united reply from environmental groups. Cooperation is also likely when it is sure to produce immediate and tangible benefits. Movement organizations are likely to cooperate to press for passage of a mutually desired piece of legislation. In some instances, organizations may actually merge to win a coalition grant. Thus, small union locals merge to obtain greater financial and organizational support from national labor organizations.

Basic Processes of Resource Mobilization Fundamental to the RM approach to social movements is the assumption that social movement organizations can be understood in terms of formal systems, or the "institutionalization and goal displacement model of organizational transformation" (Zald and Ash, 1964). What this means is that SMOs become increasingly formalized as they develop. The style of leadership, for example, comes to depend less on personal charisma and more on administrative skills. Social movement organization goals gradually shift from promoting social change to promoting the interests of the organization. In the end, fully developed SMOs function much like the formal organizations found in business and government.

As in bureaucracies, member commitment and productivity within an evolved SMO are maintained through the predictable reward structure of the organization. Some SMOs offer members salaries and room and board, while others may offer less tangible rewards, such as travel, achievement awards, and personal prestige. People take considerable time away from other concerns because the movement organization offers compensating material incentives. The RM theory suggests that member commitment is largely due to the movement organization's incentive structure; members remain committed to an SMO because they are rewarded for doing so. Rewards include *material incentives*, such as money and goods; *solidaristic incentives*, such as prestige, respect, and friendship; and *purpo-*

sive incentives, or the fulfillment of movement values. Some SMOs offer sufficient material and solidaristic incentives to maintain member commitment; in most SMOs, however, purposive incentives predominate. In practice, purposive incentives are usually manifested through quantitative achievements, such as successful demonstrations, fund-raisers, and membership drives. Thus the achievement of material rewards is essential for both member commitment and organizational success. As long as the movement can provide tangible benefits, members will remain enthusiastic. Movement organizations falter or break up when they can no longer "bring home the bacon."

Political Process Theory

People's anger and indignation do not always turn into collective protest. The political process theory tells us how people come to define and focus their discontent into socially constructed ideas that clearly articulate grievances and offer hope for successfully resolving them. The experimental work of William Gamson, Bruce Fireman, and Stephen Rytina (1982) provides a theoretical framework that identifies the ways in which people express discontent and the process through which they transform their discontent into direct collective action against authorities—how groups are able to successfully draw together and launch *protest* (see chapter 14).

Michael Lipsky (1968:1146) defines protest as "activity by relatively powerless groups, directed against a target group, characterized by showmanship, and calculated to bring third parties into the arena of conflict in a manner beneficial to the protest group." The only immediate alternative open to protest groups is persuasive protest tactics designed to appeal to the good nature of target groups and third parties. Often protest tactics are designed to harass or embarrass a target group. The publicity generated, rather than the tactics themselves, are most distressing to a target group. In order for protest to succeed, protest groups must get third parties to urge or order the target group to make concessions.

According to Lipsky, protest seldom succeeds because many external constraints operate against those who attempt to lead protest. The target group seldom capitulates and grants all—or even most—of the protest group's demands. Target groups have a wide range of tactics they can employ to waste time while projecting the appearance of change and concern. For protest groups, success often must be judged in terms other than immediate concessions from the target group. At times, success must be defined simply in terms of compelling the target group to take the protest group into account.

SUMMARY

This chapter presents three theories of collective behavior and three theories of collective action. Summary sketches of these theories are presented below. This presentation is intended to introduce the reader to the major concepts and ideas within each theory. In later chapters each theory will be discussed in greater detail.

Perspectives on Collective Behavior specify ways in which collective behavior differs from everyday social behavior carried out within basic social institutions such as the family or formal organizations such as bureaucracy.

- **Mass Hysteria Theory** defines collective behavior as aroused emotion. The crowd transforms people through processes such as social contagion, the collective impulse, or circular reactions. Major contributors to this theory are Gustave LeBon, Robert E. Park and Ernest Burgess, Herbert Blumer, and Orin E. Klapp.

- **Emergent-Norm Theory** defines collective behavior as a response to new or ambiguous social situations. Collective behavior is guided by new and emergent social norms and ephemeral roles. Members of crowds are not transformed emotionally but retain conventional motivation. This was first articulated by Ralph Turner and Lewis M. Killian.

- **Value-Added Theory** defines collective behavior as a response to social strain. Fundamental forms of collective behavior are identified as collective episodes of craze, panic, hostile outburst and norm- and value-oriented social movements. Collective behavior has many causes, including social structural factors, generalized beliefs and action of social control. This theory was articulated by Neil Smelser.

Perspectives on Collective Action emphasize similarities between collective action and other forms of social behavior. These theories are derived from the observation of crowds and from case studies of social movements and political protest.

- **Social Behavioral Interactionist Theory** accounts for the formation of temporary gatherings, frequently observed forms of collective action within gatherings, and the dispersal of gatherings. Perception control theory is used to account for purposive individual and collective action. This theory is based on the empirical and theoretical work of Clark McPhail.

- **Resource Mobilization Theory** is derived from case studies of social movements. This theory accounts for how social movements are manifested through organizations that succeed in mobilizing social networks and material resources. The dynamics of social movements is in part determined by interaction among social movement organizations. This theory was originated by John McCarthy and Mayer N. Zald.

- **Political Process Theory** tells us how people come to frame their discontent into ideas that clearly articulate grievances and offer hope for successfully resolving them. This theory also identifies the kinds of acts that clearly articulate the abuses by authorities, establish a definite sense of injustice, and increase the group's capacity to act together. Strategies of social protest are also identified. Major contributors to this theory are Doug McAdam, William Gamson and Michael Lipsky.

CHAPTER 3

STUDYING COLLECTIVE BEHAVIOR AND COLLECTIVE ACTION

Perhaps it is surprising to learn that in the 1950s, when sociologists had already completed large-scale and longitudinal studies of communities, families, voting patterns and formal organizations, only a handful of collective behavior studies had been carried out. Even these few studies had a makeshift character and appeared to have been carried out under far less than ideal circumstances. This was because researchers held the view that collective behavior is usually unanticipated and that they could not predict, for instance, the nature and occurrence of the next dance craze or clothing fad. Likewise, they could never know where the next disaster would strike or when an arrest would spark a riot.

The study of collective behavior also includes the study of crowds. Sociologists such as Tumin and Feldman (1955), who encountered an ecstatic crowd, or Myers (1948), who observed a hostile crowd, did not conduct interviews or make detailed observations while they were in the crowd and only afterwards wrote about what they saw. Finally, in the 1950s it seemed impossible to study collective behavior under controlled conditions; we could not create a revolution for research purposes, and professional codes of ethics prohibit sociologists from trying to produce a stampede panic in the laboratory.

As you have learned in the first two chapters, these views began to change in the 1960s with the emergence of the collective action perspectives. Building on the foundations of earlier collective behavior research, or working from entirely new standpoints, the field of collective action has generated a robust methodology and a large volume of research in the past thirty years. In the 1950s the field of collective behavior was correctly characterized as a field of sociology that had a weak research tradition. Even though the field of collective behavior was one of the first established in sociology, the field got off to a late start methodologically. Today, however, some of the most rigorous and innovative sociological research is to be found in the field of collective action.

Information about collective behavior and collective action has been obtained through the analysis of historical material, surveys and official statistics, experiments, participant observation, direct observation, and computer simulation. We will now review the development of these research methods that, taken together, are providing increased knowledge about collective behavior and collective action.

USING HISTORICAL MATERIAL

Consider the these lines spoken from the pulpit of a church in Holland in 1620:

> All these fools want is tulip bulbs
> Heads and hearts have but one wish
> Let's try and eat them; it will make us laugh
> To taste how bitter is that dish.

This warning was part of the moral admonition expressed against the growing tulip trade in the Netherlands at the beginning of the seventeenth century (Pavord, 1999:139–41). Surprisingly, the Dutch did not introduce tulips to Europe. Tulips were first brought to Europe in small numbers by French travelers in the early 1500s, and on a large scale by Belgian shippers in the 1560s. By 1630, tulips were cultivated throughout Europe, and the first "boom and bust" cycle of speculation in tulip bulbs had occurred in France. Still, it is the 1634–1637 cycle of tulip speculation in Holland that gave rise to the term "tulip mania" and the saying that "a fool and his money are soon parted" (Pavord, 1999).

The 1634–1637 speculation cycle was quite spectacular, but it did not appear from out of nowhere. When speculation started to peak, the Netherlands provinces were already providing tulip bulbs to the rest of the world, and a tulip futures market was well established. Further, speculation was largely confined to "breaks"—tulips that showed unique color patterns and petal shapes. Speculators as well as professional growers and gardeners for great estates eagerly sought after breaks with the hope of establishing a new tulip variety. As breaks occurred unpredictably and could suddenly appear in a bed of common tulips, the appearance of a new break would be quite a boon to the lucky owner, and so interest in common tulips also was heightened during this time period. Dutch masters were commissioned by growers to produce paintings of tulips for catalogs used to advertise inventories and bulb auctions.

The crash of the booming Dutch tulip market began in the spring of 1637 and trade was suspended in February. By mid-year, fortunes had been lost and the courts were tied up in hundreds of lawsuits resulting from the collapse. Some courts refused to hear tulip bulb cases, declaring that the courts could not be used to resolve gambling debts, and some cities set up local arbitration councils to resolve these disputes (Pavord, 1999:171). The damage to the tulip trade was short lived. By 1648, Holland dominated a strong tulip market throughout the world.

In his first "Outline of Collective Behavior" (1939), Blumer cited the "tulip mania in Holland in the eighteenth century" as an example of mass hysteria. Since then, the tulip mania example has been cited by Smelser (1962), Turner and Killian (1972), and Klapp (1972). While tulip mania is thus recognized as a class outbreak of mass hysteria or extreme form of "rapid, unwitting, and nonrational dissemination of a mood, impulse, or form of conduct," the evidence upon which this judgment is based is meager.

Only one historical account of tulip mania has ever been cited in the preceding discussions of mass hysteria—the account by Charles Mackay (1932) in the third edition of *Extraordinary Popular Delusions and the Madness of Crowds*, published in 1841 and again in 1852. Mackay makes no claims that his work represents a complete or even careful history of the events he describes, characterizing his work as "sketches" and a "miscellany of delusions . . . a chapter . . . in the great and awful book of human folly." Upon examination, little in Mackay's account of the tulip mania illustrates events of a widespread and hysterical nature, presenting entertaining anecdotes rather than detailed accounts of group processes involved in the event. Most of Mackay's chapter on tulip mania, for example, describes instances where people ate or otherwise ruined tulip bulbs—mistaking them for onions! It is difficult to reconcile the image of a nationwide, hysterical preoccupation for tulips with stories about people being unable to distinguish tulip bulbs from onions. While Mackay states that some bulbs did command extremely high prices, his accounts seem to imply that these were new or very rare varieties purchased by professional growers and serious speculators.

The use of Mackay's account of the tulip mania represents the rather casual use of historical material found within the mass hysteria/social contagion literature. It is not difficult to find colorful descriptions of past moods, diversions, instabilities, and fanaticism compatible with the mass hysteria point of view. It is from such sensationalized accounts that much of the supporting evidence for this perspective is drawn. More detailed and careful historical accounts usually reflect underlying economic, political, and social forces that shape events more than they illustrate the "hysterical" nature of events. An important question to answer at this point is: "What constitutes an acceptable level of historical scholarship?"

The Work of George Rudé

During the early 1960s, Carl Couch assigned George Rudé's *The Crowd in the French Revolution* (1959) as a required text in the collective behavior courses he taught. Couch (1968) was also influenced by Rudé's work when he concluded that crowds ". . . were no more or no less bizarre than other social systems. . . ." Rudé masterfully uses historical analysis in describing the socioeconomic composition and motives of crowds during the French revolution. Many accounts claim that the scum of French society—the ruffians, criminals, prostitutes, vagabonds, and insane—were the most active in the Revolution. Bribery and the quest for loot allegedly motivated these derelicts. Other accounts portray participants in heroic terms—the "noble poor," motivated by the lofty ideals of liberty, freedom, and equality. Rudé notes that these opposing characterizations have never been carefully evaluated from the standpoint of surviving records, most of which are preserved in the French National Archives.

Rudé examined police records for the years 1787 to 1795 and those of the revolutionary government's Committee of General Security of 1793 to 1795. These were the years of the revolutionary crowd: the preliminary skirmishes between crowds and police, the taking of the Bastille, the march on Versailles, the fall of the monarchy and the Reign of Terror, and the unsuccessful counterrevolution of 1795. These records contain lists of those killed, wounded, and arrested, and those who had complaints placed against them. Rudé notes that these records concern a minority of all participants but that the size of these records concerns a large enough group, or sample, that general conclusions can be drawn from them. Rudé also examined lists of claimants for pensions and compensation for time lost under arms during the years 1792 and 1793. During these years, the revolutionary government also conducted surveys of its police agents. In these surveys agents reported the reactions of small property holders and wage earners to the events of these years. Rudé also utilized statistical lists compiled during the revolutionary period reporting the movement of wages and the prices of bread, meat, butter, eggs, sugar, wine, coffee, candles, and soap. It is from such historical material that Rudé constructs an image of those most active in the French Revolution and draws conclusions about their motives.

Rudé concludes that the revolutionary crowds were primarily composed of wage earners, shopkeepers, small traders, housewives, craftsmen, and workshop masters. Very few of those killed, wounded, or arrested had previous police records, and, of those who did, few were for major offenses. In contrast, the leaders of the Revolution were drawn largely from the owners of large businesses, the professions, and the liberal aristocracy. While the ideals of liberty, freedom, and equality were often prominent among the expressed motives of the revolutionary crowds, the most constant motive throughout the popular uprisings of this period was the desire to obtain a stable and increased supply of inexpensive bread and other essentials. Rudé notes that police records contain very few references to bribery, or "paid participation," and he indicates that very little looting—other than the securing of weapons—occurred during these disorders.

Rudé's image of the participants in the French Revolution lies somewhere between the extremes of derelicts and noble poor. Those participating were neither riffraff nor heroes. They were mostly members of the emerging, urban, industrial social order—a new social order against whose interests the monarchy largely stood. The revolutionaries were motivated by a concern for liberty, freedom, and equality, but these motives were tempered with the practical concern for a reasonable and stable standard of living.

The work of Rudé has been widely acknowledged as providing genuine insight into the make-up and actions of crowds during the French Revolution. The question remains, however, whether the findings from this specific historical analysis apply generally to other political and industrial conflicts. One might easily suspect that the large-scale upheavals studied by Rudé are, in many ways, quite different from the various smaller and more frequent protests, strikes, military coups d'état, and localized rebellions that make up much of modern social conflict.

The Work of William A. Gamson

In order to obtain a more general understanding of the prior conditions, the dynamics, and the outcomes of political and industrial conflict, comparisons must be made among a representative sample of groups involved in conflict. This task involves three major problems. Foremost among them is specifying what constitutes a group. Once a working definition of a group is established, we must ascertain the universe of all groups that fit this definition, which involves a systematic and exhaustive search of the historical record for references to these groups. Finally, we must obtain similar amounts of necessary information about each group and the conflict in which it took part.

William A. Gamson (1975) developed a methodology to overcome these problems in his analysis of social protest. First, he developed a working definition of a protest, or *challenging*, group. For Gamson, a challenging group is involved in mobilizing a constituency among people who were unorganized with respect to a particular issue or problem. A challenging group also has a clear, external target of influence, such as employers, legislators, or police. The challenging group must have demonstrated the capacity to take such actions as petitioning, demonstrating, striking, attacking authorities, raising money, or holding meetings. Finally, challenging groups have names and a clear conception of membership in the group.

Gamson restricted his attention to challenging groups that existed in the United States between 1800 and 1945. He then addressed the task of searching history books for references to any and all groups that could possibly be considered as challenging groups. This search had to be systematic and exhaustive. A team of researchers examined the indexes of a series of general and specific histories that included the years between 1800 and 1945. The indexes were searched for the names of organizations, be they General Motors or the Iowa Socialist League, and a master card file of more than 4,500 organizations was compiled. These organizations were placed into at least one of seventeen categories, including agricultural, labor, ethnic, women, religious, professional, business, socialist/communist, peace, veterans, cranks/crackpots, and sports/recreation. These categories served as a basis for selecting general and specific history books from which descriptive information would be drawn. Seventy-five books were selected, including the *Dictionary of American History*, *The Oxford Companion to American History*, and specific histories such as *History of Woman Suffrage* by Elizabeth Stanton and her colleagues, and Louis Filler's *A Dictionary of Social Reform*. Each volume was searched for references to any of the organizations in the card file. The final dozen history books yielded minimal amounts of new information, and so the list of "all organizations in the United States from 1800 to 1945" was considered complete. From this file, a random sample of 467 organizations was selected, of which 64 met the criteria of being a protest or challenging group. These organizations and the conflicts to which they were party constituted the *database* for the rest of Gamson's analysis.

At this point, we should consider the degree to which procedures such as those outlined above can produce a "true" sample of those organizations that expressed grievances, advanced causes, and challenged authorities between 1800 and 1945. Clearly, we cannot judge how representative this type of sampling is in the same way that we judge the samples used by a Gallup poll.

We can gauge, somewhat, how representative Gamson's sample is by considering the kinds of organizations likely to have been overlooked by historians. Many "crackpot" groups, secret societies, and small, short-lived groups are likely to go unnoticed or to be considered unworthy of serious attention. Each of these types, however, is represented in Gamson's sample. Compared to the stated objectives of other groups, those of the League of American Wheelmen (1880–1905) may have received more than a few laughs. This group attempted to organize bicyclists to demand the removal of restrictions on the use of bicycles, including the prohibition of riding in the street (see chapter 8). Similarly, the Society for the Promotion of Manual Labor in Literary Institutions (1831–1833) had as its goal the improvement of physical fitness among college students. Gamson's search unearthed one acknowledged secret society—the Order of Secularists—an organization of atheists of the 1860s. Finally, nine of the groups in the final sample had brief "life spans" of three years or less. It is impossible to absolutely assess the number and kinds of groups that were not immortalized by historians. Still, Gamson's sample contains groups manifesting a wide range of interests.

There is also the question of whether Gamson located all, or a suitably large portion, of the groups actually mentioned by historians. Certainly, he consulted only a small portion of U.S. history books. Still, those examined covered a very wide range of historical interests, geographic areas, and groups. There is no noticeable bias toward overselecting books dealing with the history of a given region, such as the eastern United States, or with particular topics, such as labor and business groups. Finally, Gamson concluded his search only after reaching a high level of diminished returns, that is, when the search stopped yielding realistic amounts of new information.

The completeness of Gamson's search can be gauged through *replication*. For example, using Gamson's method of gathering historical data, would other researchers come up with appreciably more groups than Gamson did? There is no compelling reason to think that they would. However, replication would provide a greater level of confidence in this method of gathering data.

Gamson next turned to the task of ascertaining the nature and outcomes of the conflicts in which these challenging groups were involved. As it would be impossible to interview the people involved in most of these conflicts, Gamson, in effect, "interviewed" the history books.

A questionnaire containing 113 questions was composed, including the following:

- What was the size of the challenging group?
- What were the group's formal goals?
- Who were the primary antagonists of the challenging group?
- What types of police activity, such as legal arrest or illegal harassment, were directed against the group?
- What types of public relations attempts were made by the group?
- To what extent did other groups extend support to the challenging group?
- What skills did the leadership of the challenging group possess?

There were a number of questions about the outcome of the challenging group's efforts—whether they received formal recognition by employers, as in the case of trade unions, or obtained formal concessions or agreements such as the passing of requested legislation or changes in formal policy.

Researchers examined the history books for specific answers to these questions and included photocopies of relevant passages on each questionnaire. In some instances other sources, such as contracts or the minutes of challenging-group meetings, were consulted to obtain answers. These procedures involved about eighty hours of work for each questionnaire. Complete interview schedules were obtained for fifty-three of the sixty-four organizations in the sample. This is comparable to a response rate of 83 percent for a conventional survey. This response rate is generally viewed as quite satisfactory in most survey research.

The completed questionnaires were then coded in the same way that conventional interviews are coded, and the coded information was tabulated and analyzed. The information allowed Gamson to answer questions about the nature and outcomes of nearly a century and a half of protest in the United States. We will consider the findings of this study in chapter 14.

This method of historical analysis is described in much greater detail in Gamson's *The Strategy of Social Protest* (1975). These research procedures allowed Gamson to gather information systematically and comprehensively from the historical record. Much can be learned from qualitative, case-by-case historical analysis such as Rudé's. Work such as Gamson's, however, represents a quantitative approach to the historical record. Making the historical record speak in quantitative terms yields information that can be analyzed and interpreted with the statistical tools of modern sociology. In turn, quantitative information allows us to compare more meaningfully the many collective behavior events of the past with those of the present. This methodology sets a new standard of scientific rigor by which research utilizing the historical record must be judged.

USING SURVEYS, OFFICIAL STATISTICS AND ARCHIVES

Surveys and Official Statistics

A very large portion of the data used in sociology is obtained through surveys and official statistics. These are the primary sources of data in the large body of riot participation research conducted in the late 1960s and early 1970s. Altogether, the many studies of riot participation use information about or from thousands of people and dozens of disorders.

One of the first tasks in studying riots is to determine who is and who isn't a riot participant. The most obvious and frequent solution to this problem is to assume that those who have been arrested at the scene of the disorder are rioters. Most riot participation studies compare samples of respondents arrested on riot charges with a control sample of nonarrestees drawn from the community in which the riot occurred. A few studies, such as that of Strasel and Larkin (1968), simply provide a descriptive snapshot of the accused rioters by analyzing information provided by people at the time of their arrest.

In most of these studies, it is acknowledged that being arrested as a rioter does not always mean that the person has engaged in violent, destructive, or "riotous" activity. That is, there are degrees of riot involvement, ranging from being on the streets after an imposed curfew to stoning police or being caught in the act of fire-bombing a building. Some studies take the arrest charge into account. For example, Strasel and Larkin excluded curfew violators in their sample of Washington rioters; they restricted their sample to those charged with burglary II (the category for looting) and other crimes, such as assault, committed during the riot period.

A smaller number of studies utilize surveys conducted in riot communities a few weeks or months after the disorder. In these post-riot surveys, respondents indicate what they did and saw during the disorder. From this self-report information, researchers have constructed several categories of involvement, including *actives*, or persons who reported being involved in or close at hand to shootings, rock throwing, and looting. People who reported that they went out and tried to talk others into "cooling it" were classified as *counterrioters*. *Inactives* are people who reported staying at home or only observing the riot from their porches or yards.

The primary purpose and focus of riot participation studies has been to determine the personal characteristics and attitudes that dispose people to participate in riots. Studies of arrestees use information from official records made in the process of booking and pretrial investigation. For example, the D.C. Bail Agency was the source of data in Strasel and Larkin's study. The scope of the information was limited by the purpose of the bail agency, which is to determine the character, reliability, and community ties of individuals for whom a bail determination is being made. Volunteer law students and attorneys of the federal bar administered the bail questionnaires.

The information obtained for the purpose of bail determination was quite extensive and included age, race, sex, place of birth, marital status, physical and mental health, criminal records, length of residence, educational level, employment status, occupation, and take-home pay. Fifty-five relevant prisoner attributes were either listed or deducible from the original questionnaire items. In like manner, other researchers have constructed detailed socioeconomic profiles of those arrested during riots. Such information, however, has little direct bearing on the attitudes and opinions of those arrested. Arrestees' attitudes and opinions have been obtained largely through the post-riot surveys discussed above.

The post-riot surveys solicited respondents' statements about police malpractice or brutality; overt discrimination by employers, merchants, and "whites in general"; as well as respondents' political participation and expectations for the future. From these responses, researchers constructed hundreds of attitude/opinion indexes and compared them with people's involvement in rioting. We will discuss specific findings of these studies in chapter 12. Here it is sufficient to note that the results of riot participation research have been disappointing—at least as far as discovering a riot-prone personality is concerned. About all this research has shown is that, overwhelmingly, riot participants tend to be young, black, and male, as opposed, for example, to being old, white, and female. Of the hundreds of additional socioeconomic characteristics, attitudes, and opinions that have been examined, few are clearly or highly associated with riot participation. Unfortunately, the surveys and official statistics now available provide little additional information that would allow the testing of alternate explanations of riot participation.

At first thought, it seems unlikely that researchers could successfully administer questionnaires or conduct interviews within a crowd. Although newspaper and television reporters often enter the crowd to get a story, sociologists have been reluctant to enter the crowd to get their data. Quarantelli and Hundley (1969) broke new ground, however, when they conducted interviews with students during a campus disorder at the University of Ohio in 1963. Interestingly, these interviews were conducted as a pretest of methods that would be used a few months later in the first disaster studies to be conducted by the Disaster Research Center. The crowd phase of this disorder lasted almost six hours and included the blocking of vehicle traffic on streets near the campus, property damage, a protest march, and confrontations between students and police. A disorder of this magnitude and character clearly falls within the hostile outburst category of Smelser's model of collective behavior. Some data for this study were obtained with on-the-scene interviews conducted to determine the participation motives of those involved. Some interviewees attributed their presence in the crowd to feelings of hostility toward the police and university officials. The majority, however, expressed motives of curiosity, as well as desires to be with friends and share in the excitement. These findings contradict Smelser's explanation of hostile outbursts (Quarantelli and Hundley, 1969).

Adrian Aveni (1977) and a team of students also conducted field interviews within a celebrating street crowd following a University of Ohio football game. The purpose of this study was to determine social relationships within the crowd. People were randomly selected and interviewed to find out who they were with and who they had seen while on the streets. Altogether, 287 interviews were attempted, 204 of which were completed.

The studies of Quarantelli and Hundley and Aveni suggest that much more interviewing can be done in the crowd than has been assumed. This does not mean that we should interrupt looters to conduct interviews. Short of this, however, much can be done. Crowd activity is seldom as uniformly intense and focused as popular imagery suggests. Brief questionnaires can be administered, or short interviews conducted, during lulls in crowd activity. We need not interrupt a protest march to ask people questions about the assembling process or their motives for participation. Such information can likely be obtained beforehand as people are waiting for the march to begin.

Demonstration Permit Archives

Each year thousands of political, religious and special event demonstrations take place at city halls, state capitols and, especially, the U.S. national capitol in Washington, DC. Relatively few of these demonstrations are ever covered by the national print and electronic media, thereby becoming part of the larger political process. Sociologists generally use media accounts of demonstrations as a primary data source for measuring the levels and content of protest in modern democracies. An important methodological question for these studies is how the media select particular demonstrations for coverage. In order to answer this question, it is necessary to know the number and kind of demonstrations that occur within a particular venue and, subsequently, which of these demonstrations were covered by the media.

John D. McCarthy, Clark McPhail and Jackie Smith (1996) used the 1982 and 1991 demonstration permit archives of the D.C. Metropolitan Police (MPDC), the National Park Service and the U.S. Capitol Police for those years to ascertain the number, type, and size of political demonstrations occurring in Washington, DC. These records contain the expected number of participants and the location, time, and duration of each demonstration. Each permit also provides information detailing the purpose, form, and planned activities for the demonstration as well as the person or organization sponsoring the event and whether the applicants expect counterdemonstrators to possibly disrupt their demonstration.

Even though freedom of assembly is guaranteed by the First Amendment of the U.S. Constitution, political demonstrations in the nation's capitol are constrained by several guidelines. The D.C. Metropolitan Police, the National Park Service, and the U.S. Capitol Police each require that groups apply for permits to carry out demonstrations in their jurisdictions. These permit archives provide a near total enumeration of political demonstrations during the past quarter century. Demonstrations on the grounds surrounding the Capitol, House, and Senate office buildings fall under the jurisdiction of the U.S. Capitol Police, who require permits for all protests, even by a single demonstrator. Groups can also be given permits at the site of a demonstration.

The National Park Service has jurisdiction over demonstrations convened on monument grounds, the Mall, the Ellipse behind the White House and Lafayette Park across from the White House as well as most other parks in the city. Permits are encouraged for all protests and are required for protests planned for more than 25 people.

Street demonstrations outside the capitol grounds and city parks are within the jurisdiction of the D.C. Metropolitan Police. Guidelines for "public forum" demonstrations are the least restrictive, and a permit typically is not required for any peaceful protest on sidewalks and in traditional public fora that does not block pedestrian or vehicular traffic. Events involving numbers of participants or activities that block traffic do require permits. Only about one-third of protest demonstrations occurring in this jurisdiction apply for permits. The MPDC maintain a logbook of demonstrations for which permits were not issued.

Permit data from the Capitol Police were obtained by special pass, and the permit data from the National Park Service and the Metropolitan Police were readily available through the Freedom of Information Act. Researchers were not allowed to copy the original applications, but they were allowed to do on-site coding of permits. Altogether, there were 1,077 permitted political demonstrations in 1982 and 1,552 permitted political demonstrations in 1991. Somewhat over half of these demonstrations had an estimated size of 25 or fewer persons, and the average size was about a thousand participants. The estimated half-million who attended the Vietnam Memorial Dedication in 1982 was the largest demonstration in this data set.

Religious groups whose applications indicated advocating or protesting legislation or political agendas were included in the data. Excluded from the data set of political demonstrations were applicants who included "spreading the gospel" or "evangelizing" as the stated purpose of the demonstration. Also excluded from the data were over 2,500 permits for vigil demonstrations at the Vietnam memorial, since many of these "vigils" were also more or less permanent vending sites.

Examination of major print and electronic media sources indicate that about 13 percent of all demonstrations were reported by the media in 1982, and only 7 percent of all demonstrations were covered in 1991. The single most important factor in reporting demonstrations for these two years is clearly the size of the demonstration. The media cover the largest demonstrations and rarely report on demonstrations of fewer than one hundred people. From this standpoint, McCarthy, McPhail and Smith (1996:488) point out that even though a large majority of demonstrations are not covered by the media, since large demonstrations are covered, at least 80 percent of all demonstrators are covered by one or another source.

USING EXPERIMENTS

Nonadaptive Group Behavior

We noted earlier in this chapter that very little collective behavior had been produced and studied under controlled conditions. The ability to control and manipulate what is being studied is the essence of the experimental method. The lack of experimental examination of collective behavior results in part from the prevailing definitions of collective behavior. If we assume, as does the mass hysteria theory, that collective behavior involves extreme emotion, then it is difficult to justify terrorizing or otherwise exciting people for the purpose of study. If we assume, as does the value-added perspective, that collective behavior always involves structural strain and large-scale events, then experimental examination is precluded. That is, we cannot produce and manipulate structural strain and other elements of the value-added process to see if they indeed cause various types of large-scale collective behavior. At best, we can make *comparative studies* among nations experiencing different levels of political violence and civil strife. We will consider such studies by Gurr (1969) and Davies (1969) in later chapters. On the other hand, the social behavioral interactionist (SBI) perspective seems, at least superficially, more compatible with the logic of experimental examination. Milgram, Bickman and Berkowitz (1969), for example, controlled the size and activities of stimulus crowds to assess their impact on passersby.

Alexander Mintz: A Study of Panic

An early and widely cited experiment in the field of collective behavior is Alexander Mintz's (1951) study of nonadaptive group behavior. In this experiment, Mintz designed a procedure to simulate an emergency escape situation to determine the conditions under which group cooperation breaks down and individualistic, nonadaptive responses occur. Mintz placed fifteen to twenty-one aluminum cones in a large glass jug, the neck of which was large enough to accommodate only a single cone. Each cone had a string attached to it. The bottom of the jug was fitted with a valve that allowed water to enter it (see Figure 3.1).

Subjects were handed a string and told that as soon as water started to enter the jug, they could withdraw their cones. Subjects were shown that only one cone at a time could escape from the jug and that nonadaptive "jam-ups" would occur if this procedure were violated. Subjects could successfully complete the experiment if their cones escaped dry.

In the initial trials, no jam-up responses occurred and everyone escaped with dry cones. Mintz concluded that one reason for these successes was that groups usually established a "one-cone-at-a-time" plan of action in informal conversations prior to beginning each trial. In later trials, Mintz secretly recruited accomplices in the groups of subjects and instructed them to incite emotions. The accomplices were asked to swear, yell, and scream once the trial was underway. The accomplices succeeded in arousing the emotions of the subjects, but despite this disturbance no jam-ups occurred.

Mintz was able to induce jam-ups only after he forbade pretrial conversations and set up a reward-and-fine condition. Subjects received a quarter if their cones escaped dry and were fined a dime if their cones got wet. Finally, to eliminate the effects of excitement, Mintz placed a partitioned screen around the jug so subjects could not see one another. Under these arrangements, nonadaptive jam-ups occurred frequently.

Mintz's study could be characterized as a study of "panic," but this is inaccurate because Mintz dismissed emotional arousal as a key factor in the occurrence of nonadaptive group behavior. Instead, Mintz argued that the reward structure was the key ingredient in nonadaptive group behavior. From Mintz's study, it is also clear that factors of communication (pretrial conversations) and lack of mutual sensory access (the partitioned screen) greatly contributed to the incidence of nonadaptive jam-ups. (For further discussion of communication and sensory access as these factors relate to evacuation disasters, see chapter 10.)

A True-to-Life Study of Rebellion

An experimental study utilizing a more "true-to-life" situation was conducted by William A. Gamson, Bruce Fireman, and Stephen Rytina (1982). In this study, representatives of a "research organization" requested groups of subjects to engage in blatantly unethical and potentially illegal acts. Groups often encounter *unjust authority* in the real world and are forced with the decision of complying or rebelling. Gamson, Fireman, and Rytina designed their experimental study to

FIGURE 3.1: Experimental Study of Panic

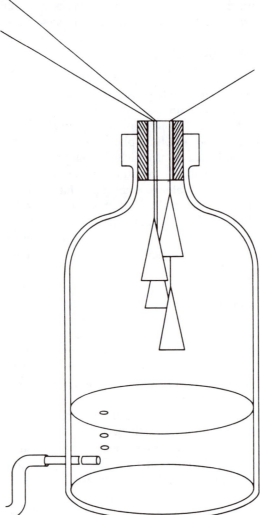

A sketch of the apparatus used to study nonadaptive group behavior, or panic, in the laboratory. Mintz (1951) found that by creating a reward structure and greatly limiting mutual sensory access among the subjects, he could produce frequent nonadaptive jam-ups of cones in the neck of the bottle.

ascertain the conditions under which groups choose and carry out rebellion.

The experimental scenario began with newspaper ads that solicited subjects for research being conducted by Manufacturer's Human Relations Consultants (MHRC). Participants would be paid ten dollars, and the research session would last about two hours. People who phoned for further information were told that the research would involve one of four topics. These topics were brand-name recognition, product safety, community standards, and research in which subjects would initially be misled about the purpose of the study. Callers were then asked to schedule an appointment for the research session.

Research sessions were held in a motel suite equipped with desks and portable videotaping equipment. When subjects arrived, they were asked to sign an agreement specifying that their participation was voluntary, that they were aware the sessions would be videotaped, and that the tapes would not be used for commercial purposes. Each participant was then paid, given a name tag, and received a cover letter that explained in general terms the aims of MHRC and the purpose of the research. Each session involved twelve people: the MHRC coordinator and his assistant, nine naive subjects, and a person who posed as a naive subject. Later in the research session this person would act to mobilize rebellion against the MHRC.

Each session began when the MHRC coordinator asked subjects to fill out a questionnaire to assess their opinions regarding large oil companies, business practices, people engaging in sexual affairs, the rights of citizens, and trust in the courts and government. Such factual information as subjects' age, sex, race, marital status, religion, and education was also requested.

When subjects completed the questionnaire, they were told that the research session would consist of a panel discussion to ascertain community values and standards for the purpose of obtaining reliable information to be used in a case coming before the federal court. The MHRC coordinator then informed the subjects of the issues involved in the particular case, which involved a lawsuit being brought against a large oil company by a service-station manager. The oil company had revoked the manager's franchise, stating that the manager was living with a woman to whom he was not married. The manager's lifestyle made him "unfit" to represent the oil company. The manager's suit charged that the oil company had invaded his privacy and that his lifestyle neither affected his performance on the job nor offended contemporary community standards. The manager further claimed that the company had taken action against him because he criticized the company's pricing policies in a televised interview.

The MHRC coordinator then asked the subjects to discuss whether they would be concerned if the manager of a local gas station pursued this type of lifestyle. Almost without exception, subjects expressed little concern with the station manager's living arrangements. The MHRC coordinator entered the room, shut off the videotape recorder, and asked the subjects to discuss whether they would do business with a person like the station manager. He then instructed three or four subjects to argue as if they were offended by the station manager's behavior. He then turned on the recorder and left the room.

After a somewhat confused and strained discussion, the MHRC coordinator entered the room and asked the subjects to discuss whether someone like the station manager was bad for the community. He then asked three more people to argue as if they were offended by unmarried cohabitation. As in the first instance, the request to act offended was not recorded.

The next time the MHRC coordinator entered the room, he asked subjects to summarize their feelings regarding the station manager's conduct. While the videotape was again stopped, he asked all subjects to act as if they were offended by the lifestyle in question.

Finally, the coordinator entered the room and asked subjects to sign affidavits stating that they were aware that the videotapes would be used in court. At the conclusion of this encounter, which was often quite abrasive, subjects were immediately informed that they had been participating in an experimental hoax. Subjects were then requested to fill out another questionnaire that asked a wide range of information dealing with what they had planned to do had this research situation not been a hoax.

Thirty-three groups participated in this study. Participants tended to be younger, better educated, and more middle class than a cross section of the adult population from the community in which the study was conducted. Still, these groups were not grossly unrepresentative of their community, which would have been the case had the groups been composed entirely of men or college students.

In almost all of the groups, some form of individual or collective resistance to the MHRC was encountered. While the person posing as a naive subject was to attempt to initiate resistance in subtle ways, subjects usually offered resistance without prompting. Resistance took various forms. Individually, subjects remained silent, disclaimed their negative statements, or acted in a sarcastic manner during the taping. Some offered open resistance by refusing to sign the final affidavits, and a few took direct action, such as seizing the participation agreements signed at the beginning of the experiment or openly threatening to seize the videotapes. Finally, some members made plans to meet later and expose the tactics of the MHRC to the courts.

In summary, four groups never developed a rebellious majority, four groups "fizzled" when the rebellious majority eventually signed the final affidavits, in nine groups the majority refused to sign the final affidavits, and sixteen groups maintained unanimous resistance. In none of the thirty-three sessions, however, did the MHRC coordinator openly threaten or intimidate subjects.

In their subsequent analysis of the videotapes, the researchers utilized Erving Goffman's (1974) symbolic interactionist terminology to analyze how rebellion developed. In chapter 14 we will consider in greater detail the development of rebellion, and how this experiment sheds light on the process. Here it is sufficient to note that necessary ingredients of rebellion include *organizing acts*, which increase the capacity of rebels to act as a unit. Groups confronting the MHRC were composed of mutual strangers. During the course of the experiment, those groups in which people engaged in friendly conversation and developed a minimal sense of solidarity and loyalty were much more capable of rebellion than those groups in which members remained strangers to one another. *Divesting acts*, which include statements that negate fears of "making a scene" and question obligations to authority, facilitate rebellion. Finally, *reframing acts* are necessary; these are acts that loudly and clearly call attention to the wrongdoings of authority.

Gamson, Fireman, and Rytina's research clearly indicates that rebellion is not easy, particularly among groups who do not share a long history of interaction. Still, their research shows that ordinary people, with no prior experience of working together, were able to openly and actively resist unjust authority. The courage to rebel seems to be in greater supply than the knowledge of how to rebel.

USING OBSERVATION

Studying Groups from the Inside

Participant observation involves a researcher becoming a participant in or member of a group in order to study the group. This method of investigation usually involves considerable time, effort, and emotional and personal commitment to the research act, and in some instances it even poses physical danger to the researcher. Why, then, would a researcher use this method of investigation? Researchers use participant observation to study groups from the inside in order to learn (1) what meanings people attach to their actions, (2) how groups are organized, (3) what the interplay between group members is, and (4) how a group takes action with respect to others.

These things are seldom visible to an outsider and may be deliberately and systematically concealed from such investigators as sociologists, the media, and police. Some aspects of group decision making and tactics may even be concealed from portions of the membership. Even though groups may often grant interviews or allow the administration of questionnaires, it is generally assumed that only superficial information can be gained by outsiders. In short, participant observation can provide information unattainable through other methods of sociological investigation.

The most important participant observation study in the field of collective behavior is that of John Lofland's *Doomsday Cult* (1966, 1977), a study of the early and largely unsuccessful days of an evangelical group that came to international prominence in the 1970s. In the beginning of his study, Lofland told members of the group, to which he gave the pseudonym "Divine Precepts," that he was a sociologist and that he would maintain the anonymity of the group in any of his later writings. Given the obscurity of the group at that time, this promise seemed quite easy to keep. Later events made the Divine Precepts and other pseudonyms used by Lofland quite transparent. Though Lofland has remained true to his initial promise and continues to use the initial pseudonym, it is quite clear that Lofland studied the American branch of the Reverend Sun Myung Moon's Unification Church, whose followers are popularly known as Moonies. Noting this, and without further comment, the Divine Precepts pseudonym used by Lofland will be maintained throughout this section.

Lofland's study began in 1962 when he was approached by a Divine Precepts recruiter to come and hear the "good news" the group had to pass along. Lofland attended a few meetings and then indicated that he did not wish to become a Divine Precepts adherent but did want to study the group. The group consented to this arrangement, and during the next thirteen months Lofland attended meetings, provided transportation, helped to set up group residences and offices, and edited some group literature. He obtained extensive biographical information and history of Divine Precepts involvement from the twenty-three people who composed the initial active core of the group. He observed the group's planning of recruitment drives and the conversion of a few new members. In March 1963, the group leader requested that Lofland either join or leave the group, so Lofland terminated the participant observation phase of his study. In all, he generated more than nine hundred pages of single-spaced typed notes and several hours of tape-recorded notes during this time. His findings regarding recruitment, conversion, and maintenance of faith were first presented in *Doomsday Cult*, dealing with the Divine Precepts' more recent history and successes. We will review Lofland's particular findings in chapter 15.

Participant observation has provided the field of collective behavior with information that would have been difficult if not impossible to obtain through other means. The observation of participants in many types of collective behavior is another valuable source of information. The accounts of major and minor revolutionary figures, for example, provide insights into the covert processes of revolutionary groups. Some accounts were intended by their writers to be widely read, such as Chairman Mao's various books of quotations and Hitler's *Mein Kampf*. Such works provide insights into the worldview of revolutionary groups. At the other end of the continuum are works that served as underground organization and training manuals for revolutionary groups prior to their wider publication. Examples include Joseph Stalin's *The Russian Social Democratic Party and Its Immediate Tasks* (1953), Kwame Nkrumah's *Handbook of Revolutionary Warfare* (1964), Carlos Marighella's *Minimanual of the Urban Guerrilla* (1970), and Abraham Guillen's *Philosophy of the Urban Guerrilla* (1973). The ideological bases of these writings are implicit and nondoctrinaire; these works, in many respects, are "how-to" books of street fighting and insurrection, providing insights into the organization and tactics of guerrilla groups.

Observing Disaster Response and Recovery

Researchers have developed methods for studying unanticipated events, particularly in the area of disaster research. The *Statistical Abstract of the United States* reveals that every year is likely to bring forty to eighty tornadoes that kill people and cause at least $500,000 in property damage. Likewise, there will be between one and two hundred floods in which lives will be lost. There will also be twenty to thirty motor vehicle accidents, railroad accidents, fires, and explosions in which five or more fatalities per accident will occur. In this sense, unanticipated events do occur at rather predictable rates. The key to studying disasters is to be prepared to do a lot of traveling on short notice.

On this basis, the Disaster Research Center (DRC) at Ohio State University was established in September 1963. The DRC was a result of the work of Enrico L. Quarantelli, Russell R. Dynes, and J. Eugene Hass. On October 31, 1963, it responded to its first disaster, a multifatality explosion in the Indianapolis Coliseum. Since then, the DRC moved to the University of Delaware in 1985 and has conducted nearly six hundred field studies in the United States, Mexico, Canada, Japan, and Italy. The DRC now maintains the world's most complete collection of materials concerning the social and behavioral aspects of disaster. This specialized library is open to scholars and emergency management agencies worldwide. The DRC hosts visiting research associates from many nations and conducts collaborative research with similar groups in Japan, Mexico, and Russia. It has also organized several multinational research conferences. The DRC has been funded from diverse sources throughout its long history and is presently supported by grants from the National Science Foundation, the Federal Emergency Management Agency, and the National Center for Earthquake Engineering Research at SUNY Buffalo. The DRC presently maintains a website (www.udel.edu/DRC/).

Field research for the DRC is conducted by teams of trained graduate research associates. These teams are prepared to leave for the site of any disaster on four hours' notice. Their field kits include DRC identification material, recording equipment, appropriate interview guides, and various information checklists. On the way to the disaster scene, team members attempt to obtain new information from radio and newspapers in order to determine the conditions they will encounter. Once in the disaster area, team members establish a communication post to coordinate fieldwork and contact the DRC headquarters. Persons interviewed are selected on the basis of their proximity to and their involvement in the

disaster. Particular attention is given to interviewing people in official and unofficial positions of authority. A careful record is kept of the names, addresses, and
organizational affiliations of all persons interviewed, in case it becomes necessary
to contact them again.

Debriefing sessions are conducted upon returning from disaster field trips. A
team member is then selected to write a preliminary research memorandum
describing the disaster, the team's field procedures, and the organizations studied. Other team members are assigned the tasks of preparing a detailed research
report and filing all newspapers, brochures, and other materials collected. A list of
all the people contacted or interviewed during the trip is compiled, and all tapes
made in the field are catalogued. One team member is selected to write appropriate letters of appreciation and handle all follow-up correspondence.

The DRC's training role should not be overlooked. Quarantelli notes that
before the DRC was established, no more than twenty sociologists had direct field
experience in the area of disaster study. Training students in disaster research
remains a high priority. The DRC has provided intense training and field experience to more than one hundred graduate students, most of whom maintain professional commitments to disaster research or to organizations such as the
National Transportation Safety Board and state civil defense agencies. DRC
alumni also worked on the President's Commission on Three Mile Island.

Observing Demonstration Gatherings

Beginning in the late 1960s, Clark McPhail and teams of graduate students from
the universities of South Carolina and Illinois developed procedures for observing
crowd activity. Initially, graduate students were sent out with tablets and pencils to
record the activities of people in shopping malls and airline terminals. The first
records were disappointing, consisting of cryptic comments and diagrams, era-
sures, and assumptions about what travelers and shoppers were thinking. No two
records were alike, even though observers had attempted to describe the same people and activities. Most of these shortcomings were overcome through practice and
recording only a few variables at a time, such as the rate and direction of people's
movement, their direction of gaze, and their manual and vocal gestures. Codes
were developed to facilitate the recording of the apparent age, sex, and ethnicity of
people being observed. Field tactics were developed for positioning observers near
or within stationary and moving crowds. Later, observation procedures were augmented by the use of 8-mm movie equipment. After this training period, observation teams were sent to dozens of rallies, celebrations, and strikes. Film and written
records were made of short-range crowd formation, verbal and nonverbal gestures, the movement of crowds from place to place, and crowd dispersal.

One might ask why sociologists should expend a great deal of effort observing
demonstrations when they could analyze the thousands of hours of video recordings of demonstrations that news agencies have in their archives. News videos capture many "human interest" events within demonstrations such as confrontations,
displays of bizarre behavior, and notable speeches. One thing that these videos do
not provide, however, is a representative picture of all the behaviors, from the mundane to the exciting, that occur during a large demonstration. People who shoot
news footage seldom attempt to obtain a "beginning-to-end" record of a demonstration. They prefer to shoot selective footage of celebrities, political figures, and

organizers, rather than other participants and spectators. Typically, edited news footage distorts the sequence of activities recorded (McCarthy, McPhail and Smith, 1996). In order to obtain systematic information about demonstrations, sociologists have to develop procedures for the firsthand observation of demonstrations.

Clark McPhail and David Schweingruber (1997) have summarized their procedures for observing and recording a *representative sample* of collective activities taking place across a large demonstration in their *Collective Action Observation Primer*. The *Primer* has been used at large demonstrations, including the annual March for Life rallies and the 1997 Promise Keepers' Stand in the Gap rally.

Prior to a demonstration, a map is made of the demonstration site to determine the general dimensions of the site and the location of buildings, monuments, speakers' stands, stages, streets, sidewalks and other prominent features within the area. This map establishes reference points to be used in describing the movements and other activities of people at the demonstration. The map is also used to select locations for observers throughout the demonstration site. The March for Life and Promise Keepers rallies have all taken place on and around the National Mall in Washington, DC. Clark McPhail and John McCarthy have utilized their own observations and maps provided by the National Park Service to develop detailed maps of the National Mall area.

Large, organized groups such as the Promise Keepers require much preliminary planning in order to stage a successful demonstration. Rallies of this type are ideal situations in which researchers can observe and record representative samples of collective activities.
© Agence France Press/CORBIS/Bettman.

Additional preliminary work includes obtaining the demonstration agenda that has been worked out by organizers and police. The agenda provides the proposed starting time of the demonstration and may contain information regarding any preliminary rallies or marches. The agenda will likely identify the order of appearance of speakers.

Teams of observers are trained before demonstrations. Their training includes an introductory lecture on gatherings and demonstrations and the purpose of observing them. Trainees are shown slides illustrating the elementary forms of collective action and the coding procedures to be used. The trainees are also shown slides and maps of the areas in which observations will be made, and they are each assigned to an observation area. Observers are taken outside and given direct experience in estimating the number of people and the density of the gathering in an observation area.

At the demonstration, observers take up their assigned locations throughout the area. Each observer is responsible for recording the behavior of all the people in his or her area. They begin by noting the number of people in their areas and the density of their congregation. By noting people's clothing, signs, banners, buttons, and other identifiers, those in the area are classified as demonstrators, onlookers/passersby, police, media, and counterdemonstrators. They observe the movement of people through their observation areas. At a specified point in time, and every ten minutes thereafter, they observe their areas for a minute and fill out code sheets to indicate what takes place during the one-minute sample.

The observers code four general categories of behavior that include nearly all observable, gross motor and vocal behavior that occurs within demonstrations. These categories of behavior are: facing, voicing, manipulation of objects and body position. Facing refers to a person's physical orientation in the demonstration and is a crude indicator of the object of a person's attention. The facing codes include simple conversation clusters and rings and arcs of spectators in which people face in converging directions. The facing codes also include people facing in the same direction, such as general monitoring, queuing and walking or marching in the same direction.

"Voicing" is recorded using categories for cheering, ooh/ohh/ahhing, booing, laughing, wailing, groans, and crying. Voicing also includes categories for speech making, conversing, chanting, singing, praying, pledging, and reciting. The observers do not attempt to code all they can hear, but just the vocalizations and verbalizations being made by people in their areas. They exclude instances of voicing that enter their areas but originate elsewhere.

When people chant and cheer, they may applaud or raise their arms over their heads and wave them in unison. People sometimes carry, raise, and wave placards as they sing. People may pass leaflets, collection containers, and food during demonstrations. People may grasp, lift, push or pull objects such as video equipment, food, souvenir carts, and strollers at demonstrations. Gestures and manual activities such as these are recorded by observers.

During demonstrations people may embrace one another or lock arms and sway together. People may kneel, sit, or lay on the ground. People may strike objects, including other people. Police may carry or drag people from the demonstration area. People may walk, run, march, or dance throughout the demonstration site. All of the gross motor activities mentioned above are included in the coding categories used by observers.

Finally, when people use physical force to damage or destroy property, or to

A. How many people are in this picture? Are the people in the rear of the crowd standing closer together than those in the front? Foreshortened perspective makes it difficult to answer these questions.

B. It is somewhat easier to count heads and judge distances between people in this picture because the camera is at a higher elevation above the crowd. This reduces foreshortened perspective distortion.

injure and kill people, this is coded as violence. Issues of intention and justification or whether it is police or civilians that first use violence are not included in coding efforts. Very few violent acts have ever been observed in marches and demonstration gatherings.

USING FILM AND VIDEO RECORDS

It is relatively easy to make film records of compact crowds in shopping malls, waiting areas of airline terminals, and on sidewalks. It is usually most convenient to shoot film from balconies or windows overlooking these areas. However, analyzing these films in order to establish the precise number of people in the crowd, their spatial arrangements, and their movements presents some difficulty. This is the problem of foreshortened perspective—a distortion in the film record that results from the height of the camera position above the surface upon which the crowd is located and the size of the area filmed. The lower the elevation of the camera and the greater the area filmed, the greater the distortion in the film record. Theoretically, we can eliminate this problem only by shooting from directly overhead. Foreshortened perspective makes people who are closer to the camera appear to be moving more rapidly than those who are farther away, even though they are moving at the same speed. Foreshortened perspective also makes it appear that shorter people who are closer to the camera are standing very near taller people who are farther from the camera, when in fact these people may be located some distance apart.

Ronald T. Wohlstein (1977) has devised a method of compensating for foreshortened perspective. His solution to this problem is of particular interest in that it involves relatively simple procedures and requires no special equipment, such as computer graphic software other than the cameras, lenses, and projectors used in making the original film record. Basically, Wohlstein's correction method involves filming a grid laid out on any large floor from the same angle and at the same magnification (or lens setting) as that of the initial film record. This creates a foreshortened matrix (see Figure 3.2) that can be marked on the projection screen, thereby providing reference points for calculating all distances in the picture. The procedure is a bit more complicated than this brief description indicates, but it has been verified to allow less than three degrees of error in estimating angles and less than a foot of error in estimating the positions of people and objects in the picture.

USING COMPUTER SIMULATION

For the past thirty years, computer assisted design (CAD) software has been increasingly integrated into the production of automobiles, airplanes, spacecraft and buildings. In the 1960s, a computer using design data could tell us approximately how much a finished automobile would weigh. Now, CAD simulation can tell us the weight, fuel economy, handling characteristics, collision safety, and much more, before an automobile is ever built. CAD simulation and modeling can also be used to locate and correct design flaws and to evaluate competing designs before expensive prototypes are built. Computer simulation and modeling are also used to forecast the weather, predict fluctuations in the stock market, and make urban land-use projections. Given such diversity, it is not surprising that people have simulated and modeled collective behavior and collective action.

FIGURE 3.2: Analyzing Photos of the Crowd: The Foreshortened Matrix

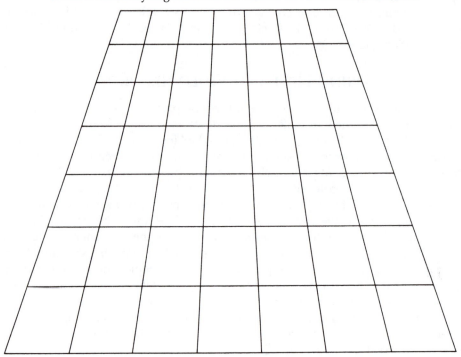

If one knows the lens setting and the elevation of the camera, a foreshortened matrix can be constructed (Wohlstein 1977). When a slide of film is projected on this matrix, accurate measures of distance between objects in the picture can be obtained.

Modeling Consensus in the Crowd

William E. Feinberg and Norris R. Johnson (1988; 1990) base their simulation model on the emergent-norm view of collective behavior. That is, collective behavior is the process through which "members of a collectivity seek information to define an ambiguous situation, generate agreements concerning the appropriate action in the situation, and develop a group response to the situation" (1990:35). The simulation model is a probability model that considers both the probability of choosing a radical or conservative course of action and the probability of moving toward or away from the center of the "crowd." Together, the level of probability of agreement and the level of probability of movement reflect the ambiguity level within the crowd. In the Feinberg and Johnson simulation model, the choices and numbers of individuals in clusters within the "crowd" influence individual action choices.

The results of multiple trials of this model show that increased suggestibility reduces the time it takes to achieve consensus in the simulated crowd. This suggests the interesting possibility that quick consensus somewhat reduces the likelihood that extreme consensus will develop. Results such as these provided by simulation show that the effect of ambiguity on consensus is more complex than is revealed by present studies of individuals and small groups.

Egress Modeling

In the 1980s *Hazard I* was developed by researchers at the National Institute of Standards and Technology's Building and Fire Research Laboratory. *Hazard I* is an integrated computer model for fire-hazard assessment, and the latest version of this software is now distributed by the National Fire Protection Association. The software is intended for use by firefighters and designers, who can input structural and performance information from planned or existing structures. *Hazard I* performs calculations to predict or model the spread of smoke, gasses, heat, and oxygen depletion throughout the building over time. This software also models the activation of heat and smoke detectors and predicts fatality and survival rates.

One portion of *Hazard I*, Exitt, simulates emergency evacuation processes for different numbers of occupants, delays in notification, decision making, behavioral interactions, and the physical capabilities of occupants. The fire-hazard model requires the specification of a complete fire scenario, including the geometry and construction of the building and the location and combustion properties of burning materials. The model also allows the user to specify both generalized and mechanical venting, which is critical in the production and travel of heat and smoke within the structure. Users must also specify the number, initial location, delay in notification, behavioral interactions, and assumed limitations of the occupants.

Hazard I then predicts the outcome of the chosen fire scenario as the eventual fate of each occupant—either the time of escape or the time, location, and cause of the fatality (National Institute for Standards and Technology, 1998). *Hazard I* variables such as the number of occupants, layout of the building, delay in notification, and the amount and spread of heat, smoke and toxic fumes have all been identified as critical factors in the success or failure of emergency egress (see chapter 10).

Marching Band Presentations

Advantage Showare® is software for designing formations and movement for marching band presentations. Virtually any conceivable formation or shape can be designed using straight lines, arcs, circles, blocks, triangles, freeform shapes, or a single player. Formations and movements can be previewed in 3-D perspective from any point around the field and any viewing angle. Player symbols, representing different instruments, sections, squads or numbers, may be used on the screen or be generated as printed charts. Most types of marching movement can be designed, including: shift, rotate, expand-contract, flex, follow-the-leader, float, and sequential drill. Information concerning step size and paths is provided.

Both sketches and detailed printouts of player paths, background charts, individual player coordinates, individual section printouts, student and director orientation charts, and charts displaying any count of the show can be printed. These are used to evaluate proposed marching band presentations and for rehearsing actual presentations.

Simulation of Behavior within Gatherings

In Powers's *Gathering Simulator* each simulated actor (SA) is programmed according to the principles of the perception control theory model (McPhail, Powers and Tucker, 1992; Schweingruber, 1995). Each SA can be assigned an individual goal, using one or more of three reference signals: (1) avoiding collisions with "disturbances" such as objects and other SAs, and/or (2) moving to a particular

X/Y coordinate, and/or (3) seeking and maintaining a specified physical distance from another SA. There is also a setting for the amount of sensitivity to error (i.e., speed of reaction) for each of the reference signals.

As many as 255 SAs can be located at specific coordinates on the field, or they can be randomly distributed throughout the field. On the screen, the SAs appear as "Ps." Each SA is programmed to control for another SA or an X/Y coordinate and may take a different path depending on the disturbances encountered during a particular "run." A "run" begins when an SA begins its movement and ends when it has reached its destination. By programming these settings for a number of actors, users are able to simulate purposive collective action such as locomotion, tracking, surges, and assembling.

Gathering Simulator presents a real-time simulation of collective action. After a few moments of watching the simulations users almost always begin to refer to the moving "Ps" as "people." Perception control theory explains collective action as the result of individuals who are controlling for reference signals that are similar or related. It is the interaction of one SA's purposive output with other SAs that yields collective action. The outcome of the above-mentioned individual goals is a ring formation of Ps at the X/Y coordinate. This simulation result is much like those described by Milgram and Toch (1969) and similar to those photographed by McPhail on many occasions.

It is interesting to note that this simulation results in a ring formation and not a scattering or jumble of SAs. It is also important to note that none of the SAs were programmed to follow a particular route to a specified destination; they were programmed to seek and find a target person. Nor were the SAs programmed to form a ring at a specified coordinate. The resulting social form is an outcome of those individuals' similar goals and their negotiation of the other SAs encountered in the course of pursuing those goals. *Gathering Simulator* has been used for professional presentations and instructional purposes and is not presently commercially available.

SUMMARY

This chapter offers an overview of the various research methods that have been used by sociologists who study collective behavior and collective action. Numerous methodological advances in the use of historical material, surveys, official statistics and archives, experiments, and participant and direct observation have occurred during the past thirty years. New methodologies have also been developed, including computer simulation.

Some *historical accounts*, such as Mackay's brief description of tulip mania, have been used to illustrate the mass hysteria image of collective behavior. More rigorous historical analysis, such as the work of Rudé, provides a model for the qualitative investigation of the composition, actions, and motives of the revolutionary crowd. Gamson developed a methodology for the systematic and comprehensive search of the historical record. These procedures yield quantitative information that can be analyzed and interpreted using the statistical tools of modern sociology.

Survey research is the most prominent method of sociological investigation. Researchers have used modified survey methods within the crowd and have obtained useful information. *Official statistics* and data from police *archives* have been used to study such diverse phenomena as riot participation and media coverage of political demonstrations.

Experiments involve the control and measurement of key variables. Theories of collective behavior employ many variables that cannot be controlled or directly measured; hence, few collective behavior experiments have been conducted. We considered Mintz's classic experiment in nonadaptive group behavior, or panic. This experiment generally has been interpreted as illustrating the impact of "reward structure" within the panic-producing situation. Mintz's study also shows how diminished sensory conditions contribute to nonadaptive responses. The unjust authority experiment by Gamson, Fireman, and Rytina further illustrates the possibility of simulating more elaborate and carefully monitored situations, thereby bringing collective action phenomena into the laboratory.

Perhaps the most important methodological advance in recent decades is the firsthand observation and recording of collective phenomena. *Direct observation,* coupled with procedures for conducting interviews within the crowd, represents the first real penetration of the crowd for the purposes of obtaining systematic sociological data. Lofland's *participant observation* of the Divine Precepts has provided valuable insights into recruitment, conversion, and maintenance of faith. There is also a wealth of observation by participants that can provide valuable insights into groups that often conceal their internal processes from outsiders.

McPhail and others have developed and used techniques to systematically observe behavior within political demonstrations and other gatherings. This research is an integral part of international research on the policing of mass demonstrations in modern democracies. This research also provides basic knowledge of the kinds of collective action that occur within gatherings of all kinds.

Computer assisted design (CAD) software is the basis of nearly all industrial production in today's electronically integrated world economy. *Computer simulation* and modeling are also used to forecast the weather, predict fluctuations in the stock market, and make urban land-use projections. It is not surprising that people have also simulated and modeled collective behavior and collective action.

Using probability calculations, Norris R. Johnson and William E. Feinberg simulated the process through which members of a collectivity seek information to define an ambiguous situation, generate agreements concerning the appropriate action in the situation, and develop a group response to the situation. The results of multiple trials of this model show that increased suggestibility reduces the time it takes to achieve consensus in the simulated crowd and that quick consensus somewhat reduces the likelihood that very complete consensus will develop.

Modern software such as *Hazard I,* used to predict or model emergency evacuation processes; *Advantage* Showare,® which assists in the designing of formations and movements for marching band presentations; and *Gathering Simulator,* a real-time simulator of locomotion, tracking, surges, and assembling have made it much easier for those who wish to research collective behavior and collective action.

In order to create computer simulations of collective behavior and collective action, researchers must carefully examine the theoretical assumptions that underlie their explanations of collective phenomena. Repeated simulations and alterations in simulation conditions can suggest ideas to researchers that are not immediately or intuitively obvious from existing theories.

PART II

COLLECTIVE BEHAVIOR AND COLLECTIVE ACTION IN EVERYDAY LIFE

CHAPTER 4

RUMOR AND COMMUNICATION

Rumors are usually thought of as unreliable stories from unknown or questionable sources that are passed indiscriminately from one person to another. Those who pass along rumors are referred to as rumormongers, gossips, or busybodies. Today, a large portion of communication that transpires on the Internet can also be described as unreliable stories from unknown or questionable sources. As only an hour or so spent surfing the Net will reveal, there is an astounding variety of topics that can be accessed quickly. The amount of information available defies quantification. Much of this information comes from unknown, or only nominally identified, individuals, groups and organizations. Some websites indicate they have been visited several thousand times within a few months.

There are hundreds of message boards and home pages that are identified specifically by their creators as a source of rumors about their topics. The Silicon Rumor Mill, for instance, is a web-based message board for people who have an interest in the computer chip industry. The Mill is a place where ". . . otherwise responsible adults sling rumor, innuendo, blatantly false and prejudiced information, silicon soap opera and worse. You'd be nuts to believe anything you read here, and certifiably crazy to base any important decisions on information from this board!" (www.gulker.com/agents/rumor.html). Likewise, The Celebrator Beer News website for microbrewers and home brewers is dubbed as a source of "Brew News, Views, Rumors and Innuendo. . ." (www.celebrator.com/celebrator/). The Supershadow site provides web users with ". . . prequel news and rumors from exclusive Lucasfilm sources and from *Star Wars* fans from around the world!" Users have only a nominal knowledge of who maintains this site, hosted by Lucasfilm insiders who are only identified by the intriguing names of "Vespon," "FireForce," "Eon," "Vecton," "Dark Ocean," "SithFox," "THX-Disciple," and "SpyLord."

While rumors can include the most fantastic, outlandish, and farfetched hyperbole, most rumors fall in line with our day-to-day affairs (Shibutani, 1966). Many rumors deal with the products we use every day. *Product rumors* usually sound plausible, but even rigorous attempts to verify them have failed. Product rumors have occurred throughout this century. In the 1930s and 1940s, for instance, rumors circulated that a leper had been discovered working in the Chesterfield cigarette factory in Richmond, Virginia. This rumor was sometimes accompanied by a companion rumor that the leper story was untrue and had been started by Chesterfield's competitors or by religious groups opposed to smoking. Even though Liggett and Meyers Tobacco Company eventually offered a $25,000 reward, the source of the rumor was never found (Jacobson, 1948).

During the 1950s, a rumor circulated that a worker in a Coca-Cola bottling plant had fallen into a vat of cola and drowned. Because of the cola's acid content, the body had been almost completely dissolved when the accident was discovered a few days later. Coca-Cola from this vat had already been distributed across the United States. Beginning in 1979, rumors circulated that McDonald's hamburgers were made out of processed earthworms. This rumor was made more plausible by bona fide news stories a few years earlier that scientists were experimenting with earthworms as a usable source of protein. Variants of the rumor included stories that scientists had perfected the worm protein and that McDonald's had secretly purchased the formula. Investigators concluded that the stories first started in Chattanooga, Tennessee. In recent years, other fast-food chains have been vulnerable to this type of rumor. Since about 1990, Procter and Gamble has been accused of using a satanic symbol for their logo and contributing portions of their profits to satanic cults.

Stories about the questionable properties of a product or a practice can potentially harm sales and damage the reputation of manufacturers. Such stories also carry the potential of damaging the sales and reputations of competitors. Consequently, the Federal Trade Commission has heard numerous cases of people and organizations spreading false information about products.

In 1981, rumors circulated that a customer was bitten by a very poisonous snake while shopping at a Kmart store in Detroit. She had been trying on a coat made in Taiwan, and the snake allegedly was in the sleeve. Somehow, it was rumored, a poisonous snake had laid eggs in bundles of clothing headed for the United States, and the snakes had hatched en route to Detroit. A similar rumor, that a woman had been bitten by a snake in the greens section of a Kroger grocery store's produce aisle, circulated in Dayton, Ohio, and was investigated by Dan Miller (1992). In both instances, variations of the rumor included reports that the victim had died or had lost an arm from the effects of the poison. No hospitals in Detroit or Dayton have ever reported treating people for snake bites received in Kmart or Kroger, nor have these stores ever been sued for this sort of harm.

Another type of rumor is the *disaster rumor*. During disasters, people must often make quick decisions based on information that comes to them in unusual ways. Sometimes this information is wrong. Occasionally, people are warned of danger when no danger is present, but they take protective action on the basis of such information. These events have been referred to as *pseudodisasters* and have been considered instances of true panic. For instance, in 1955, during Hurricane Diane, residents of Port Jervis, New York, heard and passed on numerous reports that a large dam had broken and that flooding was imminent. At one point, fire sirens were sounded to warn of the coming flood. In fact, the dam in question was holding firm. Still, nearly 75 percent of the area's residents heard these rumors, and about one-third of those who heard them made some attempt to leave the threatened area (Danzig, Thayer, and Galanter, 1958).

In 1973, people near the Barseback Nuclear Power Station in Sweden heard what they thought was a news bulletin describing a catastrophe similar to the

Three Mile Island incident. In fact, the bulletin was fictitious and had been part of a public-interest talk show dealing with the risks of atomic energy. For the next few days, radio and newspaper stories reported widespread panic reactions in southern Sweden. Later, the Swedish Board of Psychological Defense reported that the extent of the panic caused by the broadcast was much less than the media had reported (Rosengren, Arvidson, and Sturesson, 1975). In order to prevent the spread of such disaster rumors in times of crisis, the Federal Emergency Management Agency was established in 1979. It provides guidelines for community pre-planning for disaster. Pre-planning includes establishing a disaster communication center to collect and evaluate information and to disseminate accurate information during disaster.

In times of conflict, *atrocity rumors* detail vicious acts committed by one's enemies. These stories portray "the other side" in the most villainous of terms. In England during World War II, the story was often told of a family who had received a letter from their eldest son, who was in a German prisoner of war camp. The letter said that the Germans treated prisoners well, that the camp was comfortable, and that the food was "almost as good as home." The stamp on the envelope, the letter said, should be of some interest to the youngest son, Alfie, who collected stamps. Because the family had no son named Alfie, they became suspicious. When the stamp was steamed off the envelope, the family was horrified to read the message, "They have torn out my tongue." After the war, it was discovered that much the same story had circulated in Germany. This time the son was writing from a Russian prison camp, and the hidden message read, "They have cut off my feet"(Jacobson, 1948). Modern conflicts, such as the 1989 invasion of Kuwait by Iraq, the Bosnian ethnic cleansing programs, or the ethnic violence in Rwanda have also been accompanied by such atrocity rumors. Even though the actual level of interpersonal cruelty in these conflicts is extremely high, accompanying rumors of mutilations such as eye gouging, tongue ripping and amputations exaggerate these cruelties.

Atrocity rumors carry particular impact when opposing groups are in daily and close contact with one another. Such is the case with rumors that are part of race riots. Perhaps the most lurid atrocity rumors ever to circulate in the United States accompanied the Detroit race riot of 1943. After fighting broke out between groups of white sailors and black civilians on Belle Isle, one of Detroit's public beaches, rumors were spread within both the white and African-American communities. Whites passed on the story that a black had ". . . raped and killed a white woman on Belle Isle." African Americans told how white sailors had ". . . thrown a Negro woman and her baby off the Belle Isle Bridge." Adding to the atmosphere of hate, the Ku Klux Klan distributed anti-black, anti-Jewish, and anti-Catholic literature during the riot. The riot lasted little more than twenty-four hours, yet thirty-four people were killed and more than $2 million worth of property was destroyed, making this riot the most intensely violent in our nation's history.

With the growth of the Internet, *conspiracy rumors* have flourished. Anyone who regularly participates in discussion lists on the Internet is likely to encounter rumors warning patrons of viruses that can infect their computers and destroy all their files. Rumors about "web cookies," which are in actuality short pieces of data used by web servers to help identify users, have reached ". . . almost mythical proportions, frightening users and worrying their managers" (U.S. Department of Energy, 1998). Rumors have described web cookies as programs that can scan hard drives, retrieve passwords and credit card numbers, and list all the software on the user's computer. Computer viruses and such things as web cookies are seen as plots or conspiracies hatched by hacker groups, greedy corporations, or the federal government.

There are hundreds of websites dealing with alleged conspiracies. Everything imaginable is considered to be a conspiracy—by someone! The long list of conspiracies includes the assassinations of John and Robert Kennedy, Martin Luther King, Jr., and Princess Diana. Other websites claim that the Bureau of Alcohol, Tobacco, and Firearms conspired to destroy David Koresh and the Branch Davidian Church in Waco, Texas, and is conspiring to destroy survivalist and militia groups across the United States. Websites are maintained regarding the deaths of famous musicians such as Kurt Cobain (conspiracy to make his alleged murder appear as a suicide) and Tupac Shakur (his "murder" was allegedly faked, and he is alive and hiding out).

Several websites deal with federal government "cover-ups." For instance, the cover-up of the shooting down of TWA Flight 800 by U.S. military aircraft is the topic of several websites. There are web pages purporting to show that NASA has altered and edited the Mars Pathfinder mission photos to conceal such things as domed structures, towers, and even bones on the Martian landscape. Web pages speculate the federal government is covering up its study of crashed alien spacecraft in so-called Area 51. Cover-up and conspiracy rumors exist about health issues. Some web pages assert that the government and business groups created and deliberately spread the AIDS virus. Other web pages describe an alleged conspiracy between the FDA and tampon maker Procter and Gamble to hide the dangers of toxic shock syndrome.

Many rumors are passed around for a considerable length of time before they die out. Years later, they may again reappear in a slightly modified form. Rumors sometimes acquire variations as they are passed from one region of the country to another. A few rumors are truly international travelers, hopping from nation to nation. Rumors that endure for long periods of time or reappear often are referred to as *urban legends or folklore*. Jan Harold Brunvald describes dozens of urban legends, including the persistent claim that the FCC will soon propose a large surcharge for modem use and data transmission by computer (1993:188–89). Usually this message is coupled with a request for users to voice their opposition immediately to the FCC and House and Senate members. Other urban legends can be traced much further back in time, versions of which are to be found in *Grimm's Fairy Tales* and the folk tales of the Middle Ages (Brunvald, 1993:71–73).

The Loch Ness monster and Bigfoot have attained folklore status, and the web contains sites devoted to them both, as well as to numerous other strange beings. Creatures such as the Jersey Devil, the Dover Demon, the gigantic Loveland Frog, and the Maryland Goatman have become part of the identity of the communities in which they were reported. Large dinosaurs (*Mokele-Mbembe*) and fifty-foot snakes are rumored to be alive and well in Central Africa. The Caribbean islands, Central America, and South Florida Hispanic communities allegedly are home to the bloodsucking *chupacabras* (vampires) that prey on small livestock and pets. Lake Okanagan's Ogopogo, Lake Tahoe's Tessie, Lake Erie's South Bay Bessie, the Alkali Lake monster, and the White River monster bear many similarities to Loch Ness's Nessie (Shadowlands Mysterious Creatures Page, 1998).

Numerous active and frequently updated websites transmit information worldwide about the history, latest sightings and searches for these creatures. There is a high volume of visits to these websites. Years ago, these types of stories received much less attention and were only transmitted by word of mouth and in local newspapers. Occasionally, collections of such stories would be published in books such as Brunvald's. The Internet clearly provides a means of making folklore of all types come alive for young and old alike.

Before considering the classic sociological studies of rumor, it should be noted that some stories dismissed as rumors by government officials, politicians, reporters, and editors later turn out to be true. Until the late 1700s, for example, authorities dismissed the amusing stories peasants told of "lightning stones" or "thunder stones" falling from the sky. The thought of rocks falling from the sky was totally contrary to the views of the universe and creation held at the time. Even witnesses were confused by what they had seen. Norwegian peasants thought that thunder stones were useful to women in labor because they would aid in the delivery of the child. In 1795, German physicist E. F. Chladni wrote a small book advancing the argument that thunder stones were the residue of meteors that traveled through space. In a very obliging fashion, the large and widely observed meteor shower over Italy provided direct confirmation of his theory a few months later. The peasants were right—stones *did* fall from the sky! (Westrum, 1978)

As opposition to the Vietnam War grew in the United States, stories of the savage nature of the conflict began to circulate. There were abundant stories about Viet Cong atrocities, but as the war continued, stories were also told of how American troops tortured and killed prisoners and also shot or napalmed civilians. Almost always, military and government officials flatly denied these rumors, which was easy to do, considering the sources were opponents of the war. In a few instances, it was acknowledged that civilian casualties had occurred but that these had been accidents or the result of misidentification. The wanton killing of civilians was not the way Americans fought wars. Finally, in the spring of 1970, major newspapers and magazines carried stories of the Mylai 4 (Songmy) massacre. Mylai was a small hamlet in South Vietnam. On March 16, 1968 (it took nearly twenty months for the story to reach the public), five hundred women, children, and old men were shot down and bayoneted by American troops. Perhaps even more disturbing, the Mylai disclosure brought forth a number of reports about other similar incidents involving American troops in Vietnam. Mylai served to further divide an already divided nation.

It is more difficult to recognize true rumors in those situations where no previous denials have been given. Survivors of the atomic bomb dropped on Hiroshima, for instance, tried to explain the horrible destruction that had occurred. Many survivors had seen or heard reports of the incendiary raids on other Japanese cities. The total devastation of Hiroshima, however, was beyond comparison. Minutes after the bomb detonated, the smell of oil hung in the air. This led many to speculate that the lone American bomber that flew over the city before the blast had sprayed finely vaporized gasoline into the air and that the gasoline had then been detonated with an aerial flare. A prominent physician suggested that fine magnesium powder rather than gasoline had been dropped and that it had been ignited by electrical sparks from trolley cars. Another common theory held that a very large incendiary bomb called a "Molotov flower basket" scattered an enormous number of smaller incendiaries across Hiroshima and that they had been ignited simultaneously. Finally, some suggested that Hiroshima had been destroyed by the energy released when the smallest particles known to humankind were somehow split—in this case, a rumor that turned out to be true (Shibutani, 1966).

Finally, it should be noted that an initially inaccurate account of an event can be transmitted without much further distortion. After a Nova Scotia tornado, the rumor that a child died on the way to a hospital circulated throughout the disaster-struck community in the hours immediately following the tornado's impact. The girl, it turned out, had received serious injuries but was recovering. Residents of the community who had overheard police radio transmissions that claimed the child was dying were the first to pass on the news of her death. Beyond this, however, the rumor accurately portrayed the circumstances of her rescue and the extent and nature of her injuries. Once stated, the content of the rumor remained extremely consistent from one telling to another (Scanlon, 1977).

The study of rumor is a long-standing tradition in the field of collective behavior. In contrast, recent studies of collective action focus on communication and exclude rumor. This difference is not a minor shift in terminology. As the above discussion indicates, the study of rumor encompasses rumoring during mass hysterias, disasters and riots as well as folklore and urban legends. Some discussion of rumor has also given consideration to how rumoring meets the psychological needs of those who transmit rumors.

None of these issues are part of how collective action treats communication. As we shall see in this and later chapters, discussions of collective action focus on how communication is used to organize and frame the objectives of social movements and protest. The collective action perspective also looks at communication within gatherings.

RUMOR AND THEORIES OF COLLECTIVE BEHAVIOR

Mass Hysteria Theory

Discussions of mass hysteria emphasize that under conditions of intense collective excitement, people lose their ability to distinguish fact from fancy, and they become excitable, suggestible, uncritical, and irrational. Many events that have been identified as mass hysterias could aptly be described as hysterias of rumors; that is, fantastic stories come to dominate people's conversations. Orrin E. Klapp (1972:116) describes rumor as the medium of anxious hysteria. In anxious or rumor hysteria, there is no real threat to people. Imaginary threats, however, are embodied in the content of rumors that rapidly circulate through the distressed population.

The nature of rumor and the rumor process is derived from people's psychological transformations during mass hysteria. Because people are excited, they spread rumors rapidly and indiscriminately, and because they are suggestible, they pass along the most outlandish stories as fact. Because people are uncritical and irrational, they spread rumors that usually run counter to established views and the statements of authorities. Rumors are seldom accurate, but they are internally consistent—a consistency that is based not on critical consideration but on "paranoid logic" (Klapp, 1972:251).

Communication during rumor is free flowing; people willingly depart from the channels on which they rely for everyday communication. They give word-of-mouth communication the same or greater credibility than they give the established media. People may spread rumors through the use of hastily written leaflets, exchange rumors with total strangers, or pass on overheard conversations. In the deliberate transmission of product rumors, advertising agencies used teams of field workers to work stores, subways, train stops, and other places of routine public gatherings. Feigning real conversation, these workers would loudly praise or condemn a given product or manufacturer, and eavesdroppers would then pass the story on to others (Jacobson, 1948:159–86).

Stories and images fashioned by rumor usually serve the psychological needs of those who invent or pass along the rumor. According to Klapp (1972:116), likely rumor participants include the uneducated. Increasing levels of education tend to insulate people from the gullible acceptance of rumor. Other likely participants include those with pent-up hatreds, aggressions, or other tensions. Spreading rumors allows for the expression of feelings that would be otherwise held in check by psychological and social constraints.

Although people may have conscious or unconscious motives for involvement in the rumor process, participants are not totally free from group constraints. That is, motives alone do not shape the content of rumor. People tend to fabricate or distort information to fit the central theme of the rumor (Klapp, 1972:251). For example, perpetrators of violent crimes are identified as members of minority groups in the rumor process long before police investigation is complete. Evidence counter to this view is ignored. Motives for the crime, weapons used, and injuries inflicted are all molded to fit prevailing minority-group stereotypes. For instance, after Susan Smith drowned her two young sons in Sumpter, South Carolina, she concocted a story that an African-American carjacker had stolen her car and took her sons with him. This story was widely accepted at first (Squires and Greer, 1994). Moments after the bombing of the Oklahoma City Federal Building, rumors spread that "Islamic terrorists" had been connected to the bombing. The facts that emerge during investigation, however, may be quite contrary to the image of the crime conveyed by rumor. Sometimes the facts will be accepted because the rumor process has run its course and excitement has diminished. As the facts come to be accepted, few people recall the fantastic stories that circulated days earlier.

In general, people who hold this perspective view rumor as both a mechanism and a manifestation of mass hysteria. Rumor is the mechanism through which mass hysterias occur, because rumor can excite the people who participate in the exchange. Rumor also creates the bizarre images on which hysterical action is based. Rumor is a manifestation of hysteria because it clearly shows the operation of suggestibility and diminished critical ability.

Emergent-Norm Theory

For Turner and Killian (1972:32), rumor is the process through which people develop shared definitions of unstructured and ambiguous situations and is, therefore, "the characteristic mode of communication in collective behavior." In the early phases of disaster recovery, for example, there is often very little clear and certain information indicating the extent of damage, death, and injury, or the likelihood of further danger. People must evaluate and pass along information that is often incomplete or contradictory, and the group must choose between competing views of the situation. In such unstructured and ambiguous situations, rumor provides both needed information and a sense of certainty about the situation. The sense of certainty develops in part because the group attends to some features of the situation and ignores others during the rumor process. Rumor provides the basis for emergent norms that give direction to the activities of the collectivity.

Sensitization In general, communication during rumor is more open and free flowing than usual. Turner and Killian (1972:37–40) account for this in terms of increased interpersonal sensitivity within the crowd. This sensitization occurs during the milling process, which includes both "wild" and "mild" activity. An example of intense milling would be people's rapid movement and shouting as they converge on the scene of an accident, while low-key milling would be restless movements and polite but pointless conversations that occur when people wait for an overdue train. Even silence and subtle gestures can sensitize people to one another and communicate moods. Milling, in whatever form it takes, sensitizes people to those around them through the mechanism of mutual role taking.

As people become sensitized to one another, spontaneous communication usually develops between those who do not ordinarily interact. Such communication is open and unguarded, and polite conversations between strangers may be surprisingly intimate and candid. Even the norms of communication that exist between friends and neighbors may become more relaxed. For example, someone may telephone friends at mealtime or at hours later than usual to pass along information. In general, interpersonal sensitization accounts for the rapid spread of rumors.

Suggestibility Turner and Killian (1972:32–38) point out that group consensus emerges much more quickly than usual during the rumor process, which gives the appearance of increased suggestibility. It is not, however, the kind of suggestibility that occurs because of emotional arousal or diminished critical ability. Suggestibility during rumor arises because of the uncertainty of the situation. With increasing uncertainty, the greater are the fluctuations in people's judgment when they attempt to describe the situation confronting them. For example, through rumor, people may initially provide extreme estimates of the numbers of people injured in a disaster. Some may suggest that few people are injured, while others suggest that many are injured. Given such extreme initial judgments, consensus is reached in a surprisingly short time. For Turner and Killian, it is the uncertainty of the situation and not emotional arousal that increases individual susceptibility to the suggestions of others.

Selective Definition In the rumor process, the group chooses between alternate and competing definitions of the situation, closely attending some views while ignoring others. Turner and Killian (1972:47–50) point out that during the rumoring and milling that preceded some lynchings, information pertaining to the guilt and villainy of the victim was attended to very closely. On the other hand, information that suggested innocence and appeals to "let the law handle it" were ignored. The selective definition of a situation provides the basis for shared action. It provides the standards by which group behavior is judged.

Keynoting Selective definition occurs in three steps, the first of which is keynoting. Keynoting establishes the general boundaries within which later decisions will fall and the assumptions upon which proposed action is based. In the case of some lynchings, keynoting establishes that the victim is guilty and deserving of severe punishment. Keynoting also establishes that "taking the law into one's own hands" is a reasonable community response. In a sense, the fundamental assumptions are set at this stage: the victim is guilty, and a lynching is appropriate. As more people vocally agree with these propositions, other crowd members find it increasingly difficult to express views that run counter to the emerging theme. The absence of open expression of counterviews adds to the impression that keynotes are the feelings of the majority.

Symbolization The next step in the process of selective definition is symbolization. Turner and Killian argue that communication normally occurs largely through cognitive symbols. The object of cognitive symbols is separated from the feelings that the object arouses in the user. Proper names, or terms such as *my worthy opponent* or *the accused*, are cognitive symbols. Usually such terms do not call out uniform emotional responses. Selective definition involves the use of mystical symbols that do arouse uniform emotional responses among the audience. Mystical symbols include name-calling and inflammatory terms such as *commie, bastard, honkey, gook, kike,* or *nigger.* This type of symbolization simplifies the situation and neutralizes norms that might inhibit the crowd from unrestrained action toward the object of the symbol. The open and frequent use of such derogatory terms often signifies a "point of no return" in the development of collective hostile actions.

Coordination Finally, selective definition involves coordination. Statements that call attention to the separate interests of the collectivity do not permit unified action. Particularistic statements can be used to hinder the development of hostile actions. Police, for example, may call crowd members by name and ask them to leave, saying, "People like you should know better than to act this way." Ministers may remind people in the crowd that their actions are not in keeping with "what you learn in church." City officials may remind people that their actions "degrade their fine town." The effective coordinating symbol must emphasize features of the situation and identities to which a wide range of people may respond in a uniform manner.

Rumor and Crowd Action Activities and symbols that simplify the situation, eliminate ambiguity and conflicting views, and provide the basis for uniform response are the fundamentals of crowd action. Emergent norms and a sense of certainty grow together and reinforce one another. It is through the rumor process that such symbols and norms develop (Turner and Killian, 1972:55). Rumor is the characteristic mode of communication in collective behavior.

Value-Added Theory

For Smelser, rumor fills an important role in the development of collective episodes. Specifically, rumor is necessary for the development of generalized belief. Rumor is also an important part of mobilization for action. In many respects, Smelser's discussion of rumor runs parallel to that of the mass hysteria perspective.

Generalized Belief According to Smelser, beliefs that prepare people for action are present in all collective behavior, but generalized belief differs from those that are part of everyday action. Generalized belief reduces ambiguity created by conditions of structural strain. In order to reduce ambiguity, generalized belief is simplistic; it necessarily does not reflect the complexity of situations revealed by careful scrutiny. Generalized belief also prepares people for collective action by creating shared or common objects, giving focus to anxiety or discontent, and fostering consensus.

Given the nature of generalized beliefs, it is obvious how rumor is instrumental in their development. As a form of communication, rumor creates simplistic views of complex or ambiguous situations. It also creates common objects, gives focus to conscious and unconscious motives, and fosters a sense of certainty and consensus. The characterization of generalized beliefs and rumor are so similar that Smelser sometimes uses the two terms interchangeably (Smelser, 1962:82–84).

Panics are based on generalized hysterical beliefs that transform an ambiguous (and sometimes harmless) situation into a definite and potent threat. Fear-laden rumors of impending disaster, descriptions of crimes, and stories of monsters and UFOs provide the basis for generalized beliefs. Such rumors eliminate ambiguity by creating an object that is sure to harm or destroy anyone in its path. Even though these rumors foster fear, they also provide predictability and structure.

Crazes are based on hysterical wish-fulfillment beliefs. Rumors of fortunes made in land or commodity speculation reduce ambiguity in financial dealings. Hysterical wish-fulfillment beliefs portray the possibility of wealth in unrealistic terms—as a "sure thing." Rumors also play a role in the transformation of crazes into financial panics. Bankruptcy rumors, rumors that the big investors are selling, or rumors of embezzlement are enough to turn bold speculators into panicked sellers.

Hostile outbursts are based on generalized hostile beliefs. These beliefs portray the object of attack in bold, simple, negative terms. Rumor entails the use of mystical or emotion-provoking symbols. Generalized hostile beliefs also include a feeling of omnipotence—a belief that the crowd has the power to remove, punish, or destroy the object of attack. In the case of attacks against authority, these beliefs may well be unfounded. They are fostered by rumors describing the ineffectiveness of authorities or their lack of resolve to fight against the crowd. Rumors may also exaggerate the strength of the crowd or the likelihood that others will rise up with the crowd when attacks commence.

Norm- and value-oriented social movements are based on beliefs that envision the reconstruction of a deteriorating normative and value structure. These beliefs are created by rumors describing the decadence of the existing society. Bizarre stories about satanic rock groups, promiscuous sex, horrendous crimes, political corruption, dangerous environmental pollution, and wanton use of drugs portray today's society as being in dire need of drastic reform. The belief that the social movement's program is certain to bring about desired changes is also necessary for continued reform efforts.

Mobilization for Action Once generalized beliefs are in place, it is necessary to bring people into action. According to Smelser, this occurs through the action of leadership. For panics and crazes, leadership may simply take the form of models of appropriate action. Sometimes these models are concocted in the rumor process. Rumors of bankruptcy or that big investors are selling out may have no basis in fact. In hostile outbursts, leadership is often emergent and may come from people who spread reports of police brutality or pass out hate literature. The leadership of social movements can assume many of the characteristics of leadership within formal organizations. Leaders of social movements are often in a position to manipulate information through the use of planted rumors. Leaders may also have access to telephone numbers, computerized mailing lists, and the established media. Smelser acknowledges that leaders may manipulate information sent through these channels. Regardless of the way in which information is conveyed, calls to action must be expressed in unambiguous and emotional terms.

Collective Behavior and Rumor The mass-hysteria, value-added, and emergent-norm perspectives differ in many fundamental ways. In their view of rumor, however, they are much alike. The mass-hysteria perspective and, to a great extent, the emergent-norm perspective characterize rumor as conveying simplistic, often inaccurate, and emotion-provoking images of ambiguous situations. Smelser adopts this view of rumor, which fits quite conveniently with his view of collective behavior. Collective behavior is based on generalized beliefs—simplistic and emotion-provoking explanations of ambiguous situations created by structural strain.

CLASSICAL APPROACHES TO RUMOR

Rumor and Distortion: Gordon W. Allport and Leo Postman

Shortly after the United States entered World War II, rumor became a serious national concern. People told and retold stories of how our losses at Pearl Harbor were far greater than our government officials admitted. Some stories told that our entire Pacific Fleet and nearly all of our military aircraft had been destroyed and that our entire West Coast was defenseless. In fact, our losses at Pearl Harbor were greater than officials could admit publicly, so these stories were of considerable annoyance to those who had to mobilize a nation for war. Pearl Harbor stories became so troublesome that about ten weeks after the attack (February 23, 1942), President Roosevelt spoke out. His "fireside chat" radio broadcast accurately described the extent of the damage and did a great deal to restore confidence in our military situation. Still, the stories continued for months afterward. Throughout the war, government agencies such as the Office of War Information maintained active rumor-control programs. These programs included public speakers, special newspaper features such as the "The Rumor Clinic" of the *Boston Herald-Traveler*, and, of course, the "Loose Lips Might Sink Ships" posters.

During this time, Gordon W. Allport and Leo Postman carried out a series of studies on the rumor process. Allport and Postman (1965:ix) defined *rumor* as "a specific (or topical) proposition for belief, passed along from person to person, usually by word of mouth, without secure standards of evidence being presented." Even though people may begin their remarks with the phrase "It's only a rumor, but" . . . the implication is that fact is being presented.

Allport and Postman (1965:33–34) were the first to state the basic law of rumors: The intensity of rumor is the product of the importance of the subject to the individual and the ambiguity of the evidence pertaining to the topic at issue. According to Allport and Postman's law, rumor is most likely to occur when people are intensely interested in a topic and little definite news or official information is available. Rumor is unlikely when people have little interest in a topic and/or official information is plentiful.

Posters such as this one were produced by the Office of War Information during World War II as part of an active rumor-control program. © CORBIS.

An Experiment in Serial Transmission Using their definition and basic law of rumor, Allport and Postman devised an experiment to show how rumors are transmitted. Interestingly, their experiment was conducted before audiences. Allport and Postman argued that this would not contaminate the results because in real life, rumors are often passed along within groups. Further, they conducted the experiment a few times without an audience and obtained essentially the same results. They tried their experiment before a wide range of audiences including college undergraduates, army trainees, community groups, patients in an army hospital, participants in a teachers' conference, police officials, and children in a private school.

The specific procedures used by Allport and Postman have been described as creating a *serial transmission* pattern of communication. They selected six or seven volunteer subjects from the audience and sent them from the room, then selected another person to act as an "eyewitness." Next, Allport and Postman called one subject back into the room and seated the subject so that he or she could not see a picture that was being projected onto a movie screen. The pictures were usually line drawings of various scenes, including a combat scene, an accident scene, a street scene, and the interior of a crowded streetcar. The pictures included males and females, whites and blacks, signs on buildings, vehicles, clocks, and ambulances. The eyewitness then described about twenty details of the picture to the first subject.

After the eyewitness described the picture, a second subject was brought into the room and seated next to the first. The first subject then retold the eyewitness account to the second subject. Then the third subject was brought in and seated next to the second subject, who told the third subject about the picture. The researchers continued the process until the final subject described the picture. During the experiment, subjects were not allowed to interrupt or question one another or ask for repetitions. Allport and Postman justified this feature of the experiment by claiming that rumor spreaders seldom ask for clarification in real life.

In nearly every instance, the description given by the last subject bore little resemblance to the eyewitness description or the picture. Many details were lost in retelling, some details were exaggerated, and sometimes details were added that did not occur in either the picture or the eyewitness account. Still, Allport and Postman concluded that their procedure probably did not distort information as much as real-life rumoring does.

Leveling Allport and Postman noted that the distortions that occurred in the retelling of descriptions was not haphazard. Rather, three major patterns of distortion were evident from their data. The first pattern, leveling, holds that as a rumor is transmitted, it tends to grow shorter. Nearly 70 percent of the details provided by the eyewitness are lost in the course of five or six word-of-mouth transmissions (Allport and Postman, 1965:75). In particular, times of day (shown by clocks in the picture), numbers of people, names appearing on signs, and kinds of vehicles are lost. Often the final description contains no more than four or five of the original details.

Sharpening The second pattern of distortion, sharpening, refers primarily to the details that survive through a number of transmissions. Why are certain details retained? Allport and Postman attribute this selective perception and retention to the subjects' individual prejudices and interests. Very seldom are the racial identities described by the eyewitness lost during transmission. Other features of the eyewitness account are maintained when presented in a novel or odd fashion. One eyewitness described an adult as "remonstrating" a boy because the boy had stolen vegetables from a market. The term *remonstrating* was maintained through subsequent retellings. Descriptions of movement, such as running, jumping, falling, striking, or throwing are maintained fairly well. Finally, familiar symbols, such as a cross on a church or the names of popular entertainers, are maintained.

Assimilation The final pattern of distortion, assimilation, occurs when details are leveled or sharpened depending on the general theme of the story. In pictures of combat, military objects and actions are maintained more than nonmilitary parts of the picture, such as birds, clouds, or buildings. Some assimilation is consistent with racial stereotypes. In one picture, for example, a black man was shown talking to a white man who was holding what appeared to be a straight razor. In the retelling, the straight razor often ended up being held by the black man! Assimilation often reflects people's special interests. Women, according to Allport and Postman (1965), often remember clothing and signs in store windows, while army trainees and police more often remember times of day, vehicles, and weapons. Finally, some assimilation involves adding details that are not in the picture or part of the eyewitness description. This often takes the form of assuming the motives and identities of people in the pictures. Blacks were often described as "zoot-suiters" and troublemakers, while whites were often described as "defense plant workers," as "going to or coming from work," and as victims of harassment.

Discussion According to Allport and Postman, rumors are by definition inaccurate. People have little interest in ascertaining the source or accuracy of information contained in rumors, because rumoring primarily serves motives other than information seeking. Rumors help to "relieve, justify, and explain underlying tension" (Allport and Postman 1965:36–38). Rumors, for example, which portray the federal government in negative and conspiratorial terms are heartening to those who advocate greatly reduced government or separation. Rumors are a means of projecting one's own feelings; discrimination, prejudice, and even race hatred become reasonable responses in the face of rumors detailing the vicious nature of other ethnic groups. The bad conduct of others becomes a reasonable explanation of one's own negative feelings (Allport and Postman, 1965:40–41). Active involvement in rumoring is also a way to relieve guilt. Stories about the sexual misconduct of President Clinton, for example, may make our "everyday" sexual transgressions seem tame by comparison. Finally, rumoring may simply be a way of "seeking attention," "feeling important," and "filling awkward gaps in conversations" (Allport and Postman, 1965:46–47).

Allport and Postman characterize rumoring more as a process serving personal motives than as a process of information seeking or communication. In many ways, this characterization runs counter to their "basic law of rumor" that states that the intensity of rumoring is due to the importance of the subject to people and to the availability of information. After laying out the basic law of rumor, Allport and Postman say little about how to determine the importance of events and the supply information. Much of what Allport and Postman say about rumor would lead us to examine the psychological characteristics of people involved in rumoring (which is virtually everyone!) rather than the situational context in which rumors occur.

The serial transmission experiment used to study the rumor process strips away much of the context within which rumor processes occur. In everyday life, people exchange information with people they know. People can judge, at least superficially, the "reliability" of the person offering information. Further, they usually receive information from more than one person, as well as from the media, allowing for working triangulations or checks for consistency. These communication network features are totally lacking in Allport and Postman's experimental design. Finally, contrary to Allport and Postman's claim, as information is transmitted by word of mouth, people do question one another about sources and inconsistencies and do ask for elaboration. In brief, Allport and Postman's experimental design does not include conditions of _redundancy_ (more than one source of information) and _reciprocity_ (being able to question the teller of information) that are found in most real-life situations. The conditions under which Allport and Postman studied rumor are more likely to be found in a highly structured, impersonal setting than in, say, a university dormitory or party of friends. Perhaps the serial transmission arrangement produces the enormous amounts of distortion observed by Allport and Postman. Put another way, under conditions of minimal redundancy and reciprocity, almost any kind of information will be severely distorted.

It is difficult to reconcile Allport and Postman's conclusions that word-of-mouth transmission greatly distorts information with the fact that preliterate societies could store and transmit vast amounts of information, seemingly without distortion, for hundreds of generations. More to the point, in everyday life—to the discomfort of many public and corporate officials—rumors often turn out to be true.

Allport and Postman's work occurred at a time when any kind of systematic information about how the rumor process operates was sorely needed. Their work gave incentive to those whose job it was to protect vital military information, such as troop movements and cargo destinations. There was a clear need to counter fears about our military weaknesses, untrue stories that generated racial tensions, and untrue stories that undermined cooperation with such programs as food rationing. Perhaps the most important outcome of Allport and Postman's work was that it provided a stimulus for further studies of communication and rumor.

Rumor as News: Tamotsu Shibutani

Tamotsu Shibutani's (1966) interest in rumor also began with World War II experiences. Shortly after the attack on Pearl Harbor, thousands of Japanese Americans were evacuated from the West Coast and confined in relocation centers in the Midwest. Later in the war, many young men from these camps volunteered for military service, some of which was in occupied Japan. Shibutani made field notes while observing rumor processes firsthand as those around him speculated about what would happen to them next. Unlike Allport and Postman, Shibutani studied rumors in their natural setting rather than under controlled conditions. Later, he also compiled records of rumors that had occurred among other groups from the mid-1800s to the 1960s.

The classical approach of Allport and Postman characterizes rumor as inaccurate, exaggerated, or outlandish information that primarily serves the psychological needs of the people passing on the rumor; only coincidentally does rumor provide useful or accurate information. Shibutani turns the classical view around. For Shibutani (1966:17), rumor is a recurrent form of communication through which people attempt to construct a meaningful or "working" interpretation of a threatening or ambiguous situation by pooling their intellectual resources. The collective result is not necessarily inaccurate, exaggerated, or implausible. Shibutani acknowledges that rumor can relieve anxiety and be shaped by people's psychological needs. For the most part, however, rumor is primarily a substitute for news, which is usually supplied through institutional channels (see below); rumor is news that develops outside of institutional channels. In short, rumor is "improvised news."

Established Channels of Communication In everyday social life, most communication occurs through established channels. Much information is transmitted through formal or institutional channels. The term *institutional channels* refers to most of the news media as well as to the formal channels of communication that exist in bureaucracies. Institutional channels are well organized and are characterized by a stable set of rules, officers performing clearly defined roles, and well-established procedures that can be followed by interchangeable personnel. Within most institutional channels, there are fixed standards of what is acceptable news, procedures for obtaining news, prescribed routes of transmission, verification procedures, and codes of reliable conduct. Participants in institutional channels are held personally accountable for their performance, and there are agreed-upon sanctions for misconduct (Shibutani, 1966:21).

Even within the media and bureaucracies, not all routine communication is handled through established channels. Enduring auxiliary channels of communication are interwoven with institutional channels. The term *auxiliary channels* refers to the established or recurring patterns of interpersonal communication within our daily lives. Auxiliary channels are composed of family members, friends, neighbors, and work associates with whom we normally exchange and discuss information. Auxiliary channels supplement institutional channels. Within bureaucracies, for example, auxiliary channels are utilized to obtain clarification of "official" communication, correct bureaucratic errors, and resolve problems not mentioned in the "rule book." In some instances, auxiliary channels may entirely supplant institutional arrangements, as in disasters or for carrying out illegal activities such as embezzlement or employee theft. Major areas of everyday living, such as family life and most shared activities between friends and neighbors, are also constructed through auxiliary channels of communication.

Conditions Giving Rise to Rumor Allport and Postman's basic law of rumor states that the intensity of rumor is in direct proportion to the importance of the subject to the individual and the ambiguity of the evidence pertaining to the topic at issue. Shibutani (1966:57) restates this law in somewhat different terms: "if the demand for news . . . exceeds the supply made available through institutional channels, rumor construction is likely to occur." In other words, when institutional channels fail them, people move outside institutional channels for information.

Perhaps the most obvious situation in which people rely on rumor for communication is when institutional channels have broken down. This condition exists during disasters when local newspapers or radio and television stations are unable to operate or are unable to provide up-to-the-minute information. A similar situation exists when totalitarian governments shut down the media in times of political crisis.

Another situation in which people rely on rumor for communication is when the credibility of the media is suspect. This condition exists when the only media allowed to operate are government-sponsored or when strict censorship is enforced. Censorship increases rumoring, even when the censorship is voluntary and most citizens agree with it in principle. This type of situation existed in the United States during World War II. The media generally followed a policy of voluntary restraint in reporting stories having to do with the war. In principle, most Americans agreed that this policy was necessary for national security. Still, rumors circulated about disastrous military casualties, profiteering, waste, and corruption.

Finally, people rely on rumoring for news about topics that are ignored by the media because they are in poor taste, potentially libelous, or nonsensical. Through rumor, people often attempt to ascertain the exact details of mutilations in murders and accidents, the sexual and personal quirks of public figures, and UFO or Bigfoot sightings.

Types of Rumoring If unsatisfied demand for news is moderate and collective excitement is mild, then rumor construction takes place through *critical deliberation*. For the most part, people use the auxiliary channels of communication that have been established through everyday interaction. Social control, although informal, is present. Most participants retain their critical ability; reports are checked and cross-checked for plausibility and reliability of sources. The definitions that emerge tend to be consistent with cultural axioms (Shibutani, 1966:94).

Deliberative rumoring is not that different from the way we draw conclusions, arrive at decisions, and form opinions in everyday life. Shibutani (1966:94) points out that most ambiguous situations are resolved through joint deliberation and that most decisions one makes in the course of a day are predicated on unverified reports. People rely to a large extent on what they hear from others, and they usually find such information sufficiently reliable for meeting the challenges of daily life. Such information is not rumor, the term being reserved for those accounts of which one is suspicious; most information on which people base their lives, however, cannot meet high standards of verification.

If unsatisfied demand for news is very great and collective excitement is intense, then rumor construction occurs through spontaneous interchanges. Shibutani refers to this type of rumoring as *extemporaneous rumoring*. That is, people depart not only from institutional channels but from auxiliary channels as well. Reports are accepted from almost any source—acquaintances, strangers, and even overheard conversations. Under conditions of increased anonymity, personal responsibility for information is minimized. Extemporaneous rumoring departs significantly from the communication that occurs in everyday life. Under conditions of extemporaneous rumoring, the greatest amount of confusion and distortion of information occurs.

Shibutani (1966:128) argues that extemporaneous rumoring occurs only under extreme and infrequent circumstances. Even then, rumoring is not haphazard or unrestrained by previous experiences and statements of possible outcomes. Rumor content is still largely limited by considerations of plausibility. Social reconstructions, or rumors, are circumscribed by the basic culture of the group, and most rumors are consistent with cultural axioms. Implausible proposals are selectively eliminated on the basis of what seems sensible in terms of what is already taken for granted. Situations marked by intense tension and extemporaneous construction may provide the conditions necessary for the development of drastically different beliefs. This type of collective consensus is a major step in processes of social change.

Interaction during Rumor Shibutani notes that the classical view treats *rumor* as a noun rather than as a verb. In the classic sense, a rumor is an object, like a brick, that can be handed from one person to another. In Allport and Postman's study, the rumor is a "fixed combination of words" that "stimulates one person, undergoes certain modification while passing through him, and then departs to stimulate someone else" (Shibutani, 1966:8). The classical view recognizes that rumor is a social phenomenon only in the sense that more than one person is involved in its transmission; that people acting together in any enterprise are intertwined in a complex web of social relationships is ignored (Shibutani, 1966:8).

Emergent Roles in Rumoring Shibutani (1966:13) views rumor as "a collective transaction, involving a division of labor among participants, each of whom makes a different contribution." Because people involved in the development of a rumor do not have identical vocabularies, interests, and perceptions, the transaction as a whole cannot be explained in terms of individual motivations. The career of a rumor is not a process of unilinear development, as in serial transmission experiments. Instead, Shibutani suggests the collective rumor transaction involves a "division of labor" in which people occupy identifiable roles. The most obvious role in rumor development is that of the *messenger*, the person who brings pertinent information into the group. Another role is that of the *interpreter*, who tries to put the news into context and evaluates it in terms of past events and likely outcomes. Within almost any group is the *skeptic*. Occupants of this role express doubt about the authenticity of information, demand proof, and urge caution. The role of *protagonist* emerges when someone advocates one interpretation or plan of action over others. There is also the role of *auditor*, the spectator who says relatively little. This role is important because debate is frequently carried out with an eye toward winning over the uncommitted participants. Finally, there is the role of the *decision maker*, who takes the lead in deciding what should be done. Shibutani suggests that there is no necessary or close correspondence between personality types and the roles people come to occupy in the rumor process. In fact, a person may change roles during an encounter, perhaps initially occupying the role of auditor, then the role of messenger, and finally that of protagonist.

Stereotypes Shibutani takes issue with some of the stereotypes concerning the psychological processes involved in rumoring. One stereotype maintains that when confronted by rumors, people lose their critical abilities and do not verify the information on which they are acting. Shibutani notes that in normal, everyday situations, people seldom verify information before they act on it. Instead, they must rely on the taken-for-granted nature of social life. People ask total strangers for directions to important destinations; people give money to strangers, assuming they will receive the product that is promised; they accept at face value uniforms, badges, and professional diplomas. People probably could not get out of the house in the morning if they attempted to verify even a small portion of the information they act on daily!

In everyday life, people usually verify information only after they have acted on it, when events do not turn out as planned. People make inquiries when the goods they order fail to arrive, and they check credentials when hired workers fail to perform as expected. About the only time information is consistently verified beforehand is when it is someone's job to do so. There is a growing demand for the services of businesses that verify information on resumes and employment application forms.

Shibutani suggests that in problematic situations such as disasters, people can no longer rely on the taken-for-granted nature of social life. Immediate and effective action is clearly necessary, and people may actually attempt to verify more information than usual. When people act on unverified information contained in rumors, it is often because opportunities for firsthand verification are unavailable.

Another closely related stereotype is that of suggestibility: people are willing to consider and sometimes act on the most outlandish of rumors. According to Shibutani (1966:108), people are suggestible only to the extent that they uncritically accept ideas inconsistent with their own standards. In disaster situations, where survival often depends on accurate information, people usually retain their criti-

FIGURE 4.1: Serial Transmission vs. Social Transmission

SERIAL TRANSMISSION
(Allport and Postman)

Eyewitness

Serial transmission tends to distort information. In part, this is because those involved in the transmission of information are mutual strangers. Further, there is little if any redundancy in the communication network, that is, there is only one eyewitness source of information. Finally, there is little reciprocity, only one-way communication links exist between participants.

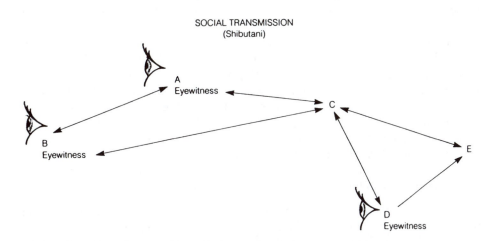

SOCIAL TRANSMISSION
(Shibutani)

Social transmission is much less likely to distort information than serial transmission. This is because many of those in the communication pattern know one another and interact frequently. Further, in social transmission there may be several eyewitness sources of information providing greater redundancy of information. Also, there is greater reciprocity among participants; most communication links are two-way and each individual can communicate with a number of other participants in this pattern. Redundancy and reciprocity provide "working triangulation," which produces accurate information.

cal abilities. People may give consideration to seemingly outlandish information because to do otherwise would be dangerous. In conflict situations such as war, rumors concerning the strength of opposing forces and battle tactics must be carefully evaluated. This "defensive pessimism" is a kind of realism that makes people consider, at least momentarily, even the most bizarre information. It also makes survival on a battlefield possible. Finally, people's critical outlook is heightened when they are aware of the possibility of being cheated or tricked. Sometimes this type of caution can result in paralyzing indecision, making concerted group action difficult (Shibutani, 1966:125–27).

The loss of critical ability, coupled with increased suggestibility, makes it more likely that people will act on information from anonymous sources. Some research indicates that information provided by anonymous sources is less likely to be transmitted from person to person than information from known sources. Rosnow and Fine (1976:63–80) discuss two experiments in which a rumor was started by a "known" and authoritative source—a teacher and a guidance counselor. A third experiment was conducted among a group of undergraduates during campus orientation. The source of the rumor was a student (assistant to the experimenter), who constituted an "anonymous" source within the group. The researchers found that rumors provided by the teacher and guidance counselor were much more likely to be repeated and passed through two or more exchanges than rumors provided by the anonymous student. These findings clearly run counter to the notion that "rumor flourishes from anonymity."

Even in crowds, the number of identifiable sources of information may be greater than we might expect. This is particularly the case for crowds that form within or near residences and workplaces. For example, neighbors may rush from their homes and gather at an auto accident in a nearby intersection. Friends and even family groups may gather at the picket lines during strikes, and friends may attend protest rallies together. Aveni (1977) surveyed a milling street crowd following a university football game and found that a majority of those interviewed (74 percent) were accompanied by one or more friends. Most (64 percent) also said that they had seen relatives and friends from class, work, residences, and hometowns on the streets after the game. Miller (1979) also found that a majority of student respondents (77 percent) were with friends while they prepared to attend a large, impromptu pep rally following an upset victory by their university's basketball team. Further, most respondents (76 percent) said they accompanied these people to the rally, stayed near them while at the rally, and returned to campus with them. In a sense, many normal, everyday social relationships are extended into the crowd and other collective behavior situations as well. These social relationships, in the form of identifiable others, give collective behavior continuity with everyday life.

Discussion Shibutani approaches the study of rumor from the standpoint of naturalistic observation rather than experiment. He conceptualizes rumor in a way quite different from the classical view of Allport and Postman. For Shibutani, rumor is in many ways like the kind of communication we use in solving everyday dilemmas. Rumor is a collective process in which people combine their intellectual resources when institutional channels of communication have failed. Then, people must rely almost entirely on the auxiliary channels of communication used in everyday interaction with family, friends, and neighbors. Under extreme conditions, people may depart from even these auxiliary channels and utilize information from any available source. Still, the outcome of rumor processes is constrained by plausibility, consideration of likely outcomes, and the people's culture. Perhaps the most significant idea in Shibutani's approach to rumor is that rumor is basically similar to the types of communication that occur in everyday life. In this sense, Shibutani's approach to rumor can accommodate both the idea that rumor is sometimes quite divergent from what most consider "accurate" accounts of events and the fact that rumors sometimes turn out to be true.

COMMUNICATION AND THEORIES OF COLLECTIVE ACTION

In many respects, rumor does not appear to be substantially different from the kind of communication that occurs in other areas of everyday life. This point is central to the "snake in the greens" rumor studied by Dan Miller:

> During a few warm days in an otherwise dreary winter a rumor spread through low-income neighborhoods on the west side of Dayton, Ohio. The rumor reported that a poor, elderly woman had died after being bitten by a poisonous snake in the produce section of a supermarket patronized by West Dayton residents. Subsequently, the rumor entered the worlds of talk radio and newspaper stories where it was characterized as outrageous and irresponsible, spread by unwitting, troubled, or malicious people. (Miller, 1992:381)

Shortly after the rumor began, Dan Miller was asked by the Kroger supermarket chain to find out how the rumor had started. Miller used a snowball sampling technique to conduct telephone interviews with 94 people who had heard or passed on the rumor. During his morning commute, he overheard bus passengers discuss the ". . . poor old woman who'd been bitten by a snake in the greens at Kroger's, and they didn't do a thing about it." Overhearing the rumor being passed on, Miller, like Shibutani, was able to gain firsthand knowledge of the rumor process. Miller reports several conclusions in his snake in the greens study:

- Rumors are not always inaccurate, nor do they grow increasingly distorted.
- The rumor did not stand alone but was used to start conversations or was embedded in extended conversations.
- Even though the rumor was stated as fact, the literal truth of the rumor was not significant to participants. No suggestibility or gullibility was evident.
- The rumor traveled through informal but enduring social networks and was not spread by social isolates.
- The rumor often was embedded in a playful interaction context that reinforced group solidarity.
- The rumor often led to talk of more serious topics, such as dissatisfaction with the supermarket and its management.
- For some people, the rumor was a metaphor that helped illustrate larger lessons: the historical relationship between the haves and the have-nots, and the belief that people have little control over or trust in the type and quality of goods and services they consume every day.
- The rumor and the rumor participants soon became objects of sarcasm and ridicule in the newspapers, on television and on radio talk shows, revealing larger social divisions and conflict.

Collective action theories approach communication primarily from the standpoint of either frame analysis or SBI's perception control theory. Neither of these orientations would argue that the communication that occurs during riots, rebellions, disasters, celebrations, or ceremonial gatherings is substantially different from communication that occurs in routine settings. Neither of these perspectives has adopted the term "rumor" to describe communication.

Designative and Prescriptive Aspects of Communication

According to both frame analysis and perception control theory, people in a given language community possess comparable repertoires of cues, gestures, words and other significant symbols which constitute a vocabulary of shared meaning. These significant symbols and shared meaning provide the basis of social behavior in gatherings and all other occasions. According to perception control theory, it is from the shared repertoire that instructions for behavior are drawn. Some instructions for behavior are cues to conduct that identify social objects with respect to which people can orient and adjust their behavior. Such instructions name, locate and denote whether objects are good, bad, dangerous, and so on. These instructions may be verbal statements, such as "The picket signs are in the blue van," or "Have you heard about the poor old woman who was bitten by a snake in the greens at Kroger's, and they didn't do a thing about it?" These instructions can establish and orient people with respect to social objects, individual goals and shared objectives and are referred to as *designations*. Likewise, framing statements create images of groups and tell us what kind of people our leaders, celebrities, enemies, work associates, and neighbors "really" are. Framing tells us who is responsible for many of life's tragedies or joys. Framing establishes what has happened, what is happening, and what is likely to happen.

Other instructions for behavior specify action with respect to social objects. These instructions tell people what to do and when activities are to begin, at what rate they are to be carried out, and when they are to end. Action specifications are referred to as *prescriptions* (Stewart, 1969). This category of instructions includes statements like "Call the police and see if anyone else saw those strange lights in the sky!" or web pages that tell people to write letters to their congressional representative opposing the Internet tax.

Designations *and* prescriptions are necessary for the organization of convergent behavior. For example, designations establish that "Molly's Craft Shop has a new shipment of Beanie Babies!" In the absence of action specifications such as "Let's hurry over there before the Beanie Babies are all sold!", designative activities alone do not provide the basis for collective action. The idea that communication contains designative and prescriptive components can offer insight into some of the problems and stereotypes identified by those who study rumors.

Rumors are idle chitchat and never amount to much. Framing or designative acts are likely to be accompanied by prescriptions for action when they identify or create an object toward which some immediate action can be taken. As such, a large portion of what we call rumor may serve simply as a conversation opener or constitute playful interaction. This is particularly true for rumors that pertain to monster sightings or to the personal lives and dealings of public figures. Rosnow and Fine (1976:81–93) refer to derogatory personal-life rumors as *gossip*. Their main criterion for classifying this type of information as gossip is its triviality. For most people in the United States, rumors about the royal family of England or about the personal lives of entertainers fall within this category. For most people, personal-life rumors are almost totally devoid of any potential for action beyond prescriptions to buy (or avoid buying) the tabloids in which these stories are published.

Occasionally, people are in a position to actually make a decision or take some action with respect to the object of the personal-life rumor. Stories about the misconduct of public officials are more likely to influence voting patterns if they are released near election time, such as Special Prosecutor Kenneth Starr's report detailing sexual encounters between President Clinton and Monica Lewinsky that was placed on the Internet just weeks prior to the November 1998 congressional elections. Likewise, derogatory stories about entertainers may either reduce movie attendance or create record sales.

Product rumors, such as the McDonald's "wormburgers" and Kroger's "poisonous snakes" rumors, may clearly generate prescriptions to avoid the product. Fundamentalist groups boycotted Procter and Gamble in the 1990s because of rumors that linked the corporation with satanic causes. Such product rumors created public relations problems for McDonald's, Kroger Foods, and Procter and Gamble but have not resulted in noticeable decreases in sales (Miller, 1992:390).

Rumors can lead to violence. Rumors are likely to be accompanied by action specifications when they occur in the context of an already established conflict. Rumors (both accurate and inaccurate) of police brutality were followed by assembling instructions and large street gatherings during the urban riots from the 1960s to the present. During wartime, atrocity rumors serve to boost recruitment, public support for the war, and austerity measures. Conversely, rumors of atrocities committed by one's own troops, such as the Mylai massacre of the Vietnam War, and rumors that United States troops were exposed to chemical and biological weapons during the Gulf War seem to create considerable dissension and debate.

Sometimes rumors spread like wildfire. Rumors about groups or individuals are more likely to be accompanied by prescriptions for action when these groups live in close proximity to one another and/or interact frequently. In the Detroit race riot of 1943, for example, two rumors—one that whites had thrown a black woman and her baby off a bridge and another that blacks had raped and killed a white woman—occurred on an evening when the streets and public beaches were congested with crowds of whites and blacks. Congestion further increased when the factory shifts changed and workers crowded onto buses and streetcars. Fighting broke out near crowded housing projects and at major intersections. Similar conditions existed in urban riots throughout the 1960s and into the 1990s.

Designative rumors are more likely to be accompanied by prescriptions for action when there is increased availability to carry out additional activities. Though people nearly always gather at the scene of accidents, fires, and disasters, assembling is more extensive when these events occur during time periods within minimum competing demands on those who assemble. Fires and accidents draw bigger crowds during noon hours, after the dinner hour, and on weekends. For most of us, holidays and vacation periods represent blocks of unstructured time during which we can schedule extemporaneous activities, such as visiting a disaster site.

Spatial availability, or proximity, can also increase the likelihood of action specifications (McPhail, 1983). Reports of arrests in progress, accidents, fires, and disasters, as well as the sights and sounds that accompany these events, are more likely to generate assembling instructions among those who are close by. Bailey and McPhail (1979) interviewed a sample of participants in a gathering at an apartment house fire and a comparative sample of people who knew of the event but did not attend. More than half (55 percent) of those interviewed indicated that they learned of the event by word of mouth. Subsequently, most of these people received suggestions to assemble from others.

Some people are likely to believe anything! Designative accounts are likely to be accompanied by prescriptions for action among people who have previously participated in activities related to the prospective object or event. Accounts of the Detroit race riot of 1943 often note that members of the Ku Klux Klan and both white and black "hoodlums" were the most likely to initiate violent attacks. Civic and religious groups were the most active counterrioters in Detroit, as well as in the riots of the 1960s. During the campus disorders of the 1960s, some people repeatedly participated in rallies and demonstrations. Years later, many of these same people spent their summers following the Grateful Dead concert tours. Finally, fundamental religious groups have been active in efforts to combat the influence of "satanic" rock and roll groups, to outlaw abortion, and to ban pornography from the Internet. This is not to say that rioters are all criminals, that the campus disorders of the 1960s and 1970s were started by "professional agitators," or that religious fundamentalism attracts only "fanatics" or paranoid individuals. Rather, these groups constitute "publics" with respect to particular issues. Websites, bulletin boards, and discussion lists on the Internet can focus on otherwise bizarre or obscure topics, from ant farms to zither making, and in short order create at least small publics around these issues.

Prior participation in events related to a given issue can result in others' identification of individuals (and groups) as likely recruits for participation in pending events of a similar nature (McPhail, 1983). Likely recruits are then targeted for instructions to participate in pending events. Interest groups often compile membership lists with names, addresses, and telephone numbers to facilitate block recruiting. In like fashion but in a less formal manner, rumors and prescriptions for action can be transmitted through the auxiliary communication channels of family, friends, work, and neighborhood groups. Occasionally, prescriptions for action are addressed to nonmembers in the form of leaflets, posters, and speeches. Thus, fundamentalist Christian groups send speakers before PTA meetings to warn against and organize resistance to "satanic music" or to coordinate support for censoring explicit sexual content from the Internet.

The resource mobilization perspective of collective action focuses on how new or emerging social movement organizations are able to recruit members and otherwise create a viable group. The Internet has proven to be a valuable resource for many nascent social movement organizations. Web sites and discussion groups have formed a staging area for people organizing everything from tax referendums to hate groups.

Internet Communication and Collective Action

One of the unique features of Lofland's study of the Divine Precepts movement (a pseudonym for Reverend Sun Myung Moon's Unification church, whose members were commonly known as "Moonies") is that he gives us a rare picture of how frustratingly difficult it can be for a group to get its message out to a receptive audience and recruit new members. The Moonies sent their first missionary to the United States in 1959. Through interpersonal contact, Ms. Lee (a pseudonym) was able to establish a core group of about a dozen followers. When Lee arrived in the United States, she had in her possession a lengthy manuscript detailing the Church's beliefs. She sent an edited (but still lengthy) version to some seventy religious magazines in hopes that it would appear as an article that would generate interest in the group. Eventually, all of the publications responded with "rejection slips, letters condemning heresy, or polite dismissals" (Lofland, 1966:67). This set the pace for what was to follow. The Moonies found that the print and electronic media consistently failed to produce the results they sought.

On at least three separate occasions the group used newspaper ads to publicize their lectures. On the first attempt, the group rented a hall for a weekly lecture series and ran an ad:

A NEW MESSAGE
Never told before. Reason and purpose of Creation—What God is going to do in the next 7 years. Lectures Mondays 7:30 P.M., January 9, 16, 23, and 30. No Charge. Bay City Lions Club Hall, 772 Clayton Street.

The first lecture was a bust. The only person who attended borrowed a copy of their recently bound Unification Church bible and never returned. The ad and the lecture series were both canceled.

After receiving an invitation to speak at another area Gospel Temple, the Moonies ran another similar ad that produced similar results. Only a few people inquired about the message and none joined the Moonies. Because of low attendance at the meetings and theological incompatibility, the Temple withdrew its invitation to the Unification Church. Further ads were canceled. Later, a successful spiritualist ran an ad announcing a series of guest lectures by Lee at the spiritualist's weekly meeting. The planned series was dropped after the first lecture.

A single-line "teaser" ad asking people to come to hear daily "New Age Revelation" lectures resulted in an occasional turnout of a few elderly ladies, which was not the response the Moonies had hoped for. Similar teaser ads to phone for "the key to perfection," to find out "why the rapid increase in suicide?," "why the vast amount of mental illness in Bay City?," and "who can stop the moral decay?" were tried and quickly proved to be a nuisance. The Moonies' phone rang at all hours, disrupting sleep, meals, and prayer. Over half of the callers hung up when the phone was answered and the rest were crank callers, lonely hearts, and people who refused to leave their names. No genuine converts were obtained. A morning radio talk show host did call the number and talked with Lee on the air for about ten minutes, thus giving the group their largest audience to date. Even though the Moonies' phone number and address were announced, the public did not respond.

Other ways were tried to access public attention. One thousand handbills were printed and distributed in January and February of 1961 containing a postal box number where one could purchase their church's bible and a phone number to call and find out about church study groups. Most were left in the doors of homes in a lower middle-class neighborhood. Not a single person responded.

The Moonies also paid for an eight-week "Age of Restoration" series of fifteen-minute spots on a small local radio station (only two of several stations would even consider putting them on the air). The Moonies had by now made audiotapes of their message, and these were played on the radio. Only two telephone calls were received in response to their the Age of Restoration series. Even so, they continued to use these tapes as a way of presenting their message.

The Moonies planned a series of five daily "Bible Week" lectures. They rented a storefront church and even built a sound truck for the occasion. For two days prior to their first meeting, members blasted the area as much as allowed by the city sound truck ordinance. Their first Bible Week audience consisted of six people, including three young boys who were asked to leave because of their loud play. They canceled Bible Week when no one showed up for the second meeting.

A large, attractive sign that announced daily lectures and meetings was built by members and hung from the second floor of the center. The first, immediate, and only response to the sign was from a city building inspector. The Moonies were told that they would have to install fire equipment, mark the exits, and make other building alterations if they planned to run a public assembly hall or they would be fined. These alterations would probably cost about $3,000. The sign came down immediately.

The Moonies tried several times to target college students for recruitment. They placed an invitation to a series of four lectures in a mimeographed monthly flyer of a small Bay City area college. The announcement also stated that a goodwill offering was to be taken at the lectures. No one came to the first lecture and the series was canceled. A teaser ad was placed in the Berkeley Campus newspaper inviting students to the center's daily discussion sessions. Several serious telephone inquiries the day the ad appeared prompted the Moonies to prepare for a large evening gathering, but only six students showed up, none of whom ever returned.

The Moonies spent nearly two months hand copying the names, addresses, religions, and nationalities of nearly 2,000 international students enrolled at Berkeley. Another two months were spent hand signing letters, addressing envelopes, and attaching stamps to 1,900 letters inviting recipients to hear about an "... event which will bring about great changes in this world within the very near future," claiming that the time spent with the Moonies "... may well turn out to be the most rewarding hour of your life." The response to the letter was minimal, dozens of students telephoned for more information, eight actually came to the center to hear the taped message, and one student joined the group.

A separate letter campaign was directed to students of German origin, inviting them to "German Night" parties without mentioning the religious aims of the Moonies. Even this deception only produced three guests at the first German Night party and seven at the last party.

The Moonies struggled for more than a decade to get their message out to a receptive audience. These days, individuals and small groups can more easily pursue an audience through the Internet and the World Wide Web, both of which became reasonably accessible to the public in the early 1990s (Zakon, 1997).

Lee received seventy rejections from religious magazines and never did get the Unification Church's views published. Today, she could have created a website, similar to the one the Unification Church presently maintains—much like thousands of other websites for large and small groups containing mission statements, position papers, manifestos, religious doctrine, and social commentary that can now be found by surfing the Net. The Moonies used newspaper ads, handbills, signs, and sound trucks in a futile attempt to entice people in their vicinity to attend their lectures and visit their center. E-mail, Internet chat rooms, and discussion lists now can more effectively accomplish the same ends drawing together people from across the world. Lee was called by the host of a morning talk radio show and was able to talk on the air for fifteen minutes. Today, small groups are able to make use of local-access television stations as well as talk radio. Just as a successful spiritualist and a Gospel Temple each offered the Moonies a chance to present their message before an interested audience, a small group's web page can now be linked to other web pages throughout the world, offering the small group a chance to build on the efforts of others.

Since the mid-1990s, communication systems such as the Internet, cable and satellite television, talk radio, and cellular telephones have made it much easier for individuals and small groups to get their message out to the world. Websites, chat rooms and discussion lists allow groups to coalesce around an incredible number and variety of issues, pastimes and problems. It is also very important to note that people participating in Internet groups can and do develop affective ties with one another. This author has participated in an Internet discussion list of about seventy people since 1996. One of the frequent contributors died in 1998. For several days thereafter, his passing was sincerely mourned with tributes, anecdotes, and even descriptions of the funeral provided by list members.

The Internet today provides the means for forming actual, face-to-face group relationships. Obviously, strangers can and do first visit in a chat room or on a list and later may agree to meet face to face. More often than not, however, people use the Internet to communicate with people known to them, such as their friends, relatives, and work associates—that is, people who communicate by way of the Internet often communicate with the very same people on a face-to-face basis. Work groups, club members, and groups of friends start discussion lists, web pages, and chat rooms that can then grow in size as new people subscribe or sign in. Some new people may become regulars and, in turn, draw in their friends or associates. The Internet does not guarantee a mass following to any individual or group. However, the Internet provides a way to quickly coalesce at least a small group of receptive individuals around almost any idea, issue, or problem. Before the advent of the Internet this fundamental step was very difficult to achieve, as is illustrated by the Moonies' recruitment efforts.

Large and small groups use the Web to plan, publicize, and coordinate their business meetings, conventions, workshops, and trade shows, as well as rallies and demonstrations. The largest demonstration held in Washington, DC during the 1990s was the October 1997 Promise Keepers' Stand in the Gap rally attended by as many as an estimated 700,000 people (see chapter 3). The Promise Keepers made extensive use of the Internet in organizing, planning, and staging this rally. Months prior to the rally they maintained a website that featured an updated FAQ (frequently asked questions), information on the events planned for the rally, travel and lodging information, and commentary. The site also contained an e-mail address for questions and answers. The virtual world of the Internet closely meshes with the real world of people and their daily face-to-face associations. The Internet provides a powerful means for forming and maintaining groups that simply did not exist until the last decade of the twentieth century.

SUMMARY

The views of rumor set forth in the mass-hysteria, emergent-norm, and value-added theories of collective behavior are not very different from the popular image of rumor. The rumor process is characterized by collective behavior theories as transmitting inaccurate, exaggerated, and dangerously simplified definitions of situations confronting people. From this standpoint, rumor is an "inferior" form of communication. This view is consistent with the idea that collective behavior is "inferior" to normal social behavior.

The serial transmission studies of Allport and Postman (1965) support and amplify the above characterization of rumor. Information transmitted serially and by word of mouth is greatly distorted in the process. According to Allport and

Postman, information is distorted because of the individual biases, fears, and misperceptions of rumor participants. A critical examination of the serial transmission model, however, suggests that distortion occurs because of the lack of redundancy and reciprocity designed into the experiment.

Shibutani's study of rumor transmission in natural settings provides additional support to the criticism of serial transmission. When people receive information from several sources and are free to question those who provide information, the amount of distortion is greatly reduced. Shibutani also suggests that people usually retain a critical stance toward information transmitted outside customary channels.

The social behavioral interactionist (SBI) perspective does not approach communication during collective action from the standpoint of rumor. Instead, collective action, or convergent activity, results from designative and prescriptive activities. Rumors are designative in character, and they establish objects toward which subsequent action can be taken. Prescriptions specify the activity that is to occur. Without additional prescriptive activity, rumors do not produce convergent activity beyond conversation.

As illustrated by the Unification Church's first unsuccessful efforts to recruit and organize members in the United States, new and emerging social movement organizations have historically had great difficulty in establishing an interested public from which they can recruit members. The growth of the Internet since 1990 has allowed thousands of such groups to coalesce publics through their websites and discussion groups. The Internet is a major, if not revolutionary, development in the history of social movements.

Rumor is one of the earliest topics studied in the field of collective behavior. Early studies assumed that rumor is an "inferior" form of communication. Collective action theories have approached communication from the standpoint of frame analysis and perception control theory and have not built on the earlier tradition of rumor.

⚔ CHAPTER 5 ⚔

MASS HYSTERIA

Mass hysterias are capricious, unpredictable, and contagious. In the theoretical frameworks of Blumer, Klapp, and Smelser, mass hysteria is the most elementary, transitory, and least differentiated form of collective behavior. Blumer ([1934] 1969) describes mass hysteria as an instance of widespread and "relatively rapid, unwitting, and nonrational dissemination of a mood, impulse, or form of conduct" that disrupts social routines and authority patterns. For Smelser (1962), panics and crazes are shaped by *hysterical beliefs,* which greatly restrict people's normal concerns to those of individual flight and escape (panic) or unrealistic wish fulfillment (craze). Mass hysteria can take almost any form, including widespread physical symptoms of nausea, dizziness, trembling, and fainting. Mass hysteria can also be manifested in widespread excitement such as fantastic rumors, rejoicing, celebration, morbid preoccupation, mourning, or fear.

Mass hysteria is transmitted through a process of mutual excitement—which Blumer calls circular reaction—during which people's behavior comes to be guided by aroused emotion rather than by social norms. The actions of people involved in mass hysteria show an alarming degree of intensity, restricted focus, and unanimity. People lose their critical abilities and begin to believe almost anything consistent with their hysterical frame of reference. These beliefs often make those involved in mass hysteria seem stupid, gullible, and dangerous.

In chapter 3 we noted that the early tulip trade in Holland traditionally has been cited as an example of mass hysteria. Events such as "mob action" (Myers, 1948) have been described as mass hysteria. A religious gathering awaiting the miraculous appearance of a saint (Tumin and Feldman, 1955) was described as mass hysteria. This event is similar to the recent gatherings at Medjugorje in Bosnia-Hercegovina, because people claim to have seen visions of the Madonna there since 1981. Dozens of Marian Groups, Associations, and Shrines are now listed on numerous websites.

Most of these "studies" of mass hysteria, however, are little more than journalistic accounts of events witnessed by their authors. In some cases, the authors happened on the event quite by accident and were not prepared to make systematic field notes. Authors who did have prior notice of an event made no real attempt to assess the relative levels of involvement among active participants, spectators, and passersby. In other words, the authors of these accounts failed to consider unanimity and intensity of involvement as evidence of mass hysteria. Instead, they concluded that they were observing mass hysteria largely because the events they witnessed struck them as being distasteful, frightening, or reflecting superstition. Beyond the frequent use of "mass hysteria" as a journalistic convention in such instances, the mass hysteria perspective has fostered very few empirical or quantitative studies. There are probably no more than a dozen mass hysteria studies in which investigators actually interviewed people to objectively compare those closely involved in the event with those having lesser involvement. These few studies and their findings address the issues we will raise in this chapter.

We will begin by describing some unusual events that later became the subjects of quantitative mass hysteria studies. Subsequently, we will see that the mass hysteria studies generated a number of questionable findings and have left several unresolved questions regarding unusual events. In the final section of this chapter we will discuss unusual events from the standpoint of collective action.

UNUSUAL EVENTS AND MASS HYSTERIA

Five unusual events involving the spread of a strange fear, affliction, or definition through a group of people are described in this section. Participants in these unanticipated outbreaks seemed to have had greatly impaired critical abilities because they rejected or ignored the "commonsense" and "official" explanations of the problem and acted on the basis of their own interpretations. Such characteristics prompted researchers to study them from the standpoint of mass hysteria. Hadley Cantril's (1966) study of the "War of the Worlds" broadcast and Donald M. Johnson's (1945) study of the phantom anesthetist are considered to be "classic" studies of mass hysteria. Each focused on the spread of fear. The Stairway of the Stars Concert (Small, et al., 1991) and the "June bug epidemic" (Kerckhoff and Back, 1968) are both investigations of mysterious outbreaks of dizziness, fainting, vomiting and other afflictions. These outbreaks were first attributed to mass hysteria by authorities who could find no physical cause for the distress. Both investigations were based on victim surveys, and each attempted to map the spread of symptoms through the group. Finally, there is the study of cattle mutilations (Stewart, 1977; 1980). This investigation used interviews with farmers and authorities in communities within which the bizarre cattle mutilations had been reported.

War of the Worlds

Probably the most widely known event to be generally considered a mass hysteria occurred on Sunday evening, October 30, 1938. Orson Welles and his CBS Mercury Theater group presented an adaptation of one of H. G. Wells's then lesser-known short stories, "The War of the Worlds," which described a nineteenth-century Martian invasion of England. The Mercury Theater adaptation was set in the present (1938) and took place in the United States. Perhaps Welles's most consequential decision was to use an "open format" during the first half of the show. Instead of using the conventional dramatic format of background music, narration, and dialogue, the first announcements of the Martian invasion took the form of simulated news bulletins, interrupting a program of dance music. Welles's second most consequential decision was to use the names of actual New Jersey and New York towns, highways, streets, and buildings when describing the movements and attacks of the Martians.

These two decisions, plus the fact that most listeners tuned in eight to twelve minutes late and therefore missed the Mercury Theater theme and introduction, set the stage for what was to follow. Thousands of people across the United States assumed they were listening to real news bulletins and public announcements. A substantial portion of these listeners became very frightened and attempted to call police, the National Guard, hospitals, newspapers, and radio stations for information. In addition, people tried to contact family members, friends, and neighbors. By the time Mercury Theater's first station break came, informing people they were listening to a CBS radio drama, most of the broadcast's damage had been done.

The next day, newspapers across the country carried stories of terrorized people hiding in basements, panic flight from New Jersey and New York, stampedes in theaters, heart attacks, miscarriages, and even suicides. During the months that followed, these stories were shown to have little if any substance, yet today the myth of "War of the Worlds" stampedes and suicides persists as part of American folklore. One clear and certain result of the broadcast, however, was a number of Federal Communication Commission regulations, issued within weeks of the broadcast, prohibiting the use of the open format in radio drama.

The Phantom Anesthetist of Mattoon

About midnight, Friday evening, September 1, 1944, police in Mattoon, Illinois, investigated a most unusual case. A woman and her teenage daughter claimed that a mysterious prowler had stood in the shadows outside an open window and sprayed an irritating gas into their house. The gas made the women nauseated and very dizzy. Mattoon police found no evidence of a prowler but were again called to the residence later in the evening when the woman's husband saw a man run from their yard.

The *Mattoon Daily Journal-Gazette* carried a front-page story of this incident the next day. The story prompted two other families to report to police that they had been gassed in their homes a few days earlier. In both instances, however, the victims had initially attributed their symptoms to other causes and had seen no prowler. On Tuesday evening two more attacks were reported, and on Wednesday three attacks were reported. There were no attacks on Thursday, but during the weekend twenty attacks were reported to police. Symptoms usually included temporary paralysis, eye and mouth irritation, dizziness, and nausea. Other Mattoon residents and a few victims claimed to have seen the prowler and described him as tall and thin, dressed in black, and wearing a black skullcap.

The thought of someone lurking about the yards of Mattoon and spraying homes with a potentially lethal gas produced considerable wariness. Mattoon police records indicate a substantial increase in the number of calls reporting prowlers during the two weeks of gas attacks. Some newspaper stories stated that townspeople were buying special locks for their windows, keeping loaded guns beside their beds, and had organized neighborhood patrols to apprehend or at least frighten off the gasser.

Newspaper coverage of these happenings was quite extensive, particularly in Illinois and the rest of the Midwest. Newspapers as far away as England made occasional reference to the phantom anesthetist. Early stories indicated that out-of-town news reporters were suffering headaches from the after-effects of the gas. A chemist from the Illinois Criminal Investigation Laboratory tentatively identified the gas as chloropictin. By September 12, many news reports began to contain elements of skepticism and sarcasm. A week later, most newspapers referred to the anesthetist story as a case of mass hysteria. The residents of Mattoon were frequently depicted as simple-minded, frightened about nothing, or seeking publicity. Altogether, twenty-nine gassing reports and about seventy prowler calls had been received by Mattoon police. Some accounts indicate that no gassing incidents occurred after September 12, while others indicate that occasional gassing incidents were reported for years afterward.

Stairway of the Stars Concert

A dozen police cars, fire trucks and ambulances were parked on the lawn of the Santa Monica Civic Auditorium late on Thursday evening, April 13, 1989. Their flashing lights illuminated the faces of hundreds of people moving about the vehicles. Many of the faces were young, some showed fear, some were crying. Police, firefighters and paramedics moved among the people on the lawn. Near a medical tent there were rows of stretchers, and many of them were occupied. It was not an earthquake or a terrorist bomb that had forced one of the largest evacuations in Santa Monica history. The Civic Auditorium had been emptied by what was to be later identified as mass hysteria.

Nearly a thousand young musicians and singers of the Santa Monica-Malibu Unified School District had rehearsed since ten o'clock that morning for the fortieth annual Stairway of the Stars concert. This was the big concert of the year for band, orchestra, and chorus students in grades four through high school. None of the musicians, or their teachers and parents, had expected this gala event to end in this fashion.

During the afternoon rehearsals, however, students and teachers had complained that the auditorium was hot, stuffy, and "smelled funny." Many students said they had to sit and rest during the day because they had headaches and felt dizzy. At least two students fainted during the day, and several students had been unable to complete rehearsal because of nausea and fever. Even though rehearsals had been difficult and uncomfortable, the classical music concert started on time.

During the concert, however, students continued to experience many flu-like symptoms, including headaches, dizziness, weakness, abdominal pain, nausea, and shortness of breath (Small, et al., 1991). Spectators also reported experiencing similar discomforts. Toward the end of the Stairway of the Stars program, some performers had collapsed or fainted and many others were too ill to continue. School officials called an early end to the concert and ordered the evacuation of the auditorium.

Police and firefighters were on hand early in the evacuation. Before the auditorium was cleared, the Santa Monica Fire Department used toxic fume detectors and found no indication of a hazard. Still, people continued to experience chest pains, coughing, shaking and chills during the evacuation. After a full search of the auditorium, while people continued to collapse and faint, the fire chief suggested that the affliction was mass hysteria.

The school district reported that 1,100 band, orchestra, and chorus members performed in the Stairway of the Stars concert. The concert was attended by an estimated two to three thousand patrons. Altogether, there may have been between four or five thousand people present at the Stairway of the Stars concert. It is unclear just how many of these people experienced symptoms. It is clear that students and teachers reported symptoms at both the morning and afternoon rehearsals. At the concert, between 200 and 250 people became ill, and somewhere between ten and seventeen students were reported to have fainted or collapsed. Nineteen students were taken to local hospitals for treatment, observation and tests.

Health experts from the Los Angeles County Health Department quickly identified the afflictions as a "classic case of mass hysteria." This was an easy diagnosis, given the symptoms. Classic mass hysterias, according to the health officials, usually affect female adolescents and preadolescents involved in stressful situations. Even though there are no pathological signs of illness, the symptoms allegedly "spread like wildfire" among girls. The feminine character of this disorder was underscored by the fact that nearly all those who fainted were sopranos!

Many parents, particularly those with daughters in the concert, objected to this diagnosis. In fact, the feminine character of the disorder was not as pronounced as first claimed by health officials. A survey of a portion of the band members taken three weeks later would show, for instance, that the most common symptom, headache, was statistically as likely to be reported by boys as girls (Small, et al., 1991). In fact, only four of the 18 symptoms measured were statistically more likely to be reported by girls. Small and his colleagues (1991:1202) found that observing a friend become sick was the best predictor of the development of symptoms.

A second Stairway of the Stars concert was scheduled for Friday night, but in spite of assurances by school and county officials that evidence of toxic fumes and materials was not found, many parents kept their children at home.

The June Bug Epidemic

In June 1962, a female worker in a southern textile mill broke out in a severe rash and complained of nausea and dizziness. The next day, several women and at least two men reported to the mill infirmary with the same symptoms. Workers insisted this ailment was caused by bites from insects that had infested the last shipment of fabric from England. During the next four days, sixty-two of more than nine hundred mill workers complained of this bug-bite syndrome and either received medical attention or were absent from work. Sixty-two ill workers was not an unusual number for a mill this large, but the type of illness was quite unusual.

At the peak of the outbreak, plant managers decided to close the mill briefly in order to locate the source of the ailments. Health officials from the mill and the Communicable Disease Center of Atlanta found only two biting insects in the entire plant. They were also unable to detect pollutants that could cause such symptoms. The mill was then sprayed for insects, primarily to soothe the fears of the workers. Management and health authorities then concurred with the earlier judgment of local physicians that the symptoms were psychogenic in nature or a manifestation of mass hysteria. Workers understandably were skeptical of this explanation, but in any event, no more bug bite ailments were reported.

Animal Mutilations

In March of 1996, an article appeared in the *St. Petersburg Times* that described the murder of 69 victims. This was only the latest in a string of such killings that began in the islands of the Caribbean.

The Weird Tale of the Goatsucker

Miami—When police arrived at the crime scene they had never seen such carnage. Lifeless victims—69 in all—lay strewn across the yards of two families in Sweetwater, a heavily Hispanic neighborhood in south Miami. But it was a Miami massacre with a difference—a case perhaps for Ace Ventura, Pet Detective.

The victims were all animals—goats, chickens, geese and ducks. Who—or what—could have done such a dastardly thing? The killer, say police and a local zoologist, was a large dog. Wrong, say local residents. It was the *chupacabras*, the Caribbean's very own Bigfoot, except this creature is a vampire-like predator whose name literally means "goatsucker" in Spanish.

Don't be surprised if you haven't heard of the chupacabras. Until this month it had never been seen or heard of outside Puerto Rico, the U.S. island commonwealth of 4 million people. For the past six months, the hideous bloodsucking beast with an oval head and bulging red-eyes—part reptile, part insect, part UFO alien—allegedly has been terrorizing the island's central mountains. But after the slaughter in Sweetwater, the chupacabras has firmly established a place in the annals of Miami make-believe. It may sound like something out of *Star Trek*, but it has gripped more than just the imagination of Hispanic Miami. For those who believe in the chupacabras, the fear is real. In some cases the attack on livestock has caused serious economic loss.

One Sweetwater woman claims to have seen it, and there have been alleged chupacabras attacks in other parts of Miami. The beast has developed a large following in Latino communities across the United States, from New Jersey to California. Authorities are taking the killings seriously—up to a point. A specialist has investigated the deaths, and a county commissioner has called for a police inquest. "It's mushroomed way out of proportion," says Ron Magill, assistant curator at Metro Dade zoo. "I'm sitting here literally in shock." (Adams, 1996)

This somewhat tongue-in-cheek account of the killings attributed to the chupacabras is in sharp contrast to the more serious newspaper accounts of cattle mutilations two decades earlier. From late August to early November, 1974, cattle producers in Nebraska and South Dakota reported to veterinarians and police cattle carcasses that appeared to have been drained of blood. In many instances, reports also indicated that the cattle's sex organs, tongues, and ears were also removed. During this episode, authorities and newspapers received between seventy-five and one hundred reports of cattle mutilations.

Speculation varied as to what or who could have caused such bizarre occurrences. In 1967 much publicity had been given to the discovery of Snippy, a dead and mutilated pony, shortly after a Colorado UFO sighting. One of the first explanations offered for the cattle mutilations was that they were the work of the occupants of spacecraft from other planets. Another explanation grew out of the reported sighting of a hairy, manlike beast in the general area of several mutilations. Zoology students from the University of Nebraska tried to track down "the thing" with absolutely no success.

Snippy the pony, one of several animals found dead and mutilated under mysterious circumstances, contributed to what some researchers consider to be mass hysteria about blood-sucking monsters or extraterrestrials. Here a forestry official performs a test for radioactivity. © Bettman/CORBIS.

Perhaps the most widely accepted explanation of cattle mutilations was that blood cult members were sneaking about and killing cattle to obtain organs and blood for their dark ceremonies. This explanation seemed quite plausible, given the lurid descriptions during 1970 and 1971 of the Charles Manson "family" and the "Helter Skelter" murders. If some cultists were able to kill and mutilate people, they could certainly do the same to cattle.

Initially, most law enforcement and veterinary authorities in Nebraska and South Dakota seemed to agree with the "mysterious mutilation" description of cattle deaths. At the peak of the outbreak, however, some authorities began to cast doubt on this explanation. Veterinarians at the Universities of Nebraska and South Dakota said that the autopsies performed on a few of the mutilated cattle indicated that the animals had died of natural causes. They suggested the mutilations and absence of blood were the combined result of small scavengers such as coyotes feeding on the dead animals, and of normal postmortem decomposition. Some authorities began to describe the cattle mutilations as a "collective delusion," posing no real danger to cattle or people.

Since this first cattle mutilation episode, others have occurred in Colorado, Illinois, Iowa, Kansas, New Mexico, Oklahoma, and Texas. During this time the Iowa Cattlemen's Association offered a $1,000 reward for information leading to the conviction of people who "steal, mutilate, or kill cattle belonging to an association member."

Other Unusual Events

Shortly after drawing blood from a dying patient, a nurse in the Riverside General Hospital emergency room became dizzy, began to tremble, and finally collapsed. Within a few minutes, five other physicians and medical workers experienced jerky movements, difficulty in breathing and dizziness, and the emergency room was evacuated. The Riverside, California, Hazardous Materials (HAZMAT) response team was called and quickly responded. This 1994 incident resulted in the hospitalization of five of the 37 emergency room workers. Eleven workers told the strange story that the blood of the dying patient gave off a strong, chemical-like odor. The HAZMAT team, however, detected no harmful fumes and decontaminated the emergency room, which reopened the next morning (Boodman, 1994). In another unusual event, a 1967 graduation ceremony at an English girls' school was halted by an epidemic of fainting. In a brief "head count" analysis of the event, Moss and McEvedy (1967) determined the approximate numbers of fainters and nonfainters in the graduating class.

The testing of nuclear weapons and the threat of nuclear war have been viewed as the anxieties underlying two other outbreaks of hysteria. Following atmospheric testing of hydrogen bombs in 1954, people in and around Seattle, Washington, began to report mysterious "pitting" damage to auto windshields. Medalia and Larsen (1958) studied the incidence of windshield-pitting reports and the spread of windshield-pitting rumors and beliefs. This incident was shortly followed by a nationwide rush to buy fallout shelter plans. Although the federal government offered free shelter plans, magazines carried hundreds of advertisements for "better" plans. Some shelter plans were indeed better than the government's, while others probably constituted mail fraud. Levine and Modell (1965) conducted a national survey to determine the characteristics of households buying fallout shelter plans and constructing shelters.

EMPIRICAL FOCUS OF MASS HYSTERIA STUDIES

Events that prompt mass hysteria studies, such as those just related, comprise three general and distinct elements. First are the *unusual and unverified experiences* of people that give the hysterical incident much of its noteworthy character—for example, interpreting a radio drama as a real news event, or being attacked by a "phantom anesthetist." Unusual and unverified experiences also include trembling, fainting, and nausea after smelling a strong odor, being bitten by a strange bug, or finding dead and partially dismembered livestock and pets. These occurrences are unusual from the standpoint of everyday experience, and they are unverified in the sense that authorities debunk or refuse to substantiate the victims' claims. Authorities are usually the first to suggest that the unusual and unverified experiences are a manifestation of hysteria.

Second, there is *mobilization* with respect to the unusual and unverified experiences. Mobilization includes such reactions as people fleeing to escape Martian attacks or workers collectively demanding that management "do something" about bug bites. Mobilization also includes the formation of neighborhood patrols to apprehend or scare off prowlers or cattle mutilators. Most often, it is mobilization rather than the unusual and unverified experiences themselves that is the most disruptive of normal social relationships.

Finally, there is the *general preoccupation* with the unusual and unverified experiences and accompanying mobilization. General preoccupations involve large portions of the population hearing about the unusual and unverified experiences and mobilization. This news serves as a topic for conversations and perhaps for arguments but little else. General preoccupation is the most extensive but least disruptive element of these unusual episodes. We will now consider the manner in which these three elements of unusual events have been approached in mass hysteria studies.

Unusual and Unverified Experiences

From a quantitative standpoint, the mass hysteria studies fail to show that unusual and unverified experiences are as widespread as mass hysteria theory suggests. In some studies, more than one table must be examined and footnotes cross-checked to determine the number of people and approximate portion of an available population who had unusual and unverified experiences. None of the quantitative studies show that even a slim majority of the available population reported such experiences.

Boodman (1994) indicated that six of the 37 people present in the Riverside General Hospital's emergency room during the blood-drawing incident received medical attention that evening, and only 11 of the 37 reported smelling the "toxic fumes." Moss and McEvedy (1967) state that about 30 percent of the students in the English girls' school incident succumbed to "hysterical dizziness, fainting, headaches, and vomiting." At most, 250 of the nearly 5,000 people present at the Stairway of the Stars concert reported symptoms of illness (Small, et al., 1991). Cantril's (1966) study of "The War of the Worlds" broadcast concludes that about 20 percent of those listening to all or part of the broadcast exhibited hysterical panic reactions. During the A-bomb fallout shelter panic of 1962–1963, only about 12 percent of U.S. households bought plans for shelters or stockpiled supplies, and less than 1 percent of households actually built a shelter (Levine and Modell, 1965). Regarding the June bug incident, Kerckhoff and Back (1968:13) concluded that about 10 percent of the first-shift textile mill workers, or 6 percent of all workers, experienced bug bite symptoms. Only 6 percent of the respondents in the Seattle windshield-pitting epidemic of 1954 reported they had any direct experience with windshield damage (Medalia and Larsen, 1958). Johnson's 1945 study of the phantom anesthetist shows that less than 1 percent of the population of Mattoon claimed to have been gassed or made prowler calls to the police. Finally, the number of cattle mutilations reported by Stewart (1977; 1980) indicates that less than 1 percent of area farmers made such reports. Quantitative studies show that the occurrence of unusual and unverified experiences within available populations is limited and, in some instances, quite rare. Nonetheless, these studies discuss the experiences as if they were being reported by a substantial majority of the available population.

Without question, listeners *were* frightened by the "War of the Worlds" broadcast; Mattoon residents *were* convinced their dizziness and nausea were caused by the phantom's gas; workers *were* hospitalized for days with rashes, rapid heart beat, and nausea during the June bug epidemic; and farmers *were* convinced their cattle had died in a mysterious manner. Those who studied these events from the standpoint of mass hysteria described these reactions as psychogenic or "mass sociogenic illness." In other words, from the standpoint of mass hysteria, fear reactions to the "War of the Worlds" broadcast were abnormally severe, given the nature of the show. Likewise, it was concluded that the physical symptoms reported in the Riverside emergency room, during the Stairway of the Stars concert, and during the phantom anesthetist and June bug episodes had no organic cause. It was also concluded that the mysterious cattle mutilations were either totally imaginary or the work of scavengers combined with normal decomposition.

Not surprisingly, these explanations fail to satisfy all of those concerned, particularly the people who had expressed fears or had reported attacks or symptoms. Parents attending the Stairway of the Stars concert, for instance, claimed that the auditorium had been hot, stuffy, and odorous the whole day. They expressed resentment at the quick diagnosis of hysteria. They felt that their children were really sick.

All the mass hysteria studies conclude that the unusual and unverified experiences had psychogenic causes. There are some major questions as to how researchers reached this conclusion. For example, in those instances where all or a majority of the victims were women, this fact alone was considered part of the proof that hysteria caused the afflictions. Johnson (1945:245) notes that "those who succumbed to the mental epidemic were mostly women. . . . This supports the above analysis and puts the 'phantom anesthetist' of Mattoon, in some respects at least, into a familiar psychological pattern." Similar logic was used in explaining the outbreaks of hysteria during the Stairway of the Stars concert and the June bug epidemic.

Victims have also challenged, as superficial or careless, authorities' searches for nonpsychogenic causes of their fears or physical symptoms. For instance, the California Department of Health Services investigation ruled that the Riverside emergency room workers were victims of a "mass sociogenic illness triggered by an odor." Personal injury lawsuits were filed against the county, however, by four of the five workers who were hospitalized the evening of the outbreak (Boodman, 1994). In the course of bringing suit a number of issues were raised. A National Institute for Occupational Safety and Health Administration laboratory analyzed a gas sample taken from the dead patient's body bag and concluded only that the compound they found does not appear in the toxicological registry. The possibility of discovery of any toxic agent was made less likely by the HAZMAT decontamination of the emergency room before the Occupational Safety and Health Administration's (OSHA) investigation was conducted. The syringe and blood sample taken from the dying woman were accidentally discarded in the course of evacuating the emergency room. The investigation by the Riverside county coroner's office was disrupted by the suicide of its chief investigator. Medical records of the dead patient and plaintiffs had not been used in the California Department of Health Services or OSHA investigations. It was argued that the persistence of symptoms such as long-term breathing difficulty, rare joint and circulation problems, and liver disorders were inconsistent with "mass sociogenic illness triggered by an odor." Finally, the Riverside emergency room had been the subject of three additional odor-and-fume complaints to OSHA since 1991 (Boodman, 1994).

In general, the mass hysteria studies give considerable weight to the hysteria explanations suggested by authorities *before* the studies were initiated. It should be noted, however, that in most of these episodes, authorities *initially* gave considerable credence to the interpretations of the victims and only began to back away from this stance later in the course of these episodes. Authorities usually act with respect to immediate, practical problems, such as getting employees back to work or restoring order in the community, rather than evaluating competing theories of collective behavior. Intense public concern and publicity accompanying these unusual and troublesome events is usually short lived, and attributing the cause of such events to "mass hysteria" is one way of laying them to rest. When they use the judgment of authorities as the primary means of ascertaining the "hysterical" nature of these events, mass hysteria studies lose a great deal of their scientific merit.

The weakness of the psychogenic explanation is perhaps most obvious when we consider the reactions to the "War of the Worlds" broadcast. Again, we should emphasize that "War of the Worlds" was not an ordinary radio drama. As previously mentioned, the first half of the show used an open format in which the entire story line was developed through the use of simulated news bulletins and on-the-scene reports. The second half of the show used a conventional dramatic format. Many discussions of "War of the Worlds" read as if listeners panicked at the very beginning of the broadcast and remained terrorized throughout the show and for much of the evening. In fact, a ten-minute segment in the first half of the broadcast caused most of the trouble.

In the days following the show, newspaper columnists and public officials expressed dismay at the "incredible stupidity," "gullibility," and "hysteria" of listeners. Many popular accounts claim that the broadcast was interrupted several times for special announcements that a play was in progress. Listeners, however, had apparently been too panicked to notice them. These extreme psychogenic assumptions are, for the most part, unwarranted and inaccurate. For example, other than Mercury Theater's one-minute introduction (which most listeners missed), the station break at the middle of the broadcast, and the signoff, there were no announcements, special or otherwise, to indicate that a play was on the air. Further, Mercury Theater was being presented by CBS as a public service broadcast, and there were no commercials from which listeners might conclude that they were listening to a drama (Houseman, 1948).

Cantril (1966) and Houseman (1948) indicate that most listeners, and virtually all of those who became frightened, tuned in Mercury Theater about twelve minutes after the broadcast began. These listeners joined the broadcast during an on-the-scene news report from a farm near Grovers Mill, New Jersey—an actual town located between Princeton and Trenton—where a large meteor had landed. Welles's careful direction meticulously created all the character of a remote broadcast, including static, microphone feedback, and background sounds of autos, sirens, and the voices of spectators and police.

Twelve minutes from the beginning of the Mercury Theater broadcast, newscaster Carl Philips (played by radio actor Frank Readick) was concluding a rather awkward interview with a Mr. Wilmuth, the owner of the farm where the meteor had landed. Phillips broke off his interview with the annoyingly inarticulate Mr. Wilmuth by providing listeners with a detailed description of the meteor. During this description, Phillips called the listeners' attention to mysterious sounds coming from the meteor and fought to maintain his composure as he described the incredible and horrible creatures emerging from the pit where the meteor had landed. Background sounds of angry police and confused, frightened, and milling spectators provided a brilliant counterpoint to Phillips's stammering narration. At this point, Phillips signed off temporarily to "take up a safer position" from which to continue the broadcast.

For what seemed a very long time, a studio piano played "Clair de Lune," filling in the empty airspace. Finally, an anonymous studio announcer broke in with, "We are bringing you an eyewitness account of what's happening on the Wilmuth farm, Grovers Mill, New Jersey." After more empty airspace, Carl Phillips returned. Apparently unsure of whether he was on the air, Phillips continued to describe the monsters. The tempo of his reporting increased until Phillips was almost incoherent. In the background, the sound of terrified voices, screams, and the monsters' strange fire weapon merged into a chaotic and hair-raising din. Then, abruptly, there was dead silence. After an unbearably long period of empty airspace, the studio announcer broke in with, "Ladies and gentlemen, due to circumstances beyond our control, we are unable to continue the broadcast from Grovers Mill. Evidently there is some difficulty in our field transmission" (Cantril, 1966:17–18). This segment of the broadcast lasted less than five minutes, but, according to later interviews, it caused most of the fright.

The technical brilliance of the broadcast aside, how could an event as seemingly unlikely as a Martian invasion readily be interpreted as real? Part of the answer to this question lies in the fact that the monsters were never clearly identified as Martians until several minutes after "Carl Phillips's" segment of the broadcast. In fact, the first announcement that the Grovers Mill monsters were part of an invading army from Mars convinced some people that they were listening to a Halloween show. It is likely that some people who became confused and frightened were reacting to actor Frank Readick's portrayal of an on-the-scene news reporter. Readick's performance had been inspired by the eyewitness description of the explosion of the zeppelin *Hindenburg*, which had occurred just a year and a half earlier on May 6, 1937, in Lakehurst, New Jersey. In this world-famous broadcast, the reporter was describing the uneventful landing of the *Hindenburg* when it suddenly exploded with spectacular and deadly force. The reporter struggled to remain coherent, and his tearful, second-by-second description was heard by millions. The day of the "War of the Worlds" broadcast, Readick spent hours listening to the *Hindenburg* recording (Houseman, 1948). His interpretation of the Martian attack created a sense of *déjà vu*. The emotion, the stammering, and even the tempo of newsman Carl Phillips's narration reminds one of the report of the *Hindenburg* disaster. Readick's blending of the real and imaginary must have been very disconcerting for those who had heard the *Hindenburg* broadcast eighteen months earlier.

After Carl Phillips's "death" and until the first station break, the broadcast consisted of a collage of news bulletins, public announcements, and on-the-scene reports. Taken sequentially, these bulletins and reports seemed to describe the Martians' utter destruction of the New Jersey National Guard, a devastating Martian advance across New Jersey, and, by the end of the first half of the show, massive nerve gas attacks on New York City. Events of such magnitude could hardly occur in a period of less than fifteen minutes. About 25 percent of the listeners who had become frightened quickly concluded that they were listening to a radio drama because of this time distortion and other internal inconsistencies of the broadcast (Cantril, 1966:106–7).

Most of the frightened listeners did not register the impossibility of a fifteen-minute sweep of the East Coast by Martians. Cantril describes these people as experiencing the most severe symptoms of panic: their critical abilities had been so disabled that they continued to believe the impossible. Cantril's data, however, suggest an alternate interpretation of this group's behavior. Quite simply, many of Cantril's interviews suggest that listeners perceived the reported events as occurring *simultaneously* rather than sequentially. Nothing in the first part of the broadcast definitely stated that the Martians who had landed at Grovers Mill were the same Martians who, moments later, were reported to be marching across New Jersey or attacking New York City. Listeners who failed to perceive a time distortion in the broadcast had not necessarily lost their critical abilities. Rather, they were perceiving the news bulletins and on-the-scene reports as an understandably confusing and disordered collage of information pouring in simultaneously from all across the nation.

The psychogenic, or hysteria, explanation of people's reactions to the "War of the Worlds" broadcast severely underplays the unique and unsettling character of the show. Cantril poses the question: "Why did this broadcast frighten some people when other fantastic broadcasts do not?" He provides a partial answer when he considers the realistic way in which the program was put together (Cantril, 1966:67–76). Houseman (1948) provides even more insight when he discusses the "technical brilliance" of the show that emerged under Orson Welles's direction. If we take into account the unique character of the "War of the Worlds" broadcast, we needn't speculate that psychogenic mechanisms caused people to lose their critical abilities and then to panic. Rather, Orson Welles and his Mercury Theater staff of excellent writers and actors not so innocently conspired to "scare the hell out of people" the night before Halloween. They succeeded in scaring the hell out of 20 percent of their listening audience.

In summary, the quantitative mass hysteria studies fail to show that unusual and unverified experiences are widespread. In some instances, these experiences are reported by a very small portion of an available population, and in no instance are they reported by a majority. The quantitative studies also fail to substantiate clearly the hysterical nature of unusual and unverified experiences. Some studies have relied almost totally on the judgment of law enforcement or medical authorities that the reported experiences are of a hysterical nature. Cantril, on the other hand, fails to take the unique features of the "War of the Worlds" broadcast into account when he concludes that the fear reactions were hysterical in nature.

Mobilization

Mass hysteria studies generally fail to distinguish mobilization as a distinct element of the episodes that prompted the investigations. Cantril, for example, alleges that panic flight occurred during the "War of the Worlds" broadcast but does not examine his data systematically to determine the extent or characteristics of this flight. Cantril also notes that telephone switchboards at CBS, local radio stations, police, and hospitals were flooded with calls from hysterical people. Again he made no systematic attempts to ascertain the nature of these calls. Likewise, Johnson (1945) noted that Mattoon residents formed neighborhood patrols during the anesthetist incident, but he did not attempt to find out when these patrols occurred or to determine their size, composition, and activities. Such types of mobilization are probably more burdensome to authorities and disruptive of social routines than are the unusual and unverified experiences themselves.

Even though the mass hysteria studies fail to examine mobilization systematically, they do present information that, when carefully considered, provides some insight into this process. Cantril's data does not document the claim that the "War of the Worlds" broadcast produced substantial amounts of panic flight. A few of his interviews, however, do suggest that some people started to pack belongings in preparation for movement before they found out the news bulletins were a play.

Cantril also received a letter from a man who had somehow heard of his investigation. The man wrote:

> I thought the best thing to do was go away, so I took $3.25 out of my savings and bought a ticket. After I had gone 60 miles I heard it was a play. Now I don't have any money left for the shoes I was saving up for. Would you please have someone send me a pair of black shoes, size 9-B. (Cantril, 1966:54)

Houseman (1948:82), too, reported that CBS received a letter from a man claiming he had spent $3.25 of his meager savings to buy a bus ticket to "go away" and asking for size 9-B work shoes. Even though the CBS lawyer advised against it, Houseman said that the Mercury Theater sent the shoes.

Cantril (1966:207–8) also notes that interviews were conducted with nine people who heard the broadcast over their car radios, only three of whom reported becoming "extremely frightened." Being in an auto presents people with an immediate means of flight. In all three instances, the drivers reported handling their cars in a reckless manner; however, none appear to have been fleeing the Martians. One driver tried to get home quickly to be with his family; another drove to "rescue" his girlfriend, and the third drove to find his parish priest. The kinds of reactions Cantril describes as "panic flight" actually appear to be similar to the efforts people usually make to contact family and friends during disasters. Additional support for this disaster reaction image comes from accounts describing unusually heavy traffic through Grovers Mill following the broadcast. Similar convergence on accident and disaster sites is quite typical and may even hinder rescue and recovery efforts. (We discuss disaster reactions in chapter 10.) There seem to have been many similarities between people's reactions to the "War of the Worlds" broadcast and people's initial adaptive reactions to real disasters. In the case of the broadcast, however, people learned very quickly that they were listening to a play.

Cantril (1966:60) notes that accounts of telephone calls flooding switchboards of radio stations, newspapers, and police stations are confirmed by statistics provided by the American Telephone Company. These statistics indicate a 25 to 40 percent increase in telephone call volume throughout northern New Jersey during, and for an hour following, the broadcast. Cantril and others cite instances where radio stations, newspapers, and police received "hysterical" calls from sobbing and incoherent people. However, Cantril's data seem to suggest that other types of calls were more frequent. Some callers requested information, such as which units of National Guard were being called up or whether casualty lists were available. Some people called to find out where they could go to donate blood. Some callers were simply angry that such a realistic show was allowed on the air, while others called CBS to congratulate Mercury Theater for the exciting Halloween program. Unfortunately, it is now impossible to determine the relative frequency of each type of call. Finally, we cannot know how many of these telephone calls were between households rather than to the radio station. It seems reasonable, however, that many callers just wanted to chat with their families and friends about the exciting show they had just listened to on the radio.

Johnson (1945:233–34) states that neighborhood patrols were established in Mattoon during the phantom anesthetist episode. In the final days of the disturbance, the commissioner of police put a note in the *Mattoon Daily Journal-Gazette* requesting that men and boys discontinue the patrols "because some innocent person might get killed." How large and how extensive these patrols were cannot be ascertained from Johnson's study. It is apparent, however, that Johnson obtained most of his information about these patrols from newspaper accounts. Later in this chapter we will show how newspaper accounts often exaggerate the number and extent of such patrols. In any event, Johnson does note that photographs of these patrols, which appeared in a number of newspapers, were posed by news photographers.

The existing mass hysteria studies tell us relatively little about mobilization with respect to unusual and unverified experiences. Cantril's study does suggest similarities between mobilization with respect to the "War of the Worlds" broadcast and reactions to disasters. Also, a portion of the phone calls made during and immediately following the show were probably for the purpose of obtaining information, volunteering services, or simply commenting on the broadcast. Johnson's study of the phantom anesthetist suggests that neighborhood patrols were not as extensive as newspaper accounts claim.

General Preoccupation

Mass hysteria studies primarily give attention to the general preoccupation element of the episodes in question. Kerckhoff and Back (1968) devote a great deal of their analysis, for example, to various aspects of the belief in bug bites among mill workers. Medalia and Larsen (1958) restrict their study to determining which groups were the most likely to believe in windshield pitting. Stewart's (1977; 1980) analysis focuses primarily on the relationship between sources of information and types of belief about cattle mutilations.

Mass hysteria studies usually begin by discussing the unusual and unverified experiences and the mobilization, which affect only a minority of the population. Then the analysis subtly shifts to the beliefs accompanying the episode, which often includes virtually the entire population. This shift from unverified and unusual experiences and mobilization to general preoccupation gives the impression that a population is almost unanimously involved in the episode. The elements of unverified and unusual experiences, mobilization, and general preoccupation, however, represent substantially different levels of involvement. People reporting unusual and unverified experiences may suffer physical symptoms as well as become targets of scrutiny by authorities. Their normal family lives and work routines may be disrupted by ridicule or by momentary celebrity status. Those involved only to the extent of mobilization also confront disruptions in normal routines, if only to the extent of irregular mealtimes and lack of sleep. However, those involved only to the extent of general preoccupation may discuss, debate, and certainly form opinions about the strange events occurring in their vicinity, but do little else. In his most recent consideration of the nature of mass hysteria, Stewart (1984) suggests we use the term *collective delusion* rather than mass hysteria to refer to episodes that involve primarily the spread of beliefs rather than physical symptoms.

When sociologists start to study the episode, perhaps weeks after it occurred, they tend to focus on the general preoccupation element. That is, studying unverified and unusual experiences and mobilization will almost certainly include finding some of the individuals involved. This in itself may be difficult and perhaps expensive. Once located, these people may be reluctant to talk to sociologists who have already concluded how "hysterical" they had been. The unavailability and reluctance to comment of gas attack victims, for example, contributed to the limited scope of Johnson's phantom anesthetist study.

Faced with such difficulties, sociologists simply may administer a large number of questionnaires or conduct telephone interviews to obtain socioeconomic information and to determine people's beliefs about what happened. Thus Kerckhoff and Back (1968:53) administered a questionnaire to mill workers, the results of which indicated that about 90 percent of the workers thought the bug bite illness had a real rather than a psychogenic cause. Medalia and Larsen's (1958) telephone survey indicated that about 95 percent of Seattle residents had formed an opinion about the cause of windshield pitting. Finally, Stewart's (1977; 1980) survey indicates a similar pattern of widespread dissemination of information and formation of opinions about the cattle mutilations.

Explicitly or implicitly, mass hysteria studies equate general preoccupation with the more direct kinds of involvement that are part of unverified and unusual experiences and mobilization. This aspect of mass hysteria studies gives the superficial appearance of demonstrating that the hysteria is affecting nearly the entire available population. While nearly all the population may be involved at the level of general preoccupation, this involvement has been shown to have little consequence. Kerckhoff and Back (1968) conducted their survey more than two months after the June bug epidemic. Almost all the workers believed that the cause of the disruption had been bug bites. The repeated denials of this view by plant managers and health authorities had done little to convince workers otherwise. More importantly, in spite of a persistent and almost unanimous belief in bug bites, work routines at the mill had returned to normal within a week of the first bug bite reports. Likewise, Johnson indicates that Mattoon residents continued to believe strongly in the phantom anesthetist months after the first attack. This belief, however, appears to have been insufficient to produce another wave of "hysteria."

In summary, mass hysteria studies have failed to substantiate either the widespread prevalence or the hysterical nature of unverified and unusual experiences and mobilization that make up the incidents under investigation. Mass hysteria studies have shown that during these episodes, there is nearly complete dissemination of information regarding unverified and unusual experiences and mobilization. This general preoccupation, or dissemination of quite interesting information throughout a population, does not necessarily reflect the workings of hysteria, nor does it seem to make a later recurrence of such incidents more likely.

EXPLANATIONS OF MASS HYSTERIA

Although mass hysteria theory states that *circular reaction* is both the cause and the mechanism through which mass hysteria is transmitted (see chapter 2), this assertion has never been examined. In part, this is because mass hysteria studies are conducted weeks and months after the episode at issue. Researchers, therefore, have no opportunity to observe the "crowd interaction" and "intense interstimulation" that are part of circular reaction. Kerckhoff and Back (1968) came closest to examining such interaction when they attempted to determine the sequence in which bug bite victims succumbed. They found that the first few victims tended to be social isolates. Then, as the affliction spread, it tended to occur more frequently within identifiable friendship groups. In the final stage, the affliction tended to occur randomly, afflicting isolates and friendship groups alike. Kerckhoff and Back (1968:115) compared this last stage to a "crowd response." Similarly, Small, et al. (1991) concluded that seeing a friend become ill was the best predictor of experiencing one's own symptoms at the Stairway of the Stars concert.

Mass hysteria studies have offered two general explanations for hysteria. The first explanation states that mass hysteria results from *social strain*. According to this view, mass hysteria is a "safety valve" that allows people to discharge, in a relatively harmless way, anxieties caused by social strains such as economic downturns or threats of war. A second explanation, not entirely unrelated to the first, is that people having certain inferior socioeconomic attributes are more prone than others to involvement in mass hysteria. In discussions of mass hysteria, researchers consistently claim that young people, women, and those having little formal education are more likely than others to become involved in mass hysteria. As the social strain explanation suggests, persons with inferior socioeconomic attributes, such as having a low income or an insecure job or owning little property, have a much greater tendency to become part of mass hysteria episodes than people not subjected to these strains. Researchers have tested various aspects of the social strain and inferior socioeconomic attribute explanations in mass hysteria studies.

Social Strain In their theoretical statements, Blumer, Smelser, and Klapp all claim that social strain is one of the necessary causes of mass hysteria. Social strain refers to the "feelings of frustration and protest over an existing mode of life" (Blumer, [1934] 1969:25), an "anxiety provoking effect of an ambiguous environment" (Smelser, 1962:141), or "tensions within individuals caused by strains in the larger social system" (Klapp, 1972:160). In all the mass hysteria studies, either directly or indirectly, researchers address the issue of social strain. Their approach, however, is to determine the nature of the strain that "caused" the hysteria rather than to learn whether strain and hysteria are actually related phenomena. That is, these researchers have failed to construct quantitative measures of social strain that can determine comparative levels of strain prior to and following the episode in question. Instead, they simply speculate about what may have concerned people prior to the event. Thus, Cantril (1966) questioned "War of the Worlds" listeners about their fears of war in Europe, and Kerckhoff and Back (1968) examined economic hardships and job satisfaction of the workers involved in the June bug incident. In this manner, almost any conceivable personal complaint or fear can be seen as evidence of social strain. Stewart (1977; 1980), for example, argued that because the price of beef was at an all-time high during some cattle mutilation episodes, this created anxiety among farmers that the price would soon drop.

Inferior Socioeconomic Attributes In all the mass hysteria studies, researchers have examined socioeconomic attributes on the assumption that certain "types of people" are more susceptible to hysteria than others. This assumption has had a considerable impact on the way in which mass hysteria studies are conducted. As previously noted, researchers have given little attention to the task of determining the nature of unverified and unusual experiences and mobilization, while they have given considerable attention to the task of determining the age, sex, economic, occupational, and educational characteristics of the available population. Consequently, the results of mass hysteria studies generally claim to show that young people;

women; and people having low incomes, low occupational prestige, and low educational attainment are more likely than others to succumb to mass hysteria.

While these studies at first glance seem to present support for the above relationships, the actual mass hysteria data consistently suggest that these relationships are quite tenuous. For example, although Medalia and Larsen's (1958) data show that women were more likely than men to believe in windshield pitting, the actual difference between the beliefs of men and women was so small that it was essentially meaningless.

In other studies, researchers seem to have forced the methods and findings a bit to fit the assumption that women are more susceptible than men to hysteria. In Kerckhoff and Back's 1968 study, for example, three of the sixty-two bug bite victims were men, one of them among the earliest and most severely stricken. But Kerckhoff and Back excluded these male victims in order to simplify the analysis. Further, they made no empirical comparisons between female victims and males whom were not affected. In the case of the phantom anesthetist of Mattoon, Johnson (1945) concluded that only 3 percent of the twenty-nine gas attack victims were males. This was inconsistent with his initial description of the episode, in which he mentioned four instances when women were with their husbands at the time of the attacks. These couples were described as being upset and showing symptoms of gassing. Had these four husbands been included among the twenty-nine gassing victims, then men would have accounted for nearly 15 percent of the reported casualties. At the beginning of his article, Johnson also noted that groups of men and boys patrolled the streets of Mattoon, but he did not include this type of male mobilization in his final analysis. In short, Johnson clearly underplayed the extent of male involvement in the phantom anesthetist episode. He concluded, "As might be predicted from the psychological and psychiatric literature, those who succumbed to the 'mental epidemic' were mostly women."

Discussion

In his 1895 work *The Crowd*, LeBon argued that crowds have the emotional qualities of inferior forms of evolution, such as women, savages, and children (see chapter 2). This statement gave rise to or at least reflected a bias that continues to the present day. Women; nonwhites; young people; and those having little education, income, or social prestige are considered the most likely candidates for active involvement in mass hysteria. Largely, the inferior socioeconomic attribute assumption has been accepted on the basis of faith and a bit of casual observation. Very few quantitative studies of mass hysteria have been conducted. Table 5.1 summarizes the variables and findings of nine quantitative mass hysteria studies. In these studies, researchers do not examine circular reaction; instead, they develop and test inferior socioeconomic attribute explanations of mass hysteria. Generally, however, the data from these studies show only minimal support for the mass hysteria image and explanation of collective behavior.

The preceding discussion places great emphasis on the shortcomings of the quantitative mass hysteria studies. However, any negative assessment of these studies must be tempered with the realization that, for the most part, they remain the *only* quantitative studies of unusual events. Since the late 1960s the focus of collective behavior and collective action research has focussed almost exclusively on the study of disaster, civil disorder, political violence, protest, and social move-

TABLE 5.1
Quantitative Mass Hysteria Studies

Study	Independent variables	Dependent variables	Percent of available population affected
Emergency Room (Boodman)	Inferred stress	Trembling, dizziness	11/37 = 30%
English Girls' School (Moss and McEvedy)	Inferred stress, gender	Fainting, vomiting	33%
Stairway of the Stars Concert (Small, et al.)	Inferred stress, gender, interpersonal contact	Dizziness, nausea, headache, fainting	20%
June Bug Epidemic (Kerckhoff and Back)	Inferred stress, gender, interpersonal contact	Fainting, vomiting, rash	20%
"War of the Worlds" (Cantril)	Inferred stress, education, gender, region of U.S.	Fear reaction, flight	20%
Fallout Shelter (Levine and Model)	Socioeconomic status, home ownership	1. Purchase fallout shelter plans 2. Building shelters	12% 1% of group (1)
Windshield Pitting (Medalia and Larsen)	Inferred stress, education, gender	Reporting wind-shield damage	6%
Phantom Anesthetist (Johnson)	Inferred stress, gender, income	Vomiting, rash, sighting of prowler, calls to police	< 1%
Cattle Mutilations (Stewart)	Income, education, occupation	Reporting cattle mutilations	< 1%

ments. Certainly research in these areas is important; however, events similar to the reaction to the "War of the Worlds" broadcast, the phantom anesthetist episode, or the June bug incident are also worth studying. As Carl Couch once put it, "The study of such seemingly strange events . . . is important, I think, precisely because such phenomena must cause us to examine more closely our assumptions about ordinary, everyday life" (personal correspondence).

Such unusual events are not a thing of the past. People still grossly misinterpret information from the media. People still see and become excited about flying saucers, or UFOs. (We will consider this particular type of unusual event in chapter 6.) People still report seeing and being frightened by "monsters" in their communities. In the next section of this chapter, we will consider a monster sighting episode from the standpoint of the collective action perspective.

COLLECTIVE ACTION AND UNUSUAL EVENTS:
THE ENFIELD MONSTER

Many of the preceding criticisms of the mass hysteria perspective and the mass hysteria studies are derived from the collective action perspective. This may not seem to be the case initially since resource mobilization theory, the political process model and frame analysis have been developed in the course of the quantitative study of social movements and political protest. The SBI and perception control perspective has been developed primarily while studying behavior within hundreds of gatherings.

However, it is from the standpoint of collective action theory, with its emphasis on the careful delineation and specification of dependent variables, that we come to break down unusual events into the components of unusual and unverified experiences, mobilization, and general preoccupation. These elements call our attention to the potentially observable aspects of odd episodes that have been confused or ignored in mass hysteria studies. The analysis of the "War of the Worlds" broadcast is an attempt to account for people's reactions in terms of "cues to conduct" rather than by relying exclusively on inferences drawn from their socioeconomic attributes.

The general standpoint of frame analysis dictates that we give credence and attention to the strange stories told by participants in these unusual episodes. Such accounts are not to be dismissed as the ramblings of overwrought individuals. Oftentimes participants in these episodes are ridiculed by media and authorities, not unlike newly formed and powerless groups studied from the standpoint of the political process model. Finally, McPhail (1991) rejects the transformation explanation of collective behavior that holds that crowds transform individuals, diminishing or eliminating their ability to control their behavior rationally.

Most of the criticisms of the mass hysteria perspective in this chapter grew out of the study of an event that had all the superficial characteristics of a classic case of mass hysteria. We will now examine this event from the standpoint of collective action.

The Episode

On Thursday, April 26, 1973, the *Carmi Times* (Carmi, Illinois) carried a story that described a face-to-face encounter with a "weird creature" in the nearby town of Enfield (population 760). The informant, Mr. M., claimed that a scratching noise at his front door at about nine o'clock the previous evening had alarmed him. When he opened the door, a three-legged creature about five feet tall confronted him. The visitor was gray, had a flat body, wide head, and two large pink eyes. Greatly alarmed, Mr. M. fired a pistol at the creature, which "hissed like a wildcat," sprang from the porch, and ran northward into the underbrush beside a nearby railroad track. Mrs. M. quickly phoned the state police, who later claimed to have discovered unusual animal tracks near the house. During the disturbance, about sixty residents of Enfield converged on Mr. M.'s property and discussed the event.

By Thursday afternoon, the news director of radio station WWKI in Kokomo, Indiana, had been dispatched to Enfield. The station subsequently broadcast reports that at least three other residents of Enfield had seen "something strange." Most prominent among the reports was that of a ten-year-old boy who lived near

Mr. M.'s house. The boy claimed that about an hour before Mr. M.'s sighting, the creature "jumped out of some bushes, stomped on his feet, and tore his tennis shoes to shreds." According to subsequent newspaper accounts, he ran home "in hysteria."

The next day, the AP and UPI news services carried the Enfield story. The *Champaign-Urbana News Gazette* ran an article claiming the investigating officers had described Mr. M. as a "rational and sober" person and that the creature's tracks were "shaped like a dog's" but had "six toe pads." The article also noted that schoolchildren told Mr. M. that they had seen a similar creature near the ballpark. The article concluded with Mr. M.'s statement that there was probably more than one of the creatures and that "they were not from this planet."

On Monday, April 30, the Carmi Times reported that Mr. M. had received more than 250 telephone calls over the weekend. One call had come from a government representative who claimed that many similar incidents had occurred since 1967 and that they were usually associated with UFO sightings. During the weekend, an anthropologist had interviewed Mr. M., examined the tracks of the creature, and decided that the tracks were definitely not those of a pet kangaroo, as some people had suggested. The April 30 article went on to note that plaster casts of the tracks had been made and were en route to an undisclosed laboratory for "closer examination." Two local men had spent the weekend searching for the creature, without success. The article concluded by suggesting that a bear may have been wandering about the Enfield area.

There was little newspaper or radio coverage of events in Enfield for the next few days. Renewed interest was shown, however, when on Sunday, May 6, Mr. M. reported to radio station WWKI that he had sighted the creature about 3:00 A.M. on the railroad tracks near his home. Later that Sunday, WWKI's news director and three companions revisited Enfield. This search party later reported that they observed an "apelike" creature standing in an abandoned barn near Mr. M.'s house. They claimed to have recorded some of the creature's cries and fired a shot at it before it ran off.

By Monday, May 7, events in Enfield were again on the wire service network, and stories appeared in the *Chicago Daily News*, the *Moline Dispatch*, the *Champaign-Urbana Courier*, and the *Alton Telegraph*. Mr. M. was interviewed on the Wally Phillips morning show over radio station WGN, Chicago. This telephone interview was broadcast live throughout the Midwest.

On Tuesday, May 8, the White County sheriff arrested five young men from outlying communities after Enfield residents complained of gunfire. The men stated that they had heard radio reports about the monster and had come to Enfield to photograph the creature. They brought shotguns and rifles "for protection" and claimed to have sighted a creature and fired at it. The hunters were charged with hunting violations and posted bond.

On Wednesday, May 9, accounts of the arrests appeared in several Illinois newspapers. The *Carmi Times* accompanied descriptions of the arrest with statements from Enfield residents expressing fears that monster hunters might accidentally shoot people or livestock. It was also suggested that some of the "experts" visiting Enfield had no academic credentials or affiliations with universities and were little more than thrill seekers. The article concluded by noting that local newspeople and law enforcement agencies continued to receive telephone calls from various magazines and from television and radio stations.

On Thursday, May 10, this author's five-person research team arrived and began to conduct interviews throughout Enfield. We left Enfield about noon on Saturday, May 12. On Sunday, an anthropology graduate student from the University of Illinois arrived in Enfield. Later that day, UPI releases quoted the student as suggesting that the Enfield monster was probably a wild ape, such animals having been reported sporadically throughout the Mississippi watershed since 1941.

On Monday morning, May 14, Wally Phillips of WGN, having somehow heard of our investigation, contacted us by phone. The interview was broadcast live, and we attempted to avoid speculating about the identity of the monster. We did, however, note the potential danger that "monster hunters" posed for local residents.

By Tuesday, May 15, almost three weeks after the first monster sighting and a week after the arrest of the five monster hunters, the *Carmi Times* included only two items concerning the Enfield monster. One item discussed the building of a calf pen by an Enfield resident who, when asked by a neighbor, claimed he was constructing a "monster pen." The other item reported that an Ohio woman was sure that the Enfield monster was her pet kangaroo, missing for more than a year. She offered a $500 reward for its return. The Enfield incident ended on these whimsical notes (Miller, Mietus, and Mathers, 1978).

Methods of Investigation

One of the most important aspects of this study was that our five-man research team arrived in Enfield *during* the episode. Within the first hour, we were struck by the discrepancy between what radio and press reports led us to believe was occurring in Enfield and what we actually saw the morning our research team entered the town. Instead of seeing anxious and agitated people milling through the streets, nervously speculating about when the monster would be sighted again, we encountered a tranquil scene of small-town community life. People greeted one another outside the post office, children were chattering as they leisurely walked to school, and the small cafe and filling station were opening for business. Friendly greetings were extended to us, and when we explained that we were in Enfield to conduct a study, the residents cooperated fully.

During the first morning, we conducted several interviews in which we attempted to assess "monster beliefs" and to administer an anxiety scale we had designed to quantitatively assess the level of social strain accompanying this event. The people we interviewed carefully answered the questions we asked them. After about two hours, however, we decided that we needed a research strategy meeting. We assembled the research team and drove to a secluded rest area a few miles outside Enfield. At this strategy session, we decided that we were clearly failing to obtain the essential who, what, when, and where information about the events occurring in Enfield. Therefore, we decided to abandon our efforts to measure monster beliefs and social strain and instead to focus on finding out as much as possible from residents about the events occurring in their community.

Enfield's street pattern enabled us to easily divide the community into four sampling areas. We used a community influential-reputational approach (Hunter, 1963) to select fourteen people to be interviewed, including Enfield's postmaster; the managers of the local recreation center, the diner and service station, and the general store; and the high school principal and teachers. Such people represent traditional clearinghouses of information in small rural communities. Also, these people occupy public positions that enable them to observe and report on the pervasiveness, intensity, and content of discussions about topics of local concern. We conducted another seventy-three interviews with people available in the four sampling quadrants. We purposely selected more people from the quadrant where the sightings took place. We also spoke with but did not formally interview a few farmers from the surrounding area and people from Carmi, Illinois. Finally, we interviewed the White County sheriff and the editor of the *Carmi Times*. From these people we obtained a sufficient amount of descriptive material to construct the following analysis.

A Collective Action Analysis of the Enfield Incident

What did happen in Enfield during those spring days of 1973? We attempted to gather as complete and detailed an account of the happenings in Enfield as possible. Our information was then organized into the previously discussed categories of unusual and unverified experiences, mobilization, and general preoccupation.

Unusual and Unverified Experiences As we interviewed Enfield residents, we saw no compelling reason to attribute the monster sightings to psychogenic causes. In part, this was because the actual number of monster sightings was much smaller than we had been led to believe from earlier newspaper and radio reports. Mr. M.'s frequent statements to the news media that "others in his community had seen monsters" created the impression that a large number of sightings had occurred. During our time in Enfield, however, we were not able to locate any of the "other people" who had seen the monster.

We did interview the boy who had his tennis shoes "ravaged" by the monster. This incident turned out to be a practical joke. The boy and his parents told us that they invented the shoe-tearing story to tease Mr. M. and to have some fun with an out-of-town newsman.

The White County sheriff told us that news stories describing the men he arrested on May 8 as a "monster hunting expedition" were an exaggeration. He described the hunters as just "out drinking and raising hell." According to the sheriff, they only mentioned the monster briefly during their questioning.

Our investigation revealed that there were perhaps no more than three firsthand monster reports. These were the April 28 and May 6 sightings reported by Mr. M. and the May 6 sighting by the WWKI news team. These three reports hardly constituted an "epidemic" of monster sightings. Such findings are consistent with those of the mass hysteria studies discussed earlier in this chapter. That is, in episodes of this kind, the number of unusual and unverified experiences is smaller than initially thought and represents only a small portion of the available population.

We also saw no need to attribute monster sightings to psychogenic causes, given the rugged woodlands surrounding Enfield. In this area of southern Illinois, it is not unreasonable to assume that Mr. M. or the radio news team had actually seen an animal. People we interviewed framed the recent events in these terms. Their accounts admitted the possibility that large dogs, calves, bears, deer, and wildcats had been sighted. Some frames suggested that an exotic pet, such as an ape or kangaroo, was the catalyst for the monster reports. Finally, some people tactfully suggested that Mr. M. had a notoriously active imagination and had probably been shooting at shadows. In any event, we interviewed only one person who agreed with Mr. M.'s claim that he had indeed seen a monster from outer space.

Mobilization The convergence of people toward or dispersal from scenes of unusual and unverified events, the formation of neighborhood patrols, and the subsequent movements of hostile or celebrating throngs are differentiated phenomena, frequently consisting of or at least preceded by *assembling processes*. A necessary condition for an assembling process is that people be notified of an event occurring at some distant location. A facilitating condition for the initiation of assembling processes is a large number of people in general proximity to one another, with a period of free or uncommitted time at their disposal. These time frames generally include nonwork hours, weekends, and holidays. For example, the first monster sighting occurred about 9:30 P.M. and was accompanied by pistol shots and the subsequent arrival of state police vehicles. About fifty to seventy-five neighbors gathered at the site of the disturbance. In contrast, no assembling processes accompanied Mr. M.'s second monster report.

Smelser's discussion of hysteria suggests that in the later stages of such outbreaks, people reach a stage of emotional "burnout" or saturation, and they become almost immune to further excitation. Events that caused great excitement earlier now seem to pass without notice. Mr. M.'s two monster sightings and the different reactions to each of them invite this type of interpretation. Our analysis, however, suggests that the quite different responses to these two sightings was due almost entirely to the kinds of cues to conduct accompanying each incident. In contrast to the first sighting, Mr. M.'s second sighting occurred at a less favorable time (3:00 A.M.), no pistol shots were fired, and no state police vehicles were dispatched. In all likelihood, many Enfield residents remained unaware of the second sighting until they read the *Carmi Times*.

The greater the distance from the location of an event, the less sensory access there is to cues that something is occurring. Persons who can neither see nor hear the event depend on face-to-face communications, phone calls, or mass media announcements for instructions that establish the existence of the event and specify movement toward (or away from) the location of the event. Newspaper stories and radio dispatches notified people throughout Illinois and parts of Indiana, Ohio, Missouri, and Kentucky of the happenings at Enfield.

An issue that must be addressed is how such extensive notification is produced. In this instance, notification of the event was facilitated by Mr. M.'s active pursuit of newspeople. For example, following the second sighting, Mr. M. called an Indiana radio station rather than the state police. Further, Enfield events may have been given play in the media because the monster stories provided some relief from other, more ominous issues. Flooding was seriously delaying spring planting in southern Illinois, the Vietnam War was still to be resolved, and Watergate disclosures were beginning to surface. Editors and station managers may have welcomed these monster stories for their contrast to an unusually long and depressing series of events.

Once people throughout Illinois and adjoining states had been informed of the Enfield events, mobilization occurred across this larger area. There were patterns to this mobilization. For the most part, news teams, anthropologists, hunters, and sightseers traveled to Enfield on weekends, when people traditionally schedule their outings. Some mobilizers, however, were clearly unencumbered by the familiar commitments of work. Four of the five hunters arrested on May 8 were unemployed, and the other hunter was on military leave.

Although mobilization processes have been acknowledged only to the extent that they represent mass hysteria, our analysis suggests an alternate interpretation. Mobilizations result from *processes of notification* through which people learn of the location of an event. Mobilizations also result from *differential availability*, or people's differential access to periods of negotiable or uncommitted time within which participation in mobilization processes can be scheduled.

General Preoccupation The rapid and widespread dissemination of all types of information, however, is a common and necessary feature of contemporary social life. A statement such as "A state police car just parked in front of Harry's house" may orient people to such events. Such necessary information is not itself sufficient for the organization of innovative or disruptive activities. At minimum, statements such as "Let's go see what is happening" must occur before further activities are organized with respect to these events (McPhail and Miller, 1973:724).

In the preceding chapter, it was noted that in order to understand the impact of communication during collective action we must also understand the circumstances under which prescriptions for action occur. Accounts of unusual and unverified events are likely to be accompanied by prescriptions when the objects established are in one's neighborhood. During the evening hours and on weekends people may have time available for extemporaneous activity. Finally, accounts of unusual and unverified events and prescriptions for action may occur within an ongoing action frame of conventional community life and among people who frequently and routinely participate in interrelated activities with one another.

In our study we sought to ascertain how accounts of monster sightings and other unusual events were used to construct activity divergent from the usual. Enfield residents seemed to be well informed of recent happenings in their town. Their frequent discussions of these events were restricted to casual conversations, jokes, and inconsequential bull sessions in homes, cafes, and other meeting places. School children had composed a few monster poems that they recited for us.

The only discussions that we know disrupted usual kinds of activities were the interviews we conducted. Business proprietors, teachers, mail carriers, and housewives stopped what they were doing to answer our questions. The only other consequences of "monster conversations" were those mentioned by a few residents who complained that their children were now "afraid to go out at night," "became frightened by small noises," and "had bad dreams." One resident reported that she cautioned her children to stay away from Mr. M.'s house because ". . . they might get shot by some fool." Finally, someone placed a barricade sign near the train tracks where the monster was first reported. The sign read "Danger! Monster Crossing!"

Of all our respondents, the White County sheriff was perhaps the most vehement in his denial that a monster had been sighted. Yet because of his organizational position, his routine activities had been disrupted more than those of any other person we interviewed. He stated that the arrests and legal dealings with the hunters, telephone calls from newspapers across the nation, and complaints from county residents had greatly hindered him and his staff in carrying out their other duties. The pre-established or institutionalized relationships within a community, rather than who believes information and who doesn't, are a key consideration in accounting for how routine activities are disrupted.

Discussion

Let's compare our study of the Enfield monster with what probably would have been done if this episode were studied from the standpoint of mass hysteria. Table 5.2 presents some comparisons between the mass hysteria and collective action perspectives.

Our analysis of a monster sighting in Enfield, Illinois, illustrates the utility of the collective action approach for understanding unusual events that in the past have been considered to be mass hysteria. With this approach we begin by ascertaining, from firsthand investigation, the general character of *differential participation* in the episode. In Enfield, only three unusual and unverified events, or monster sightings, had occurred, though newspaper and radio accounts led us to believe that monster sightings were much more frequent. With respect to mobilization, respondents reported that fifty to seventy-five people gathered at Mr. M.'s house after state troopers arrived. Fewer than ten people mobilized for the purpose of hunting the monster. Regarding general preoccupation, virtually everyone in the community discussed the event with friends and neighbors. Our data show that the type and extent of participation varied considerably. In mass hysteria studies, researchers usually fail to make such distinctions and consider these diverse types of participation as equivalent to one another. They would view all types as symptoms of mass hysteria.

We did not interpret these events as evidence that everyone "took leave of their senses" or abandoned the forms of conduct they normally use when dealing with more familiar problems. The processes of notification that accompanied monster

TABLE 5.2
The Enfield Monster: A Comparison of Two Approaches

Element	Mass Hysteria	Collective Action
Unusual and unverified experiences	Reliance on newspaper reports; monster sightings are socio- or psychogenic and the result of stress; stress inferred from current international and national events and the socioeconomic characteristics of Enfield residents.	Reliance on firsthand investigation; determination of number and circumstances of monster sightings; acknowledgement that some sightings could have been animals.
Mobilization	Reliance on newspaper reports; mobilization viewed as further evidence of mass hysteria but not examined as a separate element of episode.	Reliance on firsthand investigation; determination of extent of mobilization; examination of communication processes preceding mobilization; examination of availability.
General preoccupation	Primary focus of study; attention given to the variety of monster beliefs, comparison of beliefs, and socioeconomic attributes; most likely weak relationships are obtained.	Determination of extent to which monster information and discussions disrupted routine activity; determination of the nature of these disruptions.

reports were similar to those sights, sounds, and media announcements that inform people of street accidents, civil disorders, sports rallies, and public meetings. Mobilization processes tended to occur in the evenings or on weekends, and they involved those who were relatively unencumbered by competing institutional demands. The pervasive, community-wide discussion of monster events during this time frame did not disrupt pre-established community routines. The spread of monster information and the question of whether it was believed would have been a primary focus of a mass hysteria study.

The occupants of institutionalized positions are usually relied on by locals and outsiders to determine what is happening in a community. Monster sighting events created major problems of accommodation for local law enforcement agencies. Similar overload problems are frequently encountered by police following disasters and spectacular crimes or during presidential visits and holiday celebrations. In mass hysteria studies, researchers usually consider communication overload as evidence of aroused emotion.

SUMMARY

Mass hysteria was the first theoretical perspective within the field of collective behavior. It fostered an early interest in unanticipated, unusual, and, to some observers, senseless and possibly dangerous episodes of collective emotional displays. A few mass hysteria studies represent the first attempts to quantitatively examine collective behavior.

The collective action perspective, on the other hand, has focused on social movements, the dynamics of protest and behavior within gatherings to the exclusion of many of the traditional topics within the field of collective behavior. This is particularly the case in regard to studying those unusual events that were first studied from the standpoint of the mass hysteria perspective. In the concluding section of this chapter, it is shown that the resource mobilization, political process, frame analysis and perception control perspectives can be used in the analysis of such events.

☒ CHAPTER 6 ☒

UFOs

UFOs and aliens from outer space are very popular topics on the World Wide Web, often exceeding interest in current events. For instance, two weeks after the release of Monica Lewinsky's testimony describing her sexual relationship with President Clinton, the *Yahoo!* web search engine turned up three categories and 43 sites dealing with the Starr Report. Also, on this same day, *Yahoo!* turned up three categories and 421 sites on the home-run race between Mark McGwire and Sammy Sosa, both of whom had broken Roger Maris's thirty-seven-year-old record of 61 homers in a season. In contrast to these very popular and timely issues, the *Yahoo!* search yielded four categories and 629 sites dealing with UFOs.

UFOs and extraterrestrials have become cultural icons in the United States (Dean, 1998). Aliens have been used to market an incredibly wide variety of products including ". . . AT&T cellular phones, Milky Way candy bars, Kodak film, Diet Coke, Stove Top Stuffing, T-shirts, Rice Krispies, air fresheners, toys, abduction insurance, (and) skateboard accessories. . . ." (Dean, 1998:3). UFOs, space aliens, and alien abduction are nightly topics on talk radio (*Coast to Coast with Art Bell*) and cable television. *Entertainment Tonite*, the Fox Network entertainment news show, has devoted a number of programs to UFOs and the alien abduction experience, as has the Larry King show on Turner Network Television. A number of programs on television—*Unsolved Mysteries*, *In Search of*, *Ancient Mysteries*, *Sightings*, and *The Unexplained*—dramatize aspects of UFO experiences. The Arts and Entertainment Television Network, The Learning Channel, The Discovery Channel, and Turner Network Television air frequent documentaries dealing with UFOs. These documentaries include *"Where Are All the UFOs?"* (A&E), *"The Secret KGB UFO Files"* (TNT), The Discovery Channel's *"The Great Siberian Explosion,"* and NOVA's *"Kidnapped by Aliens?"*. Popular television shows like Fox Network's *The X-Files*, *Babylon 5* and the heritage of *Star Trek* (including the Science Fiction Channel's *Star Trek Special Edition*, *The Next Generation*, *Voyager*, and *Deep Space 9*) are all well populated with extraterrestrials.

UFOS AND COLLECTIVE BEHAVIOR

Casual observers and UFO experts alike attribute many UFO sightings to social contagion, or mass hysteria. This is a temptingly obvious characterization considering the bizarre nature of the stories provided by excited or frightened people. We will begin by identifying the range of UFO phenomena that have been recorded by governmental and civilian investigations. We will consider groups that claim to have had either enjoyable or harmful contact with the occupants of UFOs. We will then consider these phenomena from the standpoint of mass hysteria theory.

There are many references to puzzling or frightening aerial phenomena throughout the written history of human society. The legends and lore of the indigenous Australian aborigines incorporate the idea of "sky-beings," with the *Wandjina* being among the most interesting to consider. The Wandjina have been preserved in a fascinating oral tradition and in a large collection of rock paintings scattered throughout the Kimberley region of northern Australia. The paintings have received all manner of interpretations from stylized representations of a pervasive myth system to naive "ancient astronaut" theories. The Australian aborigines—"clever men" or "men of high degree"—described "celestial ascents" to meet with the "sky gods" such as Baiame, Biral, Goin and Bundjil (Chalker, 1996). Many of the accounts of the ritualistic initiation of shamans bear striking parallels to modern-day UFO contactee and abduction lore. Some contend that biblical passages such as that of Ezekiel's "heavenly wheels" represent ancient wonderment at something that today would be considered a UFO. Throughout the Dark and Middle ages, European chronicles are sprinkled with stories of great fireballs, flying ships, and even flying people. In none of these episodes does it appear that these aerial phenomena had any tremendously disruptive impact on the societies that witnessed them. Perhaps this is because unusual aerial phenomena could be easily accommodated within the prevailing religious and mystical belief systems and were viewed as a kind of omen, an angel, or a demon.

At the beginning of the twentieth century, such widely acceptable explanations were not available; new explanations and accommodations became necessary. In this chapter we will examine how UFOs became a part of our basic culture and social structure. We will first consider the types of UFO reports that lie at the heart of the matter.

HYNEK'S TYPOLOGY

Our work here is made somewhat easier by using the sixfold typology or classification system developed by astronomer and longtime UFO investigator James Allen Hynek (1972:25–35). The categories describe a continuum of strangeness of UFO reports. The most frequently reported and least "strange" events are *nocturnal lights*. Next, there are *daylight disks* and *radar/visual* reports. Finally, there are the three types of *close encounters*. Close encounters of the first kind are reports in which people claim to have had a close-at-hand experience with a UFO. Close encounters of the second kind are similar to the first kind except that tangible physical effects on the observer, on the land, or on animate or inanimate objects are reported. In close encounters of the third kind, the sighting of UFO occupants is reported. More elaborate classification schemes have been developed since 1972. Most notably there is the twenty-category Vallee classification system, which is based on the Hynek system but also incorporates those "psychic" or otherwise anomalous reports which have a connection with the UFO phenomenon (Valee, 1991).

Dr. David R. Saunders of the Center for UFO Studies began a computerized cataloguing system (UFOCAT) for UFO reports in 1967. UFOCAT draws reports from the files of UFO investigation groups, journals, and books. Although most reports concern events occurring in the United States, the catalogue includes reports from all over the world. The initial UFOCAT (1945–1973) contained nearly eighty thousand entries, and it has been updated to include more than one hundred thousand entries. UFOCAT gives us a clear indication of the very large number of UFO reports available for analysis. The following events illustrate the kinds of UFO reports that have been made through the years, categorized by Hynek's typology.

Nocturnal Lights

One of the most famous instances of nocturnal lights occurred in and around Lubbock, Texas, from August to October of 1951. The first sighting occurred about 9:30 P.M. on Saturday, August 25, when four faculty members of Texas Technical College observed a formation of twenty to thirty pale lights moving across the sky. Two more formations were observed before midnight. These sightings were reported to local newspapers but, surprisingly, no one else reported seeing these lights.

The next sightings occurred on Friday, August 31, and this time many people across Lubbock witnessed the lights. Radar at the nearby Air Defense Command briefly tracked a single object at thirteen thousand feet, traveling at nine hundred miles per hour. Further confusion arose when an amateur photographer offered to sell three photographs of the lights to the newspapers. While an analysis of the photos and negatives showed no signs of tampering, the photos themselves were dissimilar to the descriptions given by witnesses.

Weeks after these sightings, Air Force and private UFO investigators inquired into the Lubbock lights. Several people from rural areas surrounding Lubbock said that they knew the answer to the mystery—flocks of night-migrating birds. The streetlights of Lubbock illuminated the light undersides of migrating plover, giving the appearance of high-altitude, rapidly moving, luminous objects. This explanation was later verified to the satisfaction of most of the witnesses and other residents of Lubbock. Further, the Air Defense Command would not confirm the radar tracking to investigators. The Lubbock lights are now generally considered to be one of the classic cases of UFO misidentification.

Daylight Disks

On June 5, 1947, Kenneth Arnold was conducting an air search near Mount Rainier, Washington. Arnold, a co-founder of the Idaho Search and Rescue Pilots Association and an experienced mountain pilot, had taken off from Chehalis, Washington, at about 2:00 P.M. and had been flying for about forty-five minutes. Arnold was startled by a very bright flash of light as he turned his airplane toward Mount Rainier. A few seconds later, he observed another bright flash of light, which came from the vicinity of nine crescent-shaped craft flying in an echelon formation at about his altitude. Arnold watched the craft maneuver for several minutes and, using his pilot's knowledge of trigonometry, calculated their speed at more than a thousand miles per hour.

When Arnold landed at the small airport at Yakima, Washington, he discussed the sighting with airport personnel and other pilots. They speculated that Arnold might have observed guided missiles from a nearby missile base. Arnold then flew on to Pendleton, Oregon, where he tried unsuccessfully to contact the FBI. Finally he talked to the editor of the *Eastern Oregonian*, and his story was released to the wire services.

In the days that followed, Arnold was the center of considerable attention, which he neither sought out nor retreated from. Arnold described the movements of the craft as similar to that of a saucer skipping over water, and William Bequette of United Press International then coined the term *flying saucers*. Within weeks this term had become part of our language, and it is still the most popular term used to describe UFOs.

Kenneth Arnold's interest in UFOs continued after his famous sighting. In 1948 Arnold's story appeared in the first issue of *Fate* magazine. In 1952 Arnold and Ray Palmer of *Fate* magazine published *The Coming of the Flying Saucers*. Arnold also investigated several UFO sightings in the 1950s and sighted and photographed other UFOs in 1952. Arnold suffered ridicule as well as admiration during his lifetime. More than thirty years after his Mount Rainier sighting, he was still asked to "tell his story" to interested groups (Sachs, 1980).

Radar/Visual UFO Reports

UFO investigation groups such as the International Society for UFO Research find that radar/visual cases are extremely rare. Contrary to what we may think, not every bit of airspace is continuously monitored by radar systems. Airspace below 2,000 feet and over hilly terrain, for example, is not easily monitored by radar. Airports use transponder tracking systems rather than radar for most air traffic control. Finally, as the radar/visual UFO sightings reported in Ocala, Florida, on May 14, 1978 near Pinecastle Electronics Warfare Range indicate, nearby radar equipment simply may not be operating when a UFO is sighted. Pinecastle is a training facility for navy pilots. Between 10:00 and 10:15 P.M., the duty officer took two telephone calls from civilians who reported seeing bright flying objects in the area. Fearing that an air crash had occurred, the duty officer quickly ascertained that no known military or civilian aircraft were in the area.

As the tracking radar warmed up, the radar operator observed a cluster of lights moving in a northerly direction. When the radar became operational, an object was located sixty miles north of Pinecastle. Another object was located three miles north of Pinecastle, and then another three miles south. These latter two objects were observed visually, appearing as bright white and orange lights. Radar/visual contact was maintained with these two objects for about ten minutes, with the radar indicating speeds from five miles per hour to more than sixteen hundred miles per hour. Finally, the objects disappeared after circling the base. Eight naval personnel had observed the objects either visually or on radar. Civilians from nearby areas continued to make inquiries about their own sightings (Sachs, 1980:228).

Some investigators claim that this sighting was the result of bright stars, confusion over aircraft sightings, and/or faulty radar equipment. Others, however, feel that such explanations contain too many improbable occurrences. In either event, the Pinecastle incident is quite typical of the dozens of radar/visual reports made since the first one at Goose Bay, Labrador, in 1951.

Close Encounters of the First Kind

Some UFO reports involve much more than the sighting of distant objects performing puzzling maneuvers. A small proportion of UFO reports are of *close encounters*, in which people claim to have seen a UFO at an uncomfortably close range. It is
difficult to attribute these reports to the misidentification of birds or stars.

A close encounter of the first kind was reported on October 18, 1973, near
Mansfield, Ohio. Captain Lawrence Coyne and his three-man crew were returning from their annual flight physicals, flying an Army Reserve helicopter. It was
about 11:00 P.M. and the weather was calm and clear. Coyne was alerted by fellow
crewman Sergeant Robert Yanacsek that they were being paced by another aircraft on the eastern horizon. After observing what they assumed to be the aircraft's lights for a few moments, they saw the lights begin to close on the
helicopter. As the lights rapidly approached, Coyne put the helicopter into a steep
dive to avoid collision. The lights continued to close on the rapidly descending
helicopter until all four men could clearly see that the lights were on a wingless,
cigar-shaped craft. The craft took a position above the helicopter, focusing a green
spotlight on them. Meanwhile, copilot Lieutenant Arrigo Jezzi had been attempting to contact Nashville Air Control, initially to find out what other aircraft were
in the area, then to warn of their likely crash. The radio, however, had stopped
transmitting and receiving.

The strange craft stayed with the helicopter for a few moments and then
quickly departed. When Coyne regained stable flight, the helicopter was at an
altitude fifteen hundred feet higher than when they had attempted to dive. The
UFO appeared to have been able to pull the helicopter to a higher altitude. Shortly
after the UFO departed, the radio began to work properly. Some investigators
attribute this UFO incident to a near collision with a meteor and resulting cockpit
confusion. The event was witnessed from the ground, however, and the witnesses
support the contentions of the aircrew (Sachs, 1980:187–88).

Close Encounters of the Second Kind

A month after Kenneth Arnold's sighting in 1947, radio and newspapers
reported that the United States Air Force had recovered a crashed flying saucer.
The crash site was near Roswell, New Mexico, and the wreckage had been taken
to Roswell Air Force Base. Within forty-eight hours, the Air Force issued clarifications denying the recovery of a crashed flying saucer, indicating they had recovered wreckage of a large weather balloon near Roswell. Almost fifty years later, in
1994, the Air Force issued a report that claimed that this material was almost certainly from a Project Mogul balloon. The then top-secret Mogul project used balloons to loft microphones to very high altitudes to listen for Soviet nuclear tests.

Events surrounding these two days in early July of 1947 would come to be
known as the Roswell Incident and would help shape the UFO controversy from
that point onward. As the Air Force offered further clarifications and denials, flying saucer enthusiasts and the media made their first charges of a "flying saucer
cover-up." Reports that the Air Force clamped "airtight security" over the Roswell
area and that men in black suits interrogated many Roswell area citizens who had
taken items from the crash site became part of the lore of the Roswell Incident.
Recovered materials included metallic foil that would not wrinkle when crumpled
and small I-beams with "alien hieroglyphics" etched in them. The "men in black"

intimidated witnesses and confiscated their flying saucer souvenirs. One of the more bizarre claims made during the Roswell Incident was that a second crash site was found and at least one alien survivor allegedly was taken into custody by the Air Force. According to this cover-up claim, the bodies of dead aliens also were recovered and taken to Roswell Air Force Base "Hangar 18," a refrigerated facility, where a secret film of at least one "alien autopsy" was made. A British TV producer aired what was purported to be the secret alien autopsy film in 1995.

The wrecked flying saucer or saucers were reportedly taken to Roswell Air Force Base and eventually made their way to "Area 51," a remote Air Force base in the Nevada desert. It is in Area 51 that "retro-engineering" studies allegedly have been made of the alien craft. This purported work has led to discoveries that have given rise to modern electronics, high-performance aircraft and stealth technology.

Close Encounters of the Third Kind

Many people have reported being so close to a UFO that they could see occupants inside or near the object. Hynek classified sighting of occupants as a close encounter of the third kind. For instance, on October 11, 1973, Charles Hickson and Calvin Parker were fishing near the Pascagoula, Mississippi shipyards. According to their account, about 9:00 P.M. they heard a humming noise, and

This photo of debris from the Roswell crash site was believed by some to have been staged with wreckage from a weather balloon (later acknowledged by authorities to be a device for spying on the Soviets) to discourage rumors about a UFO cover-up conspiracy by the U.S. government. © Bettman/CORBIS.

moments later a translucent craft appeared near them on the riverbank. Two glowing, faceless, humanoid figures then emerged and floated toward them. Parker fainted from fright, and Hickson, although terrified, was unable to move. About a half-hour later, the pair arrived at the sheriff's office in a state of terror and confusion.

Some close encounters of the third kind involve much more than seeing the occupants of UFOs. In the case of Hickson and Parker, they were later questioned repeatedly by police, as well as Air Force and civilian investigators. Interrogating them that evening, the sheriff was firmly convinced that their terror was genuine. Lie detector tests and even hypnotic regression were later used in an effort to reconstruct and verify their experience. During this time Hickson and Parker told of being levitated into the craft, where they were given brief physical examinations. The two men were then floated back outside the craft, which disappeared a moment later after emitting a humming noise. During this time, the glowing, faceless occupants did not talk to Hickson or Parker, nor did they communicate to them through telepathy. Within weeks of the close encounter Parker was hospitalized for a nervous breakdown, and after his release he avoided publicity. Hickson, on the other hand, enjoyed a brief period of near celebrity status and appeared on several radio and television talk shows. He also sold tapes of his narration of the incident. These attempts to profit from the event led some investigators to suggest that the entire incident was contrived by Hickson to make money. However, investigators who have actually interviewed Hickson, often on several occasions, dismiss the con-man hypothesis (Sachs 1980:241–42).

Beyond Hynek's Typology

Reports of contact with the occupants of flying saucers began to appear within months after newspapers and magazines carried stories of Arnold's sightings in 1947. These reports, however, were very different from those made by Hickson, Parker, and others decades later.

During the decade following Arnold's sighting of flying saucers, many people claimed to have had extensive and pleasant social contacts with the pilots and crews of flying saucers. One of the first and more famous of these people was George Adamski, who in 1953 wrote of his experiences in the book *Flying Saucers Have Landed* (Leslie and Adamski, 1953). In his book, Adamski describes how he was picked up on eleven different occasions by friendly and very ordinary appearing "saucer people" and given rides into space. He claimed the ship and crew were from the planet Clarion. Adamski included photos and diagrams of the spaceship and, oddly, the prints left by ship commander Orthon's shoes. The well-meaning space people urged all nations to stop nuclear testing (Adamski, 1955). Until his death in 1965, Adamski maintained that these visitors from Clarion possessed both human form and high moral standards.

Contactee Groups and the Space People

In March of 1954, flying saucer enthusiasts hosted the Giant Rock Spacecraft Convention, near Giant Rock, California (A&E Home Video, 1996). About 5,000 people attended, and several contactees gave lectures and sold their own books and souvenirs such as rocks retrieved from Mars. Uniformly, contactees told stories of friendly, very humanlike "space people" who were here to help us "earthlings." Like Adamski, some contactees told of their rides on other spaceships such as *Vea-O-Mus*, a spaceship from the planet Oreon.

During this time period a number of contactee groups were formed. Perhaps the most enduring of these groups is Unarius. Supporting their venture on a monthly income from a small investment, Ernest and Ruth Norman founded the Unarius Educational Foundation in 1954 as a nonprofit, tax-exempt organization. Unarius is an acronym for Universal Articulate Interdimensional Understanding of Science. To the present day, Unarius's mission remains to prepare humankind for membership in an intergalactic federation of planets.

Ernest Norman was a scientist, electronic engineer and poet as well as, allegedly, an advanced clairvoyant. Ruth claimed to be in mental and spiritual contact with space beings. It was her mission to facilitate the landing of flying saucers on Earth. They soon adopted the names of Raphiel (Ernest) and Uriel (Ruth). Unarius came to own about 70 acres of land in Jamul, California, that were maintained as a landing site and spaceport. After spaceships failed to appear in 1977, Ruth received messages from the space people that their ships would arrive in the year 2001, a year popularized in an Arthur C. Clarke novel and the year of Ruth's 100th birthday. Presently, the landing is predicted to occur on an island that will rise from within the Bermuda Triangle. The starships allegedly will contain the Pleiadeans, our "space brothers," who are working for the benefit of humankind by visiting Earth and establishing a new age of logic and reason that will initiate a spiritual renaissance (Norman and Spaegel, 1987). According to the predictions, several starships will land on top of one another, forming the "power tower" that will serve as our link to the 32 other planets in the interplanetary confederation. The Pleiadean "space brothers" will provide 32,000 of their scientists to help us connect our nations and cities to the power tower for a limitless source of nonpolluting energy. The lost libraries of Atlantis and Lemuria will be recovered, and the Intergalactic University will be established. With the help of the Pleiadean scientists, new hospitals will be established for the treatment and cure of all our physical ailments. Finally, machines will be used to control the weather worldwide (Norman and Spaegel, 1987).

The Unarian philosophy frames reality as consisting of several planes of so-called light worlds, and we reside on one of the intermediate planes. Ernest Norman made his transition to the higher planes of light worlds in 1971. After Raphiel's death, Uriel began to receive, from higher spiritual worlds, information describing the curriculum of the interdimensional science of life, which she recorded in over 80 books of poetry, philosophy, and science that are distributed by Unarius. In 1975, she created the New World Teaching Center to pass on knowledge of the healing process of past-life therapy and the new science of reincarnation and consciousness. The Center claims to have served almost a half-million students since its inception. Ruth transitioned to the higher planes of light worlds in 1993, and now Unarius operates under the directorship of Professor Charles L. Spaegel. While awaiting the arrival of the Pleiadean space brothers, Unarius offers help and support to those with a history of drug, alcohol or mental health related problems (Unarius, 1999).

Another contactee group was Heaven's Gate. The leader of the group, Bo (a.k.a. Marshall Herff Applewhite), claimed to have been Jesus, Elijah, and Moses in his former lives. Peep, a.k.a. Bonnie Lu Nettles, was a cardiac nurse, astrologer, and spiritualist. In the mid-1970s Bo and Peep were gathering their sheep, and in

1975 they set up their headquarters in Oregon with 20 to 30 followers. Both Applewhite and Nettles were UFO enthusiasts. The group settled on the name Heaven's Gate and for the next ten years wandered though small towns and national parks of the western states. They were able to stage successful rallies at which they urged people to follow them and renounce families, sex and drugs, and to pool their money in preparation for a voyage to a higher plane of existence on a spaceship. Numbers fluctuated, but membership in Heaven's Gate probably never exceeded a hundred, and the group supported themselves with casual work and collections taken up at rallies.

Their belief system was framed in a blend of New Age spiritualism and based on different levels of existence and UFO lore. Ultimately, members of Heaven's Gate were preparing themselves for transformation to another plane of being. In 1979, Applewhite promised an August arrival of the awaited spaceship. Heaven's Gate temporarily lost membership after the spaceship failed to arrive. Thereafter, Applewhite held that the starship could arrive at any time. It would carry believers to a wondrous garden, where they would absorb cosmic energy from their coequal, the King of Kings, the Chief of Chiefs, the god who created Planet Earth. Believers would shed their earthly containers and live eternally thereafter in hairless, toothless bodies that would be free of disease and decay. Events such as the eruption of Mt. St. Helen in the spring of 1980 and major earthquakes were all interpreted as signs that the spaceship would soon arrive.

Peep died of cancer in 1985, and 1996 found Heaven's Gate renting a Rancho Santa Fe, California, mansion for $7,000 a month. Heaven's Gate made ends meet by designing websites through their Higher Source corporation. *Star Trek* terminology, such as holodecks and transporter beams, was now used to describe the expected starship. After the 1979 crisis, Applewhite had instituted a much more restrictive lifestyle within Heaven's Gate. The group now consisted of 39 members in residence, and living arrangements were communal. They adhered to dietary restrictions; alcohol and tobacco were forbidden; and a rigid daily schedule of work, eating, recreation, and sleep was maintained. The group also had taken on an androgynous, asexual way of life. Applewhite and five other men had had themselves castrated, and all members wore gender-neutral cropped hairstyles, black Nike athletic shoes, and loose-fitting jump suits.

When the Hale-Bopp comet appeared in the spring of 1997, Heaven's Gate members picked up on Internet reports that a spaceship was following the comet toward Earth. They took this as the true marker that the spaceship was arriving to take them to the next plane of existence. It was finally time to shed their "containers." Later, when a Higher Source customer entered the mansion, thirty-nine shroud-covered bodies were found. Twenty-one women and 18 men, ranging in age from 26 to 72, committed suicide by eating pudding or applesauce mixed with a lethal dose of Phenobarbital and placing plastic bags over their heads. Some members had been with Applewhite and Heaven's Gate for over 20 years. Searching the immaculately kept mansion, investigators could find no signs to indicate that members had undergone anything other than a peaceful death. Cult experts, police, and scholars examined the videos and computer disks left behind by members and generally concluded that Heaven's Gate members calmly committed suicide as an exit to what they considered to be a higher level of existence (Gleick, 1997).

In summary, early contactees described the occupants of flying saucers as friendly "space people" who wore stylish and attractive uniforms. The space people usually said they were on a mission to stop nuclear testing on Earth, in order to keep us from harm. The Unarians' Pleiadean space brothers promised to cure diseases, restore lost knowledge and ultimately bring us into full membership in an intergalactic federation of planets. Even Heaven's Gate saw the starship allegedly following the Hale-Bopp comet as the vehicle that would take them to a better life, albeit in the next plane of being. Beginning in the 1960s, however, some people began to describe UFO occupants in more sinister terms.

Aliens and UFO Abductions: Encounters of the Worst Kind

Betty and Barney Hill stopped their car to look at an unusual moving light in the sky on September 19, 1961. Barney got out of the car to use his binoculars and get a better view of the light. As the light came into focus, he could make out a strange craft of some sort, and creatures were looking at him from inside the ship. This frightened Barney, and he quickly got back into the car and sped away. The glowing craft overtook the car briefly and then flew off. The Hills called a nearby Air Force base that evening and reported the light.

This would have been classified as a close encounter of the third kind, were it not for the fact that the Hills noticed later that evening that about two hours were "missing" from the time they saw the UFO and the time they arrived home. Each began to experience bad dreams after that evening. Betty was so shaken by this event that she began to read UFO books and after a few weeks contacted the NICAP UFO investigation group. Eventually, Barney and Betty were both given medical exams by a noted specialist in neuropsychiatry. Using hypnotic techniques developed during World War II to overcome soldiers' temporary amnesia brought on by violent trauma, the Hills each recalled many of the events of the missing two hours. When the UFO overtook their car that evening, the Hills had been taken into the UFO and given frightening and painful medical examinations. Their abductors were described as small gray creatures with huge, frightening black eyes. Their experiences were recounted in the 1966 best-selling book, *The Interrupted Journey* (Fuller, 1966).

Betty and Barney Hill's interrupted journey is important to ufology (the study of UFOs) for several reasons. The Hills were the first to describe an encounter with alien creatures, not the humanoid, benevolent and smartly uniformed "space people" described by contactees during the 1950s. Their encounter was framed in terms of frightening and painful physical tests rather than as a joyride to other planets and wise council to stop nuclear testing. Their story established a scenario—an encounter with a UFO at a lonely location, abduction, frightening and painful examination, and temporary amnesia—that would come to typify most abduction claims since then, such as the Charles Hickson and Calvin Parker account described earlier.

Unlike George Adamski or the Unarians who cheerfully described their experiences with the space people, the Hills appeared to be deeply traumatized by their contact. Because of their disorientation and fear, a high level of credibility has been attributed to their abduction claim. Also, medical hypnosis was suggested as a tool in this investigation because the Hills seemed to exhibit symptoms similar to those observed in shell-shocked combat soldiers. This was the first time hypnosis would be used as an aid to the recall of abduction details.

Groups like Unarius and Heaven's Gate were established, in part, to prepare people for membership in the new cosmic order, as coequals with the space people. In contrast, abductee groups have been established both by persons claiming to have been abducted and by therapists such as Dr. John Mack (1994) of Harvard, who have worked with abductees (Dean, 1998). On the Internet, people who claim to have been abducted maintain online discussion groups, such as Shadowland. Abductee groups claim to provide social support and understanding for those who have undergone the trauma of UFO abduction.

EXPLANATIONS FOR UFOS

As the above examples show, the total UFO phenomenon has many aspects, including incidents that range from people sighting lights in the night sky to others who earnestly claim to have been taken aboard alien spacecraft against their will and given invasive, painful, and terrifying medical examinations. There are even those who claim to have been implanted with alien fetuses as part of a biological experiment by the space aliens. To these incidents and claims we must add the obvious and admitted hoaxes. After some investigation, most UFO incidents can be given an earthly explanation. Beyond this, however, there is little consensus. We will consider three explanations that have been given for the UFO phenomenon and then look at this phenomenon from the standpoints of collective behavior and collective action.

 ### The Extraterrestrial Hypothesis

The most intriguing hypothesis suggests that UFOs are spacecraft from other planets, and some UFO experts argue that there is enough evidence to accept or at least seriously entertain the *extraterrestrial hypothesis.* Thousands of people have reported seeing saucerlike, cylindrical, or other wingless craft doing aerial maneuvers that clearly surpass the performance of any known aircraft or missile. In some instances these craft have left physical traces: imprints on the ground, burned and broken shrubbery and trees, and chemical residues. In a few cases, metallic pieces of these craft have been obtained. Physical analysis has determined unusual alloy combinations, levels of purity, and density. Finally, there are the abduction incidents, in which people claim to have been taken aboard alien spacecraft. Often, victims can recall details of these abductions only through hypnotic regression. Many of these accounts have stood up well under repeated interrogation and lie detector tests.

Some reported UFO experiences presuppose the existence of psychic phenomena such as telepathy, precognition, and out-of-body and near-death experiences. UFOs, contactees, and alien abductions have also led some to suggest the existence of interdimensional phenomena such as time travel. Both Unarius and Heaven's Gate posited the existence of various planes of spiritual and physical life. From this standpoint, UFOs and their occupants are not extraterrestrial space travelers but come from other times and from higher levels of being. Valee's twenty-category UFO experience classification system includes reports of psychic and interdimensional phenomena.

Other experts argue that the evidence for the extraterrestrial hypothesis is neither clear nor convincing. We will discuss this issue in the next section. At this point, however, it is worth noting that those who oppose acceptance of the extra-terrestrial hypothesis often describe those who do as "self-styled" experts (Jacobs, 1980:123–38). Whatever else this label implies, it is a form of debunking that does not focus on the merits of the evidence.

By definition, anyone who studies UFO phenomena is a "self-styled" researcher—regardless of their conclusions. Universities do not offer degrees in UFO research, nor does the U.S. Bureau of the Census include the title of UFO Investigator as an occupational category. UFO research is a marginal and eclectic field in which experts with credentials in many fields of the natural and social sciences have participated. Further, some UFO investigations have been carried out by people who are not expert in any scientific field. Finally, UFO research has been undertaken by the federal government and private organizations. It is not surprising, then, that great diversity exists in the investigation procedures, in the handling and interpretation of information gathered, and in the conclusions reached in UFO research. Neither those who accept nor those who reject the extra-terrestrial hypothesis can lay claim to doing orthodox and flawless research.

The Terrestrial Hypothesis

If there is any consensus among UFO investigators, it is that most UFO sightings turn out to be the misidentification of stars, meteors, aircraft, and weather balloons. Atmospheric conditions such as temperature inversions may make mis-identifications more likely. Temperature inversions, in which the air at ground level is several degrees cooler than air at higher altitudes, can occasionally distort the appearance of stars and other lights and can also create weather target radar images. These often quite technical explanations are referred to here as the *terrestrial hypothesis.*

The terrestrial hypothesis is part of the "official explanation" of UFO phenomena. On January 22, 1948, after almost seven months of widely publicized UFO sightings, the United States Air Force instituted Project Sign to investigate and identify UFOs. Shortly after it began, Project Sign encountered adverse publicity and was reorganized and named Project Grudge. In March of 1952, Project Grudge was expanded and renamed Project Blue Book. Project Blue Book was continued until 1969, when it was terminated on the recommendation of a review panel headed by Dr. Edward U. Condon of the University of Colorado. The Condon Committee Report concluded that the study of UFO phenomena had little scientific merit. With the exception of the inconclusive Project Sign, all officially commissioned research adopted the terrestrial hypothesis and concluded that UFOs were not spacecraft.

Even before the Condon Committee issued its final report, some experts were challenging its conclusions. Among the concerns expressed was that as many as 25 percent of the cases reported to Project Blue Book had, after investigation, been classified as "unidentified." Defenders of the Condon Report and other official findings correctly pointed out that when investigators are unable to identify a UFO, it does not necessarily mean that people have seen an alien spacecraft.

Official reports use a similar though faulty logic. The error in this logic is most obvious in the large number of cases in which UFOs are identified as meteors. Several known meteor streams regularly pass near the earth, producing annual meteor showers in late July and early August. Even though this is a time of peak meteor activity, all bright moving lights in the sky during July and August are not necessarily meteors. The official reports, however, identify nearly all nocturnal lights and fireball UFOs occurring in July and August as meteors, concluding that no further investigation is necessary.

Similarly, official reports use the temperature inversion and weather balloon explanations in a blanketlike fashion to account for UFO phenomena. Clearly, temperature inversions can distort the appearance of bright lights and stars and also can produce false radar images. However, official reports attribute *all* UFO sightings and radar trackings occurring during temperature inversions to these weather conditions. The weather balloon explanation is frequently abused in the same manner. If a weather balloon has been recently launched within five hundred miles of a UFO sighting, then it is assumed that people saw a weather balloon.

Immediately after the Heaven's Gate suicides, commentators were almost uniform in their characterization of what was then known of the Heaven's Gate belief frame. In the context of doing an analysis and explanation of what had happened, the Heaven's Gate belief system was characterized by news commentators as "5 megabytes of soul-chilling blather," "new millennial kitsch," "New Age gibberish, edged with the glamour of sci fi," and "a mixture of New Age religion and junk culture." Clearly, these commentators were suggesting a terrestrial explanation for the tragedy.

The Hoax-Hysteria Hypothesis

Experts on both sides of the UFO controversy agree that many UFO reports are deliberate hoaxes. Most UFO photographs have turned out to be hoaxes, and some physical traces of UFOs, such as landing marks and burned foliage, have been faked to add credibility to UFO reports. England's crop circles are perhaps the most famous and easily accepted UFO hoax in recent years. Beginning in the late 1970s, patterns of downed grain began to appear in wheat fields throughout England. Patterns often took the form of stick figures, lines, and concentric circles. The study of these crop circles became known as cereology. Cereologists offered numerous UFO-related explanations for the phenomenon. Simple circles were viewed as possible UFO landing sites, and more complex patterns were viewed as possible messages from space. Finally, in 1991, after several spectacular crop circles were discovered, Doug Bower and David Chorley came forward and announced that they had made a hobby, during the previous fifteen years, of hoaxing crop circles. They claimed responsibility for over 250 circles between 1978 and 1991. The two then gave the media a demonstration of their technique by creating simple circle formations in a nearby field. Since then others have taken credit for creating crop circles. These claims and demonstrations have not convinced all observers, particularly cereologists. After many demonstrations it has been pointed out that "genuine" crop circles are more elaborate and neater than those demonstrated, and that genuine crop circles may appear within a half hour's time, much shorter than the four or five hours often required by demonstrations. Crop circles continued to appear after the 1991 demonstration. Previous crop circles were simple designs, while fractal designs now appear in wheat fields. Cereologists also claim that the downed crops in recent circles show complex weave patterns, unlike the demonstrated hoaxes (*The Crop Circular*, 1998).

Many UFOs have turned out to be pranks, such as railroad flares carried into

Thousands of UFO photographs have been analyzed by those who study UFOs. Only a very small number of these are regarded as photos of genuine UFOs. Most UFOs on film turn out to be lens reflections, dirty or damaged negatives, and other photographic artifacts. A few photos, like the one above, are simply fakes. (Photo by Grant Bogue.)

the sky by kites or balloons (Sachs, 1980:145–47). It is not surprising, then, that some investigators are unwilling to seriously consider reports made by teenagers, close encounter reports, or UFO artifacts and quickly classify them as hoaxes.

When careful investigations of close encounter sightings occur, attempts are made to ascertain the reputations of the people involved. Almost any eccentricity or disorderliness can be used as grounds for classifying the report as a hoax. If witnesses have an interest in science fiction literature or ties to a UFO organization, then their accounts are routinely challenged on these grounds. This "reputational analysis" is essentially intuitive and at times has verged on character assassination.

People who make UFO reports are frequently overwhelmed by news reporters and UFO investigators. Their integrity is directly challenged and they are often severely ridiculed. In some cases, the notoriety has been so severe that witnesses have quit or lost their jobs and moved to another community. The negative responses invariably encountered by witnesses have given investigators reason to doubt some of the hoax "confessions." Admitting to a hoax is one way to end an unpleasant situation.

Some close encounter sightings have been classified as likely hoaxes primarily because witnesses have tried to capitalize on their stories. UFO witnesses, for example, have appeared on television and radio talk shows and have sold their stories to publishers. A UFO Center is maintained in Roswell, New Mexico, and the town celebrated the fiftieth anniversary of the event in 1997. Nevada Highway 375, which passes near Nellis Air Range (Area 51), was unofficially designated the Extraterrestrial Highway for the opening of the 1996 Fox Film *Independence Day*. Although the profit motive can serve as a reason for a hoax, many UFO witnesses who attempt to profit from their stories appear to do so hesitantly and often only at the urging of others.

The *National Enquirer* and many magazines and organizations offer prizes for the best UFO story of the year, the best UFO photograph, or physical evidence of UFOs. This "bounty hunter" approach to the UFO question encourages hoaxes. Knowledge about UFOs would be greatly furthered if these resources instead were used to train investigators and to support ongoing research programs.

Some UFO witnesses have steadfastly adhered to their stories through repeated interrogation by police, UFO investigators, and psychiatrists. Since Barney and Betty Hill's medical hypnosis, hypnotic regression has often been used to allow witnesses to recall the details of their experiences. Hypnotic regression is used in many areas of conventional psychiatry (although recently the practice has become increasingly controversial) to get people to recall repressed or forgotten incidents from their childhood, battlefield experiences, or other traumatic occurrences, and information so obtained is generally assumed to reflect the reality of earlier experiences. On this basis, then, investigators have concluded that "something very real and very frightening" has happened to some UFO witnesses. Although this conclusion may be valid in some instances, it must be noted that people other than UFO witnesses can be made to "recall" UFO abductions under hypnotic regression (Lawson, 1980). Naive subjects give vivid, detailed descriptions of the interior of spacecraft and also express confusion and fear. There are many similarities between these descriptions and those provided by other UFO witnesses. That people can vividly "recall" imaginary events through hypnotic regression has rather far-reaching implications, not only for the study of UFO phenomena but for the field of psychiatry as well.

Finally, there is the mass hysteria explanation of UFO phenomena. Project Blue Book, for instance, attributes some UFO sightings to mass hysteria. In many ways, UFO phenomena seem to fit the "rapid, unwitting, and nonrational" characteristics of mass hysteria. UFO investigators have noted, for example, that on nights shortly following major UFO sightings, groups of people gather excitedly to watch the lights of radio transmission towers. Even when people report a sighting as a hoax, others in the vicinity will fervently claim to have seen the UFO. In the next section of this chapter, we will give a more detailed consideration to UFO reports as mass hysteria. We will also consider the classic laboratory studies of group influence and suggestibility done by Asch (1958).

While the question "What are UFOs?" must remain unanswered, we can state unequivocally that interest in UFOs has become an enduring feature of our basic culture and our social life. In the final section of this chapter, we will look at UFOs from the standpoint of collective action by tracing the social history of UFOs. We will also consider the origins and dynamics of the many UFO organizations that have flourished since the 1950s. We will trace the level of public awareness and perception of UFOs as measured by national polls and, finally, consider the UFO as a cultural icon.

The Mass Hysteria Perspective

Neil J. Smelser and Orrin E. Klapp cite UFO phenomena as one of several manifestations of mass hysteria. In a strict sense, Smelser does not regard UFO phenomena as value-added panic or as a collective flight based on a hysterical belief. He does, however, describe outbreaks of UFO sightings as involving widespread terror, bodily symptoms of fright, anxiety, and fantastic beliefs (1962:142). In keeping with Smelser and the value-added explanation of panics, Graebner (1998:21) attributes the UFO scare of 1947 to foreign policy frustrations, fears of attack, and the developing cold war.

In contrast, Klapp identifies outbreaks of UFO sightings as enthusiastic contagions that give evidence of magical wish fulfillment. It is assumed that space visitors are benevolent and intend to use their knowledge to benefit humankind.

Smelser and Klapp argue that UFO sightings are decidedly episodic in their occurrence, strongly suggesting the work of contagion. Klapp (1972:133) uses data reported by Dr. J. Allen Hynek to support this view. This same data is summarized in Table 6.1, which also includes the source of the information and the yearly differences in UFO sightings.

Table 6.1 shows three major UFO waves, peaking in the years 1952, 1957, and 1966. The year-to-year fluctuations in the number of UFO reports are not as extreme as the hysteria explanations imply. The peaks of 1957 and 1966, for example, represent less than a doubling in the number of UFO reports from the previous year. In fact, in only one instance does the number of UFO reports show marked fluctuation. From 1951, the number of UFO reports increased more than tenfold in 1952 and then dropped to less than a third that number in 1953.

The year 1952 is often referred to as the year of flying saucer hysteria. It should be noted, however, that in March 1952, Project Grudge was expanded and upgraded to Project Blue Book. Project Blue Book was given more publicity, the number of field investigators was substantially increased, and investigation procedures were made more rigorous. Some of the increase in UFO reports, particularly during the summer of 1952, is due to the improved reporting and recording procedures of Project Blue Book. It should also be noted that during Project Blue Book's sixteen years of full operation, the annual number of reports obtained always exceeded 186, the largest yearly total obtained through Project Grudge. Rather than showing peaks of hysteria, Table 6.1 shows the effects of improved reporting and recording procedures between 1947 and 1968. This table also shows that the incidence of UFO reports is fairly constant and is not as erratic as those who offer the hysteria hypothesis have suggested.

Since the end of Project Blue Book, UFO reports have been tabulated and investigated by a number of private UFO organizations such as the J. Allen Hynek Center for UFO Research and the Mutual UFO Network. The tallies compiled by these organizations indicate that UFO sightings are reported at a fairly steady rate of ten to twenty per month across the United States. More are reported worldwide. These numbers are somewhat higher when such things as crop circles and claims of alien abduction are taken into account. There have been peaks of UFO reports in each decade since the 1970s. UFOs are not, as some suggest, merely a quaint part of the popular culture of the 1950s and 1960s.

What about the hundreds of sightings that are classified as close encounters? In close encounters, witnesses report being within fifty feet of the landed UFO, and

TABLE 6.1

Pattern of UFO Sighting Reports in the United States, 1947–1968

Air Force project source	Year	Annual total reported sightings	Percent increase or decrease from the preceding year
—	1947	79	—
Sign	1948	143	+ 81
Grudge	1949	186	+ 30
Grudge	1950	169	− 9
Grudge	1951	121	− 28
Blue Book	1952	1,501	+ 1,140
Blue Book	1953	452	− 70
Blue Book	1954	429	− 5
Blue Book	1955	404	− 5
Blue Book	1956	778	+ 93
Blue Book	1957	1,178	+ 51
Blue Book	1958	590	− 50
Blue Book	1959	364	− 38
Blue Book	1960	514	+ 41
Blue Book	1961	488	− 5
Blue Book	1962	474	− 3
Blue Book	1963	399	− 16
Blue Book	1964	526	+ 32
Blue Book	1965	887	+ 69
Blue Book	1966	1,060	+ 20
Blue Book	1967	937	− 12
Blue Book	1968	392	− 58

SOURCE: Original data reported in *Christian Science Monitor*, April 2, 1970, by Dr. J. Allen Hynek, then director of Lindheimer Astronomical Research Laboratory, Northwestern University.

in a few instances they report entering the UFO. Can people grossly misperceive aircraft, streetlights or other common objects so close at hand? Some UFO investigators have attributed close encounter experiences to group-induced hysteria (Menzel and Boyd, 1963:138). That is, under conditions of emotional stress, great excitement, and group pressure, susceptible people lose their critical abilities and see things that aren't there.

Group influence and suggestibility long have been topics of experimental investigation. The nature of suggestibility as demonstrated in the laboratory is quite different from that assumed in the hysteria explanation of close encounters. It should also be noted that in about half of the close encounters, witnesses report that they were alone at the time of their experiences.

The classic studies of group influence and suggestibility conducted by S. E. Asch (1958), for example, indicate that naive subjects can be made to misperceive something as simple and unambiguous as the length of lines. In Asch's study, naive subjects were each placed in a group of eight, whose members previously had been coached to give false judgments as to the length of lines. Each member, in turn, was to announce aloud which two of five lines were the same length. Faced with unanimous announcements of incorrect judgments, 25 percent of the subjects remained independent in their judgments and gave entirely correct answers. However, another 25 percent of the subjects capitulated to the group by making incorrect judgments in one-half or more of the trials.

Are some of the very dramatic and strange close encounter reports the result of similar processes of suggestibility that distort the witnesses' judgment? This seems unlikely if we further consider the Asch studies. Nearly all of the subjects who yielded to the unanimous majority later reported that they did so because they thought they had "misunderstood the instructions" or "didn't want to ruin the experiment," even though they had clearly perceived the majority response as incorrect (Asch, 1958:176–79). Those who report close encounters do not indicate that they are trying to appease other witnesses who are wrong in their judgments.

Finally, Asch conducted a series of trials where the majority was not unanimous. The presence of even a single dissenter almost totally eliminated the compliance effect (1958:179–80). Reports from witnesses to the same close encounter usually contain conflicting elements and alternate interpretations. As Asch's studies show, these inconsistencies eliminate extreme compliance with the group.

Laboratory findings regarding social influence illustrate what Turner and Killian refer to as the *normative constraint* that operates in groups and crowds (1972:21–25). People's actions do influence one another. In natural settings, however, these actions are not uniform enough to produce the extreme influences claimed by the mass hysteria explanations of UFOs and other collective behavior phenomena.

Alien abduction accounts are even more intense and dramatic than most close encounter reports. The mass hysteria explanation has not been advanced to account for such reports. Instead, critics have posited that alien abduction reports are a result of psychopathology or fantasy proneness (Bartholomew, et al., 1991). Nickell (1996) examined thirteen of John Mack's abductee cases and concluded that all thirteen cases evidenced one or more characteristics of fantasy proneness such as susceptibility to hypnosis, vivid waking dreams, claims of dual identity and past lives, and claims of receiving messages from higher beings.

Mass hysteria, group influence, and suggestibility have all been offered as an explanation of both collective and individual UFO reports. While the number of UFO reports fluctuates from year to year, these fluctuations are not so dramatic as to suggest the presence of waves of mass hysteria. It is also difficult to reconcile laboratory studies of group influence and suggestibility with what is known about the dynamics and circumstances of actual UFO and alien abduction reports. While mass hysteria is characterized as a transitory social phenomenon, UFOs have been part of our popular culture for over half a century. In the next section, UFOs will be discussed from the standpoint of collective action, beginning with the social history of UFOs.

THE UFO AS COLLECTIVE ACTION

The collective action perspective has been developed in the course of studying social protest, demonstrations, and social movements. These phenomena may seem greatly divergent from UFO sightings and UFO organizations. The following discussion, however, is an attempt to apply the social action perspective to a new range of phenomena. The collective action perspective is based on the careful examination and description of the events to be explained, whether the events be protest demonstrations or UFO sightings. We will begin this section by considering the social history of UFOs and how these phenomena have been framed in social discourse. The modern idea that UFOs are the vehicles of space travelers began to emerge just before the beginning of this century. By the 1960s, this idea was fully developed and amply reflected in our popular culture. In the 1970s the discourse on UFOs was elaborated to include sinister elements such as alien abductions.

The first modern UFO flap occurred during the winter of 1896, when thousands of people reported seeing mysterious airships hovering, cruising, or racing in the skies across the United States. Many explanations were offered at the time, such as secret inventions, hysteria, and hoaxes. Although a few people attributed the airships to visitors from other planets, this explanation did not become popular for another forty years.

Mystery Airships

The first repeated sightings of UFOs in the United States took place in November and December of 1896 and March through May of 1897. Sightings were reported in nineteen states, from California to West Virginia. The most common term used to describe the reported objects was *airships*. Many of the descriptions would seem to describe dirigibles, zeppelins, or blimps. However, the first known dirigible flight in the United States did not occur until three years later, and the first practical dirigible, the *California Arrow*, was not flown until 1904. In the 1890s there was a general expectation that someone would soon invent a successful, powered flying machine. Many patents had been issued, and dozens of inventors, including the Wright brothers, were busily experimenting with powered flight. It is unlikely that such experiments were the cause of numerous and widespread airship reports, although "experiments" was one of the most popular explanations offered at the time. In much the same way that UFOs are currently explained, several astronomers stated that bright stars had been mistaken for "mystery airships." Some people argued that the airships were hoaxes, and indeed some of the later incidents proved to be so. A few suggested that the airships were advertising gimmicks for cigarettes or circuses. Finally, some skeptics attributed the sightings of airships to gullibility, stupidity, or too much whiskey.

An extraterrestrial explanation was occasionally suggested: the airships were exploration vehicles from Mars. The "canals" of Mars had been discovered about twenty years earlier, which led to the belief that Mars had an earthlike climate and intelligent life. This explanation, however, was not as popular as that of the "secret inventors" (Jacobs, 1975:28–29).

Dozens of encounters with the airship crews also were reported. A few witnesses described the crew as monsters who spoke a strange and frightening language. Most witnesses, however, described the crew as gentlemen who introduced themselves as inventors. Often, the airship crews mentioned the confidential nature of their flying machine and asked witnesses not to tell others about what they had seen. Another common theme to the encounters was that the aircrew requested food and water or borrowed tools.

While most accounts described what possibly could have been dirigibles, zeppelins, or blimps, several accounts were similar to more recent descriptions of UFOs. A few airships were described as egg-shaped, metallic, and able to accelerate "like a shot out of a gun." Reports of night sightings often mentioned bright, pulsating, white, orange, red, and blue lights. There were some reports of airships flying in formation.

The airship sightings did not precipitate government-sponsored investigations or the founding of any private investigation groups. In fact, it appears that the airship mystery was soon forgotten, perhaps because the "mystery airships" never returned. Also, the airship reports were soon to be outdone by news stories and pictures of the successful flights of the Wright brothers and other early air pioneers. The airships of 1896 and 1897 probably received more consideration after 1947 than when they occurred.

Foo-Fighters, Ghost Rockets, Flying Saucers

The twentieth-century history of the UFO began during World War II when Allied, German, and Japanese aircrews reported being intercepted, followed, and occasionally harassed by fireballs and disk-shaped objects. Aircrews referred to the phenomenon as "foo-fighters" and considered them to be enemy secret weapons of some sort. The United States Fifth Army's explanation was that foo-fighters were mass hallucinations induced by the stresses of air combat (Jacobs, 1975:35–37).

In 1946 "ghost rockets" were reported in Sweden and continued to be reported throughout Europe until 1948 (Sachs, 1980:123). These cigar-shaped UFOs and fireballs were given some attention by the United States and Swedish military, primarily to find out if the Soviet Union was conducting rocket experiments. It was generally concluded that most of the ghost rockets were misidentified aircraft.

In early 1947, many people across the United States began to report UFOs to their local authorities and newspapers. These reports were given scant attention until Kenneth Arnold's sighting of nine "flying saucers." At first the press reported sightings in a straightforward manner. This stance soon became more cautious, and in spite of the great amount of UFO or flying saucer activity reported, no concrete evidence for the existence of these strange craft was obtained. Caution changed to open skepticism and ridicule as some blatantly absurd reports were given and numerous hoaxes were revealed. Finally, the UFO phenomenon fell into further disregard as followers of the occult and other marginal groups began to adopt and adapt UFOs to their particular interests (Jacobs 1975:xi). To the present day, the established media have maintained a skeptical stance toward UFO reports. What attention is given is usually in terms of human interest, hysteria, or "silly season" stories (Jacobs, 1975:278).

The Air Force Projects

The "mystery airships" of 1896 and 1897 were forgotten as soon as the glamour of early aviation captured the public imagination. After World War II, however, flying saucers became a matter of much greater concern to the United States government and to numerous civilian groups that sought to answer the flying saucer question.

Despite early and growing skepticism, the United States Air Force instituted Project Sign in January 1948 in order to ascertain the nature of flying saucers and to determine whether they presented a threat to national security. In 1950 Project Twinkle was undertaken to obtain photographs of the green fireballs frequently being reported in northern New Mexico (Sachs, 1980:261). The Washington Air National Guard equipped aircraft with cameras to obtain pictures of UFOs. These projects came under immediate criticism as either "extremely inadequate, given the scope of the problem" or a "waste of taxpayers' money." None of these UFO projects, however, were ever top-priority Air Force projects, and they were poorly funded. Project Twinkle was terminated after only six months of operation, and no photographs of fireballs were obtained. At one point, Project Blue Book had only two field investigators and was briefly directed by an enlisted man.

UFO Organizations

A large number of groups have, in one way or another, mobilized around UFOs. Groups have engaged in studying UFOs and UFO witnesses and have pressured the U.S. Congress for funds to "answer the UFO question," or to break the government's conspiracy of silence on UFOs. Other groups are passing along messages from the space visitors, or helping the victims of alien abductions.

Various UFO organizations have maintained membership and programs over an appreciable length of time. There are three major types of organizations. UFO *investigation groups* are bureaucratic in nature and are often headed or advised by credentialled scientists interested in studying UFO phenomena. The general membership of such groups includes field investigators and those who simply receive periodic mailings. The second type of UFO organization is the *contactee group*, whose leaders and members claim to have been contacted by people from other planets. The stated purpose of these groups is to spread the messages given them by the extraterrestrials. The third type of UFO group is the UFO *cult* (Buckner, 1965). These groups are leader-centered and claim that God (or other supreme beings) sends UFOs for the salvation of humankind. Investigation, contactee, and cult groups have little in common beyond their general interest in UFO phenomena and are frequently at odds with one another.

Investigation Groups The first civilian UFO investigation group to be established was the Aerial Phenomena Research Organization (APRO). APRO was established in 1952 by Coral and James Lorenzen, and it had a staff of seven, with a five-person board of directors. At its peak, this group claimed to have about fifty professionals in the physical and social sciences as advisers. APRO was established, in part, out of dissatisfaction with the procedures used by the Air Force in investigating and reporting UFO phenomena. APRO is international in scope; in the 1970s it claimed about three thousand members and five hundred field investigators in the United States and fifty other countries. Independent of APRO, Coral and James Lorenzen authored and coauthored several popular books about UFOs. APRO ceased operations in 1985 with the death of the Lorenzens, but it was reestablished a year later in Illinois as a not-for-profit organization by William Heft. Heft was the director of APRO's Phoenix, Arizona chapter. Under Heft's administration, APRO has sought to follow the direction first established by the Lorenzens, and today APRO once again claims worldwide membership and has started a mailing list. APRO maintains websites and groups in Illinois, California, and Texas.

In 1956, the National Investigations Committee on Aerial Phenomena (NICAP) was established by T. Townsend Brown. Marine Corps Major Donald E. Keyhoe became director of NICAP in 1957 and served until 1969. Keyhoe often brought NICAP into controversy with frequent charges that the Air Force was engaging in a cover-up of the UFO phenomenon. In part, this was because Keyhoe saw NICAP as having a dual role: investigating UFO sightings and lobbying for congressional and scientific investigations of the UFO phenomenon (Jacobs, 1975:145–57). In the early years, the board of governors of NICAP included U.S. senators, businessmen, and military officers. Prior to the Condon Committee Report, NICAP claimed more than twelve thousand members worldwide. In the 1970s NICAP claimed a membership of about four thousand members and about seventy-five field investigators across the United States (Sachs, 1980:213). In the 1980s NICAP's files were placed under the care of the Center for UFO Studies. NICAP's original monthly newsletter, the *UFO Investigator*, is now maintained as a web page.

Walter H. Andrews, Jr., John Schuessler, and Allen R. Utke established the Mutual UFO Network (MUFON) in 1969. Today, MUFON is under the director-ship of Walt Andrus and claims to be the largest international UFO research orga-nization in operation. MUFON has an advisory board of professionals in the physical and social sciences and claims more than five thousand active members and investigators. MUFON chapters are maintained in almost every state and in several nations. MUFON sponsors annual UFO symposiums for scientists, engi-neers, and authors and publishes the 24-page monthly *MUFON UFO Journal*. MUFON maintains several active websites and discussion lists.

In 1973 Dr. James Allen Hynek founded the Center for UFO Studies (CUFOS). The Center has no official position regarding the nature of UFOs; its goal is to pro-vide both a public source of reliable UFO information and an international clear-inghouse to which people can report their UFO experiences without fear of ridicule (Sachs, 1980:52). The computerized catalogue of UFO reports mentioned earlier (UFOCAT) is maintained by CUFOS and is available to those studying UFOs. MUFON assists the Center in its field investigations. The Center is not a membership organization; it is composed of invited scientists and other academ-ics who are willing to actively investigate and study the UFO phenomenon. The monthly *International UFO Reporter* is available by subscription, and the Center maintains an active website and discussion list. Presently the Center is identified as the second largest UFO study group in existence.

For nearly thirty-five years, Dr. James Allen Hynek was an advocate for the sci-entific study of UFOs. Dr. Hynek was an astronomical consultant to Project Grudge and Project Blue Book from 1948 to 1968. Hynek was also chairman of the Depart-ment of Astronomy and director of Dearborn Observatory at Northwestern Uni-versity from 1960 to 1975. He directed CUFOS from its beginning in 1973 until his death in 1986. CUFOS is now named the J. Allen Hynek Center for UFO Studies.

The UFO investigation groups described above are all nonprofit organizations. Critics often charge that these groups have a vested financial interest in keeping the UFO controversy alive, but this charge appears to be largely unfounded. Some of the most successful movies of the last twenty years, such as *Close Encounters of the Third Kind, E.T., Alien* and its sequels, *Independence Day, Men in Black, Contact*, and even the *Star Trek* and *Star Wars* series, had to do with UFOs. UFOs have proven to be money makers for movie studios and advertising agencies much more so than for UFO investigation groups.

Contactee Organizations Contactee groups frequently claim to have been given messages from, or given missions to perform by, the occupants of UFOs. UFO investigation groups have largely refused to investigate the claims of con-tactees because of their apparent likelihood of being hoaxes. At the beginning of this chapter two contactee groups were described: Unarius and Heaven's Gate. Several other contactee groups also have succeeded in mobilizing a substantial membership and maintaining organizational continuity over time.

The Amalgamated Flying Saucer Clubs of America (AFSCA) was founded in 1959 by contactee Gabriel Green. At the urgings of visitors from Alpha Centauri, Green ran as a candidate for the California legislature in 1960 and the presidency of the United States in 1972. AFSCA claimed fifty-six hundred members world-wide during the 1970s and more than a hundred unit directors. AFSCA maintained no formal investigative program; instead, it held that flying saucers obviously originated from our own solar system and from other galaxies; "space people" have fed false information to our probes of the solar system to make us think the planets are uninhabitable. The mission of AFSCA was to assist the space people in their efforts to contact the leaders of the world. AFSCA maintains that the space people offered solutions to most of our planet's problems, but our world leaders refused to take their advice because to do so would decrease their own power and influence; hence AFSCA's help was needed.

For a period of at least twenty years, AFSCA sold tape-recorded messages from the space people, books, photographs, and even bumper stickers. One of the popular bumper stickers read, "Flying saucers are real, the Air Force doesn't exist" (Sachs, 1980:13). This group is probably defunct or no longer operates under the name of Amalgamated Flying Saucer Clubs of America.

The National Investigations Committee on UFOs (NICUFO) was established in 1967 by contactee Frank E. Stranges. Initially, this organization was patterned much along the lines of NICAP. The purpose of NICUFO was to investigate contactee cases that generally have been ignored by other UFO investigation groups. NICUFO claimed to have proven that UFOs come from Earth and from other planets and that UFOs have been on Earth for at least four thousand years. NICUFO has a board of directors, but it consists largely of contactees, including Donald Fry, Gabriel Green's running mate for the presidency in 1972. At that time, NICUFO claimed about one thousand members. Membership rights and benefits include a 10 percent discount on all NICUFO literature; a 20 percent discount on NICUFO-sponsored conventions, workshops, and lectures; and a subscription to NICUFO's *Confidential Newsletter*.

The National Investigations Committee on UFOs is no longer in existence. However, 1995 found Frank Stranges delivering a lecture at a MUFON convention where he told of Valiant Thor, a spaceman from Venus, who lives in a flying saucer called *Victor One*, which Stranges says is currently parked below the surface of Lake Mead near Las Vegas. The saucer, about 300 feet in diameter, contains a swimming pool, steam room, laboratory, library and kitchen. Floor plans of *Victor One* were for sale at the lecture for $5. Stranges also had available the *Interspace Link Newsletter*. The subscription price was $75 a year, the subscription form must be signed in the presence of a notary public, and the applicant must further agree to hold the contents of the newsletter in strictest confidence.

UFO Cults Heaven's Gate quickly acquired the negative label of "cult" in the 1970s, and the suicides of their members in 1997 reenforced collective fears of cults and their seemingly mysterious power over susceptible people. To many, it seemed remarkable that a cult could be formed around a belief in spaceships and alien beings. While Heaven's Gate seemed quite unique, similar groups had existed in the past. While UFO beliefs were central to the action frames of these groups, they also laid claim to being religions and to being in contact with higher spiritual realms. These groups also centered on leaders who claimed to receive guidance from superior beings. At least one group, established in 1960, Mark-Age, continues to operate.

In 1947 the Universal Industrial Church of the New World Comforter was established by contactee Allen-Michael. The church had about seventy-five members, and the group claimed to maintain telepathic contact with space people. According to the group, the purpose of UFOs is to bring peace, freedom, and security to Earth through Uni-Communism. The system of Uni-Communism would grant to each person ample food, clothing, shelter, and care. The church sought out people who had had UFO experiences and could no longer cope with society. According to the church's precepts, Christ was a Venusian contactee, and the people from Venus provided Christ with much assistance (Sachs, 1980:349). This group was active at least into the 1970s but is now likely defunct.

The Universaurian Foundation was established in 1962 by contactees Zelrun W. Karsleigh, LeRoy Roberts, and A. H. Albrecht. Karsleigh claimed to be in telepathic contact with space people and served as the main guide for the foundation. The Universaurian belief system included the dissemination of information provided by the highly evolved space people, who desired to eliminate the fear and misery that exists on Earth. If this failed, the space people promised to transport selected and perfected people to other planets before Earth was destroyed.

In the late 1970s the Universaurian Foundation claimed 420 members in Portland, Oregon; Syracuse, New York; and Phoenix, Arizona. A library of UFO, scientific, and religious books was available to members. Chapters met three times weekly throughout the year except in August and sponsored speakers on the topics of UFOs, extrasensory perception, and other interesting subjects. *The Voice of Unarius*, the group's monthly magazine, presented and discussed the latest messages from the space people (Sachs, 1980:349–50). It is likely that this group no longer exists.

Mark-Age was established in 1960 by Charles B. Gentzel and Nada-Yolanda. These contactees claim that Nada-Yolanda, also known as Pauline Sharp, is the present earthly speaker for the spiritual government of the solar system. Christ, or Sanada, is part of the program of earthly enlightenment being conducted by the spiritual government, and he is scheduled to return to Earth by the year 2000. UFOs have guided earthlings throughout our evolution and in the year 2000 will help us attain a new cycle of fourth-dimensional existence (Sachs, 1980:189). Forty years since it was founded, Mark-Age maintains an active website and continues to provide its members and other interested people with meditation tapes, home study courses, and counseling and training in the ways of the New Age.

UFO investigation groups, contactee groups, and cults have proved to be enduring social phenomena. The life cycle of many protest groups can be measured in months (see chapter 14). In contrast, some UFO groups identified in this chapter, such as the Universal Industrial Church of the New World Comforter, endured for decades; others, such as MUFON or Mark-Age, have maintained continuity of action for nearly half a century and are presently active and popular among UFO enthusiasts. Some groups are bureaucratic in form and operation, while others are definitely leader centered. From the standpoint of collective action, UFO groups may share some similar characteristics with protest groups.

Like more prosaic social movement organizations, UFO organizations compete for money, membership, and other tangible resources. A few benefactors, such as Robert Bigelow, a wealthy Las Vegas real estate investor who has actively sponsored research in UFOs and other paranormal topics, can provide financial resources for some groups. A 1998 Stanford study, the first independent review of UFO phenomena since 1970, was initiated by Laurance S. Rockefeller and supported financially by the LSR Fund. Organizers and members of these groups have occasionally written popular and profitable books that helped these organizations continue operations, but for the most part these organizations are far from lucrative undertakings. UFO organizations compete for members among UFO enthusiasts. Like other social movement organizations, UFO groups form alliances or challenge one another's positions and programs.

Public Awareness of UFOs: National Polls

The first national poll to include UFO items was done by the Gallup organization on August 15, 1947, less than eight weeks after Kenneth Arnold's widely publicized sighting. As shown in Table 6.2, the poll indicated that fully 90 percent of the adult population had heard of or read about UFOs. By comparison, fewer people were able to recognize pictures of Dwight D. Eisenhower (83%) and Douglas MacArthur (76%). This poll offered little to support the notion, however, that the United States was in the grip of a flying saucer hysteria or scare. The most frequent answer given to the follow-up question "What are flying saucers?" was

TABLE 6.2
Public Awareness and Definitions of UFOs (1847–1996)

Gallup poll question	Response	Percent by year							
		1947 flying saucers	1950 flying saucers	1966 UFOs	1973 UFOs	1978 UFOs	1987 UFOs	1990 UFOs	1996 UFOs
Have you ever heard of or read about flying saucers [UFOs]?	Yes	90	94	96	95	93	88	90	87
Are flying saucers from other planets?	Yes	1	5	—	—	—	—	—	—
In your opinion are they something real or just people's imagination?	Real	—	—	46	53	57	49	47	48
Do you think there are people somewhat like ourselves living on other planets in the universe?	Yes	—	—	34	46	51	50	46	38

SOURCES: *The Gallup Poll: Public Opinion 1935–1971*, Vols. 1 and 3 (New York: Random House, 1973), pp. 666, 911, 2004. *The Gallup Poll: Public Opinion 1972–1977*, Vol. 1 (Wilmington, DE: Scholarly Resources, 1978), pp. 213–15. *The Gallup Poll: Public Opinion 1978* (Wilmington, DE: Scholarly Resources, 1979), pp. 161–63. *The Gallup Poll Public Opinion 1987* (Wilmington, DE: Scholarly Resources, 1988), pp. 52–53. *The Gallup Poll: Public Opinion 1990* (Wilmington, DE: Scholarly Resources, 1997), pp. 206–7.

"optical illusions, imagination, and hoaxes" (39%). Less than 5 percent of those polled indicated that UFOs were Russian secret weapons or alien spacecraft. Later in the poll, people were asked what was the most important problem facing the United States, and 45 percent of the respondents indicated either inflation or foreign policy. Less than 1 percent mentioned flying saucers. On May 20, 1950, the Gallup poll again asked about flying saucers. This time 94 percent had heard of or read about UFOs. Five percent of these people said UFOs were "something from another planet" or "Russian weapons." While almost everyone knew about flying saucers, few perceived them as a threat.

The Gallup poll did not ask UFO questions again until May 8, 1966. This time "UFO" was substituted for "flying saucer" and additional questions were asked. Ninety-six percent of the national sample had heard of or read about UFOs, and 5 percent of these people claimed to have seen a UFO. Pollsters asked whether UFOs were real or imaginary. Forty-six percent said UFOs were real, 29 percent said they were imaginary, and the rest had no opinion. This question was ambiguous compared to that of the earlier polls in which people were asked, "What are flying saucers?" People who claimed that UFOs were real may have had in mind "real" optical illusions as well as "real" spacecraft. As shown in Table 6.2, Gallup Organization polls since mid-1966 show some consistent patterns. Depending on how questions are phrased, 50 to 80 percent of the U.S. population believes that there is intelligent life elsewhere in the universe. About 90 percent of the U.S. population has heard of UFOs, and about half the U.S. population believes they are real. It also appears that better educated adults are more likely than others to believe in UFOs. The Gallup polls conducted in 1966, 1973, 1978, and 1987 revealed that about 45 percent of those with less than a high school education believe in UFOs, while 60 percent of the college educated believe in UFOs (see Table 6.3).

When asked, "Have you, yourself, ever seen anything you thought was a UFO?" about 10 percent of the population answered "yes" (Gallup, 1996:207). Questions asked in a *Time/CNN* (1997) survey indicate that if respondents were to meet an extraterrestrial, 44 percent said they would expect to be treated as friends, while 26 percent think they would be treated as enemies. This poll also found that about 2–3 percent of the population feel they may have been abducted by aliens. The same *Time/CNN* poll shows that 80 percent of Americans think the government is hiding knowledge of the existence of extraterrestrial life. A 1996 Gallup Organization poll similarly found that 71 percent of the public agrees that the U.S. government knows more about UFOs than it is telling us (Gallup 1997:207). Considering poll results such as these, it is not surprising that UFOs have posed a continuing public-relations problem for our government, and for the Air Force in particular, ever since Kenneth Arnold reported his flying saucers in 1947.

UFOs as a Public Relations Problem

Shortly after Kenneth Arnold's report hit the airwaves and newsstands, the Air Force was asked to explain what Arnold had seen. News reporters, public officials, and ordinary citizens wanted to know if flying saucers were real, if they came from other planets, and if they posed a threat to our national security. A few weeks later, people were asking if the Air Force had recovered a crashed flying saucer, or saucers, from the New Mexico desert.

TABLE 6.3
UFO Beliefs and Education Levels

Gallup poll question	Response	Level of education	Percent by year			
			1966	1973	1978	1987
In your opinion are [UFOs] something real or just people's imagination?	Real	College	51	62	66	56
		High School	51	55	57	44
		Grade School	33	41	36	—
Do you think there are people somewhat like ourselves living on other planets in the universe?	Yes	College	37	58	62	57
		High School	38	47	53	35
		Grade School	25	39	24	—

SOURCES: *The Gallup Poll: Public Opinion 1935–1971*, Vols. 1 and 3 (New York: Random House, 1973), pp. 666, 911, 2004. *The Gallup Poll: Public Opinion 1972–1977*, Vol. 1 (Wilmington, DE: Scholarly Resources, 1978), pp. 213–15. *The Gallup Poll: Public Opinion 1978* (Wilmington, DE: Scholarly Resources, 1979), pp. 161–63. *The Gallup Poll Public Opinion 1987* (Wilmington, DE: Scholarly Resources, 1988), pp. 52–53. *The Gallup Poll: Public Opinion 1990* (Wilmington, DE: Scholarly Resources, 1997), pp. 206–7.

By 1953 the Air Force was satisfied that most UFOs were misidentifications, hysteria, or hoaxes and did not pose a threat to national security. Consequently, the UFO phenomenon was as much a problem of public relations as it was a problem to be investigated (Jacobs, 1975:89–107). There seemed to be no real need to continue Project Blue Book other than to avoid the outcry from UFO buffs and organizations if the project were canceled. Chief among these advocates was Marine Corps Major Donald E. Keyhoe, director of NICAP, who frequently charged that the Air Force was engaging in a cover-up of the UFO phenomenon, and he lobbied for congressional and scientific investigations (Jacobs, 1975:145–57).

Project Blue Book was continued until 1969. After 1953, sighting investigations were carried out as training exercises for Air Intelligence Service Squadron personnel. Thereafter, Project Blue Book involved little more than compiling air intelligence reports and investigating a few of the "unidentifieds."

In 1957 the number and kinds of UFO reports again brought the UFO phenomenon to public attention. While the Air Force argued that these were nothing more than the usual misidentifications, hysteria, and hoaxes, private UFO organizations pushed to have congressional hearings. The purpose of hearings was to upgrade the scientific study of UFOs and to get the Air Force to disclose what it really knew about UFOs. By late 1957, however, the number of UFO reports was beginning to decline, and so did congressional enthusiasm.

In 1966 the number of UFO sightings returned to the 1957 level. On April 5, 1966, the House Armed Services Committee held the first and to date the only open hearing on UFOs. It was decided at this brief meeting that a scientific committee should be appointed by the Air Force to investigate selected UFO sightings and evaluate Project Blue Book.

By the end of 1968, the number of UFO sightings had declined to their lowest level since 1959 (see Table 6.1). It was in the context of lower-than-usual UFO sighting reports that the Condon Committee issued its congressionally mandated report. The report concluded that the Air Force had done an excellent job of studying UFOs and that UFOs had a number of terrestrial explanations. The Condon Committee Report concluded that there was no longer any reason to continue Project Blue Book.

After the Condon Committee Report, many UFO organizations underwent a rapid and marked decline in membership. Several UFO magazines went out of business (Jacobs, 1975:256). The number of UFO reports submitted to private UFO investigation groups indicated that there had been a clear decline in UFO sightings from the levels of the 1950s and 1960s. Many felt the UFO had departed the American scene.

THE UFO AS A CULTURAL ICON

The decline in UFO sightings, however, was only temporary. By 1973 the number of UFO reports approached those of 1952, 1957, and 1966. This time the Air Force remained outside the controversy, which was easy because the disputes accompanying UFO sightings had calmed considerably. In 1973 the media seldom ridiculed UFO reports, and charges of hoax were less frequent and less bitter. There were many reasons for this change in public reaction. UFO sighting reports had become tame stuff compared to what had, since 1966, become commonplace to the American public. The report that someone had observed an automobile-sized, egg-shaped object take off at high speed seemed much less dramatic to the millions of people who had watched live television coverage of several *Saturn V* launches. The report that someone had observed humanoid pilots scampering around their UFO hardly compared to the drama of watching Neil Armstrong take the first step on the surface of the moon. The occasional blurred photos alleged to be UFOs couldn't hold a candle to the brilliant photo essays of the Gemini and Apollo space missions published in *Life* magazine. Any possible threat the UFOs posed now seemed to be matched equally, or even to be exceeded, by those of our own making. We were discovering the worldwide threat of pollution and continually were being reminded that we had finally created nuclear arsenals clearly capable of destroying our planet.

The scientific study of UFOs also seemed to have attained a degree of respectability not enjoyed earlier. Perhaps this was because scientists had succeeded in demystifying themselves in the eyes of the public. During the late 1960s and early 1970s, there was an increase in the number of celebrity scientists. People such as Jane Goodall, Marlin Perkins, Jacques Cousteau, and Carl Sagan allowed the American public to see scientists as quite likable, articulate, and dedicated people, in marked contrast to the "egghead" image given to scientists during the 1950s. Their popular books and television shows greatly increased public awareness of the nature of scientific investigation and the scope of scientific interests. If scientists studied the social life of chimps, catalogued the density of ocean plankton, and speculated about the nature of antimatter and black holes in space, then why not study UFOs?

The books of James Allen Hynek seriously addressed the methodological and analytical problems involved in studying UFOs. Previous serious discussions of UFOs were primarily devoted to, for example, how temperature inversions could produce false radar images (Menzel and Boyd, 1963). Hynek's *The UFO Experience: A Scientific Enquiry* (1972) clearly stands apart from earlier books written about UFOs. It presents, foremost, a scientific methodology for classifying and studying UFO reports.

The Interrupted Journey, describing Barney and Betty Hill's abduction by aliens, was published in 1966 and was a bestseller. For many, this book described a "one-of-a-kind" encounter with space aliens. Twenty-one years later, in 1987, *Communion* and *Intruders* were published, each a bestseller and each describing numerous alien abductions and medical experiments that were allegedly part of a larger and sinister pattern of intrusion into human society by aliens. The late 1980s also saw tremendous growth in cable television. Needing to fill over a hundred viewing channels, UFOs and thousands of other topics were pressed into service by new and established studios and local stations. In the wake of rapid growth of cable television, the Internet provided outlets for UFO enthusiasts of all persuasions. Benefactors provided monies for UFO-related activities. With the need to fill vast amounts of television time and the seemingly unlimited capacity of the World Wide Web, the Roswell Incident, Area 51, and alien abductions are once again topics of congressional debate and investigation panels of scientists convened at Stanford University.

The character of the UFO phenomenon has changed through the years. When people first began to report strange airships in the sky, it was largely attributed to mysterious inventions, hysteria, or hoaxes and was promptly forgotten. The next time large numbers of people reported strange craft in the sky, it was treated as a possible threat to national security and worthy—though just barely—of official investigation. Much controversy and bitter debate surrounded the UFO phenomenon until the mid-1960s, when the government concluded its UFO studies and the number of UFO reports decreased substantially. When large numbers of people began to see UFOs in the 1970s, much had changed. Scientists who expressed interest in studying UFOs and the people who reported them were subject to less ridicule than before. Most UFO reports seemed less fantastic now that people's frames of reference had been expanded to include the drama and spectacle of real space travel.

As noted above, in order to fill the expanding number of television channels in the 1980s, new forms of programming were hastily adopted. In this context of rapid innovation, the traditional distinction between programming and commercials quickly broke down with the introduction of infomercials. Likewise, in an effort to fill the new channels, around-the-clock, continuous news sources proliferated and the distinction between news and entertainment quickly blurred. Speculation regarding lurid scandals and bizarre conspiracies, once the fodder of supermarket tabloids, now came into our homes, at any time, under the guise of legitimate news investigations and special reports. As the number of cable channels grew, centuries-old legislation and customs also gave way to bring courtroom proceedings into our homes as entertainment. (If the entertainment intent is in doubt, we find it interesting that the coverage of the courts heavily favors criminal and civil cases having prominent violent and sexual content over such things as title transfers and real-estate transactions.)

The basic theme of nearly all investigative and courtroom reports is that nothing is as it first appears. Nightly news now uncovers one conspiracy, malfeasance, and deception after another. News networks maintain websites to augment their programming. Individuals and groups maintain websites and discussion groups that review and integrate these events and generate discussions of new issues. Such uses of cable television and the Internet can be readily interpreted as cultural lag. Some critics describe the end result as "junk" or "trash" culture, wherein the truth is whatever the government is hiding from us and what the respectable media are afraid to reveal.

It is into this context that UFOs were drawn in the last quarter century. Now, much of what appears about UFOs on the Web has to do not with UFOs but with the nature and extent of government conspiracies and plots to hide the truth about Roswell, Area 51, Apollo 13, the Mars rover, Heaven's Gate, and so forth. The harshest criticisms come from UFO groups themselves as they question the motives, practices, and conclusions of other UFO groups. Jodi Dean (1998) characterizes UFOs as a cultural icon or action frame, which since the 1980s has come to embody far more than interest in the possibility of extraterrestrial visitors. UFOs have come to reflect and express the deep paranoia of the present times. UFOs are but one of many deep secrets that the government (or—depending on the source—big business, the United Nations, the Jews, or the Muslims) or the aliens themselves are keeping from us. UFOs are a way of expressing the human tendency to fear and hate anything alien, whether extraterrestrial or earthly. Of course, these fears are manufactured in the course of creating compelling news and entertainment. UFO discourse, like the discourse of many other cultural items today, is a paranoid discourse of fear and anger. The idea that "space people" are here to help us died with the members of Heaven's Gate.

SUMMARY

There are references to puzzling and often frightening aerial phenomena throughout recorded history. In recent years people have attributed such UFO occurrences to extraterrestrial visitors. The modern UFO era started with the mysterious airships of the 1890s and reached its full development with the flying saucer terminology of the late 1940s and early 1950s. This chapter began with a description of some typical UFO incidents in a now-familiar classification scheme first set forth by J. Allen Hynek: nocturnal lights, daylight disks, radar/visual sightings, and close encounters.

There probably have been more than a quarter million reported sightings of UFOs since 1947. Some UFO investigators claim that all UFO sightings result from the misidentification of such familiar objects as aircraft and stars, the effects of certain atmospheric conditions, hysteria, and hoaxes. Other UFO researchers conclude that a sizable number of UFO reports are genuine and that the extraterrestrial hypothesis cannot be dismissed. The investigation of UFO reports is difficult; neither camp can lay claim to having the superior research methodology.

One perspective of collective behavior identifies outbreaks of UFO sightings as a type of mass hysteria. For Smelser UFO flaps represent widespread terror, and for Klapp they represent hysterical wish fulfillment. An examination of UFO reports indicates that fluctuations in the annual volume of reports is not as extreme as is suggested by the definition of mass hysteria. Some of this fluctuation is certainly due to the procedures used in obtaining reports. Asch's (1958) classic line-judging study illustrates that group influence is capable of distorting people's judgment. The conditions that led to distorted judgment in Asch's study, however, are seldom found during UFO sightings.

The collective action perspective offers some insights into the social nature of UFO phenomena. Present explanations have emerged through a process of collective definition, or framing. The explanations offered for the "mystery airships" included stars, hysteria, hoaxes, and visitors from Mars. These explanations have become more elaborate during the course of subsequent outbreaks of UFO sightings.

Following World War II, when flying saucers were seen as posing a possible military threat, numerous governmental and private organizations have sought to study them scientifically. Although official government interest has ceased, private groups continue to study UFO-related phenomena.

The Gallup polls indicate that UFOs have become a permanent feature of popular culture. About half the adult population believes that there is intelligent life similar to ours on other planets and that UFOs are real. There are few major differences in these beliefs that can be accounted for in terms of people's level of education.

UFOs have provided the basis for investigative, contactee, and cult groups. Some of these groups originated shortly after the first sightings of flying saucers in 1947 and are still active today. Some groups succeeded in mobilizing thousands of members and used bureaucratic and leader-centered organizations. Groups compete for members and obtain financial support from their members as well as from several benfactors.

UFOs have posed a public-relations problem for governmental and military agencies since 1947. Cable television and the Internet have had a profound impact on the UFO phenomenon. Through cable television and the Web, UFOs have become a cultural icon, framed in terms of governmental conspiracies and other manufactured fears.

⚔ CHAPTER 7 ⚔

FADS AND FASHION

About a quarter to five in the morning, our buses pulled into the parking lot of the Country Dining Room. We had left the high school about seven hours earlier, on the first leg of our band's trip to Chattanooga, Tennessee for the symphonic band competition. My wife and I were chaperones for bus number three, and we had been able to doze only a bit during our late-night ride. Still, all the band members had been very well behaved and had settled in for a quiet ride about half an hour after we left the high school. This was our scheduled breakfast stop, and I welcomed the chance to get out and stretch my legs, even though it was still dark outside and there was a light, cold rain falling. The driver then announced that we had arrived sooner than expected and that the restaurant was not yet open.

I looked out the window and noticed that about ten people were already standing by the doors under the Country Dining Room's old-fashioned-style front porch. I said to my wife that this should be taken as a sign that the Country Dining Room served great breakfasts. As the band members began to stir, we announced that we would have an hour and a half for breakfast and that there would be a change of drivers. A small cheer went up for Tom, the driver, who had brought us safely to our destination.

Once more I looked onto the porch of the Country Dining Room, and now there were at least twenty men, women, and children standing by the doors. Again I told my wife that this was a *really* good sign that the Country Dining Room served good breakfasts. Then I told her how truck drivers and bus drivers *always* know the best places to eat. As the restaurant doors were opened, even more people converged onto the porch. I told my wife that this place must be *great!* About fifteen minutes later, after I had ordered pecan pancakes, I mentioned to the waitress that the Country Dining Room must serve good breakfasts, since there had been a crowd waiting at five in the morning. The waitress smiled and assured me that although the Country Dining Room did indeed serve wonderful breakfasts, the people at the door had been there to buy the new shipment of Beanie Babies! (And, yes, it was a very good breakfast.)

Fads, such as the Beanie Babies, and fashion were among the earliest concerns of sociologists. This may seem surprising, because most of us view fads and fashion as part of the "lighter side" of social life. George Simmel (1904), however, argued that fads and fashion play an important role in modern society. Through fads, people can experience a "sense of identity and unity" with groups to which they aspire or belong. Fashions, from the latest ready-to-wear collection from Paris to Chicago gang colors, are expressive symbols that communicate people's status and prestige within society. Thorstein Veblen (1912) noted that through conspicuous adherence to fashion, people find a socially acceptable way to advertise their wealth to others.

With respect to fads and fashion, most theories of collective behavior take the classic statements of Simmel and Veblen as their starting point. They depart from these statements, however, in their emphasis on the apparent spontaneity, novelty, and intensity of fads and fashion. While the classic theories emphasize the integrative aspects of fads and fashion, theories of collective behavior usually emphasize the disruptive aspects.

Fads and fashion occur within nearly every sphere of social life in modern society, most obviously in the areas of clothing, personal adornment, and grooming. Commentators often note that the dress and decoration of women are more prone to fads and the whims of fashion than those of men, although such differences are probably overstated. Men had their white buckskin shoes, bolo ties, DA haircuts, and lamé shirts in the 1950s. If they dig far enough into their closets, many men can still find narrow ties and belts, madras shirts, and perhaps even a Nehru jacket they wore in the 1960s.

If one ever remodels an old house, many remnants of past fads and fashions of interior decoration come to the surface. Alternating layers of wallpaper and paint tell us what designs and colors were "in." During the late 1950s, vivid pink and black bathroom tile was popular. In the 1960s, vivid, solid colors were the thing, and beautiful woodwork and cabinets were painted to match the walls. Flawless hardwood floors were covered with wall-to-wall shag carpets. Stained and etched glass, once casually discarded from American homes, returned as a popular decorative item.

Some fads center on novelty items. If we search through our closets, garages, and basements, we are likely to find hula hoops, lava lamps, woodburning sets, beaded curtains, beanbag chairs, pet rocks, Rubik's cubes, and deely boppers. Although now we would not have the nerve to sell many of these things at a yard sale, they were once prized possessions.

There are also activity fads. These include the dance marathons of the 1930s, the jitterbug contests of the 1940s, and the eating contests, panty raids, and phone-booth stuffing of the 1950s. In the early 1960s a Kennedy family tradition, the twenty-mile hike, was copied around the country. The 1970s brought us toga parties and streaking. Break dancing was part of the 1980s scene; moshing and crowd surfing marked the 1990s.

THREE KINDS OF FADS

In this chapter we begin with descriptions of three separate kinds of fads. First is the fantastic burst of sales of citizens' band (CB) radios in 1976 and 1977. What began as another 1970s "fad," the debut of the personal computer, made the transition from just another popular useful product to one of the mainstays of our daily lives. The next type of fad episode is the *novelty product fad*, which centers around items that have little practical value for the user, as illustrated by the frenzy over Cabbage Patch Kids dolls during the Christmas season of 1983. In these days of mass consumerism, this type of fad seems to deluge us every holiday season in such guises as Tickle Me Elmo dolls and Furbies. Finally, the *activity fad*, in which variations of an activity are publicly displayed, usually within a crowd setting, is exemplified by the streaking phenomenon of 1974. One of the more popular activity fads during the last decade of the twentieth century, moshing, is also discussed.

Useful Products

CB Radios Citizens' band radios came into use on October 4, 1958, when federal regulations were changed to permit their operation. Licensing was much less stringent than for ham radios, in part because they were designed to have a range of less than ten miles. Taxicab companies and local delivery services were the first businesses to use the CB radio extensively; noncommercial and recreational uses were rare. The growth in CB licenses and sales was steady, holding at about one hundred thousand licenses and radios a year.

Annual sales suddenly increased about twentyfold during the gasoline crisis of 1973. During that year, 2 million CB licenses were issued, most of them to long-distance truck drivers who found that CBs helped them locate filling stations that sold diesel fuel. The CB also proved valuable in keeping truckers informed about road conditions and accidents and for relaying emergency messages. Also, the CB was a welcome diversion for truckers who just wanted to talk to one another during the long hours on the road. Soon, truckers had evolved their own jargon, nicknames or "handles," and rules of CB etiquette.

Motorists who spent a great deal of time on the highways, such as sales representatives and commuters, began to use CBs. Farmers put radios on their tractors and trucks. They were very useful for relaying messages between house and field, coordinating fieldwork, and herding livestock. Farmers and ranchers also used CBs to organize night patrols when theft and cattle rustling became more common.

The greatest increase in CB sales came in 1976, when more than 11 million CB units were sold. Most commentators attributed this increase to the fifty-five-mile-per-hour national speed limit that was enacted that year. The CB radio was used to thwart police enforcement efforts. Truckers and motorists began to "convoy," or drive in large groups at high speeds. Drivers of oncoming vehicles were able to notify speeders of the location of police in time for the convoys to slow to "double nickels."

That year, CB radios began to appear on everything from family autos to bicycles and golf carts. There were also numerous spin-off items, including jewelry boxes, banks, cologne bottles, and salt and pepper shakers designed to look like CB radios. Toy CB radios were sold for use on tricycles and kiddy cars. Model truck kits appeared on the shelves of hobby shops. Numerous books on CB jargon were published. Elaborate locking and alarm systems were marketed to prevent the theft of CBs.

CB jargon invaded popular speech. Tractor-trailer rigs became "eighteen wheelers," state police became "smokeys,"and exceeding the speed limit became "putting the pedal to the metal." The term 10-4 was often substituted for saying yes, of course, or all right. People adopted "handles" like the truck drivers, calling themselves such names as Vitro, Big Red, Hotshot, The Professor, Rubber Duck, Ditch Witch, and Squirrelly Shirley. "QSL" cards were originally created to be send by one CB operator to another as a confirmation of reception. Often comically illustrated, these cards that proclaimed operators' handles and locations became popular collectibles among CB buffs.

Songs about truck drivers and truck driving, such as C. W. McCall's "Convoy," broke out of the country-and-western field and into the Top Ten. Television shows such as *B.J. and the Bear* capitalized on the CB radio-truck driver-state police theme. The second most popular film of 1977 was Burt Reynolds's *Smokey and the Bandit*, in which truckers used CB radios to evade the police.

CB clubs were established across the nation. Some of them were primarily social in nature, allowing people who talked over CBs to meet face to face. These clubs also allowed people to exchange the latest technical information, make trades, and purchase equipment in large volume. Other clubs, such as Radio Emergency Action Citizen Teams (REACT), were established to relay emergency information and monitor weather. These groups often sought to work closely with police in the area of surveillance and disaster assistance.

In addition to evading enforcement of the fifty-five-mile-per-hour speed limit, CB radios were put to other "outlaw" uses. Burglars used CB and scanner radios to monitor police transmissions, and CB prostitutes used the radios to proposition truckers and motorists in or near interstate rest areas (Klein and Luxenburg-Ingle, 1980a; 1980b). Finally, during this period CB radios became a very popular theft item (Gutschenritter, 1977). They were stolen and hocked from coast to coast, and some thieves were arrested with hundreds of stolen CBs in their possession!

CB radios presented other problems as well. Some operators illegally modified antennas so that they could skip their signals over hundreds of miles. Some cheaply built, poorly maintained, or damaged CB sets interfered with radio, television, and stereo reception. The use of CB radios near construction sites posed the threat of detonating explosives. Many people were electrocuted and injured or killed in falls while erecting antennas. CB radio clubs worked to promote CB etiquette and a positive image within the community. They also urged the safe use of radios and reported "skippers" to the authorities. Still, in many communities, CB radios came to be regarded as a nuisance. General interest in CB radios began to decline during 1978, and by 1980 some commentators were claiming that the CB phenomenon was dead (Keerdoja and Sethi, 1980). This was an exaggeration, of course. Tens of thousands of new-generation CB radios are used today, augmenting cellular phone technology.

The CB radio was the first item that gave many Americans a "hands-on" experience with an electronic item other than a simple radio, television, or record player. Soon many homes would be inundated with cable television converter boxes, VCRs, component stereo systems, programmable appliances, calculators, and personal computers.

Personal Computers In January of 1975 a small Albuquerque company, Micro Instrumentation and Telemetry Systems (MITS) sold their first "personal computer kits" to be assembled from some stock items used in mainframe computers. During the previous six months, no orders had been placed for their product, but immediately after their little computer appeared on the cover of *Popular Electronics* magazine, sales took off. MITS had optimistically planned to sell 800 kits in 1975. By February, however, they were taking orders at the rate of 400 a day. Within six months several other companies were making direct copies of the MITS computer. By 1978, small personal computers were being made by dozens of new companies including Osborne and Commodore. Radio Shack, a long-time provider of electronic kits for hobbyists, brought out their own brand of personal

---

Reflections: Adapting to the Personal Computer in Mid-Career

Initially, home users purchased most personal computers. As the capabilities of the early machines increased, they were introduced into the workplace. Like many, this author's first use of a personal computer occurred at the office. One of my colleagues had been using an Apple computer (32K) at home for a few months and convinced the dean to purchase a computer for the sociology office. The computer soon arrived, and the departmental secretary did not want to learn how to use it. I was writing a text-book at the time (*Introduction to Collective Behavior, 1/E*) and had completed four chapters in eight months using a typewriter. I began to use the Apple for word processing and completed the remaining eleven chapters in the same amount of time. By then I had bought my very own Franklin computer (64K and Apple compatible!), and our office had two Apples. Of course, the secretary now used the computer, as did a few other faculty members. Within six years nearly all members of the department were using computers for word processing. Some memorable comments heard during this time period included:

"We shouldn't be making so much fuss over trendy things like personal computers."

"Backup files? I don't need backup files."

"You shouldn't ever need more than 125K."

"What's the Internet?"

Like most people in the early 1980s, none of our faculty had any previous experience with personal computers in graduate school. Although the university began to offer workshops to teach faculty word processing, nearly all faculty acquired their computer skills on their own, at the office, or on their computers at home. Likewise, faculty began to use the Internet in their homes before it was available at the office. Early innovators taught others how to use the technology, and few utilized workshops. The personal computer is the one item that has most altered how we do our work. It is ironic to note that those of us who entered academia before 1980 largely taught ourselves how to use this technology.

---

computer. A small California company, Apple, marketed their first computer. None of these early participants imagined the vast capacity for rapid growth of the personal computer market (Osborn, 1984).

Novelty Items

Cabbage Patch Kids In 1974 a very flexible synthetic fabric was introduced to the home needlecraft market. The material was used for making dolls (Poly Dolls). With proper stitching, one could make chubby but hauntingly lifelike faces, hands, and feet. Soon craft shows and bazaars across the country featured dolls that were crafted to look like grandmas and grandpas as well as infants.

Georgia artist Xavier Roberts established Original Appalachian Artworks in 1977 and began to sell "little people." He moved his sales/showroom into a former medical clinic in Cleveland, Georgia. Because the dolls were handcrafted, no two were identical. Further, depending on the quality of the sewing, the size of the doll, and the clothing, prices ranged from about $50 to $1,000. At Roberts's "hospital," dolls were "delivered" from under cabbage leaves by employees dressed in nurses' uniforms. New "parents" of the little people had to vow undying love for their new dolls and were given adoption papers. Many of the most expensive dolls were bought by adults for themselves. By 1983 Roberts had sold more than two hundred thousand dolls.

Coleco Corporation and Original Appalachian Artworks negotiated a licensing agreement that allowed Coleco to market their version of the doll under the label of Cabbage Patch Kids. By using the latest robot technology, Asian manufacturers were able to retain the handcrafted appearance of the original dolls while manufacturing them in mass quantities. Cabbage Patch Kids were introduced in February 1983 and sold for about $30. Coleco also included adoption papers. If purchasers returned the papers, they received a note of thanks and, a year later, a birthday card for the doll.

Initially, retailers placed modest orders for the 1983 Christmas season. It did not appear that Cabbage Patch Kids would sell any better than other dolls, and it was also feared that the season would be characterized by generally weak sales. Coleco, however, set out on a nationwide advertising blitz, and by mid-November retailers were placing new orders. As Christmas approached, Coleco was scrambling to meet demand. In regions where dolls were in very short supply, ads were stopped altogether out of fear that false advertising charges would be brought by consumer groups. At this point, Coleco was chartering planes to bring in two hundred thousand dolls a week from their Hong Kong factories.

These cherubic little dolls seemed to inspire very un-Christmaslike spirit in holiday shoppers. In Charleston, West Virginia, a near riot was reported when about five thousand people crowded into a department store that had advertised a new shipment of dolls. In Wilkes-Barre, Pennsylvania, a woman broke her leg in a disorderly crowd waiting for a department store to open. Some stores set up special Cabbage Patch waiting lines in an effort to end shoving matches and angry squabbles between customers.

It is not surprising that a black market in Cabbage Patch dolls began to emerge. Newspapers carried classified ads offering dolls for resale at grossly inflated prices. Those who knew how to make the dolls capitalized on their skills in the weeks before Christmas. Advertisements offered counterfeit dolls at prices as high as $200. In New Jersey, the FBI arrested counterfeiters with more than one thousand dolls in their possession.

There were other ways to cash in on the Cabbage Patch Kids. Stores that were able to acquire only a few dolls used them as promotional items. One store, for example, kept their dolls in the vault of a local bank and used them as prizes in a daily drawing. Churches and civic groups raffled off the dolls. Charity auctions were held, with reports that some dolls brought as much as $1,500. Predictably, sales declined after Christmas, but by then Coleco had sold nearly 2.5 million Cabbage Patch Kids. No other doll has ever sold so well in its first year.

It was 1990 before the Teenage Mutant Ninja Turtles approached anywhere near the Christmas time popularity of the Cabbage Patch Kids. The figures were also coordinated with a holiday Teenage Mutant Ninja Turtles movie and television show. The 1993–1994 season brought us the Mighty Morphin Power Rangers, again with a movie and television show tie-in.

 Tickle Me Elmo Dolls

Tickle his tummy once to make him giggle,
twice to make him laugh longer.

Tickle him a third time
and he shakes with laughter!

Tyco's Tickle Me Elmo doll was, by far, the most popular and sought-after gift of the 1996 Christmas season. By comparison, the 101 Dalmatians and Space Jam figures that were tied in with movies and had been heavily promoted in the fall were also-rans in the race for the Christmas gift dollar. Of course, Elmo had been a Sesame Street star for years. The first 300,000 copies of Elmo were nearly all sold by mid-October. By Thanksgiving, people who had bought Elmos earlier in the season were reselling them at incredible prices, and air freighters were bringing in new supplies from Chinese factories. Elmo dolls were offered for sale privately in newspapers and on dozens of websites. In a few stores, as supplies trickled in, customers and clerks came to blows over Elmo dolls. In gestures more character-istic of the Christmas spirit, however, numerous Elmo dolls were auctioned to benefit charitable groups across the country. In total, a million Tickle Me Elmo dolls were sold between August and Christmas of 1996.

Tickle Me Elmo, clearly the most popular toy of the season, was the precursor of what have now been dubbed audio-animatronic toys—including what have been called "virtual pets." Using a combination of sensors, microprocessors, servo- and electric motors, gears and speakers, these "pets" can respond to out-side stimuli. If you touch them or talk to them, they will (depending on the toy) talk back to you, giggle, sing, sneeze, meow, bark, hoot, and/or move in a variety of ways. Such toys are the results of recent breakthroughs in artificial intelligence and robotics. Bandai marketed a line of small, keychain-style virtual pets in 1997. An added feature of these pets was that they had to be "cared for" by their own-ers or the pet would suffer a "virtual death" and cease to operate. These pets could be "resurrected" several times before they died permanently.

The most successful virtual pet to date is Hasbro Toys' Furby, a fluffy, owl-like doll that sells for about $40. Furbies can talk to one another in their own Furbish language, are capable of "learning" English, and also will get sick if not cared for properly. Furbies were the hot toy for the 1998–1999 Christmas season. Pokémon topped the 1999–2000 Christmas wish list for many youngsters.

Unlike previous novelty-item fads, the success of Tickle Me Elmo and subse-quent virtual pets has generated a noticeable backlash. Newspapers have carried editorials claiming that these products represent consumerism at its worst. Other editorials have claimed that virtual pets are likely to seduce children into not car-ing about real pets or treating real pets like toys. Numerous "Hate Elmo" and anti-Furby websites have also been created.

Activities

Streaking What would you do if you were eating lunch and someone ran naked through the restaurant? What would you do if you saw a small crowd of nude people running down the street? In early March of 1974, you probably would not have been perplexed. Rather, you would know immediately that you had just witnessed a "streaking." Total or partial nudity had been familiar for many years on and about college campuses, taking the form of "mooning" pranks and initia-tion rituals. Still, the volume of these activities combined did not equal that of the rash of streaking that occurred from February 11 (the acknowledged date of the first true streak) until March 15, when no one seemed to care anymore.

Evans and Miller (1975) concluded that one or more streaking incidents occurred on at least 123 colleges and universities during the outbreak. In addition, dozens of restaurants, shopping centers, high schools and junior colleges, a few state legislatures, and at least one baseball training camp were streaked. For a time, nothing was sacred, as Wall Street, St. Peter's Square, and the Eiffel Tower were also streaked.

Evans and Miller discerned a pattern in the campus streaking incidents. On any given campus, a daring individual or small group would streak, often at night. Rumor and local media usually made the incident widely known by the next day. After that, other streaks occurred, climaxing in a preannounced streak-in. These streaks usually drew large crowds and the media to await the first sign of bare bottoms, tops, and everything else. During these streaks, innovations such as streaking on bicycles, motorcycles, roller skates, and wheelchairs occurred. Nude dancing, stripteases, and mass moonings were interspersed in the festivities. "Streak-ins" usually lasted about two or three hours. Afterward, smaller, unannounced streaks would occur. After a few days, the cycle occurred again. After about the third streak-in, interest faded rapidly, and students used their spare time to pursue other things.

Streaking was generally restricted to the college-age population, although streakers as young as eleven and as old as sixty-five occasionally appeared. Streaking was most likely to occur on or near large public universities. There was no discernible pattern of diffusion among universities. Small universities and private institutions, as is usually the case, had a much lower incidence of streaking. Streakers were predominantly male, although women were well represented. For the most part, it was a lighthearted episode. Police made few attempts to capture or arrest streakers, and campus authorities made little effort to put a halt to the activity (Evans and Miller, 1975).

Numerous explanations were offered, though none seemed particularly convincing. Evans and Miller suggest that streaking may have reflected a general attitude of disdain for existing social conditions. Beyond this, they suggest that it was simply a lot of naughty fun.

Moshing Typically, concerts by groups such as Nine Inch Nails, Pearl Jam, Moist, Bad Religion, Pantera, and music festivals such as Lollapalooza include "mosh pits" sometimes enclosed by four-foot-high barricades. Inside the pits, sweating, reeling moshers thrash about, slam against each other and the barricades, or try to climb up to the stage to get within reach of the band.

Moshing had its predecessor in the slamdancing of the 1970s, in which concert-goers bounced off one another to the beat of fast rock music. It can be mostly sweaty fun with the exception of bruises, cuts and the occasional sprained ankle or dislocated shoulder. Still, deaths and injuries have occurred in mosh pits with unpadded barricades. In 1994 two young men died and two others were left quadriplegic in separate crowd-surfing and stage-diving accidents. In 1997, a 17-year-old girl died in a stage-diving incident at a Dublin Smashing Pumpkins concert.

At most concerts today, tighter security has put a stop to stage diving, and security people monitor the pit barricades and are prepared to pull moshers to safety if they appear in distress. Barricade crashers will be sent to the side of the stage, where they'll be given a cup of water to avoid dehydration and a lecture on moshing safety. Medic stations and waiting ambulances now are commonplace at all-age concerts. Many of these precautions are required by fire ordinances, insur-

Moshing is a popular activity in many music clubs. Although to the uninitiated it seems like a dangerous and violent activity, most moshers say they're just enjoying themselves. © Barry Lewis/CORBIS.

ance companies, and concert promoters. In 1996, Pearl Jam and their concert managers were successfully sued for injuries received by a concert-goer who was trampled and knocked unconscious after the band encouraged fans to rush to the mosh pit. This and other lawsuits have also contributed to "safe moshing."

✳ THE NATURE OF FADS AND FASHION ⵜ

Numerous attempts have been made to define both fads and fashion, and there are several common elements to these definitions. For example, both fads and fashion are part of "conspicuous consumption" and occur with respect to superficialities (for example, Simmel, 1904; LaPierre and Farnsworth, 1949; Lofland, 1981; Schaefer, 1983). The superficial nature of fads and fashion does not refer to the degree of excitement or to the financial and emotional investments found in them. Rather, it refers to the likelihood that fad and fashion items will be outmoded and replaced before their serviceability ends. Because of this aspect of fads and fashion, we see perfectly usable clothing and furniture being discarded or sold at yard sales because they are "out of fashion."

Additionally, fads and fashion follow much the same pattern of development and decline (e.g., Penrose, 1952; Meyersohn and Katz, 1957; Lofland, 1981). This pattern is characterized by an initial *latent period*, in which the object of the fad or fashion is known only within a limited and often small group. Then there is the *breakout period*, during which the first group introduces or other groups "discover" the fad item. Next there is the *peaking period*, in which use of the new item is defined as a fad or fashion and people enthusiastically adopt it as such. During the peaking period, competing items, such as other forms of recreation or fashion, are ignored. Innovations on the theme of the fad, such as contests for the first, best, or most, occur frequently. Finally, there is the *decline period*, in which the fad or fashion rapidly fades. In the case of fashion, it is always replaced by something else. Use of the fad or fashion item may totally disappear or again be restricted to a small group.

Finally, fads and fashion serve much the same ends in society. Simmel (1994) argued that human beings possess two competing impulses—unity and differentiation. First and foremost, people desire a secure feeling of acceptance or belonging to groups of which they are a part (unity). Second, people desire a sense of self-identity and autonomy (differentiation). Fads and fashion can accommodate these competing impulses more or less simultaneously. Personal involvement in a fad or adherence to a particular fashion communicates a sense of unity, comradeship, and belonging to a group. Involvement also sets individuals apart from the "rest of society" and establishes them as "trend setters" or at least "in tune with the latest happenings" in society. Fads and, in particular, fashion communicate a sense of one's own personal identity and social status. Fad and fashion, then, give people a clear sense of both unity and differentiation.

How do fads and fashion differ from one another? To begin with, the concept of fashion is most often applied to dress, grooming, and personal adornment. Discussions of fads typically include these areas but are seldom limited to them (Sann, 1967). Several discussions emphasize that fads are less predictable, and their life cycles shorter and more intense, than fashion (for example, LaPierre and Farnsworth, 1949; Penrose, 1952; Lofland, 1981; Schaefer, 1983). Fads are also seen as more trivial than fashion. *Fashion* may manifest trends that allow a person to wear a style of clothing for a few seasons and still remain in step. Clothing *fads*, on the other hand, seldom last more than a few months. Fashion usually communicates economic status much more clearly than fads do. Finally, some have argued that fashion is more enduring than fads. Fashion often comes to characterize historical periods, whereas most fads are soon forgotten, leaving little trace of their passing.

Social Origins of Fashion

Style Simmel (1904) was among the first to argue that fashion, as a dynamic means of social differentiation, does not exist in primitive social systems. For Simmel, primitive social systems include tribal systems or caste systems such as those of India and Sri Lanka. A caste system is characterized by a nearly total absence of social mobility from one group to another. People's social status is strictly ascribed at birth, and everyone is expected to remain within their caste throughout their lives. Primitive social systems also include what Simmel referred to as "classless" societies, such as the hunting and gathering societies of many American Indians or the early horticultural societies of New Guinea. The social structure of these societies is assumed to be relatively simple and undifferentiated. These groups are very small; they generate little economic surplus. Consequently, there are few differences in wealth among members.

Primitive societies are therefore characterized by little social differentiation. In caste systems, social differentiation is not only limited, it is also inflexible. Simmel offers a twofold explanation for the kind of social differentiation found in primitive societies. First, he assumes that the imitation impulse is much more developed among primitive people than is the differentiation impulse. According to Simmel, the primitive mentality mistrusts and even fears that which is new or different. For Simmel, the development of the impulse toward differentiation is a mark of civilized people. Second, the imitation impulse is reinforced by a heightened need for unity within primitive societies that arises because primitive groups are more directly subject to the adversities of nature, such as disaster, disease, and famine than are more civilized peoples. Only a united and highly cohesive group can stand against such constant testing.

Saying that fashion does not exist in primitive social systems does not mean that clothing, grooming, and personal adornment are unimportant. In these societies, both obvious and subtle differences in dress and decoration convey such important dimensions of social status as one's age, kinship, marital status, occupation, past exploits, and religion. These styles, however, are dictated by tradition and are relatively unchanging. They do not exist as a dynamic or variable means of conveying status. Primitive societies utilize more or less permanent differences in style, rather than fashion, as a basis of limited social differentiation.

Fashion and Social Differentiation As societies grow in size and their technology becomes more complex, there is an accompanying pressure toward social differentiation. Some people learn new skills, others remain masters of old skills, and innovators create the skills of the future. Greater differences in wealth develop among members and become ingrained in the social structure. New opportunities for power present themselves. According to Simmel, all these conditions heighten the need for increased social differentiation. Further, it is a need for social differentiation of a new sort—a type that is flexible enough to reflect constantly changing social relationships.

Fashion meets this need. Various elites attempt to differentiate themselves from others by way of new or exotic items of dress, grooming, or personal adornment. Because the elite are in an enviable position with respect to other groups in the society, many try to copy the styles of the elite. Simmel notes that in modern societies, it may take very little time before large numbers of people are also using the same colors, fabrics, hem lengths, and trouser styles as the elite. In order to successfully differentiate themselves from others, people must change styles. Simmel refers to this constant cycle of change in styles as fashion. In modern and wealthy societies, the fashion cycle is institutionalized. Fashion sections become a regular feature of newspapers, and a plethora of fashion magazines appear on the magazine racks of grocery stores, book stores, and newsstands or are available to individuals and businesses by subscription. Fashion houses compete with one another each season for the nod from the elite at fashion shows, which are also major media events. Manufacturers constantly race to bring the "latest" fashion to the racks of the clothing and department stores of the world. An enormous volume of this fashion also is made available through mail and electronic ordering systems.

Fashion and Psychological Diversity Simmel claimed that women are far more conscious of fashion than men are, in part because there is less psychological diversity among women, as a group, than among men. The limited psychological diversity of women contributes to their adherence to fashion or the "social average." On the other hand, Simmel argues that fashion gives women compensation for their lack of clear status position in a society where so much of individual identity rests on occupational skills and profession. For his time, Simmel set forth a rather contemporary-sounding hypothesis, namely, that as women acquire more equal footing with men in terms of occupational and professional opportunities, fashion would become correspondingly less important to women.

The Natural History of Fads

Just as there are many predictable elements to the fashion cycle, so are there regularities in the origins, growth, and decline of most fads. Penrose (1952), Meyersohn and Katz (1957), and many others have attempted to trace the "natural history of fads." What follows is a composite of these discussions.

Latent Period Meyersohn and Katz (1957) conclude that fads are not born but are rediscovered. That is, fads often involve items that were once commonplace among limited constituencies such as ethnic, regional, or occupational groups, or collectors and hobbyists. For example, one of the most successful novelty items of all time, the hula hoop, started as a bamboo hoop used in gym classes in Australia. A plastic version was introduced into the United States in 1958 by the Wham-O Manufacturing Company, and before the fad subsided a year later, 30 million hula hoops had been sold (Sann, 1967). Many of the moves in break dancing, the urban phenomenon of the 1980s (for example, backspins, swipes, knee spins, and splits), come from a very athletic style of dancing found among southern rural blacks that dates back to the 1930s. If one looks carefully, nearly every fad can be found to have its mundane predecessor.

Breakout Period The latent period ends when the fad item is adopted by groups outside the original constituency. This early diffusion occurs primarily through interpersonal contact, with media playing a secondary role. Diffusion is enhanced when members of the original constituency actively promote the new item. For example, CB radios were originally sold almost exclusively through truck dealerships, at truckstops and service garages, and through specialty catalogues. Once groups other than truckers started to purchase the radios, manufacturers recognized their wider sales potential. By the time the national speed limit was enacted, CB radios were just beginning to be found in department stores.

Early adopters often take their cues from the original users. Motorists who bought CB radios mimicked the truckers' style of using it, often with hilarious results. Coleco took great care to retain the Cabbage Patch Kid ritual established by Xavier Roberts.

In the breakout phase, originators and early adopters are usually ignorant of the extent to which the use of the object has spread. Adoption reaches a point, however, when people cannot help but notice that something is happening. At this point, a statistical fad becomes a real fad (Meyersohn and Katz, 1957).

Peaking Period Fad dynamics are closely connected to the working of the media during the peaking period. It is difficult to imagine a modern fad apart from the media. Indeed, if we consider the descriptions of what could be considered one of the earliest fads, namely, Holland's tulip mania of the 1600s, we find that the media of the day played an important role in its development. Numerous written tracts, the precursor of modern newspapers, condemned the booming tulip trade. While moralists railed against the trade in their tracts, tulip merchants whet their customers' appetites with beautifully illustrated catalogs, pamphlets, and brochures to advertise their wares or the offerings at upcoming bulb auctions. These items, far more numerous and attractive than the moralist tracts, represented one of the first uses of the print media for mass advertising and marketing. Some exceptional catalogs were sought after because of their artistic merit and became the seventeenth-century equivalents of a bestseller (Pavord, 1999:151–55).

The peaking phase begins when the media acknowledge and name the fad. Diffusion then occurs through both interpersonal and media channels. Usually a groundswell of adoption occurs immediately after the fad is given a name and attention by the media.

Later adopters are likely to be more innovative than earlier adopters in their use of the fad item. Later adopters still tried to mimic truckers when using CB radios, for example, but they were less concerned with CB etiquette. Before the CB radio, truckers customarily used Channel 19, and Channel 9 was reserved for emergency use. As more and more motorists acquired radios, Channel 19 became virtually useless for truckers, and Channel 9 was often used for idle chatter. New CB users frequently interrupted or "walked over" the transmissions of serious users. Other kinds of innovations occurred as well. CBs were mounted on all sorts of vehicles, including bicycles and skateboards! Others began to interfere, using nuisance innovations such as "skipping" and illegally powerful radios. Young children transmitted without supervision.

At their peak, fads may produce a large "coattail" effect. This includes writing popular songs about the fad and quick merchandising to capitalize on the fad. Some merchandising, such as counterfeit Cabbage Patch dolls, may be illegal; other merchandising, although legal, may be blatantly opportunistic. Manufacturers rushed poorly designed and cheaply built CB radios and accessories into production. During the Davy Crockett fad of 1955, the coonskin motif was used to sell everything from toy guns to refrigerators.

It is not surprising that as the fad peaks, original users often come to view the fad with contempt. Truckers were infuriated by novice and thoughtless users. The Cabbage Patch fad created a shortage of Poly Doll fabric, which raised the ire of needlecrafters across the land.

Decline Period Some fads fade slowly, while others disappear overnight. Widespread adoption creates the conditions for a fad's decline. A theoretical "saturation point" is reached, beyond which the fad ceases to be a novelty; then, adherence to the fad becomes the mark of the nerd. Knowledge that all fads ultimately die can be a self-fulfilling prophecy, as merchants delay or reduce orders for fad items in anticipation of the fad's passing.

The natural history of fads is such that fads rarely leave substantial traces of their passing. Items that once were eagerly sought are discarded or put away in closets, basements, and garages. If any traces remain, it is because use of the fad item has returned to the original constituencies of the latent phase.

Discussion The natural history of fads describes social phenomena with which we are all familiar. Still, efforts to describe a typical pattern of fad growth and decline have focused on *product fads*. It is somewhat difficult to apply this natural history to *activity fads*, such as goldfish swallowing or streaking, which often have little if any commercial aspects. The natural history of fads fails to explain why fads sometimes remain highly localized events. Many fads occur only within the boundaries of a high school, college campus, or region of the country and fail to catch on elsewhere.

Finally, the natural history of fads suggests that fads are so trivial that they seldom leave traces of their passing. It must be remembered, however, that numerous items that have fundamentally transformed our lives were initially regarded as fads. A small sampling from this list includes automobiles, airplanes, movies, radio, television, and business and home computers. Other fad items remained to enrich our leisure time, including ten-speed bicycles, games such as Monopoly and Scrabble, barbecue grills, Polaroid cameras, and Frisbees.

The natural history of fads emphasizes their trivial nature, and indeed many fads are trivial. On the other hand, fads are also an important component of cultural diffusion. (For more information on the diffusion and adoption of innovation through social networks, see Coleman, Katz, and Menzel, 1957; Snow, Zurcher, and Eckland-Olson, 1980; and Rogers, 1962.) We will now examine fads and fashion from the standpoint of theories of collective behavior.

FADS AND FASHION AS COLLECTIVE BEHAVIOR

Simmel only hinted at the unpredictable, irrational, and wasteful aspects of fads and fashion, focusing instead on their consequences for social integration and differentiation. Others, such as Tarde (1903) and Park and Burgess (1921), reversed this focus and instead described fads and fashion primarily as a form of social pathology. Sapir (1937), for example, identifies fads as something unexpected, irresponsible, or bizarre and socially disapproved. Viewed in this manner, fads and fashion clearly fall within the domain of collective behavior.

Mass Hysteria Theory

According to Herbert Blumer ([1934] 1969), fads are a form of mass hysteria, characterized by collective excitement that attracts and infects spectators and bystanders. As they catch the spirit of the fad, participants lose their self-consciousness and become attentive only to the immediate situation. For Orrin E. Klapp (1972), fads and fashion represent a temporary subordination of individual identity to mass identity. Fads and fashion are not a source of group solidarity, as Simmel suggests, but a pathological loss of self-identity to the group. For Blumer, such mass hysterias as fads are caused by underlying conditions of social unrest, such as economic uncertainty and fear of war. For Klapp, an important underlying cause of fads is boredom with the social relationships found in modern society.

Klapp states that recent fads and fashions are fundamentally different from those of thirty or forty years ago. Fads such as goldfish swallowing barely exceeded the limits of acceptable conduct. Fashions such as designer jeans still function much as Simmel suggested—as a means of communicating status. Recent fads and fashion, however, have left the range of tolerated freedom and threaten the basic norms of society. Fads and fashion no longer communicate status; they threaten to destroy status. Thus, goldfish swallowing gave way to panty raids, which in turn gave way to public nudity in the form of streaking. The CB fad had an "outlaw" character not found in earlier fads. Today's evolutionary by-products of "punk" fashion reflect a level of hostility and decadence heretofore unwitnessed in America.

According to Klapp, fads and, to an extent, fashions serve a safety-valve function for society. They allow people to act on tensions and impulses in a way that leaves the basic social institutions intact. If, however, tensions (including boredom) become extreme, then even safety-valve outbursts can threaten the social structure.

Young people often use fashion to define their independence and, sometimes, their defiance of societal norms. © Nik Wheeler/CORBIS.

The mass hysteria perspective emphasizes the lack of predictability, seeming irrationality, intensity, and infectious nature of fads and fashion, constituting a form of social pathology. Still, even social pathology can serve a hidden positive function for society. Fads and fashion can help release collectively felt tensions while leaving the social structure intact.

Value-Added Theory

According to Neil Smelser, collective episodes of fads and fashion are common instances of the *craze*, or mobilization for action based on a positive wish-fulfillment belief. Such beliefs embody a greatly inflated view of the craze item's worth and blind people to possible alternative and substitute items in their environment. Crazes can occur in the economic sphere of social life and include speculative booms in securities, land, and commodities as well as "get rich quick" schemes such as chain letters (Sann, 1967). In the political sphere, crazes take the form of bandwagons for political candidates and utopian schemes such as the Townsend retirement plan of the 1930s (Sann, 1967).

For Smelser, fads and fashion largely operate in the expressive sphere. They are, as Simmel suggests, a means of expressing differential prestige and status. Fads and fashion, and their status-expressive components, enter into all aspects of social life, including clothes, architecture, vehicles, conversation, and the arts. They can even extend into medical treatment (Penrose, 1952) and psychotherapy (Rosen, 1979).

Fads and fashion are collective episodes caused by the combined effect of a number of societal conditions that Smelser identifies as the value-added components. How these components combine to produce fads and fashion will be the focus of the following discussion.

Structural Conduciveness The most general necessity for fads and fashion is a differentiated social structure in which people are formally free to openly express their economic and social status. This view runs parallel to Simmel's view of fashion in modern social systems. Even in highly differentiated societies, however, people may not be free to use dress to communicate status. Clothing styles may be set by laws (sumptuary legislation) that prohibit the wearing of certain items or the use of certain products by the masses. In regimented societies such as the People's Republic of China, dress may be restricted largely to workers' uniforms. Military dress is severely restricted, and, to a certain degree, school dress codes may limit the spread of fads and fashion.

Fads and fashion are encouraged in societies with marketing systems that can disseminate products rapidly. Research and development is given high priority in economies in which inventions can be rapidly translated into new consumer items. These social systems can also produce less expensive versions of nearly any product. Fashion behavior may be more structured than fad behavior: in the fashion industry leadership is fairly well defined, and a responsive marketing system is geared to a seasonal fashion cycle.

Structural Strain Structural strain may be a more or less permanent feature in an open and differentiated society, taking the form of an ingrained status consciousness that carries over to such things as clothing, autos, and home furnishings. The rapid availability of cheaper copies, as well as institutionalized fashion cycles in these areas, virtually guarantees that such items will lose their uniqueness and exclusiveness.

Strain is heightened by the uncertainty of when to abandon a particular fashion item. The upper classes desert a fashion as soon as it no longer differentiates them from others who have adopted it. For the less affluent, the fashion item represents a relatively larger investment, and they will endure greater stress before abandoning it. Strain also results from the uncertainty of which new item will be adopted in the next fashion cycle.

Generalized Belief Smelser describes this aspect of fads and fashion as a "wish-fulfillment fantasy." Elements of this belief are an implicit part of open and differentiated societies. For example, the get-rich-quick mentality is an established cultural belief that does not have to be created for every speculative outburst. Likewise, the desire to be "in fashion" is a stable attitude shared by most people. These beliefs need only be excited and sharpened by the presence of other conditions. This underlying state of "psychological readiness" explains why fads and fashion are perhaps the most volatile and frequently observed episodes of collective behavior.

Mobilization for Action For Smelser, mobilization for fads and fashion often occurs through preexisting channels. This is most obvious in the case of fashions. Leadership is already established in the form of fashion houses and reputable designers who service a fairly definite and exclusive clientele. In turn, these designers rely on a responsive and widely based system of distribution.

In the case of fads, the media are quick to cover such matters as a source of light filler for the news. Likewise, manufacturers, merchandisers, and retailers are constantly alert for unexpected opportunities to capitalize on collective whims. Beyond this, leadership in fads is largely by example. Public figures can give tremendous impetus to fads.

As a type of hysteria, fad and (to a lesser degree) fashion interaction is characterized by imitation and suggestion. Once leaders have started a fad or fashion, much interaction is among anonymous individuals. Fad and fashion are also characterized by a type of intensity not found in other forms of social behavior. A seemingly irrational and mindless attitude emerges that takes the outward form of abandonment or inattention to other suitable and less expensive alternatives to the current fad or fashion.

Smelser also notes that fads and fashion consist of real and derived phases. For fashion, the real phase consists of the adoption of styles among the upper classes. The derived phase is characterized by a substantial "trickle-down" of the fashion into the lower classes and its abandonment among the upper classes. For fads, the real phase consists of the early adoption of an item, its subsequent labeling as a fad, and the groundswell of adoption that follows immediately thereafter. The derived phase is characterized by innovations on the fad theme and coattail effect, such as the indiscriminate use of the Davy Crockett motif.

Action of Social Control Authorities rarely intervene in fads or fashion. Exceptions occur when laws are violated in the course of the collective episode. For example, the Interstate Commerce Commission (ICC) tried to force trucking companies to remove CB radios when drivers used them to evade enforcement of the speed limit (Klein and Luxenburg-Ingle, 1980a). The FBI arrested counterfeiters of designer jeans and Cabbage Patch dolls. Local police sometimes made attempts to arrest streakers (Evans and Miller, 1975).

Other forms of social control are inherent in fads and fashion. Speculative booms are kept from getting totally out of hand by the inevitable apprehension over grossly inflated prices. Fads decline because of loss of novelty caused by widespread adoption and the exhaustion of opportunities for innovation. Both fads and fashion are held in check by the desertion of leaders. Finally, fashion cycles are regulated by the approach of the new season.

Discussion The value-added approach to collective behavior characterizes fads and fashion as a type of hysterical craze. Smelser restricts fads and fashion to the expressive sphere of social life. Following Simmel, Smelser characterizes them as a means of expressing status and prestige in an open and differentiated society.

Unlike Simmel, Smelser argues that fads and fashion contain elements of hysteria. Fads and, to some degree, fashion are unpredictable in their incidence and content. Both are based on widely held fantasies. Fads and fashion lead people to ignore other immediate opportunities for gratification and gain. Leadership is largely through the mechanism of imitation and interaction among anonymous individuals.

In other respects, the value-added model complements the natural history of fads described earlier. The real phases of mobilization roughly correspond to the latent and break-out stages of fad development. The derived phases of mobilization correspond to the peaking stage. Finally, Smelser's comments about the social control of fads and fashion run parallel with descriptions of the decline of fads.

Emergent-Norm Theory

Turner and Killian (1972) argue that fashion tends to reinforce established status distinctions. Items such as oceangoing yachts, Paris originals, private jets, and Rolls Royces do not trickle down to the less affluent. Less expensive substitutes for these items serve more to mark one as a member of an anxiously aspiring group than to convey higher status. Fads, on the other hand, may establish status and prestige at variance with the conventional scale, because pacesetters of a fad can come from any social stratum. Today's nerd can become tomorrow's champion at skateboarding, dancing, or video games.

Turner and Killian state that most descriptions of fads tend toward overdramatization. Further, fads are equated more closely with the compact crowd than is justified. In the compact crowd, mood and attention are sustained in part because participants have no chance to relax and survey their own behavior. The fad, however, is sustained with constant interruptions, as people attend to their families, jobs, and community.

Fad involvement can be intermeshed with other activities partly because it does not consist of simple, mindless imitation. Recruitment is not through the interaction of anonymous individuals but through interaction nets that already exist in neighborhoods, schools, and workplaces. These nets account for the selective clustering of fad adoption. Social support found in these nets is essential for maintaining the fad and justifying the behavior of the faddist. Likewise, indifference or opposition to a fad is not treated with much toleration. Fads are accompanied by strong informal pressures to participate and penalties for those who resist. The "selective inattention" that is part of fads is not due to contagion that blinds people to other opportunities for amusement or gain. Instead, it results from the normative constraint that operates in all areas of social life.

Fads are characterized by differential involvement. Some participants are firmly committed and actively involved, while others' involvement is short-lived and sporadic. Still others restrict their involvement to spectatorship and kibitzing. Finally, some take an exploitative attitude and attempt to capitalize on fads.

There is a tendency to emphasize the spread of fads among people who are somewhat detached from the stable aspects of society, such as adolescents or those with little education and low incomes. Turner and Killian argue that no abnormal degree of isolation or insecurity is necessary for faddish behavior. People do, however, trivialize the behavior of adolescents and others of low social standing. Thus we often describe clothing styles among teenagers as "fads" while adults adhere to "fashion."

Finally, Turner and Killian suggest that the dynamics of fads also apply to the transmission of important cultural items. They present Penrose's (1952) analysis of the growth and decline of therapies within the practice of medicine. Likewise, the growth of "deviant epidemics" such as anti-Semitism, vandalism, or recreational cocaine use follow many of the same lines as fads. Fads and fashion are one of the ways that social change is brought about.

FADS AND FASHION AS COLLECTIVE ACTION

McPhail has yet to specifically address fads and fashion. Still, many elements of his social behavioral/interactionist (SBI) approach are immediately applicable to issues raised in the previous discussions. Like the emergent norm approach, the SBI approach sets forth a differentiated view of fad behavior. Fads generally involve crowds—from those gathered at a panty raid to shoppers waiting to buy Cabbage Patch Kids—that are preceded by assembling processes. A wide variety of activity occurs in fad crowds, ranging from people stuffing themselves and others into phone booths to idle conversations.

Assembling Behavior

Not all fad activity transpires in gatherings, but when it does, it is preceded by assembling processes. One of the last and largest panty raids at the University of Iowa occurred in late April of 1967. Early in the week a 2:00 A.M. fire alarm had roused about seven hundred male students from their dormitory and sent them into the streets. It was a cold and misty evening, and as the students huddled gloomily, a basketball player shouted, "Panty raid! Panty raid!" About fifteen students left the crowd and headed toward the women's dorms. Campus police stopped the small group, however, and ordered them back to the dorm in a threatening and abusive manner. That morning at breakfast, the dining hall was the scene of heated conversations. Students took the earlier actions of the police as a challenge. If they were going to threaten fifteen pajama-clad guys who were clowning around, the students would show them on Friday night what a *real* panty raid was like.

During the next two days, word-of-mouth assembling instructions were augmented by notes and signs on classroom walls and in dormitory hallways. These signs announced the location of a gathering place from which the raid would be launched. They also announced the time at which the gathering would commence, which, incidentally, was about fifteen minutes after the closing of campus-area taverns and the library.

A crowd of five to six hundred formed at the gathering place and then moved toward the women's dormitories. They were stopped by state police at an intersection about three blocks from the dormitories and near the fraternity row. The crowd at the intersection, as well as chants, cheers, shouts, and the flashing lights on police cars, created a focal point for further assembling. In about twenty minutes, the crowd had grown to nearly five thousand by drawing members from passersby and residents of fraternities and other off-campus residences. Additionally, "messengers" had left the crowd and returned with people from more distant locations. Finally, the police dropped their barricade, and thousands of people dashed toward the dormitories.

The crowd that milled about the dormitories was not composed exclusively of young college males. Many female students were in the crowd, as were teachers, townspeople, reporters, and police. The crowd seemed composed primarily of small groups of people who arrived together and apparently knew one another, rather than of isolated individuals. Chants of "Pants! Pants! Pants!," applause, and numerous loud cheers were raised as undergarments, sheets, pillowcases, sanitary napkins, and trash were thrown from dormitory windows. Most of the items were caught before they hit the ground.

Police kept people away from dormitory doors and off fire escapes. As groups moved from one dormitory to another, many clusters of people engaged in happy conversations. A large portion of people in the crowd simply stood around and watched the spectacle. After about an hour, the crowd began to thin as contingents returned to the men's dormitories or moved off quietly in other directions. The great panty raid of 1967 was over.

Timing of Fads

The timing of fads is not as random or haphazard as some claim. The SBI perspective suggests that fad activities are interspersed with other activities, including those of family living and work. While fad activities do sometimes disrupt or supplant ordinary routines and schedules, on the whole, they usually mesh rather well with these demands. This is because people typically carry out fad activities with family members, roommates, friends, neighbors, and others they know well and with whom they associate on a day-to-day basis. Further, involvement in fad activities peaks during lunch hours, evenings, weekends and at other times when people are likely to have free time. Perhaps this is why many conclude that fads leave no trace of their passing.

Many fads occur on college campuses. Paul Sann (1967) describes an admittedly nonrandom sample of these fads. Of the ones that include dates, descriptions indicate that the fads struck in late May and early June. Nearly all of the streaking incidents occurred during the week of Saturday, March 2, to Saturday, March 9, 1974 (Evans and Miller, 1975). The panty raid described above occurred on a Friday night in late April. As one reflective student put it, "These things occur after midterms, when it's too soon to start booking for finals."

Fad Origins

What about the origins and promotion of fads? The SBI perspective cannot tell us why one item becomes a fad while similar items fail to do so. Of course, other collective behavior perspectives do not tell us this either. The SBI perspective does suggest, however, that fad items are not adopted in a "mindless" way, as is often suggested. In the case of CB radios, hula hoops, pocket calculators, or Frisbees, there may be no nonfad item of immediately comparable use that is ignored. Even novelty items are purchased with hard-earned money and then used intensively with family, roommates, friends, and neighbors. Compared to other recreational costs, fad items may be a "good deal" or at least a comparable value. Finally, fad items frequently provide people with happy and long-remembered experiences.

Is it possible to promote any single product and turn it into a fad? The answer appears to be no. Most product fads are aggressively promoted by an organization keyed to quick and flexible market responses. This explains little, however, because many nonfad items are promoted in the same way. Once an organization has inadvertently produced a fad item, it often tries to come up with another and has little success in doing so. Wham-O seems to have the best track record in this regard, having introduced the hula hoop, Frisbee, and superball. The ability of Wham-O executives seems to be intuitive: they play-tested the hula hoop on children in their own neighborhood and at cocktail parties—a far cry from anything scientific.

While there seems to be no sure-fire formula for producing fad items, sometimes fads reveal or perhaps create new markets for further exploitation. The CB radio certainly helped to increase the electronic sophistication of the American public. People who initially couldn't fathom the workings of even the most elementary electronic devices were soon able to talk confidently about coaxial cables, band widths, amplitude, the finer points of antenna design, and rules of the Federal Communications Commission (FCC).

Many people went into business for themselves by retailing CB radios. Merchants who had sold nothing more sophisticated than toasters broke into the CB market. Electronic specialty shops such as Radio Shack, Allied Electronics, and Pioneer Electronics enjoyed tremendous growth and became household words during the boom. As CB sales faded, these merchants began to stock other electronic items, such as video recorders and business and home computers.

Decline of Fads

It is often argued that fads decline because of "psychological satiation." Fads reach a point of diminishing returns that minimizes the novelty of adoption: people become bored or exhausted, and they regain their senses. Little else seems to explain the decline of activity fads such as panty raids and streaking. For product fads, however, other explanations are possible. The decline in CB sales, for example, can be explained in terms of an obvious decline in utility. That is, at the peak of the fad, novice users, skippers, and walkovers greatly reduced the usefulness of radios for on-the-road communication. Further, by 1978, sunspot activity had reduced the range and clarity of CB transmissions. Many CB units simply wore out after more than a year of intense use. They were not replaced, in part because people were traveling much less than they were in 1976. Inflation and unemployment also cut deeply into the disposable income of the main cohort of recent CB adopters, middle- and low-income blue-collar workers. Clearly, this explanation does not apply to decline in sales and use of novelty items such as hula hoops or deely boppers.

Marketing Schemes and Fads

One evening, Nick was looking through the Star Wars figures at Wal-Mart. He was examining a Han Solo figure, imagining a battle with Darth Vader. An older man intruded on his fantasy and told Nick that this particular Han Solo figure would be a very good purchase, since it would likely increase in value in the next few years. The helpful shopper strongly urged Nick not to unwrap the figure as it would decrease its value as a collector's item. Nick's mom, herself a knowledgeable collector of salt and pepper shakers, was annoyed by these comments since she knew Nick just wanted a toy. Since the mid-1980s children and parents alike have been confused by the blurred distinction between popular toys and bona fide collector's items.

People have collected toys for most of the twentieth century. They began the serious collection of Mattel's Barbie dolls in the 1960s. This activity arose more or less independently of Mattel's marketing efforts. By the 1980s, however, special-edition Barbies were being created specifically for the collectibles market. The Cabbage Patch Kids were the first toys that utilized the collectibles tie-in with their product's premiere. Perhaps this is because the Kids first originated in the crafts market. In any event, Coleco emphasized saving the Kids' birth certificates, tags, and boxes, or not ever taking the doll out of its box, in order to retain its "collector's value." Ty's Beanie Babies have developed the idea of a collectible novelty item to the extreme. Their strategy of limited production runs, limited distribution, and publicized "retirements" of certain Babies is clearly calculated to create and sustain a collectibles market.

The distribution of some toys is also closely coordinated with the release of movies. Perhaps the first instance where this was the case was the release of Star Wars figures shortly after the premiere of the first *Star Wars* movie in 1977. Similar strategies have been used with later movies such as *Alien, Batman, Teenage Mutant*

Ninja Turtles, and *Jurassic Park*. The reprise of the Star Wars figures in 1996 was coordinated with the twentieth anniversary re-release of the movies, and utilized the collectibles marketing strategy. The JC Penny Christmas catalog, for instance, featured the Star Wars line of collectible figures. In 1999, the Star Wars "prequel," *The Phantom Menace*, also featured collectibles tie-ins. Discussions of contemporary novelty product fads need to take into account the schemes used to sell such items. The traditional characterization of a fad as collective behavior included the idea of the spontaneous generation of enthusiasm for a novelty item. Following this characterization, we should give attention to those novelty items that enjoy enormous sales and widespread popularity apart from any extensive, well-planned marketing scheme. Such items are rare.

Fads, Fashion and Violence

Trends in Music We usually associate fads and fashion with the lighter side of social life, but sometimes fads and fashion are perceived as threats to the social order. Early rock and roll, as it emerged in the 1950s, was seen both as a fad and as a threat to the youth of America. Many male rock performers such as Elvis Presley, Jerry Lee Lewis, Chuck Berry and Little Richard were editorially branded as bad influences on youths. Rock and roll music was likewise condemned as too sexual and quickly became associated—fairly or not—with another new social problem, namely, juvenile delinquency. Like the Zoot Suiters of the previous generation, a particular style of dress and grooming became associated with a disorderly lifestyle. Duck-tail or DA hairstyles, black leather jackets, blue jeans, and engineer boots were publicly attacked as delinquent attire.

In the 1960s and 1970s, the long hair and flamboyant costumes of rock stars did nothing to assuage parents' fears about the influence of rock music on their children. The situation was exacerbated by veiled (and sometimes not-so-veiled) references to drugs and sex in the lyrics of the popular music of the time, a trend that continued into the 1980s.

In the 1990s, gangsta rap music, gang colors, and a saggy, baggy look in casual clothing also became closely associated with crime and violence. Misogynistic lyrics shocked audiences with their sometimes openly violent message. West Coast hip-hop music began to take on ominous characteristics in 1986. The short-lived band from L.A.'s Compton district, NWA (Niggaz Wit' Attitude), is usually credited with ushering in hip-hop's gangsta era. NWA was produced and managed by solo rapper Eazy-E, and its members included future gangsta stars Dr. Dre and Ice Cube. Early on, NWA established a particular "gangsta look" by wearing baggy "prison blues," the silver-and-black colors of the bad-boy L.A. Raiders, and unfashionable Jheri-curl hairstyles. Their 1986 album *Straight Outta Compton* went platinum and immediately obtained mainstream attention when the track "Fuck tha Police" was condemned by the 200,000-member national Fraternal Order of Police. Gangsta rap videos brought vivid imagery and explicit lyrics about murder, drugs, misogyny, and other realities of the inner cities into American homes by way of the newly formed MTV cable channel.

True to the image of gangsta rap, performers and producers seemed to be constantly embroiled in street crime. Snoop Doggy Dogg was acquitted of a murder charge. Death Row Records president Dr. Dre served time for assault. Tupac Shakur served eight months of a one- to four-year sentence for first-degree sexual abuse of a female fan and was murdered before he could face his second charge of carrying a concealed weapon. Death Row CEO Marion "Suge" Knight, a 6-foot-4 inch, 315-pound former college defensive lineman, was accused of physically intimidating competitors.

No style of American music has ever touched off such intense controversy as gangsta rap. Gangsta was the central focus of 1994 U.S. Senate hearings into profane music lyrics. Testimony included the concern that these lyrics were patently offensive to most community and family values. Tipper Gore urged that the record industry adopt an age-grading system for lyrics. Eloquent critic C. Delores Tucker, chairwoman of the National Political Congress of Black Women, contended that gangsta music is directly responsible for violence, drug use, and misogynistic actions toward women. Tucker and former education secretary William Bennett led a loose coalition of civil-rights activists and clergy in opposition to gangsta rap. They urged shareholders to sell their stock in any companies that profit from sales of gangsta rap such as Time-Warner and Canada-based Seagram Co.

Gang Colors The Chicago police recognize at least 45 criminal gangs operating within the city. The more notorious gangs include Pachucos, El Rukns, Gangster Disciples, Black P Stone, Latin Kings, and Vice Lords. These gangs operate outside Chicago as well. Other recognized gangs have names like Ashland Vikings, Bishops, Campbell Boys, Harrison Gents, and the Insane Popes. There are also the Latin Eagles, Latin Avers, Latin Saints, Latin Lovers, Souls, and the Maniac Latin Disciples. Each of the 45 gangs have created their own "colors." Items such as crowns, crescents, stars, and pitchforks represent a modern-day heraldic system for urban gangs. Gangs in northern California use the colors red and black and wear caps of the Oakland Raiders, San Francisco 49ers, and the Chicago Bulls. Skinheads popularized the Doc Marten lace work boot, and the Crips wear British Knight athletic shoes. Some gang colors derive from high schools of prominent members (Leet, Rush, and Smith, 1997).

Casual Clothing During the 1980s massive changes in casual fashion began with the introduction of designer-label blue jeans that had been manufactured in low-wage regions of Asia, South America, and the Caribbean. This clothing, however, retailed at correspondingly higher prices than regular blue jeans in stores. At about the same time advances in graphic design technology brought us messages, pictures, and corporate logos associated with sports, leisure and entertainment on our t-shirts, jackets, and sweatshirts. The 1990s brought us designer athletic gear from makers such as Reebok, Nike, and Starter. Starter Corporation designs, licenses, and markets apparel bearing the names, logos and insignia of sport teams and leagues. JC Penney, Wal-Mart, and Kmart began to market their versions of designer wear.

The ethic of individuality became commercialized as all types of casual wear were advertised as a way of expressing one's individual tastes, concerns, and identity to others. The message T-shirt became a way of publicly declaring personal interests and preferences. Wearing the logo of a multinational corporation such as Coca-Cola or Nike on one's shirt, cap, or jacket was advertised as a way of expressing one's individuality. Corporations succeeded in convincing people to actually pay, and pay well, to wear company advertising.

Casual wear intruded into settings previously reserved for formal wear. Baseball caps with team logos and athletic shoes began to be worn with tuxedos at weddings, funerals, and high school proms. The penetration of designer fashion into casual wear, particularly for teens, was problematic. Concern was expressed by parents at the high cost of designer-label clothing and athletic gear compared to their nondesigner equivalents. Teen shoplifting seemed to grow in direct proportion to the availability of designer garments, caps and athletic shoes in malls. Fighting and even murders having to do with the theft or disputes over expensive clothing and shoes were reported.

Many parents and school administrators claimed that there was a clear relationship between the statements being made by wearing casual clothing styles, increases in school discipline problems, and declining academic performance.

School Dress Codes In response to concerns expressed by numerous groups and the results of recent studies and trials, President Clinton did the unprecedented urging of the adoption of uniforms in schools in his 1996 State of the Union address. Shortly thereafter, the *Manual on School Uniforms* was sent out by President Clinton's Secretary of Education to each of the nation's 16,000 public schools. According to the Manual, school uniforms can save money, make schools safer, and give the school an overall neat look. These claims mirrored those of schools throughout the country. Many California schools adopted uniforms or dress codes in 1994. Such dress codes discourage oversized clothing and prohibit shirts or hats which have references to sex, drugs or alcohol. Bare midriffs and shorts are prohibited. In general, the intent is to adopt a school clothing program that will simplify proper dress and ensure a businesslike climate dramatically different from that of the beach or skateboard park.

Dress codes prohibited certain personal clothing statements such as "baggin'" to extreme proportions and "saggin'" so low that pants are "under the crack of the rear end." This style is clearly a form of gang dress. Studies or patterns of gang involvement among Hispanic and black adolescent males indicated that the popular conception of "gang dress," the wearing of saggy, baggy clothing and gang colors, was indeed one of the activities associated with close gang involvement (Curry and Spergel, 1990).

In the 1990s, public schools across the country adopted stricter dress codes or uniforms because of violence and other problems associated with the wearing of gang colors, and pricey, casual costumes. Advocates of these changes claim that uniformity in dress is a great peacemaker and contributes to a better learning environment. President Clinton cited the most publicized school uniform program, that of the Long Beach, California, school district. This district reported a halving of fighting incidents, and substantial decreases in thefts, sex offenses, assaults, and even drug cases during the first year of the program. Other schools in Baltimore, Cincinnati, Dayton, Detroit, Los Angeles, Miami, Memphis, Milwaukee, Nashville, New Orleans, Phoenix, Seattle, and St. Louis have reported the most dramatic reductions in such problems in recent times as a result of adopting uniforms as the school dress code.

While fads and fashion are often a reflection of social silliness, they may also reflect more serious social concerns. Do the lyrics of gangsta rap, as well as some other types of music, incite some people to attack police or commit suicide as critics claim? Do misogynistic lyrics endanger women in our society by weakening the norms against rape and other physical abuse? Can new styles of clothing be used to establish and reinforce social boundaries that result in gang violence and hate crimes? The answers to these questions will become increasingly important in the twenty-first century.

Fads, Fashion and Social Solidarity

As the previous discussion indicates, fads and fashion may be composed of collective action that results in social division and antagonism. On the other hand, some elements of popular culture can also contribute to social solidarity. Sometimes fads can take the form of reviving earlier popular or traditional forms of action. Swing dancing enjoyed a popular revival in the 1990s, and along with it, a revival of dance bands and a style of dancing that requires lessons to learn. In a similar fashion, traditional Irish step dancing has enjoyed a revival, most notably with the very successful tours of the *Riverdance* production. Traditional Irish dancing provided a workable social bond between groups that were otherwise deeply divided and in conflict with each other.

> Something magic happened in *The Point* in Dublin on April 30, 1994, when Michael Flatley and Jean Butler astonished us with the power and the poetry of their hard-shoe dance. To see *Riverdance* was to be part of a remarkable moment of popular culture. Seen live, the moment was simply burned into memory. It was a moment when an audience of 3,000 shot to its feet in ovation as if propelled by an external force. The full-throated roar of acclaim and the thunder of applause physically impacted on the eardrums. The statistics of *Riverdance*'s subsequent commercial impact are not enough to explain the wave of passion released that night. The roar of approval still resonates in the memory. It came from deep, deep down.
>
> —Joseph Meehan (1996)

In the United States, *Riverdance*'s popularity coincided with their national tour and the release of the *Riverdance* video. This event capped what had been a steady growth in interest in Celtic culture in the United States with movies such as *Braveheart*, *Rob Roy*, and *The Crying Game*, and the popularity of new-age singers such as Enya. *Riverdance* inspired numbers of people to learn Irish hard-shoe step dancing. This was particularly the case in Northern Ireland, where the traditional dances had not been practiced to the extent that they were in the Republic of Ireland. Many dancing classes in Northern Ireland were taught by Catholics from the south. The dance came to bond Catholic and Protestant participants by their common heritage and in a common undertaking.

Irish dancing was one feature of the growing peace process instituted to end sectarian violence in 1996. The peace efforts were damaged when a terrorist group, identified only as The Real IRA, set off a bomb in the town center of Omagh, Northern Ireland on August 15, 1998, killing 28 people. The condemnation of this act was immediate and bipartisan. The dancing groups continued to flourish in the aftermath, and the peace process, while damaged, continued to move forward.

SUMMARY

Fads and fashion were among the earliest concerns of sociologists. Simmel and Veblen, for example, saw fads and fashion as a way of communicating status within open and differentiated societies. Others, such as Tarde and Park and Burgess, emphasized the seemingly contagious and irrational nature of fads and fashion. These later views brought fads and fashion into the field of collective behavior.

The mass hysteria perspective emphasizes the irrational and disruptive aspects of fads and fashion. Klapp, for example, argues that modern fads and fashion work more to destroy status distinctions than to reflect them.

The value-added perspective views fads and fashion as a type of hysterical craze. Fashion represents the most nearly institutionalized form of craze behavior. Fads and fashion arise from stresses in the social system, namely, concerns over the expression of status. Both are based on common cultural fantasies: the hope to get rich quick and the desire to be in fashion. Mobilization during outbreaks of fads and the fashion cycle is largely through imitation and interaction among anonymous individuals. Internal mechanisms of social control keep fads and the fashion cycle in check.

The emergent-norm perspective presents a differentiated view of fads and fashion. Fashion functions more to reinforce status distinctions than to allow people to express higher status. Fads allow people to attain a type of status and prestige that is at variance with the conventional scale. The intensity and uniformity of fad behavior are often exaggerated. Differential participation in fads and fashion can range from committed involvement to spectatorship to exploitation. People conform to fads and fashion because of normative constraint rather than contagion and mindless imitation. Fads and fashion can occur in important as well as trivial areas of human endeavor, and they can be an important source of social change.

The collective action perspective also presents a differentiated view of fads and fashion. Fad activity often occurs in temporary gatherings, which form through the same assembling processes as do other prosaic gatherings. Many, if not most, participants in fad crowds are accompanied to the scene by family members, roommates, friends, and neighbors. For those in the crowd, fad-related activity is neither unanimous nor continuous. Participation in fad activity is intermeshed with the demands of routine and previously scheduled activities. Consequently, fad activities peak during lunch hours, in the evening, and on weekends, when people have free time at their disposal.

Fads and fashion are part of the larger political and economic processes. Fads can create and enlarge distribution systems and open potential new markets. The decline of fads is due in part to competing demands. Since the 1980s coordinated marketing schemes have packaged movies, television shows, and novelty items together. Collectibles markets are created for some novelty items when they are introduced to the public.

Global manufacturing of clothing and advances in graphics technology greatly transformed casual clothing in the last quarter of the twentieth century. More so than ever, clothing can be used to communicate status and social standing. The ethic of individuality has been commercialized. Some casual clothing portrays a dangerous or criminal status and has been adopted by juvenile gangs. Casual wear has intruded into settings traditionally reserved for more formal wear, such as the public schools. Dress codes and uniforms have been widely adopted in the 1990s as a response to this trend. Finally, some activity fads, such as Irish dancing, can contribute to social solidarity.

⚔ CHAPTER 8 ⚔

SPORTS

Sports are an important part of social life. The feeling of belonging to a group, which is a fundamental ingredient of social life, is served by sports. People who associate themselves with sports teams, whether as athletes or as fans, gain a feeling of identity that is heightened by rivalry within sports (Figler, 1981:19–24). From pre-school through college, sports programs are an important component of our educational system. Sports are there for the stated purpose of creating and maintaining desirable attitudes and behaviors of fair play, competitiveness, respect for authority, teamwork, self-control, and the drive for achievement.

Virtually all of us have been a spectator to a sporting contest. Millions of Americans participate in sports through teams organized at work or at church. Some of us are officials in state and national sports associations. Some of us work hard to promote obscure sports. Some of us are team managers, cheerleaders, and ushers. Sports play such a large part in the lives of so many people that police spend more time controlling crowds at sporting events than they do at political demonstrations.

SPORTS AS COLLECTIVE BEHAVIOR

Gary Marx (1980) identified problems within social systems, undifferentiated groups, communication processes, group emotion, social influence and interaction, and behavior outside of traditional culture as the six major concerns within the field of collective behavior (see chapter 1). Sports encompass at least three of these traditional concerns.

Spectator violence at sporting events is often used as an example of group emotion. Fighting over the outcome of a game or the possession of a small trophy seems somehow more irrational and hysterical than fighting over more consequential things such as political autonomy, land, or oil.

The chants and cheers of spectators at sporting events are examples of direct, immediate, and highly involving forms of social influence and interaction. While some chants and cheers are traditional, many are improvised on the spot. The crowding of spectators appears to increase chanting and cheering.

The historical development of many sports includes behavior that falls outside traditional culture. Sports often represent novel or innovative behavior that contrasts sharply with the everyday demands of work and family obligations. Sports help bring forth people's potential for self-organization, creativity, and expression. Sports create heroes for neighborhoods, schools, towns, cities, states, and nations.

We will begin this chapter by examining spectator violence, primarily British football (soccer) hooliganism. More is known, perhaps, about British football hooliganism than any other form of spectator violence, because Britain's Football Trust has provided financial support for football-related research since 1982 and in 1987 established the Sir Norman Chester Centre for Football Research, located at Leicester University. Centre scholars have traced the history of football-related disorders from 1863, the year the Football Association was founded in England, to the present day (Dunning, Murphy, and Williams, 1988). Since 1970, researchers have attempted to observe football hooliganism systematically, and recently cross-cultural studies have been carried out (Murphy, Williams, and Dunning, 1990). The Football Trust and the British government have consulted with scholars in efforts to devise strategies and tactics to curb football hooliganism.

SPECTATOR VIOLENCE

In order to understand hooliganism, it is necessary to mention some of the features of British football grounds and football crowds. Most stadiums are located in mixed commercial and residential areas and are immediately surrounded by shops, pubs, and homes. Stadiums are accessible by bus, and many are less than a five-minute walk from train stations. Some stadiums, like those in the United States, have parking lots. Unlike sports facilities in the United States, large numbers of spectators watch British football while standing on inclined sideline and end-zone terraces. Since the 1960s the end-zone terraces predominantly have been occupied by male spectators between the ages of 14 and 25, the people most likely to take part in hooliganism.

British Football Hooliganism

Hooliganism at sporting events is a widespread form of collective behavior, particularly among the English. Within the first weeks of England's 1985 football season, a number of matches had been marred by disorder. At the Sunderland-Chelsea match, for example, Chelsea supporters invaded the playing field (or pitch) in an effort to stop the game. Mounted police were used to clear the pitch. Autos, nearby homes, and businesses were vandalized as crowds departed the grounds.

On April 13, 1985, the Luton-Millwall football match was disrupted by spectator violence. Even though this match was televised and violence was more extensive than at earlier season matches, a number of familiar aspects of football hooliganism were present. Spectator violence was anticipated by both police and fans days before the match. The violence occurred almost exclusively among the "fighting crews" (a largely unwanted contingent of team followers that generally seek out their counterparts accompanying opposing teams) and police, while the majority of fans remained uninvolved. Those who fought used fists, feet, and missiles, but the use of knives or firearms was not reported. Fighting occurred before, during, and after the match, on and off the football grounds. Some of those who fought received injuries, and arrests were made.

Police anticipated problems with hooliganism at the April 13, 1985 match between First Division Luton Town and Third Division Millwall. To begin with, Luton was playing for its first Football Association Cup semifinal in 26 years, and Millwall, with ten straight wins, was making its bid to become the first Third Division club to reach two semi-finals. Further, Millwall supporters also had the longest standing record of violence in the Football League, stretching back to 1900. Earlier in the season, Millwall fans fought on the terrace during the Bristol City game and afterwards damaged pubs and the special fan train that British Rail had scheduled to take them to and from the match. Finally, Millwall was a London team and their fighting crews, the "Bushwhackers" and the "Nutty Turn Out," considered Luton Town to be a bunch of yokels. Young men spoke of the likelihood of *aggro* (violence) as they anticipated Millwall's takeover of a "country boy team and a country boy town."

Large numbers of Millwall supporters departed for Luton Town by rail. Travelers at London's St. Pancras station complained of crowds of as many as 200–300 drunken Millwall supporters behaving in a loutish, hooligan fashion and terrorizing others standing on the platform throughout the morning and early afternoon. As sporadic fighting broke out in the streets and pubs of Luton, it was obvious

A British football hooligan displays "aggro" with skull and crossbones; the lettering on his sign depicts dripping blood. Vandalism, assault, and general mayhem are common among young male spectators at soccer games. © Reuters Newmedia Inc./CORBIS.

that the number of visiting fans would far exceed early police estimates. Also, members of fighting crews from other London clubs such as Chelsea, West Ham and Tottenham Hotspur were reported to be converging on the stadium.

As game time neared, over 8,000 visitors were in, or entering, the Luton grounds. Minutes before kickoff, Millwall fans crashed the gates into the already crowded visitors' sections, and hundreds of Millwall fans ran onto the playing field. Millwall's manager urged fans to return to their allocated areas over the P.A. and then helped police direct people off the pitch. Complaining of the disorder, some people left for home before the game began.

In spite of the pre-game invasion, the game started on time but was stopped after thirteen minutes of play when fighting broke out between members of the overflow Millwall crowd and Luton supporters. Millwall supporters again rushed onto the field. Play resumed 25 minutes later, after police and club officials cleared the pitch and quelled the fighting.

Surprisingly, the game was played to completion, even though there was sporadic fighting in the stands and terraces, objects were thrown at Luton players, and the pitch had to be cleared of fans once again during the second half. As the game neared its finish, it was obvious that losing Millwall was unable to take over the "country boy team" as they had boasted, and winning Luton fans offered up a number of taunting chants to that effect. When the final whistle blew, about 500 Millwall fans charged into the Luton terraces and stands and onto the pitch. Police immediately moved against these people, and the resulting battle lasted for over an hour. The majority of spectators in the stadium, however, remained in their seats—many afraid to leave because of the fighting. Nearly 700 seats were ripped out of the family stands and thrown at police, while nightsticks and dogs were used to move Millwall supporters off the pitch and toward exits. Trash fires were started on the visitors' terrace.

Outside the stadium, waves of Millwall hooligans dodged police lines and ran through the streets, smashing windows of homes, stores, and autos. Some cars were overturned. A few Luton residents were attacked and injured by Millwall supporters. Vandalism and fighting even continued on the train that was returning Millwall supporters to London. In spite of the presence of British Rail police, the interiors of several special soccer coaches were wrecked. Before the evening ended, 31 police and 16 others were injured, 33 were arrested, and over $100,000 in property damage was reported.

The next day, many newspapers devoted more headlines to the Luton-Millwall fighting than to Prime Minister Thatcher's meetings with Soviet Premier Gorbachev (Williams, 1985). For the first time in history, a Prime Minister became directly involved in the problems of football! Prime Minister Thatcher strongly condemned the previous night's hooliganism, demanded "instant action to smash hooliganism," and also demanded a report from the Football Association outlining an "anti-hooligan campaign" within a week.

A number of popular explanations have been offered for violence such as accompanied the Luton-Millwall match. For instance, newspaper editorials have pinpointed both beer consumption and permissiveness as causes of hooliganism. Academics, on the other hand, suggest more complex explanations.

Outlet for Social Strains

One explanation of spectator violence is that rough contact sports such as football and hockey provide an acceptable outlet for personal aggressions that cannot otherwise be expressed in everyday society. The verbal assaults, fighting and riots that accompany many sports contests provide a "safety valve" for the release of social strains that would be expressed in other, more harmful ways, such as political violence.

The mass hysteria and value-added theories of collective behavior strongly suggest that sports are an outlet for individual frustrations and social strains (Klapp, 1972; Smelser, 1962). Both theories state that aggressions and strains that are released through sports are less damaging to the society than if they were discharged by way of protest or revolution. Along similar lines, others characterize spectator violence as essentially a ritualized expression of aggression that only creates an illusion of physical violence and injury (Marsh, 1978). Marsh contends that British football hooliganism involves little serious physical violence and little serious physical injury. Football hooliganism is in keeping with the "rough" character of working-class standards of conduct. This ritualized aggression is preferable to "real" forms of aggression such as political violence. Courts, politicians and police may be more tolerant of spectator violence than of strikes by workers or political protest. Perhaps this is because authorities often define sports riots as "letting off steam" rather than as a threat to their political position.

Jerry M. Lewis (1989) examined newspaper accounts, photos, radio and television reports, and government reports of Belgium's Heysel soccer stadium riot (discussed later in this chapter) to ascertain the sources of social strain that brought about the violence. During this incident, Lewis suspects that social strain may have been created before Liverpool supporters attacked Juventus fans, by insults directed at the English, England, the Queen, and Britain. Such insults would have created strain at the level of societal values: nationalism and patriotism. Lewis was unable to conclude with certainty that this type of social strain was created prior to the outbreak of fighting. It appeared much more likely to Lewis that the fighting was preceded by strain at the normative level. That is, the major source of normative strain was an attack on a young Liverpool fan who, unfortunately, got into the adjoining Juventus section of the terraces. This led a small portion of the Liverpool crowd to take action. Fighting led to surging, which was described as a swirling river of bodies. At this point there were probably relatively few injuries, and there was nothing to dramatically distinguish this event from dozens of other hooligan episodes. Moments later, however, a stadium wall collapsed, dropping hundreds of the surging fans into a terrible pileup in which over 400 people were injured and 39 others killed.

Do the disorders and riots that accompany many sports contests provide a safety valve for the release of social strains that would be expressed in other, more harmful ways, such as political violence? While the theories of Smelser, Marsh and Klapp suggest this is the case, there is a problem with this view: Sports violence may actually reinforce other violent tendencies in a society. The "safety valve" theory does not recognize that disorders and riots that accompany sports contests can be very destructive, and they can escalate into wider political conflict. In short, the "safety valve" theory does not tell us at what level violence and disorder cease functioning as a safety valve and, instead, become a genuine threat to the society.

Spectator Violence as a Cultural Trend

The alternate point of view to the safety valve theory is that spectator violence is a reflection of broader cultural trends and can reinforce other violent tendencies in a society. Sports violence is not a safety valve. Disorders and riots that accompany sports contests can be very destructive, and they can escalate into wider political conflict. Studies undertaken by Eric Dunning, John Williams, and Patrick Murphy of The Sir Norman Chester Football Research Centre support this latter point of view. They suggest that football hooliganism is deeply rooted, widespread, and contains real as well as ritualized violence (Dunning, et al., 1988). Hooliganism poses an economic threat to the game in many countries. The costs of controlling sports violence is a major part of police budgets.

Spectator violence at football-like games has been documented as early as the fourteenth century, when a number of Royal edicts banned the game. The term "hooligan" was coined in the nineteenth century to describe criminal and disorderly people, including those attending football matches. It is also clear, however, that in England there was a marked decrease in spectator disorders from 1920 until the early 1950s (Dunning, Murphy and Williams, 1986). There is some factual basis, therefore, for claims that these were "the good old days" of British football against which today's problems compare so unfavorably.

The mid-1950s saw an increase in spectator disorders at football matches. Media attention to these events increased when England was selected as the host country for the 1966 World Cup Finals. In fact, as the Finals approached, officials voiced nearly as much concern about what would happen on the terraces as they did about what would happen on the field. Preoccupation with the possibility of disorder, and the accompanying publicity and glamour of the World Cup aimed at the youth market, unintentionally established the soccer fields of Great Britain as a focal point for the disorderliness present in their young, "rough," lower-working-class male subcultures (Dunning, et al., 1988).

The mid-1960s saw ad hoc match-day alliances being formed between groups of young men drawn largely from local working-class housing estates and suburbs. These supporters staked out the goal-end terraces of football grounds as their territory and managed to exclude from them, much more successfully than before, older spectators and rival fans. The development of these "youth ends" and their role in defending local masculine reputations and territories helped to produce a national network of gang rivalries focussed on football. For the young men involved in these groups, their own performance in overcoming or intimidating rival "firms" (or crews) began to become more important than the performance of the players they had come to watch. Today, most serious confrontations between rival fans no longer occur over territories inside grounds. Instead, rival groups sometimes try to meet outside before or, more often, after matches. In 1991–1992, around 5,000 arrests were made at league football matches, an average of 2.4 per match.

During the 1980s police and football clubs responded to hooliganism by using more police at games, routinely detailing between 75 and 250 officers at Premier League matches. Police escorted visiting supporters to and from their transport, and then out of town. Stewards and private security firms were more recently employed to reduce the numbers of police needed inside club grounds. In the early 1980s police began to search fans entering the terraces for missiles and weapons, while some clubs banned known troublemakers from all games. Luton banned visiting supporters from games in 1986–1987, with a drastic decline in attendance and revenues. This experiment was halted the following year. These measures have minimized fighting on the terraces but are costly and interfere with orderly spectators' enjoyment of the game.

Police control also displaces fighting from the terraces into the stands and onto the streets outside the stadiums (Dunning, et al., 1986). During the 1980s hooliganism included invasion and damage of stands, battles between opposing fans near train stations and bus parking areas, and the vandalism of homes, businesses, and autos near football stadiums. Wider controls probably encouraged the formation of "fighting crews" in recent years. The most cohesive—and combative—of these crews include West Ham's "Inter City Firm," Chelsea's "Headhunters," Manchester United's "Red Army, " and Leicester's "Baby Squad." These fighting crews have a more or less active core of members who share a combination of team, neighborhood, family, and ethnic loyalties. On match days the crew's reputation is on the line: prestige is to be gained by intimidating other groups and "making them run," as well as hand-to-hand fighting.

The English were the most obnoxious and unwelcome fans present during Spain's 1982 World Cup, at least according to the world's press (Williams, et al., 1984). Other European countries began to call their own football-related disorders "hooliganism" and "the English disease," particularly once their young fans began to mimic the notorious fighting crews (Williams, 1986).

In 1985 British teams were banned from European competition. Altogether, 1985 was a very bad year for British football. After the Luton-Millwall fighting, government, police and the Football Association feverishly debated the hooligan problem and possible solutions. The Millwall club was fined £7,500 (about $11,000 U.S.), and Luton was ordered to install fences between the stands and the pitch. If any hopes were raised that such measures were sufficient to end hooliganism, they were dashed by the events of the next few weeks.

On Saturday, May 11, police battled spectators at the Birmingham City-Leeds United match. Police were bombarded with bricks, rocks, and roof tiles torn from a refreshment stand during the game. As the match ended, hundreds of Leeds fans ran onto the pitch from the terraces. In the battle to clear the pitch, police used a baton charge to push people toward the exits. Near one exit, a person was killed and 236 others were injured when a brick wall toppled as hundreds of people were pressed against it.

While police and spectators clashed at Birmingham, 56 people died in a fire at the Bradford City football grounds. The fire started in trash that had accumulated under the grandstand. The old wood structure was completely enveloped in flames within four minutes. First newspaper reports stated the trash was ignited by a smoke bomb tossed by a hooligan. The committee of inquiry, however, later dismissed this as a cause of the tragedy (Popplewell, 1985:5). Nonetheless, the Bradford fire was seen generally as harming British society and harming the game of football. A sense of profound national crisis descended on England (Lewis and Veneman, 1987).

Stories of death and injuries at Bradford and Birmingham were still to be found in the British papers when, eleven days later, the world was shown dramatic television pictures of death and suffering at Heysel Stadium, Brussels, Belgium. Fighting had broken out between spectators at the Liverpool Soccer Club and Italy's

Turin-Juventus match. Spectators attempting to distance themselves from the fighting between English and Italian fans, or to leave Heysel Stadium altogether, were crushed against a stadium wall. In a haunting repeat of the Birmingham City tragedy, the wall collapsed, 39 people died, and nearly 400 people were injured.

Whether or not Liverpool fans provoked the Heysel fighting, they clearly received most of the blame for doing so. Television sequences of the rampaging Liverpool fans, movingly interwoven with pictures of the dying and the injured, were broadcast worldwide. Interviews with a few callous Liverpool supporters returning from Brussels were also aired. These fans expressed anger at police, football officials and Italian fans, but very little sympathy for the casualties. Sharp and immediate condemnation was directed toward Liverpool fans in the world's popular press. Within days, the Union of European Football Associations (UEFA) banned all English club teams from continental play for an indefinite period.

The Prime Minister's war on hooliganism intensified after Heysel. A number of new football-related offenses and alcohol restrictions were specified in the Public Order Act of 1986. To enforce the new laws, police expanded their use of video surveillance of football crowds. Undercover police officers infiltrated hooligan "gangs" in order to secure evidence against their leaders. In addition to these measures, financially strapped football clubs came under considerable pressure to implement costly, computerized membership plans.

The European ban of English teams was not completely lifted until the spring of 1989. With tragic irony, on April 15, 1989, a few weeks after English teams were given full status, 95 people died in a crush at Hillsborough grounds. In the early moments of the quarter-final match between Liverpool and Nottingham Forest, Liverpool fans surged against the hooligan fencing that was put in place shortly after Heysel. Later, the official inquiry (Lord Chief Justice Taylor Report) condemned the fencing, but by then virtually all hooligan fencing had been voluntarily removed from grounds across England. Lord Chief Justice Taylor proposed the elimination of terraces and to make England's major football grounds "seating only" facilities. Following Hillsborough, the 1989 Football Spectators Act was passed, providing restrictions on the carriage and consumption of alcohol at football grounds, and also the banning of football offenders from matches. The Act provides penalties for racist abuse and missile throwing and makes trespass onto the playing area illegal. Finally, the Act is used to prevent hooligan offenders from travelling abroad to watch English matches. Offenders have to report to special locations in England when matches are being played abroad.

During the 1990s many football grounds, with the help of ground improvement grants, were refurbished and converted to "seating only" facilities, eliminating the terraces accommodations. Various "members only" plans were implemented, and efforts were made to encourage family attendance at matches. In 1998, Rupert Murdoch and Sky Television made a $1 billion offer to buy England's largest football club, Manchester United. The resulting clamor (involving Murdoch, Sky Television, the Office of Fair Trading, the Monopolies and Mergers Commission, and the Secretary of State for Trade and Industry) destroyed any remaining illusions that football was still a community-based sport. Hooliganism, however, persisted and attained levels not seen since the 1980s. The media gave extensive attention to English hooligans during major football-related disorders during the 1998 World Cup, hosted by France and drawing record attendance. The Brits did, indeed, distinguish themselves among the hooligans from several countries. Their activities prompted many to urge that U.K. Prime Minister Blair pull England out of the competition, and the hooliganism clearly endangered the British Football Association's campaign to get the Fédération Internationale de Football Association (FIFA) to select England as the site for the 2006 World Cup (Palmer, 1998).

The research of Dunning, Murphy, and Williams has led them to the conclusion that football hooliganism is a social phenomenon deeply rooted in British society. They point out that there has never been a period in the history of modern soccer when spectator disorderliness has been entirely absent from Britain. Since the 1970s, football hooliganism has become an established part of "aggressive masculinity" that is a primary working-class social characteristic. Aggressive masculinity carries with it a sense of territorial identification and proprietorship that extends to the "home end" terraces and the surrounding streets.

THE QUEST FOR EXCITEMENT VS. THE CIVILIZATION PROCESS

Elias and Dunning (1986) place sports in a central position in their analysis of how societies operate. They contend that two major forces operate within society: the quest for excitement and a counterforce, the civilization process. Like George Herbert Mead's work, Elias and Dunning's "quest for excitement" is based on the assumption that humans are continuously active. Humans thrive on spontaneity, physical movement, and activities that give full play to the senses. Humans create and seek out pleasurable excitement. Play, games, and sports represent a significant portion of pleasurable excitement in society. Some aspects of conflict and battle also generate pleasurable excitement. Some sports, such as games of football, represent mock battles.

The essential aim of the civilization process, on the other hand, is the control of pleasurable excitement. Pleasurable excitement must be channeled into ends dictated by the family, the community, the workplace, or the state. While the civilization process affects all aspects of human social behavior, it is not monolithic. Not all areas of social behavior are civilized at the same rate. The civilization process does not uniformly impact on all groups within society. Further, the civilization process is not irreversible; de-civilization processes can occur.

For sports, the civilization process represents a continuous pressure to accommodate sports to the more ordered parts of society. This pressure is manifest in such things as rule standardization and record keeping. The process also engenders a sharp distinction between player and spectator as the spectator's role degenerates into a passive, vicarious enjoyment of the game. Media such as radio and television further separate the spectator from the action.

Sports are often co-opted by authorities to enhance their own popularity and power. A central theme of participation in the Nazi party of Germany during the 1930s, for example, was preparation for the annual Nuremberg games. Today, the governments of the world directly or indirectly sponsor "national teams" and compete for world prominence in nearly every organized sport. This, in turn, represents an enormous subsidy to the manufacturers of athletic equipment, alcoholic beverages, breakfast cereals and sports media.

Present-day hooliganism in Britain represents territoriality and aggressive masculinity. It is also costly and threatens the welfare of the game. Viewed in a broader context, however, hooliganism, and spectator disorderliness in general, represents a failure of the civilization process to completely control the quest for excitement. Spectator disorderliness can also be viewed as an effort of people to force themselves back into a more active, enjoyable, and exciting role in "the game."

Extreme Sports and the Quest for Excitement

During the summer of 1998, ESPN broadcast the X-Games from San Diego. The concept of the X-Games production was to get younger viewers to tune into the ESPN network. The show featured competition in a number of the alternative, extreme sports (or Xtreme sports) that have proliferated since the mid-1980s. The X-Games featured competition in eight Xtreme sports. There were competitions in street, half-pipe (a long, semicircular ramp on which the cyclists, skaters or skateboarders perform aerial tricks), downhill skateboarding, in-line skating, and bicycle stunt riding. Sport climbing, in which contestants ascend walls and other obstacles, was also featured. Competitions in the two- and four-person street luge were held. The X-Games also included sky surfing, in which sky divers perform aerial tricks on a snowboard while free falling from a height of 10,000 feet. Finally, competitions in barefoot water-ski jumping and wakeboarding, in which contestants kneel on boards and are towed by boats while performing jumps and spins along the course, were televised. Many of these activities were considered to be "junk sports" or were unknown even a decade earlier.

Xtreme sports is a term applied to a wide variety of activities, many of which would not be considered sports in the traditional sense. The X-Games did not include other Xtreme sports such as bungee jumping, hang gliding, parachuting, white-water rafting, mountain biking or jet-ski racing.

The 1998 Winter Olympics were held in Nagano, Japan and were broadcast worldwide by ESPN. Snowboarding, free-style skiing, and short-track speed skating were added to the traditional winter sports in an effort to increase interest in the games, particularly for American and Canadian audiences. American and Canadian teams were expected to do better in these Xtreme sports than European teams who usually dominated traditional winter sports.

The visibility and popularity of Xtreme sports has resulted from processes quite unlike those involving traditional sports such as football or baseball. Traditional sports evolved from folk games that, over many decades, acquired formalized rules, referees, and play associations. These established sports then acquired professional players, team owners, and finally, highly marketable media and trademark rights (Dunning and Sheard, 1979). Xtreme sports, on the other hand, do not have their roots in folk games, nor are they to be found in high school athletic programs. Instead, Xtreme sports have been introduced to the general public in a very short period of time, by way of cable television, carefully planned media campaigns such as the X-Games, and corporate marketing schemes. Xtreme sports have been, from the outset, professional activities—that is, the first skateboarders, in-line skaters, and trick bicyclists to attain any popularity were people who were paid to exhibit both their skills and their sponsors' products. For the most part, Xtreme sports are not team sports but are sports for individual competitors or exhibitors.

Xtreme sports are extremely oriented to an adolescent audience and style of consumption. Half-pipe sports in particular have teenaged professional champi-

Extreme sports such as snowboarding, sky surfing and in-line skating are popular with younger enthusiasts, and many of these events have been added to traditional winter sports as Olympic events.

ons. One would hardly conclude that the Super Bowl is a way to sell football helmets or that the NBA playoffs are designed to sell basketballs. In contrast, Xtreme sports are used to directly market equipment like skateboards, snowboards, trick bicycles, in-line skates, and all the accompanying helmets, clothing, and other accessories. While watching and participating in Xtreme sports can be part of a "quest for excitement," these new sports are also part of a "quest for money."

Professional Wrestling: A Most Unique Category of Sport

Local Saturday-night wrestling shows were one of the most popular items during the early days of television. By the mid-1960s, however, wrestling had all but disappeared from television, being replaced by network programming. Wrestling made a sudden and unexpected comeback in the mid-1980s when cable television expanded to more than a hundred the number of channels previously available, channels that required programming—any type of programming—to fill them. Professional wrestling fit the primary need of cable television: it was comparatively cheap to produce in large volumes of air-time. A single evening's exhibition of matches could be cut, spliced and edited to produce several television shows. Professional wrestling could also be merchandised in the form of videotapes, action figures, clothing and magazines. When pay-per-view television was introduced in the 1990s, it allowed large wrestling "championship" galas to be produced, enjoyed, and afterward marketed on videotape. The resurgence of professional wrestling, so closely tied to cable television production, led many to question whether it was a professional sport. Surprisingly, doubters included Vince McMahon, Jr., the leading promoter of professional wrestling, who concluded in an interview on the ABC television news magazine *20/20* that professional wrestling was perhaps not a legitimate sport but that ". . . professional wrestling and the World Wrestling Federation is a most unique category" (Maguire and Wozniak, 1987:262).

Maguire and Wozniak (1987) suggested that "there is . . . ample support for thinking of professional wrestling as something other than, or something in addition to, sport. Usually this something is defined as theater, drama, or, in more current terms, media production" (1987:263). During the 1980s, professional wrestling differed tremendously from mainstream professional sports through the obtrusive use of racial and ethnic stereotypes. Maguire and Wozniak examined content analysis data of World Wrestling Federation broadcasts and wrestling magazines over a 12-month period (June 1984–June 1985). They concluded that the open and unfettered use of racial and ethnic stereotypes clearly set professional wresting apart from professional sports and also contributed to the appeal of these media productions. The free and open use of these stereotypes was more akin to what was seen on "trash television and radio" than what was seen in mainstream, professional sports where broadcasting such stereotypes was anathema. In a sense, professional wrestling represented a special venue for the free and open display of racial and ethnic stereotypes. Profession wrestling media productions appeared to be immune from the inquiries and objections that occurred in mainstream media where racial and ethnic stereotyping was systematically and actively discouraged. (Maguire and Wozniak, 1987:263).

The Strange World of Professional Wrestling

In the last decade the world of professional wrestling has changed dramatically. Whereas the WWF used to attract fans by promoting sharp contrasts of good and evil and highlighting time-worn racial and ethnic stereotypes, today's success formula is much different. Five factors help explain the current popularity of the two dominating alliances, the WWF and the WCW (World Championship Wrestling). First, professional wrestling has become more spectacular than conventional sports entertainment. In what other sport can viewers see a competitor throw a lightning bolt and set a man on fire? This has happened in professional wrestling and makes the exploits of athletic heroes such as Mark McGwire or Tim Duncan look tame by comparison. Second, in an era when most sports and television programming generally look to curb violence, pro wrestling celebrates it. Violence sells! Third, professional wrestlers have not gone on strike or left one city for another as have many other big-time professional athletes. Accordingly, professional wrestling fans are perhaps more loyal than fans in other sports. Fourth, today's wrestling star fits neither a "good guy" nor "bad guy" profile, but reflects both qualities. This may resonate well with the widespread contemporary view that humans (even heroes) are a mix of good and evil. Lastly, the WWF and WCW have used state-of-the-art special effects (e.g., pyrotechnics) to attract and hold fan interest.

Contributed by Brendan Maguire
and John Wozniak

Maguire and Wozniak used insights from cultural anthropology, phenomenological and Marxist sociology, and the psychoanalytic tradition to explain why these stereotypes were so marketable. Professional wrestling represented an area within cable television where a much more open and free expression of racial and ethnic stereotypes was tolerated. The 1990s have seen a trend away from such stereotypes and toward the theatrical display of violence. As was earlier the case with racial and ethnic stereotypes, the current displays of violence clearly seem to surpass what is tolerated elsewhere.

SPORTS AS COLLECTIVE ACTION: AMERICAN GRIDIRON FOOTBALL

Clark McPhail provides us with the most extensive database of collective action research available. His work spans three decades and has relied on a developing methodology to systematically observe and record collective action in public gatherings (see chapter 3). For a number of years, McPhail has observed spectator behaviors at home football games at the University of Illinois at Urbana-Champaign (UIUC). His observations inside the stadium reveal that football games represent a complex tradition of differentiated and purposive collective action (McPhail, 2000).

From the standpoint of perception control theory, the individual human being is a closed-loop, negative-feedback control system. (See Appendix.) Purposive collective action occurs when two or more people adjust their ongoing actions to make their current perceptions correspond to similar or related images in their minds. In terms of a UIUC Saturday football game, this means that people adjust their ongoing actions with respect to their images of familiar and traditional actions such as cheering, singing, and applauding. More complex actions include football plays, the halftime show, or card stunts. Most people come to the games with images of these activities already in their minds, because they have previously engaged in these actions or discussed, rehearsed, practiced, or seen others engage in these activities. These similar or related images are sometimes retrieved independently by individuals, as in cheering, applauding, or booing. Sometimes these images are retrieved interdependently through interaction with companions. Often, these images are provided by third parties such as quarterbacks, coaches, band conductors, stunt directors, or the public address announcer.

Collective Action and The Football Team

A Saturday afternoon's Big 10 football game is the result not only of the efforts of the players but of the coordinated actions of the coaching staff, physical trainers, and the equipment team. Also, a team of officials (referee, umpire, head linesman, line judge, chain crew and others) collectively monitors the play and coordinates the play on the field with regard to the established rules. The stadium in which the game is played must be maintained and prepared for each game by teams of grounds and maintenance workers. During the game the public order team, ticket sellers, ushers, and food and souvenir vendors are at work. The press box contains hundreds of people, including the director and staff of the university sports information service, coaches, journalists, technicians, security, and food service workers. The coordinated actions of many teams are required to produce a

Saturday Big 10 football game. How does this coordination come about?

As previously mentioned, perception control theory views each person as a closed-loop, negative-feedback control system. Since we do not have the capacity to read one another's minds, the interaction and conversation between two or more people is not and cannot be a closed loop, regardless of the frequency, intimacy or history of their interaction. However, because we can see and hear one another, describe things and activities to one another, and repeat, rehearse, and practice activities, people can collectively *approximate* a closed, negative-feedback loop. That is, through communication and practice they can engage in highly complex forms of collective action. It is also within the venue of a college football game that we find some of the most complex and elaborate collective action ever recorded. A series of successful football plays and the halftime field show far surpass in complexity and precision any collective action observed within demonstration gatherings.

McPhail (2000) provides descriptions of how the football team and coaching staff interact in the effort to "close the loop" and produce complex and successful plays and game plans. In order to develop simple or complex plays, a play is diagrammed and described in excruciating detail by coaches. Both players and coaches watch videos and film that show how the play is "supposed" to work. Finally the play is rehearsed at practice. The play is repeated over and over, and McPhail stresses how repetition is essential in developing complex collective action.

A football game is composed of a repertoire of offensive and defensive plays and special team plays. Coaches who have observed their own teams at practice as well as videos of the next opposing team devise game plans for the upcoming contest. Game plans include projections and approximations of what the other team may do. Regardless of the amount of repetitions during practice, there are always unanticipated consequences during a game. Each team is likely to introduce variations that are calculated to offset its opponent's strongest offensive or defensive formations and plays. Opposing team plays as well as weather, injuries, fumbles, decisions by officials, interceptions, and misdirection introduce resistance and disturbances, thereby necessitating compensating adjustments in the actions of players and coaches. McPhail points out that third parties—the coaches in the press box who have an overall view of the field and access to instant video replays—identify the corrections that must be made to accomplish the objectives of scoring points or stopping opposing plays. These corrections are communicated by closed-circuit telephone to the head coach on the sidelines.

Collective Action by the Band

The 260-member Marching Illini Band is one of the most highly regarded college bands in the world. Their pre-game and halftime shows represent elaborate examples of collective action, including the marching band itself, thirty-seven flag team members, a team of twenty-eight precision dancers, two baton twirlers, and three drum majors.

The complexity of the pre-game and halftime shows far surpasses the complexity of any single play carried out by the football team. The shows include the band playing a number of songs from stationary and moving formations. Coordinated marching by the band is used to create formations of rows, columns, parallel arcs, rectangles, circles, pentagons and five-pointed stars as well as formations that spell out block letters. The flag team and precision dance team carry out simultaneous collective actions coordinated with those of the band.

McPhail (2000) describes the "closing of the loop" that results in performance of these complex shows. Purposive collective action occurs when two or more people adjust their ongoing actions to make their current perceptions correspond to similar or related images in their minds. Individual members of the band, flag team and precision dance team arrive at the Illini Marching Band camp ten days before the start of fall semester. The majority of these individuals have already participated in the previous season's band or teams. New members bring with them extensive experience in excellent high school marching bands. All can sight read musical scores and share a large vocabulary of musical and marching terminology, as well as several years of similar experiences.

The band director provides each band member with a handbook, *The System: A Marching Band Guide for the University of Illinois Marching Illini*. This handbook provides a standard drill vocabulary including verbal commands (and other signals) for stationary and parade movement, postures and different marching steps, as well as the fundamental march commands. Fundamental to the handbook is a textual and graphic notation system that will be used to design, teach, rehearse, and refine marching drills. The notation system is keyed to the football field's grid system and details the spacing of individuals to create the arcs, blocks, and line formations used in the shows. The handbook is a set of common instructions provided to people by a third party, the band director.

While people cannot read one another's thoughts, they can be instructed to create particular mental images in their minds. The director wishes the band to produce "a dark, full, and loud symphonic sound." McPhail describes how the director and section leaders work to impart this sound to the band. Producing the Illini sound requires that each musician have a "mental concept" of the sound and also repeated and frequent exposure to the quality of sound the band is trying to produce. Section leaders provide reference sounds that the members hum in order to produce the mental concept of the pitch. Members then tune their instruments to closely approximate the reference pitch that is in their minds. This procedure is repeated prior to each performance.

McPhail also describes how the band puts together their field shows. Field shows are choreographed by way of computer-generated instructions for each section of the band (see chapter 3). These instructions detail the kind, rate, and direction of movement. All movements are keyed to a shared reference signal, the ever-audible cadence beat provided by the percussion section. Components of the field show are described, walked through, and then repeatedly practiced at the summer camp. Drill, practice, and rehearsals continue daily during fall semester. A final rehearsal is held on Saturday morning before the game. During rehearsals and performances individual members of the band cannot hear all the sounds or see all the movements of the other band members. Overhead observers on portable towers and the press box monitor the sounds and movements of the band members and compare them to reference images. These overhead observers then provide instructions for the correction and adjustment of individual or collective action. The observers may also instruct band members when "That's perfect! That is the way to do it!"

McPhail notes that the musical and marching actions that band members fit together into collective actions (pre-game and halftime shows) concede nothing in complexity to those of the football teams. These are extremely complex sequences of sounds on musical instruments that have required years of instruction and practice to master, not to mention the intellectual and physical skills required to learn and execute the complex and complementary manipulation and locomotion actions that constitute marching drills. There are probably more incomplete passes, broken plays and fumbles in a football team than mistakes in the pre-game and halftime shows. The band, however, neither plays nor marches against opposition and the disturbances that opposition introduces (McPhail, 2000).

Collective Action by the Student Card Stunt Section

Several large universities throughout the United States have card stunt sections in their stadiums, where individuals are given sets of printed instructions for the manipulation of square sheets of cardboard or plastic with contrasting colors on each side. Since 1969, when the first computer-designed stunts and computer-prepared instructions were introduced, the number and complexity of card stunts has increased.

McPhail (2000) provides a history of card stunts in the United States. Card stunts appear to be a University of Illinois invention. In 1910, during a game against the University of Chicago, undergraduate males wearing orange caps sat together and arranged themselves so that the orange caps formed the block letter "I." This was an occasional practice, and after the First World War, students wore orange hats and bibs. The first card stunt occurred in 1927 as an addition to the repertoire of the 900-member cheering section. Card stunts were not used from 1939 until they were reintroduced in 1946. By that time other schools used card stunts, and in 1947 the student chairperson of the stunt section introduced a more elaborate stunt system developed at the University of Southern California. The present Block-I is a section of 1,022 seats on the east side of the stadium. The design, preparations for and coordination of the Block-I stunts are the responsibilities of a student committee known as the Blockheads (McPhail, 2000).

Tickets for the Block I area are reserved for students who want to participate in the Block I activities. Season tickets are sold to students who sign a Block I contract that lists home game attendance requirements, arrival times, and code of conduct. Students also receive an instruction pamphlet with graphics illustrating how to hold and manipulate cards. There is only one rehearsal session before the first game. Instructions for specific card stunts are distributed to Block I members a few minutes before the beginning of the halftime show. The instructions list card colors and manipulations for the numbered stunts. The stunt director and section leaders communicate with closed circuit telephone and depend upon "third-party" monitors who provide feedback instructions for adjustment.

Collective Action by Fans

McPhail's systematic analysis of film and videotape records of fans collectively cheering the successes and lamenting the failures of their team shows that they are able to do so almost instantaneously, simultaneously, and without prior consultation with their companions or prodding by their cheerleaders (McPhail, 2000). On the other hand, even among groups of ardent supporters, there is no continuous and mutually inclusive collective action, let alone continuous attention to the game. The behavior of fans includes collective purposive actions regarding the game, their team, a team member, the band, cheerleaders, and officials. The behavior of fans also includes purposive individual actions such as stretching, yawning, buying and eating refreshments, or reading the program. The behavior of fans fluctuates between collective and individual action.

Webster's Ninth New Collegiate Dictionary defines a fan as an enthusiastic devotee of a sport or performing art, usually a spectator. McPhail generally uses the term "partisan" rather than "fan" to refer to the majority of onlookers to sports contests. While the term "partisan" does connote enthusiasm for a sport and team, McPhail introduces the terminology to help emphasize that there is wide variation among onlookers at sports contests. Some onlookers, such as security personnel, vendors, or technicians, may or may not be fans of the sport and team. Those who may be classified as partisan to the outcome of the game include the members of each team who are not on the field as the game proceeds. These partisan onlookers include the first team defensive or offensive players, special team players, and the reserves. On the sidelines are also coaches, trainers, and student managers who have a preference in the outcome of the game and cheer the gains and lament the losses during the course of the game.

Partisan spectators are the people who attend all the home games and travel to away games or follow the away games on radio and television. These are the people who attend pep rallies and greet the home team when they return from road trips. This group includes students, faculty, and staff members of the school as well as the local community and area residents who identify themselves as fans of the team and band. A surprisingly large portion of these partisan spectators is made up of the family members, friends and acquaintances of the football players and members of the marching band.

The majority of individuals who attend football games do so in the company of a family member, friend, or acquaintance. These small companion groups assemble together, remain together through most of the gathering, and then leave together at the end of the game. McPhail notes that it is a mistake to conclude that because any one member of these companion clusters is a fan of the game or team that all the other members are fans as well. Some members attend because they would rather be with their companions than be left at home, because they find the spectacle of the game interesting, or they want to watch the band. These people are likely to join in cheering the successes of the team but are less likely to lament the failures. These people may not perceive or appreciate the individual or collective athletic skills displayed on the field. They may, however, greatly appreciate the halftime show.

McPhail distinguishes between collective vocalization—oohs, aahs, yays, moans, and laughter—and collective verbalization—singing and chanting—that occur within gatherings. In sports gatherings, we see tremendous variation in these phenomena. In U.S. sports, we hear more collective vocalization, oohs, aahs, yays, boos and shouting than we do collective singing and chanting. At British football matches, however, collective singing and chanting is much more evident than just yelling. Willam J. Fellows (1985) states that some of today's British football songs have been sung since the 1890s. He also points out that it is not uncommon to hear over a hundred songs, and nearly twice as many cheers and chants, during a game.

In the United States, National Football League games played in enclosed stadiums have been delayed by sustained shouting. Home team supporters yell so that the visiting center and wide receivers cannot hear the quarterback's signals. This interference can create offsides and jumbled plays. The 1989 "noise rule" created a yardage penalty against the home team if spectator noise is judged to be excessive. When the Detroit Lions were given penalties in their Silverdome, however, many observers contended that most of the noise came from the visiting Chicago Bears fans. The noise rule has proven to be an unsatisfactory solution to the noise problem.

In Great Britain, singing and chanting is a traditional part of football. Over the last thirty years, hooligan singing and chanting has become a more obvious part of this repertoire. Hooligan songs differ from other traditional football songs in that they are generally abusive, sadistic, or crude. The Portsmouth Song is reported by Fellows (1985) as being sung on the Fratton Park terraces by the Portsmouth supporters. Versions of this abusive song, always depicting opponents as slum dwellers who search their garbage cans (dustbins) for food, are sung across Britain. Sadistic songs, such as the Chelsea and Everton songs, threaten or describe violent attacks.

Game announcers and broadcast technicians keep the worst of the songs and cheers from being heard over the air. In the United States, dirty songs and chants are seldom a problem. Rarely do we hear of an event such as occurred in 1985, when Tigers president Jim Campbell closed the 10,000-seat capacity bleachers at Tiger Stadium for a month because of profane chanting. The "Bleacher Creatures" began a few weeks earlier to chant a popular Miller Lite beer commercial. One side of the Creatures would stand and yell, "Less filling," then the other side would rise and shout, "Tastes great!" These alternating yells were great fun until the chant evolved into "Fun cue" and "Eats hit" a few games later (Nash and Zullo, 1986).

A Hooligan Songbook

Portsmouth Song

> In the (Millwall) slums
> They look in the dustbin for something to eat
> They find a dead cat and they think it's a treat
> In the (Millwall) slums

Chelsea Song

The Chelsea singers challenge opposing fans to come into their terraces (The Chelsea Shed) where they will be kicked around.

> I was born under the Chelsea Shed
> Boots are made for kicking
> Guns are made to shoot
> Come up into the Chelsea Shed
> and we'll lay in the boot

Everton Song

(Sung to London teams)

> He's only a poor little Cockney
> His face is all tattered and torn
> He makes me feel sick
> So I hit him with a brick
> And now he doesn't sing any more.

Variation in Collective Singing

William J. Fellows (1985) concludes that football singing and cheering has its own character, and it differs substantially from the vocal and verbal activities that accompany other sports. He bases this conclusion on years of personal experience at football matches and a systematic analysis of recordings of football singing and cheering during the 1982–1983 football season. Recordings were made prior to and during Pompey matches at the Fratton End of Fratton Park, Portsmouth, England.

Fellows identified a number of factors that contribute significantly to the type and amount of fan singing. There are a number of background factors, such as rivalries or league standings, that influence collective singing at any football match. These situational circumstances are distinct from factors of play, such as scoring or fouls, that also contribute to variations in singing.

Local and Traditional Rivalries One of the most important factors determining the level of singing and cheering in a match is the existence of a local or traditional rivalry. Fellows identifies a number of local rivalries, or "jewels of the game." Many, like the rivalry between Manchester United and Manchester City, are cross-town rivalries. Traditional rivalries also exist between cities that are some distance apart, such as the rivalry between Liverpool and Everton. Rivalries usually mean bigger home gates (more paid admissions) and a large number of supporters traveling to the away matches. Opposition fans are well represented, and competitive singing is an established feature of the game.

Championship Matches The national championship, or the FA (Football Association) Cup, historically has been a prime factor in determining public arousal; hence crowd size especially where knockout (team elimination) and home advantage features are combined with other special factors such as local or traditional rivalry. The Southampton game is not such a good example of this, as the same level of interest would probably be expected on the basis of traditional rivalry alone.

Time and Occasion The time and occasion of a game is another factor which may contribute significantly to the amount of singing and chanting. Games played during holiday times such as Christmas, New Year, and Easter are traditionally ones which draw larger than average crowds, and when local or traditional rivals will often be played.

Opposition Fans Large numbers of opposition fans increase the amount of singing and chanting that occurs. Fellows (1985) notes that the presence of 9,000 Southampton fans at Fratton Park was undoubtedly a significant feature of the match in which, before the game even started, there were 251 songs. The reputation of the opposition may be in terms of their singing and their "hardness," or their fanaticism. Teams that have "reputations" draw big crowds and encourage singing and chanting.

Mutual Respect and Distaste Fans tend to have respect for the fans of some clubs and distaste for the fans of others. Fellows (1985) points out that there is a certain amount of mutual respect between Chelsea and Pompey fans, for instance, and that Pompey fans have respect for fans of Leeds and Newcastle. On the other hand, there is mutual distaste between Portsmouth and Southampton fans. This distaste is shown in Pompey's broad repertoire of "we hate scummers" chants and songs.

Local Issues Local issues, particularly controversial issues, can lead to much singing. Fellows (1985) notes that when Pompey sacked (fired) their manager Bobby Campbell and replaced him with Alan Ball, fans were upset about this sacking and doubly upset with the appointment of Ball, who was an ex-Southampton player (and hence a "scummer"). At the next game, when Pompey was winning easily and did not require much vocal support, the fans turned their attention to the managerial issues and sang these words to various tunes:

> "There's only one Bobby Campbell"
> "You can stick your Alan Ball up your arse"
> "Bring back Bobby Campbell"
> "We love you Bobby, we do"
> "Alan Ball's a scummer, la la la la"

A few weeks later, when Pompey was losing and Alan Ball made an unpopular coaching decision, derisive songs were again sung, including words such as:

> "Alan Ball's a wanker"
> "If you all hate scummers, clap your hands"
> "Bring back Bobby Campbell"
> "Bobby Campbell's blue and white army"
> "If you all hate Ballie, clap your hands."

Factors of Match and Play

The background factors identified thus far constitute situational phenomena that contribute significantly to the type and amount of fan singing. However, Fellows (1985) notes that background factors do not exist in a vacuum and that singing and chanting is mediated in a dynamic interaction between this framework and many moment-to-moment incidents as the match is played.

Critical Density Fellows (1985) suggests that for singing and chanting to operate with any unity there has to be a "critical density" of fans present, both in number and in concentration. Critical density is the numerical concentration of fans which can be provoked into a specific "unity" manifested in collective singing and chanting. Fellows suggests that this critical density will vary from one match to another. For example, at every match, singing and chanting may be heard from a crowd of 2,000 at the small Colchester club. However, when Pompey visited Liverpool for a League Cup game in 1980 there were 17,000 Liverpool fans but very little singing from them. Since Liverpool's average gate is well above 30,000, the number of fans at this game was below a critical density. It may also be interesting to consider that the "critical density" of away supporters may be a great deal less than that needed at home games.

Along similar lines, McPhail suggests that collective yeaaas, applause, booos, ohhhs and ahhs are extremely simple forms of collective action that result from two or more individuals independently controlling for similar reference signals— that is, attending to scoring points, stopping the opposition from scoring points, or winning the game. It is the sights and sounds of others (and their number and location) doing the same that result in adjustments in the intensity, volume, or duration of applause and cheers.

Cheerleaders While collective yeaaas, applause, booos, ohhhs, and ahhs are extremely simple forms of collective action, McPhail repeatedly asserts that for sustained and complex collective actions to occur, two or more people must either interact with one another to interdependently develop similar reference signals and directions for behavior, or they must adopt those reference signals and directions from a third party. If sustained and complex collective actions such as songs and chants are to occur for a football crowd, spectators must adopt reference signals and directions from "cheerleaders." Cheerleaders deliberately attempt to manipulate verbal and nonverbal symbol sequences to produce collective action by members of the gathering. They do so by carefully selecting significant symbols, by stating those symbol sequences simply and repeatedly, and often by making them redundant across sensory modalities—audible, visible, and sometimes tactile.

Cheerleading is generally a combination of previously rehearsed and improvised signals and directions. Cheers coordinated with clapping, foot stomping, standing, sitting, or rocking are likely to have been rehearsed by cheerleaders. Reciprocal cheers, where fans are asked to echo or repeat the cheerleader, also are likely to have been rehearsed by cheerleaders. Of course, some cheers are "rehearsed" through repetition at previous games and matches or at rallies beforehand.

Fellows suggests that the importance of cheerleaders lessens with increases in the level of crowd arousal. With an increase in frequency volume and tempo of collective vocalization, it may be more difficult for spectators to adopt reference signals and directions from any third party, including cheerleaders. The actions of cheerleaders and the actions of the crowd seem disjointed under these conditions. The cheering and singing of the fans tend to become less complex and to merge with the simple forms of collective action such as yeaaas, applause, booos, ohhhs and ahhs.

Team Performance Fellows (1985) argues that team performance is one of the most important factors contributing to singing and chanting. The excitement of goals and other match incidents can create an atmosphere that may provoke much more singing and chanting than would otherwise occur due to the factors already mentioned. He notes that the Swansea game, for example, was watched only by 7,400 people (the lowest crowd of the season), and yet the 5–0 win provoked a total of 73 songs. A similar situation occurred in the Brighton game that was won 5–1 despite being 0–1 at halftime. A total of 82 songs were recorded in the second half, which is the highest total recorded by Fellows throughout his study.

Precipitating Match Events

McPhail notes that scoring points, stopping the opposition from scoring points, and winning the game provide the "reference signals" for simple vocalizations and more complex verbalizations. From the data gathered during his study, Fellows identified many specific match events that precipitated cheers and songs. Fellows notes, for instance, that pre-game activities such as players and officials inspecting the pitch, the players' warm-up, and the arrival and acknowledgement of ball boys are occasions for cheers and songs, as are announcements such as player of the month and halftime scores, the carrying of displays or advertisements onto the pitch, and the introduction of home and opposition teams are accompanied by collective vocalization.

In addition to scoring points and winning, the game regularly provides other reference signals for cheering and singing. Traditional songs and chants occur at the toss-up, line-up, and kickoff. Good play, including skillful dribbles and passes, are accompanied by collective vocalization. Likewise, poor play and mistakes are occasion for collective derision directed against the team or particular players. Applause, cheers, and songs accompany good sporting conduct such as helping up an opponent from the ground. Injured players leave the pitch and substitutes are brought on to collective singing.

Infringements or fouls on players, player tussles and aggression, and booking or sending off players are reference signals for rowdy songs and cheers. Collective taunts, as well as songs, accompany disputable decisions and penalties.

Close misses, corners, free kicks, throw-ins close to the goal and saves by goalies are occasion for ooohs, ahhs, and moans as well as singing and chanting. Of course, goals nearly always precipitate cheers, applause, singing of club songs, and the chanting of the game score, such as "Two–nil!"

Often when police enter the grounds they are greeted with derisive chants, cheers, and songs. "Here we go!", sung to the first notes of John Phillip Sousa's *Stars and Stripes Forever*, is often sung over and over as police move into the crowd to remove flags, banners, or to arrest or remove fans. "Here we go!" may also be sung when fights break out among fans. It seems to be a perennial favorite, as it was sung during fighting between English fans and others at the 1998 World Cup in France.

The approach of halftime and the end of match are times when scores are chanted or sung. Additionally, chants such as "You're gonna get your fuckin' heads kicked in" occur at or near the end of the game as a threat to visiting fans who will soon be making their way to buses or train stations. Victories that advance clubs to the FA cup may be flaunted with lyrics such as "We're going to Wembly with our willies hanging out." Victories over traditional rivals may be emphasized with boastful ditties like "We'll be running 'round scummers with our willies hanging out."

Fellows (1985) argues that football singing and cheering has its own character, and it differs substantially from the vocal and verbal activities that accompany other sports. He provides a vivid description of football singing and the background and game events that sequence this activity. Clearly, cheering and singing accompany other sports, and these collective activities are keyed to pre-game activities, both good and bad play, controversial calls by officials, and victory and defeat. Quite likely, the amount of football singing at each game substantially exceeds the vocal and verbal activities that accompany other sports. Rousing traditional school, team, or club songs are part of many sports. With British football, however, a significant proportion are "hooligan" songs with an abusive and sadistic content. With football singing, a number of songs are deliberate taunts to specific teams and people, including managers, coaches, and players. Much football singing is improvised at the match, and such extensive improvisation is not seen in the singing that is part of other sports.

SPORTS AS SOCIAL MOVEMENTS

The origins and growth of sports can be examined from the standpoint of social movements, even though we often think of a sport as a game that was "invented" by a particular individual. Many sports have their own invention myths: the game of baseball was "invented" by Abner Doubleday; basketball was "invented" by Reverend James Naismith; rugby was "invented" by William Webb Ellis, and so forth. Some of these invention myths, rugby's for instance, have little if any factual basis. It is of greater importance, however, to note that invention myths obscure the fact that "invented" games had earlier variants and that they "evolved" more so than they were "invented" at a particular moment in time (Dunning and Sheard, 1979).

The early development of many sports contains elements of informality that are also characteristic of the early history of other social movements. Many games evolved as part of collective celebrations of saints' days and holy days and were closely identified with people's regional identities and trades (Dunning and Elias, 1972). Games were played between neighboring villages or between guilds such as masons and shoemakers. Games were a means of settling old scores. These games had simple, improvised rules rooted in local customs. There was little distinction made between "player" and "spectator" in these communal experiences that often degenerated into savage brawls. The evolution of these early forms into modern sports roughly parallels the process of "increased formalization" that has occurred in many political movements.

Like other social movements, sports movements have been opposed by established authorities. In fact, the majority of references to football in medieval English sources come from royal and civil edicts banning the game, or from records of court cases against offenders. Dunning and Elias (1972) cite twenty-three edicts against football between 1314 and 1615. The ban issued by King Edward III in 1365 noted that football was one of the "vain games of no value" and that able-bodied men "shall in his sports use bows and arrows" to greater ensure protection of the kingdom. A long list of games and sports, at one time or another, have been condemned, outlawed and even actively suppressed. Authorities have resisted American football, soccer, rugby, hockey, boxing, auto racing, bicycling, and in general, women's athletics. These sports movements were resisted because, in the judgment of authorities, the games were too dangerous, wastes of time, immoral, or improper conduct for ladies and gentlemen. In turn, members of sports movements have utilized tactics of mass organization, persuasion, petition and protest to change the stance of authorities.

The Bicycle: From Fads to Social Movements

Sidney Aronson (1951) begins his classic sociohistorical analysis, "The Sociology of the Bicycle," by noting that the bicycle came to America three times. The first two times, in 1819 and 1869, the introduction of the bicycle took the form of a fad. In 1879, however, the bicycle came to stay, and its use created one of the major popular movements of the time.

The idea of the bicycle, a human-propelled, two-wheeled vehicle, may date back to the time of the Egyptian empire, and bicycles were probably "invented," after a fashion, many times since then. There is, for instance, a clear reference in the 1665 diary of John Evelyn to English craftsmen making a "wheele for one to run races in" (Smith, 1971). Later, French and German craftsmen made their versions of the "wheele." It was not until 1819 that the English "dandy horse"—also known as the "hobbyhorse" and "swift walker"—came to the United States (Smith, 1971). Built of wood and iron and weighing about 150 pounds, the dandy horse was a juggernaut. The front wheel was steerable, it was propelled by walking while straddling the crossbar, and the greatest speed could be attained on the dandy horse by coasting downhill. In fact, the dandy horse appeared to have been used primarily as a downhill coaster. For two or three years, hills in Boston, New York and Philadelphia became gathering places for daring—and wealthy— young men and admiring young women.

It was not until 1866, nearly fifty years later, that the bicycle once again hit the streets of the United States. That year the velocipede or "boneshaker" was introduced from France. The boneshaker had pedals on the front wheel that allowed the machine, with considerable exertion, to be propelled over level ground. The seat was also supported by a steel spring. Otherwise, there was little difference in construction or weight between the boneshaker and the dandy horse. The boneshaker, however, had a greater impact on the communities in which it was used. The French inventor of the velocipede, Lallement, made an unsuccessful attempt to finance a velocipede factory. The numbers of enthusiasts grew rapidly as riding schools were established, and older men began to ride as well. There was a corresponding reaction against these new developments. In New Haven, Lallement and others were arrested for frightening horses with velocipedes. Critics condemned the machines as a health hazard when reports of concussions, broken limbs, ruptures, and sprains mounted. Ministers began to preach that Sunday velocipede riding profaned the Lord's Day.

By 1870, it was clear that the boneshaker was going the way of the dandy horse. Both had enjoyed less than five years of popularity. Opponents of these contraptions had hardly breathed a sigh of relief when, in 1876, the first high-wheeled, "ordinary" bicycle was exhibited by its English manufacturer at the centennial exposition in Philadelphia. The ordinary bicycle was an entirely different machine than the boneshaker. Made of steel tubing instead of wooden timbers, it was graceful in appearance. Weighing less than half the weight of a boneshaker and having solid rubber tires, the "ordinary" was far more maneuverable and comfortable to ride. Because the ordinary was one of the exhibition's most popular attractions, a Baltimore firm, Timms and Lawford, began to import the English bicycle. A few months later, Colonel Albert Pope of Boston converted his shoe factory to a bicycle import house and riding school. From the outset, it was impossible to meet demand with imports. In 1878, Pope manufactured the "Columbia" model ordinary, widely held to be the first bicycle manufactured in the United States, even though it was a close copy of the English design. Other bicycle manufacturers, including the Victor Bicycle Company, were soon producing their own versions of the ordinary. Because of its strength, reliability, and maneuverability, the racing potential of the ordinary was immediately realized and competitions flourished. By 1880, it was clear that the ordinary would be around much longer than either the dandy horse or the boneshaker.

The resistance to bicycling was renewed with more vigor than ever before. Sunday bicycle riding and racing were again vehemently denounced from pulpits across the country. Ministers condemned the growing practice of young men and women cycling without chaperones. The high-wheeler was blamed for a clear trend toward tighter, shorter, more revealing clothing, including knickers for men and bloomers and trousers for women (Smith, 1971). These changes in customary fashion were denounced as sinful and immoral. Adding to their earlier concern with concussions, broken limbs, ruptures and sprains, physicians expanded their list of the physical dangers of bicycling to include facial paralysis for men and sterility for women (Aronson, 1951). Arrests mounted as people were charged with frightening horses with their ordinaries. Many cities and towns passed increasingly restrictive bicycling ordinances against riding in parks and on streets.

Reacting to this resistance, bicycling began to take on the characteristics of a social movement. There was a concern for formalization. Hundreds of local bicycle clubs were formed across the country and worked against restrictive ordinances. These clubs also promoted tour outings, picnics, parades, dances, charity balls, fashion shows, and racing. In 1880 the League of American Wheelmen emerged as an organization dedicated to promoting the "general interests of bicycling, to ascertain, defend, and protect the rights of wheelmen, and to encourage and facilitate touring" (Smith, 1971:12). The League initiated a vigorous campaign for the elimination of restrictive ordinances and the improvement of streets and roads. The League also undertook to regulate racing, and in 1882 awarded the first national championship to George W. Hendee (Nye, 1988).

There was an effort to improve the image of bicycling and to counter criticism. In 1881, Charles E. Pratt published *The American Bicycler*, the first handbook for cyclers. Pope and other bicycle manufacturers underwrote new bicycle publications, including *Bicycle World*, *The Wheel*, and *Wheelman*. These publications contained advertisements for the newest models, technical reports, racing news, and the exploits of the adventurers who were attempting to ride their bicycles around the world. Pope also offered prizes to physicians who published the best articles promoting bicycle riding as a positive aid to good health. Additionally, Pope financed numerous court cases challenging restrictive ordinances.

In 1887, when the ordinary was at the zenith of its popularity, the Victor Bicycle Company introduced their version of the "safety bicycle." The Victor Bicycle established the basic design for bicycles of the present day. The Victor Bicycle had two wheels of the same size, a diamond frame made of steel tubing, and a chain drive. Within a few years, Victor and other manufacturers had introduced pneumatic tires, lighter frames, ball bearings, and the coaster brake. The ordinary was no match for the safety bicycle, which immediately proved to be faster, cheaper, more comfortable and safer than the ordinary. Soon people who never had the courage, stamina, and coordination for the ordinary were avid riders of the safety bicycle. Women clearly preferred the safety bicycle and rapidly became a substantial portion of the bicycle market.

When the safety bicycle was introduced, there were 27 shops making bicycles in the United States. Nine years later, in 1896, there were over 500 manufacturers. By then, Smith (1971) estimates, consumers had spent over $300 million on bicycles. Spin-off enterprises flourished, including hundreds of riding academies, many offering rental plans. Riders had spent over $200 million on bicycle lights, locks, training wheels, cycling shoes, gloves, and clothing.

Involvement with the bicycle peaked in 1898, when early in the year the market slumped. The number of U.S. manufacturers began to decline, and the price of bicycles fell. Interestingly, the price decline made bicycles a popular gift for children, and the number of juvenile riders began to increase. In 1899, the League of American Wheelmen lost membership when it split on the issue of Sunday racing. Sponsors and promoters were in favor of Sunday athletics of all sorts (Nye, 1988). The League voted to abandon racing and to devote the organization to the development of touring. It changed its name to the American Road Makers in 1900. Another smaller organization, the National Cycling Association, moved quickly to promote bicycle racing. The number of cycling publications declined sharply after 1899.

Social movements are often evaluated in terms of their lasting accomplishments. Obviously, the bicycle has become a permanent item in our material culture. Clearly, the League of American Wheelmen, a social movement organization, accomplished much toward meeting its goal of promoting the general interests of bicycling and continued, even after changing its name, to advocate the improvement of roads in the United States.

It was the bicycling movement of the 1890s that introduced us to a number of new ideas and practices. For the first time, women were recognized as major consumers of a major product. New advertising and marketing strategies for bicycles were targeted specifically at women. Cycling clothing for women was the first large-scale instance of spin-off merchandising. When "the 'sundries' cost more than the wheel," money was to be made in promoting the use of these new, daring, and liberating fashions.

Female models began to appear at gala sales expositions. These expositions, in turn, were developed around a new idea—the highly publicized introduction of a new model bicycle each year. The idea of the media campaign was pioneered with the bicycle. With a new model each year came consumers' first experience with planned obsolescence. A market in used bicycles was created, as consumers became familiar with terms such as "trade-ins" and "year-end clearances."

Assembly-line production methods were perfected at the giant Overman bicycle factory. Leading manufacturers built nationwide distribution and service networks. The first widespread instance of installment buying in the United States made bicycles available to more people. It is not surprising, then, that the bicycle movement prepared the country for things to come. In 1899, the Annual Cycle Exhibition at Madison Square Garden was renamed the Annual Cycle and Automobile Exhibition. Colonel Albert Pope personally exhibited an electric automobile made at his Columbia Bicycle Works.

Crisis Resolution: The Gridiron Football Movement

After witnessing a bit of Americana such as the Rose Bowl festivities, it is hard to imagine that gridiron football was once barely tolerated on U.S. campuses. It is also hard to imagine that "Rough Rider" President Theodore Roosevelt, in 1905, demanded that the eastern universities save football from the "brutality and foul play" that threatened the game. Roosevelt's voice was one of moderation compared to the clamor of thousands who demanded that the game be banned immediately. The end of the 1905 season saw 18 dead and 189 seriously injured on the playing fields, and football was banned at Columbia, Northwestern, Union College, California, and Stanford (Lawrence, 1987).

The earliest mention of a football game was in 1761, when notes of a Princeton faculty meeting included their irritation with students "playing at ball" (Lawrence, 1987). By the 1870s football was being played on campuses across the United States. Many traditional rivalries, such as those among the Ivy League universities of Brown, Columbia, Cornell, Dartmouth, Harvard, Pennsylvania, Princeton and Yale, were well established. Still, football was a game for enthusiasts and held little mass appeal. At many games players outnumbered spectators. Occasionally, small admissions were charged, but they did not constitute important sources of revenue for the universities.

In 1876, the first clear effort to formalize the football movement in the United

States occurred. The Intercollegiate Athletic Association, whose founding members were Columbia, Harvard and Princeton, was formed. In many respects this was a student organization, consisting of student players, coaches, and managers. Few full-time university faculty were members or even marginally involved in this organization (Lawrence, 1987). The objectives of this organization were to promote the game of football through the standardization of rules, the keeping of records, and the establishment of leagues. This organization never fully realized these goals and collapsed in 1894.

Seemingly resistant to formalization at the turn of the century, the game of football was much different from the game played today. Although some universities were beginning to sense its potential as a money maker, the game was still viewed as a nuisance by most administrations. There were few generally accepted rules and a wide range of plays were allowed or, more accurately, not forbidden. Consequently, the game began a clear drift toward roughness. For instance, "mass play" was not forbidden and began to appear in the 1890s. Perhaps the most notorious mass play was the "V-trick." Also called the "wedge" or the "flying wedge," this play began when players locked arms, forming a wedge around the ball carrier, and charged down the field. Once formed, the wedge was unstoppable, and opposing players who tried to break it up were often injured. Other bizarre plays were not forbidden, including plays in which the ball carrier was thrown over the line of scrimmage to gain yardage or score goals. Handles were sown onto uniforms to allow throws of greater height and distance. Obviously, these plays were a source of broken necks and other serious injuries. There were also "dirt plays" in which the offensive lines threw dirt in the faces of the defense when the ball was snapped.

Compared to today's scientifically designed equipment, players during these years had scant protection. Most men played without helmets, and only shin pads were worn. Add to this a vagueness in the rules covering hitting, kicking, gouging, and tackling, and it is easy to see how early football generated far more serious injuries and deaths than today's game. Even so, the toll in death and injury of the 1905 season was shocking. At Roosevelt's insistence representatives of Harvard, Yale, and Princeton met at the White House in October to formulate rule changes that would reduce the "brutality and foul play" that had come to characterize the game.

In late December, representatives of 62 other colleges met to deal with the safety issue and formed the Intercollegiate Athletic Association of the United States. Unlike the earlier Intercollegiate Athletic Association, the IAAUS was composed primarily of faculty members and university officials of the participating colleges. This more stable membership allowed for effective long-range planning and agreement on standardizing the rules of play. Immediate changes, such as the banning of mass plays and making the forward pass a standard part of the game, quickly brought about a drastic reduction of fatalities and injuries. With the rapid transformation of football into a more acceptable sport, the IAAUS began to standardize rules for other collegiate sports as well as to develop guidelines for tournaments and championships. These early successes also contributed to a rapid rise in member colleges. In 1910, the IAAUS changed its name to the National Collegiate Athletic Association, which regulates college sports to the present day.

Those involved in the events of 1905 probably never imagined that the game would ever evolve into a multibillion-dollar "industry." Nor were they likely to imagine that, like other industries, there would someday be clear lines of economic conflict drawn between owners and "workers": the players. These processes came into sharp focus during the 1987 National Football League players' strike. Whereas strikes in mining and manufacturing were somewhat commonplace, the players' strike represented a new and controversial social reality (Schmitt, 1991). The owners of the NFL teams created replacement teams of non-union players, who began season play. Games by the replacement teams counted fully in the league standings. Replacement games were televised, minimizing the economic impact of the strike on owners. There were many strike issues, but the public failed to side with the players primarily because they had difficulty identifying with the plight of highly paid players (Schmitt, 1991). Media practices, including televising the games and generally describing the replacement teams as legitimate contestants, worked against the players.

SUMMARY

Sports encompass three traditional concerns in the field of collective behavior: First, there is spectator violence and the group emotion this seems to entail. While spectators do occasionally exhibit violent actions at sports contests in the United States, British soccer fans have earned a reputation since the 1960s for being among the world's most violent. In this chapter we considered the extensive research done by sociologists under the auspices of Britain's Football Trust, through the Sir Norman Chester Centre for Football Research. Findings of the Centre suggest that soccer hooliganism is not simply a contagious, emotional discharge caused by social strains as suggested by the mass hysteria and value-added theories of collective behavior. Instead, the work done by Dunning, Murphy, and Williams of the Centre characterize soccer hooliganism as a cultural trend.

British football hooliganism constitutes a genuine threat to the well-being of the game. Hooliganism seems to follow some rather predictable patterns and is engaged in almost exclusively by groups popularly known as fighting crews. Conflict between crews is an expression of what Dunning, Murphy, and Williams term "aggressive masculinity" and is deeply rooted in the working-class lifestyle. Soccer hooliganism has generated numerous control efforts including intensive policing of matches, banning of British teams from European competition, the passing of restrictive football spectators' legislation, members only admission to matches, and the building of physical barriers to prevent playing field invasions. The use of physical barriers, or hooligan fences, resulted in 95 deaths during a surge of spectators at the Hillsborough grounds in 1989.

Sports also encompass behavior that falls outside traditional culture. Elias and Dunning note that many of our modern spectator sports, such as baseball, soccer and gridiron football, have their roots in folk games. They have evolved into their modern form as part of the civilizing process. In their transition to their contemporary forms, these sports were frequently seen as dangerous to the social order and at some point in their development were actively suppressed by authorities. The Xtreme sports of the 1990s, such as skateboarding, in-line skating, sky surfing and street luge, appear to be developing along much different lines. Since their very beginning, these sports have been highly promoted by the manufacturers of their accoutrements and accessories, and by the media.

Finally, the chants and cheers of spectators at sporting events are examples of direct, immediate, and highly involving forms of social influence and interaction.

More so than any other sociologist, Clark McPhail has examined the collective action within sports gatherings. Using perception control theory, McPhail analyzes how a football team puts together plays and practices them, how a band puts together and practices its field show, and how a card stunt section creates its routines. All of these collective actions are part of a complex patchwork quilt of activity that, taken together, constitute a contemporary college football game. McPhail also examines the collective action of fans, particularly the collective vocalization and verbalization as they lament the failures and cheer the successes of their team and cheer the halftime performances and card stunts. This chapter also presents the work of William J. Fellows (1985), who examined the collective and oftentimes competitive singing of spectators at English soccer matches.

PART III

COLLECTIVE BEHAVIOR AND COLLECTIVE ACTION
THREATS TO THE SOCIAL ORDER

CHAPTER 9

MIGRATIONS

Maja Vindovic sobs quietly outside her ransacked home in the hills above Drvar, in western Bosnia. Forced to flee for her life during the war, she and her family have returned to their two-story stucco house, which now looks like a wrecking crew has trashed it. Members of Impact Teams International (ITI), an independent humanitarian aid agency, try to comfort Vindovic. By getting this far, to her own front porch, she's won a victory in this war no one can win. But the devastation that greets her is overwhelming.

The house is without windows. The front door has been ripped out of the frame and lies on the stoop. Inside, shirts, dresses, pants, dishes, towels—anything that can be stored on a shelf or in a drawer—are strewn across the floor. In the kitchen, a stove, its connections torn from the wall, blocks the entrance. Cabinets are toppled and shoved out of place like dice shaken on a table. A blue enamel pan, encrusted with food, juts surrealistically out of an exposed drawer in a counterless cabinet. No room is spared. Looters have stolen furniture, electrical fixtures, wiring, even wood from the walls. This is wartime's welcome wagon.

Before the war, Serbs lived in Drvar and its surrounding villages. The Vindovic family is Serbian. During the war, Croats drove the Serbs out and occupied the undamaged homes that remained. The Bosnian Croats who now live in Drvar were themselves forced to relocate there. Many of them had been refugees in Croatia. This was not their first forced move. . . .

Many Bosnians simply want to live in peace. They never thought of themselves as Serbs, Muslims or Croats, and they don't want to now. They're simply Bosnians. For many it is hard to retain this attitude with the same innocence as before, but every so often an opportunity to relate human to human appears like serendipity knocking at the door.

Two families talk around a coffee table in a home in Drvar. The tableau is warm and nostalgic, a pleasant visit between friends. Or so it seems. What makes this group unusual is its composition.

One family—a mother, child and grandmother—is Croatian. The other—a husband, wife and mother-in-law—is Serbian. The Croatian family lives in the house where the Serbs used to live. Now the Serbs have returned to visit and see if they can return permanently. They have asked the ITI peacekeepers to go with them, fearing harassment by the new neighbors.

The faces around the table are strained and weary. Each person knows the other has problems much the same as their own. The man speaks from the

231

heart, restrained yet impassioned. The mother listens and responds in turn. The little boy sits between the two. Whether or not he understands the import of this adult conversation isn't particularly important. What he's learning about tolerance and understanding is.

As the visit ends, the man says, "A Croat family and a Serb family talking here together. This is a historic moment." But this "historic moment" has a bitter epilogue, one that reveals the emotions of a war of displacement. Before leaving the house, the Serbs are threatened by a neighbor who yells, "When I get my home back in Banja Luka, then you can come back." (Lasdon, 1998)

Human migrations are usually sad occasions. People who leave their native lands have often been uprooted by disaster, war, famine, poverty, or, as in Bosnia, Kosovo, and Rwanda, ethnic strife and racial hatred. People who migrate seldom travel first class, and hunger, disease, and death are usually the migrants' constant companions. Migrations of thousands of miles have been accomplished on foot. Migrations by sea are usually carried out under miserably crowded, unsanitary, and dangerous conditions. Many vessels that brought Irish immigrants to North America in the 1840s were called "coffin ships" because of the high death tolls incurred during the voyage. Hundreds of Haitians have died trying to sail to the United States in overloaded and poorly provisioned open boats. In the process of migration, families are separated and broken. The migrants' sense of ethnic identity is challenged. Migrants are often viciously exploited—they are sold shoddy goods and impure foods and sometimes are simply robbed of their meager resources. Those who migrate are seldom welcomed by the receiving country.

In this chapter we begin with a description of two migrations. First, we will consider the migration of the Irish to the United States in the 1840s and 1850s. This was one of Western society's greatest migrations, precipitated by famine and political upheaval. We will then consider the migration of Cubans to the United States—the Freedom Flotilla of 1980. This was one of the largest influx of immigrants into the United States since the 1840s and illustrates how migrations acquire political overtones. Next we will briefly consider migrations as mass behavior, and finally we will examine migrations as collective action.

THE IRISH MIGRATION

The migration of the Irish is one of the largest migrations in human history, and probably Europe's greatest migration. During its peak years, 1846–1855, more than 2 million people migrated from Ireland and England to the United States and Canada. The reasons for this migration are many and deeply rooted. People stood in three distinct relationships to the land in Ireland. First, there were the *landlords*, many of them residing in England, who owned 80 percent of Ireland's farmland. Below the landlords were *leaseholders* and *middlemen*, who seldom actually farmed the land but used it as a source of rental income. The *tenants* and *farm laborers*, who paid rents to the leaseholders and middlemen, actually farmed the land.

This system was quite inefficient as far as food production was concerned, but it did serve other purposes. The landlords were free to pursue other interests, such as politics and hunting, while the leaseholders and middlemen were able to obtain a substantial return on their capital by squeezing the tenants and laborers. Finally, the tenants and laborers were able to earn a meager subsistence from the land. Access to a little plot of land and the garden crops it could produce was all that distinguished this group from the paupers who wandered the countryside or sought charity in the cities. As the middle of the nineteenth century approached, things began to change. For the leaseholders and middlemen, the dawning industrial revolution and expanding trade were beginning to suggest better uses for land and capital. The status of the tenants and laborers became increasingly precarious.

Disaster struck in the spring of 1846, when the potato and most other food crops were destroyed by blight. Starving and unable to pay their rents, thousands of laborers were dispossessed. When the blight reappeared in 1847, the leaseholders and middlemen rapidly began to divest themselves of their properties and seek other investments. Meanwhile, thousands of Irish died of starvation and disease. The British Parliament did little to ease their plight, largely because of the almost universal assumption then popular among Western governments that feeding starving people destroys their character and encourages idleness.

A few positive efforts were made, however. Grain imports were increased, causing a rapid drop in the price of corn. But regardless of how much the price of corn fell, it was still too expensive for the Irish. A program of soup kitchens was started, but this program was weakened by corruption from the beginning and did not provide even minimal nutrition to those who depended on it. Finally, in 1847, in an effort to increase relief funds, Parliament extended England's Poor Laws to include Ireland. Under the Poor Laws, landlords were charged a rate, or tax, based on the number of paupers residing in their county (Smith, 1962:36–37). Ironically, this law did much to hasten and enlarge the emigration.

Suddenly faced with the possibility of being taxed according to the number of paupers residing in their county, landlords felt that it would be cheaper to pay passages to the United States and Canada than to pay the rates. To "encourage" tenants and laborers to accept passage, a policy of "shoveling out" and "tumbling of houses" was undertaken. Landlords hired gangs of toughs to evict tenants and laborers. Families, infants, widows with children, the elderly, and the sick or dying were thrown from their cottages. Their personal belongings were often destroyed or stolen in the process. Then, amid tears and protests, the cottages were "tumbled," or smashed to the ground. Some gangs boasted of being able to tumble sixteen cottages in a day. Some tenants built *scalpeens*, or temporary shelters, from the wreckage of their cottages. A few landlords did not use such brutal tactics, instead offering their tenants passage and traveling expenses if they would agree to leave. Whether tenants agreed to leave or were shoveled out, passage to the United States and Canada seemed a better alternative than the disease-ridden workhouses.

Most emigrants probably never realized that the landlords had no legal basis for compelling them to leave Ireland. This private program of deportation was a major factor in the early stages of the Irish migration. Some landlords deported as many as two thousand people. When large numbers of tenants were leaving, landlords chartered ships rather than buying passages. After leaving their former tenants in Quebec, Halifax, New York, or Boston, landlords loaded their ships with cargo for the return voyage to England, allowing them to offset some of the charter costs. Parliament took little notice of this private deportation program. In one instance, a landlord eloquently defended his actions to Parliament by noting that his former tenants would prosper in the United States and Canada and would therefore buy more British goods than if they had remained in Ireland. Perhaps he was correct.

After 1850, private deportations declined in importance as word came back from the United States and Canada from those who had emigrated earlier. Brothers, sisters, sons, daughters, cousins, and husbands wrote frequent letters to their families describing life in the new lands (Schrier, 1958:18–42). More important, they sent money and tickets to their families. More than $3 million was sent back to Ireland between 1847 and 1856 (Coleman, 1972:204).

The Irish migration was not typical of most migrations because about equal numbers of men and women emigrated. Initially, larger numbers of men were emigrating, but the number of women and children among the emigrants began to increase rapidly after 1850. Then, single women began to emigrate in appreciable numbers, as demand for Irish maids began to grow among affluent families in the United States.

The emigrants left from the ports of Belfast and Liverpool. Here, they were preyed upon by "runners" who stole the baggage of those waiting to board ships. An emigrant's baggage sometimes contained all his or her worldly possessions, and its loss could mean tragedy. Runners also separated emigrants from their money by selling them counterfeit ship tickets and worthless medicines to prevent everything from seasickness to cholera. They referred emigrants to dishonest merchants and boardinghouse operators. The crimes of the runners became so outrageous that Parliament instituted several investigations and, at one time, even considered establishing a government-run emigration facility.

More than 90 percent of the emigrants traveled steerage class. These accommodations are discussed later in this chapter; here it is sufficient to note that steerage conditions were dangerous. There were passenger laws designed to protect emigrants somewhat from the avarice and blatant disregard for life and limb shown by booking agents, captains, and crews. However, it was virtually impossible to enforce most of these laws, even if funds had been made available to do so. One law, for example, forbade swearing by the passengers in order that a wholesome atmosphere be maintained aboard ship.

Emigrants Become Immigrants

Irish immigrants arrived primarily at the ports of Quebec, Halifax, Boston, and New York. Immigrants had to wait aboard ship, sometimes for almost a week, until Immigration Authority doctors examined them. If typhus or cholera were found, the ship would be immediately quarantined for one month. The ill among the immigrants were sent to military hospitals, such as Wards Island in New York Harbor. In these facilities whole families perished. The quarantine procedures were only partially effective. Runners, even more predatory than those of Belfast and Liverpool, boarded and departed from waiting ships at will. The bedding and clothing that had been soiled during passage, and other possibly infected refuse, were thrown overboard before doctors arrived, washing ashore within hours. Sometimes, to speed Immigration Authority clearance, the ill would be smuggled off before the doctors arrived. Captains and crew were unlikely to report suspected typhus or cholera deaths in order to avoid being held in quarantine. Consequently, Quebec, Halifax, Boston, and New York were swept by outbreaks of typhus and cholera in 1847, 1849, and 1852.

The Irish appeared an unsavory lot when they climbed upon the docks of New York and Boston. Malnutrition, near starvation, and the six to fourteen weeks spent in the crowded filth of steerage had all taken their toll. Additionally, about one-third of the immigrants were illiterate (Schrier, 1958:20). The most common fear expressed in Boston and New York was that they would soon become paupers. While a surprisingly small proportion of these immigrants became indigent, still, within a short time the majority of those receiving public assistance in New York and Massachusetts were Irish immigrants.

Boston, being smaller than New York, was particularly hard pressed by the arrival of the Irish, some of whom were coming by foot and rail from Canada. Bitter concern was expressed that Britain was turning the United States into another Botany Bay by sending convicts among the emigrants. In an effort to deter immigration and to fund relief efforts, Boston and New York imposed $2.00 and $1.50 head taxes, respectively. In addition to the head tax paid by each immigrant, bonds were demanded for aged, injured, ill, or any other immigrant that authorities thought might become a pauper. Obviously, this left a great deal to the discretion of the authorities.

The Supreme Court decided against head taxes in 1849 and pauper bonds in 1875. Both the tax and bond were viewed as unconstitutional restraints on commerce (Coleman, 1972:231–35). In 1847 citizens petitioned the Massachusetts Legislature to spend less money on immigrants. By 1854 the Know-Nothing Party had made Irish immigration a national political issue. Local Know-Nothing leaders provoked attacks on Irish laborers and Catholic churches. But the party, which disseminated anti-Irish and anti-Catholic literature from 1850–1856, collapsed in 1856 after it was soundly defeated by the new Republican Party.

Anti-Irish and anti-Catholic sentiment ran deep but was diffused in part by the growing national division over slavery. The sons of these immigrants would fight and die in the American Civil War. After the war, those arriving from Ireland would be joined by emancipated African Americans, Scandinavians, and Chinese. Together, these immigrants would build a railroad across a continent.

Initially, the Irish migration began as a response to disastrous crop failures in Ireland. While some landowners bankrupted themselves in an effort to provide for their tenants, the effects of the famine were largely unmitigated by any comprehensive food relief program. The lack of information and political resolve has contributed to the effects of famine throughout history. In 1992 the United Nations Department of Humanitarian Affairs (DHA) was created to provide a rapid and coordinated response by the U.N. system to natural disasters and major complex emergencies. This department's mission is to coordinate U.N. action, send assessment teams into trouble spots, and publish situation reports. The DHA makes appeals for funding humanitarian relief programs and monitors the status of donor contributions.

THE FREEDOM FLOTILLA

During 1979, about one hundred thousand Cuban Americans visited their homeland. For most, it was a chance to renew family ties. For some, it was also a chance to show off the prosperity they had attained in the United States. The designer jeans, pretty dresses, digital wristwatches, and cameras drove home to many Cubans that their economy was still unable to provide, even in short supply, goods that were readily available in most American shopping centers. This glimpse of prosperity came at a time of high unemployment for the Cuban people. Blight had ruined the sugar and tobacco crops, and most sugar mills and cigar factories were closed until the next harvest.

In the early months of 1980, small groups of Cubans began "fence hopping"—entering the Peruvian and Venezuelan embassies to seek political asylum. Most of these people stated they wished to leave Cuba to join their families in the United States. Stories of these incidents appeared occasionally in the U.S. press as interesting little vignettes that illustrated the discontent of Cubans with their political system. Finally, on Easter weekend of 1980, a group of Cubans entered the Peruvian Embassy to request political asylum. Cuban officials attempted to remove these people and, failing to do so, issued a public statement that any other Cubans who were unwilling to work and live within the socialist system could join those at the embassy and leave Cuba. Within forty-eight hours, about fifteen hundred people had converged on the Peruvian Embassy. By midweek, this number had grown to more than five thousand persons. This number of people so overloaded the Peruvian Embassy that it soon represented a health and safety hazard. By the end of the week, arrangements had been made for the transfer of these people to Havana Airport for flights to Costa Rica, France, Venezuela, West Germany, and Peru. The United States reluctantly agreed to accept thirty-five hundred of the Cubans.

By now, the Peruvian Embassy had become a focal point for large, daily, anti-defector demonstrations. Those leaving were being characterized as selfish people who were selling themselves for a pair of designer jeans. President Castro publicly described the emigrants as delinquents, antisocial elements, bums, parasites, homosexuals, gamblers, and drug addicts. He cautioned the governments admitting these Cubans that they were opening their doors to a flood of people that would be hell for them. Despite such denunciations, Cuban officials attempted to provide the emigrants with safe passage to the airport. Still, those leaving were harassed and attacked along the way. At least a thousand emigrants remained in the Peruvian Embassy during the last week of April.

The focus and character of this unfolding event changed considerably when Cuban officials ran newspaper notices stating that anyone who had relatives willing to pick them up could leave Cuba. The place of departure was Mariel Harbor Naval Base, thirty miles west of Havana. Telephone lines were flooded as Cubans tried to reach relatives in the United States. As soon as the news of Mariel Harbor spread through Miami, anti-Castro groups began to organize the Freedom Flotilla. Dozens of Cuban-American work boats and yachts departed on the two-hundred-mile voyage to pick up relatives. Within days, these boats were joined by hundreds of others, including those who were charging up to $1,500 per relative brought from Cuba.

Mariel Harbor became heavily congested, and the Cuban Navy had to oversee harbor traffic and the loading of emigrants. This was interpreted as harassment by those returning from Cuba. Initially, boats were picking up the relatives of Cuban Americans who chartered them. As the numbers of Cubans converging on the harbor increased, officials began to demand that returning boats be fully loaded with emigrants. Consequently, many people were disappointed that after chartering a boat to Cuba, they had to return with a boatload of strangers, sometimes without the family members they had set out to find.

The first Cubans to arrive were given sixty-day parole visas and, if needed, room and board. This procedure soon became impractical as thousands more Cubans arrived. A receiving area was established at Miami's Tamiami Park, where Cubans were screened by FBI and immigration officials. It was soon apparent that about half of those arriving had no relatives in the United States. Private relief agencies began to mobilize sponsorship drives for these people. The World Council of Churches, Refugee and Migration Service worked with local churches in support of the refugees, helping to provide both emergency and long-term assistance, including sponsorship. Also, in cooperation with local churches, the Council advocated on behalf of the newly arrived. The Council also provided public information and training and facilitated meetings between churches on refugee issues. Still, the processing of refugees was so slow that the population of the receiving camp climbed steadily.

The United States had initially agreed to accept thirty-five hundred refugees, but by May 20, almost ten times this number of Cubans had arrived by boat. By the first of June, over sixty thousand Cubans had arrived. Additional refugee camps were set up at Key West, Florida, and Fort Chaffee, Arkansas. Newspapers predicted that another two hundred thousand refugees would be arriving. Increasingly frequent complaints were being expressed that a large portion of the refugees were "common criminals." Cubans released from the reception centers were given food stamps, housing, and, often, jobs in restaurants and hotels. African American leaders in Miami began to complain that it was easier for a Cuban refugee to get food stamps and a job than it was for most American citizens. Even the Ku Klux Klan started to hold anti-Cuban rallies.

In mid-May, U.S. officials began seizing boats in Miami Harbor in an effort to reduce the number of arrivals. This was met with bitter protest from boat owners and parts of the Cuban-American community. Countercomplaints were voiced that the refugee situation was having a negative impact on the South Florida tourist trade: people did not wish to vacation amid such turmoil. Refugee sponsorships by relief organizations were beginning to decline. For many Americans, the height of ingratitude seemed to have been reached when about one thousand of the seventeen thousand Cuban refugees at Fort Chaffee rioted. The Cuban complaints included detention with violent criminals, poor treatment by authorities, and poor living conditions at the camp. In mid-June, the U.S. Coast Guard finally imposed a full blockade against the Freedom Flotilla, greatly slowing the arrival of refugees, but by then at least one hundred thousand refugees had arrived.

The aftermath of the Freedom Flotilla was bittersweet. Obviously, thousands of people benefited materially by coming to the United States. However, in early June of 1980, Miami was shocked by three days of rioting, chiefly by African Americans. More than thirty people died, and about $90 million of property damage was sustained. Afterward, black leaders complained of the seemingly preferential treatment given the Cubans by state and voluntary welfare organizations. It was also noted that during the height of the Freedom Flotilla, boatloads of Haitians were being detained and even turned away from U.S. shores. (The economic and political conditions in Haiti were even more severe than in Cuba; however, all the Haitian refugees were black.)

Cuban officials likely allowed and probably encouraged an appreciable number of habitual criminals and derelicts to depart from Mariel Harbor. Sporadic outbursts occurred at Fort Chaffee, where more than a thousand "unplaceables" were detained until 1985. Finally, hundreds of refugees requested to be returned to Cuba, and at least one airliner was hijacked to Havana by refugees.

Similarities Between the Irish and Cuban Migrations

The Irish migration during the Great Famine and the Cuban migration during the Freedom Flotilla occurred more than a century apart, yet there are similarities in the two migrations. Both were carried out by people facing stark economic conditions, but who had been given a glimpse of substantially better conditions elsewhere. Further, neither group was fully welcome in its homeland. Both migrations illustrate the importance of family ties. Both groups were exploited during their departure and journey to the new land. The Irish were exploited for what little wealth they carried with them; the Cubans, for propaganda purposes in the game of international politics.

Neither group was fully welcome in the land of its choosing, and they were viewed as potential burdens on the welfare services of the United States. The arrival of both groups precipitated civil disorders. Both groups were feared to contain common criminals (and both groups did). In each instance, however, the general public overlooked the fact that the offspring of common criminals sometimes become some of our more upstanding citizens and, sometimes, noteworthy politicians. Finally, in both instances, a small number of those who emigrated soon decided to return to their homelands. The two or three thousand Irish per year who chose to return were relatively free to do so. The Cubans who wish to return, however, are hindered in their efforts by the modern intricacies of foreign relations and extensive bureaucracies.

MIGRATIONS AS COLLECTIVE BEHAVIOR

Blumer identifies migrations as one of several kinds of *mass behavior*, which he characterizes as the behavior of groups composed of anonymous individuals responding in parallel fashion to a common event or idea (1939:78). Within the mass there is little if any communication, coordination, or control. There may be a sense of pursuing a common goal, but instead of generating a sense of cooperation in the mass, a sense of competition arises. The mass behaves in terms of anonymous individuals working to answer their own needs. The form of mass behavior is determined by individual lines of activity rather than by concerted action.

Turner and Killian's brief discussion of migrations proceeds much along the lines set forth by Blumer. Turner and Killian discuss migrations as part of the *diffuse crowd*, which also includes such phenomena as fads, crazes, and deviant epidemics (1972:111–41). They characterize migrations as involving "a certain amount of social contagion and *we feeling* (or group solidarity), even though in the final analysis, the activity remains primarily individualistic" (1972:136).

Most collective behavior discussions, then, characterize migrations as homogeneous and individualistic in nature. From this standpoint, migrations are motivated by people's overblown, hysterical images of a "promised land" where they will find unlimited opportunity or at least shelter from their current misfortunes. There is minimal cooperation and much competition among migrating people, caused either by the excitement of reaching the promised land or by the desire to get there before others.

Perhaps it might be fruitful to analyze some migrations from the standpoint of mass behavior. The 1849 gold rush to California may have involved unrealistic views of attaining wealth and may have been characterized by individualistic competition. We could consider the drift of U.S. population to the Sun Belt states in terms of individual or family decisions made with respect to such things as rising energy costs in the northern states and increased job opportunities in the South. These migrations, however, are not typical of most human migrations.

MIGRATIONS AS COLLECTIVE ACTION

Migrations are complex and differentiated phenomena. This characterization is fundamentally the opposite of the mass behavior characterization. Migrations arise from multiple rather than single causes, and they involve concerted behavior rather than homogeneous, individualist action. Migrations involve various expressed motives from numbers of sources rather than a single, compelling vision of the promised land. Migrations involve *dispersal process* and *collective locomotion*, which were discussed in chapter 2.

Migrations can be seen as taking place along a continuum. At one end of the continuum are groups who set out proudly and with great fanfare to go to a new land of opportunity. Examples of this extreme form of migration are hard to find, although this may not be too inaccurate a characterization of some wagon train departures heading West from St. Joseph, Missouri in the 1840s and 1850s. At the other end of the continuum are migrations that are aptly described as a *forced dispersal* of people with little regard for their welfare or ultimate destination. Perhaps the most extreme form of this kind of migration since World War II was Pol Pot's Khmer Rouge forced dispersal of the urban populations in Cambodia in 1975.

Other migrations result from people fleeing racial and ethnic conflict, or an ethnic group being attacked and expelled by another group. It was in Bosnia in the early 1990s that we first heard the term "ethnic cleansing" to refer to the expulsion of Muslim Croats from predominantly Serbian towns and villages. The Serbs are largely Eastern Orthodox Christian. In addition to expulsion, Serbian forces imprisoned many military-age male Croat refugees, and some expulsions were accompanied by mass killings. United Nations forces were used to restore order in Bosnia.

While Muslim Albanians make up 90 percent of Kosovo's population, Serbia is internationally recognized as having control over Kosovo. In 1996, Albanians established the Kosovo Liberation Army (KLA). The KLA succeeded in expelling Serbs and establishing a number of KLA-controlled areas in Kosovo. However, in February of 1998, arch-nationalist and Serbian president Slobodan Milosevic sent Serbian army troops to take back KLA-controlled areas of Kosovo. This military operation soon deteriorated into a pattern of ethnic cleansing and government-sponsored violence against Albanian civilians. Tens of thousands of Albanians were driven from Kosovo, and mass killings occurred while U.N. peace efforts floundered. Finally, NATO resorted to military action in the spring of 1999 when it launched an air campaign against the Serb army. Initially, the air campaign seemed to intensify Serb attacks against Albanians, and many critics doubted whether air attacks could halt ethnic cleansing. After 78 days of bombing, Serbia finally agreed to sign a U.N.-approved peace agreement with NATO on June 9. The U.N. and NATO quickly set about several difficult tasks including the resettlement of returning Albanians, disarming KLA and Serbian militias, and preparing housing for the approaching winter.

Migrations are often a byproduct of racial and ethnic conflict. The breakup of the nation of Yugoslavia, for instance, has been accompanied by nearly a decade of continuous ethnic strife, particularly in the former provinces of Bosnia and Kosovo. Muslims, Christians, Croats, Serbs, and Albanians each have been both victor and vanquished in this bitter conflict. Even before violence flared in Kosovo in 1998, about 600,000 displaced people were living in the former Yugoslav territory or in other European nations, particularly Germany. Similar ethnic conflict has generated even larger numbers of displaced persons in east Africa, particularly in the Rwanda region.

REFUGEES AND INTERNALLY DISPLACED PERSONS

The term "refugee" refers to a person who flees his or her country due to persecution or violence. The 1951 United Nations Refugee Convention adopted a uniform definition of refugees and specifically demanded that they be protected. An "internally displaced person" (IDP) is a refugee who did not—or could not—flee to a neighboring country but rather remained inside his or her own country. IDPs flee for much the same reasons refugees flee—persecution, human rights abuse, or civil war. There is no international instrument or treaty that defines internally displaced persons or provides for their protection.

Statistics on refugees and internally displaced persons are often inexact and controversial. One country's refugee is another's illegal alien. Today's internally displaced person may be tomorrow's refugee. As such, government tallies cannot always be trusted to give full and unbiased accounts of refugee movements. Statistics compiled by the United States Committee for Refugees (1997) as well as the United Nations High Commissioner for Refugees (UNHCR) indicate that the worldwide population of refugee and IDPs has been somewhere between 13 and 18 million people since 1987.

These numbers reflect statistics on two categories of uprooted people: asylum seekers who are awaiting a refugee status determination, and refugees who are unwilling or unable to return to their home countries because they fear persecution or armed conflict. Counting refugees accurately is difficult. In emergency situations it is often impossible to ascertain numbers reliably. In large-scale refugee situations, people move in and out of refugee camps, often without notifying UNHCR or the local authorities. "Closed" camps, where the movement of residents is subject to control, are an exception. Only a few of the industrialized countries maintain a refugee register from which the increases and decreases in the refugee population can be established. Information on asylum seekers once they have been granted refugee status, including spontaneous departures, emigration and cessation of refugee status, is usually unavailable.

Statistics can become outdated quickly as a result of sudden new arrivals or departures. Significant forced displacements may go un- or underreported. Thus, in a number of instances, UNHCR is unable to establish or verify the total refugee population in the country but can only collect information on those refugees with whom their office has come into contact. Increases in the refugee population are generally more accurately recorded than decreases, and in countries where refugees are assisted by UNHCR, refugee numbers may be overestimated (UNHCR, 1998). Given such difficulties in counting and monitoring trends in the numbers of displaced persons, it can be concluded with caution that since 1995, the world trend has been, happily, toward reduced numbers of uprooted persons.

Dispersal Processes: Mobilization and Departure

Flight from a disaster area is an infrequent occurrence. Authorities who attempt to evacuate people from threatened or dangerous areas often encounter resistance. Following even partial evacuations, people usually attempt to return to their communities before it is entirely safe to do so. In short, it is usually difficult to get people to leave their homes and community for even short periods of time.

Given the normal tendency for people to remain in their home community, even under extremely adverse conditions, what gives rise to migrations? If we can make any generalization, it is that many migrations have been preceded by the sudden appearance of circumstances that, for all practical purposes, make it impossible for people to continue their traditional or accustomed way of life. It is obvious that human beings are extremely adaptable to changing circumstances. But if the change is sudden, stark, and far reaching, the capacity to adapt can be exceeded.

Many human migrations have followed disasters of such magnitude that large areas were rendered virtually uninhabitable by the survivors. The only natural forces seemingly able to produce disasters of such scope are disease and climatic shifts; the only human-made force is war. The migration of the Irish to the United States was precipitated by a disastrous potato blight that for three consecutive years, 1846–1849, totally devastated Ireland's food production. For the past twenty years, areas of eastern Africa have been swept by intense drought, destroying areas that for thousands of years produced crops; provided grazing land for cattle, goats, and sheep; and supported large populations. The migration of starving people to the refugee camps of Somalia was the result (Kohl, 1981:756–75).

A Red Cross worker aids drought victims. In the twentieth century, portions of eastern Africa were swept by intense drought that caused the migration of starving people to refugee camps like this one.

The impact of disasters is increased by the failure of governments to make concerted efforts to alleviate the plight of those affected. In Ireland, for example, the colonial government and Parliament made no provision, aside from the workhouses, for the tenant farmers and farm laborers who were first affected by the famine. In eastern Africa, the countries of Ethiopia, Kenya, and Somalia continue to devote substantial portions of their national resources to fighting border wars, while drought refugees swell the refugee centers in Somalia to more than 2 million. The occupants of these camps are mainly women, children, and old men. Young men have joined or have been forced to join the armies of Kenya, Ethiopia, and Somalia, or they have migrated farther north, seeking work in the Arabian Peninsula oil fields. Kenya and Ethiopia view international relief efforts as "indirect military aid," relieving Somalian men of their familial obligations so that they can go off to fight (Kohl, 1981:761). Migrants often face desperate situations in terms of securing their livelihood, when governments are unwilling or unable to help them.

Authorities Initiate Migrations In some instances, authorities may be hostile rather than simply indifferent to the migrants. Landlords tumbled cottages to "encourage" dispossessed tenants to accept passage out of Ireland. The armies of Somalia, Kenya, and Ethiopia steal the sheep, goats, and cattle of Somalian migrants. Finally, some migrations result from open attacks on minorities by majority religious, political, or ethnic groups.

The practice of driving out the unwanted provides some of the grimmest historical examples of "righteous" brutality. If the victims survive the initial attacks, numbers of them migrate to different areas. Thus millions of people who were identified with the United States during the Vietnam War have been driven out of Laos and Cambodia and into refugee camps in Thailand. Likewise, almost a half a million people left the southern part of Vietnam after the war, migrating by boat to Hong Kong and Malaysia. Some of these "boat people" eventually found their way to Europe and the United States.

The migrations that are considered in the above examples resulted from authorities encouraging the migration of undesirables or using violence in an attempt to expel them. Sometimes authorities attempt not to expel a group but to enslave or exterminate them. In these instances, groups migrate in spite of the efforts of authorities. Perhaps the clearest example of this type of migration was people's escape from Nazi-controlled areas of Europe between the years 1936 and 1945. Hundreds of thousands of Jews, Catholics, and other eastern European groups escaped through the underground. Those migrating needed fake passports, travel permits, and places to hide, eat, and rest, as well as transportation. Groups such as the Society of Friends, also known as the Quakers, have a long history of providing such things out of humanitarian concern. Other groups have provided these services at high cost.

Migrations Initiated in Other Ways Certain migrations are initiated out of despair and hunger. During the twentieth century, vast areas of Africa and Asia periodically have been swept by famine. Daily, hundreds of emaciated and starving people come out of the desert areas of Kenya, Ethiopia, and Somalia or the jungles of Laos and Cambodia and arrive at refugee camps. People are starving in areas that once exported food or at least provided an adequate livelihood. Today, because of war and fractured social structures, food production is one-tenth of what it was formerly. Large populations simply have been cast adrift to fend for themselves.

Clearly, not all migrations involve the breakdown of social structures or harassment by authorities. Some groups initiate migration on the basis of requests and other information from those outside their country. Countries with a high demand for labor may advertise abroad for workers. Even after the worst of the Irish famine years, wealthy American families continued to advertise and pay passage for Irish women to serve as maids. Fruit and vegetable growers throughout the United States utilize temporary farm laborers from Mexico. The *brasero* program is frequently criticized as exploitation and is opposed by the United Farm Workers and religious groups. England, France and Germany utilize temporary workers imported from southern and eastern Europe and North Africa to regulate their nation's labor supply. Arabian oil fields employ workers from all over the world. Initially, many of these work agreements are viewed as temporary, both by the host country and by the migrant groups. The host country sends the migrants back once they are no longer needed; the migrants plan to return to their homes and families once they have earned a considerable amount of money. Often, this is just what happens; occasionally, however, migrants establish social ties and remain in the host country.

Collective Locomotion: The Journey

The mass behavior conception of migration emphasizes the contagion and excitement among migrating people as they individualistically strive to reach their destination. Turner and Killian point out that aroused emotion is not sufficient to sustain a social movement (1972:247–50); rather, organizational structure and a program of action are necessary to sustain it. In like manner, it seems clear that excitement is not sufficient to sustain a migration. Once a migration is underway, excitement quickly gives way to weariness and thoughts of decent meals and soft beds (cf. Walker, 1966). Any additional excitement that occurs en route is usually caused by fear for one's survival. As with social movements, a degree of social structure and cooperation is needed to sustain a migration.

The Flight of the Nez Percé On June 17, 1877, Companies F and H of the United States First Cavalry attempted to force a group of 650–750 Nez Percé Indians onto Idaho's Fort Lawpi Indian Reservation. The ensuing battle of White Bird Canyon was a culmination of this and earlier disputes. Thirty-four soldiers were killed and seven wounded. Only two warriors were wounded, and no Nez Percé were taken to the reservation.

Following the battle, the group decided to make a break for the Canadian border in the hope of obtaining sanctuary. The band was led by several chiefs, including Joseph, Looking Glass, and Yellow Wolf. For the next eleven weeks, this band of warriors, women, children, and elderly were pursued by at least ten separate U.S. Army units of infantry, cavalry, and artillery.

Their flight took them across some of the most rugged terrain in North America. The Nez Percé fled southward, down the Bitterroot Mountain range between Idaho and Montana, then bore eastward into Wyoming and through what is now Yellowstone National Park. Then they headed northward through the mountains of central Montana. When they were within sixty miles of the Canadian border, they were overtaken in the Bear Paw Mountains. Here, the Nez Percé held off a cavalry and artillery siege for three days in freezing rain and snow.

Finally, the main body of Nez Percé, led by Chief Joseph, surrendered. Chief Looking Glass had died in the siege, and Chief Yellow Wolf and a few dozen Nez

Percé who had been separated from the main group escaped into Canada. Altogether, 418 Nez Percé surrendered, including 147 children, 65 elderly, and more than 40 wounded. In the eleven weeks since they left White Bird Canyon, this group had traveled more than seventeen hundred miles (Beal, 1963).

Throughout this ordeal, the Nez Percé social structure and discipline endured. This was a major reason that they were able to successfully evade the U.S. Cavalry for so long. Chiefs Joseph, Looking Glass, and Yellow Wolf maintained their authority and acted as strategists, frequently seeking advice from other chiefs and subchiefs in the group.

The Nez Percé engaged the U.S. Cavalry eleven times in addition to the battles at White Bird Canyon and the Bear Paws. The warriors' success in these battles was due to their coordinated offensive and defensive maneuvering. Effective in their own right, the warriors' tactics were additionally confusing to the soldiers because the Nez Percé were not "fighting like Indians." Finally, a factor in their evading the U.S. Cavalry was the Indians' ability to set up and strike camp quickly and to gather food on the move. This was quite an accomplishment for a group that was not traditionally nomadic. Most of the responsibilities in this area were assumed by women, children, and the elderly (Beal, 1963).

Steerage The transportation of migrants is usually quite lucrative, as exemplified by the steerage accommodations aboard ships. During the age of the great ocean liners (1850–1950), first- and second-class passengers were referred to as ladies and gentlemen, while third-class, or steerage, passengers were referred to as males and females. Until the 1920s, virtually all steerage passengers from Europe to the United States were emigrants, in part because steerage passage cost a small fraction of what other accommodations cost. Nonetheless, steerage fares represented one-third of the shipping company revenues and more than half their profits during the age of the great liners (Maddocks, 1978:58).

Between 1850 and 1920, more than 30 million people had crossed in steerage, mostly under wretched conditions. There were usually only two toilets for the entire steerage section, and the canvas bunks were only eighteen inches wide and frequently four tiered. Agents often overbooked steerage, adding to the crowding. Such close confinement contributed to the filth and stench as well as to the spread of disease. Death rates ran as high as 10 percent on some voyages.

Steerage passengers were kept strictly apart from the other passengers: they were boarded and departed from separate gangways. If any above-deck areas were made available, they were the small freight-handling decks. First- and second-class passengers enjoying their fine meals, entertainment, and recreation facilities were often quite unaware of the disease, filth, and misery on the decks below them. At the end of the voyage, steerage passengers were required to scrub and dry the steerage areas before leaving ship.

These distinctions were maintained under all conditions, including disasters at sea. During the sinking of the *Titanic* on April 15, 1912, armed crewmen guarded the passages leading up from steerage decks and only opened them after most of the lifeboats were away. The old nautical rule of "women and children first" was replaced with "steerage last." In all, 1,503 men, women, and children died in the sinking of the *Titanic*. Twelve percent of the women and only one child in first- and second-class died, 40 percent of the women and 53 of the 76 children in steerage died. The survival rate of men in first class was greater than that of children in steerage (Broom and Selznik, 1968:175). The heavy death toll among steerage passengers in the *Titanic* disaster was not atypical. Emigrant ship passengers have represented the bulk of those lost at sea throughout maritime history.

Exploitation of Migrants Those who exploit migrants are not just the petty criminals, typified by the runners who preyed on Irish immigrants. Such exploitation can become virtually institutionalized as established groups profit from the migrants' plight, and if laws are broken in the process, the legal restitution to migrants is slow in coming. In 1834 Alabama speculators were paying Creek landowners about ten cents on the dollar for their estates. As the Creek people were to be removed by the U.S. Army to the Oklahoma Indian territory, it was a buyers' market. Speculators urged the Creeks to sell quickly before the artificially depressed prices went even lower. The federal government largely ignored this early white-collar thievery (Jahoda, 1975:143–59).

In 1837 the Chickasaw people were being removed from Mississippi to the Oklahoma Indian territory. For this unwanted action, the Chickasaw were obliged to reimburse the United States government for the expenses of transporting them westward. Rations were to be provided by private contractors. Altogether, the Chickasaw paid about $200,000 for spoiled pork, flour, and corn and were billed another $700,000 for rations they did not receive. It took the Chickasaw people fifty years to obtain settlement from the government for the food not delivered, spoiled food, and baggage lost during their removal (Jahoda, 1975:172).

Even today we find that illegal immigrants to the United States, particularly from Mexico and Central America, are exploited on both sides of the border. In Mexico, they are at the mercy of those who lead groups of illegal immigrants across the border. Once across the border, illegal immigrants are exploited in sweatshops and fields. Many are employed illegally in the service economy, working in the homes of the wealthy or in restaurants and hotels.

Migrations: Arrival

For many migrants today, a difficult journey often ends in an indefinite stay at a refugee camp. Cubans from the Freedom Flotilla were detained at Fort Chaffee, Arkansas, for nearly three years. Some refugees were intimidated and attacked by the violent among them. Although all but a handful of the refugees eventually found sponsors, it was a long and emotionally draining wait. The legal status of some refugees remained uncertain for many years.

While the accommodations at Fort Chaffee were austere, some refugee camps have been little more than "dying grounds." In the last half of the twentieth century, the most notorious of these have been located in Thailand, Somalia, Ethiopia, Uganda, Zambia and Rwanda. In these camps residents did not receive enough food to sustain life over an extended period of time, and most people who arrived ill or in the advanced stages of starvation died. In these camps, population densities at times exceeded fifteen hundred people per acre, overburdening the water supply and sewage facilities. Outbreaks of tuberculosis, measles, dysentery, and malaria were common. When food and water trucks were delayed by as little as a few hours, the death rates rose dreadfully. Little is known about the social organization of these refugee camps.

At the other end of the continuum are immigrant communities within host countries. In cities across the United States, there are neighborhoods named Germantown, Little Poland, Little Italy, El Barrio, or Chinatown. Within these communities native languages are spoken, native newspapers are published, traditional foods are served, and other native customs and social relationships are maintained. These communities provide recent and many not-so-recent immigrants with employment, information, companionship, and a place to either find relief from the pressures of assimilation or avoid assimilation altogether. Within these communities, immigrant organizations such as the Puerto Rican Young Lords Party or the Chinese *tongs* provide everything from a political voice to illegal goods and services. In many respects, immigrant communities are more cohesive and complex in their social organization than the larger communities surrounding them (Schaefer, 1979:289–328). Immigrant communities clearly are not distinguished by a sense of individualistic competition, which is part of the mass behavior characteristic of migrations.

Refugee Camps An enormous number of Palestinian refugees were created in 1967 by the six-day war in the Middle East. Nearly half of the world's refugees reside in the Middle East. Palestinian refugees and Jewish settlements have been the basic barrier to peace in this region since 1967. While some refugee camps gradually took on the characteristics of permanent settlements in the region, other camps were relocated by Israeli security forces. One such camp, Sumoud, consisting of about five hundred people living in tents and shacks, was destroyed in the spring of 1998. This camp had been previously broken up a year earlier. Many of the residents of Sumoud took shelter in an unfinished school building with no water or sanitation and were later moved out by authorities. The Sumoud Camp Council has long demanded a place to live in Jerusalem for a reasonable rent that suits their economic situation. The Council has petitioned for the right to live without the permanent threat of ID card confiscation or the loss of social welfare (Israeli National Insurance), and to have access to state health insurance. A number of Palestinian rights organizations have supported Sumoud residents and their demands (BADIL, 1998).

In fluid situations, refugee camps have been set up by refugees themselves, without help from governments, nongovernment organizations (NGOs) or the United Nations (UNHCR). Camps may be set up in areas the refugees deem as "safe," or at locations where exhaustion, hunger, epidemic, or weather put an end to their flight. The United Nations has established food, water, and sanitation standards for refugee camps. UNHCR attempts to monitor all refugee camps and work with government and nongovernment organizations to provide immediate support to camp residents and to work toward the return of refugees to their place of origin. Where return is not an option, the UNHCR works to find some other place of permanent residence for refugees.

In its work, UNHCR greatly relies on NGOs, such as Impact Teams International in Bosnia. Organizations such as Council of Churches Refugee and Migration Service and the International Catholic Migration Commission (ICMC) work closely with the United Nations Children's Fund (UNICEF) in the interests of displaced children. These church organizations are nondenominational in their day-to-day workings. The International Federation of Red Cross and Red Crescent Societies, through 169 national societies, cares for refugees and internally displaced persons outside areas of conflict. The secretariat mobilizes the International Federation's own financial and in-kind contributions and health, social welfare, logistics, and managerial staff to supplement Red Cross and Red Crescent Societies' and UNHCR's resources. The Federation has observer status to the U.N. General Assembly.

The European Council on Refugees and Exiles (ECRE) is a council of 60 NGOs including the International Organization for Migration (IOM), representing 68 countries, and The European Legal Network on Asylum (ELENA), an NGO consisting of legal counselors. ECRE and its member NGOs assist refugees and are concerned with refugee and asylum policy. ECRE monitors national and international developments, promotes legal and information networks, and advocates progressive standards for the treatment of refugees and asylum seekers. The International Organization for Migration (IOM) was established in 1951 to arrange resettlement processing and transportation of refugees and migrants. IOM conducts related programs for medical screening, language training, and cultural orientation.

In addition to the organizations mentioned, there are literally thousands of other NGOs that operate to aid refugees, internally displaced persons, and asylum seekers. Some of these NGOs properly could be viewed as "emergent organizations," arising during a particular conflict or famine and having limited organizational structure. Other NGOs are church based and attempt to recruit or convert those they assist. NGOs often compete with each other for resources while attempting to render assistance to the displaced.

SUMMARY

This chapter began with descriptions of two migrations: the Irish migration to the United States in the 1840s and the Freedom Flotilla migration of Cubans to the United States in the spring of 1980. Although these two events are separated by over a century, they are similar in several ways: both groups left countries with economies and governments that were under severe strain from agricultural failures. Those who left were not fully welcome in their own countries. Both groups endured great hardship during their travel and encountered resistance upon their arrival in the United States.

There are perhaps between 15 and 30 million displaced people throughout the world today. They are migrants who have fled from drought, war, and religious and racial hatred. It is this kind of migration that is of interest to those who study collective behavior. Historically, though, the collective behavior literature has had a great deal to say about riots, rebellions, and revolutions but relatively little to say about the migrations that often accompany them. Blumer and Turner and Killian discuss migrations from the standpoint of mass behavior and the diffuse crowd. From this point of view, migrations are similar to fads and crazes; that is, they involve aroused emotions, mass hysteria, and are homogeneous and individualistic phenomena.

The collective action perspective suggests an alternate point of view. Migrations are complex and differentiated phenomena involving processes of dispersal and collective locomotion. We have briefly considered the social conditions and the actions of authorities and the migrants themselves that are necessary for initiating dispersal. Collective locomotion, or the actual journey, involves varying degrees of social organization. Part of the character of migrants' journeys results from the vulnerability of migrants to exploitation by established groups. Migrants today live under a wide range of conditions, from disease-ridden refugee camps to largely self-contained immigrant communities within many cities in the United States. They are assisted by governments, NGOs, and the United Nations.

⚒ CHAPTER 10 ⚒

INDIVIDUALS IN DISASTER

It's kind of hard for us to remember that this euphoria and this success is for a film that's based on a real event that happened, where real people died, that shocked the world in 1912. I'd just like everybody to go with me for just a second. I'd like to do a few seconds of silence in remembrance of the 1,500 men, women, and children who died when the great ship died. And the message of *Titanic*, of course, is that if the great ship can sink, the unthinkable can happen, the future's unknowable. The only thing that we truly own is today. Life is precious. So during these few seconds, I'd like you to also listen to the beating of your own heart, which is the most precious thing in the world. Join me for seconds of silence.

—James Cameron, accepting the award for Best Picture,
1998 Academy Awards

One of the most successful movies of all time is about a disaster: James Cameron's 1998 film, *Titanic*. The film won 11 Oscars, in the categories of directing, art direction, cinematography, costume design, film editing, original dramatic score, original song, sound, sound effects editing, visual effects, and of course, best picture. Not since 1959 when the film *Ben-Hur* also won eleven Academy Awards has a movie done so well. *Titanic* also received four Golden Globe Awards as best dramatic motion picture, motion picture director, original score and original song. *Titanic* was a box-office phenomenon, grossing $601 million, surpassing its closest rival, *Star Wars* (1977) by $140 million. The movie was released on video in the summer of 1998 and enjoyed massive sales. Costumes, jewelry, and props used in the Cameron film, as well as items salvaged from the wreck, are today highly prized.

Although the *Titanic* sank in 1912, this event continues to resonate to the present day. Cameron's *Titanic is* the latest of several movies, including *A Night to Remember* (1958), *The Unsinkable Molly Brown* (1964), and *Raise the Titanic* (1980), that feature this disaster in some fashion. Dozens of film and video documentaries concerning the disaster were made. Discovery of the wreckage in 1985 inspired a flurry of new documentaries, newspaper features, and coverage in *National Geographic*.

Since the discovery of its resting place, the *Titanic* has become the focus of a struggle between those who would preserve the site as a memorial and those who have interests in salvaging items from the wreck. A joint French and American scientific expedition led by Dr. Robert Ballard used robot and manned submersibles to explore and photograph the wreck site during 1985–1986. No items were removed from the wreck, and Ballard did not claim salvage rights to what he considered to be a cemetery. In 1986, *RMS Titanic, Inc.* was formed by an international group to recover, preserve, and display *Titanic* artifacts. *RMS Titanic, Inc.* was granted the exclusive salvor-in-possession rights to the ship, and recovery began in 1987. Since then, thousands of artifacts, including a 20-ton section of the hull, have been recovered by *RMS Titanic, Inc.* These items are now on display in several museums and in traveling exhibitions throughout the world. Some items are now also in the hands of private collectors.

People are still greatly fascinated by the *Titanic* disaster, even though it happened nearly a century ago. Other great disasters are also commemorated and remembered as major events in the history of cities and towns throughout the world. The great fires of London and Chicago, the Galveston and Johnstown floods, and the great San Francisco earthquake are but a few of the disasters that have attained permanent historical significance. People in the Atlantic and Gulf Coast states have developed a "hurricane culture" within which specific decades are remembered with reference to notable hurricanes. The 1960s gave us Donna, Carla and Camile, the 1970s featured Agnes and Frederic, the 1980s had Juan, Gloria and Hugo, and the 1990s shuddered under the impact of Andrew, Fran and Floyd. Family histories are replete with hurricane stories. People have developed nearly ritualistic behavior in preparing for and riding out hurricanes. The hurricane party is a social custom unique to the Eastern and Gulf Coast regions of the United States.

Disasters fascinate people because they are often important landmark events in a nation's history. Disasters are sometimes the primary impetus for major and progressive social reforms. After a disaster zoning rules and building codes may be strengthened, fire departments may be upgraded, or disaster planning may be implemented. Finally, disasters are often major events in family histories and in our own lives.

RESPONSE TO DISASTER

The agents of disaster, of which the sinking of the *Titanic* is a classic example, include fires and explosions, floods, tornadoes, hurricanes, and earthquakes, as well as airplane crashes, train wrecks, and the sinking of ships. Disasters often strike without warning, and when they do, people face unexpected and unfamiliar problems that demand direct and prompt action. There is the obvious problem of sheer survival at the moment when disaster strikes. During impact, individuals must confront and cope with their fears while at the same time looking to their own and others' safety. After disaster impact, people encounter numerous problems demanding life-and-death decisions as they carry out rescues and aid the injured. During disasters people must make do with what is at hand: people with needed information are missing; utilities have been knocked out; shelter is in short supply; and transportation systems are in shambles. *Improvising* is the key activity in disaster response. In this chapter we will examine how individuals improvise to cope with the many problems that are created by disasters.

Of course, a range of other problems accompanies disasters. These problems are confronted by *organizations, communities,* and *societies.* Police and fire departments, for example, are usually the first organizations to respond to disaster, undergoing important transformations as they do so. Communities are also transformed by disaster. In particular, communities are greatly altered as outside agencies and organizations arrive to provide assistance. Finally, some societies are better able than others to channel resources to disaster-struck regions. We will consider these problems in chapter 11.

In this chapter we focus on *individuals* in disaster, beginning with the description of multifatality evacuations. Tragedies such as the 1974 Gulliver's Discothèque fire in Port Chester, New York, and the 1977 Beverly Hills Supper Club fire in South Gate, Kentucky, are sometimes described as *stampede panics*—part of the popular imagery often used to refer to fatal theater, nightclub, and hotel fires. Neither of these fires killed as many as the worst building fire in our nation's history, Boston's Cocoanut Grove fire in 1942, that killed nearly 500 people.

Fire and Multifatality Evacuations

Gulliver's Disco Gulliver's Discothèque in Port Chester, New York, was a popular establishment that catered largely to a young adult clientele. Patrons entered Gulliver's on the ground floor, which contained a bar, dining area, and an enclosed kitchen. Just inside the main doors was a narrow flight of stairs that descended into another bar and a dance floor known as the Pit. The split-level layout seemed to add character to the establishment.

A few minutes past midnight on July 1, 1974, more than three hundred people were packed into Gulliver's. The band finished their last set at about 12:50 A.M., when the club manager told the band to ask everyone to leave because a fire had broken out in the building adjoining Gulliver's. The low-key announcement urged everyone to remain calm and leave carefully. Some patrons began to leave the Pit and other areas of Gulliver's and went outside to watch the fire next door. The smell of smoke began to spread throughout Gulliver's, and increasing numbers of people began to leave in an orderly manner. Suggestions were made that people remove their high-platform shoes to avoid ankle injuries on the stairs. Regular patrons began to move toward basement exits, guiding others unfamiliar with the layout of the building. A majority of those in the Pit, however, remained and continued their conversations and drinking.

Ten minutes later, at least one hundred people remained in Gulliver's and the band again announced that everyone should leave. Then, dense black smoke erupted from the ceiling and fire exploded across the dance floor and bandstand. Large air-conditioning units tore away from the ceiling and crashed into the crowd below. Orderly dispersal became impossible. Blinded and choking patrons exiting up the stairs began to collide with people leaving the ground floor. Others stumbled and fell on the stairs. People moving to the basement or dining room exits became disoriented in the noise and smoke. Unsure of the location and condition of exits, two couples dropped to the dance floor and covered their heads with jackets.

The local volunteer fire department received the call at 1:07 A.M. and responded quickly. When the first units arrived, flames had already broken through the roof of Gulliver's, and most who were to survive had already made their way to safety. Firefighters entered the building and rescued a few semiconscious people, including the two couples on the dance floor. The next day, headlines across the nation described terror-stricken crowds and panic stampedes for the exits. In all, twenty-six young people died.

Beverly Hills Supper Club The Beverly Hills Supper Club in Southgate, Kentucky, was one of the region's most popular night spots. On Saturday evening, May 28, 1977, between 2,400 and 2,800 patrons had come to the club for banquets and stage entertainment. About half the occupants were in the Cabaret Room to watch the featured stage show. The fire started in a small, unoccupied service room and burned for some time before being discovered by club employees. The employees unsuccessfully tried to extinguish the fire, and it was several minutes before a call was placed to the fire department or patrons were notified of the fire. Most of the patrons were evacuated safely with the assistance of the employees. Notification of patrons in the Cabaret Room and the upstairs Zebra Room occurred after the evacuation by others was well underway. Most of the 164 deaths occurred in the Cabaret Room (Best, 1977). Within hours of the fire, specialists from the National Fire Protection Association (NFPA) joined the Kentucky State Police and began what would be a two-week, on-site investigation of the fire. Ultimately, the investigation would come to include personnel from the Kentucky State Police and Fire Marshall's Office, the National Bureau of Standards, the National Fire Prevention and Control Administration and the Southgate Fire Department. Police interviewed the owners and employees of the club, and a survey questionnaire obtained information from several hundred survivors. Because of this extensive investigation, we know much about the development of the Beverly Hills Supper Club fire and people's behavior during the escape period.

Large-Scale Accidents

Sea Disaster Friday night, March 6, 1987, the passenger and freight ferry *Herald of Free Enterprise* capsized outside the Belgian harbor of Zeebrugge with the loss of 189 lives. The number of people aboard the *Herald* when it left port will never be known. At that time, most ferry lines, including Townsend Thoresen, did not make passenger lists, and ticket sales did not accurately reflect the number of people aboard. Some survivors may not have checked in at disaster reporting centers, and some bodies may have been washed out to sea. The formal investigation report estimated that there were 539 people aboard the *Herald* (459 passengers and 80 crew), which is about 60 less than the newspapers' estimate of nearly 600. At least 189 people (151 passengers and 38 crew) are known to have died. Still, it is clear that about two-thirds of those people aboard the *Herald* were able to escape, under particularly terrifying and difficult conditions. The 8,000-ton roll on/roll off ferry had inadvertently left the harbor with its 20-foot-wide bow doors open. As the ship picked up speed, waves broke over the scoop-shaped loading ramp, and hundreds of tons of water entered the vehicle deck. This caused the bow to dig even deeper into the water, swinging the ship nearly 140 degrees from its direction of travel. The *Herald of Free Enterprise* then rolled onto its port side, coming to rest on a submerged sand bank, leaving the entire starboard side above water. The capsizing occurred in less than 30 seconds. Had the *Herald* been half a mile further to sea, it would have been in deep water and capsized totally, probably killing everyone aboard.

As the ship tipped, people were thrown across lounges, down hallways and through glass partitions. The emergency lighting system failed. In the dark, people clung to tables, stairs, partitions, and door sills to keep from dropping into the freezing water. Many of those in the water drowned immediately or, because of the cold and their injuries, were immobilized by shock or suffered heart attacks. Moments after the ship came to rest, a few passengers and members of the crew broke out windows and climbed onto the side of the ship. Those who escaped immediately took ropes and tools from the lifeboats but, without lights, they were greatly hindered in their efforts to rescue people struggling in the total darkness below (*The Times*, 1987b, c).

Ships and boats quickly converged from all over the harbor. Police and military forces also arrived within minutes of the capsizing. The Belgian crisis plan for the harbor was activated when the first mayday was received from the scene. This proved to be a very effective plan, and within fifteen minutes of the rollover more than 100 Red Cross workers and 30 of 35 available ambulances were at the quay. The first survivors were soon on their way to hospitals (Vandenbussche, 1988:27–29).

The crisis plan established clear priorities for the survivors. The hypothermic and seriously injured were bundled in blankets and on their way to hospitals by ambulance within 60 seconds of being brought onto the quay. Only one of these casualties died later in the hospital, a clear indication of the effectiveness of the quayside operation. The less seriously injured were treated and transported to the hospital on city buses. Uninjured survivors were taken to a predetermined reporting center by bus. At the reporting center survivor lists were compiled and phone calls made to families. The rescue plan effectively kept the media away from survivors, and early disaster-related information was released through crisis plan officials.

Air Crash Eastern Airlines Flight 401 from New York crashed into the Florida Everglades twenty miles west of Miami International Airport at 11:42 P.M. on December 29, 1972. The jetliner, a Lockheed Tristar, carried 176 passengers and crew and hit the swamp at more than two hundred miles per hour, totally disintegrating as it cartwheeled for almost two thousand feet. Nearly all of the passenger seats ripped loose and, with their occupants, were scattered in a path six hundred feet long. Investigators later classified the crash as nonsurvivable, yet seventy-three people did survive.

The impact of the crash was sufficient to rip people's clothing from their bodies. Moments after the crash, conscious survivors found themselves injured, completely or nearly naked, wet, cold, and surrounded by darkness and devastation. There was no moonlight and the temperature was in the mid-forties. Deep saw grass, mud, and sharp shredded aluminum made walking difficult and dangerous. It would be almost thirty minutes before the first rescuer located the crash site and an hour before the first survivors would be removed to hospitals.

Survivors reported two major concerns as they waited for help. Their first concern was to give aid and comfort to those near them. Prominent among the most active survivors were the flight attendants. They gave aid and comfort to the injured and dying, often while they themselves were in great pain. They helped in the early stages of rescue. One flight attendant began to gather survivors near a prominent chunk of wreckage. She reminded people not to light matches or cigarette lighters in spite of the cold and darkness because of the danger of igniting spilled fuel, then located cushions and placed them to warm and protect the severely injured. In an effort to distract people from their injuries, she led them in singing Christmas carols. Unable to walk because of her severe internal injuries, another attendant took the job of holding and comforting an infant.

The second concern among the survivors was freeing those trapped in the wreckage and locating specific individuals. A New York clothes buyer who had survived uninjured freed two flight attendants trapped in their seats. Then he went through the wreckage and collected cushions and loose clothing and distributed them to the injured. Another passenger who had suffered only a leg wound searched for her husband until she found him alive but trapped in the wreckage. For the next hour she comforted and protected her husband, found clothing and cushions for the injured, and gave directions to the rescuers. At one point she refused to be evacuated and protested loudly that her husband was still trapped. Not until her husband was on his way to the hospital did she agree to be evacuated. After receiving treatment in the hospital, some of the flight attendants helped console the families of victims. They considered themselves valuable employees of Eastern Airlines, doing a job they had been trained to do, as best they could.

Our four examples clearly show that people can make effective adaptive responses during disaster and that they can show concern and even compassion for one another in disaster's aftermath. We usually assume quite the contrary: that people panic during disaster and that they are unable (and perhaps unwilling) to help themselves or others. These two quite differing viewpoints will be examined from the standpoint of the research done over the last forty years by various investigators, including those from the Disaster Research Center.

DISASTER: LEVELS OF ANALYSIS

We have used the term *disaster* rather freely up to this point. Some researchers, such as Dennis E. Wenger (1978), have tried to use the term more precisely, partly in order to provide a means for distinguishing clear levels of analysis in the study of disasters. The first level of analysis is that of *interpersonal* responses, which includes interaction among individuals and small groups. Events such as the evacuation of Gulliver's and the crash of Flight 401 are described and analyzed at this level. The next levels of analysis are those of *organizational, community,* and *societal* responses to disaster, discussed in chapter 11.

Wenger uses the terms *emergency* and *crisis* for the classification and analysis of disasters. In general terms, emergency situations are those in which traditional and existing social arrangements are sufficient to overcome the problems posed by disaster agents. On the other hand, crisis situations are those in which new social arrangements must be forged in order to overcome these problems.

At the first level of analysis, that of interpersonal response, emergencies refer to those situations in which group norms and relationships, though perhaps strained, are still able to cope with events. An unexpected death of a family member, for example, usually entails traveling on short notice, arranging temporary lodging, and providing meals. Established family ties as well as the traditional roles of host, hostess, pallbearer, and sympathy giver are called into play. These resources are usually sufficient to carry out a successful funeral.

The term crisis refers to those situations in which established group relationships and norms are not sufficient to cope with events, and new roles, relationships, and ways of dealing with the problem must be established immediately. In the case of Gulliver's, band members found themselves playing an unfamiliar but essential role in crowd dispersal. Some people found themselves assisting strangers to exits not normally used in exiting the nightclub. Unable to see or hear, some patrons found themselves blindly groping along crowded halls in mortal peril.

Some survivors of Flight 401 found themselves giving aid and assistance to flight attendants, while others had to make the unsettling decision as to who was alive and most in need of help.

At the level of organizational and community response, the fire at Gulliver's and the crash of Flight 401 represent emergencies. In these instances there were perhaps unusually large numbers of casualties, and, in the case of Flight 401, the crash site was quite inaccessible. Still, police and fire departments, hospitals, and the Coast Guard had adequate equipment at their disposal and tactical resources sufficient to the task.

At the level of societal response, large-scale disasters represent an emergency but not a crisis. Established federal relief programs are soon brought into operation. Recovery proceeds much as it has with earlier floods throughout the nation. From the standpoint of Wenger's analysis, the United States has faced few if any societal crises caused by natural disaster. The Dust Bowl drought of the 1930s perhaps came the closest to being a societal crisis. It produced large-scale economic disruption in the farming sector and migration from the hardest-hit regions. Many national agricultural extension services were initiated as a result of the drought. Other nations, however, have not been so lucky. Droughts, floods, famines, plagues, and earthquakes have periodically devastated the nations of Europe, Asia, Africa, and South America. Crises at the level of societal response usually entail crises at all other levels of social integration.

Table 9.1 illustrates Dennis E. Wenger's approach to the classification and analysis of disaster, using examples from chapters 9, 10, and 11. Wenger (1978) suggests classifying disaster events in terms of their impact on social integration. Emergencies can be handled within the framework of existing norms, roles, and resources within groups, organizations, communities, and societies. The response to crisis events, on the other hand, involves new or emergent norms, roles, and alterations in the use and distribution of resources. This framework is probably of little use to people stacking sandbags during a flood or to community groups planning their disaster preparedness program. However, it can be put to good use in efforts to systematically survey and evaluate the field of disaster theory and research.

TABLE 9.1
Disasters and Social Integration

Events	Interpersonal		Organizational		Community		Societal	
	emergency	crisis	emergency	crisis	emergency	crisis	emergency	crisis
Unexpected death of a family member	yes	no	no	no	no	no	no	no
Gulliver's fire	yes	yes	yes	no	no	no	no	no
Crash of Flight 401	yes	yes	yes	no	no	no	no	no
Farmers' rescue of air crash survivors	yes	yes	yes	no	yes	no	no	no
Johnstown flood	yes	yes	yes	yes	yes	yes	yes	no
Potato famine in Ireland (1840s)	yes	yes	yes	yes	yes	yes	yes	yes

PANIC AND DISASTER

Most theories and research dealing with interpersonal responses to disaster concern the issue of *panic*. Theories of collective behavior differ substantially in their views regarding panic. The mass hysteria and value-added perspectives view panic as a necessary ingredient in situations like the evacuation of Gulliver's or the reaction of passengers following a devastating air crash. Further, panic is seen as responsible for the sense of confusion and personal helplessness within communities confronted with disaster. On the other hand, the emergent-norm perspective minimizes the role of panic in disaster situations. Apparently, non-adaptive responses and confusion are not the result of panic but are the properties of emergent groups and definitions of the situation. From the standpoint of the SBI perspective, activities commonly referred to as panic, such as fatal stampedes toward exits, are better understood as behavior organized under adverse and deteriorating sensory conditions.

The "Grip of Terror" Defined

The mass hysteria and value-added perspectives consider panic to be a frequent interpersonal response to disaster. The absence of panic in these situations is taken as a stroke of luck. According to the mass hysteria perspective, pre-disaster anxiety, milling, and circular reaction produce panic. From the standpoint of the value-added model, whether one is considering a stampede panic such as Gulliver's evacuation or a financial panic such as the stock market crash of 1929, panic is rooted in hysterical beliefs. Under conditions of structural conduciveness (insufficient exits) and structural strain (strident warnings of danger), hysterical beliefs can arise that restrict people's attentiveness to their environment. People's attention becomes narrowly focused on escape and self-preservation. Thus people shove and trample others in their efforts to get to the main exit while ignoring side exits that are clear. For both the mass hysteria and value-added perspectives, the outward manifestations of panic are *intense personal terror, uncontrolled individualistic flight*, and *emotional shock*.

Intense Personal Terror During and shortly following disasters, individuals are seized by terror that strips away their veneer of socialization. People may lose their ability to speak coherently, and their behavior may appear random and ineffective. On the other hand, terror may cause people to act on the basis of unvarnished, short-term self-interest. People may become oblivious to their normal responsibilities to family, friends, jobs, and community. Gripped by such terror, disaster victims have no inclination to cooperate with others or to give aid to those who are suffering.

In the hours immediately following the capsizing of the *Herald of Free Enterprise*, recall that the media did not have access to the survivors who had been taken to hospitals or to the reporting center. Police and military sources provided only limited information to the media. Newspapers, therefore, turned to psychologists and psychiatrists to speculate about what had happened aboard the *Herald* when it capsized. Virtually all of the initial stories described intense personal terror. *The Times* of London quoted a psychiatrist's description of mass panic and chaotic fighting to get out of the sinking ferry with little heed for women and children as a typical response to such a disaster (*The Times*, 1987a). The psychiatrist went on to state authoritatively that survivors would feel completely helpless and would be too traumatized by the event to have any considered thought for others.

According to this expert, most people would have panicked within seconds. They would have started shouting and screaming, crying, running around aimlessly, and behaving totally out of control. He noted that the darkness and the water would exaggerate people's natural feelings of claustrophobia, adding to a compulsive desire to get out of danger. A psychologist explained to *The Times* that the initial psychological signs of panic come after a massive increase of adrenaline, produced through fear (*The Times*, 1987a). The heart starts racing, the body sweats effusively, and all senses are heightened to exaggerated proportions. A person so affected would jump at the slightest provocation, such as a feather brushing by. He went on to conclude that everyone on the ship would have experienced a primitive "fight or flight" response similar to that experienced by a terrified animal. The greater the terror, the greater the desire to run away, but at the same time the increased adrenaline would boost aggressive feelings; hence the theorized skirmishes between passengers fighting to escape. In some respects, these discussions were used as "filler" because of the meager amount of news from the *Herald* and Zeebrugge. Similarly, articles describing effects of hypothermia appeared in several British newspapers.

Uncontrolled Individualistic Flight The second manifestation is uncontrolled individualistic flight (or panic flight) from real or imagined danger. Panic flight contributes substantially to the death, injury, and disorder that accompany disaster. The uncontrolled and individualistic nature of flight is indicated by such things as movement toward only a few of several possible exits and people being knocked down and trampled. Panic flight may occur as a response to little more than the word *fire* spoken in a crowded auditorium (as described by Klapp in chapter 2—see the box on the mass hysteria perspective and women). The exodus of survivors from Hiroshima and Nagasaki, the movement of people during and shortly following the 1938 broadcast of the "War of the Worlds," and the migration from Ireland during the potato famine are some of the events cited as large-scale panic flights.

The likelihood and extent of flight are increased if people have experienced anxiety or other kinds of emotional strain prior to the disaster. Explicit or strident warnings of impending danger can produce sufficient anxiety to cause terror and panic flight even if the threat fails to materialize. The fear that warnings of danger can produce panic flight in nightclubs, theaters, and hotels has often resulted in the issuing of ambiguous and low-key warnings of fire or, in some cases, no warnings at all.

Postdisaster Emotional Shock The final manifestation of panic is the emotional shock that sets in shortly following disaster. Symptoms of this shock include incoherence, spatial and temporal disorientation, and helplessness. Emotional shock significantly reduces the capacity of disaster victims to engage in rescue work, to repair damage, or to find food and shelter for themselves. Civil and military authorities and disaster assistance organizations expect to encounter helpless and passive people at the scene of disasters. Let's examine these manifestations of panic to see if they actually occurred in the disasters mentioned earlier in the chapter.

The "Grip of Terror" Examined

Is panic an essential component of disasters, as the mass hysteria and value-added perspectives suggest? Put another way, are disaster victims usually gripped by terror that strips away concern for others? Are disaster victims likely to experience shock that severely limits their ability to cope with the aftermath of disaster? In light of much disaster research and consideration of incidents such as those described at the beginning of this chapter, the answer to these questions is a qualified *no.*

Terror Reactions During disasters, people exhibit a remarkable degree of composure and concern for family, friends, neighbors, and strangers. During the evacuation of Gulliver's, band members remained on the bandstand, urging people to leave and to remove platform shoes to avoid injury. Three of the band members died in the final seconds of orderly dispersal when flames shot across the bandstand. Flight attendants such as those involved in the crash of Flight 401 are trained to help passengers from their seats, down escape chutes, and away from the plane in the vital moments following air crashes. Attendants have carried out these activities while injured, being showered by flying glass and metal, and facing the very real danger of violent explosions. Following the 1977 runway collision of two 747s at the Los Rodeos Airport in the Canary Islands, passengers assisted attendants and one another in getting out of and away from the burning planes. A few passengers returned to the flaming wreckage several times to lead others to safety.

Fritz and Marks (1954:79), in their summary of early disaster research conducted by the National Opinion Research Center (NORC), note that less than 2 percent of disaster victims usually exhibit "highly or mildly agitated states involving uncontrolled behavior" during the time of disaster impact. In addition, the National Opinion Research Center collected data to ascertain if women are more likely than men to exhibit these manifestations of panic. The data show that women are more likely to be perceived and described by men as displaying panic. When self-reports are compared, however, they show that women are no more likely than men to describe themselves as having experienced panic.

In direct contrast to the earlier opinions of the experts, one of the first survivors of the capsized *Herald* to be interviewed by *The Times* described the eerie quiet that descended on the ship after it turned over. Survivors were amazed at the silence. There was some shouting and crying but not continuous screams of terror. People remained quiet to listen for other trapped passengers. Rescue started immediately as people made their way, crawling and climbing hand over hand, up the tables, chairs, benches, and anything else that was above water. Human bridges were formed across hallways, and people carried infants in their teeth as they climbed to safety.

As more news came from Zeebrugge, hardly any further mention was made of panic. Instead, articles in *The Times* (1987b) and the *Daily Telegraph* (1987) told of the heroism and selflessness of passengers and crew. Although articles occasionally mentioned people who had failed to help others, or of men who had shown little concern for women and children, when asked if the rule of "women and children first" was followed on the *Herald*, one woman replied, "This is not the *Titanic*, you know!" The irony of this remark is that the old norm of the sea was probably better adhered to on the *Herald* than on the *Titanic*, where the survival rate of men in first class was greater than that of children in steerage. When the last of the bodies were recovered from the *Herald* four weeks later, it was noted there was a preponderance of middle- and older-aged men among the casualties. This may have been a result of the "women and children first" norm, but it is also likely that older men were the least able to survive their immersion in cold water and died of shock and heart attacks.

Uncontrolled Individualistic Flight Stampede panics occur very seldom among large numbers of people gathered in nightclubs, theaters, hotels, or auditoriums. As was the case for the fire at Gulliver's, initial reports of these events often mention terror-stricken crowds and death by trampling. Later reports of the same event usually include stories of people maintaining presence of mind and acting with a concern for others. Most apparent trampling deaths later prove to have been death from asphyxiation and from poisonous fumes in the smoke. This is not to say that no one has ever been trampled in a surge as a large number of people evacuated a building; however, injuries and deaths of this sort are far fewer than injuries and deaths from smoke and flames.

It is difficult to find clear, documented instances of panic flight from communities. On the other hand, as previously mentioned in chapter 9, it is well documented that authorities find it difficult to evacuate communities. Substantial numbers of people refuse to evacuate, evacuate too slowly, or leave for locations other than those specified by authorities (Drabek, 1969). Often, people attempt to reenter the community before all danger has passed (Fritz and Mathewson, 1957). Such behavior is clearly in evidence during technological disasters, such as the accident at the Three Mile Island nuclear power plant. These problems have caused many to seriously doubt the adequacy of most community evacuation plans.

Nonflight movement following disasters has often been inaccurately described as panic flight. For example, Cantril's analysis of the "War of the Worlds" broadcast described panic flight as part of the hysterical aftermath (see chapter 5). Cantril (1940) presented interviews wherein people reported they were frightened and confused as they moved about on foot or in automobiles during and shortly following the broadcast. These interviews also indicated that people were not fleeing for their lives. Instead, interviewees reported they were going to the homes of parents, fiancées, or friends. This concern with contacting others is a common response among disaster-struck populations and should not be equated with panic flight. That same evening, interestingly, the residents of Grovers Mill, New Jersey (the small town where Martians were reported to have landed), claimed that an unusually large number of automobiles drove through their town. This is very similar to the convergence of people on the scene of disasters, which is a frequent component of disasters but can hardly be termed panic flight.

In 1973 similar inaccurate reports of panic flight followed the broadcast of a fictitious news bulletin announcing a nuclear power station accident in Sweden. Later investigation requested by the Swedish Board of Psychological Defense found that less than 10 percent of the population had misinterpreted the program as real (Rosengren, Arvidson, and Sturesson, 1975). A small number of these people (less than 1 percent of the population) subsequently attempted to contact friends or family. There was no evidence of panic flight.

Johnson, Feinberg and Johnston's (1994) examination of data from Kentucky State Police depositions taken from 342 survivors of the Beverly Hills Supper Club fire indicates that panic flight did not occur. This important finding needs to be put into context. Uncontrolled individualistic flight was held to a minimum, perhaps in part because of the extensive social bonds that were found throughout those gathered in the nightclub on the evening of the fire. Nearly 90 percent of those present were accompanied by their spouses or other family members. Ten percent indicate they were with a dating partner, and 40 percent were part of a friendship group. Almost half of the respondents were also part of a secondary group, such as a corporate-sponsored banquet. The most common pattern of social grouping was that of a married couple with friends, usually another married couple. The next most frequent patterns were: married couples alone, and married couples within a secondary grouping (the corporate banquet). Social ties to others bonded nearly everyone in the club, and many were embedded in dense networks with multiple bonds. Only five individuals (1.5 percent) reported no ties at all.

Collective Flight The Johnson, Feinberg and Johnston study (1994) tested three competing explanations of collective flight. The first is the classic, "grip of terror" panic flight model. As stated earlier, panic flight is a likely and immediate response to danger. During panic flight, people have little or no regard for social bonds, which suggests, for example, that husbands will push their wives and children aside to scramble to safety. The second model of collective flight is the "social model" in which people become very concerned with social ties in times of danger and look to the safety of the social group. During flight, people will try to escape with their family and friends and will assist others, even if it means increasing danger to themselves. The social model suggests that social ties can withstand extreme levels of stress. Finally, there is the severe threat model that suggests people initially will try to escape with their family and friends and will assist others. When there is extreme danger and an immediate threat of total entrapment, however, social ties will break down and panic will ensue.

In order to test these competing explanations of collective flight, transcripts were coded for each mention of an action that reflected concern for other group members. This *social response* measure included expression of concern for another group member's safety or concern over involuntary separation from a group member. Social response also included delay in exiting, or returning, in an effort to assemble the group as well as efforts to stay together; directing, leading, lifting, or carrying group members; and exiting together. These items were summed to create a social response index ranging from nonsocial (score = 0) to being highly concerned for others (score = 7).

Transcripts were also coded to create a measure of entrapment threat. Some respondents reported that they were able to walk directly out an exit, unhindered by others or by smoke and flame. These people perceived very little threat (score = 0). People experienced mild threat if they were forced to file through exits behind others (score = 1). Those patrons whose first choice of exit was blocked by people, smoke, or flames experienced moderate threat (score = 2). Some patrons reported that they were unable to exit without crawling under smoke or over people who had fallen, while others were carried from the building. These patrons were classified as experiencing severe threat (score = 3).

Since patrons in some areas of the Beverly Hills Supper Club were able to exit directly and were not exposed to smoke or flames, data analysis was done using the 253 patrons who were in the Cabaret Room, the three adjacent Crystal rooms,

Beverly Hills Supper Club room definitions for exit analysis

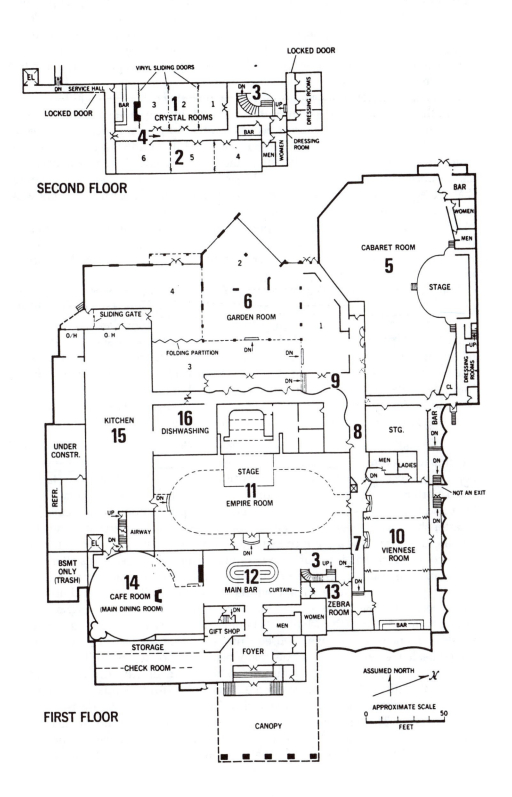

and the Empire Room, in all of which there was severe threat. All of the 253 patrons in these rooms reported at least one primary or secondary group bond, and most reported multiple, linked ties. Social response scores clearly indicate that greater concern for group members was expressed as the threat of entrapment increased. Patrons fled as members of groups, often hesitating in an effort to stay together or to assist one another. When separated, they expressed concern for the whereabouts and safety of others.

These findings generally support the social model of collective flight from danger. In the Crystal rooms, however, the main exit, by way of a circular staircase, was in flames by the time patrons became aware of the fire. Here, patrons were trapped for several minutes until an employee led them down a narrow service stairway and out through the kitchen. In the Crystal rooms, there was decreasing social concern with increasing threat (the severe threat model). It should be noted that the erosion of social concern was not total and that concern for others was shown. It was also in the Crystal rooms that the lights failed and exit was by way of a dark, narrow hallway, thereby preventing actions (such as hesitating to join one's spouse in order to escape together) that would later be coded as social responses. Most of the casualties occurred in the Cabaret Room. Here, the concern for social ties remained strong throughout.

The study by Johnson, Feinberg and Johnston (1994) provides strong support for the idea that social ties endure during collective flight from danger. Their findings lead to the rejection of the "grip of terror" image of immediate, unregulated, and nonsocial panic flight. People survived this disaster because social concern for others prevailed. People helped their spouses, friends, and work associates to safety and cooperated with them in the use of stairways, hallways, and exits. Ironically, the evidence suggests that some people died because of the strength of interpersonal social ties. Some people reentered the building in search of loved ones, and others died because they would not abandon others in their flight to safety.

Postdisaster Emotional Shock Emotional shock in the hours following disaster impact, contrary to the views of the mass hysteria and value-added approaches, occurs rarely; when it does, it is short-lived and affects relatively small portions of the population. For the early NORC studies summarized by Fritz and Marks (1954), the largest percentage of a population experiencing postdisaster shock was 14 percent (22 percent of the women and 5 percent of the men). We can state with some assurance that since then, there have been no documented instances in which a majority of a population exhibited shock reactions after disaster. Characteristically, the first rescue and recovery efforts are made by members of disaster-struck communities. These efforts are usually quite direct and effective, partly because of the survivors' familiarity with their community. Neighbors, for instance, are familiar with each other's families and know who is having weekend guests and who is out of town. Consequently, they know better than rescue crews from outside the neighborhood how many people to look for in a collapsed home or who is actually missing. When numbers of homes are destroyed, survivors construct makeshift shelters or move to the homes of nearby friends and relatives. Communities often underutilize the shelter facilities provided by disaster assistance agencies. The temporarily homeless either avoid the shelters altogether or use them for only a short time. If the option exists, survivors usually prefer to sleep in a real bed and have hot meals at the home of a nearby relative rather than sleep on an army cot and eat peanut butter sandwiches in the high. (McLuckie, 1970). Civil and military authorities receive complaints from . who resent the curfews, traffic rerouting, and parking restrictions impose. authorities to maintain order (Demerath and Wallace, 1957).

Disaster investigators note that survivors report experiencing grief, depression, despair, headaches, loss of appetite, sleeplessness, and nightmares in the weeks following disaster. However, these emotional and physical reactions are not so acute as to be considered postdisaster shock, and they usually do not substantially hinder a community's recovery efforts. Further, the same kinds of reactions follow the death or injury of family members and friends or the loss of property in nondisaster situations.

Posttraumatic Stress Disorder Rather than giving in to the fears, grief, and various manifestations of panic, as the mass hysteria and value-added perspectives suggest, people usually occupy themselves with the problems of rescue and recovery. Some researchers have tried to ascertain the consequences of this denial of emotion in the immediate aftermath of disaster. Roth (1970) suggests that there are cultural differences inherent in the degree to which people express emotion during disaster. The Greek peasant women who stand about wailing and crying following an earthquake are not gripped by hysteria. Rather, they are giving vent to their emotion in a culturally prescribed and potentially healthy manner. Findings usually suggest that initial denial of emotion, a characteristic found in many Western cultures, may contribute to later feelings of guilt, depression, or neurosis (Kinston and Rosser, 1974; Perry and Lindell, 1978). Since posttraumatic stress disorder (PTSD) first entered the psychiatric lexicon with the third edition of the *Diagnostic and Statistical Manual of Mental Disorders* (*DSM-III*, American Psychiatric Association, 1980), numerous investigations have concluded that exposure to life-threatening stressors leads to PTSD in persons of all ages (Davidson and March, 1996; March et al., 1996). Earlier, Erickson's (1976) study of a Buffalo Creek dam collapse pointed out that severe guilt feelings and depression plagued survivors for several months after the disaster. Silber, Perry, and Bloch (1957) suggest that children are quite susceptible to long-term adjustment problems if they become separated from their parents during a disaster or if they are not allowed to talk freely about their experiences and fears afterward. Today, these problems would likely be labeled PTSD.

The Consequences of the "Grip of Terror" Myth

The mass hysteria and value-added perspectives cite panic as a fundamental cause of deaths during evacuation disasters. Postdisaster shock necessitates the use of National Guard and other organizations to take care of, and make decisions for, the "helpless" survivors. Nearly a half-century of research has cast great doubt on panic as a viable explanation for people's behavior in most disasters. Still, the grip of terror persists in our popular imagery of disaster, and in the views of some behavioral scientists. The persistence of the grip-of-terror image creates unrealistic expectations about people's reactions to disaster. The grip of terror serves as a self-fulfilling prophecy, and it provides an expectation and justification for nonadaptive or selfish behavior during a disaster. The grip of terror is a way of "blaming the victims" and transferring some of the responsibility for disasters and multifatality evacuations from owners, operators, and incompetents to the victims. Finally, the grip of terror inhibits disaster planning and preparedness. In many U.S. communities, citizens may hold the view that there is nothing that can be done about panic. With such views, disaster planning and disaster drills are likely to be given low priority. The more productive stance that much can be done by way of up-to-date safety codes, disaster planning, and drills has grown only slowly in the United States. This view has produced a decline in fire-related deaths in the United States over the last twenty years, but crisis and disaster planning are given much more emphasis in Europe and Japan (Karter, 1996).

MEDIA REPORTING OF DISASTERS

Henry Fischer (1988; 1994) did a content analysis of disaster reporting found in *Time Magazine* from 1944 to 1985. This analysis identified a number of "myths" or journalistic conventions that were frequently used to report disasters. For instance, collective flight from danger was likely referred to by the media as a "panic," and surges as "stampedes." Deaths and injuries were often referred to as "trampling" deaths and injuries. Even though the documented amount of looting at disaster sites is low and is much less than that of looting during civil disorders, magazine articles routinely alluded to the occurrence of looting in their descriptions of disaster scenes. The media often portrayed the mobilization of the National Guard as using "martial law" to "stop" looting, even when the Guard's duties primarily consisted of search and rescue, traffic control, shoring up buildings and clearing debris. Referring to the use of the National Guard as "martial law" is a common misnomer, since martial law—the suspension of the U.S. Constitution and the imposition of military rule—has never been declared in the United States.

News stories frequently describe communities as "evacuated" and note that emergency shelters are overwhelmed. The full evacuation of communities is rare, and people generally return to their communities before all danger has passed. The use of public shelters is sporadic. Studies of shelter use following recent California earthquakes, for instance, reveal that the majority of displaced people find shelter with family and friends outside the disaster-struck area. Those who use shelters generally do so as a matter of convenience, and for short periods of time. Some people live in the open or quickly return to their homes after makeshift repairs are made. In general, early news story estimates of deaths, injuries, and extent of damage were too high.

The convergence of people upon disaster scenes includes those seeking the whereabouts and safety of family and friends, volunteers offering assistance, and job seekers hoping to be hired to help in the clean-up and rebuilding. Media reports often referred to these people as "crowds" of "sightseers" or potential looters.

Decades of disaster research have shown that following disaster, altruistic behavior is observed frequently (see below) and that social bonds within a community are enhanced (see chapter 11). In contrast, Fischer's (1988; 1994) content analysis generally showed that disasters are reported from the standpoint of a community breakdown model. News stories indicate marked deterioration in community ties following disaster and an increase in deviant or antisocial behaviors. *Time Magazine* stories often alluded to price gouging for items such as fresh water, food, and building materials. Fischer actually investigated one such report and found that the mentioned items were being given away.

Fischer contends that between 1944 and 1985, the media conveyed several myths in their reporting of disasters. These myths appeared as journalist/ ventions used to write interesting, concise, and resonant stories about d..... Fischer noted that these myths were more likely to be part of the reporting of *natural* disasters, and the human-interest stories associated with them, than in the reporting of *technological* disasters, such as industrial accidents.

Todd Bernhardt (1997) did a comparable content analysis of *Time Magazine* disaster stories printed between 1985 and 1995 to ascertain the extent of such stereotyping in more recent disaster reporting. For this time period, Bernhardt identified 98 natural disaster stories and 163 technical disaster stories. Of these 261 stories, 128 were reported on disasters that occurred within the United States and 133 reported on disasters that occurred elsewhere in the world. Approximately 30 percent of these stories were follow-up stories appearing at least six weeks after the disaster. Follow-up stories contained revised damage estimates, reports of the findings of boards of investigation, outcomes or dismissals of court actions, and pertinent regulatory changes.

The text of these articles was coded for the appearance of *individual, adaptive description*. This would include reports by survivors, recovery workers or others, which indicated their thoughts, comments, and actions that would indicate effective coping with the disaster, and the use of terms such as "surge" instead of "stampede." Articles were also coded for the appearance of *organizational adaptive description*. This would include comments indicating expanding or extending functions of organization, networking with other agencies, solving problems, or limited success in dealing with some problems. Stories were also coded for "neutral," nonsensational reports of death and destruction. Stories were coded for the occurrence of analytical discussion of cause and effect of the disaster. Finally, articles were coded for *disaster stereotyping*. This would include reports using terms such as "panic," "craze," "stampede" or "screaming crowds," as well as mention or discussion of the breakdown of social order, lack of concern for others, failure to help others, and speculation about looting (including measures taken to prevent looting). Gratuitous descriptions of injuries were also classified as disaster stereotyping. Since an article might contain reports of individual and organizational responses, casualty estimates, analysis of causes, and disaster stereotyping, a total of 454 items were coded.

The content analysis indicated that stereotype reports constitute only about 5 percent of all reports, and that stereotypical reporting is in decline. That is, since 1985, we read fewer reports of terrorized, stampeding crowds, widespread looting, and social breakdown. On the other hand, we also find that there are comparatively few reports that contain organizational (12%) and individual (8%) adaptive description. The preponderance of disaster reporting focuses on ascertaining or discussing causes and effects (48%), or death and destruction estimates (32%).

Since 1985, nearly all of the stereotype reports (N = 16) concern international disasters and not domestic disasters. This does reflect a bias toward reporting international events in stereotypical terms since they compose 51 percent of the sample.

Emergency Evacuations and Collective Action

During a fire at the MGM Grand Hotel, guests reported getting dressed, finishing baths, notifying roommates and others of the fire, and trying to determine the location and size of the fire prior to attempting to leave the hotel (Bryan, 1983). During the fires at Gulliver's Disco and the Beverly Hills Supper Club, patrons continued to drink, dine, or dance after being notified of the danger of fire. Those who began to evacuate these facilities with their spouses, dating partners, and friends started to do so in an orderly manner. That is, they moved toward the exits known to them, and they did not push and shove one another. Similar behaviors are reported to have occurred at the outset of most multifatality evacuations.

Screaming, yelling, and other subsequent activities that occur during these evacuations, such as surges toward exits and hallways or pushing and shoving in stairwells, can be better understood as behavior organized under quite adverse and rapidly deteriorating ecological and sensory conditions. Perception control theory and the SBI perspective offer characterizations and explanations of many of the kinds of activities involved in multifatality evacuations.

Collective Locomotion

Collective locomotion toward exits in an emergency is typically impromptu and improvised. It develops out of gatherings that are already involved in activities such as watching a stage show, dining and drinking, or dancing. The main routes of egress, usually by the same route used to enter the structure, are known to most of those gathered; however, other routes of egress, such as through service exits, kitchens, or loading docks, may be known only to a handful of others. Goffman (1963) makes the distinction between "front-stage" and "back-stage" spaces of public buildings such as restaurants, clubs, hotels and theaters. The front-stage spaces are where the public is welcome and the social encounter unfolds. Front-stage spaces of theaters include the lobby, concession area, and auditorium. The front-stage spaces of restaurants include the bar, dining rooms, and buffet lines. Often, exits from front-stage areas are marked as such and can be easily seen by patrons.

The back-stage spaces include loading and storage areas, employee offices and locker rooms, and food preparation areas. Goffman notes that strong social norms and rules dictate that patrons restrict their movements to the front stage-spaces of public places. Routes to back-stage spaces are not likely to be known by patrons and may be designated as "employees only." In emergency evacuations patrons are not likely to invade back-stage spaces or use exits from these spaces unless directed or guided by third parties, such as employees or firefighters.

Purposive collective action, in this case collective locomotion through buildings and exits, occurs when people adjust their ongoing actions to make their current perception correspond to similar or related images in their heads. In terms of collective egress, this means that people adjust their ongoing actions with respect to their images of the physical layout of their surroundings and the location of exits. They must also adjust their behavior in terms of their images of the egress movements of others. These images are retrieved independently by individuals, and interdependently through interaction with companions. These images may also be provided by third parties who know the building's layout or the location and extent of the threat. These third parties include regular patrons, employees, and firefighters. Third-party instructions have been shown to be very critical to the development of coordinated movements during successful evacuations as well as multifatality evacuations. In the case of the MGM Grand fire, guests also utilized "survival" images previously gained from television, radio, movies, and periodicals, such as "Do not use the elevators," "Use wet towels on face," "Feel doors before opening," and "Think before acting" (Bryan, 1983).

Egress movements are generally initiated in the direction of exits by people following instructions to leave the area. En route, collective movement will most likely change in velocity, spatial alignment, tempo, and direction. These adjustments may be generated by the interaction of participants en route, e.g., "We can't get out this way. Let's go through the storeroom!" Evacuation is accomplished by additional instructions that specify orderly movement, such as "Let's go!" "Don't shove," "Watch your step, these stairs are steep," "Remain calm," or "Use the other exit." To varying degrees, people can see one another and monitor the rate, direction, and progress of movement. In multifatality evacuations, many factors operate to disrupt and prevent orderly movement. Adjustments may also occur in response to deflections or resistance introduced by barriers, narrow hallways and stairwells. Adjustments in collective movement may be produced by disturbances introduced by smoke or noise.

In his characterization of emergency evacuations, McPhail notes that people initially provide quite rational instructions for dispersal or escape, and move in the direction of exits known to them or suggested to them by the movements of others (McPhail, 1983; McPhail and Wohlstein, 1986). To varying degrees, people can see one another and monitor the rate, direction, and progress of movement. Thus, escape movement is initially coordinated and adaptive rather than individualistic and nonadaptive. While emergency evacuations start out coordinated and adaptive, they may become confused, and as a result escape movement ceases. When this happens, some injuries and fatalities may result from crowding pressure, although generally most injuries and fatalities occur through the action of the disaster agent.

Milling within Gatherings

Even during egress, successful collective locomotion is not continuous or uniform. Individuals and small groups are intermittently stationary and mobile. Clusters alternate between observing and talking about the people, activities, and objects around them. Some people approach, join, and remain with or leave other individuals and clusters. It is this intermittent stability and movement, observation and conversation, within and between clusters, that traditionally has been referred to as "milling." It is in this process of locomotion and clustering, of observation and conversation, that people assess "what's going on?," "what's coming next?," and "what should we do?" The milling process contributes to the construction of shared reference images of the situation (McPhail and Wohlstein, 1986:449).

Surges within Gatherings

Surges consist of the more or less simultaneous movement of adjacent persons over short distances, in the direction of some object, approaching or leaving the gathering, or toward some event developing elsewhere within the gathering (McPhail and Wohlstein, 1986:448). During emergency evacuations, surges have been reported toward exits, and toward groups of people waiting to exit through doors, hallways, or stairs. There have been surges away from venting smoke and flames and surges toward areas of temporary safety, such as balconies or atriums.

The Life Safety Code

The Life Safety Code of the National Fire Protection Association specifies standards for the construction, protection, and occupancy features of buildings classified as places of assembly. The intent of the code is to minimize danger to life from fire, smoke, fumes, or panic, before buildings are vacated. The code specifies the number, size, and arrangement of exit facilities sufficient to permit prompt escape of occupants from buildings in case of fire and like emergencies. The code recognizes that life safety is more than a matter of exits; accordingly, it deals with various matters of building operation that are considered essential to life safety.

The Life Safety Code provides a comprehensive set of standards that may be adopted by localities with the force of law. Life Safety Code standards are also used by underwriters and insurers. The National Fire Association's investigation of the Beverly Hills Supper Club fire identified the following facility and operational deviations from the Life Safety Code (Best, 1977):

- The club did not have an automatic sprinkler system, a fire detection system, or an alarm system. Consequently the fire developed for a considerable time, discovery was delayed, and the fire spread through other concealed spaces.

- There was no evacuation plan establishing fire emergency procedures for the club. Employees were not schooled or drilled in duties they were to perform in case of fire.

- The number of people in the Cabaret Room exceeded almost triple the number of occupants that the room could safely accommodate. The number of occupants of the club was more than double the number of people that the building could safely accommodate.

- The capacity of exits for the club—and especially for the Cabaret Room—was not adequate for the number of occupants in the building at the time of the fire.

- The interior finish in the main corridor exceeded the allowable flame spread for places of assembly and contributed to the rapid spread of the fire.

MULTIFATALITY EVACUATIONS

Hardly a week goes by that we do not read or hear about an emergency evacuation. News reports of hotel, nightclub, or theater fires in which everyone escapes are usually quite brief, while multifatality evacuations are given lengthy treatment. In nearly all of these latter descriptions, at least some note is made of successful and initially quite orderly movement from danger. People initially provide instructions for dispersal in the direction of exits that are either known to them (people usually leave through the doors they entered) or suggested to them by the movements of others. We'll now turn our attention to the immediate circumstances that contribute to the breakdown of this orderly movement.

Overcrowding

Perhaps the most common and immediate circumstance of multifatality evacuations is overcrowding. It is difficult to judge the extent of overcrowding when conditions are initially described as "standing room only," "packed to the rafters," or "overcrowded." In some instances, however, we can assess overcrowding in terms of a building's fire code occupancy limit or licensed seating capacity. When we apply either criterion, it becomes clear that drastic overcrowding precedes most multifatality evacuations. Sixty young people were killed and 162 were injured in the 1998 fire at the Macedonian Association Halloween dance in Gote-borg, Sweden. The ballroom was on the second floor and some people died in the surge toward the exit. Other youths scuffled with police in attempts to get in and try to help friends. An estimated 400 people were at the dance, even though the facility had approval for a maximum of 150, according to the detective leading the disaster investigation

No specific fire code occupancy limit had been established for Gulliver's Disco. Crowds at Gulliver's were typically described as packed or standing room only. In the case of the Beverly Hills Supper Club disaster, on the night of the fire the nightclub had nearly double the number of occupants the building could safely accommodate (Best, 1977). Further, the Cabaret Room, where most of the fatalities occurred, was packed to nearly three times what the room could safely accommo-date (Best, 1977). One gets a vivid picture of disastrous overcrowding in the case of Boston's Cocoanut Grove fire of 1942. In all, 492 people died, which was 32 *more* people than the club's licensed seating capacity of 460 (Velfort and Lee, 1943). Per-haps as many as 1,200 people—about three times the licensed capacity—were in the nightclub when the fire broke out. It does not seem an exaggeration to suggest that for multifatality evacuations, the number of people involved usually far exceeds either the commonsense or the legal occupancy limit of the facility.

One immediate consequence of extreme overcrowding is the increased poten-tial for breakdown in front-to-rear communication (Quarantelli, 1957). When peo-

A fireman surveys the ruins of the fire that destroyed the Cocoanut Grove nightclub. In multifatality evacuations, such as this one in which 492 people died, overcrowding is usu-ally the major factor contributing to the high death toll. © Bettman/CORBIS.

ple are standing shoulder to shoulder in large crowds, their straight-ahead and peripheral vision are blocked by those around them. Most people in a densely packed crowd cannot see exits or at least cannot see if known exits are blocked. We all know how difficult it is to carry on conversations in crowded nightclubs, restaurants, waiting rooms, and theater lobbies. Also, it is very difficult to hear announcements in crowds unless the speaker is using some sort of voice amplification device. In the absence of audible verbal instructions (e.g., "Everyone on the west side of the aisle should use exit number four"), people receive cues to the direction of movement from the movements of those directly in front of them. At the center of the crowd, these movement cues can be quite contradictory. People move first in one direction and then in the other, losing their sense of orientation. It is not surprising, then, that movement in densely packed crowds toward a single exit, toward closed exits, or toward blind walls, seems "nonadaptive."

Another consequence of extreme overcrowding is a corresponding increase in the time necessary for dispersal. Occupancy limits for public buildings are established in part through consideration of the time needed to move a given number of people through available exits. Obviously, dispersal time increases directly in proportion to the number of people in the building. In addition, extreme overcrowding, as noted above, can result in slower and less direct movements toward exits than would be the case for smaller numbers of occupants. In this sense, exceeding the legal occupancy limit by 30 percent may actually double or triple the time needed for evacuation (Pauls, 1977).

Fortunately, the *Herald of Free Enterprise* was not overcrowded, even though it was overloaded with cargo. Darkness, rather than overcrowding, made it difficult for people to see one another. People escaped by way of windows on the starboard side of the ship. The number of people able to climb up tables and partitions was never sufficient to produce a substantial jam at the exit.

Limited Time for Dispersal

Under ideal conditions, given the number of occupants and the number and capacity of available exits, it could take at least ten minutes to evacuate a building such as Gulliver's. Fire can spread throughout a building at an even faster rate; multifatality fires often engulf the occupied areas of a building in as little as one to five minutes. These fires often burn for some time prior to their discovery, building up tremendous amounts of heat and smoke in stairwells, within walls, and above suspended ceilings. Contained fires such as these suddenly vent and explode into the oxygen-rich atmosphere of the open spaces of the building. The heat flash can ignite combustible material several yards away, allowing the fire to race down hallways and jump from room to room. Normally, air must contain at least 15 percent oxygen to sustain consciousness. These fires lower the oxygen level inside a building to less than 5 percent almost instantly. The fires that swept Gulliver's and the Beverly Hills Supper Club were of this nature. The fire at the Cocoanut Grove was fed by highly combustible Christmas decorations strung throughout the occupied areas of the nightclub.

Burning plastics, acrylics, and solvents generate extremely toxic fumes. In the Beverly Hills Supper Club, toxic fumes were generated by burning carpet padding and wall paneling (Best, 1977). Fumes swept through the Cabaret Room so rapidly that patrons died while still seated at their tables. The rapid elimination of

oxygen limits the amount of time during which evacuation can occur. Automa
sprinkler systems prevent fires from reaching the venting stage described abov⌐,
and some sprinkler systems automatically transmit alarms to the fire department.
No such systems existed in the Gulliver's, Cocoanut Grove, or Beverly Hills Supper Club fires. The National Fire Protection Association has noted that there are
no recorded instances of fires killing three or more people in buildings equipped
with operating sprinkler systems.

The above discussion concerns multifatality evacuations during fires, but similar points could be made about other situations in which the time available for
evacuation is limited, such as on a sinking ship. Multifatality evacuations occur
when the spread of fire, fumes, or some other real threat makes the time available
for evacuation appreciably less than the minimum time it would take to evacuate
people under ideal conditions.

In the case of the *Herald of Free Enterprise*, the only real constraint on the time
available for dispersal was the cold. The water temperature was at or slightly
below freezing. Autopsies showed that many people who plunged into the cold
water suffered immediate heart attacks or deep shock. The people most likely to
survive in the water longer than others had an excess of body fat but were otherwise healthy. Still, five minutes of continuous immersion in the freezing water
rendered even the hardiest people nearly helpless, and twenty minutes in the
water was fatal. Hundreds of life vests floated to the surface moments after the
capsizing, yet they were useless to many floundering in the water because their
cold-numbed hands were unable to untangle the vests and put them on properly.
Likewise, people were unable to tie or hold on to rescue ropes.

Instructions for Dispersal

As mentioned earlier, people provide quite rational instructions for dispersal in
the direction of the exits known to them. In the case of Gulliver's, at least three or
four minutes elapsed between the band's first announcement of the fire and
requests for dispersal and their second set of instructions, given immediately
prior to the fire's venting. At least fifteen minutes elapsed between the discovery
of the fire in the Beverly Hills Supper Club and the first call to the fire department
(Best, 1977). It should be noted that club employees had no training or drill in the
duties they were to perform in case of fire (Best, 1977). Accounts indicate that
employees made only one announcement of the fire to patrons during this
interim. Dispersal began immediately after this announcement, but it was sparse
and relatively slow. From the accounts of these and other multifatality evacuations, it is apparent that the first announcement of the fire and the instructions for
movement were low key and somewhat equivocal (such as, "We think there is a
fire in the building; maybe everyone should leave"). In retrospect, valuable dispersal time was lost because of the delay in announcing the fire to patrons and the
use of low-key announcements to avoid panic. Immediate, frequent, and unambiguous announcements—such as, "There is a fire in the building; the fire department will arrive shortly; please leave immediately through the exits to the east
parking lot"—would have occasioned earlier and more complete evacuation.

We should not equate prompt notification and the use of clearly audible, direct,
and unequivocal instructions with yelling "Fire!" in a crowded theater. Strident
instructions are not usually unequivocal instructions. Unequivocal instructions

clearly identify the threat, specify immediate movement, identify exits, and, if possible, direct portions of the crowd toward separate exits. In the darkness of the capsized *Herald of Free Enterprise* disoriented survivors moved toward the sounds of others, and in general played a terrifying game of blind man's bluff. Movement was hindered by ignorance of the ship's layout. Those giving the clearest instructions for movement were crew members familiar with the maze-like layout of the ship. Their help in guiding passengers toward the improvised exits contributed greatly to survival.

Use of Exits

Descriptions of multifatality evacuations sometimes mention exits that are locked or otherwise unusable. Such instances of entrapment are documented but are certainly not common to most multifatality evacuations. More often, it is simply the case that some exits are not used. Seldom are occupants of a building aware of all exits, particularly in buildings such as restaurants, where patrons are restricted to the public areas. It was noted, for example, that one exit from Gulliver's was from the kitchen. Although five other exits were suggested and used, survivors complained that they had no knowledge of the kitchen exit. Commenting on the exodus from Gulliver's, a firefighter pointed out that during such emergencies people usually attempt to leave public buildings through the same doors they entered. When rapid and generally orderly movement is occurring through a known and nearby exit, people are not likely to strike out through an unfamiliar building in search of other exits. Moments later, when dense smoke suddenly obstructs their vision and it becomes difficult to breathe, people are unable to search for other exits.

Another common feature of buildings within which multifatality evacuations have occurred is that many of the exits could not be reached by short-distance, straight-ahead movement. In Gulliver's, for instance, people could exit from the Pit only by moving up a narrow flight of stairs and out the main doors or by going downstairs and out through basement exits. In the Beverly Hills Supper Club, people could only reach some exits by using intersecting hallways (Best, 1977). Streams of people met at these intersections, creating traffic jams. In the Cocoanut Grove, the main exit was through revolving doors that became jammed with bodies shortly after people started using them. It is in these places of crowd extrusion that many fatalities occur, including the infamous "trampling deaths." In all likelihood, death by actual trampling is rare; however, people may be knocked down and immobilized in these areas until they are asphyxiated. Occupants' limited knowledge of available exits and exits that can be reached only by negotiating long hallways, stairs, and other obstacles are common circumstances in multifatality evacuations. Probably all survivors of the *Herald of Free Enterprise* escaped by way of windows on the starboard side. Townsend Thoresen had been considering replacing the glass windows with stronger plastic windows prior to the *Herald* capsizing. Had strong windows been in place, escape by kicking out windows may have been impossible. As rescue time elapsed, the use of ropes to lift people up to the windows became less and less effective. Simple harnesses that could be used by cold-numbed hands would have been of considerable help in getting people out of the *Herald*. The official inquiry report recommended that footholds be designed into the walls and ceilings of passenger areas to facilitate movement if the ship is at an extreme angle.

Sensory Interference

In order for people to initiate dispersal movement and to successfully negotiate hallways, stairs, and exits, they must be able to provide movement instructions to one another and to visually monitor each other's movements. Multifatality evacuations usually entail conditions of sensory interference that severely limit the possibility of providing audible instructions and visually monitoring the movements of others. Human bodies make excellent sound diffusers. Additionally, the shuffle of feet, extraneous conversations, and even the movement of furniture as people initiate movement create substantial background noise. Consequently, once numbers of people initiate movement in overcrowded buildings, it becomes increasingly difficult to provide additional, audible instructions for movement. During the evacuation of Gulliver's, the instructions provided by the band were mentioned by survivors. Standing somewhat above the crowd on an elevated stage and using sound equipment, the band members were in an acoustically advantageous position to make themselves heard above the rising din. In the case of fires, resulting explosions and rumbling flames provide additional background noise with which movement instructions must compete. In the final moments of evacuation from Gulliver's, air conditioners were crashing loudly to the floor and interfering with audible instructions for movement.

Visual monitoring of the movements of others is restricted in crowded areas. Those at the rear of a crowd, for example, cannot see that an exit is blocked or that people have fallen on the stairs ahead of them. Consequently, people at the rear keep moving, which results in crushes and pileups near exits and stairways. Streams of people may converge head-on or at right angles in hallways. Again, those farther back in the crowd are unable to see the resulting jam-up and keep moving.

Visual monitoring is often made difficult or impossible by the spread of smoke throughout a building by air-conditioning ducts or other conduits, such as stairwells and suspended ceilings. Even emergency lighting systems are useless in dense smoke. Even if smoke does not create a total blackout within the building, it can be as irritating to the eyes as tear gas, creating blurred vision or temporary blindness. When people are unable to see others or their immediate surroundings, their movement toward exits becomes increasingly disorganized. Careful attention to building design and the selection of building materials, as well as the use of air-conditioning systems that shut down automatically during fires, could do much to alleviate the sensory interference caused by smoke.

The almost total darkness inside the *Herald* was the single greatest sensory interference faced by survivors. Rescuers and survivors were angered by the failure to bring sufficient lighting aboard the *Herald* during the hours of the rescue. Lighting that existed was provided by a few flashlights brought aboard by divers. Noise from the Belgian Air Force helicopters used to remove survivors from the *Herald* made conversation almost impossible. In the last hours of the rescue, the helicopters were ordered away so that rescuers could listen for trapped survivors.

Discussion

The mass hysteria and value-added perspectives of collective behavior cite panic as a fundamental cause of deaths during evacuation disasters. Although much research casts great doubt on panic as a viable explanation for people's behavior in most disasters, multifatality evacuations such as the Cocoanut Grove fire or Gulliver's Disco are still considered by many to be instances of true panic. Stampede panics seem to give clear evidence that people lose both their normal attentiveness to the environment and their concern for others. In some instances, people may trample those standing between themselves and safety. Early writers, such as Strauss (1944), suggested establishing programs of anti-panic training, but for the most part such programs would be possible to implement among civilian populations.

The SBI perspective of collective action, in contrast, suggests that multifatality evacuations result from potentially avoidable circumstances, including tremendous and often illegal overcrowding, the unusually rapid spread of fire or some other lethal agent (which greatly limits the time for evacuation), and dispersal under severely adverse sensory conditions. Few if any multifatality evacuations have occurred in buildings where occupants were not crowded and who faced a threat that allowed reasonable time for dispersal and otherwise posed little threat to life and limb.

ALTRUISM AND DISASTER

In contrast to the "grip of terror" stereotype of people's general disregard for others, disaster studies frequently document people's high level of concern for and generosity toward disaster victims. In chapter 11, we will discuss a disaster that occurred over 40 years ago, during which Iowa farmers risked their lives to remove survivors from the gasoline-drenched wreckage of an airliner. Many farm women carried their families' warmest blankets to the crash site with little concern that the blankets would be permanently soiled with bloodstains, mud, and oil. Few blankets in which survivors were sent to hospitals were ever returned. In the days following the crash, warm meals and hot coffee were provided by civilians, around the clock, to state police and aviation officials. Finally, farmers provided tractors, loading equipment, and labor during the removal of the wreckage. Families received little reimbursement for their efforts, although reimbursement seemed to be of little concern to these people. They took pride in their generosity.

Looking at the generosity and concern extended to disaster victims today, one can see that the open display of concern for others is not a thing of the past. In 1993, armies of volunteers turned out to fight the largest and most significant flood event ever to occur in the United States. During June and July of that year approximately 600 river forecast points in the Midwestern United States were above flood stage at the same time. Nearly 150 major rivers and tributaries were affected. Still, the numbers of volunteers were sufficient that, at times, they were sent home because they were not needed.

In October of 1998, Hurricane Mitch tore across Central America. This hurricane of biblical proportion killed at least 9,000 people and devastated property across Honduras, Guatemala, El Salvador and Nicaragua. Weeks after the hurricane, thousands of Central Americans were missing and millions were homeless. Governments and nongovernmental organizations (NGOs) from across the world shipped clothing, shoes, medicines and other emergency supplies to this region. Other critical relief needs that were met through this massive effort included those of volunteer physicians and nurses as well as medicines, clothes, shoes, blankets, canned food, powdered milk, soap, toothpaste, home-repair tools, and agricultural tools. Altruism also may be reflected in the low incidence of looting during disasters.

Disasters present ample opportunities for looting: homes are broken open, and people's possessions are scattered about streets and fields. But looting during disasters is quite rare (Quarantelli and Dynes, 1969). During civil disorders, looters may enjoy a degree of community support, but during disasters, looters are thoroughly condemned by authorities and community members alike. What little looting occurs is usually done by outsiders who converge on the community after the disaster.

In the case of the farmers' rescue of the air crash survivors, the farmers assumed a protective stance with respect to the victims' property. As the rescue of the injured and the recovery of bodies progressed, scattered luggage was placed in a pile and a cardboard box was kept nearby for smaller items, such as watches, jewelry, purses and billfolds, and some loose money. Several farmers walked among the rescuers, directing them toward the box of valuables when such items were found. Reasonable and effective precautions were taken to recover the property of victims. Still, items of jewelry were lost while victims were transported to hospitals and morgues, and some valuable items were scattered across the field or lost in the twisted wreckage. Unfortunately, the loss of these items was usually attributed to "looting." Perhaps the only items of possible value that the farmers removed from the crash site were scraps of aluminum or bolts, to be kept as a reminder of a very significant event in their lives.

Stress Explanations of Altruism

Discussions of disaster-related altruism usually claim that this concern and generosity are seldom shown in nondisaster situations. If this is indeed the case, then what causes disaster-related altruism? Some discussions attribute this altruism to the stress of anxiety and guilt generated by the disaster (Wallace, 1957; Martin, 1964). Immediately following disaster impact, survivors can look about them and see the capricious nature of what has happened. A tornado, for example, may level homes on one side of a street yet inflict little if any damage to homes on the other side. Floods may carry away entire neighborhoods while only flooding basements on the other end of town. Many of the survivors who have been injured can look around and see others in greater pain and, perhaps, the dead. Some disaster studies claim that survivors initially tend to underestimate their personal losses and to feel that others have suffered greater loss (Fritz, 1961; Cranshaw, 1963). Given this, survivors experience initial feelings of anxiety and guilt as to why God or circumstance has spared them from the greater suffering they perceive others have experienced. Giving assistance to others substantially reduces these stresses. Unfortunately, there have been no real attempts by researchers to systematically study this explanation of disaster-related altruism.

Situational Explanations of Altruism

During the 1960s, there was considerable interest within the field of social psychology in the issue of bystander intervention. This research was directed toward ascertaining the conditions under which people would come to the aid of victims of physical assaults, accidents, and seizures. These studies were prompted by the murder of Catherine "Kitty" Genovese in 1964 (Rosenthal, 1964). Genovese was knifed by a man as she walked to her apartment building in Kew Gardens, Queens, New York. It was almost 3:30 A.M., the street was deserted, and the neighborhood was asleep. When the attacker struck, Genovese screamed and lights went on in the windows above the street. An onlooker shouted down, "Let that girl alone!" The attacker walked away, only to return as soon as the lights went out. Genovese screamed when he knifed her again, and he left as soon as people came back to their windows. Genovese made her way to the doors of her building, where the attacker found her and stabbed her once more. It was probably not until after the last attack that one of her neighbors called the police. When officers arrived, she was dead and her murderer was gone.

Why didn't any of the thirty-eight witnesses to the killing of Kitty Genovese come to her aid? Why didn't her neighbors call the police immediately instead of nearly thirty minutes after the first attack? Why did only one person call? The bystander intervention research indicates that people usually do render aid in emergency situations but only when certain immediate circumstances are present (Latané and Darley, 1968; Wheeler et al., 1978). First, there must be clear and unambiguous distress cues within the situation. Though Genovese screamed and called for help, a number of witnesses reportedly interpreted her sounds of distress as a quarrel rather than a murder. Neighbors looking from their windows did not have a clear view of what was going on in the shadows.

Second, witnesses must perceive some responsibility for the victim's fate. This is most likely to occur when the number of witnesses is small or the witnesses constitute a social group, such as a family, work or recreation group, or friendship group. Witnesses are also more likely to assume responsibility if they know the victim. As the number of unassociated witnesses increases, the likelihood of giving assistance to the victim decreases. Latané and Darley describe this as "responsibility diffusion," in which each witness assumes that someone else will come to the aid of the victim or that someone else has already called the police, fire department, or ambulance. In the case of Kitty Genovese, the person who finally called the police knew her personally.

Third, there is the effect of modeling. If the first bystanders seem to be unconcerned, later bystanders pick up on these cues from those who were there when it started and are less likely to give assistance. Often, the first person to give assistance precipitates helping behavior on the part of a number of bystanders. Finally, there is the ability to help the victim. Competence based on first-aid training, knowledge of crisis situations, and even martial arts skills increase helping behavior in situations that demand intervention.

Disasters create nearly ideal conditions for eliciting helping behavior. Signs of distress and the need for assistance are obvious and plentiful. Little is ambiguous about shattered homes and open wounds. Those injured, trapped, or missing are known to their neighbors. The role that family, work, neighborhood, and friendship groups play in giving assistance to others is well documented. Often, there is little need to worry about whether someone else has called the police or fire department, as these agencies may have had forewarning, or at least certain knowledge, of the disaster from many sources. Within moments of the disaster's impact, there are numerous models of helping behavior. Finally, the ability to help victims may involve little more than the ability to push aside fallen branches or other debris, give someone a blanket, say a few comforting words, and call for help.

In the later stages of disaster recovery, altruism seems to give way to more selfish concerns (Taylor, Zurcher, and Key, 1970). In part, this is because the immediate needs of rescue and assistance have been met, and the more diverse needs of long-range community recovery are emerging. Such needs as home-repair financing usually give few outward cues of distress. The altruism of people possessing skills relevant to this kind of assistance, such as local insurance agents and adjusters, comes into play in later stages of disaster. These people may work exceedingly long hours investigating and processing insurance claims so that victims get prompt financial relief.

SUMMARY

Panic is a traditional part of the popular image of people's response to disaster. We need not search too long or too hard to find descriptions of theater, hotel, or nightclub fires that mention human stampedes toward exits and trampled bodies in hallways and stairwells. Panic is an almost instantaneous response to both real and imaginary threats. Part of American folklore includes the panic that resulted from the 1938 "War of the Worlds" broadcast. Even today, descriptions of this event mention suicides and terrorized flight from New Jersey and New York. This popular imagery has led to the reluctance to give warnings in emergency situations in an effort to prevent panic.

The panic image of individual responses to disaster is central to the mass hysteria and value-added perspectives of collective behavior. Panic is caused by circular reaction or hysterical beliefs that restrict people's attention to their environment. These theories present a "grip of terror" image of disaster response—that is, during disaster impact, people's attention focuses on their own survival, and they lose all concern for the well-being of family, friends, and neighbors. Panic flight is instantaneous, and people are trampled or roads and highways become clogged by traffic as a result. Finally, emotional shock sets in following disaster, and people become unable to carry out rescue and recovery work.

Even the early disaster response survey by the National Opinions Research Center (NORC) indicated that panic as depicted in the "grip of terror" image was a poor representation of people's actual response to disaster. Since the early 1960s research by the Disaster Research Center has consistently showed that victims of disaster retain their presence of mind during disaster; retain concern for family, friends, neighbors, and community; and are very active during the rescue and recovery phase of disaster.

This research-based view of individual responses to disaster is reflected in both the emergent-norm and collective action approaches to disaster response. The emergent-norm view, for example, characterizes disaster response as highly normative in character and suggests that people become more rather than less responsive to the needs of friends, family, neighbors, and their community. The SBI perspective clearly applies to the classic stampede panic situation. In multifatality disasters, death and injury seldom if ever are a direct result of panic. Instead, death and injury are an unavoidable outcome of evacuation under unusually adverse conditions. Adverse conditions include extreme overcrowding, very limited time for dispersal because of the rapid spread of fire or deadly fumes, sensory interference caused by overcrowding, noise, and smoke, late and/or ambiguous warnings of danger and inadequate dispersal instructions, and, finally, poorly accessible exits. The panic explanation blames the victims for the unfortunate outcome of multifatality evacuations. The SBI perspective, on the other hand, points out preventive measures that can be implemented through building codes, fire code regulations, and emergency procedures for management and staff of hotels, restaurants, nightclubs, and other enclosed facilities that accommodate large gatherings.

Contrary to the assumptions of the "grip of terror" explanation, a close examination of people's response to disaster reveals that people usually show high levels of concern and generosity toward disaster victims. One explanation of disaster-related altruism emphasizes the anxiety-reducing effect of this altruism, but this would be very difficult to test in the field. Studies of bystander intervention, on the other hand, suggest some rather specific factors that probably promote disaster-related altruism. During disaster, there are numerous and obvious distress cues. People often face disasters with their relatives, friends, and neighbors in the community. These social groups are more likely to render assistance to people in distress than are groups composed of mutual strangers. Disaster presents opportunities for meaningful assistance to people possessing even limited helping skills. Finally, during disaster, there are usually numerous models for rendering assistance to those in need.

The bulk of early disaster research examined interpersonal responses to disaster and was conducted by the Disaster Research Center. Today there are hundreds of governmental and private disaster or disaster-related research organizations worldwide. Much recent research focuses on organizational and governmental responses to disaster.

CHAPTER 11

ORGANIZATIONS, COMMUNITIES, AND SOCIETIES IN DISASTER

We were eating supper when the phone rang. Our son, Ben, was calling to tell us to turn on the television. News stories were being broadcast from Plainfield, Illinois, which had been struck by a killer tornado that afternoon. Our friends of many years, Carolyn and Roger, and their three children, lived in Plainfield. It was difficult to comprehend the devastation that we saw on our screen, and we began to fear that our friends could be injured or dead. We realized that it would be pointless to try to telephone them, but later in the evening we were able to talk with Carolyn's mother. She told us that everyone in the family had escaped injury, and we later learned this was due in part to the grandmother's quick action. She had brought the children into the house when the sky turned green and had made the children "hit the deck" just seconds before the house started to come apart.

The tornado that struck Plainfield on August 28, 1990 was one of the strongest tornadoes ever recorded by the National Weather Service. It resulted from an unexpected storm pattern that traveled from the northwest to the southeast, an unusual track for tornadoes. Several tornadoes occurred along this path, beginning at about 1:45 P.M. near Rockford, Illinois. The most developed of these tornadoes struck Plainfield, and it consisted of four funnels that rotated around the perimeter of a massive central funnel. This incredibly intense tornado type is characteristic of many "killer" storms because it produces a particularly brutal twisting, shearing and ripping effect on whatever is in its path. It killed 28 people in Plainfield but was not the deadliest tornado ever to strike in Illinois. The twister that tore through Oak Lawn and Belvidere in 1967 and killed 58 people holds this awful record.

On the morning of August 28, 1990, the weather was predicted to be hot and humid, with some chance of rain and slightly cooler temperatures in the afternoon. By early afternoon, however, a major thunderstorm system with two huge cells had developed over south central Wisconsin. The system moved southeast into Illinois, gathering strength. Tornadoes were on the ground for nearly two hours, cutting a path of destruction across five counties and leveling most of Plainfield, before the National Weather Service issued its first tornado warning. In the months that followed, the National Weather Service reassessed its tornado tracking and warning system and made several structural and operational improvements.

When disaster strikes, individuals usually look first to the safety of themselves and those around them. Soon, however, people become aware that they are also members of organizations, communities, and societies and that these relationships have an impact on their activities. For instance, people often must try to get time off from work to clean up their houses. People also experience a heightened community spirit as they pitch in to restore their neighborhoods, and they become aware of how much they take community-based services such as clean water and emergency health care for granted. Finally, people find that they must comply with bureaucratic demands and seemingly unnecessary red tape to obtain federal disaster relief funds.

In this chapter we examine organizations, communities, and societies in disaster. We will begin by considering the Johnstown, Pennsylvania, flood of 1977 and the recovery efforts that emerged in the weeks following the flood. These efforts involved the coordination of the resources of many volunteer, private, and governmental organizations into an effective assault on the damage caused by the disaster. In the second instance, a farming community quickly organized an effective rescue of the survivors of an airline crash. For some farmers, this rescue involved placing their own lives on the line to save people they did not know and would likely never see again. In the days that followed, the community assisted state police and aviation investigators working at the crash site.

Finally, we will look at the "thousand year flood" of the Mississippi and Missouri Rivers in 1993. This is the largest flood ever recorded in the United States, and it devastated 16.4 billion dollars worth of property. This disaster was so costly and affected such a large geographic area that it created far-reaching problems for our society. Federal agencies such as the Federal Emergency Management Administration and the National Weather Service had to reassess their operations and priorities while dealing with this devastation.

ORGANIZATIONS IN DISASTER: THE JOHNSTOWN FLOOD

At about 7:30 P.M. on Tuesday, July 19, 1977, it started to rain throughout the Conemaugh Valley of Pennsylvania. In Johnstown, residents welcomed the thunderstorms as relief from a week-long heat wave. By 5:00 A.M., however, 11.8 inches of rain had fallen. According to the National Weather Service, a rainfall of this magnitude had never been recorded on the North American continent and was likely to occur only once in ten thousand years. During the night, six dams in the Conemaugh Valley had burst or been topped by floodwaters. The death toll was alarming: seventy-three known dead and eighteen missing. More than a thousand homes were damaged or destroyed. Stores and other businesses were heavily damaged. Public buildings such as Johnstown's David A. Glosser Memorial Library and the War Memorial Arena were flooded. Highways, bridges, and railroad lines were washed out. The official property damage estimate was nearly $250 million.

During the first hours of the rain, people's main concern was with the blockage of storm sewers and basement flooding. By midnight, however, people's concerns turned to sheer survival. Water entered the ground floors of homes, and people moved to attics and rooftops. At about 1:00 A.M., dams began to burst and walls of water swept through the already flooded communities of the Conemaugh Valley. In the steel mills, anxious workers tried to call their homes, but telephone lines had been washed out. Widespread power outages occurred. In Johnstown, residents of the Grand Hotel moved to the upper floors as water rose in the streets outside. Throughout Johnstown, more than three thousand automobiles floated down streets and into rivers. Some cars were occupied, and people died attempting to wade from their cars to higher ground. Thousands of accounts could be given of people spending a frightening night without light, transportation, or telephone. Lightning flashes showed people eerie glimpses of rising, rushing water filled with debris from shattered homes, uprooted trees, and, occasionally, bodies. Throughout the night, people were concerned with their immediate safety, but they could do little about the deteriorating conditions around them.

The rain stopped about dawn, which revealed a scene of unbelievable destruction. Distant communities were just becoming aware of the disaster, and assistance was rendered rapidly and generously. Those arriving to help, however, found that the residents of Johnstown and nearby communities had already begun recovery efforts. Ham radio operators were functioning as dispatchers for the many recently formed work and rescue crews, and they continued to play a critical role by coordinating recovery efforts until telephone service was partially restored days later. Small boats and large trucks were being used to move those stranded by the water to safety. Throughout the morning of the flood, National Guard helicopters transferred blood and medical supplies from the disabled refrigeration units of the Johnstown Red Cross center to a milk warehouse outside the city.

By noon, the Salvation Army was trucking three thousand hot meals from Pittsburgh to Johnstown. Throughout the next nineteen days, the Salvation Army operated twenty-five emergency vans, distributing sandwiches and coffee to work crews. The Salvation Army also sponsored chicken barbecues and provided hot meals at refugee centers. During this period, other groups, such as the Mennonite Disaster Service, Catholic church groups, and even a Baptist choir from Birmingham, Alabama, provided assistance. Some groups limited their assistance to a particular segment of the disaster-struck population or to a particular task. For example, some groups sought out and assisted the elderly or invalids who could do little heavy cleanup work. Groups from Penn State University helped with the salvage efforts at the library.

Refugee centers were quickly set up in schools, churches, and even a convent, and they also functioned as daycare centers for children when parents returned to the family homes to assess damage and start the cleanup. Volunteers took children to playgrounds and also provided entertainment for them in the refugee centers. Despite the many refugee centers available, many people elected to stay in the upstairs of their homes without electricity or telephone while they cleaned out the ground floors and basements.

In the days following the disaster, the chief concern of most people was the cleanup, work that was made even more tedious by the oppressive heat and humidity that continued across the Conemaugh Valley. Furnaces, washers, dryers, and freezers were ruined and had to be removed from basements. Basements and ground floors had several inches of mud in them and furniture was ruined. Removing mud-soaked sofas, rugs, and mattresses was heavy, hot, and depressing work. Time after time, people would pause and look sadly at a mud-drenched memento such as a family photo album or a souvenir from a summer vacation. The loss of mementos was perhaps more depressing than the loss of less personal but more expensive items such as autos or furniture. Many people and groups from the Wilkes-Barre community offered informal assistance and advice gathered from their experiences with recent floods. They told residents of Johnstown, for example, not to immediately repaint walls, because mud would continue to seep from them for months afterward. They informed residents which kinds of furniture could be successfully dried out and restored and which items should be discarded.

In retrospect, some recovery efforts were ill-advised and ineffective. Perhaps people tried to resume normal activity too soon—five days after the flood, gasoline fumes in the storm sewers exploded, destroying a store, killing one person, and injuring six others. Following the flood, there was a persistent but probably unfounded fear of looters. In general, however, the effectiveness of the recovery efforts in Johnstown was comparable to that of formal and more structured organizations that respond to unusual but less devastating situations.

COMMUNITIES IN DISASTER: RESCUE OF AIR CRASH VICTIMS

Sunday, August 24, 1954, had been an unusually stormy day across northern Iowa. The farming community ten miles south of Mason City had been experiencing thunderstorms throughout the afternoon; finally, at about 4:45 P.M., a very brief but violent thunderstorm struck, dropping at least an inch of rain in ten minutes. As this last storm rapidly subsided, one farm family sat down to supper. They had just begun to eat when they heard their dogs barking and then a knock at their door. When they went to the door, the family was surprised to see a drenched and mud-spattered young woman standing on their porch. The woman looked at them and stammered, "We crashed . . . we need help," and then collapsed. Going to her aid, the family noticed the wreckage of an airliner strewn across their nearby pasture. The crash of Braniff Flight 152, carrying nineteen passengers and a crew, was the worst domestic airline crash of 1954. For this farming community, the next few hours would be remembered and discussed for years to come.

The young woman, who had walked nearly a quarter of a mile with a compound fracture of the ankle, was a flight attendant and the only crew member to survive. As soon as she had been moved to a couch, the farm wife telephoned the hospital in Mason City, informing them that an airplane had crashed and that ambulances were needed immediately. She then called other neighbors and the state police.

The first farmer to arrive at the crash site could hear crying and talking inside the crushed fuselage, but he was unable to find a way inside the wreck. Another farmer soon arrived and was immediately sent to bring heavy jacks and chains to the crash. The third farmer to arrive was a rather small man, and he located a hole in the fuselage and was able to squeeze inside. He shouted to the others who were arriving to keep all cars, trucks, and tractors up on the road and not to smoke because the fuselage was filled with several inches of fuel. One semiconscious woman was pinned in the wreckage in such a way that her face was partially immersed in the fuel, and she was in immediate danger of drowning. Almost all of the remaining passengers had been jammed into a heap in the front of the fuselage by the impact. Another rescuer was able to squeeze into the wreck, and together the two men began to reposition the survivors.

Numbers of rescuers were now arriving with jacks, chains, ropes, and pry bars to separate the wreckage enough to begin removing survivors. As they set about this task, other farmers drove back to the nearest farms and removed barn doors and wooden gates to serve as improvised stretchers. Farm wives had set up a collection center for blankets, pillows, bandages, and hot water and were bringing these to the crash site. Less than fifteen minutes had elapsed since the flight attendant had knocked on a stranger's door for help.

As the first survivor was being removed, a state police car and an ambulance arrived. The trooper and ambulance crew expressed surprise and regret as they told those at the crash site that they had interpreted the emergency call as the crash of a light plane and not an airliner. Immediately, calls were sent out for more ambulances and state police.

In the meantime, farmers continued their rescue efforts. Many farmers and their wives had taken first-aid classes at one time or another and were also knowledgeable about back injuries. Consequently, survivors were moved carefully after being secured to barn doors and gates. The survivors were gathered together a safe distance from the fuel-soaked wreckage and were cared for and comforted by their rescuers. Ten people were taken from the wreckage alive, but two died before reaching the hospital. Another victim, a sixty-eight year-old man, died two days later.

By 7:00 P.M., all survivors and bodies had been transported to surrounding hospitals. Throughout that night and the next week, many of the farm families provided meeting places, coffee, and food for state police, firefighters, reporters, and aviation officials. Farmers assisted in removing the wreckage from the field after the crash investigation was completed. Finally, for years afterward, some farm families and survivors exchanged letters, cards, and even Christmas gifts.

SOCIETIES IN DISASTER: THE MIDWEST FLOOD OF 1993

The hydrometeorological activity leading up to "The Great Flood of 1993" actually began in the fall of 1992. Autumn rain and heavy winter snow produced near saturated soils. Persistent and heavy spring storm systems followed over the entire Midwest. By April the soil throughout the Midwest could absorb no more water, and serious flooding began. There was some respite in May, but the pattern of heavy rains resumed in mid-June and continued throughout July and into August. Some areas received more than 1.2 meters of rain during the period. The duration, extent, and intensity of the flooding made this event the flood of the century. Flood waters remained in many areas for nearly 200 days, which is very unusual for this part of the North American continent. At one time during the flooding, Vice President Gore referred to the state of Iowa as the United States' sixth Great Lake.

Record flooding occurred along dozens of rivers, including the main stems of the Mississippi and Missouri Rivers. Nine states, more than 15 percent of the contiguous United States, were flooded. The social disruption caused by the flood is difficult to comprehend. Finalized estimates are that more than 50,000 homes were damaged or destroyed and that flooding displaced approximately 54,000 people. Hundreds of towns were impacted with at least 75 towns totally and completely under flood waters. More than 15 million acres of farmland were inundated. Given such devastation, it is surprising that only 50 lives were lost in the flooding. Flood damages amounted to $15 billion. Put in perspective, the United

States usually sustains only about $2 billion in annual flood damage. The dollar loss of flooding in 1993 created major budgetary problems for federal and state governments.

ORGANIZATIONAL RESPONSES TO DISASTER

When Roger arrived at the Naperville Eagle Food store where he worked, he was immediately informed that a powerful tornado had just hit Plainfield. His coworkers wished him well as he left immediately to pick up Carolyn. Carolyn, a Naperville elementary school teacher, was preparing her classroom for the start of fall classes the next day. Roger told Carolyn the disturbing news, and within minutes, they were speeding on their way home to Plainfield. Neither Roger nor Carolyn was expected to stay at work under the circumstances, and they had both received words of hope and concern from their coworkers and supervisors.

The emergent-norm perspective emphasizes that people become acutely aware of their social ties and commitments to others during disaster. Disaster research repeatedly documents this characterization. With heightened salience of interpersonal ties, many people are confronted by the dilemma of having to choose among the various roles they occupy. Lewis Killian (1952) was the first to discuss the more common dilemmas in his analysis of multiple-group membership during disaster. Perhaps the most common conflict encountered is between the demands of primary groups such as family, friends, and neighbors and the more instrumental and impersonal demands that are part of one's association with most formal organizations. Put in less abstract terms, people must choose between their loyalty to family and friends and, usually, loyalty to their jobs. Disaster research shows that people usually give priority to the needs of family, friends, and neighbors (Killian, 1954; Barton, 1969). Such actions clearly create problems for organizations, particularly if the majority of workers leave factories, offices, and stores unattended while they check on the whereabouts and safety of their families and friends. Further, effective disaster responses depend on at least some people, such as police, fire, and hospital personnel, giving priority to their formal roles within organizations.

Organizations and Personnel Allegiance

Problems of personnel allegiance are minimized for those organizations with clearly defined roles in areas of community protection and disaster response. These organizations include police and fire departments, utility companies, and hospitals (Dynes, 1970). Occupants of roles in these organizations have a clear perception of the necessity for continued operation of the organization during disaster. Many members of these organizations receive training that specifically emphasizes job priority during disaster. Sometimes this training includes family disaster planning. Knowing that their families have first-aid kits, stockpiles of food and water, emergency shelters, and agreed-upon evacuation plans, police, fire, and hospital workers have some assurance that their families can cope with disaster in their absence. Community members may also pressure members of relevant emergency organizations to stay on the job (Dynes, 1970). Implicit pressure is exerted when community members approach these people for assistance. Failure to give assistance is likely to be interpreted as cowardice, laziness, insensitivity, lack of professionalism, or an attempt to "cheat the taxpayer."

Problems of personnel allegiance are much greater for organizations with no clear potential for disaster assistance, such as factories, department stores, or entertainment and recreational facilities. People who work in such organizations are seldom given disaster-related training. In some factories, emergency shutdown procedures may be ignored as workers rush home to be with their families during a disaster (Killian, 1952). Many organizations of this type may simply cease operation during the initial stages of a disaster (Dynes, 1978).

Personnel allegiance may not pose such extreme problems when workers and supervisors receive early and unequivocal notice that their families and neighborhoods are in no immediate danger. Sometimes this can be inferred simply by knowing the nature and location of the disaster (Killian, 1952). When disaster strikes the workplace and nearby communities, personnel allegiance is more likely if workers have close personal ties with one another. In these instances, people are more likely to give assistance to their friends and relatives at the workplace before leaving for home. At the same time, workers are more likely to be concerned about the well-being of the workplace, at least as far as it concerns the safety of the trapped and injured. Efforts to extinguish fires, secure dangerous industrial chemicals, and properly shut down machinery are more likely in these situations.

Sometimes problems of personnel allegiance are aggravated by the actions of supervisors. Supervisors with close personal ties to their subordinates are more likely to give priority to workers' concerns than to the interests of the organization (Killian, 1952; Haas and Drabek, 1973). Often, supervisors have received little instruction as to organizational priorities in the event of disaster. Confronted with the choice between the oftentimes implicit and unstated demands of the organization and the immediate and unequivocal demands of their subordinates, it is not surprising that supervisors fail to enforce organizational interests. New supervisors or those with few personal ties to their subordinates are more likely to enforce their perception of organizational interests (Killian, 1952).

Means of Organizational Response

In an ideal sense, formal organizations have rather clear-cut boundaries in terms of the tasks they usually perform, definite membership, formal roles, and established lines of authority. Disasters may distort the form and operation of organizations from this ideal. Organizations often confront tasks far different from those they usually carry out. During disaster, the membership of organizations may change. Some members are injured or dead, while others have temporarily defected to aid their families. Occasionally, disaster may actually increase organization membership, as auxiliary personnel are activated or people volunteer their services. Formal roles and lines of authority are altered as organization members are faced with the necessity of making decisions normally made by others.

The earliest research done by the Disaster Research Center (DRC) sought to document organizational responses to disaster. In the 1970s Russell R. Dynes integrated the early findings into an "ideal type" description of organizational response to disaster. Much of the following discussion is based on this work.

Dynes (1970) developed a convenient fourfold typology of organizational response to disaster. One dimension of this typology is the nature of the *tasks carried out by organizations* in the wake of disaster. Some organizations respond to disaster by carrying out many of those *regular tasks* that the organization frequently and routinely performs in the course of their regular, day-to-day operation. For police departments, regular tasks revolve around the protection of life and property and maintaining order. During disaster, police still maintain a direct role in carrying out these tasks. They aid the injured, search for trapped or missing people, and direct traffic around or through the disaster area. Fire departments also carry out familiar tasks of fire suppression, rescue, emergency medical services, ambulance transport, and hazardous materials (HAZMAT) response.

Other organizations respond to disaster by carrying out what, for them, are *nonregular tasks*. The emergency tasks may be carried out because they bear some relationship to the organization's physical resources or to its routine tasks. During the Johnstown flood, for instance, operators of a refrigerated milk warehouse were called upon to store blood and perishable medical supplies. Schools were temporarily turned into shelters for the homeless. Following the Plainfield tornado, UPS donated trucks and drivers to haul clothing, cleaning supplies, canned goods and other items to emergency shelters. The Joliet Township Animal Control Center provided a service for pets lost in the tornado. They compiled a list of missing pets and provided shelter and care for stray animals until they were reclaimed.

The second dimension of Dynes's typology is the nature of *organizational structure* utilized in disaster, that is, whether organizations use their *old and established* structure or develop *new and untried* structures. For police and fire departments, disasters may involve little if any change in organizational structure. Fire officers may work double shifts, and such routine tasks as making fire safety inspections may be discontinued; overall, however, the authority structure of the department and role expectations remain the same. Other organizations may experience substantial alterations in their structure as they respond to disaster. Utility companies, for instance, may shift a large portion of their organizational resources to the task of restoring water, gas, electric, and telephone service. Twenty-four-hour crews were called in throughout northern Illinois to restore utilities in the Plainfield area. Insurance companies established temporary claim centers in Plainfield. The City of Chicago sent heavy equipment and workers to Plainfield. In such instances, supervisory personnel may be temporarily transferred from the office to the field, and clerical staff may be asked to help load utility vehicles. Organizations such as the Red Cross and the Salvation Army may undergo substantial transformations as they coordinate their efforts with state and national offices.

Finally, there are the many emergent organizations, such as neighborhood cleanup crews and temporary communication centers. For instance, after Roger had found that his children were uninjured and he had assessed the extensive damage to his house, he then joined together with a group of his neighbors who were going around the area shutting off gas lines. Groups such as these do not constitute formal organizations. Still, they must resolve the problems of task priority, command and authority, communication, and resource allocation in order to mount effective rescue and recovery efforts.

Established Organizations Dynes's typology of organizational responses to disaster is presented in Table 11.1. There are four types of organizational responses. Type I groups, or *established organizations*, respond to disaster by performing familiar tasks and utilizing old and established structure. Typically, these organizations, such as police and fire departments, HAZMAT response teams,

TABLE 11.1
Organizational Response to Disaster

Type of Organization	Disaster-Related Task Performance	Disaster-Related Structural Alterations	Example
Type I: Established Organizations	Performance of many familiar tasks; demand for services is greatly increased	Few structural changes; changes that occur are largely the result of increased demand for organization's services; tasks carried out by existing personnel	Police, Fire departments, HAZMAT teams, National Guard
Type II: Expanding Organizations	Performance of familiar tasks; prepared to carry out disaster-related tasks	Major structural changes due to disaster-related tasks and integration with other groups and volunteer or auxiliary personnel	Utility companies, Red Cross, Salvation Army, affected trauma centers and coroner's office
Type III: Extending Organizations	Performance of largely unfamiliar disaster-related tasks	Major structural changes due to disaster-related tasks; existing personnel carry out tasks	Local construction companies, student organizations such as fraternities, sororities, or other service organizations; church-affiliated assistance groups
Type IV: Emergent Organizations	Performance of unfamiliar disaster-related tasks; emergent	Emergent structure; shifting, temporary membership	Neighborhood rescue and cleanup crews; volunteers not affiliated with or representing a group or organization

hospitals, and the National Guard, are clearly expected to play a primary role in disaster response and recovery.

Expanding Organizations Type II groups, or *expanding organizations,* respond to disaster by expanding their membership and expanding the scale of their operation during disaster. The American Red Cross is a good example of an expanding organization. The Red Cross's day-to-day activities are typically carried out by a core of volunteers and paid workers who maintain training programs in the areas of first aid, water safety, and accident prevention. When the Red Cross swings

The American Red Cross is a good example of an expanding organization. During a disaster, less active members and volunteer workers fill out the ranks to provide aid to victims of floods, earthquakes and other catastrophes.

into action during disaster, numbers of less active, and perhaps less prepared, members and volunteers join this active core. When this occurs, the organization may encounter problems of membership discipline and coordination. Further, in large-scale disasters, national officers and personnel may arrive at the scene and oversee the operation of the local chapter. Rivalries may soon develop that hinder the coordination and reconciliation of the diverse aims of local, regional, and national levels of association in these organizations.

During a disaster, utility companies may be overwhelmed by tasks that they routinely perform on a much smaller scale. These tasks include debris removal, major repairs, and transportation of supplies. To perform this unusual volume of familiar tasks, work hours and the number of shifts are expanded. Mutual aid agreements may come into play, and local utility workers and managers will be joined by their counterparts from communities across their region.

The St. Joseph Medical Center is located within a mile of the areas damaged by the Plainfield tornado. The tornado struck at just about the time of the trauma center shift change. Day crews stayed on and supplemented the arriving afternoon staff. A number of nurses and physicians from other hospitals also arrived and offered to help in the first hours after the storm. The physical therapy room on the second floor of the hospital was taken over as a holding area for survivors with minor injuries and those awaiting word of friends and family members being treated downstairs. Altogether, more than three hundred injured people passed through this expanded facility from other hospitals (*Herald-News*, 1990).

Extending Organizations Type III groups, or *extending organizations*, extend the scope of their operations to include nonregular tasks while retaining much of their predisaster structure and personnel. Examples of extending organizations include voluntary groups such as local Boy Scout troops who serve coffee, run errands, and perhaps heft sandbags during disaster. Student organizations from Penn State University worked to salvage books at the Glosser Memorial Library following the Johnstown flood. In early stages of disaster recovery, construction companies frequently make their equipment and personnel available to those searching the debris for survivors. While extending organizations retain much of their predisaster structure, decision making tends to occur at lower levels of organizational authority than is the case in day-to-day operations (Quarantelli, 1970).

Emergent Organizations Type IV groups, or *emergent organizations*, are typified by the neighborhood rescue and recovery teams that form almost immediately following disaster impact. Occasionally, these groups assume the qualities of formal organizations, with definite task specialization, definite membership, and clearly defined roles and authority relationships. Typically, these emergent groups are built around interpersonal relationships that are part of preexisting work groups, families, and neighborhood association patterns.

Turner and Killian (1972) point out that an "ephemeral and temporary" division of labor emerges among community members following disaster. This division of labor arises while carrying out tasks such as rescue and transporting survivors to hospitals. Emergent groups may be highly involved in the later clean-up work, including removing fallen trees, mud, broken glass, and wreckage of buildings. Volunteer work crews are also formed to transport and distribute fresh water, food, and clothing and to provide transportation for community members.

Louis A. Zurcher (1968) participated in and studied such work crews following a Kansas tornado. Zurcher notes that some work crews emerged from preformed groups, such as the Mennonite Disaster Services, and civic clubs such as the Veterans of Foreign Wars. Other work crews consisted of residents who were strangers to one another prior to the disaster. These work crews emerged about thirty-six hours after the tornado struck and were relatively small, usually consisting of fewer than fifteen people. Zurcher described those who joined as people who had no "preempting obligations to help specific relatives, friends, or neighbors" and had found "appropriate channels for their motives to volunteer." One might speculate that in addition to the obvious opportunity to help one's neighbors and community, disasters give some people an opportunity to dramatically justify their earlier purchase of four-wheel-drive vehicles, chain saws, and CB radios.

During the Midwest flood of 1993, prisoners from minimum-security facilities in several states volunteered to work at sandbagging levees. These people put in many days of backbreaking work before being returned to prison. On weekends and holidays throughout that early summer, thousands of volunteer groups converged on flood-threatened communities to assist with the hot, heavy work.

Discussion

Turner and Killian make frequent use of disaster-related examples when they present the emergent norm perspective of collective behavior. For Turner and Killian, disaster turns people's concerns to the repairing and maintaining of personal ties and organizational relationships. Dynes's typology of organizational response summarizes the kinds of changes that have been observed among different organizations as they work to meet the challenges imposed by disaster. In brief, the organizational changes that occur during disaster are related to the tasks the organization regularly performs, or is prepared to perform, as well as to the organization's structure prior to disaster.

Established organizations carry out familiar tasks and undergo minimal restructuring during disaster. These groups have clear and traditional roles in disaster recovery. Expanding organizations are prepared to carry out familiar tasks but must expand or alter their structure to do so. Expanding organizations, such as the American Red Cross, often have traditional roles in disaster recovery. Extending organizations accomplish nonregular tasks during disaster with essentially the same structure used in their day-to-day operations. Extending groups generally have no traditional role in disaster recovery. Finally, emergent groups form at the scene of disaster to meet the most immediate demands of rescue and, later, to play an active role in neighborhood cleanup and recovery. These groups emerge out of family, work, and neighborhood networks of interpersonal association. Typically, these groups last only a short time and dissolve toward the end of the disaster recovery period.

INTERORGANIZATIONAL RESPONSES TO DISASTER

Just as disaster brings about temporary changes *within* organizations, it also brings about many changes *among* organizations. Before disaster, the relationship between the police department and the local Red Cross chapter may be quite indirect. For example, some police officers may take first-aid refresher courses offered by the Red Cross. During disaster, however, the relationship between the police department and the Red Cross chapter may be more immediate and direct. Police officers and Red Cross volunteers may work side by side while rescuing people. These organizations will probably see the need to exchange information with one another. Police may be asked to provide vehicles and officers to assist in Red Cross efforts to distribute food and clothing. Police concerns for security and traffic control may directly conflict with Red Cross volunteers' desire to have free access to the disaster site. A wide range of interorganizational changes has been documented. Dynes (1978) has condensed these findings into an overall summary of interorganizational responses to disaster.

Communication   The first interorganizational response to occur following disaster is usually the joining together of organizations for the purpose of communication. Immediately following disasters, survivors gather together and exchange information about injuries and property damage. Often, they gather near prominent landmarks or places offering shelter or adjacent to areas accessible to emergency vehicles. Many of the injured are brought to this gathering place for aid and transportation to hospitals. Others gather here to inquire about the missing and injured. This site emerges as the operations center for further rescue and recovery work. Representatives of various organizations converge on this site and expand the scope of its operations. Probably the first organization to be represented is the police, followed by hospital personnel. Short-wave and CB radio clubs may also set up equipment at this location, further enlarging the communications link to the outside. Later, the Red Cross, Boy Scouts, church groups, and private vendors may also converge to provide food and coffee to those in the operations center and to neighborhood work crews.

Recovery Task Coordination and Resource Allocation Another interorganizational response emerges to deal with the substantial problems of recovery task coordination and resource allocation. Looking after the injured is usually given clear priority in disasters. Once this task is in hand, however, there is often considerably less consensus regarding the next priority. Should city work crews, for example, be assigned to help utilities restore electrical and telephone service, or should they help the municipal water department? Representatives of the organizations involved in disaster-related activities meet and reach a working consensus regarding community priorities. Temporary lines of authority are established among representatives of city work crews, utilities, and groups under contract to provide cleanup services. Representatives of voluntary organizations and emergent work crews may also seek or be requested to provide input into these decisions. This group functions around the clock to settle procedural problems as they arise.

Disaster-Related Scarcity A third type of interorganizational response arises to deal with disaster-related scarcity. Hospitals may trade thermometers for antibiotics in an effort to meet immediate postdisaster medical needs. Suppliers may be asked to make special deliveries of surgical equipment. Private pilots and corporations may be asked to make their aircraft available for transporting medical supplies and personnel. City governments may approach county agencies and private contractors for the use of heavy equipment. In disaster, organizations unfamiliar with one another tend to avoid communication. Usually, organizations see if they can obtain assistance from their old suppliers and clients before initiating new relationships. As each organization restores contacts with its suppliers and clients, a web of functional integration is established that facilitates disaster response.

Excess Resources Interorganizational responses also arise to deal with the surprising problem of excess resources. Following many disasters, communities have been swamped with unsolicited aid in the form of food, clothing, and various other tangible items (Fritz and Mathewson, 1957). Money, food, clothing, medicine and supplies began to arrive in Plainfield from dozens of sources within hours of the disaster. The Soviet Embassy in Washington, DC, contacted Illinois Governor James Thompson's office and offered to send aid. The Soviet Union wanted to repay aid given by the United States in 1998 following earthquakes in Soviet Armenia. The vacant Weiboldt's store in Joliet was volunteered as a major collection point for the large volume of donated clothing, cleaning supplies, canned goods, dishes, flashlights, cases of soft drinks, toilet items, diapers and toys that were arriving. Kodak donated 700 cameras for use by victims to record damage done to homes for insurance purposes. Other corporations donated many items and also made nearly a quarter of a million dollars in monetary contributions, including over $50,000 obtained by a WGN Radio and Television fundraiser.

Donated items can be of immediate use to disaster victims. Much, however, is not. Donated goods often arrive in amounts far greater than what is actually needed. Some items are either not needed at all or are unusable. There are instances in which disaster victims have been shipped truckloads of unlabeled and damaged canned goods, gigantic tennis shoes, used magazines, defective electric fans, and lice-infested used clothing. In some cases, disaster victims were asked to pay shipping costs. Perhaps some of these gift givers view disasters as an opportunity for tax deductions or as a dumping ground for unwanted items. Even if they are given an opportunity to refuse these gifts, disaster victims frequently accept them in an effort not to appear ungrateful. In any event, unsolicited goods add to disaster site congestion and may disrupt the local economy. More important, from the standpoint of organizations, the storage, sorting, and distribution of unsolicited goods may absorb the services of people and material resources that could be used for more essential tasks. The distribution of donated items, whether they are critically needed or not, can cause conflict between organizations, as well as between organizations and the general populace.

Means of Interorganizational Response

Interorganizational responses occur with respect to problems of restoring communication, task coordination and resource allocation, disaster-related scarcity, and control of excess resources. How do organizations get together in the wake of disaster to solve these problems?

Prior Planning One means of interorganizational response is through prior planning. Some communities maintain disaster-preparedness and evacuation programs that specify the roles that many community-based organizations will play in disaster response. Prior planning for disaster is now supported through the Federal Emergency Management Administration (FEMA). This is particularly the case since the introduction of Project Impact, FEMA's initiative to make participating communities disaster resistant. Disaster plans often assign police primary responsibility for sounding warnings, making evacuation decisions, and establishing postdisaster communication with organizations outside the affected area. Firefighting priorities are established for the fire department. Some city governments have standing contracts with private construction firms for the temporary use of heavy equipment in the event of disaster. Church and civic groups may make their own plans for distributing donated goods. Prior planning includes hazards assessment, or the identification of likely disaster agents and scenarios for the community. Prior planning also includes developing lists of medically trained people in the community and the specification of duties for plan personnel—making an inventory of community ice supplies, for instance. Evacuation routes are identified in prior planning, and the locations of primary and secondary emergency operations centers are specified.

Planning for disaster does not guarantee that all problems of interorganizational coordination can be eliminated. As communities grow and change, these programs can quickly become obsolete. Further, planners of disaster preparedness programs cannot anticipate all community needs created by disaster; nor can they know the capabilities of emergent groups. Some community organizations will be totally unaware of disaster plans. Finally, many communities have no disaster plans at all. Fortunately, there are other means of interorganizational response.

The Emergency Domain In addition to prior planning, organizations get together by way of organizational goals and leadership decisions. Dynes refers to this as association on the basis of legitimate claims on the emergency domain. Established groups such as police and fire departments, hospitals, and utility companies, as well as many expanding groups such as the Red Cross and Salvation Army, have clear and undisputed claims on the emergency domain. These organizations will be among the first to contact one another in the event of a disaster.

Extending and emergent organizations have a less clear claim to the emergency domain. Their role in disaster response may be dictated by circumstance rather than by any generally recognized claim to the emergency domain. One example is the milk warehouses that were used to store blood following the Johnstown flood. Fast-food outlets may extend their hours as the demand for quick meals increases. Boat clubs, snowmobile clubs, and four-wheel-drive clubs may provide rescue and transportation services during floods and blizzards.

The degree to which the leadership of these groups can integrate their activities with those of police, hospitals, and other organizations with clear claim on the emergency domain will determine the success of these groups' claim to legitimacy. They may be viewed as providing a valuable service, or they may be seen as a nuisance. Even emergent cleanup crews are occasionally seen as an annoyance by the police and National Guard, who try to control movement within the disaster area.

Finally, some organizations make no claims on the emergency domain. High schools cancel athletic events, theaters and department stores close, and bridge, garden, and literary clubs cancel their meetings. In part, these organizations cease operation because of personnel defection to organizations with greater claim on the emergency domain. When these organizations once again begin to operate, it usually denotes the end of the disaster period.

Supplier-Client Relationships Another means of interorganizational response is by way of previously established supplier-client relationships. These relationships provide a network of association that can be partially or totally activated following disaster. This usually occurs in response to problems of disaster-related scarcity. Dynes suggests that there is a tendency to initiate few new supplier-client relationships for the purpose of disaster response. In part, this may be due to the difficulties that organizations have in judging one another's reliability and competence during disaster. Further, disaster frequently creates the need for special orders, processing, delivery, and means of payment. Shipments of items needed at the scene of the disaster must be given priority, while shipments of unneeded items must be postponed until clients are ready to receive them. Such special needs are best met through long-established supplier-client relationships.

Personal Contact Finally, interorganizational response is carried out through personal contacts between organizations. Some people occupy what Dynes describes as "boundary roles" and others have called "gatekeeper roles"; such people are in frequent contact with people in other organizations. Top executives, trade association members, and high-ranking public officials, for example, have almost daily contact with representatives of other organizations and are in a good position to assess the disaster response of these organizations. Following disaster, occupants of boundary roles know when and where to contact members of other organizations. Finally, people in these roles may be able to call in favors during the crisis. Boundary personnel belong to two or more organizations. Police officers, for example, may also be members of the Red Cross or short-wave radio clubs or may be leaders of Boy Scout troops. Boundary personnel are in a good position to integrate the responses of these organizations. People with extensive or unusual patterns of friendship represent another type of boundary personnel. These people can help initiate contact between organizations and perhaps play a major role in subsequent joint efforts of the organizations.

Discussion

Immediately following the impact of disaster, people's primary concern is with the well-being of family, friends, and neighbors. People usually rely on their own resources in their first efforts to give aid to those around them. As time passes, however, they turn to the organizational resources of the community. Some organizations, such as police and fire departments, hospitals, utility companies, and the Red Cross and Salvation Army, have immediate and traditional roles in disaster response. The resources of other organizations are also brought into play to assist and supplement those of the organizations with primary responsibility. Interorganizational responses usually revolve around the problems of communication restoration, task coordination and resource allocation, disaster-related scarcity, and the control of excess resources. Organizations work together on the basis of prior planning, legitimate claims on the emergency domain, previously established supplier-client relationships, and personal contacts between organizations.

Often, the restructuring of organizations in the aftermath of disaster seems ineffective and chaotic. Such outward appearances are deceiving. The temporary organizational structure is more unified in terms of goals and more controlled by central authority than the predisaster structure. These qualities allow those in the new structure to make more rapid decisions, take more direct action, and resolve problems more quickly than they can under the conventional organizational structure.

COMMUNITY RESPONSES TO DISASTER

From the examples and discussions presented above, it is obvious that disasters and people's responses to them produce a number of *functional* and *structural* changes within communities. Dennis E. Wenger (1978) has presented an overall summary of community responses to disaster. Much of the following discussion is based on this framework and analysis.

The term *community* is sometimes used to mean the same thing as *neighborhood* or to refer to a certain category of people, as when we speak of the Latin community. In Wenger's analysis, the term *community* refers to an entire town or city having a definite legal boundary. In the case of rural communities, the term refers to the legal boundaries of county government, which figure importantly in disaster response. The legal boundaries of a community usually circumscribe the authority of organizations involved in disaster response. Police and fire departments, for example, cannot indiscriminately cross municipal boundaries to render assistance to nearby communities.

A general finding of disaster research is that communities begin to rebuild almost immediately after disasters. Three days after the twister struck Plainfield, for example, Uwe F. Koehler, a professor of architecture at Ball State University, brought students to Plainfield to study the effects of tornadoes. He wanted to show students the effects of tornadoes on structures, and to look at patterns in the debris. However, much of the debris had already been bulldozed and some trucked away for burning (*Herald-News*, 1990).

Community Functions

In order to provide an overall framework for his summary of community response to disaster, Wenger begins by identifying five basic community functions. These functions are generally accepted by sociologists as constituting the normal, day-to-day outputs and concerns of community life. When we state that disasters disrupt community functions, we mean that some community activities can no longer be carried out and that people must suddenly assign new priorities to many activities. Further, people strive as much as possible to restore community functions to their predisaster state.

These functional and structural components of community life are generally taken for granted within the communities in which they operate. That is, community functions are carried out concurrently, with little concern for overall priorities. The elements of community structure order activity in such a manner that community functions are carried out on a continuing basis. Disasters disrupt this fluid nature of community life. In disaster, people must immediately consider the priority of community functions, and they must alter community structure accordingly.

Production, Distribution, and Consumption The first community function we'll consider is the very broad range of activities that revolve around the production, distribution, and consumption of goods and services. The financial livelihood of most families in a community depends directly on participation in the production and distribution of goods and services. Further, the manner in which these functions are carried out determines a great deal within any community. The tempo of community life, for instance, is set by the hours of factory shifts, store hours, and the office hours of professionals. Likewise, the tempo of family life is determined by work hours, mealtimes, and the scheduling of shopping trips, music lessons, and medical appointments. Finally, types of production facilities in a community are related to possible disaster outcomes. Communities with oil refineries, nuclear reactors, chemical plants, or underground coal mines, for example, are more likely than others to have disaster contingency plans.

Following disasters, normal production, distribution, and consumption activities are typically given low priority. Factories and many retail stores cease operation during the early stages of disaster recovery, while facilities with clear relevance to the immediate crisis are given priority. As the earlier discussion of extending organizations indicates, disaster-related operations are usually quite different from normal operations. Disasters overload and often cripple transportation facilities, so trucks, buses, vans, and autos are pressed into emergency service to take the injured to hospitals or transport the dead to morgues. Police may allow only emergency-related traffic into the disaster area while halting or rerouting normal commercial traffic. The reopening of factories, stores, offices, and normal traffic routes usually denotes the end of the initial recovery period.

Socialization Another community function is that of socialization. Central to this function is the operation of public and private schools. In addition, many organizations within a community provide various types of specialized training, be it in ballet, childbirth preparation, or firearm safety.

Socialization functions are given low priority during early stages of disaster recovery. Schools are often turned into emergency shelters and distribution centers. In some cases, schools are unable to function normally because area transportation facilities are in shambles. The reopening of schools also signals the end of the initial recovery period.

Participation Communities also provide opportunities for participation in social life. This function, which is interconnected with those previously mentioned, is performed by community elements that provide opportunity for association and interaction. One's job, for example, provides opportunity to associate with others in an instrumental fashion for the production of goods and services. Business lunches, coffee breaks, executive retreats, and softball leagues provide opportunities for workers to associate in a noninstrumental fashion. Recess and school carnivals and picnics provide opportunities for children, parents, and teachers to interact in a less structured fashion. Recreation programs extend opportunities for community participation to preschoolers and senior citizen groups.

The social participation function of community life takes on increased visibility and priority in disaster. This is the case even though conventional forms of community participation such as work and school have been temporarily suspended. Disaster fosters social participation in other ways. Immediate demands are created by the tasks of rescuing and transporting the injured. Cleanup crews emerge, and volunteer groups, such as the Red Cross or Salvation Army, are activated.

There are also some less obvious channels of social participation. The elderly, for example, may be drawn into more intense community involvement as their neighbors, at least for a time, show greater concern for their physical and emotional welfare. Older people may also be requested to look after children during later recovery efforts. For months after the Plainfield tornado, for example, Carolyn and Roger's children often spent weekends with grandparents while they worked on their house.

Teenagers, who occupy many marginal roles in community life, often find opportunities in disaster to fill more central roles in emergency social systems. Form (1958) notes that teenagers ran errands, carried emergency supplies, and even transported the dead and injured to hospitals following a Michigan tornado. Teenagers and young adults often constitute a major portion of the work force recruited to heft sandbags during floods.

Finally, in the days following disaster, neighborhood groups and organizations sponsor fish fries, chicken barbecues, and other communal functions that sometimes impart a festival-like atmosphere and help to dispel the depression that accompanies cleanup efforts.

Social Control Maintaining conformity to community standards and protecting life and property are social control functions within community life. Police and fire departments are charged with primary responsibility in this area, while additional social control functions are carried out by regulatory agencies and probation and parole offices.

The Plainfield disaster provides an opportunity to investigate the alterations that can occur in the social control function during a disaster. After Roger picked up Carolyn at her school, they sped back to Plainfield. In the brief amount of time since the twister had struck, police had set up roadblocks, stopping all but emergency vehicles from entering the area of destruction. Carolyn and Roger were stopped about a mile from their home and told they could not enter the area. They explained very emphatically that they lived in Plainfield and they were going in to find their children. The police allowed them to proceed on foot into the Lily Cache subdivision where their home was located and one of the most heavily damaged areas of Plainfield. Even before they reached their home, they met friends and neighbors who told them that their children were unharmed, but that their home had been wrecked.

Social control functions, particularly vehicular and pedestrian traffic control, are given high priority during disaster. These functions are essential to ensuring that available emergency vehicles have access to the disaster site, and that pedestrians are kept away from such things as downed power lines or broken gas mains. Police priorities also include the prevention of looting. The generally recognized low incidence of looting during disaster may be due to police efforts, in addition to the lack of significant social support for such activity (Wenger, 1978). Some social control activities may be relaxed during disaster; specifically, some research suggests that police assign lower priority to making arrests for traffic offenses, drunkenness, and disturbing the peace (Wenger, 1978).

Church groups usually take an active social control role in storing, sorting, distributing, and, in some cases, disposing of donated goods. A major social control function for police, and other groups as well, is dealing with the convergence of people and donated goods to the disaster site. Traffic control problems are often aggravated by sightseers and outsiders who have come to the community to volunteer their labor.

Mutual Support Organizations such as community mental health centers and family welfare services are formalized community efforts that meet the needs arising from individual and group crises. Less formal organizations, such as drug and alcohol rehabilitation programs that provide counsel to troubled teenagers, also meet this function, as do families and friendship groups, particularly at times of childbirth, illness, or death.

The social support function of community life emerges as a clear priority during the early stages of disaster recovery. For a time, life in the community becomes emotionally and physically intimate. Neighbors who may have hardly spoken to one another now share fears, hurts, and hopes. Outward signs of support and caring, such as pats on the back, hand holding, and hugging, are more frequent than usual.

Perhaps this intimacy arises because there is an increased reliance on face-to-face communication in the emergency social system. Further, there are fewer social barriers to communication in the emergency social system. Damaged houses, for example, no longer provide seclusion for their occupants. Clothing that is borrowed, torn, or mud-stained is unlikely to convey social standing. The elderly who seldom venture from their homes may be quite literally thrust into the social life of their neighborhood by disaster. Community response to disaster takes on an intimate and supportive character in part because many of the facades and tactics we use to isolate ourselves from others no longer operate.

A major mutual support concern within a community is sheltering the homeless. Communities provide temporary shelter in gymnasiums, auditoriums, and church basements. These public shelters are almost always more than sufficient to meet the needs of the homeless, because many people make their homes available to relatives and friends who need shelter (Dacy and Kunreuther, 1969). Social relationships established in public shelters are likely to reflect mutual support, even between ethnic groups who have previously experienced mutual antagonism (Fritz, Rayner, and Guskin, 1958). However, research also suggests that the longer these temporary living arrangements are maintained, the greater the likelihood that disharmony will develop.

Another mutual support function to emerge during disaster is that of victim-advocate. After disaster, many victims must deal with insurance companies, find sources of credit, perhaps seek public aid, and, in general, deal with a number of private and governmental agencies. For many, this is an unfamiliar, first-time experience. Though most disaster victims can handle these difficulties by themselves, some cannot. Increasingly, church groups are recognizing this need and including victim-advocate programs as part of their disaster assistance planning (Bush, 1979). Victim-advocates help people deal with private and governmental agencies in the aftermath of disaster. In particular, victim-advocate programs target the elderly, the non-English-speaking, the poor, and small businesses for their services. A few victim-advocate programs provide volunteers to assist in the repairing and rebuilding of homes and businesses.

Finally, some mutual support efforts take the form of programs that provide long-term counseling to disaster victims. Months after a disaster, some people still need to ventilate their fears and feelings about what happened. Often, these people were injured, had family members killed, or sustained major property losses. Also, some parents may need to discuss the adjustment problems of their children in the wake of disaster. These programs pull together volunteers with skills in the areas of personal and family counseling, such as clergy and social-work students (Bush, 1979).

Community Structure

Community structure provides the means through which the above functions are carried out in a regular and predictable fashion. Wenger identifies four important features of community structure.

The alterations in community functions summarized earlier by Wenger entail corresponding alterations in community structure. When there are forewarnings of danger, as with hurricanes, some structural changes may occur before disaster strikes.

Cultural Values and Beliefs Values are collective definitions of what is good, just, and worthy of achieving. In modern, ethnically and occupationally diverse communities, there is a minimal consensus of values; many divergent values are pursued simultaneously within the community. Despite this marked diversity of values, however, beliefs in modern communities tend to reflect an "individualistic-activistic" stance toward life. That is, individual efforts on one's own behalf are seen as the best way of relating to the world. Further, it is believed that the individual pursuit of self-interest and personal gain generally contributes to the overall good of the community.

Disaster brings about a temporary consensus of values and a change in beliefs. Disaster focuses community concerns on humanitarian values of care for the injured, aid for the homeless, and the protection of life over property. Diverse materialistic values, for the moment, are of secondary importance. At hardly any other time are people in a community as united in their concerns for the well-being of others.

Beliefs in the utility of self-interest shift to beliefs in the benefits of working for the common good. Beliefs about self-reliance become tempered with the recognition that some needs are best met through the generosity and cooperation of others. In later stages of disaster recovery, beliefs about the cause of disaster may become important. This is particularly true for such technological disasters as mine explosions, refinery fires, or hazardous chemical spills. In these instances, much postdisaster concern centers on the assignment of blame. Those deemed responsible may escape censure if they can clearly demonstrate predisaster competence and concern for safety. If not, these people are likely to be charged with incompetence and greed (Drabek and Quarantelli, 1967). Such charges may permanently alter the relationship between organizations and the community.

Normative Structure Normative structure refers to the explicit and implicit guidelines for behavior that exist within a community. As is the case with values, normative consensus is relatively low in communities with high ethnic and occupational diversity. Still, some general normative guidelines exist, the most important of which are the traditional rights and concerns that accompany property ownership. There is also a tendency to judge collective decisions in terms of long-range consequences and cost effectiveness. There are also those norms that constitute distinctions of status. These norms regulate interaction between the rich and the poor and between men and women, and they usually tend to establish nonegalitarian patterns of interaction between these groups.

Most changes in the normative structure during a disaster are related to the use of property. Emergent norms often override the traditional rights and concerns that accompany property ownership. Immediately following disaster impact, all kinds of goods are appropriated for the use of rescuing and transporting the injured. People who own tractors, trucks, boats, and airplanes are often confronted with demands to assist in rescue efforts. Few owners deny these requests, even though the wear and tear on their equipment may be substantial. Other goods and equipment are pressed into service in a manner that would constitute theft in nondisaster situations. For example, people may break locks of company equipment sheds in the early stages of disaster response. Later, most if not all items commandeered in this fashion are returned.

Another type of norm to emerge in the early stages of disaster response is that of immediacy: disaster victims want action, the sooner the better (Bruning, 1964). During this stage of disaster response, relatively few decisions are made in terms of long-range consequences or overall cost effectiveness. Rather, decisions are made and judged in terms of immediate effectiveness. Sometimes, for example, casualties are brought to hospitals in subcompact cars, while four-wheel-drive trucks are being used to carry a few pints of blood to aid stations near the disaster site. This is certainly not a cost-effective or even convenient use of resources. But in terms of immediate effectiveness, it works: casualties are getting to the hospital, and blood is getting to the disaster site.

Disaster responses may alter norms that regulate interpersonal relationships. Emergent norms in this area tend to be more egalitarian than those prior to disaster. Patterns of association based on distinctions of high and low social status are temporarily abandoned; that is, the rich and the poor are more likely to treat each other as equals during disaster. Further, norms that regulate relationships between ethnic groups are much less salient. Finally, women may temporarily take on roles normally carried out by men.

Organizational Structure The formal ties among organizations whose primary activities are carried out within and for the community are part of community organizational structure. These include the organizational ties between the police and fire departments or between hospitals, patients, and local sources of medical supplies and other services.

Another element of community organizational structure is the extent of ties to organizations outside the community, many of which are hierarchical in nature, such as the relationship between local welfare agencies and state departments of welfare. In these types of relationships, the local community organization is in a subordinate position.

Modern communities have extensive ties with nonlocal organizations. To the extent that these ties predominate, those between local organizations are less central to the overall functioning of the community. Further, extensive ties between local subordinate organizations and distant superordinate organizations reduce community autonomy.

During disaster response, alterations in organizational structure usually take the form of an overall strengthening of a community's internal and external organizational ties; that is, the number and intensity of contacts between organizations substantially increase. Dormant ties are reactivated and new ones are sometimes initiated.

The strengthening of organizational ties is quite obvious when communities have some forewarning of disaster, as when a community braces itself for a hurricane. This preimpact stage is characterized by intense interorganizational contact within a community. Local hospitals take stock of their supplies and contact each other regarding last-minute needs. Police departments issue statements to radio and television stations, while factory and business personnel contact police and radio stations to inquire about the severity of winds and danger of flooding.

The preimpact stage is also characterized by greater contact with organizations outside the community. Police and fire departments maintain closer contact with the National Weather Service. Hospitals reaffirm mutual aid agreements with hospitals outside the community. Local Red Cross chapters contact state organizations to discuss impending needs, and National Guard units are placed on standby alert.

Interorganizational ties within a community remain strong during and immediately following disaster impact. However, ties to organizations outside the community may be temporarily weakened or broken. This may be due to temporary isolation caused by damage to telephone lines, collapsed bridges, or flooded highways. To the degree that the external ties are broken, community autonomy is increased. This temporary isolation and autonomy can be a positive factor in early disaster response. Community needs are more easily given priority over the interests or policies of distant superordinate organizations. For instance, it is easier for extending organizations to loan personnel and equipment when the home office is unable to voice objections. It may even be possible to conceal the extent of this community assistance.

In the later stages of disaster recovery, external ties are once again intensified. This is particularly true for expanding organizations such as the Red Cross, which receives money, supplies, supervisory personnel, and volunteers from regional headquarters. On the other hand, the added presence of outside organizational personnel increases the likelihood that the needs of these organizations will take precedence over local interests. That is why the later stages of disaster response are often marked by greater amounts of dispute and bad feelings.

Power Relationships According to many sociologists, power relationships in modern communities typically follow the pluralist pattern. That is, there are several sources of power within any community, and there are many conflicting interests among people and organizations with power. Consequently, the power relationships within a community are seldom directed toward a common objective. Some sources of power, such as police, fire, and welfare departments, operate in clearly defined areas. Other sources of power, including property ownership, possession of scarce skills and knowledge, interpersonal influence, and political parties, operate in less clearly defined areas. Power derived from these sources is often exercised indirectly and intermittently.

Community disaster response usually involves a temporary alteration in power relationships. The pluralistic pattern of power relationships is replaced by a more centralized, regimented, and authoritarian power structure. Following disaster, representatives from city government, police, volunteer organizations, and private business work together to deal with the problems of recovery task coordination and resource allocation. This grouping may be an ad-hoc association or the result of disaster pre-planning. For a time, this group occupies a central authority role within the community. Typically, this group is quite unified in terms of recovery goals. Such centralized authority, goal consensus and regimentation seldom exist in everyday situations.

Power is also used in a more authoritarian fashion in the disaster-struck community. Given the sense of urgency in the early stages of disaster response, few people object to the orders they receive from the police. Authoritarian structure is most clearly seen when military organizations such as the National Guard are used in disaster recovery. Community members may be required to get travel permits in order to go to their homes in the disaster area. Curfews are imposed as a precaution against looters or as a means to discourage sightseeing. Initially, community members view these authoritarian measures as necessary or at least tolerable. In the later stages of disaster recovery, however, travel permits, roadblocks, and curfews may actually impede recovery efforts. Consequently, community members come to regard authoritarian measures as disagreeable and voice their objections.

Finally, there is the issue of emergent leadership during disaster. What are the personal characteristics of those who assume unusually active roles in disaster situations? According to the findings of disaster research, the effective community leader usually possesses disaster-related skills and has previous experience with disaster. In addition, these leaders have limited ego involvement in the situation. This means that people who know their families and property are safe are more likely than others to tend to the larger needs of the community. Research also suggests that those who already occupy leadership positions are likely to extend their leadership functions during disaster. For example, business leaders, chiefs of police and fire departments, and hospital administrators are more likely than others to assume major leadership roles in disaster recovery. In part, this may be because community members demand that people in these positions play a major role in disaster recovery.

Discussion

Much of our discussion so far would lead us to believe that disasters bring out the best in people. People do not panic but respond effectively to even the most terrifying situations; people tend to be altruistic in disaster; organizational priorities can quickly shift to meeting the immediate needs of the community; communities display a degree of harmony seldom seen in everyday situations. In Plainfield, for instance, much of the debris had been gathered and relief centers were about ready to close only two days after the tornado struck.

As communities enter the later stages of disaster recovery, we see that once again, people begin to give priority to even minor individual and family needs and show less concern for the lingering problems of others. Immediately after the tornado, friends invited Carolyn, Roger, and their children to live with them until they could move back into their home. The family stayed in their damaged home until after Christmas, when the contractors were finally able to start work. By then, however, the invitations had been forgotten or implicitly withdrawn. During the rebuilding the children stayed with grandparents, and Carolyn and Roger stayed with another family. These arrangements were very inconvenient and fostered many disagreements.

Invariably, stories circulate about people who lost nothing but received large amounts of aid and others who lost everything and received no aid. Relief agencies are charged with inefficiency and callousness. As organizations resume their normal operations, the full cost of the disaster comes into focus. City governments look at budgets that have been severely depleted or totally overrun. Earlier antagonisms that had been set aside emerge again. Political opponents charge one another with using the disaster situation for political gain. Groups within the community may object to proposed reconstruction plans.

In the days following the Plainfield tornado, people had to ascertain their insurance coverage, and obtain loans and contractors to repair or rebuild their homes. Such dealings can be frustrating under the best of conditions. Even though contractors from over a wide area offered their services to Plainfield residents, it took many families several weeks and even months to obtain a contractor. For some families, rebuilding began within days of the tornado. Other families, like Carolyn and Roger, made enough temporary repairs that they were able to return to their homes, sometimes without heat, water, and electricity until they could rebuild. For Carolyn and Roger, rebuilding began after Christmas. The builder they initially hired, like some other builders, took on too many jobs after the tornado and was unable to start the work as promised. The delay was very frustrating and depressing for the family.

Fortunately, disaster research shows that postdisaster disharmony also passes. Disaster nostalgia replaces emotional intensity. People tell their children how they fought the great Midwest Flood of 1993, or how they were never so frightened as when they saw the tornado coming. Within a few years, lives will have been resumed, organizations restored, and monuments may be erected to commemorate the victims and volunteers (Wright et al., 1979). The Lily Cache subdivision of Plainfield was about twenty years old when it was devastated by the tornado. Like many subdivisions that were built in the 1970s, Lily Cache had a rather plain appearance. All the homes in the subdivision were single-story, four-bedroom dwellings with the same, or mirror-image, floor plans. After the tornado, many two-story homes were built. Carolyn and Roger enlarged their living room and added a two-story addition to their home. We brought them some trees, shrubs, and bedding plants to replace those lost in the tornado. By the late summer of 1994, only a year after the tornado flattened much of Plainfield, new roof lines, new colors, and new landscaping gave the rebuilt areas a much more attractive and interesting appearance. Plainfield was not as plain as it once was.

⭐ SOCIETIES IN DISASTER

Compared to what we know about individuals, organizations, and communities in disaster, we have relatively little specific knowledge about societies in disaster. Perhaps this is because we use a number of terms other than disaster to refer to calamitous events of sufficient scale that they produce noticeable changes in the operation of an entire society. Instead of calling these events disasters, we call them droughts, famines, plagues, and wars.

⭐ Dynes's Typology ⭐

Dynes (1975) has offered a classification of societies in terms of their vulnerability to disaster. In quite general terms, Dynes views the societal response to disaster as a result of population size, economic base, and the extent of coordination between organizational levels in the society. Taking these factors into account, Dynes identifies three types of societies with characteristic patterns of response to disaster.

Type I Societies These societies have small populations and are organized in terms of family, kin, and clan or tribal relationships. The economic base of these societies is food gathering. Dynes characterizes these societies as having a tenuous ecological base, which makes them quite fragile and lacking in resources for adapting to disastrous situations. Consequently, disaster can produce considerable disruption and social change in these societies. In the most extreme cases, disaster can totally destroy these small, fragile societies.

Type II Societies These societies have larger populations than Type I societies. Their economies are based on some sort of farming that regularly generates economic surplus. Consequently, Type II societies have some, though limited, ability to replace resources lost through disaster. Social organization is somewhat more complex in Type II societies and is based on villages that are integrated into regional forms of association, such as kingdoms and empires. Disasters produce moderate amounts of disruption and social change in Type II societies.

Type III Societies These societies have large populations and highly complex and integrated social structures, such as nation-states. They have considerable physical resources and surplus to replace what is lost through disaster. Type III societies also have agencies, such as the Federal Emergency Management Administration, that are directly concerned with disaster response. Consequently, disaster produces relatively little social change and disruption in Type III societies.

SOCIETAL CONSEQUENCES OF DISASTER

Dynes's threefold typology roughly follows the distinctions usually made between hunting and gathering, farming, and industrial societies. For Dynes, the impact of disasters is inversely related to the degree of modernity and technological development within a society. The "primitive" hunting and gathering societies are much less capable of coping with disaster than more "advanced" societies.

Dynes's view is clearly in keeping with conventional ideas regarding the relative capabilities of these societies. In the following sections, we will reexamine this view and present some alternate ideas.

Hunting and Gathering Societies

The species *Homo sapiens* emerged some fifty thousand years ago. Since then, more than 90 percent of human social experience has transpired within hunting and gathering societies. Although this way of life has often been characterized as fragile and ecologically tenuous, the hunting and gathering form of association has endured for nearly five hundred centuries. Only in about the past ten thousand years have other forms of human association emerged to challenge this way of life (Fagan, 1976).

Clan and tribal associations among hunting and gathering groups temporarily brought sizable populations together for the purposes of hunting, butchering, and drying meat, as well as trade (Wormington, 1957). The primary structural unit of day-to-day association, however, was the family band. These microsocieties usually consisted of fifteen to forty people and seldom had more than one hundred members. As groups approached this upper limit of size, they broke into smaller groups and went their separate ways. When the first farming groups emerged, about ten thousand years ago, the world's population stood somewhere between 5 and 10 million people. This sparse population, however, was divided into more than one hundred thousand small hunting and gathering societies (Lenski and Lenski, 1978).

The way of life in these small societies was characterized by almost continuous travel as they followed the seasons and herds of migrating animals. These groups did not build permanent dwellings. Igloos, yurts, tipis, and huts were either abandoned or dismantled and carried with them when the group moved on. It is quite likely that all the clothing, tools, and weapons that any one of these groups possessed could be packed into a small trailer.

How did disaster agents such as storms, droughts, fires, flood, and diseases affect these societies? Quite likely, hunting and gathering groups had no clear perception of disaster apart from their daily problems in living. What little evidence there is to support this assertion comes from studies of hunting and gathering groups that survived into the twentieth century. These include Eskimo groups, the !Kung bushmen of Africa, Indians of Central and South America, and some groups in the South Pacific Islands. Though these groups have words to refer to storms, floods, epidemics, and misfortune, they have no words that have an equivalent meaning to disaster (Jones, 1971). Obviously, individual hunting and gathering groups were annihilated by flood, fire, volcanic explosions, and disease. This does not mean, however, that disaster agents usually caused widespread and substantial alterations in these societies. Rather, the mode of existence of hunting and gathering groups, in many respects, minimized the impact of these disaster agents.

In an economy based on hunting and gathering, every unit of energy put into the system in the form of hunting and gathering activity yields about 1.5 units of energy output in the form of food calories. Therefore, a hunt that yielded meat with a caloric value of 15,000 units involved the expenditure of 10,000 calories by the hunter, for a net gain of only 5,000 calories (Kemp, 1971). Further, in a band of twenty people, there were probably no more than five prime hunters. Under these conditions, hunting and gathering groups lived with the constant peril of starvation. The injury of a hunter, or the failure of a hunt, could represent a disaster for the group. The way of life in hunting and gathering groups was structured in such a way as to eliminate, as much as possible, this potential for disaster.

Most hunting and gathering groups are perhaps better described as gathering and hunting groups—that is, gathering was usually their primary and most constant source of food. All members of the band helped in the gathering of vegetables, grains, bird eggs, fruits, nuts, and berries. Insects, rodents, and reptiles were also part of the diet of hunters and gatherers. This wide range of food items better ensured that people would not go hungry too often.

As noted above, the injury or death of a hunter could severely reduce a group's food supply. Consequently, the hunting methods used by these groups were quite unlike the techniques used by today's recreational hunters. Hunters rarely engaged dangerous game in mortal combat, and when they did, it usually had ceremonial overtones. (Today's African bushmen, for example, occasionally hunt lion to prove their courage, and so they use only a single spear.) Everyday hunting methods for early hunters and gatherers relied heavily on the use of entrapment, poison, and the taking of small, young, or disabled animals. In Europe, hunters stampeded mammoths, bison, and wild horses into bogs where the animals became trapped in the mud. In North America, hunters stampeded large game over cliffs or into gullies (Wormington, 1957). In Africa and the jungles of Central America, hunters developed a variety of poisons for use in the hunt. Eskimos used whalebone blades embedded in frozen meat to rupture the stomachs of polar bears. Many of these techniques resulted in substantial overkill, which may have contributed to the extinction of several animal species. However, these techniques ensured that the hunter would live to hunt another day.

Hunting and gathering societies were constantly on the move, following animal herds and gathering seasonal plant life along traditional migration routes. Their high mobility served to reduce the impact of localized weather conditions, such as floods and drought. These groups were often able to travel up to thirty miles in a single day and more than two hundred miles in a week. With their high degree of mobility, hunting and gathering groups could easily flee from immediate dangers or leave regions that were not to their liking.

It is easy to visualize a situation, such as a flash flood, in which a hunting and gathering group could lose most of its material possessions. This loss would not create as severe a hardship for hunters and gatherers as it would for people in other kinds of societies. Almost every member of a hunting and gathering band possessed basic survival skills. In a short period of time, nearly all the material goods necessary for the group's well-being could be fashioned from raw materials immediately at hand. Once they reached a place of comparative safety, the hunting and gathering band would quickly turn to the tasks of building fires, shelters, and tools. Within hours, the group would be warm and dry and have serviceable spears, bows, and arrows.

The hunting and gathering way of life served to keep human populations dispersed. Even in the most favorable environments, population density rarely exceeded three people per square mile. Not only were hunting and gathering populations sparse, contact between groups was infrequent. These ecological conditions inhibited the spread of contagious diseases such as smallpox, cholera, and plague.

The hunting and gathering way of life was ecologically suited to the environments in which it flourished, much more so than the ways of life that were to follow. Even so, hunting and gathering groups often faced severe hardship, and few of us today could successfully adapt to this way of life.

The most disastrous occurrence for hunters and gatherers was contact with other social forms. Hunters and gatherers seldom have been able to compete effectively for territory and other resources used by farming and industrial societies. Most often, hunters and gatherers retreated into lands that other societies considered worthless. With decreased mobility and increased population density, hunters and gatherers often fell victim to starvation and disease. The most obvious instance of this process was the concentration of the Native American populations onto reservations, which began shortly after European colonies were established in the New World. Throughout the world, the process of concentration was often accompanied by vicious exterminations (Jones, 1971). Even benevolent gestures such as introducing modern tools into their material culture often resulted in the destruction of hunting and gathering groups (Sharp, 1952). Of the thousands of hunting and gathering groups that once existed, fewer than three hundred survived into this century. The destruction of these groups and their habitats has accelerated. In all likelihood, no hunting and gathering groups will survive into the twenty-first century (Lenski and Lenski, 1978).

 ## Farming Societies

The first farming societies emerged about ten thousand years ago in various parts of the world. Horticultural societies farmed the jungles, tilling small garden plots with digging sticks and hoes. Agricultural societies farmed the open lands, using plows and draft animals. Both types of farming societies sometimes used irrigation systems. Farming represented a tremendous shift in the energy flow within societies. Every unit of energy put into farming yields about fifteen or twenty units of energy output in the form of food calories (Rappaport, 1971). Compared to hunting and gathering societies, farming societies generated economic surplus. Both horticultural and agricultural farming were accompanied by the growth of permanent settlements—villages, towns, and cities—and drastic increases in population density. Farming was also accompanied by the emergence of larger political units, such as cities, states, empires, and nations.

Although this way of life produced surplus, it also increased the potential for disasters, particularly those associated with crop failure. In farming societies we see the expansion and formalization of religion. Asking the gods to deliver a good harvest was a central theme in early religions. In the Mayan and Aztec empires of Central America, human sacrifice was used to coax the gods into cooperation. The Mayans also took some matters into their own hands by constructing an elaborate system of wells and cisterns to carry the empire through the dry season. These wells and cisterns took on religious significance. Human sacrifices were carried out at the wells, and some of the Mayans' finest architecture and art was devoted to the construction and decoration of wells and cisterns. Activities such as these, carried out in farming societies, can be viewed as structural responses to disaster.

Unlike the temporary camps of the hunters and gatherers, permanent settlements are vulnerable to a number of disaster agents. Archaeological excavations reveal that many ancient villages were destroyed by earthquakes and floods. The majority, however, were destroyed by fire. In some cases, new villages were built upon the ashes of the old, only to be destroyed by fire once again. Whether by wind, fire, or water, the archaeological record offers ample evidence that the end of most ancient villages was disastrous.

Occasionally, archaeological digs reveal that settlements were abandoned while still intact. This and the predominance of burned villages suggests that epidemics may have been responsible for the extinction of many ancient villages. Early farming settlements were so spatially compact that, even though they seldom contained more than one hundred residents, the population density usually exceeded that of the worst slums of modern cities. This very high population density, coupled with a near total lack of sewage facilities, created ideal conditions for the spread of plague, cholera, and smallpox. Surviving descriptions of Europe's plague years often mention that villages were burned and abandoned when they were struck by disease.

Compared to hunting and gathering societies or industrial societies, early farming societies were probably the least able to respond to disaster. To a large degree, early political systems, particularly empires, were systems designed to systematically exploit and drain the resources within a given region for the benefit of the central authority. When outlying towns were struck by disaster, they could expect little organized assistance from the central authority. Even if the central authority sought to provide assistance, it was severely hindered in its efforts by slow and unreliable transportation systems. There are places in the world today where material and political conditions are hardly better than those confronting ancient farming societies. It is in these areas that the impact of disaster is most keenly felt. Since World War II, following disasters, people in these countries often receive more help from external sources, such as the United Nations, NGOs, and the foreign humanitarian assistance programs of industrialized countries, than from their own governments.

Industrial Societies

Several definitions of industrial society exist. According to their common elements, an industrial society is one in which (1) less than half of the population is directly engaged in farming, (2) most wealth is generated through industrial production, and (3) more than 2,000 kg of coal-equivalent energy is consumed annually per person. According to the definition, Japan, Taiwan, Mexico, Canada, the United States, and nearly all the nations of Europe are industrial societies.

Early industrial societies continued the trend of growth and population concentration found in farming societies, and their cities were as unsanitary and disease-ridden as the towns in farming societies. Today, the urban centers of industrial societies are considerably cleaner and safer than they once were. People no longer live in constant fear of mass epidemics of deadly contagious diseases. This relative safety depends upon complex and expensive systems of sewage disposal and carefully monitored programs of inoculation and public health measures. Were these complex systems to break down, as would likely be the case in the event of nuclear war, survivors would soon experience firsthand the horrors of the epidemics of the past.

In industrial societies, many agencies have direct and indirect roles in disaster response and recovery. In part, this is the result of increased awareness of industrial societies' tremendous structural interdependence of regions, organizations, and functions, and the need for some mechanism to quickly repair breaks in this social fabric. The existence of disaster-related agencies also presupposes that industrial societies anticipate and plan for a given amount of disruption and loss from disaster agents.

The Federal Emergency Management Agency was founded in 1979, in order to
create a comprehensive national program of disaster mitigation, preparedness,
response and recovery. Before FEMA was established, Civil Defense and dozens
of other federal and state agencies responded to disaster on a disaster-by-disaster
basis. Many services were duplicated, while some problems were ignored (Timko,
1998).

   FEMA may work with up to 28 federal agencies to provide assistance following
a disaster. FEMA also cooperates with many NGOs, including the American Red
Cross. FEMA even cooperates with the Humane Society of the United States to
assist household pets, farm animals and wildlife during disaster. State and local
governments must request aid through a presidential declaration of disaster or
emergency. Typically, the president or a high-ranking presidential representative
visits the disaster site before making the declaration. Federal assistance is usually
financial, but the federal government may also be asked to mobilize resources
from any number of federal agencies and to participate in the response. This is
when the government implements the Federal Response Plan.

   To coordinate the federal efforts, FEMA recommends and the president
appoints a coordinating officer for each state that is affected by a disaster, and a
FEMA field office is set up near the disaster scene. It is from there that the federal
and state personnel work together to carry out response and recovery functions.

   While industrial societies may develop an awareness of their complex structure
and the need for some mechanism to quickly respond to social disruptions caused
by disaster agents, the mechanism may, in itself, become a source of societal contention (Timko, 1998). Thus, FEMA budgets and programs have become a focus of
partisan political disputes since their inception.

   Industrial societies increasingly press into disaster-prone areas. For millions of
years, hurricanes have battered the Eastern seaboard of the United States, the Gulf
of Mexico, and the eastern coast of Central and South America, all now heavily
populated. The ancient Mayans in the Yucatan adapted to this feature of the environment by building villages and cities well inland or on high ground (Kurjack,
1971; Sanders and Marino, 1970). Even today, those who live near these sites are
seldom harmed by hurricanes. Recent settlement patterns in this area, however,
clearly favor beachfront development. Resorts, hotels, business, private homes
and other coastal developments—and the people in them—now fall victim to
disaster. The consequences of this trend were driven home to us in the last days of
October of 1998, when a tropical disturbance in the Southwestern Caribbean grew
to become the fourth most powerful hurricane ever measured in the Atlantic and
the most deadly Atlantic storm in the last 200 years. Hurricane Mitch scored a
direct hit on the nation of Honduras, causing over 7,000 deaths, destroying 80 percent of the nation's agriculture, sweeping away 94 bridges, and leaving nearly 20
percent of the people without homes (Honduras Institute of Tourism, 1998).

   Similar things can be said about modern U.S. settlement patterns on the Gulf of
Mexico. Over 6 million people now live in southern Florida, once the home of a few
hunting and gathering bands. The city of San Francisco is built over the San
Andreas fault line, another disaster-prone area. In 1906, San Francisco was heavily
damaged by earthquake and resulting fires. Much additional damage occurred
when dynamite was used to blast a firebreak across the city because water lines
were ruptured by the quake. The effects of the disaster resulted from the combined
effects of the disaster agent and the lack of disaster preparedness in the community.

During the four-year period between September of 1989 and September of 1993 the United States sustained over $50 billion in disaster-related damage. In 1989 Hurricane Hugo caused $7 billion in damage, becoming, for a short while, the costliest hurricane on record. Another $7 billion was lost a month later in the Loma Prieta, California, earthquake. Hurricane Andrew struck Florida and Louisiana in August, 1992, killing 52 people and leaving a quarter of a million people homeless and $20 billion in damage. In 1993, the great Midwest flood occurred with a price tag of nearly $17 billion. Disasters of such magnitude were unprecedented and certainly called for the largest FEMA response in its history. The FEMA budget and planned disaster funding proved to be insufficient to meet these demands. Special funding was authorized by Congress. During this tumultuous period FEMA received criticism from many quarters, which prompted a major organizational review (Timko, 1998). The results of this review were to place greater emphasis on disaster prevention and the reduction of loss. The review also showed that existing FEMA operating procedures were found by ordinary citizens and state and local officials to be little understood and very cumbersome.

After this thorough review was made of all programs and evaluation-related documents, FEMA adopted the strategic planning model of disaster response. FEMA drafted its first strategic plan in 1994. Strategic planning generally means that, more so than previously, FEMA will emphasize disaster prevention and reduction of loss and respond to disaster in a prompt and systematic fashion. The plan specified three strategic goals. The first goal is to protect lives and prevent the loss of property from all hazards. It is the intention of FEMA to reduce the risk of loss of life and injury from hazards by 10 percent and the risk of property loss and economic disruption by 15 percent by fiscal year 2007. The second strategic goal is to reduce human suffering and enhance the recovery of communities after disaster strikes. As part of the strategic plan, FEMA will work to reduce human suffering from disasters by 25 percent and increase the speed with which individuals, businesses, and public entities are enabled to recover from disasters by 20 percent. The third strategic goal is to insure that FEMA serves the public in a timely and efficient manner. To reach this goal, FEMA has simplified many of its earlier operations and increased the speed with which it begins to make its presence known in disaster-struck communities. It has sought to become more accessible to the general public, and to be more informative regarding its mission and day-to-day operation. Included in these efforts is the maintenance of a very informative website.

Much of FEMA's effort to reduce the risk of loss of life and injury from hazards and the risk of property loss and economic disruption has occurred by way of what became known in 1998 as Project Impact. From 1988 to 1998, FEMA spent $20 billion to help people repair and rebuild their communities after natural disasters. Insurance companies also spent additional billions in claims. As a result of disaster, businesses lost revenues; employees lost jobs; and other government agencies spent millions more. Worst of all is the terrible loss of human life caused by disaster during these years. The increasing number and severity of natural disasters since the 1980s prompted FEMA to take action to reduce the threat that hurricanes, tornadoes, severe storms, floods and fires impose upon the nation's economy and the safety of its citizens.

Project Impact represents a fundamental shift in the way FEMA deals with disasters. Project Impact is designed to help communities protect themselves from the devastating effects of natural disasters by taking actions that dramatically reduce disruption and loss. In 1995, for instance, Hurricane Marilyn swept over the Virgin Islands and killed 11 people. Marilyn also cost FEMA $450 million and insurance companies another $750 million. In 1998, an even stronger hurricane, Georges, slammed into the Virgin Islands. Because the Virgin Islands implemented and enforced a stringent building code that ensured new buildings were constructed to be stronger and safer after Hurricane Marilyn, there were no fatalities. Georges cost FEMA less than $50 million in federal disaster aid and repairs. Private insurance companies had to pay out less than $5 million.

Project Impact, in which FEMA lends technical support to communities already trying to become "disaster resistant," operates on the damage-reduction approach, basing its work and planning on decisions made at the local level. Therefore, private and long-term efforts and investments in prevention measures are essential. At the outset, pilot communities were selected across the country to demonstrate the benefits of the damage-reduction approach. FEMA offers expertise and technical assistance from the national and regional level to local communities. FEMA has used all the available mechanisms to get the latest technology and mitigation practices into the hands of the local communities. The first Illinois community to participate in Project Impact was Carbondale, in southern Illinois, approximately 100 miles southeast of St. Louis. It has a population of 28,000 and is the home of Southern Illinois University, the town's largest employer. The town is also home to a large healthcare center, recreational boat manufacturer, appliance manufacturer, and Veterans Administration Hospital. Carbondale is the largest city in southern Illinois and sits on the New Madrid Fault Zone complex. Current estimates place the risk of a damaging earthquake in southern Illinois at 50 percent over the next 20 to 25 years. Carbondale also lies in the Midwest's "Tornado Alley" and often experiences severe spring and summer thunderstorms and associated tornadoes. The potential for tornado and wind damage from these storms is significant. The area is subject to flooding from tributaries of the Big Muddy River, but because of its aggressive floodplain management program, there have been no repetitive losses under the National Flood Insurance Program definition of repeat claims.

A Letter from St. Croix

Washington, October 30, 1998

In the wake of Hurricane Georges, a U.S. Virgin Island resident took the time to tell FEMA how the agency helped her family become disaster-resistant and withstand this latest storm:

> While your agency is here on St. Croix again, we would like to take this opportunity to thank you for the grant our family received in 1995 after Hurricane Marilyn completely destroyed our mobile home. With those $25,000 tax dollars we purchased a geodesic dome kit and combined it with a $10,000 loan from the SBA, and we were able to finish our new home sufficiently to withstand Hurricane Georges in 1998.
>
> We suffered no damage to our structure at all, although at our 700-foot elevation we probably felt a few 150-mph gusts. We built to withstand another category 4 storm like Hugo. We are another FEMA success story and do thank you for all your efforts. (Federal Emergency Management Administration, 1998)

In keeping with Project Impact, the city has been an active and successful participant in the National Flood Insurance Program (NFIP) since the 1970s. According to FEMA, local officials have consistently demonstrated a high degree of knowledge about flood loss-reduction strategies, and the city has acquired flood-blighted properties using its own resources. These properties have been retired from business uses. The city has a seismic safety requirement in its building code and enforces extraterritorial jurisdiction out into the rural countryside. Spring tornado awareness campaign literature is given out in all the public schools. Active Local Emergency Planning Committees monitor hazardous materials storage and transport. The fire and police departments are equipped with HAZMAT equipment.

Because of rapidly rising human and monetary costs, FEMA is trying to get people and their property out of harm's way. In some instances this may entail paying residents to relocate or helping communities to prevent disasters. Assisted through FEMA, the entire southern Illinois town of Valmeyer relocated to the top of a bluff after most of the town was washed away in the 1993 Midwest flood. FEMA also announced (1998) plans to cut off federally subsidized flood insurance to those who repeatedly get wiped out—and to make premiums more expensive for those who choose to live in areas that are repeatedly flooded.

The growth of industrial societies has also increased the likelihood of technological disasters, the potential scope of which is limited only by our imaginations (Vacca, 1974). Some immediate concerns are worth mentioning. The transportation of poisonous or explosive chemicals has resulted in many fatal disasters and emergency evacuations, while the transportation of liquefied natural gas (LNG) poses a disaster threat of incredible magnitude. Ships carrying thousands of tons of LNG routinely enter New York Harbor and the East River. Although it is claimed that the explosion of a fully laden LNG tanker is unlikely (but not impossible), the explosion—if it did occur—would be larger than the atomic explosion over Hiroshima. Some have even speculated that an unexpected explosion of an LNG tanker in New York Harbor might be mistaken for a nuclear explosion and accidentally trigger a nuclear war. Contingency plans call for firefighters to abandon the harbor area and begin fighting fires four miles inland (Mostert, 1974). Several large oil tankers have exploded in various oceans of the world. These explosions have been less powerful than the explosion of an LNG tanker would be. Still, had one of these explosions occurred in a populous area instead of in a remote loading terminal or at sea, it would have constituted one of the largest disasters ever to befall an industrial society.

There are also silent disasters posed by the disposal of dangerous chemicals. The Love Canal disaster illustrates this problem. In 1980, the scale of contamination of homes and schools built over the abandoned Hooker Chemical waste dump was discovered to be sufficient to have caused chromosome damage among Love Canal residents. By then, hundreds of people had already been evacuated from their homes in the Love Canal area. President Carter visited Niagara Falls to sign the special appropriation bill that provided the funding for permanent relocation for all nine hundred families who wished to leave. Still, residents sustained physical injury, financial losses and emotional trauma. Had Love Canal been hit by a tornado or flood, there would have been rebuilding loans, insurance coverage and many other resources available to them. However, since Love Canal was destroyed by a dump for hazardous materials, assistance was meager and a long time in coming. While victims of tornadoes and floods received outpourings of sympathy and aid, victims of Love Canal were often labeled as "agitators" and "troublemakers."

In contrast to communities like Plainfield, which recover from *natural* disasters in an amazingly short period of time, it was almost twenty years before a small section of Love Canal was declared safe for resettlement. FHA home insurance was made available to returnees in 1992. In 1995, Occidental Petroleum took over full operation and maintenance of the chemical waste treatment plant at Love Canal, after agreeing to pay over $225 million in state and federal cleanup costs.

One outcome of the Love Canal disaster is that it dramatically calls attention to the fact that, even today, industrial societies have little control over the amount of lethal industrial byproducts they generate. Love Canal has also shown that we have virtually no social mechanism, apart from the profit motive, to substantially reduce the amount of chemical dumping. Finally, Love Canal has shown us that the costs of cleaning up even small chemical dumps are well beyond the budgets of most local governments. Undoubtedly, a large portion of these costs will have to be shared by the federal government or directly assessed to the industries that did the dumping. Even then, the cleanup costs may equal or surpass the $90 billion spent to put men on the moon. Ultimately, we may find that some dumps cannot be cleaned up, and communities will have suffered irreparable damage. As with Love Canal, the dump areas will be paved over and surrounded by chain-link fences. Even then, underground water supplies will be highly contaminated.

Finally, there is the slow disaster. For decades scientists have warned of ocean pollution, but little general concern has been shown, in part because it is difficult to "show" people clear evidence of damage to the oceans. Even major oil spills can be cleaned up, and later studies show that the oil has little lasting impact on ocean life—at least, this is the case where oil spills occur infrequently. In areas where oil and other chemical dumping is routine, the surrounding ocean areas are dead. The degree to which the oceans can sustain this present burden is debatable. The problem with slow disasters is that when the first dramatic signs of danger appear, it may be too late to prevent disaster. Those who study the ocean's ecological system fear that by the time they convince nations that the oceans are dying, it will no longer be possible to save the oceans.

Other slow disasters include air pollution and the accompanying acid rain and global warming. In December 1997, the nations of the world met in Kyoto, Japan, to negotiate a treaty that sets mandatory limits on greenhouse gas (CO_2) emissions. The outgrowth of the conference was the Kyoto Protocol, a treaty that mandates the amount by which each country must reduce these emissions. In the case of the United States, these emissions must be reduced by more than one-third from levels occurring in the base year of 1990.

There is also concern with the degree of genetic standardization of world food supply beyond the range of human experience. Since the 1960s, nations have come to rely on fewer genetic varieties of rice, soybeans, wheat, and corn. As food crops become more standardized, the possibility arises that a few crop diseases could spread worldwide and destroy a large portion of the food supply. Since the 1980s we have recognized that the destruction of the world's rain forests holds the potential of creating a worldwide ecological collapse.

We have seen how difficult it is to get families to evacuate their communities in the face of such obvious threats as flood and fire. How, then, can we get people to take seriously those threats that now manifest only subtle and conflicting signs of danger? This is particularly troubling when there are groups that oppose preventative action in these areas. One such group is the oil industry's Frontiers of Freedom Institute, founded by former U.S. Senator Malcomb Wallop. The Frontiers of Freedom group contends that global warming is a bogus issue publicized by "hysterical, global warming doomsayers." The FFI cites studies that predict higher CO_2 levels will result in more rainfall, longer growing seasons, and increased agricultural output. They maintain that remedial actions such as those proposed in the Kyoto agreement are based on partial and faulty science and would be catastrophic to the U.S. economy and sovereignty (Wallop, 1998).

In some respects, industrial societies are well equipped to respond to and recover from disaster. They have rapid and reliable systems of communication and transportation, as well as economic surplus that can be used to tide people over while disaster recovery efforts are underway.

Industrialized nations have many organizations with a clear responsibility for disaster response and recovery. In the United States we have FEMA, the Red Cross, the Salvation Army, and the Mennonite Disaster Service. The National Weather Service monitors and reports on dangerous storms. The National Guard and U.S. Army Corps of Engineers restore essential services and clear debris. Financial assistance for disaster victims is made available through the Federal Disaster Assistance Administration and the Small Business Administration. The Farmers' Home Administration provides disaster relief loans to farmers. There are literally hundreds of NGOs worldwide, with hundreds of thousands of volunteers, that offer assistance to victims of disaster.

However, industrial societies have created new kinds of disasters with air and water pollution and the disposal of hazardous wastes. These "disasters in disguise" have been created almost exclusively by the industrial social order. Industrial societies have not adapted to this type of disaster as well as they have to natural disasters. Had Love Canal been hit by a tornado, for example, residents would have received all sorts of immediate and long-term aid from a number of sources. As it was, however, it took months of petition and protest before government agencies would acknowledge the existence of a problem. Even then, some public officials stoutly denied that the high rate of miscarriages, birth defects, cancer, lung disease, and genetic abnormalities were the results of the chemicals buried under Love Canal. It took nearly five years of agitation before the president of the United States declared Love Canal a federal disaster area, and it took an act of Congress before the government agreed to buy up the homes. It is too soon to tell whether industrial societies possess the adaptability and resources to prevent or recover from these disasters of their own making.

SUMMARY

In this chapter we have examined disasters from the standpoint of responses made by organizations, communities, and societies. From the standpoint of organizational responses to disaster, such efforts involve varying degrees of change in organizational structure. Many of these changes can be understood in terms of an organization's expected and official role in disaster response. Organizations with a clearly defined and immediate role in disaster response undergo fewer internal changes than other organizations do. Supplier-client and interpersonal contacts between organizations are of immediate importance in establishing interorganizational responses to disaster.

At the community level of analysis, social participation, social control, and mutual support functions predominate in community responses to disaster. Disaster response also produces a temporary but obvious convergence of community values, beliefs, norms, and power structure. Organizational ties within a community are strengthened through intense interaction. For a short period of time, communities enjoy greater autonomy because of weakened ties to external organizations. Finally, communities usually demonstrate remarkably rapid and complete recovery from disaster.

At the societal level, different types of societies have experienced and responded to disasters in many ways, according to their population size, economic base, and extent of coordination between organizational levels. In all likelihood, hunting and gathering societies of the past had no conception of disaster apart from the problems they faced on a daily basis. The small size, great mobility, and sparse distribution of these groups greatly alleviated the effects of most natural disaster agents, such as hurricanes, floods, droughts, earthquakes, and disease. Most members of hunting and gathering societies possessed essential survival skills. Further, these groups could make nearly all their material possessions from raw materials near at hand. Consequently, these groups quickly were able to replace much of what was lost through accident or disaster.

Historically, farming societies have been seriously disrupted by disaster. Epidemics spread quickly through very densely populated villages, towns, and cities of early farming societies. The compact and crowded construction found in early settlements presented fire hazards and was vulnerable to earthquakes. Early farming societies were established in floodplains where floods could destroy both crops and settlements. The regional coordination within early political systems was often ineffective, and as a result, disaster-struck areas received little if any assistance from central authorities. Today many small farming societies are still defenseless from the disaster agents of the past and are dependent upon disaster relief from external sources, such as the United Nations, other governments, and hundreds of NGOs that specialize in disaster aid.

Public health measures in industrial societies have greatly reduced the impact of infectious disease. Most industrial societies also possess disaster-response organizations that mobilize rapid and effective assistance and, like FEMA, attempt to limit disaster losses due to natural forces. Still, urban growth in industrial societies increasingly has pressed into floodplains, geological fault zones, and coastal areas that are regularly battered by hurricanes. Disaster-recovery costs for government and private insurers have risen dramatically in these areas. Finally, industrial societies have created new kinds of disasters with air and water pollution and the disposal of hazardous wastes. Governments, the public, and disaster-response organizations generally have been slow to recognize pollution and hazardous materials as disaster agents. It is too soon to tell whether industrial societies and existing disaster-response organizations will be able to cope as readily with large-scale technological disasters as they have with the traditional disaster agents.

ᴀ CHAPTER 12 ᴀ

INDIVIDUALS AND RIOTS

I felt a strong sense of déjà vu as I watched rioters drag a man from his truck, beat and kick him, and finally throw a cinder block at his head. This was April 29, 1992, and I was watching television coverage of a riot occurring in South Central Los Angeles. Earlier in the day, four Los Angeles Police Department officers had been acquitted of the beating of Rodney King, another brutal event that had been televised repeatedly during the trial.

It was with the same dreadful fascination that I had watched other riots on television nearly thirty years earlier. Our "long, hot summers" began in 1963 with the Bedford-Stuyvesant and Harlem riots in New York City. The next year brought the Los Angeles Watts riot of 1964, and the cry "Burn, baby, burn" entered the popular vocabulary. Chicago burned in 1965, and Omaha in 1966. There were weeks of rioting in Newark, Detroit, and Milwaukee in 1967. Immediately in the wake of Martin Luther King's assassination in April of 1968, there were more or less simultaneous riots in 125 urban areas, including Washington, DC, where massive vandalism, looting, and arson occurred within a mile of the White House (McPhail, Schweingruber, and McCarthy, 1998). Beginning in the mid-1960s, dozens of university campus demonstrations against the Vietnam war ended in disorder, mass arrest, and, in a few instances, shootings. On September 9, 1971, inmates at New York's Attica Correctional Facility took hostages and rioted. Forty-three inmates and hostages died when authorities retook the prison by force four days later.

Virtually all cities in the United States with populations of over 100,000 experienced a riot during this era. Disorders had been given extensive television coverage. It was through the experience of watching live television coverage that most Americans vicariously experienced riots. These images were stark and intense, shaped not only by riot events themselves, but also through journalistic conventions, the commentary of reporters, and editorial policies.

An atmosphere of national crisis developed during this era. U.S. presidents appointed three national commissions between 1967 and 1970 to investigate riots and demonstrations. The first of these commissions, the Kerner Commission, reported in 1968. The report recommended major changes in police and community relations. It recommended, for instance, that public officials establish new mechanisms, such as police and civilian review boards, to offer redress of grievances against police. The Commission also recommended new initiatives in police

315

training and tactics. These included comprehensive and continuing training for civil disorder prevention and control and the elimination of "abrasive" policing practices. Finally, the Commission criticized the use of deadly force and recommended the use of minimum, necessary force in controlling situations. The other Commissions also made recommendations along these lines, providing the basis for what is now known as the public order management system (POMS) (McPhail, Schweingruber, and McCarthy, 1998).

Public order management systems seem to have proven effective. Since 1971, there has been a marked decline in riots. Our campuses and prisons have also remained comparatively free of disorder. Given the high level of public disorder experienced between 1963 and 1971, the decades since then have been quite calm. Still, Miami's Liberty City area experienced a riot in 1980 that left 17 people dead (Ladner, Schwartz, Roker, and Titterud, 1981). The 1992 Los Angeles riot left 52 dead, over 2,000 injured, and $1 billion in destroyed property (Useem, 1997).

Most people agree that riots involve crowds and injury or the threat of injury to people or property. Beyond this, there is little agreement. Civil and military authorities in the United States must act on the basis of legal definitions of riots. To authorities, riots are a form of collective behavior that is by definition against the law. In the next chapter, we will briefly consider some of the legal definitions of riots used in the United States. Sociological characterizations, however, are more elaborate, divergent, and certainly less exact than legal definitions. We will discuss how the mass hysteria, emergent-norm, and value-added perspectives of collective behavior characterize riots. We will then consider riots from the standpoint of collective action.

A very large volume of riot-related research was accumulated during the late 1960s and early 1970s. Even today, sociologists often return to this data with new questions and ideas (McPhail, 1994). In order to explore this large body of research, we will examine riots from the standpoint of individual participation and, in the next chapter, from the levels of organizational, community, and societal responses to riots.

TYPES OF RIOTS

Sociologists frequently refer to four types of riots: communal riots, commodity riots, protest riots, and celebration riots. *Communal riots* are characterized by collective violence between opposing racial or religious groups; they are also commonly referred to as "race riots." The antagonists are usually civilians, and conflict starts over some contested area, such as a neighborhood, beach, or factory (Janowitz, 1968). Police may inflict casualties as they attempt to keep opposing groups apart, but most injuries and deaths result from attacks by civilians on one another. The United States experienced waves of communal rioting in 1919 and 1943 (McPhail, 1994:2). One such riot, the 1943 Detroit riot, will be described below. Prison riots of the 1980s and 1990s generally involved prisoners attacking prisoners (Maguire and Radosh, 1999).

In *commodity riots*, the object of attack is more clearly the property rather than the people of another racial or religious group. In commodity riots, violence is directed primarily at the buildings, merchandise, and equipment of another group. In the 1700s, workers who smashed the machinery being brought into factories to replace them, housewives who overturned grocery stalls during the

"bread riots," and African Americans who looted and burned white-owned businesses in the ghetto in the 1960s were involved in commodity riots. Although
commodity riots do involve isolated attacks by civilians on one another, most violence occurs between civilians who are attacking or looting property and the
authorities who are trying to stop them.

In *protest riots*, violence centers on a specific government policy. England's Gordon Riots of 1780, America's anti-draft riots during the Civil War, and some anti-
Vietnam War disorders fall within this category. Generally, the contending groups
in a protest riot are civilians and the police or military attempting to quell the disorder. The actions of citizens usually take the form of rowdy disobedience of government representatives. Occasionally, citizens attack police with clubs, rocks,
bricks, or other projectiles. Sometimes civilians attack government property that
symbolizes the issues involved. Rarely do civilians use firearms or such weapons
as Molotov cocktails. Authorities inflict nearly all casualties and injuries as they
attempt to restore order in political riots.

The April 1968 riots following the assassination of Dr. Martin Luther King are
sometimes characterized as political riots, even though they involved extensive
violence against property in the form of vandalism, looting, and arson. The dozens of campus disorders and the Weathermen group's four "Days of Rage" in
October 1969 are clearer examples of political riots. In 1969, the Weathermen, an
anti-war group, engaged in violence against Chicago police and against the properties of the state and corporations who profited from the Vietnam War (McPhail,
1994:2). Finally, inmates protested items such as inadequate food, blankets, clothing, and prison policies and rules during the Attica prison riot of 1971 (Maguire
and Radosh, 1999). Earlier prison riots were also protest riots. As previously
noted, more recent prison riots are better characterized as communal riots.

Celebration riots may be the most frequent form of rioting. Participants are fans
of a team that has won a championship or defeated a traditional rival. Their targets are accessible properties that belong to no particular group or category. The
acts of celebration include chanting, singing, gesturing, clapping, pounding
upon/rocking/overturning cars, breaking bottles or windows, setting afire trash
cans and overturned cars, and looting. Rioting is not always associated with, nor
should it always be attributed to, anger, rage, deprivation or despair.

We begin this chapter with a description of a communal riot and a protest riot.
We will then consider riots from the standpoint of each of the general theories of
collective behavior. Each presents a different view of the nature of riots and the
activities of which they are composed. We will review and discuss research that
was conducted to test the value-added theory of hostile outbursts. Finally we will
review the riot participation literature that was designed to find out who riots.

Communal Riot: Detroit, 1943

During the 1920s, Detroit was the fastest-growing metropolitan area in the
United States. In 1928 nearly 90 percent of Detroit's blacks and more than half of
the whites were newcomers. The majority of those moving to Detroit were from
the South. Leaving the traditionally white-dominated social order of the South,
whites and blacks moved into a new social order in which they competed, on
much more equal terms, for jobs and housing. The first racial conflicts occurred in
the mid-1920s when African-American families moved into all-white neighbor-

hoods. In a few instances, terrified blacks shot at the crowds that taunted them and threw bricks, rocks, and coal into their homes (Levine, 1976). In 1941 racial clashes occurred in Detroit when African Americans were used as strikebreakers at the Ford River Rouge Plant. Racial clashes occurred at Northwestern High School later that year. Early in 1942, there were racial disturbances at the Sojourner Truth housing project.

As our nation's war effort strengthened and Detroit became known as the "arsenal of democracy," many hoped that these ugly events were a thing of the past. For a time, it seemed that the war had drawn the races together. Everyone working together—that was what democracy was all about.

The racial truce was broken Sunday evening, June 20, 1943. Like the Los Angeles "zoot-suit" riots a month earlier, the Detroit riot began with fights between white sailors and nonwhite civilians (Turner and Surace, 1956). Fighting started at about 10:30 P.M. at Belle Isle Park, a public beach. Sailors from the naval armory and young African-American men were the first to land punches on one another. Large numbers of people were on Belle Isle at the time. The weather was fine, and for many it was the weekend before high school graduation. Within ten minutes, hundreds of people were involved in the fighting. From the beginning, it was white against black. Those who tried to leave Belle Isle had to pass over Belle Isle Bridge, and white youths and sailors turned the bridge into a gauntlet for escaping African Americans. Many of the first casualties to be brought to hospitals were injured on or near the bridge.

Just what happened in these early moments of the disorder is unclear. Some reports indicate that police did little to disperse crowds or break up fights, particularly when blacks were getting beaten. African Americans who ran to police for protection often received none. This display of police indifference may have contributed to the spread of the disorder. Within an hour, fighting between wandering groups of whites and blacks were occurring over a wide area beyond Belle Isle Park (Lee and Humphrey, 1968:72–79).

Both whites and blacks repeated accounts of how the fighting started. For the whites, fighting started "because Negroes had raped and killed a women on the Belle Isle Bridge. . . . because Negroes had attacked some white girls while they were swimming at Belle Isle," and . . . "because the Negroes tried to throw the whites off Belle Isle." For African Americans, fighting started "because a bunch of white guys killed a Negro woman and her baby at Belle Isle Park." . . . "because the whites threw a Negro woman and her baby off the Belle Isle Bridge," and . . . "because the whites tried to throw the Negroes off Belle Isle." These stories of where and why fighting was occurring were disseminated widely by word of mouth and by public announcements in nightclubs and at the gates of factories (Lee and Humphrey, 1968:27).

The fighting increased in intensity when the factory shifts changed. Between midnight and 2:00 A.M., African Americans going to or returning from work were attacked. In some areas, whites systematically stopped streetcars to search for black targets. Likewise, at least one streetcar loaded with white workers was stopped by a group of African Americans, who then severely beat some passengers. Groups of whites formed outside two all-night theaters and beat blacks that attempted to leave. Police watched passively for some time before they attempted to disperse the crowd or warn African Americans inside the theaters (Lee and Humphrey, 1968:28).

At about 3:00 A.M., groups of African Americans began to vandalize and loot white-owned stores in the predominantly black Paradise Valley area near Belle Isle. In retaliation, whites began to overturn and burn autos driven by blacks. Many of the occupants were beaten before they could escape.

At 4:00 A.M., the Detroit police commissioner held a meeting with the mayor, the U.S. Army commander of the Detroit area, the FBI agent in charge of the Detroit area, a captain from the state police, and the Wayne County sheriff. At this meeting, the army commander informed everyone that troops could be on patrol within an hour of their call-up. When the meeting ended at 6:30 A.M., however, it had been decided that the rioting was slowing and federal troops would not be needed.

Had the police commissioner received better information, he would have known that the rioting had not slowed. Looting and car burnings continued. Hospitals contained growing waiting lines of injured, and at 6:15 A.M., the first death was recorded: an African-American man bled to death; the source of his wounds was unknown.

By 9:00 A.M., a black delegation from the Detroit Citizens' Committee met with the mayor of Detroit and urged him to use federal troops to stop the rioting. A prominent African-American minister began to tour the Paradise Valley area with a sound truck, urging people to return home. The governor arrived in Detroit at 11:00 A.M. and called for federal troops, but he was told that troops could not be used unless he declared martial law. The governor felt that the declaration of martial law was an extreme step, and he declined the offer of federal troops. During this time, blacks continued to loot, whites continued to overturn and burn cars, and blacks and whites were attacked and beaten.

At noon, the mayor attended the Detroit Citizens' Committee meeting. The president of the United Automobile Workers' Union spoke out strongly against the rioting. Later in the day, the union would call an emergency meeting of shop stewards to "intensify the Union's educational program for building labor unity between men and women of all races." Some committee members suggested that they urge the governor to declare martial law and send in the troops. Others suggested, instead, that an African-American auxiliary be formed to assist police in stopping the riot (Lee and Humphrey, 1968:32).

About 1:30 P.M., high schools began to dismiss their students for the day. Some students converged on Woodward Avenue, the area of heaviest violence. Other students simply tried to make it home without injury. Finally, white and black youth, quite peacefully, watched the Metropolitan League baseball championship at Briggs Stadium (Lee and Humphrey, 1968:35).

At 3:00 P.M., a civilian peace patrol was established under the authority of the office of Civil Defense. The patrol was composed of about 250 volunteers, black and white. The patrol had no power of arrest and was instructed to confine itself to monitoring activities, giving assistance, and offering persuasion. Even though the rioting was still very intense and attacks frequent, more individuals were beginning to act as "counterrioters." A white minister and his son drove around, confronting groups of whites that were stalking blacks. He quoted scripture and argued with the crowd while his son escorted African Americans to their cars. Likewise, blacks helped whites get out of dangerous areas. A group of church, labor, and youth leaders met and issued a joint statement urging the use of federal troops, requesting that radio broadcasts ask people to stay off the streets, and appealing to the newspapers to avoid inflammatory stories (Lee and Humphrey, 1968:35–37).

Despite the efforts of counterrioters, violence continued, and as late afternoon approached, it accelerated. A crowd of nearly ten thousand people gathered near city hall on Woodward Avenue. Several attacks occurred as African Americans were taken off buses and streetcars that passed through the area. Anti-Jewish hate literature was being passed about. Unsubstantiated but inflammatory statements were broadcast over the radio. It was announced, for example, that state police were watching for carloads of "armed Negroes headed for Detroit from Chicago" (Lee and Humphrey, 1968:38).

At about 6:30 P.M., the governor declared a state of "modified" martial law in the counties of Wayne, Oakland, and Macomb. His order also banned the sale of alcoholic beverages and closed all amusement places at 9:00 P.M. until "further notice." A curfew was imposed from 10:00 P.M. until 6:00 A.M. for people "not going to or coming from work." Finally, the governor's order prohibited the carrying of arms "of any sort" by anyone other than police.

While the paperwork to implement the governor's declaration was being completed, rioting continued. At about 8:30 P.M., police and residents of a mission hotel exchanged gunfire for several minutes while a crowd of nearly one thousand spectators watched. As white crowds moved into the black residential section of Paradise Valley, they were met with volleys of rocks and an occasional shotgun blast. An African-American man was attacked and beaten unconscious near the federal building. The U.S. Army commander for the Detroit area witnessed the beating from his office window and sent officers to rescue the victim (Lee and Humphrey, 1968:41).

Federal troops did not move into the streets until nearly 9:00 P.M. Within an hour, however, two full battalions of military police patrolled the streets of Detroit. By 10:30 P.M., the rioting had stopped almost everywhere. It wasn't until nearly midnight that President Roosevelt signed the form authorizing the use of federal troops in Detroit! For the most part, the Detroit riot of 1943 was over.

Compared to many urban disorders, the Detroit riot of 1943 was a very short riot—violence lasted little more than twenty-four hours. The intensity of the violence, however, has seldom been witnessed: thirty-four people died (twenty-five blacks and nine whites), and more than one thousand people received injuries at the hands of others. More than eighteen hundred people were arrested and charged with offenses ranging from manslaughter to traffic violations. Absenteeism from work during the riot decreased wartime productivity by nearly half. About $2 million worth of property damage occurred: buildings were damaged, stores looted, and cars were destroyed. Finally and interestingly, in the factories of the "arsenal of democracy," whites and blacks continued to work side by side without incident as violence carried the day outside. A month later, the U.S. Attorney General attributed this to effective union discipline.

Protest Riot: Kent State University, 1970

On May 4, 1970, after three days of disorder, Ohio National Guard troops fired on students at Kent State University. The shooting lasted for about ten seconds. Thirteen of the sixty-seven rounds fired hit people: four students were killed, and nine were wounded. As the news of the killings spread across the nation, disorders intensified on other campuses.

The disorder at Kent State was part of a nationwide wave of protest that began on Thursday, April 30. That morning President Nixon announced that American and South Vietnamese troops were entering Cambodia to destroy enemy sanctuaries. The decision to invade Cambodia was one of the best-kept secrets of the war. There were none of the usual rumors, leaks, denials, or discussions that made many events of the war "old news" by the time they finally happened. For several months, Nixon had also publicly pursued a policy of "winding down" the Vietnam War. The news of the Cambodian invasion came as a tremendous shock and disappointment to people who were hoping for smaller combat losses and American troop withdrawals. Consequently, protest of the invasion came quickly. Thursday evening protest rallies were held at Princeton, Rutgers, and Oberlin College. Within days, some form of protest had occurred on almost two-thirds of the colleges and universities in the United States. Most protest was peaceful. At more than one hundred universities, however, protest turned disorderly and violent, severely hindering university functioning. Dozens of universities were either closed temporarily or dismissed early (Peterson and Bilorusky, 1971:15–69).

At Kent State, a brief, peaceful protest rally was held on the commons—a field near large dormitories and major pedestrian walkways—at noon on Friday. The ROTC building was located on the northwest edge of the commons. The presence of large gatherings of students on or near the commons was not unusual. This ecological feature of the Kent State campus was critical to what followed (Lewis, 1972:66).

It is unlikely that the Kent State administration anticipated further rallies or disorders. On Friday afternoon, the president of Kent State left for Mason City, Iowa. The first disorder started Friday evening, near the campus. At about 11:00 P.M., students barricaded a street on which several bars were located. Soon, a bonfire was started in the street, and students began to harass passing motorists. Initially, city police did not interfere. As complaints mounted, however, the city police decided to close the bars, in hope that students would return to campus. Instead, angry patrons left the bars and began to mill in the streets. Soon antiwar chants were raised, and students threw rocks and bottles at one another and at police. Some in the crowd of about twelve hundred people broke store and office windows. The police chased the crowd toward the campus and, at about 2:00 A.M., finally dispersed it with tear gas. The crowd did about $30,000 damage, and sixty arrests were made.

All day Saturday the campus was calm. Rumors circulated that Weathermen radicals, Hell's Angels, and Black Panthers were headed to Kent State to help battle police. Local merchants claimed they received threats. At about 8:00 P.M. a crowd began to gather on the commons, and within an hour more than one thousand students and others were present. Observers, including Jerry M. Lewis (1972), indicate that no violent plans were openly proposed. Still, people began to throw rocks at the ROTC building. After several windows were broken out, burning trash was thrown inside. At 9:00 P.M., the fire department arrived. Students cut the fire hoses and threw rocks at the fire crew. The fire trucks retreated, and at 9:30 P.M., campus police dispersed the crowd with tear gas. Shortly, the Ohio National Guard arrived on the commons under orders to protect property. At this point, they could do little more than watch the ROTC building burn.

Throughout the remainder of the disorder, communication between the guard and university officials was meager. Officials were frequently indecisive and offered the guard few guidelines as to what they expected from them. In turn, the

While most anti-war demonstrations in the 1960s and 1970s were peaceful, they sometimes erupted into violence. A standoff between the National Guard and student protesters at Kent State University resulted in four fatalities. © Ted Streshinsky/CORBIS.

guard seemed to take actions that seemed arbitrary and unilateral. In a sense, university officials took a hands-off policy once nearly two thousand guard troops entered the campus. The only mediators between students and the guard were the unofficial student and faculty monitors.

Once the crowd had been dispersed from the commons, there were no further confrontations on Saturday night. On Sunday morning, Governor Rhodes arrived at Kent State. After a brief tour and an inspection of the ruins of the ROTC building, he denounced the students as "the strongest, well trained, militant group ever assembled in America." The university president returned to Kent and met briefly with the governor at the airport. At 4:00 P.M., the university issued orders prohibiting all forms of demonstration, "peaceful or otherwise."

On Sunday afternoon, the guard used tear gas to scatter a crowd near the president's house. On Sunday evening, a few hundred students marched down Main Street toward the center of Kent. They were stopped at the northwest corner of the campus by a line of guard. Students sat down in the street and asked to meet with the mayor and university president. While they waited, they chanted vulgar and familiar protest chants: "One-two-three-four: we don't want your fucking war," "Hell no, we won't go," "Fuck Nixon," "Pigs off campus, pigs off campus," and "Strike, strike, strike." After an hour and a half, the guard told students they were in violation of the curfew and then used tear gas. The noise of helicopters, the flash of searchlights, and general commotion continued nearly all night.

On Monday morning, students returned to classes, and it seemed as if the university might return to normal. The university president left campus at about 11:45 A.M. to dine with four university vice-presidents. At about the same time, a crowd began to gather on the commons. No organized protest or demonstration was attempted, though some students began to taunt the guardsmen who were posted around the shell of the ROTC building. Shortly, students were told they were in violation of Sunday's order prohibiting demonstrations, and the riot act was read. Tear gas was then used to disperse the crowd.

One group of students descended a shallow hill that led to a nearby football practice field. They were followed by about seventy National Guard troops wearing gas masks. Other students remained in the general area of the commons. Students on the field began to throw rocks and chunks of dirt at the guard, who responded with tear gas canisters. In the open space of the football field, the gas was ineffective. Soon students were throwing the canisters back at the guard. Students who had gathered in a parking lot north of the field and on a veranda of a campus building west of the field watched and cheered. After tossing tear gas canisters back and forth, the guard reformed their lines, knelt, and leveled their rifles at the students. Students responded with taunts and the chant "Shoot, shoot, shoot!" The guard abruptly turned and marched off the field and back up the shallow hill. When they reached the top, near the veranda, they turned and fired.

When the shooting started, people scattered, fell to the ground, and hid behind trees, buildings, or parked cars. When the shooting stopped, few students ran from the area. Instead, people began to cluster around the fallen. Other students began to group together and move slowly toward the guard. Shouts of "Murderers! Murderers!" were raised. The troops who fired were immediately ordered from the area, and the remaining troops assumed a formation to move against the crowd. For a moment, it looked as if another clash was about to occur. Then faculty marshals moved between students and the guard. Faculty pleaded with students to leave the area and with the guard officers not to charge into the students. There was a standoff situation until ambulances started to arrive. After the dead and injured were removed, the size of the crowd diminished. Shortly, Kent State University was closed by order of its president and the Common Pleas Court of Ohio.

Levels of Analysis

Riots can be studied and analyzed in terms of individual activity as well as organizational, community, and societal responses. Each level of analysis poses different problems and questions. At the individual level of analysis, many questions revolve around the issue of riot participation. McPhail (1994:6) notes that at this level of analysis, most explanations of riot participation have been couched in terms of "individual predispositions," or attitudes, motives, and beliefs that lead people to participate in a riot.

Attitudes, motives, and beliefs have traditionally been measured by questionnaires containing attitude scales administered to arrestees or residents of riot communities. In some studies, attitudes, motives, and beliefs have been inferred from the socioeconomic characteristics of arrestees and residents without the use of attitude scales. It is assumed, for example, that unemployed persons are more likely to feel deprived and frustrated and therefore more likely to participate in riots than others. Finally, riot participation has been examined in terms of demographic attributes (and attitudes and motives inferred from them). Young men, for example, are considered to be more impulsive and daring than others are and hence more likely to participate in riots. In the case of the urban riots of the 1960s,

African Americans were considered to be more deprived and frustrated than other groups and thus more likely to participate in these riots.

The study of riots can be approached from the standpoint of organizational responses, as is Useem's (1997) study of the 1992 Los Angeles riot. How, for example, do police departments plan and mobilize for riot control? What are some of the common riot control tactics of police, and what are the outcomes of these tactics? What roles do civilian organizations play in riots? Some militant black organizations were suspected of starting urban disorders during the 1960s. Were such suspicions warranted? The role of black organizations, particularly of civil rights and church groups in efforts to limit and calm disorder, are much more apparent. We must also consider the media. How do the media report disorder? Does media coverage facilitate the spread of disorder from one community to another, as some critics claim? Does media coverage intensify violence? How does the picture of disorder presented by the media influence decisions made by the police and lawmakers? Finally, how did the experiences of the 1960s and 1970s with student and urban disorders alter organizational responses to these types of events?

Examining riots from the standpoint of communities raises other kinds of questions. Much attention has been given to the question of whether we can ascertain a community's potential for disorder. In other words, are there "riot-prone" communities? Sociologists have attempted to find out what particular blend of community socioeconomic and demographic characteristics are related to the occurrence of riots (Spilerman, 1976). There is also the "pressure cooker" characterization of communities and riots. Does the occurrence of a riot relieve social pressures in a community and thereafter decrease the probability of further riots and other forms of social protest or political violence?

Finally, there is the issue of societal responses to riots. Are there meaningful differences between societies in the manner in which they respond to riots? Some have suggested, for example, that there are major differences between police responses to riots in the United States and Great Britain. Similar differences have been suggested between the responses of "modern" and "developing" nations. What, if any, are these differences? We must also consider other, more general responses to riots. One response to the riots of the 1960s was the establishment of the National Advisory Commission on Civil Disorder. President Lyndon B. Johnson appointed this commission, composed of governors, mayors, lawyers, and even a couple of sociologists, to study the riots. The commission was charged to determine the causes of urban riots and suggest ways to prevent further riots. This produced a major shift in policing tactics, away from policies of escalated force, and the development of public forum and protest law (McPhail, Schweingruber, and McCarthy, 1998).

When confronted by riots, other countries have established similar commissions to study and recommend responses to riots. Still other societies have shown little interest in studying riots. Instead, they have established special police units to suppress rioting, have formed secret police units to infiltrate civilian organizations, or have relied on martial law to keep order. What leads one society to study riots and another to turn to violent suppression and the suspension of civil liberties?

There are a number of levels of analysis from which we can examine riots. This chapter focuses on individual participation in riot activity. In chapter 13, we will consider organizational, community, and societal responses to riots.

RIOTS AS COLLECTIVE BEHAVIOR

Each of the general theories of collective behavior presents a different image of individual participation in riots, and each presents a different explanation for participation. Many of our stereotypes regarding people's behavior during riots come from the mass hysteria perspective. We will begin by examining this perspective and riot stereotypes.

Mass Hysteria Theory

Descriptions of riots and mob action are frequently used to illustrate the mass hysteria perspective of collective behavior (LeBon, [1895] 1960; Blumer, 1957; Myers, 1948; Klapp, 1972). During riots, we supposedly witness the most extreme instances of contagious mental unity. Normally law-abiding people are stripped of their veneer of socialization; rioters are extremely suggestible; they are irrational and destructive. Even sociologists who otherwise find the mass hysteria perspective of little utility often use such terms to describe rioters and rioting behavior.

Such characterizations are indeed tempting, particularly when we are describing the actions of those with a different social and ethnic heritage or political views from our own. Rudé's study of the riots of the industrial and French revolutions does much to dispel the mass hysteria characterization of riots. These crowds did not act without provocation; their destructiveness was not indiscriminate or uncontrolled; their acts were not totally devoid of political and economic purpose (see chapter 3). Certainly, these riots are not representative of all riots, but Rudé's work does point out the futility of trying to match any extreme characterization with riots in general.

Carl Couch (1968) examined some of the common stereotypes of crowd behavior, most of which originate in the mass hysteria characterization of riots. Couch argues that if crowds are as suggestible as claimed, authorities could control riots simply by suggesting that rioters disperse and go for a cold swim. During riots, including those described at the beginning of this chapter, a number of responses occur when police order crowds to disperse. Contrary to the unruly image of riotous behavior, some people do in fact disperse or at least move away from the police. Some in the crowd may be unable to leave the area because others are blocking their way or because no escape routes are available. Some fail to hear or otherwise take note of the dispersal orders. Finally, some people in the crowd may taunt authorities or openly defy the dispersal order. Occasionally, some in the crowd may even order the police to go away and leave them alone! Conformity with the instructions of authorities and one's colleagues is more likely in socially structured environments, such as bureaucracies and primary groups. In crowds, whether it is a riot or an audience, compliance with instructions will usually be less complete. Couch (1970) suggests that this is because there are greater difficulties in monitoring the behavior of others, gaining attention and acknowledgment of others, and acting together in the crowd.

Emergent-Norm Theory

Turner and Killian discuss many processes that occur within riots. For them, a riot is not something that "just happens" because of internalized hatreds, excitement, or suggestibility. Turner and Killian (1972:154–58) discuss the manipulation of crowds in a variety of situations. Riots, or a collective attack against people or property, are developed through emergent definitions of what is appropriate behavior. Thus, the people being attacked must be vilified and shown to be deserving of whatever they get. During the Detroit riot, for example, the Ku Klux Klan distributed anti-black and anti-Jewish hate literature. Once the scope of the violence had spread far beyond that of punishing any particular individuals who may have started trouble on Belle Isle, new justifications for violence emerged. In the later stages of the riot, violence was justified as a rightful way to "show the niggers their place." At this stage, violence was being defined as a means of intimidating and controlling an entire group of people.

The emergent-norm perspective suggests that within the mob there is a degree of structure. This structure is usually not rigid, nor does it necessarily exist prior to the crowd. We will discuss emergent organization within riot crowds in greater detail in chapter 13. Here, it is sufficient to note that descriptions of the Detroit riot concluded that the groups of whites and blacks that roamed around the city searching for victims had their origins in neighborhood gangs. These gangs were mobilized and expanded to include new people during the riot. Some gangs appeared to be content with harassing or roughing up their victims, while others seemed to adopt a pattern of administering severe beatings or openly attempting to kill their victims.

As we shall see in chapter 13, the emergent-norm perspective of Turner and Killian emphasizes the definitions that groups develop and apply to one another. Within riots and other conflict situations, standards of behavior develop that serve to limit or increase the level of violence. Finally, Turner and Killian emphasize the emergent character of conflicting groups within the riot situation.

Value-Added Theory

Smelser breaks down the field of collective behavior into the craze, the panic, the hostile outburst, the norm-oriented social movement, and the value-oriented social movement. Crazes and panics are often followed by hostility, which in turn can provide the starting point for more general norm- and value-oriented social movements (Smelser, 1962:271–74).

The Hostile Outburst Smelser (1962) defines the *hostile outburst* as mobilization for action under a hostile belief. His concept of the hostile outburst encompasses most riots, but not all hostile outbursts take the form of rioting. For Smelser, hostile outbursts can take the form of widespread public outcry for the punishment of offenders, petitions to governments, demands for impeachment, the distribution of scathing pamphlets, and the threat of rioting. For instance, the aftermath of the Cocoanut Grove fire included a hostile outburst of editorials, accusations, and inquiries in an attempt to assign responsibility for the tragedy (Velfort and Lee, 1943).

For Smelser, hostile outbursts manifest all five value-added components: structural conduciveness, structural strain, generalized hostile belief, mobilization for action, and action of social control. Each component contributes to the overall nature and outcome of the hostile outburst.

Structural Conduciveness Structural conduciveness refers to the most general social boundaries within which collective behavior operates. Structural conduciveness that facilitates hostile outbursts includes (1) the structure of responsibility during conditions of strain, (2) the presence of channels for expressing grievances, and (3) the possibility of communication among the aggrieved (Smelser, 1962:227).

Prior to a hostile outburst, a structure of responsibility must exist that allows people to identify a clear target for their hostility. Hostilities may often appear to focus on an arbitrary target but seldom on an ambiguous one. In some situations, there are obvious targets for hostility, such as elected officials who have clear authority and responsibility within a particular area of social concern. President Hoover was the target of much blame and outcry at the beginning of the Great Depression. He had inherited what seemed to be a vigorous national economy, and he appeared to take a laissez-faire attitude as the Depression grew. Sometimes an accused criminal becomes the target of hostility, as in the case of a lynching. This is particularly true when the accused had a prior reputation as a dangerous person or a troublemaker. People who have firsthand familiarity with the accused's reputation are likely to be among the most immediately involved in the lynching. Finally, a structure of responsibility exists in communities having longstanding racial or ethnic cleavages. Almost anything can be readily blamed on minority groups.

Hostile outbursts are made more likely by the presence of channels for expressing hostility. Opportunities to openly express hostility arise when authorities are unable or unwilling to prevent hostile outbursts (Smelser, 1962:231–36). Retreat or hesitation by police in the early stages of disorder is likely to increase disorder (Useem, 1997). At times, the knowledge that police and other authorities are sympathetic to their aims can encourage people to express hostility. The knowledge that local police wouldn't shoot whites contributed to the incidence of lynching of blacks (Cantril, 1941).

Opportunities to express grievances and anger, short of open violence, can preclude hostile outbursts. Even token concessions to petition and protest can give the aggrieved a sense that they can achieve their ends through institutionalized channels. Token concessions can also function to divide an otherwise united opposition. The abrupt closing of channels for protest and the elimination of other means of handling dissatisfaction often precede outbreaks of collective violence (Smelser, 1962:236–40).

Finally, hostile outbursts are facilitated by communication among the aggrieved and immediate accessibility to objects of attack. The areas of cities in which urban riots occur provide nearly optimum conduciveness to hostile outbursts. Population density, coupled with an almost around-the-clock continuous street life, greatly facilitates face-to-face communication and assembling. Residential dwellings interspersed with or very near to commercial buildings present immediate opportunities for looting and destruction of commercial property.

Structural Strain The next value-added determinant is structural strain. The most frequent source of strain in the origin of hostile outbursts is deprivation, which, for Smelser (1962:245), can be "real or threatened, absolute or relative." Deprivation is most likely to be a source of structural strain when it can be easily attributed to the actions of a definite person or group, a change in organizational policy, or other definite normative changes. Historically, either the imposition of new taxes or the withdrawal of long-standing or promised privileges has often preceded collective violence. The raise in oil prices by OPEC nations in 1972, for example, triggered angry protest throughout the United States. Not all student protest in the 1960s and early 1970s was directed against the Vietnam War. Other protest, such as the free speech movement and protest against dress codes, restrictive dormitory rules, and job recruiting on campus, reflected a substantial shift in the lifestyles of young people. Conflicts of values are an enduring source of structural strain within communities having clear economic, ethnic, and political cleavages. Value conflicts between Catholics and Protestants, for example, have been a longstanding source of collective violence in Ireland. Finally, Smelser identifies the lack of information as a source of structural strain. Inadequate communication contributes to the strains that lead to scapegoating and the spread of outlandish rumors. Misinformation or the lack of information has preceded many types of collective violence, such as lynchings, violent labor disorders, and rebellions.

Generalized Hostile Belief The next value-added component of hostile outbursts is a generalized hostile belief. The conditions of structural conduciveness and structural strain are usually sufficient to create a level of "free-floating or broadly focused" aggression within society (Smelser, 1962:249). We see this type of aggression in the vague fears and intolerance that often exist between religious, racial, or ethnic groups. Protestants, for example, fear and resent the supposed political power of Catholics, while Christians resent the economic power of Jews. Whites maintain negative stereotypes about the lifestyles of African Americans.

This aggression is aggravated and thrown into sharper focus by precipitating events that confirm or justify existing hatreds and fears. The Gordon Riots of 1780, for example, were sparked by a parliamentary measure extending the rights of Catholics. For weeks, London was torn by rioting as Protestants demanded a rescinding of these rights (Rudé, 1964:57–59). Smelser (1962:249–52) also notes that sharp new deprivations, the sudden closing of an opportunity for peaceful protest, and rumors can also serve as precipitating events.

Finally, a precipitating event may include some obvious "failure" that demands an explanation and assignment of responsibility. In this sense, hostile outbursts do not necessarily include physical violence against persons or property. In December of 1998, for instance, a well-intentioned Brooklyn third-grade teacher, Ruth A. Sherman, was threatened, denounced as a racist, and subjected to antiwhite taunts and slurs in a meeting with angry parents. A few days earlier, Ms. Sherman had read the critically acclaimed children's book *Nappy Hair* to her mostly black and Hispanic third grade class. *Nappy Hair*'s African-American author, Ms. Colivia Herron, was inspired by the stories her uncle had told at family gatherings when she was a child. Written in the call-and-response style used by Ms. Herron's uncle, *Nappy Hair* was a literary celebration of the African-American heritage and sought to turn something historically negative—nappy hair—into something positive by celebrating its attributes. After the heated meeting, Sherman asked for, and received, transfer to another school out of fear for her safety. Both Herron and School Chancellor Rudy Crew supported Sherman's use of the book. Later Chancellor Crew said that it was unfortunate that a group of ill-informed residents had succeeded in driving a white teacher from her classroom for using the book.

Although the precipitating event sharpens the focus of aggression, a generalized hostile belief is necessary for a hostile outburst. The generalized hostile belief assigns blame to a specific agent, group or person. It further includes a desire to punish or remove the responsible agent. Finally, the generalized hostile belief includes a sense of omnipotence—the actual feeling on the part of the aggrieved that they have the power to accomplish their aims (Smelser, 1962:101–9). Smelser points out that this feeling of omnipotence is usually quite unjustified, although it may be fostered when authorities refrain from the use of force or act indecisively in the early stages of an incident. For Smelser, the feeling of omnipotence accounts for those situations in which unarmed civilians attack armed police. This feeling can be at considerable variance with the realities of the situation.

Mobilization for Action Given an aroused and angry group, the next value-added component in a hostile outburst is the mobilization for action, in which Smelser (1962:253–54) emphasizes the role of leadership. Leadership may simply consist of a model—the person who strikes the first blow, throws the first rock, or fires the first shot. Or the leader may be a person who deliberately urges others to hostile action. Finally, groups and organizations may assume a leadership role in the developing conflict. This includes groups such as the Weathermen, who organized war protests on American campuses.

Another factor in the mobilization for a hostile outburst is the preexisting structures that provide channels for action. Simply put, Smelser (1962:255–56) argues that causal gatherings of pedestrians or tavern customers are likely to exhibit hostility in the form of an "uncoordinated brawl." Hostile actions are more likely to be structured when they are based on preexisting organizational relationships, such as the authority and committee structure of a trade union. Factories may be surrounded, picket lines maintained, and food and entertainment provided to workers standing picket duty. The outbreak and carrying out of hostilities will usually follow a "hostility curve" (Smelser, 1962:257–61).

Smelser divides hostile outbursts into real and derived phases. In the initial or real phase, hostilities focus quite narrowly on the precipitating event and the specific conditions of social strain. Initial hostilities, however, may create conditions of structural conduciveness for the expression of additional hostilities. Hostilities then broaden in scope, taking in many issues besides the precipitating event, and other groups and people are drawn into the conflict. This is the derived phase of the hostile outburst. In this sense, the Watts riot of 1965 was but a preliminary phase in the more general wave of hostility that swept the United States in the 1960s.

Action of Social Control The final value-added component is the action of social control. The response of authorities to hostilities is a determinant not only of the intensity and duration of disorder but also of its content and character. Useem (1997), for instance, contends that the Los Angeles Police Department was unable to make coordinated and effective responses during the first six hours of the riot, and this allowed the disorder to continue and to spread. If police are indecisive in the first stages of disorder, the crowd may develop a false sense of power or feeling of omnipotence. In addition to conventional crowd control responses, authorities can plant counterrumors to dissipate generalized hostile beliefs. Legal and economic concessions can be made that reduce structural strain.

Evaluating the Value-Added Approach to Riots

Smelser (1962:385–86) describes the value-added components as creating the necessary conditions for the occurrence of collective behavior. This means that when we observe collective behavior, we should also be able to find evidence of each of the value-added components. If we observed collective behavior and could not find evidence of a generalized belief, for example, then we would know that this component is not necessary for the occurrence of collective behavior. Such evidence would lead us to reject or at least modify the value-added explanation of collective behavior.

There is disagreement among sociologists as to whether the value-added components create the necessary conditions for collective behavior. This is particularly true when we consider hostile outbursts, or riots. There are two studies, for example, that apply the value-added model to the analysis of campus riots. The first disorder, which was studied by Quarantelli and Hundley (1975), followed the arrest of a female student for jaywalking. It lasted for about six hours and included substantial property damage, civil disobedience, the harassment of police, and a protest march. Because there were no attacks, injuries, or arrests, there is some difficulty in distinguishing such hostile outbursts from what Smelser calls a "mere disturbance of the peace" (Quarantelli and Hundley, 1975:382–84).

Jerry M. Lewis (1972) studied the Kent State incident described earlier in the chapter. These two studies reached quite different conclusions regarding the adequacy of the value-added explanation of hostile outbursts.

Table 12.1 summarizes and compares the findings of these two studies. Both studies found evidence for structural conduciveness, structural strain, and action of social control. But Quarantelli and Hundley did not find evidence of a hostile belief; further, the mobilization process that occurred during the disorder did not develop in the manner described by Smelser (Quarantelli and Hundley, 1975:374–81). Lewis did find evidence of a hostile belief, and he agreed with Smelser's description of mobilization. These inconsistent findings and conclusions merit further discussion.

Quarantelli and Hundley note that while some students taunted police, there was little indication that they felt omnipotent or felt that they had the power to "remove or punish" city police. In fact, a wide diversity of beliefs was in evidence. Some students were at the scene to "be with friends," to "see what was happening," or to "make observations for a collective behavior course." A few students indicated that the protest might serve to air grievances and eventually improve relations between students and police. Finally, some students expressed concern that nothing would come out of the protest except "trouble for students." Such a diversity of views is indeed contrary to Smelser's description of a generalized belief.

TABLE 12.1
Hostile Outbursts: Tests of the Value-Added Components

Value-added component	*Study*	
	Lewis	*Quarantelli and Hundley*
Structural conduciveness	Yes	Yes
Structural strain	Yes	Yes
Generalized hostile belief	Yes*	No
Mobilization	Yes	No
Action of social control	Yes	Yes

*See Table 12.2.

Much of Lewis's support for the existence of a generalized hostile belief came from a survey conducted among Kent State students weeks after the disorder and killings (1972:64). The survey classified respondents as nonattenders, observers, and participants (see Table 12.2).

Nonattenders—those who were absent from the scene of the shootings—were more likely than others to think that the National Guard would fire on students. Those who participated seemed to be convinced that the guard wouldn't fire. There were many more observers at the scene of the shootings than participants. On the basis that bullets do not discriminate between observers and participants, these two categories could be combined into the category of attenders. When the Lewis data is examined in this fashion, as it is in Table 12.2B, the difference between attenders and nonattenders is not as great. Further, the data did not include nearly six hundred respondents who were at the scene of the shootings but were classified as "counterdemonstrators" and "others." Given this possible alternate interpretation of the data and this omission of respondents, one cannot say that thinking the guard would fire on students kept students away from the scene of the shooting. Finally, even if this relationship was more distinct than it is, it tells us little about generalized hostile beliefs. Thinking that the guard would not fire as it attempted to control unarmed students seems quite reasonable; it can hardly be described as a feeling of omnipotence.

Quarantelli and Hundley (1975:377–81) note that mobilization during the campus disorder involved more than modeling, or the deliberate agitation of students by radicals. Most mobilization seemed to occur through friendship channels, while other mobilization was simply the result of passersby stopping to talk with others in the gathering. The activities within the gathering did not correspond to what Smelser terms the *real* and *derived* phases of mobilization during disorder. During the last three and a half hours that the gathering was assembled, people did little more than stand around a bonfire. Police and university officials in and around the crowd were generally ignored.

Smelser takes a very broad view of structural strain. That is, structural strain

TABLE 12.2
Two Interpretations of Generalized Hostile Belief Data

*A. Data as Presented by Lewis (1972)**

Did you think that the National Guard would fire on students?

	Participants	Observers	Nonattenders
Yes	5	129	513
No	509	1,746	2,346
Uncertain	27	280	807

*B. Lewis Data Collapsed to Show Relationship between Attenders and Nonattenders***

Did you think that the National Guard would fire on students?

	Attenders	Nonattenders
Yes and uncertain	441	1,320
No	2,255	2,346

*This relationship is statisticaly significant (p < .001) but weak (Cramer's V = .16).

**This relationship is statistically significant (p < .001) but weak (φ = .22).

can be real or threatened; it includes both absolute and relative material deprivation; norm and value conflict can produce structural strain. Inadequate communication can produce structural strain. Conceptualized so broadly, it seems that almost any circumstance can be interpreted as causing some type of structural strain. Not surprisingly, then, both studies found evidence for structural strain prior to and during the disorders. Quarantelli and Hundley (1975:373–74) inferred structural strain from the long-standing opinion among students that police were negatively biased in their dealings with them. Lewis (1972:61–62) argued that the simple presence of National Guard on the Kent State campus represented the primary source of structural strain for students.

Likewise, the students' open defiance of the university's ban on rallies was a source of structural strain for the guard. Beyond these few inferences, none of these researchers attempted to develop or empirically test Smelser's ideas about structural strain; they did not, for example, attempt to find out whether there had been a rising level of structural strain prior to these disorders. Smelser also claims that collective behavior is in part an effort to reduce conditions of strain within the social system. But these researchers did not try to determine if strain was lower after the hostilities than it had been at the beginning. In short, the researchers simply assumed that structural strain was present during the disorder. They did not attempt to develop or test specific propositions about the role (if any) of structural strain in the playing out of these hostile outbursts.

These two studies highlight some of the major problems with the value-added approach to hostile outbursts, or riots. In particular, there is difficulty with the generalized hostile belief component. Smelser (1962:226) states that "participants in an outburst must be bent on attacking someone considered responsible for a disturbing state of affairs." What can be said, then, of counterrioters, many looters, or people whose participation is brief and perhaps largely due to their proximity to the disorder? In riots we encounter hostile beliefs and behavior, but these are intermingled with and often subordinate to other kinds of quite different attitudes and actions (Quarantelli and Hundley, 1975:384).

Smelser views mobilization primarily in terms of actions taken to excite the emotions of the aggrieved. He devotes relatively little attention to how these social relationships and activities actually bring people together and are used to carry out a course of action. Smelser defines structural strain so broadly that virtually anything can be taken as an indication of structural strain. More recently, several attempts have been made to better define and empirically study structural strain. Tilly (1975) summarizes these efforts and concludes that existing models of structural strain tell us little about the occurrence of disorder and political violence. Gamson, Fireman, and Rytina (1982:8) argue that violence is not an eruption of latent tensions and frustrations; rather, it is an outcome of a more or less continuous process of mobilization and conflictive interaction.

RIOT PARTICIPATION STUDIES

Few events of the twentieth century inspired as much sociological research as the urban disorders of the 1960s. It was assumed that a careful comparison of rioters and nonrioters would tell us what attitudes, beliefs, and tensions led people to riot. Some people thought that this research would allow us to predict when riots were likely to occur and, perhaps, provide the means for preventing riots. In general, riot research fell far short of these goals. Although riot research provides answers to some rather important questions, it does not answer the questions researchers originally set out to answer.

McPhail (1971) reviewed ten studies of major urban disorders occurring between 1965 and 1967. The riot participation studies were carried out following riots in Watts (1965), Omaha (1966), Detroit (1967), Milwaukee (1967), and Newark (1967). The first task in these studies was to determine who had actually taken part in the riot. Classifying people as participants and nonparticipants in a riot is not as simple as classifying people as male and female or as young and old.

Each study developed one or more measures of riot participation, of which the most frequently used was arrestee status. Six of the studies compared a sample of respondents arrested on riot charges with a control sample of people from the community in which the riot occurred. This type of comparison is not entirely satisfactory. Some sociologists have suggested that people who commit the most violent acts are also the most likely to evade police, while many of those arrested, such as female looters, are probably the least wary and least experienced at evading apprehension. In short, arrestees are not a representative sample of those who participated in the riot in one manner or another. Because of this problem, researchers developed other measures of riot participation that did not rely on arrestee status. These measures were based on self-reports. Respondents selected from neighborhoods in which riots occurred were asked what they did, what they saw, and whether they considered themselves to be riot participants. On the basis of these self-reports, comparisons could be made among people the researchers classified as rioters, nonrioters, and, in some instances, counterrioters.

Many sociological discussions of hostility, rebellions, and riots, such as Smelser's value-added model or Davies' J-curve of rising expectations, suggest that social deprivation leads to frustrations that are vented in acts of aggression. Variants of this idea, at least in the 1960s, were part of the "common knowledge" within the behavioral sciences. Consequently, almost all riot investigators sought to ascertain the hostile beliefs, negative attitudes, and frustrations that led to riot participation. Some of these psychological attributes were measured directly with attitude/opinion questionnaires. In other instances, individual tendencies to riot were inferred from people's socioeconomic attributes, such as income and education levels, and demographic characteristics, such as age, sex, and ethnicity. These various measures of people's predispositions to participate in riots are summarized in Table 12.3.

Altogether, these ten studies tested 287 separate relationships between some predisposition to riot and a measure of riot participation. Of the 287 relationships, 268 (93 percent) were either not statistically significant or were of weak magnitude. This means that nearly all of the predispositions to riot turned out to have little if any association with riot participation! Even the associations with the most immediate bearing on the deprivation-frustration-aggression explanation of riots showed a similar pattern of weak relationship (McPhail, 1971:1063–65).

Only seventeen relationships were of moderate strength, and most of these were between opinions that police frequently mistreat blacks and arrestee status. These relationships held for both black and white arrestees. Such findings seem to suggest that negative opinions about police lead to riot participation, but McPhail cautions that this interpretation may be incorrect. It seems likely that many of the negative opinions about police were generated when people were arrested, held in jail, and charged with crimes. In other words, negative opinions about police may have

TABLE 12.3

Riot Participation Studies: Independent Variables and Their Strength of
Association with Riot Participation Measures

	Strength of Association				
Independent Variables	*Not Significant*	*Weak*	*Moderate*	*High*	*Total*
Attitude statements	18	55	6	0	79
Social relationships and interaction	26	31	1	0	58
Socioeconomic attributes	22	34	1	0	57
Experiences and opinions of discrimination	15	30	5	0	50
Demographic attributes	5	18	4	2	29
Political participation	5	9	0	0	14
Totals	91	177	17	2	287

SOURCE: Adapted from Clark McPhail, "Civil Disorder Participation: A Critical Examination of Recent
Research," *American Sociological Review* 36:1062.

been a result rather than a cause of riot participation. This interpretation seems
likely because lower associations were obtained between negative opinions and the
self-report measures of riot participation that did not include arrestee status.

The only independent variables to show a fairly consistent and strong association with riot participation were age, sex, ethnicity, and education level. Young
black males who had not completed high school were more likely than others to
participate in riots. These relationships are open to two quite different interpretations. We might immediately assume that young people are more daring than
older people are and that blacks are more disenchanted than whites with the
political climate. We might also assume that males are more daring and aggressive than females and that greater educational attainment makes people more
rational and less likely to riot. McPhail suggests an alternate interpretation that is
not based on these stereotypes. He suggests, simply, that these people are more
available for riot participation by virtue of the large amount of uncommitted time
that results from "being young, black, male, and without educational credentials"
(1971:1069; 1994:10–11). Subsequent studies of the 1980 Miami riots yielded similar results (Ladner, et al., 1981; McPhail, 1994).

Given the meager findings of the riot participation studies, we need not conclude that they were a waste of time and money. If nothing else, these studies
strongly suggested that we must attempt to explain riot participation in terms other
than individual attributes. McPhail (1971; 1994) uses the phrase *monolithic conception of riots* to describe the way in which sociologists traditionally approach the
study of riots and riot participation. Sociologists (as well as journalists, politicians,
and anyone else with an opinion on the subject) frequently describe riots as if they
consist of a unitary type of human action such as running or swimming. To say that
someone is running or swimming conveys a specific image and meaning that we all
recognize. The monolithic conception uses the term *rioting* as if it conveyed a similar unitary meaning. We talk about people who are rioting in much the same way as

we talk about people who are running or swimming—as if rioters were carrying out a unitary activity called rioting. Orders are given to "stop the rioting," "rioters" are to be arrested, and sociologists study "riot participation." In addition, the monolithic conception of riots led researchers to seek and find those particular hostile attitudes and beliefs that were commonly held by all or most riot participants.

RIOTS AS COLLECTIVE ACTION

From the standpoint of collective action, riots are complex and differentiated phenomena (McPhail, 1971; Wohlstein, 1982; McPhail and Wohlstein, 1983). Riots are also socially constructed—that is, the starting point of a riot is often quite arbitrary. Descriptions of riots provided by the National Advisory Commission on Civil Disorders, for example, note that most of the riots were preceded by many abrasive confrontations between police and residents of riot areas in the months and weeks before the riot. The confrontations identified as the "flashpoints" or "precipitating events" of many riots appear to be very similar to these earlier incidents (Snyder, 1979; McPhail, 1994). The media have often described disorders as riots before police and other officials have designated them as such (Useem, 1997:375). In some instances, the police have had difficulty contacting mayors and governors to inform them that a situation was out of control and that additional assistance was needed. The "beginning" of a riot involves not only disorder but also an emergence of consensus among police, mayors, governors, and usually the media.

The collective action perspective acknowledges the consensual nature of identifying events as riots. Ideas about the attitudes, hostile beliefs, and other social pressures that are claimed to produce riots must be reconciled with observed actions before a given event is declared to be a riot. Such consensus is not automatic, nor does it necessarily occur given a specific amount of violent or disruptive behavior. During the 1960s, people were quite sensitized to the issue of riots. The National Advisory Commission noted that many of the events that were then being called riots would have probably been considered simple disturbances of the peace years earlier. On the other hand, many of us can recall instances, such as the celebrations after winning athletic championships, in which people were injured, looting occurred, and property damage was considerable. When these events are described as riots, city officials quickly deny the charge. These are not riots; they are enthusiastic displays of civic pride! Finally, there are instances in which strikers or protesters demonstrate their views in a rowdy or aggressive manner but do not inflict injuries or destroy property. Many of these events are considered to be riots, however, as legal interest is shown in the violent *intent* of those taking part in demonstrations.

Further, the diverse activities that constitute rioting are not continuous. During the Watts riot of 1965, the 1967 riot in Detroit, and the 1968 riot in Washington, DC, activities such as looting, arson, and rock throwing peaked during the hours of 10:00 P.M. and midnight. These activities steadily declined through the early morning hours until noon, then again gradually built up through the afternoon and early evening (McPhail and Wohlstein, 1983). Crowds are not continuously present, and such violent acts as assault occur sporadically. Looting usually occurs in the first hours of the disorder and is often quite selective: appliance and liquor stores may be hit, while pawnshops may be left alone. National Advisory Commission data indicate that most property damage and attacks against police or troops occur during evening hours. In the mid-morning hours, the streets in the riot area may be nearly deserted. Such dramatic fluctuations in the kind and amount of activity in communities during riots are not recognized within the monolithic conception of riots.

McPhail characterizes riots and rioting as very complex phenomena that are sufficiently infrequent to permit ready and easy familiarization with all that is to be explained (McPhail, 1994:7). In an effort to deal with the complexity of riot phenomena, Wohlstein (1984) and McPhail (1994) suggest aims for future riot research. New research should examine the *assembling processes* that are part of the disorder. Research should seek to determine under what circumstances and by what processes people converge on the area where rioting develops or is already underway (McPhail, 1994:7). Researchers should determine how people first hear of the disorder, what they are doing at the time, and their location. Such information can tell us the sources and sequences of assembling instructions that route people to the scene of the disorder. It can also tell us what types of activities compete with or preclude riot participation. Finally, this type of information is necessary in order to determine what role, if any, proximity plays in riot participation.

Why do people assemble? There is seldom any single purpose for all riot participants; instead people assemble for multiple and diverse purposes, including to see and hear what people are doing at the scene, and to accompany or locate a family member or friend. Some people may converge on a riot location for the purpose of protesting the precipitating incident, and/or to assault the person or property of those identified as responsible for the precipitating incident. Some people converge on riot locations to loot. Finally, in nearly all disorders some people converge on riot locations to advocate nonviolence (Knoph, 1969b).

New research should also focus on *riot area activities*. We should seek to determine the range of individual and collective, of nonviolent and violent, activities in which people engage in the riot area (McPhail, 1994). The behavior of a person during a riot may consist of a wide variety of both violent and nonviolent activities. A person may throw rocks at police at one intersection and help police aid an injured person at another. People who engage in violent, destructive, or antisocial acts do not do so continuously during their presence at a disorder. Further, many conventional and routine activities are considered to be antisocial when they occur during a riot. In many communities, for example, people routinely loiter on street corners, in front of taverns, and in parks. During riots, such gatherings are usually forbidden and may be broken up by police. The massive amounts of property damage that occur during many riots may result from relatively few violent acts on the part of relatively few people. Once a firebomb has been lobbed into a building, for example, flames spread quite rapidly without any further attendance from rioters. Many people in the riot area may do little more than walk around and look at the damage that has occurred. Finally, some people's activities may revolve around protecting their property or some types of community property, such as recreation centers, and urging other people to "go home and calm down." In short, people engage in a wide variety of activities during a "riot," none of which is inherently "rioting" behavior.

Perception Control Theory

McPhail has made extensive reviews of films and videotapes of rioting in progress in the 1965 Watts riot and 1992 South Central Los Angeles riot and has made use of his field observations of riots in the 1960s and 1970s, and on the reports of other scholars' field observations. Regarding riot area activities, McPhail (1994:12) concludes:

- Every individual in the riot area does not engage in violence.
- Those who do engage in violence—vandalism, looting, arson, or assault—do not do so continuously or exclusively.
- Despite repeated references to "mob violence" the majority of violent acts are carried out by individuals or small groups, not collectively by all or even most of the larger gathering.
- Riots are not a uniform blanket of continuous and mutually inclusive violence. Riots are patchworks or kaleidoscopes of individual and collective, nonviolent and violent, alternating and varied actions.

When violence occurs in riots and other gatherings, it usually takes the form of vandalism, looting, arson, and assault. McPhail (1994) applies perception control theory to explain individual, interpersonal and collective violence against another person—such as the violence directed against trucker Reginald Denny by four young African-American males described at the beginning of this chapter. McPhail (1994), Tilly (1978), and others distinguish between outcome violence and intended violence. *Outcome violence* occurs when individuals act, alone or together, to control for their perception of some nonviolent goal, such as locating a family member who may be at the scene of disorder. During their search, they may encounter resistance, such as a police roadblock, or a disturbance, such as members of a rival group, or an abandoned store. At this point, they attempt to avoid, overcome, oppose, or eliminate that disturbance. The outcome of these corrective efforts may be violent—assault, looting, or arson—even though the original purposes were not.

Intended violence results when people act alone or together to control for their perceptions of the reference signal of a violent goal. They act to make their perceptions match their goal of violating—through intimidation, assault, injury, or by killing—another human being. It is then that people seek to make their behavior match their reference signal, or perception of how such acts are to be carried out. During some of the first violent demonstrations against the Vietnam War, student protesters lacked clear images or reference signals for violence against property and persons. Their attempts at vandalism appeared almost comical. Students carried rocks to demonstrations in picnic baskets, and retrieved their rocks after breaking store windows because they had not brought enough rocks. Protestors developed reference signals for far more effective techniques of vandalism in the next few years. Members of the Weathermen, for instance, began to wear heavy protective clothing and helmets to demonstrations. They identified targets for vandalism in advance and worked in squads. Instead of rocks, they used chains and batons to break windows and were able to inflict massive amounts of property damage during the 1969 Chicago "Days of Rage."

McPhail (1994:23) notes that the work of Eric Dunning, Patrick Murphy and John Williams (1986; 1988) provides a persuasive explanation for the violence of England's football hooligans. Their research suggests that many hooligans have grown up in working-class families in which they witness physical violence, and in which they are often the recipients of physical violence. More importantly, they are often coached in violence by parents, by older siblings and peers to become skilled at using violence and to enjoy the successful practice of violence. Soccer-related violence even has its special name: *aggro*. Hooligans act to make their perceptions match their goal of aggro. Targets of aggro are typically their counterpart supporters of rival teams, and the rules are "we" versus "them," not unlike the stereotypical categorization of members of one racial, language, or religious community by members of another (McPhail, 1994:23).

McPhail (1971; 1994) suggests that we no longer view riots as the outcome of individual motives and beliefs or the socioeconomic attributes of the communities in which riots occur. Instead, he suggests that we first examine assembling and the activities that occur at riot locations. To date, we know comparatively little about these features of riots, and McPhail (1994:7) suggests that we "ransack the limited descriptive data that are available on riots and rioting." This includes locating and carefully examining film and videotapes of rioting in progress made during nearly every major urban disorder during the 1960s and those since then. If possible we should try to create detailed, hour-by-hour accounts of what people actually do during the time frame of the riot. We already know that people defy and attack police, destroy property, and loot during riots. We still know little about the immediate circumstances that bring people to carry out such activities. We know even less about people's activities when they are not confronting police, destroying property, or looting.

Finally, Wohlstein (1982) and McPhail (1994) both point out that we need to know how people become involved in competing activities that may take them from the scene of the disorder. That is, we need to examine *dispersal processes* to ascertain when and how people leave, and possibly return to, the riot area. Dispersal processes include people leaving the riot area because of pending work or family activities at other locations. People may also leave the riot area because of the actions of the police. In the next chapter, greater attention will be given to dispersal process when we examine riot control tactics used by police, the National Guard, and the U.S. military.

SUMMARY

In this chapter we have focused on theories of collective behavior and collective action that pertain to individual participation in riots. In general, theories of collective behavior characterize riots as unitary phenomena, and that "rioting" is an activity like walking, running, or swimming. Theories of collective behavior also explain riot participation as the result of the frustrations, hostile beliefs, anti-social attitudes, and inferior socioeconomic attributes of participants. These were the prevailing views of riots and riot participation that guided riot research in the late 1960s. A review of this research shows that measures of frustration, hostile beliefs, anti-social attitudes, and most socioeconomic characteristics were unrelated, or only weakly related, to measures of riot participation.

The collective action perspective sets forth a differentiated view of riots. That is, riots are composed of a wide variety of purposive activities, some of which are anti-social and some of which are pro-social. Few activities at the scene of a disorder are ever displayed by all of those present, nor are any of these activities continuous. Unfortunately, previous research has told us very little about the assembling processes that precede riots, the wide variety of activities that occur at riot locations, and the competing activities that take people from the scene of the disorder. Some insight may be gained in these matters by developing methodologies for examining existing film and videotapes of rioting in progress.

★ CHAPTER 13 ★

ORGANIZATIONAL, COMMUNITY, AND SOCIETAL RESPONSES TO RIOTS

During August 1965, the Watts area of Los Angeles was torn by nearly a week and a half of rioting that began on Wednesday evening, August 11. Most of the violence and destruction occurred during the next five days, but the police curfew was not lifted until August 22. By then, thirty-four people were dead and hundreds were injured. Nearly four thousand people had been arrested in connection with the rioting. Hundreds of businesses in Watts had been burned or looted. It had taken a massive police response to end the rioting. The Los Angeles Police Department, hundreds of state police, and more than thirteen thousand California National Guard had been used in Watts.

Watts is often thought of as the prototype of the hundreds of urban riots that occurred in cities across the United States during 1965–1972. These riots can be classified as *commodity riots* (McPhail, 1994). Relatively little violence occurred between African-American and white civilians. Instead, African Americans attacked and looted white-owned property in their neighborhoods. Most of the violent conflict occurred between black civilians and police, National Guard, and, occasionally, federal troops.

In this chapter we will examine how social control organizations respond to riots. The disorderly and violent acts that later become identified as the start of a riot may be very similar to many other events that routinely occur within a community. As the number of violent acts escalates and the number of people involved increases, police and other public officials come to the consensus that things have gotten out of control or that a riot is occurring. We will examine the legal definitions used by authorities to distinguish rioting from other kinds of activity. We will then briefly consider the kinds of changes that occur within police departments as these organizations take action to stop the rioting. We will also consider the kind of organization that emerges among community members. Some of this emergent organization is *antisocial*, as people work together to thwart police and carry out looting. Other emergent organization is *prosocial*, as groups go into their community to urge calm, care for the injured, locate the missing, and monitor police-civilian contacts. We will also consider the kinds of crowd-control tactics that are used by police and National Guard during riots.

What kinds of communities are likely to have riots? During the 1960s, it seemed that rioting was epidemic and that no ethnically mixed community would escape such violence. Sociologists have examined the city-to-city spread of disorders to see if certain community characteristics contributed to the outbreak of violence. We will examine the research that was designed to measure the "riot proneness" of communities.

What kinds of changes occur within communities during and following riots? Interestingly, there are some striking similarities between community responses to riots and community responses to disaster. There are some important differences as well. In this chapter we will look at community responses to riots within the framework developed by Wenger (1978) for the analysis of community responses to disaster.

Are there important societal or cultural differences in the ways nations respond to riots? In some nations, rioting is routinely quelled by the use of lethal fire, while other nations use lethal force only as a last resort. Some governments respond to widespread rioting by suspending all civil liberties and instituting martial law, while other governments try to muddle through, leaving civil liberties intact. Some governments, such as those of Great Britain and the United States, have spent considerable amounts of money to study the problem. We will examine some of the sociological explanations of these differences in societal response.

First, we will consider the Watts riot of 1965. As noted above, it was the first large-scale riot of the 1960s and is seen by many as the prototype of what was to follow. Every summer during the next seven years found areas of major cities in flames. The Watts riot was typical in another way. Police, plagued with communication problems, had great difficulty in mounting effective riot control in the first hours of the disorder. Public officials who were needed to make important decisions were unavailable at critical times. Finally, police and National Guard decided to use high-powered weapons in Watts, which greatly added to the death toll.

THE WATTS RIOT: AUGUST 11–22, 1965

Descriptions of the Watts riot generally agree that the event that triggered the first violence was the traffic arrest early Wednesday evening, August 11, of a young African-American man, Marquette Frye (Cohen and Murphy, 1966; Conot, 1967). From the moment a California Highway Patrol motorcycle officer pulled Frye over, only a block from his home, the arrest had gone wrong. To begin with, the arrest attracted an unusually large number of spectators. It had been a very hot afternoon, and people were enjoying the coolness of the evening on the sidewalks, streets, and front porches of Watts.

At first, the spectators were quite passive. When Frye began to verbally resist arrest, police shoved him; then Frye's brother and mother loudly intervened. By now, other officers had arrived at the scene of the arrest, and their vehicles added to the congestion. Nightsticks were used on the Frye brothers, and their mother was manhandled into a police car. Spectators began to jeer the police. When police attempted to leave, they were spat upon. An officer waded into the spectators to apprehend the spitter. He struggled with a young woman wearing a beautician's smock that unfortunately looked like a maternity dress. The sight of a police officer manhandling a pregnant woman infuriated the crowd. Police called for additional assistance, and soon there was a large tangle of police vehicles and angry civilians. Finally, forty-five minutes after Frye had been pulled over, the police attempted to leave the area. Retreating police vehicles were sent on their way with a barrage of rocks, bottles, and obscenities. Shortly thereafter, the crowd broke into several smaller groups and dispersed.

By 9:00 P.M., large but casual crowds had gathered at nearby intersections with Imperial Highway. People stood in groups on the sidewalks; others loitered in front of stores and filling stations. Children darted about and threw rocks at one another. Soon, police began to patrol these crowds, and by 10:00 P.M., nearly one hundred officers were on hand. Obscenities and insults were directed at police as they stood about near the crowds. Shortly, people started to throw rocks at police and passing cars. Police then attacked with nightsticks in an effort to clear the crowds from the south side of the highway. Again and again, police charged, people scattered, and crowds reformed some distance from the police and resumed their taunts and rock throwing.

Soon, the violence escalated. At the intersection of Avalon Boulevard and Imperial Highway, crowds began to smash windows of cars. A station wagon used by a television crew was overturned and set on fire. Residents of Watts who were trying to restore calm suggested that traffic be stopped. Police refused, claiming that they lacked authority to close the highway. Shortly after midnight, traffic increased as factory shifts ended. Crowds began to surround cars and pound on them after breaking their windows. Some white motorists jumped from their cars and fled toward police. A few of the whites were beaten, but African Americans helped others out of the area. The abandoned cars were overturned and set on fire.

During this first evening of violence, at least two dozen African-American and white civilians were injured, seventeen police received hospital treatment, and twenty-nine people were arrested. By 2:30 A.M. Thursday, police had dispersed the crowds and assumed that the disturbance was over.

On Thursday morning, welfare workers called clients and urged them to keep their children off the streets. It turned out to be another hot day, however, and by noon crowds had begun to gather in Watts. Thursday evening started out much like the night before, with rock throwing and attacks on vehicles. Police attempted to disperse crowds while refusing to halt traffic along Imperial Highway. Crowds attacked both police and firefighters. Looting began, and on Thursday evening one store was set on fire. After a night during which scores were injured and arrested, police again assumed that it was all over. The worst had yet to come.

Friday was even hotter than the days before. Looting began early in the morning and at about 1:30 P.M., the first firebombing occurred. Soon, because of the firebombs and brisk winds, entire blocks of Watts were burning. The primary targets of firebombs were white-owned businesses; residences and African-American-owned businesses were usually spared. Fire department crews were unable to check the flames, in part because crowds often attacked them. Looting continued as buildings burned.

Late in the afternoon, police began to fire over the heads of crowds. The shooting soon became lethal. The first person to die was an African-American man standing in front of a barber shop. He was killed by a stray bullet fired a block away. The next person to die was a police officer, killed by the accidental discharge of another officer's shotgun. By 9:00 A.M. on Saturday, eighteen people had died in Watts.

The California National Guard was officially called up Friday afternoon, but the first thousand-man contingent did not move onto the streets of Watts until 11:00 P.M. This was not nearly a large enough contingent to contain the rioting. The guard could do little more than scatter looters and set up roadblocks. The darkness and lack of familiarity with Watts further hindered their efforts. As dawn approached, however, the rioting quieted.

All day Saturday, the National Guard continued to arrive, until maximum strength was reached Saturday evening. Firebombing and skirmishes continued throughout the early afternoon and into the night. The National Guard fired on looters and autos at roadblocks. By late Saturday night, another twelve people had been killed.

Sunday was quiet. Some looting continued as people sifted through the burned-out shells of buildings. In the stores that had received little damage, proprietors and their help remained to discourage looters. Sunday evening was also quiet.

On Monday arrests continued, and a young looter was killed, but for the most part Watts remained quiet and few crowds gathered anywhere. Tuesday, August 17, was quiet as well. That evening at 10:00 P.M., the first National Guard units were withdrawn from Watts, and on Sunday evening, August 22, the last guard left Watts. Monday, eleven days after the arrest of Marquette Frye, the evening curfew was lifted. The Watts riot was officially over.

LEGAL DEFINITIONS OF RIOTS

Mobs, mob action, unlawful assembly, and *routs* are terms that in federal, state, and municipal criminal law have the same or nearly the same meaning as *riot* (Williams, 1962). In general, all these terms refer to gatherings of three or more people who share a clear intent to do violence, to terrorize, and to otherwise disturb the peace to achieve their ends. The ends may be unlawful, as is the case with looting, destroying property, or interfering with the working of city government. In some instances, the ends may be lawful, as is the case with a political rally. If, however, the rally is staged in a "violent and tumultuous" manner, it can legally constitute a riot.

In some instances, riot and mob action statutes include reference to the unlawful and violent "exercise of correctional or regulative power" by assemblages of people. The actions of vigilante groups and lynch mobs fall within this category.

Some statutes attempt to define riot participation. In general, riot participants are those who remain at the scene of a disorder following an official "reading of the riot act," or orders to disperse. Under some statutes, remaining at the scene of a riot does not make a person a rioter. Some word or gesture, even if the language is not violent, that indicates a willingness to assist the rioters must be manifested before the person can be declared a rioter. Under a few statutes, people who remain at the scene and act to suppress or calm the rioting are considered to be nonrioters.

Compared to other areas of American criminal law, riot and unlawful assembly statutes are quite vague and subject to wide interpretations. A few clarifications, however, are worth noting. In some towns having ordinances against Sunday movies, theater owners and patrons have been prosecuted under unlawful assembly statutes, but these cases were dismissed because the patrons did not display "violence, terror, or tumult." Likewise, peaceful marches usually do not constitute unlawful assembly. Finally, some cities have attempted to prosecute groups of streetcorner loiterers as unlawful assemblies. Such antiloitering laws were passed as a measure against violent street gangs. These cases were also dismissed due to a lack of "violence, terror, and tumult," even though loiterers occasionally hindered other pedestrian traffic (Cohen, 1998).

Some of the riot participation studies discussed in chapter 12 equated riot participation with being arrested and charged as a rioter. Although these people may be considered rioters in this sense, they may not be rioters in a sociological sense. When police use mass arrests in dealing with disorder, many of those arrested have engaged in no violent acts or, at least initially, have had no negative attitudes toward police and other authorities. Some of those arrested were simply in the wrong place at the wrong time.

ORGANIZATIONS AND RIOTS

Once police and other public officials have reached a consensus that "things have gotten out of control" or that a "riot" is occurring, several kinds of organizational changes occur, many of which are similar to changes that occur during disasters. Some sociologists have even suggested that riots are a type of disaster (Form, 1958; Tierney, 1994). This approach has some merit when one considers the similarity of organizational responses to both riots and disasters.

Social Control Organizations

Although crowd control is a routine task for police, the control of violent or openly hostile crowds is not. Hence police departments take on many features of expanding organizations under these conditions (see chapter 11). Like expanding organizations during disasters, police departments undergo organizational changes as they extend shifts and, in some cases, activate auxiliary police units. As is the case during disasters, police departments may also strengthen their ties to other police departments in nearby areas. This strengthening of ties occurs as other police departments initiate contacts to find out what is happening in the riot area or as police departments anticipate the exchange of personnel or equipment. Local departments may initiate contact with state police in the early stages of the riot, informing them of the status of the situation. State police may then take officers off routine patrols and assign them to the riot area as observers or advisers. If state police are fully activated for riot duty, substantial organizational changes occur in local and state organizations as these two agencies coordinate their efforts. The riot-related changes that occur within police departments are probably not as makeshift as those that occur in other expanding organizations during disaster, because police departments usually have clearly specified contingency plans for riot control.

These organizational changes are important to an understanding of how and when a given type of disorder becomes defined as a riot. In the Watts riot, for example, coordinated and extensive organizational responses were delayed for several hours, while arson and looting continued. A major reason for this delay was the difficulty encountered in reaching the governor's office for the purpose of activating the California National Guard. The police and mayor of Los Angeles decided that the rioting could no longer be controlled during the second day of the disorder, but Governor Edmund G. Brown, Sr., was on a European trip and did not return to Los Angeles until the fifth day of the riot. Officials contacted Lieutenant Governor Glen Anderson, who insisted on personally visiting the riot area before calling up the guard. It wasn't until 5:00 P.M. on Friday, August 13, the third day of the disorder, that the guard was officially called out. Prior to the official call-up, however, the guard had been assembling in various armories. Still, they did not arrive in Watts until after 10:00 P.M. Initially, about 1,200 troops were used. But in the darkness and on unfamiliar streets, the guard could do little more than chase looters away from stores. More troops were brought in, until nearly 60 percent (or 13,500 troops) of the California National Guard patrolled the riot zone (California Governor's Commission Report on the Los Angeles Riots, 1965).

Delay in appropriate police response was also noted by the National Advisory Commission as a contributing factor in the growth of many other riots during the 1960s. Delays were attributed to many causes. One frequently mentioned cause was the inability of police officers to recognize "precipitating incidents." As we noted earlier, most precipitating incidents are discovered after the fact—in the weeks and months following the disorder—as police, city officials, media, citizen groups, and sometimes sociologists try to figure out what "really" happened. This "Monday-morning quarterbacking" is perhaps thought provoking, but it is of little utility to the police units in the field. Most precipitating events had little to set them apart from other routine events in the community. Here it is suggested that the delay of appropriate police response in the case of riots is a feature of organizations and the relationships between them rather than the result of "poor judgment" or "lack of sensitivity" on the part of individual police officers.

The response of organizations other than police and National Guard also warrants some note. Fire departments were overwhelmed with calls during many of these disorders, and crowds at the scene of the fire often attacked crews who answered alarms. In some instances, fire departments refused to answer calls in the riot area unless the police or the guard escorted them in. At times, police gave priority to protecting fire crews over making arrests or breaking up looting crowds. During some of the major disorders, hospitals near the riot zone were overwhelmed with injuries, and ambulance service was difficult and at times impossible. As in disasters, many of the injured arrived in private vehicles or on foot. The riot-related overload produced organizational changes within hospitals quite similar to the ones that accompany natural disasters. Finally, the breakdown of normal transportation facilities often accompanies both disaster and disorder. Bus and taxi service within the riot area was usually discontinued in the first hours of the disorder, often at the order of police. Sometimes, however, bus and taxi companies made this decision on their own, after vehicles were damaged or drivers refused to enter the riot area. Bus and taxi service was often not restored until weeks after the riot, and their absence may have actually prolonged the disorders, because many residents of the riot area could not get to work (Lee and Humphrey, 1968; Bullock, 1969).

Emergent Organizations

Looting crowds have been characterized as "individualistic" (Turner and Killian, 1972). That is, in the looting crowd there is little cooperation among members, and there is a sense of urgent individual competition as people try to grab the most valuable items and escape with as much as they can carry. Contrary to this characterization, however, there appears to have been a considerable amount of emergent organization among looters during the urban disorders of the 1960s. Some people, for example, told others where various types of goods were available for the taking. Looters often exchanged goods, trading beer and wine for shoes or small appliances for clothing, and some looted items appear to have been stockpiled for later redistribution (Cohen and Murphy, 1966).

In some of the riots, police and fire department personnel were fired on by civilians, which led some to portray sniping as a "new pattern of violence" that characterized the riots of the 1960s (Janowitz, 1968; Masotti and Corsi, 1969). McPhail and Wohlstein (1983) note that other research ran counter to this characterization. For example, Knoph (1969a) found that in only two of the twenty-five reported incidents of sniping during July and August of 1968 were police killed. In nearly half the reported incidents, police later denied that sniping had occurred, and in other incidents snipers missed police or only inflicted minor injuries. In these incidents, civilians used low-powered weapons, and the shootings appear to have been individual impulsive acts rather than well-thought-out plans to pin down or kill police. The National Advisory Commission on Civil Disorder (1968) also concluded that most of the incidents thought to be "sniping" were actually city and state police forces shooting at each other.

Emergent organization among looters and the fear of snipers led the National Advisory Commission to investigate charges that large-scale riots were carefully planned uprisings or conspiracies. The commission (1968:89) concluded that "the urban disorders . . . were not caused by, nor were they the consequence of, any organized plan or 'conspiracy.'" This conclusion does not mean, however, that there was an absence of emergent organization within communities during the riots.

Riots, like disasters, confront people with many problems. Some people probably discuss what they would do if a riot starts in much the same way that they discuss what they would do if disaster strikes. Emergent organizations frequently solve anticipated and unanticipated problems very effectively. Although previous planning is only one component of their actual response to these problems, the effectiveness of emergent organization gives the appearance of careful prior planning. We are most tempted to assume prior planning when an emergent organization temporarily foils the objectives of formally organized groups, such as the police, or accomplishes ends that are usually viewed as antisocial.

Ironically, the most obvious emergent organization among people in riot areas was directed toward prosocial ends. There may be fundamental similarities between the crowds that roam the streets during riots and the groups that carry out rescue and recovery activities during disaster. Both types of groups appear to form through the use of pre-existing family and friendship ties and residential patterns. During the riots, emergent organization was evident among those who transported the injured to hospitals and among those who worked to locate the missing at hospitals, jails, and morgues.

The National Advisory Commission found that positive civilian social control efforts developed in eighteen of the twenty-four disorders they examined. In these and other disorders, counterriot groups were usually composed of ministers and church members, city employees, and members of youth gangs (cf. Knoph, 1969b). The efforts of these groups were similar to those of the Watts Non-Violent Action Committee, which worked to calm the violence in the later stages of the riot (Cohen and Murphy, 1966:130). The committee also distributed leaflets during the disorder, urging residents to report to them any instance of police brutality (Cohen and Murphy, 1966:112–13). In several disorders, emergent groups took up weapons to protect fire department crews and ward off looters. Finally, people established rumor control centers that functioned to provide accurate information during the disorders (Knoph, 1975).

ESCALATED FORCE AND CROWD CONTROL

Several "how-to" books have set forth principles and tactics of crowd and riot control. In a manual prepared in 1947, Joseph P. Lohman presented six general principles of crowd control. These principles raise issues and advocate methods that are clearly reflected in later crowd-control manuals used by police and military personnel. Each of the three national commissions that were appointed to investigate civil disorders called escalated force tactics into question. Each report strongly suggested that escalated force tactics result in the excessive use of force by police which can, in turn, magnify turmoil and incite further violence.

Assumptions

Escalated force principles of crowd control are based on at least three assumptions. First, it is assumed that police have a sufficient number of officers at hand to carry out crowd-control tactics. Second, it is assumed that the officers present can act as a coordinated unit. These first two assumptions are problematic. In the early stages of many riots, a major problem confronting police is getting sufficient numbers of officers to the scene of disorder. It may take large police departments several hours to become fully activated for riot duty. The first officers to arrive at the scene of a developing disorder may have little advance information as to the nature of the situation. As was the case in the Watts riot, officers may arrive in an uncoordinated fashion, from many directions, thereby adding to the congestion and confusion at the scene.

The third assumption on which common crowd-control principles are based is that police are able to foretell the future. That is, some crowd-control principles instruct police on ways to respond to milling crowds and precipitating events. Milling crowds may be breaking no laws, and they do not necessarily constitute an overt threat to life or property. Quite simply, a milling crowd may not be a matter of police concern. We have noted above that a precipitating event may initially appear no different from other routine events in a community. It would indeed be helpful if police could tell beforehand which types of crowds and events would eventually turn into riots. Almost always, however, such insight is gained after the fact.

Principle One Lohman's first principle of crowd control embodies all three of the above assumptions. The first principle is the *removal or isolation of the individuals involved in the precipitating incident before the crowd has begun to achieve substantial unity*. The removal of individuals from crowds increases in difficulty with the size of the gathering and the number of people to be removed. Those involved in the precipitating event are most likely to be at the focal point of the crowd—in the center. At times, these people will resist removal or at least chant, sing, or be verbally abusive as they are being removed. In turn, these activities are very likely to increase the focus of the crowd. The verbal gestures of those being removed provide cues to others in the gathering, and chants, jeers, and obscenities may be shouted by a majority of the onlookers. The removal of persons from the crowd may in fact produce the "substantial unity" Lohman describes.

In practice, Lohman's first principle of crowd control suggests that police should use care in the location and circumstances in which they detain citizens in public places. If the option exists, police should carry out these contacts away from pedestrian flow or gatherings that could become focused on them. If arrests are necessary, they should be carried out quickly and with minimal displays of force. Police should operate on the assumption that once a crowd begins to gather, it will continue to increase in size, at least until the arrest is completed and police have left the area. They should try to develop a sense of how fast the crowd is growing and use this awareness when they make decisions in the field. The use of computers to check drivers' licenses, vehicle registrations, and outstanding warrants has shortened the time needed to make a routine traffic arrest. Priority codes, to be used when rapid assembling is occurring, could further shorten this response time.

Police may be able to anticipate the kind of response arrestees will make in the event they are removed from the gathering. If highly visible and vocal responses are likely, this will probably produce greater focus within the gathering. At this point, alternatives to arrest and removal should be considered. A verbal warning or a ticket to appear in court may be a prudent substitute for a street arrest. In any event, police should be aware that their calls for additional assistance are likely to produce additional assembling by civilians. A few extra officers may be of little help in controlling a gathering of greatly increased size.

Principle Two Lohman's second principle of crowd control is the *interruption of communication during the milling process by dividing the crowd into smaller units.* This principle can be carried out only with a sufficient number of police officers at the scene. Further, unless these officers can act as a coordinated team, attempts to divide the crowd will probably result in further disorder. James Hundley (1968) noted that police in riot situations usually failed to divide the crowd; instead, they usually attacked along a frontal line in an attempt to push the entire crowd out of a contested area. In an open area such as a park or a university mall, breaking a gathering into smaller groups may be difficult if not impossible. In an open area, the crowd simply parts in front of the police units, envelops them, and regroups behind them. This situation existed immediately prior to the National Guard's shooting of students at Kent State (Lewis, 1972). Lohman's second tactic is more workable in an enclosed area with several narrow exits, such as a street. Police units can approach the gathering from opposite ends of the street. As the police units draw together, people can disperse through divergent side streets, alleys, and across yards. Dispersed in this fashion, people are less likely to immediately regroup and confront police (Momboisse, 1967:428–35).

Principle Three Lohman's third principle of crowd control is the *removal of the crowd leaders, if it can be done without the use of force.* Before crowd leaders can be removed, they must be identified. In some instances, this can be quite a simple matter. Leaders may be well-known personalities, as when Dr. Martin Luther King led protest marches, or they may carry bullhorns and wear armbands, special hats, or clothing that sets them apart from the rest of the crowd.

Often, however, the identification of crowd leaders is not so simple. In crowds that confront police during riots, leadership is often emergent and transitory, provided by people who give instructions that others near them follow (Turner and Killian, 1972:80–95). Such leaders are often people with the loudest voices or people who are at some prominent location in the crowd where they can be seen and heard by many others. Their influence on the activity of the people near them is often incomplete and of momentary duration. During the Watts riot, for example, the movement of crowds from one location to another was preceded by shouts of street addresses or store names.

Identifying leaders (or shouters) in this type of situation is quite difficult, and arresting and removing an individual considered to be a leader is not likely to halt such activity. Momboisse (1967) suggests that when it is not advisable to remove emergent leaders, police can sometimes limit their influence. In some situations, for instance, prepared scripts or music played over loudspeakers can jam the internal communication upon which emergent leadership is based. Also, if police know some of the people within the crowd, they can call upon them to help control it. If members of the gathering are unknown, individuals can be appointed or called upon to assist police. Occasionally, police can circulate through the gathering, saying things to individuals that counter the suggestions being made by other crowd members. Momboisse refers to this type of activity as rumor control. Also, police can provide instructions for immediate activity that can counter the instructions of emergent leadership. During one of the last great "panty raids" at the University of Iowa in 1967 (see chapter 7), state police circulated through the crowds who roamed the streets near the women's dorms. They urged young men to "have fun" but "stay off fire escapes" and "don't damage property."

The removal of a boisterous and prominent member of a gathering often produces a temporary focus within the gathering and creates further crowd-control difficulties. Momboisse refers to particularly conspicuous emergent leaders as "agitators." If these agitators cannot be removed from the gathering, police can, without being verbally abusive, say things to deflate them in the eyes of the crowd. Pointing out an obviously inaccurate statement made by agitators, or questioning their motives, can accomplish this objective.

Principle Four Lohman's fourth principle of crowd control is *distracting the attention of the crowd from its focal point by creating diversions at other points*. This tactic is particularly effective if the gathering loses membership as it moves from one location to another.

This principle can be illustrated by an event that occurred during Hiroshima Days, a week of antinuclear protest in New York City, in August 1970. Several hundred protesters marched to a bandshell in Central Park for a rally. The rally did not start promptly, however, because two competing antinuclear groups began a strident debate onstage to determine which group should be first on the program. As the debate wore on, a few who had marched to the park left the rally. This movement accelerated when a Trinidad steel band began to play within earshot of the bandshell. Thirty minutes later, many more than half of those who had first gathered at the rally were assembled around the steel band. The steel band ended their set with a very upbeat number; then the musicians abruptly grabbed their instruments, dashed to an old station wagon, and sped out of the park.

Many in the audience were surprised by the band's rapid departure. As this gathering broke into small conversation groups, dispersal began. Only a small portion of the audience returned to the rally. Whether the presence of the band was a coincidence or simply clever crowd control by the New York Police Department is not known. In either case, it illustrates Lohman's fourth principle of crowd control.

Principle Five Lohman's fifth principle of crowd control is *preventing the spread and reinforcement of the crowd by isolating it*. To begin with, police can advise people to stay away from the riot area through public announcements and news coverage. When police attempt to physically isolate a crowd, much depends on where the crowd is located. A university administration building occupied by a few dozen students protesting dormitory rules can be isolated rather easily. Likewise, small mining towns can be isolated by police during labor disorders.

On the other hand, the Los Angeles Police Department and nearly 13,500 California National Guard were not able to totally isolate Watts. The street pattern of Los Angeles is based on the grid pattern typical of most American cities. The Watts area probably has more than thirty thousand possible entry and exit points, such as major highways, streets, alleys, and yards (California Governor's Commission Report, 1965). Likewise, movement in and out of the Detroit riot area, although difficult, was not impossible (Stone, 1969).

Much of Momboisse's discussion of riot control details effective tactics for isolating riot zones in the urban area. He views containment as a defensive tactic, however, and cautions that containment must not become the sole objective of riot control (1967:401–2). Efforts to encircle a large area can greatly disperse police forces and leave them vulnerable to attack. Often, encirclement will fail because of the great mobility of rioters. Even when near total isolation can be achieved, it can have a negative effect. People in the riot area may be reluctant to leave if they think that police are guarding all routes in and out of the riot area. Ultimately, the successful isolation of large urban areas depends on the cooperation of the majority of the citizenry.

Principle Six Finally, Lohman suggests the *show of force* as a principle of crowd control. Large numbers of police, who display weapons with a clear readiness to use them when disorder is imminent, can intimidate potential rioters. The show of force can make the actual use of force unnecessary.

Momboisse (1967:326) points out that the show of force is likely to succeed when the number of potential rioters is small and police have greater numbers. It is most effective when dealing with people who have had little previous contact with police or experience with disorder. In general, however, Momboisse cautions against the use of the show of force. The show of force is usually carried out by police making a grand entry into the scene of the disturbance. The movement of large numbers of police, accompanied by sirens, flashing lights, and police vehicles, can provide a focal point for and initiate assembling processes. Quite simply, the show of force can increase the size of gatherings as it is carried out.

Further, the show of force can infuriate rather than intimidate. Those in an angry and unruly crowd can easily interpret the show of force as police overreaction and brutality. The show of force by police can provide cues for a show of force by those in the gathering. There are many instances in which the arrival of police reinforcements apparently triggered, or renewed, violence. In Boston, on September 8, 1975, loud and unruly crowds had gathered at public schools during the first week of a newly instituted racial busing plan. The "grand entry" of eighty National Guard troops produced further assembling at one school. Shortly, the cursing crowd started to throw rocks at the guard and began to damage buses. Dozens of arrests followed. It is difficult to determine the amount and type of force that must be displayed in order to intimidate people and not infuriate them. History gives us many examples of people attacking tanks with sticks and bricks or taunting ranks of soldiers armed with fixed bayonets. Momboisse suggests that police should, as a rule, display no more force than they are authorized and prepared to use in any particular situation.

Momboisse's approach to crowd control, according to Clark McPhail (personal communication), represents traditional public order policing policies and practices in the United States until the early 1970s (McPhail, Schweingruber, and McCarthy, 1998). Momboisse's approach was appropriated from Lohman, who was a student of Herbert Blumer. All three assumed protestors' cognitive processes were crippled by virtue of their crowd membership. This was Lohman and Momboisse's justification for police use of force to control crowd members who were "unable to control themselves" (Schweingruber, 2000). The implementation of this policy was characterized by an initial show of followed by a progressive escalation of force to compel dispersal by gatherings of people who did not comply with police orders.

The Lohman and Momboisse approach provoked more disorder than it prevented. Police agencies that had to deal with demonstrations on a daily basis at the United Nations in New York City and at the White House and U.S. Capitol in Washington, DC began developing what McPhail and McCarthy (1998) call the "negotiated management" of protest events. Supreme Court decisions in the 1970s and 1980s mandate police respect for protestors' First-Amendment rights. Police communications with protestors before, during and after protest events and police regard for and insistence upon protestors' capacity to police themselves combine to minimize confrontations and other disorderly developments that might otherwise require police intervention.

Confrontation Management

The experiences with escalated force between 1964 and 1970 led to an overall reassessment of the policing of crowds involved in celebrations, protest, demonstrations, and civil disorders. The outcome of this reassessment is the current policy of confrontation management (McPhail, Schweingruber, and McCarthy, 1998). This policy did not materialize during a think-tank exercise but resulted from consideration of numerous insights gained in the field. By the early 1970s, some police organizations were already employing more effective tactics that were based on communication and diffusion rather than escalated force. For example, some departments learned that the use of large, stationary formations of police should be avoided when possible. Often, such formations provide focal points for assembling processes, particularly when formations block normal routes of travel or are used to secure buildings. Crowd-control options are greatly reduced in the dense and focused gatherings that are produced. Instead, if possible, small mobile teams of officers should be used to patrol these areas. Volumes of traffic, which can be monitored by police, should be allowed to move through these areas.

Rather than the show of force, Momboisse (1967) suggests a strategy of force in reserve. This may have been part of the Iowa Highway Patrol's planning in dealing with the University of Iowa disorder that followed the killing of students at

Kent State in May 1970. When the Highway Patrol arrived in Iowa City, there already had been two days of disorder. One campus building had been burned, the ROTC building had been heavily damaged, and about three hundred students had been arrested. Across the campus, students speculated as to when the state police would arrive. Beginning at about noon on the second day of the disorder, individual patrol cars each carrying two officers began to cruise the streets near the center of campus. The police cars evoked stares from students but little else. By mid-afternoon, however, there were at least three state police cars per block in the campus area. Had the Highway Patrol used the grand entry, students who had been awaiting their arrival probably would have assembled at the center of campus. Instead, the patrol had, without flashing lights and blaring sirens, slowly and quietly saturated the campus area with a considerable number of state police. They had not created a focal point for assembling by students.

A few days earlier, students had established a protest-command center in an apartment building near campus. Here, students compiled information regarding the movement of campus and city police. Student protest marshals were dispatched from their command center to locations where police-student confrontations were occurring. The student marshals attempted to maintain order by urging students to be calm and police to refrain from the use of force. The command center also provided a place for student leaders to meet with one another and to plan organized protest activities. The field commander of the Highway Patrol visited the student command center on the afternoon of the patrol's arrival. He informed students of the patrol's objectives and gave them some advice on how to better carry out their marshaling efforts. Finally, he told students that he would be at the patrol's command center, at a motor inn on the outskirts of Iowa City. He told students they were welcome to visit the patrol's command center and that he would be available for consultation.

When students arrived at the motor inn, they saw a parking lot full of state police cars, buses, communication trailers, and a large number of officers. Although few of the officers who patrolled the campus were wearing riot helmets or carrying riot batons, the students could see rows of helmets and batons on display at the control center. Momboisse would describe this tactic as force in reserve. At the scene of disorder, police and riot control equipment are not displayed in a manner likely to produce a focal point for assembly or needlessly antagonize civilians. Procedures are established, however, that make it clear to civilians that considerably greater force is near at hand.

Momboisse (1967) emphasizes the importance of maintaining communication between police and civilians during disorder. Even during the most severe disorders described in this chapter, authorities were able to recruit assistance from civilians in the riot area. Recognized community leaders, as well as members of youth gangs, put forth great effort urging people to return to their homes (National Advisory Commission, 1968:177–78). By maintaining communication with civilians, police gather valuable information that can be used to evaluate rumors.

The Iowa Highway Patrol initiated and then maintained communication with students at the University of Iowa during the disorder described above. At this time, there were frequent reports that the Black Panthers and the Hell's Angels would soon arrive in Iowa City to help students battle police. The Iowa Highway Patrol quickly was able to dismiss this information as "rumor and fancy" because of their ongoing communication with students and student leaders. The Highway

In riot situations, police should be trained to respond in a manner that avoids raising the level of conflict. The manner in which this policeman presents himself flaunts "symbols of conflict" (e.g., the black uniform, large weapon, mask and helmet) that can inadvertently escalate the level of violence in sensitive situations.

Patrol was also able to inform student organizations of the guidelines governing street crowds, rallies, and arrests during the period of disorder. Likewise, student protest leaders were able to inform the Highway Patrol of their plans for pending rallies and demonstrations. Many misunderstandings were worked out in conferences rather than in street battles.

Finally, Momboisse frequently suggests that police must be sensitive to the level of conflict in which they are involved, and they must respond in a manner that communicates police readiness without unnecessarily raising the level of conflict. Police control the use of many different "symbols of conflict," including riot helmets and face shields, riot sticks, various types of firearms, and even armored personnel carriers. Certain types of activities also symbolize conflict. The wedge formations police use to break compact gatherings into smaller groups and lines of troops in kneeling positions, with rifles leveled and aimed, are symbols of conflict. How these symbols are selected and used by police can play an important role in the development of conflict.

At times, police can reduce the level of conflict by refraining from the use of symbols of conflict. Prior to the Iowa Highway Patrol's arrival on the campus of the University of Iowa, there had been an increasing spiral of conflict. Communication between students and campus and city police had broken down entirely. The local police patrolled the county courthouse lawn with automatic weapons. Tear gas had been used against crowds of students, and more than $100,000 worth of property had been destroyed. Across campus, students spoke of the pending arrival of the state police. It was said that they would enter the city in armored personnel carriers and use 50-caliber machine guns against students. Some students collected rocks for throwing and bottles for molotov cocktails and even discussed ways of obtaining firearms and gas masks.

The Highway Patrol failed to validate the dramatic spirit of conflict that was emerging. Their entry into the campus was unobtrusive, and they did not wear riot gear when they were on campus. Seeing the state police in regular uniforms and patrolling the campus with two-person teams was a marked contrast to what most students had expected. After their arrival on campus, little property damage occurred and mass arrests ceased. The Highway Patrol's crowd-control tactics were in sharp contrast to those used at Kent State. From their first movement onto the Kent State campus, National Guard troops wore full riot gear and carried rifles. They repeatedly used riot formations in their confrontations with students. Finally, even if by accident, the ultimate symbol of conflict was utilized—lethal gunfire.

COMMUNITIES AND RIOTS

Sociologists have attempted to answer two kinds of questions about communities and riots. The first question is that of "riot proneness" and whether some cities are more likely than others to experience riots. The second question is that of determining the kinds of changes that occur within communities during and following riots.

Riot Proneness

One of the first studies to empirically examine the question of riot proneness was that of Lieberson and Silverman (1965). These researchers compared seventy-six cities that experienced race riots between 1913 and 1963 with a matched sample of seventy-six nonriot cities for that same time period. They selected nonriot cities for their size and proximity to the riot city. Lieberson and Silverman concluded that riot cities were more likely to have a high level of economic competition between the races and municipal governments that were unsympathetic and unresponsive to African-American problems.

This type of paired comparison analysis was not possible for the decade of the 1960s, when at least 820 racial incidents were recorded by various sources. Of these incidents, 341 disorders were described as involving "significant instances of black aggression" or "riots." Simply put, there were not enough nonriot cities to construct a matching sample for riot cities!

Faced with this difficulty, Seymour Spilerman (1970) developed a different kind of analysis. Instead of comparing riot and nonriot cities, he compared the actual distribution of riots with hypothetical distributions generated by mathematical models. Spilerman began his analysis by noting that there were 673 cities with populations greater than twenty-five thousand in 1960. Then Spilerman identified the way in which 341 riots would be distributed among these 673 cities, assuming that riots were random events and each city had an equal probability for disorder. Under these hypothetical conditions, 405 cities should have no disorders, 206 cities should have only 1 disorder, 52 cities should have 2 disorders, 9 cities should have 3 disorders, and 1 city should have 4 disorders.

The actual distribution of riots was significantly different from this hypothetical distribution. In fact, 504 cities had no disorders, 93 cities had one disorder, 36 cities had two disorders, 19 cities had 3 disorders, and 21 cities had 4 or more disorders. This comparison shows that despite the greatly increased number of riots in the 1960s, they were not random occurrences.

The Riot Reinforcement Model Using more elaborate mathematical procedures, Spilerman created other hypothetical distributions. He constructed a hypothetical "riot reinforcement" distribution in which the occurrence of a riot in a city would make it more likely that the city would experience further riots. The riot reinforcement model suggests that the initial disorder would generate interracial hatreds and mutual preparations for further violence. Spilerman also created a "negative reinforcement" distribution in which the occurrence of a riot would decrease the likelihood of further riots in that city. The negative reinforcement model assumes that a riot would result in the release of accumulated tensions and provide evidence of the futility of violence. Finally, Spilerman created a "geographic contagion" distribution in which the occurrence of riots in nearby communities would contribute to a city's riot proneness. None of these hypothetical distributions matched the actual distribution of riots.

The hypothetical distribution that most closely matched the actual distribution of riots was based on the assumption that communities have different underlying disorder propensities. In one sense, this was the same conclusion that was reached earlier by Lieberson and Silverman (1965). However, Spilerman rejected their conclusion that the important differences between communities were black-white economic competition and unresponsive city government.

Spilerman (1970:642) examined eighteen community attributes and their relation to the number of disorders within the community. He used, for example, the percentage of dilapidated housing as a measure of social disorganization and the size of the city council as a measure of effective political structure. He also examined income, unemployment, and median levels of education as indicators of absolute and relative deprivation. Low correlations were obtained between these measures and the number of disorders in a city. The only measure that was strongly associated with the number of disorders was the absolute number of African-American residents in a city. Spilerman (1970:645) concluded that "the larger the Negro population, the greater the likelihood of a disorder. Little else appears to matter." Spilerman explains this conclusion in terms of a nationwide pattern of African-American discontent sufficient to overwhelm the impact of local conditions (Spilerman 1970; 1971; 1976). The number of African Americans in a city increases until a "critical mass" is reached, and disorder follows.

Differentiated View of Riots Spilerman's findings run largely counter to McPhail's differentiated view of riots. The differentiated view clearly suggests that some city environments provide greater likelihood than others do for assembling processes and, in turn, disorders (McPhail, 1971). The age structure and unemployment rates of a population are crude indicators of people's relative availability for involvement in disorder. The character of residential patterns and patterns of traffic flow create conditions of greater or lesser proximity among available people. The availability and proximity of persons create a favorable precondition for assembling processes. Street arrests are one source of assembling cues that often denote hostility. Face-to-face communication networks within the community transmit and augment these cues. Spilerman did not examine such factors as these in his analysis.

Factors in the differentiated view of riots are important because they constitute an "immediate interactional environment" for people (McPhail, 1971:1072). The immediate interactional environment for the urban disorders of the 1960s was typically a mixed residential and commercial area of a city. Most riot areas were more densely populated than the rest of the city, and more than 80 percent of the residents were African American. In these areas, the greatest number of people were killed, injured, or arrested, almost all property damage occurred, and police concentrated their greatest control efforts. Outside the riot areas little damage occurred, and few arrests were made. It follows from the differentiated view, therefore, that the riot area, not the entire city, is the proper unit of analysis.

Spilerman, however, used the riot city as his unit of analysis. Granted, when comparing cities, there seems to be little besides the size of the African-American population that distinguishes one riot city from another. Comparing riot areas, however, may reveal substantial differences in, for example, age structure and unemployment rates. Likewise, street arrests may be considerably more frequent in some riot areas than in others. Street patterns and residential patterns may create quite different degrees of conduciveness for assembling among riot areas.

David Snyder (1979) conducted a study of the urban riots between 1961 and 1969 that used the predominantly African-American census tract area, or "ghetto," as the unit of analysis. Further, Snyder attempted to examine variables suggested by the differentiated view of riots. He assumed that the likelihood for instructions to assemble was a function of the number of police-resident contacts within the ghetto, and he created a variable that would reflect the probable number of these contacts. The "area-contact-interaction" variable was based on the number of police, the number of blacks in the ghetto, and the size of the ghetto relative to the rest of the city.

Instructions to assemble are more likely to result in assembling if many people hear or see them. Snyder constructed a "spatial availability" variable, which was the number of street intersections within the ghetto. The greater the number of street intersections in the ghetto, the greater the likelihood that people will see and hear assembling cues. Snyder also suggested that further studies include the density and type of residential dwellings in the ghetto. Widely dispersed housing and high-rise housing are relatively less conducive to assembling than dwellings clustered close together.

People are likely to assemble when they have few or no competing commitments. Consequently, Snyder constructed a "temporal availability" variable, which consisted of the number of ghetto residents between the ages of fifteen and thirty-four, the number of unemployed residents, and the number of people who recently moved into the ghetto. These people are generally assumed to have greater amounts of unstructured or uncommitted time at their disposal than others.

Assembling is more likely to be extensive when face-to-face communication links spread assembling cues throughout the ghetto area. Snyder used the population density of the census tract as a crude indicator of these communication links, and he suggested that future studies take into account communication barriers, such as rivers, highways, or railways that intersect many ghetto areas.

Snyder admits that his measures of ghetto characteristics are nearly as crude as Spilerman's citywide measures. Further, information about predominantly African-American census tracts was available for only 244 of the 341 disorders included in Spilerman's study. Even so, Snyder's differentiated variables are more closely associated than Spilerman's with the number of disorders occurring in ghettos. The differentiated view of riots, according to Snyder, clearly shows that some ghettos are more riot prone than others. This is not because some ghettos have greater levels of discontent than others. Rather, some ghettos have significantly greater numbers of police-citizen contacts that can be easily observed by ghetto residents. Further, Snyder's analysis suggests that ghettos with younger populations, high unemployment, and many new residents are more likely than others to experience disorder. These people are more likely than others to be on the streets with nothing to do.

Finally, Snyder's analysis confirms the idea that assembling and resulting disorders are likely to occur in ghettos where news can be transmitted rapidly among the residents. High population density, large numbers of people on porches and sidewalks and in the streets and parks, and few ecological barriers to face-to-face communication seem to be clearly associated with a ghetto's riot proneness.

Community Responses to Riots

Riots and people's response to them produce a number of functional and structural changes within communities. Many of these changes are documented in the riot studies conducted during the 1960s. In order to present these findings systematically, we will use Dennis E. Wenger's (1978) framework for analyzing disaster-related community changes.

Functional Changes Wenger identifies four community functions in his discussion of community responses to disaster (see chapter 11). The first function is the wide range of activities that constitute the production, distribution, and consumption patterns of community life. The second function includes the activities and organizations that carry out child and adult socialization. The third community function is participation. Work, school, voluntary service organizations, kin, and friendship groups provide opportunities for instrumental and noninstrumental participation in community life. Finally, there is the mutual support function. Families, as well as formal organizations, provide psychological and material support during times of stress.

Riots, like disasters, produce important and noticeable changes in these normal community functions. Wenger notes that the type of production facilities in a community is related to possible disaster outcomes; similarly, the proximity of residences to streets, stores, and factories is a major factor in a community's conduciveness to riot (Snyder, 1979; McPhail, 1971). Further, the timing of production, distribution, and consumption functions determines the tempo of community life. Work hours and vacation schedules determine when substantial portions of a population have free time at their disposal. The majority of urban riots began or reached their peak during evenings and on weekends (National Advisory Commission, 1968:71, 360–406). During the "long, hot summers" of the 1960s, riots most frequently occurred during the vacation months of July and August.

After disasters, communities often face the problem of distributing unsolicited gifts of food, clothing, and other useful items. No such generosity is shown to riot communities. In fact, some resources, such as bus and taxi service, may be withheld from the riot area for some time after order is restored.

The restoration of production, distribution, and consumption functions signifies the end of the disaster period and is often accomplished within a surprisingly short period of time (Wright, et al., 1979). In contrast, community functions are restored slowly following riots. In some riot areas, such as Newark, New Jersey, and Watts, the burned-out shells of buildings still stand, years or even decades after the disorder. The rebuilding of riot communities is often hindered by a serious lack of property insurance in the areas where riots occurred. The National Advisory Commission (1968:305–12) noted that in some areas nearly half of the commercial businesses had neither fire nor theft insurance prior to the disorder. Unlike the case with disasters, no direct federal "riot assistance" was immediately available to finance reconstruction. After the riots, residential and commercial insurance rates often tripled. The high cost or total unavailability of insurance decreases the rate at which commercial property within the ghetto can be bought and sold, greatly hindering the ghetto's recovery. Finally, some commercial properties in the ghetto may, for all practical purposes, be abandoned after riots.

Socialization functions are of secondary importance to community life during disasters. Schools may be dismissed in advance of hurricanes or blizzards. Similarly, some schools were dismissed when "a riot was likely." Although this precaution was well intentioned, many of the children and teenagers who were released from school eventually became involved in disorders. Schools, daycare, and recreation centers were seldom looted or vandalized, even though they contained valuable items (Berk and Aldrich, 1972; Quarantelli and Dynes, 1968).

During disasters, the participation and support functions of community life are heightened. There is some evidence that similar things happen during riots. Quarantelli and Dynes (1968) point out that the looting that occurred during the urban disorders of the 1960s was carried out by residents of the community. Further, their actions received a great deal of community support. This is in sharp contrast to the looting that occasionally accompanies disaster. Outsiders usually carry out disaster-related looting, and community members condemn their actions. Some suggest that during riots local criminal gangs often initiate looting. In the later stages of a riot, it is clear that people from all age and income segments of the riot area carry out looting with little competition or conflict. Small groups and families, often with the encouragement of bystanders, carry out looting quite openly. Surveys conducted after riots indicate a substantial support for these activities, even among nonparticipants (Thomlinson, 1968; Oberschall, 1968).

Riot-related opportunities for participation in community life were increased where youth patrols were organized by police, city officials, churches, members of local antipoverty agencies, and autonomous "black power" groups (Knoph, 1969b). Sanctioned youth patrols were used in at least eighteen major cities during 1967 and 1968, and their size ranged from twenty (Pittsburgh) to nearly five hundred (Newark). They assumed a variety of official and unofficial names, including White Hats (Tampa), Peace Monitors (San Francisco), Youth Alliance Security Patrol (Boston), and the Soul Patrol (Providence, Rhode Island). These groups provided a "socially approved" activist role for many youth gangs. Patrols guarded against vandalism, tried to calm crowds, monitored police activity, and offered general assistance, such as providing coffee for police, aiding Red Cross workers, and evacuating people from burning buildings (Knoph, 1969b:18).

The National Advisory Commission (1968) took a largely negative view of the youth patrols, noting that they had no clear and legitimate authority and therefore contributed to the confusion during riots. Further, the commission characterized the youth patrols as ineffective in preventing violence. Knoph (1969b:8), who studied the youth patrols in great detail, came to the opposite conclusion, stating, "In the . . . cases where information is available, youth patrols were extremely effective in handling crowds and reducing tensions."

In most cities, following a major riot, job training programs, neighborhood improvement associations, and youth-oriented programs were initiated (Bullock, 1969:51–103). Most of these organizations were short lived, and few are active today. For many people, however, a riot provided a stimulus for a few months of increased community participation.

We know relatively little about the degree of personal support shown toward residents who suffered as a result of a riot. Quite likely, friends and neighbors offered sympathy to the injured and even to those who were arrested; looted food and clothing may have been offered to people in need. Little compassion was shown, however, to the merchants who were burned out or looted. In fact, some stores that had been looted were burglarized shortly after they reopened (Cohen and Murphy, 1966).

Structural Changes Wenger (1978) identifies four structural elements of community life in his discussion of community responses to disaster: the community's value and belief system, social norms, organizational structure, and power relationships. Disasters usually produce an increased consensus of values and beliefs within a community. For a brief period of time, humanitarian values and beliefs in the effectiveness of cooperation become central to community life.

There appears to be a similar growth of consensus and alteration of community values and beliefs during riots. For a brief period of time, activist values and beliefs become central to community life. From the end of World War I until the 1960s, riots of a racial character in the United States had value and belief overtones of race warfare (Grimshaw, 1968). During these riots, inaccurate rumors of cross-racial assaults upon women and children were used to justify attacks on members of the other race. For the most part, groups of white civilians hunted down and attacked blacks that were outside "their area of the city." Sometimes, whites actually invaded the black areas of the city, attacking people and property (Grimshaw, 1960).

This pattern of conflict was not typical of the disorders during the 1960s. The antagonists were largely residents of African-American communities and the police and National Guard. Rumors of cross-racial assault of women and children were not a substantial ingredient of these disorders. Blacks concentrated their attacks primarily on property rather than on people. There were no attempts to invade white communities.

Grimshaw attributes these marked differences to the ideology that inspired the riots. While the overwhelming majority of African Americans expressed fear and dismay at the burning, destruction, and loss of life during the riots, they did not see the riots as purposeless, nor were they unsympathetic to the rioters (Thomlinson, 1968). The majority of a national sample of blacks saw the riots as a way to call attention to their problems, express their discontent to whites, improve their conditions, and end discrimination (Thomlinson, 1968). Many African Americans viewed the riots of the 1960s as a revolt by blacks against intolerable conditions.

Following disasters, most changes in the normative structure are related to the use of property. Heavy equipment may be appropriated to rescue and transport the injured. Under other circumstances, this might well be considered theft. Quarantelli and Dynes (1968) point out that a similar normative transition took place during riots of the 1960s. A very broad cross section of community residents, not just the "criminal element," took part in looting. Further, the looting was carried out openly and with enthusiasm. Looters were also rather selective: their most frequent targets were grocery stores, followed by furniture, clothing, and liquor stores. Banks, schools, manufacturing plants, and private residences were largely ignored.

Because of this open, enthusiastic, and selective character of looting, Quarantelli and Dynes concluded that it was normatively regulated. They suggest that this looting represented "situations of temporary and localized redefinition of property rights" (1968:8). This means that few looters and bystanders viewed the ransacking of local stores as simple theft. Instead, they saw their actions as a type of "justice" in which today's looting equalized years of past mistreatment by white merchants. Looting was seen as a means of communicating to the broader society that something was fundamentally wrong about the marked inequality of the American economic system.

Disasters produce a temporary weakening and then a strengthening of ties between the community and outside organizations. A similar pattern occurs for riots. Initially, the riot community may be isolated by police and National Guard from surrounding areas, although this isolation is usually not complete. Many goods and services provided by outside organizations may be withheld from a community during and for a time following the riot. After order is restored in a riot community, ties to organizations providing social services may be increased. The National Advisory Commission (1968) recommended a marked upgrading of job training, remedial education, and community development programs within riot areas in an effort to prevent further riots.

Finally, power relationships become more authoritarian during disasters. Similarly, authoritarian patterns of power use occur in riots, most obviously in the riot control efforts of police and National Guard. Moderate African-American organizations, such as the NAACP, were able to wield power in a more authoritarian fashion following riots, in part because more of the white community felt that moderate organizations represented the "responsible leadership" of the African-American community.

SOCIETIES AND RIOTS

Although the majority of demonstrations and protest events are both legal and orderly, some situations escalate into riots where vandalism, looting, arson, and other illegal acts of violence against property and person occur. Napoleon claimed that the most effective means of stopping riots was a "whiff of grapeshot." Contrary to Napoleon's view, however, having access to lethal force does not solve all the problems of crowd control in riot situations. Increasingly, authorities may hesitate in using wholesale lethal force out of fear of international sanctions. On December 10, 1948, the United Nations General Assembly adopted the Universal Declaration of Human Rights without a dissenting vote. This was the first multinational declaration that mentioned human rights by name. Since then, the Declaration has become a worldwide standard by which to judge the actions of authorities, worldwide. In the preamble to the Declaration, it is stated:

> Whereas the peoples of the United Nations have in the Charter reaffirmed their faith in fundamental human rights, in the dignity and worth of the human person and in the equal rights of men and women and have determined to promote social progress and better standards of life in larger freedom,
>
> Whereas Member States have pledged themselves to achieve, in co-operation with the United Nations, the promotion of universal respect for and observance of human rights and fundamental freedoms, . . .

Among the human rights and fundamental freedoms enumerated by the Declaration (Article 20) is the right of everyone to freedom of peaceful assembly and association. Article 29 of the Declaration further states that everyone shall be subject ". . . only to such limitations as are determined by law solely for the purpose of securing . . . the just requirements of morality, public order and the general welfare . . ." in a democratic society. Articles 20 and 29 would seem to preclude the unrestrained use of force by authorities against their citizens.

Human Rights Issues

The Declaration of Human Rights became more salient internationally when, in 1961, a group of lawyers, journalists, writers, and others, formed the Appeal for Amnesty. The founders were offended and frustrated by continued human rights abuses, such as the sentencing of two Portuguese college students to twenty years in prison for having raised their glasses in a toast to "freedom" in a bar. The Appeal for Amnesty took out newspaper ads that told stories of "prisoners of conscience" who had been jailed for peacefully expressing their political or religious beliefs, and called on governments everywhere to free such prisoners. It called for strict impartial, non-partisan appeals to be made on behalf of these prisoners and any who, like them, had been imprisoned for peacefully expressed beliefs. The Appeal shortly adopted the name Amnesty International and, during the 1970s, gained permanent observer status as an NGO at the United Nations. In 1977 it was awarded the Nobel Peace Prize for its work.

Amnesty International prepares frequent reports on the status of human rights that are read by legislatures, state departments and foreign ministries around the world. It prepares press releases on human rights abuses and victories for the world press. Amnesty International and U.N. recommendations provide a forum in which the human rights records of nations can be meaningfully compared. It is increasingly difficult for governments to ignore this information. The United States and many other countries have threatened to withhold and, at times, actually have withheld foreign aid and trade concessions out of concern for violations of human rights. Likewise, the World Bank shows concern for human rights and political stability in making and extending loans to nations.

Even world corporations have sought to make human rights an important component in business decisions. Most noteworthy, perhaps, is the human rights campaign of Reebok Corporation. Reebok began its campaign for human rights in the late 1980s after seeing reports on the working conditions in the factories of suppliers for Reebok and other sports and casual wear labels. These reports cited several areas of concern including child labor, the exploitation of women, and dangerous working conditions. In 1988 Reebok joined with Amnesty International in sponsoring the Human Rights Now! international concert tour. The annual Reebok Human Rights Award was also created that year to recognize young people's efforts in the area of human rights, and the fortieth anniversary of the U.N. Declaration of Human Rights. In 1992, The Reebok Foundation joined with the Lawyers Committee for Human Rights and musician Peter Gabriel to create Witness, a program to arm human rights groups with the tools of mass communication such as video cameras and fax machines. Since then, Witness videos have documented police brutality in Nigeria; exhumations of mass graves in Bosnia, Guatemala and Haiti; as well as providing graphic evidence of "ethnic cleansing" of Rwandese refugees by Hutu militants and the abuse of street children in Honduras and Guatemala.

Reebok also set forth and adopted their own human rights production standards. Reebok continues to seek compliance with these standards by their contractors, subcontractors, suppliers and other business partners. Reebok seeks business partners that allow Reebok full knowledge of their production facilities and uses affirmative measures, such as on-site inspection of production facilities, to implement and monitor these standards. These standards include a non-discrimination policy and a sixty-hour-a-week limit on working hours and overtime, and prohibition of forced or compulsory labor and the use of child labor. The standards specify that business partners shall strive to assure employees a safe and healthy workplace that does not expose workers to hazardous conditions.

Reebok seeks business partners who are committed to the betterment of wage and benefit levels that address the basic needs of workers and their families as much as possible. Reebok will not select business partners that pay less than the minimum wage required by local law or that pay less than prevailing local industry practices (whichever is higher). Reebok seeks business partners that share its commitment to the right of employees to establish and join organizations of their own choosing. Reebok recognizes and respects the right of all employees to organize and bargain collectively. Every factory producing Reebok products will publicize and enforce a nonretaliation policy that permits factory workers to speak with Reebok staff without fear of retaliation by factory management. Finally, Reebok takes strong objection to the use of force to suppress any of these standards and will take any such actions into account when evaluating facility compliance with these standards.

In 1996, the Apparel Industry Partnership, consisting of Reebok, Nike, L.L. Bean, Liz Claiborne, Wal-Mart, and many other apparel makers and labor and human rights groups met with the Justice Department's antitrust division. The Partnership sought department approval to get together and set voluntary, humane production and labor standards and to develop a labeling and advertising plan to inform consumers which companies abide by them. In addition to the corporations and groups already mentioned, the Partnership included the following: Business for Social Responsibility, Interfaith Center on Corporate Responsibility; International Labor Rights Fund; Karen Kane Inc.; Lawyers Committee for Human Rights; National Consumers League; Nicole Miller; Patagonia; Phillips-Van Heusen Corp.; Retail, Wholesale and Department Store Union; AFL-CIO; Robert F. Kennedy Memorial Center for Human Rights; Tweeds Inc.; Union of Needletrades, Industrial and Textile Employees; and Warnaco Inc.

In spite of, or maybe because of, horrendous human rights violations by governments since the 1970s, human rights are now much more salient in international dealings. The United Nations, the World Bank, hundreds of NGOs and churches, many strategically important corporations, and nearly all national governments now subscribe to the idea of universal human rights. Many formal and informal sanctions are likely to be imposed against governments that use unrestrained force against dissenting and even rebellious citizens. Finally, governments using unrestrained force against segments of their population risk military intervention by United Nations and other international peacekeeping forces. For instance, during the 1990s, both the United Nations and NATO intervened in the ethnic cleansing occurring in the Bosnia and Kosovo regions of the former Yugoslavia.

The Use of Force

The stigma of having a "poor human rights record" and the resulting sanctions may restrain authorities in their use of force against their citizens. A number of other constraints have also been identified. Turner and Killian (1972:160–61) note that even in totalitarian regimes, some police and soldiers may feel a sense of sympathy for those they must suppress. In these extreme instances of totalitarian control, ethnic, religious, or regional identities may inhibit the unrestrained use of force against rioters.

Other factors also operate to restrain police in their use of force in riots and uprisings. In the later stages of revolutions, for example, police may refuse to fire on or otherwise suppress crowds in the name of an authority that may soon be deposed. Such defections and mutinies of the military and police have signaled the end for many governments throughout history (Rudé, 1964; Tilly, 1975).

In some instances, the use of force may be curtailed by the simple realization that it may enlarge the scope and intensity of disorder. The unrestrained use of force against one group may bring other groups into the conflict. This can happen, for example, in labor disputes. The violent suppression of workers in one industry can bring about sympathy strikes by workers in other industries.

The use of lethal force by authorities has often served as a justification for the use of lethal force by their victims. The blatant use of force on street crowds can also change the nature of conflict. Open, relatively unorganized, and isolated defiance can give way to more broadly based and organized resistance. Further, the aims of this resistance may change from relatively nonviolent reform to violent, total revolution. Stalin, for example, pointed out how the whips and saber blades of the czar's Cossacks served to infuriate and radicalize the pre-revolutionary street crowds of Russia (Stalin, 1953).

The use of force may also be ruled out because of its costs. The cost and difficulties in using the latest weapons to quell their own citizenry may give some governments pause. These resources of terror can be put to better use (such as intimidating nearby nations), particularly when less forceful means of crowd control offer promise of success.

Finally, the use of force may be restrained when authorities are dealing with disorders involving high-status or popular groups within the society. Students were shot and killed on at least three separate occasions during the student disorders of the 1960s and 1970s. In two instances—those at Jackson State, Mississippi, and Orangeburg State, South Carolina—the student body was almost totally African American. The other incident, of course, was at Kent State, Ohio, a predominantly white university. Although there were numerous demonstrations at Ivy League and Big Ten universities, lethal force was not used at these schools, and on the whole, student riots were treated in a much more restrained fashion than the urban riots of the time or the labor riots of earlier decades.

Cultural Differences

It has often been suggested that there are cultural differences in the ways that societies view the use of harsh tactics of crowd control. It is suggested, for example, that English bobbies seldom use firearms in crowd control, in part because they are dealing with a more "civilized" or "reserved" populace. Urban disorders in England, such as the 1981 riot in London's Brixton district, have occurred in areas where recent, often non-English-speaking, immigrants have settled. In Brixton, violence occurred for nearly a week, with much arson and looting. Only one casualty occurred, however, when a boy was struck and killed by a police vehicle. The Brixton riot presents a sharp contrast to the thirty-five deaths that occurred during the Watts riot or the thirty-nine fatalities of the Detroit riot of 1967.

Such differences, however, can only be attributed to cultural factors in the most general sense, if at all. There are more immediate considerations. First, it must be noted that a fair number of the casualties that occurred during riots in the United States were not the result of direct police action. For example, two civilians died in Detroit when they walked into downed power lines (National Advisory Commission, 1968). In Watts, some people died in fires, and the only police officer to die was killed by the accidental discharge of his partner's shotgun (Conot, 1967).

Not all civilians who were injured or killed by police gunfire were deliberately shot while committing crimes. Numbers of people died simply because high-powered weapons were often used in densely populated urban areas. Police frequently fired over the heads of looters without taking direct aim. Sometimes, police shot in the general direction of buildings that they suspected to contain snipers (National Advisory Commission, 1968). Some National Guard and police units had little riot training or experience, and at times, these units discharged their weapons without orders to do so. In Detroit, troops fired 201 rounds, and in

Newark, National Guard and police fired 13,326 rounds, including 50-caliber tracer bullets (National Advisory Commission, 1968). Many of those who fell were not intentional police targets. Rather, the stray bullets and ricochets that hit people were fired from weapons hundreds of yards away. Perhaps the development of more precise and less lethal weapons is in order.

In recent English riots the majority of injuries were inflicted upon the police, while in the United States during the disorders of the 1960s police sustained only about 10 percent of the fatalities and less than 30 percent of the injuries (National Advisory Commission, 1968:66–67). It seems that the English are willing to tolerate injured police more readily than dead civilians.

Finally, it should be noted that English crowd-control tactics have not always been so refined. Rudé, for example, documents the brutal character of riot control tactics used in England during the industrial riots of the eighteenth and nineteenth centuries (Rudé, 1964). The vicious responses of British authorities to the naval mutinies of the eighteenth century are also well documented. It seems, therefore, that no group is "culturally immune" from the use of harsh riot control tactics.

Normative Constraint

The reliance on harsh and brutal riot control tactics seems to occur when neither side feels a normative constraint on its actions toward the other party (Turner and Killian, 1972:161–62). These conditions may be approached within political systems that deny fundamental rights of property or dissent to groups within their midst. Such disenfranchised groups are usually held in low regard throughout the society. The use of violent suppression is likely to occur at the slightest provocation on the part of the low-status group. Further, this suppression will probably be approved of or at least not objected to by the dominant groups in the society. In fact, the brutal actions of authorities may simply be a "legal" or "formalized" version of the same suppression informally used by the dominant groups in their normal dealings with the outcast group.

The response of authorities to many Indian uprisings on the North American frontier exemplify this type of situation, which still exists in those parts of the world where some industrializing societies confront hunting and gathering or horticultural groups. These small groups are being exterminated at the slightest provocation; in extreme instances, those being attacked may not even be considered to be part of the human race. The nineteenth-century extermination of native Tasmanians by European colonists is one such example. Some of the victims were used for dog food.

This lack of restraint is also seen in those settings where longstanding or traditional antagonisms exist between control agents and crowd members. Thus we see many instances where brutal suppression is directed against the members of religious and racial minorities. Often the most brutal actions are taken by auxiliary police or militia composed of local residents. The 1990s brought us intense ethnic violence in many parts of the world. Yugoslavia disintegrated into ethnic conflict between Croatian, Serbian, and Bosnian partisans. Ethnic violence between Hutu and Tutsi groups swept the lakes region of Africa. These and other conflicts were nearly unbelievable in their unrestrained ferocity. Violence was inflicted on civilians by civilians. Police, militia, paramilitary and rebel groups carried out violent campaigns against their opposite counterparts as well as displaced civilian groups. Domestic and international groups that worked for peace in these areas were at times virtually powerless to halt the carnage.

Finally, restraint is less likely to be shown in regions that are isolated from the public eye. Some discussions of riot control claim that the presence of the media contributes to the intensity and spread of violence. To a limited extent, this may be the case. However, media coverage can also serve to limit disorder. Studies of urban disorders show that about half of those people who eventually became involved in the disorder heard their first news of the disorder by word-of-mouth or were at the scene of some of the earliest confrontations (National Advisory Commission, 1968: Singer, Osborn, and Geschwender, 1970). They were not brought to the event on the basis of news coverage. Further, most news coverage contained appeals to people to remain calm and stay out of the riot areas.

Both authorities and civilians are likely to show restraint in the presence of the media. During the expulsion of demonstrators from the steps of the Pentagon in October 1967, for example, federal troops repeatedly ceased clubbing demonstrators and demonstrators stopped throwing trash at the soldiers when the television cameras were turned in their direction. The most ugly and brutal suppression of humans usually occurs far from the eye of the media. The death squads of authoritarian regimes carry out their atrocities on country roads and in isolated jungle clearings. Local authorities have often attacked news teams from the United States and other countries. Their news reports also have been closely censored. The bloodiest labor confrontations in the United States occurred deep in the mountains of Appalachia or in the small mining towns of the West and received little media coverage.

As noted in the previous chapter, between 1963 and 1972 virtually every city in the United States with a population of more than 100,000 residents experienced at least one riot. Student demonstrations and riots occurred on most major campuses in the United States, and students were killed during campus disorders in Mississippi, South Carolina, Ohio, and Michigan. Since 1972, however, there probably have been no more than five disorders of such magnitude in the United States. What happened?

In the previous chapter we considered the explanations of riots offered by collective behavior theorists. These explanations emphasize social strain that engenders frustrations and hostile beliefs that erupt into outbursts of rioting. Riot data gathered at the time provided little empirical support for these ideas. Subsequently, more elaborate analysis of this riot data has yet to yield substantively significant findings (McPhail, 1994). Since 1972, there has also been no substantial shift of material wealth toward the poorest groups in society and, in fact, these groups may be relatively worse off today than in the mid-1960s. It would be very difficult to argue that there has been a decline in other frustrations for these groups, or that their aspirations have lowered substantially. So, again, we must ask: What happened? Why did rioting cease so abruptly?

The collective action perspective calls attention to a fundamental change in the politics of contemporary democracies that began in the 1970s. There has been a trend toward increased institutionalization of collective action, particularly in advanced industrial democracies (Meyer and Tarrow, 1998). This means that since the 1970s, social protest has moved from being a sporadic feature of democratic politics to becoming a perpetual element in modern life. Today, protest is employed more frequently, by more diverse constituencies, and is pressing a wider range of claims than ever before. Most important, professionalization and institutionalization may be changing the social movement into an instrument of conventional politics (Meyer and Tarrow, 1998:4). This idea will be discussed further in the last two chapters.

One of the first outcomes of this process of institutionalization of protest was a substantial shift in the tactics used by police in dealing with civil disorders. Three presidential commissions, The National Commission on Civil Disorder, The National Commission on the Causes and Prevention of Violence, and The National Commission on Campus Unrest, noted that police actions were pivotal in the development of riots and disorder (McPhail, Schweingruber, and McCarthy, 1998). The commissions noted that the excessive use of force for handling disorder often has the effect of magnifying turmoil and not diminishing it. Since deadly force frequently incites further violence, only the minimum force necessary to effectively control the situation should be used. While most police departments used the escalated force model described earlier, the commissions noted that few communities had adequate numbers of police officers *trained* to deal with major crowd control problems. The reports recommended that all levels of police personnel receive comprehensive and ongoing training for civil disorder prevention and control. The commissions also recommended that officials implement fair and effective continuing programs to redress civilian grievances against the police. Departments should also devise plans to identify and eliminate abrasive policing policies (McPhail, Schweingruber, and McCarthy, 1998).

In 1967, the Department of Justice directed the United States Army Military Police School at Fort Gordon, Georgia to develop a civil disturbance orientation course (SEADOC) for civilian police officials. SEADOC trained police officials in the use of escalated force tactics of crowd control. SEADOC was halted in April of 1969, three months after The National Commission on the Causes and Prevention of Violence issued its report. SEADOC II training began a year later, and this training reflected the recommendations of the National Commission. SEADOC II training for civilian police officials emphasized the "confrontation management" style of controlling civil disturbances. New key elements in this training included lectures emphasizing that civil disorders can take many forms and that police should retain a high degree of flexibility and selectivity in their response to civil disturbances. Field operations should rely on the rule of "minimum necessary force," and arrests should only be used as a last resort and then be carried out in a manner to avoid injury. Firearms are not to be used to prevent offenses, such as looting, which are unlikely to cause death, bodily harm, or endanger public health or safety. Shoot-to-kill orders are not authorized (McPhail, Schweingruber, and McCarthy, 1998:62–64). SEADOC II training and lectures have acknowledged that earlier policing methods risked contributing to disorder, and the new confrontation management style sought to prevent police overreaction. Finally, it has been acknowledged that confrontation management requires extensive training and periodic retraining and practice.

Confrontation management also relies on the use of current public order technologies. This includes computers, databases and field communication systems. Defensive technologies include protective clothing for officers. Offensive technologies include batons, tear gas, pepper sprays, rubber bullets and specialized firearms.

In 1992, Los Angeles experienced a level of rioting not witnessed for decades. Why did this occur? According to Useem (1997), the rioting was a result of the LAPD being caught "flat-footed" during the first six hours of the riot. Even though the LAPD was committed to a policy of confrontation management, it failed because of several reasons. The first police to enter the immediate area of disorder were, quite simply, vastly outnumbered and overwhelmed. Effective communication between the field command post and the station was never fully established, and an alternate (and also disorganized) command post was established a few blocks away. This duplication resulted in the loss of unity of command. Emergency equipment arrived in the confrontation area in an uncoordinated fashion and caused traffic jams. Large numbers of police personnel arrived at the field command post, only to experience 45-minute delays in receiving assignments. Squads dissipated as they waited and could not respond immediately when they finally did receive assignments. These were many of the same problems that were experienced decades earlier in the Watts riot!

SUMMARY

Riots, like disasters, produce a number of changes within and among community organizations. When faced with the problem of controlling hostile crowds, police departments, fire departments, hospitals, and public transportation lines take on many features of expanding organizations. Counterrioters, looting crowds, and crowds opposing or assisting police are similar in process and structure to the emergent groups in disaster.

We considered six principles of crowd control used by police organizations. These principles of escalated force assume that police have sufficient numbers of officers at hand and that these officers can be deployed in the field in a coordinated fashion. Escalated force principles also assume that police will be able to identify incidents that are likely to precipitate riots and take action before crowds achieve unity. These assumptions are often the most problematic aspects of crowd control. We used the differentiated view of riot behavior to evaluate these crowd control tactics.

Communitywide riots produce a number of changes that are similar to those produced by disaster. During and after riots, such community functions as production and socialization are given less priority, while social control, participation, and mutual support may be strengthened in ways similar to those of communities coping with disaster. We noted some exceptions to this pattern. Following riots, for example, there is little evidence of convergence of unsolicited goods into the impact area. Also, the restoring of pre-riot production, distribution, and consumption functions is slow compared to the recovery of communities after disasters.

Finally, we gave some consideration to the ways in which societies respond to riots. Some societies respond with severe repression, while others are much more accommodating or at least far less violent in their responses. Since the 1960s a greater concern for human rights has tempered the use of unrestrained violence against civilian populations by their leaders. In the United States, there was a major shift in the manner in which authorities responded to civil disorder between 1964 and 1972. Authorities moved away from tactics of escalated force and toward those of confrontation management. In the following chapters we will discuss how these more recent policies are part of a trend toward the institutionalization of protest within contemporary industrial democracies.

⚒ CHAPTER 14 ⚒

PROTEST

In May of 1992 residents of Whiteside County, Illinois were becoming aware of a plan by the Whiteside County Board to allow Waste Management, Inc. (WMI), the world's largest landfill operator, to site a landfill in an area of prime farmland. The new landfill was intended to replace a county-owned and operated landfill that had not only outlived its usefulness, but also contained many hazardous chemicals and "hot spots" where leaking buried metal barrels were expelling toxic, lethal substances. Clean-up costs were estimated to be in the multimillions of dollars. Whiteside County officials scrambled for solutions and found their options limited. They eventually decided to accept a proposal from WMI to help them close the hazardous 40-acre landfill and build a new, 229-acre landfill adjacent to the old site.

The process of siting the new landfill had been covered by local and regional media for more than two years before any protesters appeared to question the decision. The first protesters were an elderly couple who owned farmland near the landfill site. Their presence at a monthly board meeting was quite innocuous. They asked a few questions and left the meeting.

By the next month the numbers of protesters had grown. Dozens of people attended the next monthly board meeting, carrying pickets and demanding to be allowed to speak to the county board. Their request was denied because they had not followed board protocol that required advance notice for a place on the agenda. The growing group had circulated petitions protesting the new landfill and wanted their concerns heard by board members. They angrily left the board meeting. Several of the group had emerged as leaders, and during the next weeks they gathered information and recruited new members.

The protesters were attempting to enter the political arena with little or no knowledge about how to effectively challenge decisions that affected them, but they were united in their commitment to protest the landfill. The group quickly made advances. They adopted CARL (Citizens Against a Regional Landfill) as their name and developed a statement of purpose. They began organizing public informational meetings with experts in environmental degradation, and they began accepting donations to help defray the expenses of running a protest group. Within three months of their organizational debut, the group had hundreds of people supporting their cause and about a dozen core workers.

The group faced its toughest challenge at a state-mandated public comment meeting where WMI was slated to provide information to prove it met Environmental Protection Agency standards for constructing a landfill. The meeting time and place had to be changed at the last minute to accommodate the hundreds of people who turned out for the meeting. Most were there hoping to protest the landfill. WMI was well-prepared for the meeting with a panel of expert witnesses who testified the landfill would meet health and safety requirements.

CARL members were not as prepared. They failed to bring expert rebuttal witnesses, and most of their prepared testimony was disallowed because it was considered irrelevant by a presiding court officer. CARL members were allowed to do little except present a petition signed by 1,500 county residents who opposed the landfill. CARL members had not anticipated such formal proceedings, and had clearly not done their homework to learn the scope of the meeting. Many of the protesters did not understand the technical, scientific information being represented by WMI witnesses. The crowd was unruly at times, and some protesters were threatened with expulsion. The meeting was extended from one day to two days, and at the close, the testimony was forwarded to the Illinois Environmental Protection Agency for review and a decision on the acceptability of the WMI proposal.

Following this meeting, the protesters grew frustrated and hostile. Members of the county board and their families were threatened with physical harm by anonymous callers. The tension lasted for about a month, and then the IEPA ruled in August 1992 that WMI met all the criteria and would be granted a permit if the county board made a final vote to approve the landfill. Until this point, of 27 county board members, only one had publicly stated his opposition to the landfill. CARL members warned that board members would lose their seats in the next election if the siting was approved.

The board set the final vote for October. Prior to this meeting CARL members hastily hit upon a new strategy. They hired a legal representative to speak to board members prior to the vote. The evening of the vote arrived and hundreds of people, mostly protesters, crowded into an auditorium to hear the decision. Local and county police were posted throughout the building because of increasing numbers of threats against board members.

CARL members and their attorney were granted the right to speak, and for more than three hours the group's lawyer and members pleaded with the board members to deny the contract to WMI. The question was called for a vote, and board members approved the contract, 18 to 7. Two members were absent from the meeting. CARL members booed and some shouted obscenities, but police moved into the crowd and it dispersed.

CARL members said after the meeting they would continue with a legal appeal. They did appeal to the Illinois Pollution Control Board, but their appeal was denied in January, 1993. At this point CARL members still had the option for further appeal in the civil courts, but the group took no further action. The elderly couple who had started the protest and continued as leaders throughout the movement said someone else should take over the fight and leadership of CARL. No one did, and the protest was over.

—contributed by Adell V. Newman

Not In My Back Yard (or NIMBY) protests have proliferated in the United States during the 1990s. The CARL protest described by journalist Adell V. Newman is typical of many of these protests. CARL came about as a response to the closing of an old, exhausted, and dangerous landfill that had been built and operated by the county. A private corporation would operate the new landfill with limited ties to the community in which it would operate. Similar NIMBY protests have occurred in communities throughout Illinois, Iowa, Missouri, and Wisconsin in efforts to halt the building of very large hog production facilities by agribusiness corporations such as Land O' Lakes. These facilities, often referred to as mega-hog farms, are designed to house over ten thousand hogs. Animal wastes are typically processed in large lagoons at the farm site. Landfills and mega-hog farms are opposed by local residents because of quality-of-life issues, such as smell, appearance, and the contamination of groundwater. These incidents, as well as the two more detailed accounts that follow, are all examples of *social protest.*

AN EXAMPLE OF LOCALIZED PROTEST

In May of 1983, during the last week of school, seven teachers in Campus, Illinois, were abruptly informed that in the fall they would be transferred to other schools in the district. The teachers had not been consulted beforehand, nor were they given reasons for the transfers. The reassignments posed hardships for the teachers and angered many students and parents.

Much of what followed revolved around the transfer of a very popular sixth-grade teacher, Mary Sidmore, from Washington School. Shortly after the school board's plans were announced, townspeople were surprised to see a noon-hour demonstration by Washington School students protesting Sidmore's transfer.

A concerned parent, Joan Wallace, presented a petition to the president of the Campus school board on May 27. The petition carried the signatures of more than one hundred Washington School parents, and it requested a special meeting to consider the transfer of Mary Sidmore. The petition was denied the same day that it was presented. The president agreed, however, to put the matter on the agenda of the board's regular meeting, a month later, if officially requested to do so.

Joan Wallace then called a meeting of parents to discuss the transfers. Washington parents were notified by telephone, and others by radio announcements. The meeting was well attended by Washington School parents, but few attended from other schools. At the meeting, Wallace was appointed spokesperson for the group, which decided to take the transfer issue before the June school board meeting. A number of parents also agreed to write letters to the editor of the local newspaper in an effort to widen community opposition to the transfers. Others agreed to personally contact board members and express their dissatisfaction with the reassignments. Finally, the group decided to contact parents at other district schools and try to persuade them to speak out against the transfers.

While preparing for the board meeting, Joan Wallace discovered that according to Board Policy 1069, the transfers were the responsibility of the district superintendent, not the board. The board president told Wallace that little could be accomplished at an open board meeting and suggested that she talk with the superintendent of schools behind closed doors. In the conference with the superintendent, Wallace was told that his decision to transfer teachers was based on administrative considerations and that the reasons for specific transfers were confidential. When Wallace said that this was not a satisfactory explanation, the superintendent stated calmly that Mary Sidmore and the other teachers should consider themselves lucky to still have jobs. The closed-door meeting ended on this discordant note, and it was agreed that the matter would be taken before the board.

While they prepared for the board meeting, the parents' group decided to point out that the unilateral transfer of teachers for "administrative" rather than academic reasons was inappropriate. They also decided to request that Board Policy 1069 be amended to include input from the board members, teachers, and concerned parents when transfers were being considered. Finally, they suggested an alternative plan that involved only two transfers rather than seven.

On June 20, the board of education held their monthly meeting, and more than two hundred parents attended. Shortly before the meeting, Joan Wallace learned that the transfers were not on the agenda; instead, she was scheduled to speak as a "visitor" to the meeting. Wallace was one of the first speakers. After she delivered her statement, the board referred Policy 1069 to their policy committee, which was scheduled to meet a month later. The board did not discuss the transfers or solicit questions from the audience; it simply moved on to other business. While the concerned parents looked on, the board discussed and approved a raise in administrative salaries and the renewal of a food contract. The board also discussed energy conservation measures, admission prices to athletic events, and requests for leaves of absence. Finally, near the end of the meeting, a disgruntled parent, Lawrence Tanner, spoke from the floor. He pointed out that the board was acting in an extremely arrogant manner by not even discussing the issue of teacher transfers, even though two hundred people had come to the meeting for that purpose. The meeting was then adjourned.

After the meeting, it was clear that little had changed. The board had referred one of its policies to a committee that would meet in three weeks, but it had not explained the reasons for the transfers or taken notice of the parents' alternate plan and, obviously, the transfers would be carried out in the fall. As Joan Wallace observed later, "The board's best weapon was absolute silence."

Three weeks later, the policy committee met and discussed Policy 1069. Nothing was changed. Mary Sidmore asked to appear before the board for an explanation of her transfer. Her request was denied. In the fall of 1983, four people ran for the school board with the support of many Washington School parents. Two of them were elected.

This protest was, in many ways, similar to the NIMBY protest described earlier. These protests were carried out by people who had little, if any, previous experience with protest; the protests were of short duration; and both failed to achieve their initial aims.

AN EXAMPLE OF PROTRACTED PROTEST

In the spring of 1890, representatives of the American Miners' Association, the Miners' National Association, and the National Federation of Miners and Mine Laborers held a convention. In the days that followed the three unions decided to merge, and the United Mine Workers of America was founded under the leadership of John McBride. Ironically, at about the same time, Samuel T. Brush of Carbondale, Illinois, was organizing the St. Louis and Big Muddy Coal Company, which sank its first shaft into the rich coal fields near Carterville, Illinois. At the very outset, Brush stood firm: there would be no unions at his mine. Soon, the St. Louis and Big Muddy would be the most productive underground coal mine in Illinois. A clash between Brush and the United Mine Workers was inevitable (Angle, 1975:89–116).

Sam Brush was not an outgoing man, and he was quite puritanical in his personal conduct. Though he was often described as a tactful manager who was always ready to remedy any grievance of those who worked for him, he did not pay his employees well. St. Louis and Big Muddy Coal Company miners were paid subsistence wages of about $20 a month, and most of them rented company houses for $5 a month. The miners also worked under rules specifying that they would forfeit all pay due them and be evicted from company houses if they joined a union or went on strike.

In April 1894, John McBride declared that wages in the nation's mines had "sunk below the limit of human endurance" and called a nationwide strike. At that time, the United Mine Workers had fewer than 11,000 members and only 300 members in Illinois. Still, 130,000 unorganized miners, including those at the St. Louis and Big Muddy mine, joined the strike. The mine owners held firm. The strike collapsed two months later, and miners returned to work across the nation. Those at the St. Louis and Big Muddy mine held out to the end, returning to work after fifty-six days at their previous wages (Angle, 1975:93–97).

Although the strike did little to increase the wages of miners, it brought many new members to the United Mine Workers. The St. Louis and Big Muddy miners, however, remained unorganized. In May 1897, Illinois mine operators announced new wage reductions, and another strike seemed imminent. The United Mine Workers called the strike for July 4. Workers at the St. Louis and Big Muddy mine ignored the strike call. On July 15, Sam Brush announced that he would raise wages if workers would stay on the job. Workers agreed, and they kept their promise, even though they received heavy pressure from strikers in nearby counties. That year, the St. Louis and Bug Muddy Coal Company mine produced more coal than any other mine in Illinois (Angle, 1975:95).

The strike of 1897 was a success. In October, mine operators yielded and promised wage increases, the first in nearly ten years. During January 1898, workers at the St. Louis and Big Muddy Coal Company were able to form a United Mine Workers local without Sam Brush's knowledge. In March, Illinois mine operators and the United Mine Workers announced their agreed-upon wage increases. They were substantially higher than what Brush was paying, and he refused to meet them. Eight percent of his miners struck.

For six weeks, Sam Brush ran the mine with a reduced workforce. Finally, he called the union's strike committee and delivered an ultimatum: unless they returned to work within five days, he would bring in African-American miners he had recruited in Tennessee. Preparing for trouble, Brush hired more mine guards and stockpiled arms and ammunition. He even mounted a Gatling gun near the mine entrance. The strikers held firm, and on May 20, about 150 black miners and their families arrived by train. Nearby mines soon announced wage cuts and plans to import black miners. The strike spread.

Strikers picketed and sometimes blocked roads leading to the mines. Numerous attempts were made to persuade the strikebreakers to walk out. A few defected and joined the strikers; others simply left the area. Brush continued to import African Americans for replacements rather than rehire his former workers. Many strikers spent the winter of 1898 living in tents. A new union local was established at the St. Louis and Big Muddy mine, again without the owner's knowledge.

The St. Louis and Big Muddy Coal Company continued to operate, but output was way down from the previous year. The company was near bankruptcy and receivership when Brush announced that he would pay his workers more than the Illinois union-operator scale and institute an eight-hour workday but would not recognize the union.

For nearly a year, there had been little violence in the St. Louis and Big Muddy Coal Company strike. Then, Sam Brush discovered that a new union had been organized among the nonstriking workers, and he summarily fired three of its leaders. Others in the union demanded that the three be rehired, and Brush refused. On May 15, 1899, half of the miners walked out.

On June 30, a small crowd of strikers met the train bringing in thirty more black miners to replace strikers and deserters. Quite likely, a striker fired the first shot, and guards, mine officials, and passengers immediately returned fire. Within seconds about twenty people were wounded, and one passenger was killed. Brush was also on the train; he shot at the strikers and escaped uninjured. The train pulled out of the station under fire and made it to the mine.

Later in the day, several hundred men surrounded the mine, and shooting continued through that afternoon and into the night. Toward morning, the mine guards and strikebreakers counterattacked. Strikers obtained more weapons and ammunition during the day, and it looked as if a major battle was about to occur. Shacks that had been hastily built for the blacks who had joined the strike were burned. The Williamson County sheriff managed to keep the opposing forces apart until two hundred state militia arrived in Carterville on July 2 and restored order.

The St. Louis and Big Muddy mine continued to operate through the summer, and the militia left Carterville on September 11. The next day, Sam Brush was attacked and beaten. A week later, fighting broke out between black strikebreakers and white strikers at a tavern in Carterville. The fight escalated into shooting, and five strikebreakers were killed.

The militia returned to Carterville and was kept there until trials were held for those accused of the murders of June 30 and September 15. Much in the trials focused on the conflict between mine operators and the union rather than on the guilt or innocence of the accused. The juries returned not guilty verdicts in all the trials. The last trial ended on March 4, 1900, and at its conclusion the judge admonished those in the crowded courtroom to forget the hatreds that had led to the Carterville tragedies (Angle 1975:102–12).

The judge's hopes came to pass. Sam Brush and his sons operated the St. Louis and Big Muddy Coal Company mine with nonunion blacks for another six years without major incident. Still, turnover was high, security costs were high, and output was uncertain. Finally, in 1906, the mine was sold to the Madison Coal Company, which renamed it, simply, the Madison Number 8. The Gatling gun was removed, and Madison Number 8 was worked from then on under contract with the United Mine Workers of America.

THE PROTEST CONTINUUM

In general, protest leaders are neither professional agitators nor people greatly skilled in the political process. At least this is the case at the outset. Those who have little recourse to more effective means of influencing the political process carry out protest. Protest often fails, and when it succeeds, it often does so in terms other than the initial goals. Occasionally, however, protest can result in the acquisition of considerable influence in the political process.

All of the incidents described above fall somewhere along a continuum of protest. At one end of this continuum is the highly *localized protest*, such as the landfill protest. This type of protest involves comparatively few people, receives little attention outside the communities in which it occurs, relies on tactics of petition and persuasion, and lasts only a few days or weeks. At the other end of the continuum is *protracted protest*, such as the twelve-year struggle by miners to obtain union recognition from the St. Louis and Big Muddy Coal Company. What began as a strike over specific grievances at the coal mine quickly came to embody the nationwide conflict between employers and organized labor. This type of protest is waged for very high stakes, which is perhaps why extreme hatreds and bloodshed often mar such protest. It is fairly easy to see how protest at this end of the continuum can be viewed as a component of social movements. In much of this chapter, we will focus on protest at the "modest" end of the continuum. In chapters 15 and 16, we will consider more extensive instances of protest from the perspective of social movements.

Protest as Collective Behavior

The mass hysteria, emergent-norm, and value-added theories of collective behavior describe and explain protest in much the same way. In describing protest, each emphasizes that protest is an expression of localized grievances, such as dissatisfaction with the actions of a local school board or an employer's intransigence. Small homogeneous groups trying to accomplish seemingly modest and definite aims or goals carry out protest. When protest moves beyond clearly local concerns, draws upon a more diverse constituency, and seeks broad or multiple goals, it is transformed into a social movement.

In explaining protest, the general theories view protest as a result of some sort of social unrest or social strain. These theories acknowledge that resistance by authorities can crush protest, but they emphasize that such resistance is more likely to transform protest. Resistance can draw other dissatisfied groups into the conflict, make protest more disruptive and violent, and broaden the goals of protest.

Mass Hysteria Theory

Herbert Blumer (1957:24) briefly notes that protest is a form of social unrest that is characterized by "feelings of frustration . . . over an existing mode of life and a consequent readiness to lash out in violent forms of attack on targets symbolizing that mode of life." Orrin E. Klapp (1972:206) defines protest as a more or less rational, verbalized expression of grievances, usually in terms of injustice. Protest aims at telling what is wrong and finding means to remedy a problem, and it brings the pressure of public opinion upon the existing system and its officials. If a clear and immediate remedy is lacking, protest becomes the early stage of a social movement.

For Klapp, the public perception of protest is an important determinant in its outcome. If protest takes the form of orderly petition and patient willingness to accept compromise solutions, public opinion is likely to be favorable. The more protest is recognized as legitimate, the more quickly the grievances of the protest group are set right.

Protest can be perceived as an illegitimate threat to the social system, particularly when it takes the form of disruptive demonstrations, strikes, boycotts, name-calling, and/or violence. Public opinion then pressures authorities to make no concessions and to deal severely with the protest groups. Such harsh control responses by authorities are likely to channel protest into more general social movements.

In Klapp's view, protest is an outgrowth of social strain and accompanying tensions. Consequently, other opportunities for expressing tensions serve as a safety valve that can reduce the incidence of protest. Institutionalized opportunities for tension release accompany violent sports such as boxing, wrestling, hockey, and football. Other institutionalized opportunities include holidays, national celebrations, and religious services. Klapp suggests the establishment of a national "tension monitoring agency." He also suggests building more safety-valve institutions through greater investment in leisure and religious institutions.

Emergent-Norm Theory

Turner and Killian (1972:420) make a distinction between primitive and modern protest. *Primitive* forms of protest do not actually bring about changes in the organization of society; they merely exact concessions within the existing structure. This type of protest is characterized by "Robin Hood" groups and by the localized disputes over the ownership of livestock and farm produce that characterized medieval society (Hobsbaum, 1959). These primitive forms of protest pitted one local communal group against another (Tilly, 1969).

The linkage of groups beyond the boundaries of local communities into classes, ethnic groups, age groups, and other broad constituencies characterizes *modern* protest. Unlike participants in primitive protest, participants in modern protest can generate a shared conception of changing the structure of society. Modern protest, therefore, can be transformed into general social movements.

Value-Added Theory

Protest is not one of the collective episodes identified by Smelser. Instead, he encompasses protest within hostile outbursts and norm- and value-oriented social movements. Hostile outbursts such as riots may be preceded and followed by the expression of specific community grievances. Protest is also the incipient phase of social movements.

Lack of opportunity for protest is one condition of structural conduciveness that contributes to hostile outbursts, while opportunity for protest is one condition of structural conduciveness that contributes to the development of social movements.

Often, generalized beliefs develop in the context of protest. In the case of blocked protest, generalized hostile beliefs are formed that later lead to attacks on authorities or on other groups within the community. In the case of social movements, protest experiences can lead to beliefs that much greater changes in the social order are necessary to accomplish group ends.

Some hostile outbursts grow out of confrontations between authorities and people already mobilized for protest. Mobilizing people for localized protest is often but a dress rehearsal for the massive mobilizations that are part of norm- and value-oriented social movements. The action of social control is often constrained by public opinion. Nonviolent forms of protest are likely to create favorable public opinion. Social control is then inclined to take the form of redressing grievances and other kinds of accommodation. Further, discontent is also likely to remain narrowly focused on specific grievances, a characteristic of norm-oriented social movements. Disruptive or violent protest, however, often engenders negative public opinion that in turn encourages suppression by authorities. As we will explain in chapters 15 and 16, suppression is likely to move the discontented in the direction of value-oriented social movements.

PROTEST AS COLLECTIVE ACTION

The collective action perspective takes a micro-approach to protest. Specifically, this perspective examines how demonstrations, marches, and rallies are organized, how these are controlled by their leaders and civil authorities, and how they are terminated. Clark McPhail has conducted extensive firsthand studies of demonstrations, marches, and rallies in Washington, DC, and other major eastern cities. He has also made an extensive review of published studies that focused on individual participation in civil rights, student, antiwar, and antinuclear protests as well as religious rallies. (We will discuss McPhail's work in the context of social movements in chapter 15.)

Findings about demonstrations, marches, and rallies can be generalized to other forms of protest, such as petition campaigns, boycotts, strikes, and even violent confrontations. To date, however, few attempts have been made to do so.

The Origins of Protest

Anger and indignation do not automatically translate into social protest. People often become upset by the actions (or inaction) of public officials and government agencies, businesses, and employers. They may complain to their families, friends, neighbors, and/or work associates, and some may write sharply worded letters to their local newspaper, congressional representative, or Better Business Bureau. Although people often talk of confronting employers, government agencies, and other authorities, collective protests such as petition campaigns, demonstrations, marches, picket lines, strikes, and boycotts seldom materialize.

William Gamson, Bruce Fireman, and Stephen Rytina (1982) devised an experiment wherein thirty-three groups confronted a situation in which collective protest was an appropriate response. (Details of the experiment are presented in chapter 3.) Although all 33 groups took issue with the conditions facing them, only 16 groups succeeded in drawing together and offering unanimous collective resistance. Gamson's study provides important insights into the origins of social protest.

Confrontations with Unjust Authority

In Gamson's experiment, people volunteered for what was described as a survey of community values being conducted by an organization called Manufacturers' Human Relations Consultants (MHRC). At the beginning of the experiment, subjects were paid $10 by the MHRC representative and asked to sign a participation agreement in which they were informed that their responses would be videotaped for later use in a trial. They were then asked to give their opinions about unmarried couples living together. In none of the groups were strong objections to unmarried cohabitation expressed. Then the MHRC representative asked members of the group to act as if they were "very offended" by cohabitation. The MHRC representative was asking people to commit perjury! At the conclusion of what was usually a stormy and abrasive encounter, the MHRC representative attempted to get group members to sign affidavits stating that they were aware that the videotapes would be used in court.

All thirty-three groups started the experiment in a *compliant* manner. That is, the participants attempted to carry out the requests of the MHRC representative to the best of their abilities and in a cheerful and enthusiastic manner. In all the groups, the tone of the interaction changed substantially as soon as the subjects were instructed to act as if they were offended by cohabitation.

An early and common response was *evasion*. Participants did not confront the MHRC representative directly but instead failed to perform in the correct or desired manner. Participants acted as if they were offended but used very sarcastic tones, talked with obviously fake accents, or talked in the third person. Others claimed that they were "poor actors" and remained silent when it was their turn to speak. Evasion did not constitute a combined effort to resist the unjust request of the authority. These individuals, however, clearly sabotaged the intent of the authority because their affected testimony would be useless in court.

Another common response was to *challenge the context* of the encounter. Participants questioned the representative's conduct and attempted to renegotiate the conditions of compliance. Participants often asked the representative to explain why they were being asked to act offended. They asked questions about the MHRC and its relationship to the defendant in the trial, a large oil company. Some participants asked if they would get to view the tapes later or be able to state on camera that they were not giving their true opinions.

Challenging the context usually merged into *dissent*. Participants loudly rejected the representative's justifications and criticized the MHRC. A few participants stated that the representative was asking them to commit perjury, and some compared the encounter to Watergate. In general, dissent represented a clear shift in the direction of the encounter.

All but four of the groups reached the stage of open and loud dissent. In many respects, however, dissent is but a simple outcry against the directives of authority. When they were presented with the final affidavits, dissent subsided in thirteen groups. In four of these groups, a majority signed the affidavits, and in nine groups, a minority signed. To successfully challenge authority, groups had to turn the unorganized babble of dissent into collective protest.

Gamson and his colleagues observed three types of protest in this experiment, the most elementary of which was collective *resistance*. Resistance involves not the concealed intent of evasion but the open and stated refusal to perform as authorities command. In the MHRC encounter, resistance took the form of a group's unanimous refusal to sign the final affidavits. Sixteen of the groups passed the threshold of boisterous dissent and openly and unanimously refused to sign the affidavits.

A more developed form of resistance to authority is *preparation for future action*, in which participants attempt to do more than openly disobey authority; they make plans to act against the authority. Nine of the sixteen groups exchanged names and phone numbers and agreed to meet after the MHRC session. When asked later, they stated that their intent was to collectively contact the Better Business Bureau, judges, lawyers, and newspapers to "blow the whistle" on the MHRC.

For five of these groups, refusal to sign the affidavits and plans for future action did not seem sufficient, so they took *direct action*. Direct action involves attempts to immediately sabotage and destroy the authority system. In these five groups, members seized the original participation agreements and the final affidavits, and members of one group threatened to seize the video equipment as well!

From the results of their experiment, Gamson and his colleagues have developed an explanation of how groups are able to successfully draw together and launch protest against authority. The protest may well fail to better the plight of the group, but at least it has been launched.

What Types of People Protest?

Many sociologists explain collective behavior phenomena in terms of types of people and the attitudes they carry with them. Gamson and his colleagues, however, found little relationship between people's successful protest in the MHRC encounter and their attitudes toward government, big business, or protest in general. But they did find some differences in terms of the previous experiences of people within the groups. A number of people had previous organizational experience as officers in voluntary associations. Many of the participants were college educated, and some stated that they had taken part in political demonstrations and strikes. Individuals with these previous experiences were not evenly distributed throughout the groups. Eleven groups had deficits in one or more of these areas. Four of these groups failed to voice dissent, and none of them successfully managed to mount protest, while about half of the groups with full assets collectively failed to resist the MHRC representative.

Groups composed of people who have had few previous experiences that contribute to the organization of protest seem to have great difficulty in translating dissent into collective resistance. On the other hand, having access to these resources is certainly no guarantee that protests will materialize. The necessary ingredients for group protest seem to be kinds of acts that severely challenge authority, free the group from fears of "making a scene," and increase the group's capacity to act as a unit.

Types of Protest Activities

At the beginning of their encounter with the MHRC, participants had no reason to suspect that the MHRC was something other than what it appeared to be. They thought that the MHRC was a legitimate business enterprise that was following standard professional procedures and paid above-average compensation. As the encounter unfolded, however, it became apparent to many that their initial impressions were in error. As Gamson and his colleagues described it, it became apparent that the MHRC was working on behalf of its oil company client to suborn perjury. It was collecting material that could distort the true nature of community standards in a trial.

Reframing In the descriptions of encounters provided by Gamson and his colleagues (1982), it appears that in nearly all of the groups the participants sensed that something was wrong as soon as the MHRC representative asked them to act offended. Almost immediately, people began to act evasively and to question the representative about his instructions. What did not happen immediately in some groups, and what failed to occur at all in others, was a clear verbalization of just what was wrong with the representative's request. Gamson and his colleagues refer to such verbalizations as *reframing*.

Reframing involves *attention calling*—words and deeds that clearly point out what the authority is doing or about to do in the encounter. Attention calling keeps the authority's actions from passing unnoticed. In many of the groups, people called attention to the fact that the MHRC representative was asking people

July 4, 1776
The Unanimous Declaration of the
Thirteen United States of America

In 1776, it was not at all clear to the newly formed Congress of the United States that the anger and indignation felt by many colonists would actually lead them to take action against King George III, his troops, and the British colonial administration. The time was at hand to articulate colonial grievances and to propose a plan of action. The Declaration of Independence was penned over a period of about two weeks and underwent several drafts and corrections before the final draft was approved and signed. This document enumerated recent and abrasive actions of the Crown and denounced them as violations of fundamental human rights. Declaring our national independence was cast as the only just and reasonable redress of these grievances.

Gamson, Fireman, and Rytina's (1982) study of protest shows that in order for protest to occur, reframing acts must focus attention on the conduct of authorities, thereby removing the acts of authorities from the taken for granted part of social life. Further, the acts of authorities must be cast as a violation of the shared moral principles of those who protest. The Declaration identified dozens of repeated *injuries* and *usurpations* carried out by the King. These offenses ranged from very general complaints of harming the economic interests of his subjects to specific charges such as the convening of legislative bodies at unusual, uncomfortable, and distant locations with the intent of fatiguing colonists into compliance with his measures. King George was also charged with using mock trials to protect the British and mercenary troops from punishment for the murder of colonists. The King was charged with disbanding Colonial legislatures, declaring their laws invalid, and intimidating judges. The Declaration notes that the King had harmed domestic tranquility by causing insurrections among the colonists and inciting Indian attacks along the frontiers. These are but a few of the charges detailed in the Declaration. In fact, about half of the Declaration's text is devoted to enumerating charges against the Crown.

The Declaration notes that the many enumerated offenses of the King clearly depart from the taken-for-granted, self-evident part of social life, namely, life, liberty, and the pursuit of happiness. These acts are labeled as a violation of the shared moral principles of those who protest—acts of absolute despotism and tyranny that rendered the King unfit to rule.

Participants in protest must also engage in divesting acts that declare them free from further obligations to obey authority. This type of contract voiding is found in prominent phrases of the Declaration that proclaim that the United Colonies are rightfully free and independent states, and that all allegiances and political connections to the British Crown are totally dissolved.

Finally, those opposing authority must build unity within the group. The Declaration is identified as *The Unanimous Declaration of the Thirteen United States of America*. All through the document the parties are referred to as the United States; the term "we" is used throughout in referring to the declarers. The final sentence of the Declaration of Independence is a pledge of unity: *And for the support of this Declaration, with a firm reliance on the protection of divine Providence, we mutually pledge to each other our Lives, our Fortunes and our sacred Honor.*

not to express their true feelings. Some drew attention to this when they expressed concern that these instructions were not on the videotape. Others drew attention to the representative's request by claiming that they were not good actors or by deliberately overacting. Participants made this seem like a great departure from their initial understanding of what they were to do in the encounter.

Reframing also involves *altering context* through acts that apply the injustice frame to what is happening. In the MHRC encounter, people pointed out that the representative was asking them to distort community standards. Others made reference to Watergate, and in a few encounters, participants forcefully informed the group that they were being asked to commit perjury. Reframing acts, which break down an encounter's sense of legitimacy and replace it with a sense of injustice, usually occurred within the context-altering and dissent phases of confronting authority. Groups in which reframing acts occurred early were much more likely to translate reframing into successful protests than groups in which reframing occurred later or not at all.

Divesting Acts Another important class of activities, *divesting acts*, typically follows or occurs with reframing acts. Divesting acts are "declarations of independence" that sever people's obligation to authority. Groups in which such acts occurred early were more likely to launch unanimous protest than those in which these acts occurred later or not at all. In the MHRC encounter, divesting took the form of *contract voiding*. Participants challenged the representative by noting that his requests violated the terms of the participation agreement. In some groups, these claims were reinforced by offers to return the MHRC money and by threats to walk out.

Divesting acts also *negate fear of making a scene*. In many groups, one or more participants suggested "going along" with the MHRC and then forgetting the whole thing. These suggestions were quickly countered in some groups by reminders that the MHRC requests were unethical if not illegal. In several instances, a general spirit of rowdiness that developed in a group reduced fears of making a scene.

Working Together In addition to reframing and divesting acts, most of the sixteen successful groups showed an early and clear internal rapport that allowed them to work together nearly as a team. This rapport consisted of *loyalty building* and internal *conflict managing*.

An act that contributes to loyalty building is *consensus calling*. Participants can say things that make the group aware of its shared outlook. Because the issues were so blatant in the MHRC encounter, the discovery that everyone agreed did not provide a great boost to group solidarity. Nonetheless, in most of the unsuccessful groups, the possibility of collective resistance was not even discussed. People seemed to decide individually whether to obey or disobey the representative. In successful groups, the issue of collective disobedience was often raised early and discussed openly.

Another contributing factor to group loyalty is *protest humor*. In the MHRC encounter, humor, sarcasm, and irony were a means by which the group created its own solidarity in opposing the representative. In addition, humor also served a divesting function by contributing to the rowdy atmosphere of some groups. Once a wide-open atmosphere was established, there was little decorum left to lose in scenes created by open defiance of the representative.

Shared collective orientations toward protest were created most openly and directly by people *speaking for the group*. In the MHRC encounter, a number of people adopted the role of spokesperson. Often these people were the most straight-forward with their comments to the representative. The spokespersons took the initiative in using the words *we*, *our*, and *us* when talking to the representative; they were also the initiators of many reframing and divesting acts. Successful groups often had more than one spokesperson. Without a spokesperson, few groups succeeded in unanimously opposing the representative.

Managing Conflict In many of the groups, some people openly disagreed about how to interpret the representative's actions and explanations. In other groups, people advocated compliance with the representative. In most of the successful groups, disagreements were resolved early and compliance suggestions were countered right after they occurred. These groups contained unofficial diplomats who not only recognized and quelled disagreements quickly but also strengthened group solidarity in the process. Groups that failed to unanimously oppose the representative also failed to recognize and resolve disagreements in the early stages of the encounter.

Discussion

Anger and indignation do not automatically lead to protest. Gamson, Fireman, and Rytina's study of protest under controlled conditions shows that a number of acts must occur together in order for protest to occur. Anger and indignation, if they are necessary for protest at all, must occur in the form of evasion, challenges to the context of authority, and open criticism and disapproval of authority. Even these are not guarantees that sustained protest in the form of resistance, preparation for future action, or direct action will develop.

Participants in protest must engage in reframing acts that focus attention on the conduct of authorities, removing the acts of authorities from the part of social life that is taken for granted. Reframing also includes identifying the acts of authorities as a violation of the shared moral principles of the participants.

Participants in protest must also engage in divesting acts that in one way or another declare them free from further obligations to obey authority. Divesting acts also free participants from the fear of bringing their discontent into the open and creating a public scene. Finally, participants in protest must build loyalty to their group. All of these components identified in the study of response to unjust authority can be found in the Declaration of Independence of the United States of America.

PROTEST AS A POLITICAL RESOURCE

Gamson's study of unjust authority shows that reframing, divesting, and unifying acts are needed to transform anger and indignation into protest. Once people initiate protest, however, they must pursue effective tactics of contention in order to make gains. Gamson's (1975) historical analysis of protest in the United States, from the early 1800s to 1945, sought to reveal the group characteristics and protest tactics that lead to success. The sampling techniques used in this study are discussed in chapter 3. Gamson selected a sample of sixty-four challenging groups that ranged in size from several hundred to more than a million members. Some of these groups were organized along bureaucratic lines and gave formal status and duties to their members. This sample was drawn from the history books and would not include small groups such as the parents who protested local teacher transfers, or the CARL group that opposed the regional landfill. Challenging groups used a wide range of tactics to accomplish their aims, ranging from petition and the formation of new political parties to the tactics of disruption and violence. Some challenging groups initiated violence, attacking authorities or other groups, while others resorted to violence only when attacked by authorities. Some challenging groups were the passive recipients of violence, and a number of challenging groups managed to avoid violent confrontations altogether.

Challenging groups made gains by winning acceptance and representative status in the political arena. Some challengers were asked to appear before governing bodies as legitimate representatives of a constituency. Others entered formal negotiations with government or employers. Sometimes governing bodies and businesses formally recognized in writing that these challengers were legitimate representatives. Finally, challengers were sometimes offered formal membership and positions of status in the organizational structure of government or business. Other challengers obtained new advantages for the group and its constituency. Some challenging groups sought the passage of legislative packages. Some of these, such as income maintenance plans, would have benefited people other than members of the challenging group, while other packages would have benefited only the challenging group. Some groups sought concessions from business, such as hiring agreements, wages, and prices paid for farm products. Some groups were granted acceptance but were unable to convert their newfound roles into tangible gains for the constituency. Other groups simply did not seek acceptance themselves but were able to get significant parts of their goals enacted. Finally, most challenging groups failed totally. Only about a quarter of the groups in the sample made clear gains.

Gamson found that bureaucratically organized groups with centralized authority were more likely than other groups to succeed in terms of acceptance and winning new advantages. These challenging groups were the least hindered by factionalism. Nonbureaucratic and decentralized groups seldom succeeded in gaining acceptance or new advantages. Gamson also found that large group size helped to obtain acceptance, although group size had little relationship to gaining new advantages. Small groups were as likely to achieve new advantages as were larger groups. The most successful challengers were *selective incentive* groups that offered some tangible benefit for contributions or imposed an effective dues structure on members. These groups also tended to be bureaucratically structured and have centralized authority. *Solidaristic* groups had minimal criteria for membership, allowed nearly anyone to join, and depended on voluntary contributions from members. Solidaristic groups thus tended to be rich in membership but poor in financial resources and also seldom successful. *Privileged* groups obtained most or all of their financial support from philanthropists, often also utilizing other resources of the philanthropist such as newspapers, housing, or land. Privileged groups were only slightly more likely to achieve success than solidaristic groups.

Some groups focused their efforts on a single goal, while others sought several goals simultaneously. Surprisingly, Gamson found little difference in success for groups that pursued a single goal and those that pursued several. A goal of some challenging groups was to displace or replace public officials, government agencies, and employers. Although none of the challenging groups had displacement as their only goal, those that included displacement seldom succeeded in obtaining acceptance or new advantages.

Most challenging groups attempted to make use of the peaceful tactics of persuasion and petition, and some groups relied on these tactics exclusively. Some groups responded passively when arrested or attacked. Challenging groups that used the peaceful tactics of persuasion and petition had few successes, and groups that responded passively when violence was used against them had the fewest successes. Groups that used disruptive tactics such as name calling, marches, demonstrations, and boycotts achieved greater successes, and those that used violence were the most likely to succeed. Perhaps because they understood what authorities had in store for them, some challengers initiated violence. Other groups used disruptive tactics and responded with violence when arrested or when otherwise provoked by authorities or employers. Not all these combative groups gained acceptance or new advantages, but most did. In particular, the groups that were well organized, had clear authority structures, and had strong member discipline were the most likely to succeed.

For many, the above findings may seem counterintuitive and disturbing. In this regard, Gamson's study covers the years 1800–1945, and his findings may not be wholly applicable to the protest that has occurred since the passage of the National Labor Relations Act of 1935. The National Labor Relations Act (Wagner Act) guaranteed workers the right to organize and bargain collectively. Prior to its passage, virtually all picketing, boycotting, and strikes could be stopped by injunctions enforced by police action. There was a significant decrease in labor violence after the National Labor Relations Act was passed (McPhail, McCarthy, and Schweingruber, 1998). Since 1945, Gamson notes, there have been profound changes in American society that have created a radically different environment for challengers. These changes include an alteration in policing strategies used in responding to protest. Another important change is a much greater intrusion of the media, particularly television, into the arena of protest (Gamson, 1990, pp. 145–179).

In this chapter we have characterized protest as a localized event that is focused on concerns of the immediate community. Protest leaders are seldom professional agitators or people greatly skilled in the political process. Protest is carried out by groups who have little recourse to other, potentially more effective means of influencing the political process. The typical life span of a protest group may be measured in months, from the first enthusiastic organizational meeting to the time when a meeting is called and no one comes.

In large measure, this view is derived from Michael Lipsky's description of protest. Lipsky (1968:1144) defines protest as "activity by relatively powerless groups, directed against a target group, characterized by showmanship, and calculated to bring third parties into the arena of conflict in a manner beneficial to the protest group." The character and outcome of protest is determined by interaction among relatively powerless (protest) groups, target groups, and third parties.

Relatively Powerless Groups

Membership in a relatively powerless, or protest, group is usually small and drawn from a narrow, or localized, constituency—parents in a school district, members of a neighborhood, students of a university, or employees of a business enterprise. Seldom is membership in a protest group national or even statewide in scope, and only occasionally is a sizable majority of the potential constituency active in the group. Given that protest groups are typically formed from very narrow and small constituencies, few members of the group have had any previous experience with protest.

Money The financial resources of a protest group are usually very limited. Some constituencies can use personal savings or take out loans to support their protest efforts; but other constituencies, such as unemployed workers, may be financially destitute. This means that protest groups are limited in terms of their ability to afford mailings, telephone calls, and reimbursements for travel, meals, and hotel bills. Often, they cannot afford offices. Thus many protests are organized out of basements, garages, and living rooms. Finally, protest groups often cannot pay for legal assistance and technical advice.

Since the 1980s, there has been a trend toward formalization of protest groups (McCarthy and McPhail, 1998). Protest groups that register with the state as nonprofit organizations may enjoy substantial reductions in postage for bulk mailings, for example. Those who provide financial support to registered groups may also receive tax benefits for doing so. Still, smaller groups such as the Washington School parents may find such formalization impractical or of little immediate benefit. These groups are confronting issues that will be resolved or moot before they can obtain nonprofit status or derive benefits from this status. Further, the benefits of nonprofit status are more likely to accrue to larger groups that are organized to carry out action over extended periods of time. Small nonprofit organizations may seldom have enough mail volume to qualify for bulk rates.

Access to Power Brokers Protest groups have limited access to such power brokers as mayors, members of Congress, corporate leaders, university presidents, and heads of federal and state agencies, although occupants of these positions play important third-party roles in the resolution of protest. Power brokers often have had no prior dealings with protest leaders or their constituencies, and protest leaders are rarely at liberty to casually call or obtain appointments with power brokers. Members of protest groups seldom have informal relationships with power brokers.

Access to Media Protest groups typically have difficulty in getting media coverage for their side of the story. Reporters may have little interest in getting the background of a protest; instead they are at hand during the crisis phase of protest, when leaders are the busiest. The leader must often meet with the press with little preparation, and in order to maintain the interest of the press, leaders may need to make more radical statements than they would like.

The Internet and World Wide Web offer protest groups a medium through which they can publicize their side of the story. Today, hundreds of small activist groups do just that through numerous political Usenet groups, websites, and America On Line (AOL) chat rooms. Right-wing extremist web pages are more high-profile and sophisticated than those developed by local groups (Hill and Hughes, 1998).

Public Forum Law During the 1960s, protesters were routinely denied access to areas such as parks, streets, and sidewalks for rallies and marches. Police frequently halted demonstrations and speeches because of offensive content. Such practices greatly limited relatively powerless groups and often contributed to violent confrontations (McCarthy and McPhail, 1998: 83–85). However, the legal doctrine that defines the rights of protesters and how protest is regulated by authorities has continued to evolve since the 1960s. In general, there has been a trend toward greater protection of First Amendment rights of free public assem-

Protest is characterized by showmanship. University professors do not usually think of themselves as members of a relatively powerless group. When faced with declining enrollments, shrinking budgets, and threats of layoffs in the 1980s, faculty found they had very little influence with university administrators and governing boards. On some campuses, faculty groups turned to protest in an effort to press their concerns. Many of these groups soon affiliated with national organizations such as the American Federation of Teachers and the National Education Association. (Photo by Grant Bogue).

bly and free speech. That is, Public Forum Law provides protesters with broader access to public spaces today than it did when Lipsky discussed relatively powerless groups in the 1960s.

When carrying out protest activities, protestors now have greater access to *traditional public forum* areas such as streets, parks, sidewalks and those other spaces that traditionally have come to be used for expressive activity. First Amendment activities in these areas can be limited only by reasonable and narrowly drawn time, place, and manner restrictions. Street marches and other special events between the hours of 7:00 and 9:30 A.M. and 4:00 to 6:30 P.M. may be restricted if these events will substantially interfere with rush-hour traffic. Demonstrations in the White House area are restricted. Restrictions are placed on such things as the size and structure of speaker's platforms, volume of sound equipment, and size and construction of picket signs. These restrictions are independent of the content of protesters' messages (McCarthy and McPhail, 1998:87).

In general, *private property* is not considered to be a public protest forum. This has become an issue in cases such as the Hare Krishnas' efforts to recruit members and carry out acts of worship at airports, fairgrounds, malls and sports arenas, and pro-life demonstrations that deny access to abortion clinics. U.S. court decisions in the 1980s made some clarifications. *Limited Public Forums* consist of government property that has been opened specifically for the purpose of expressive activity. They include places such as airports, university meeting spaces, municipal theaters, and state fairgrounds. Reasonable restriction on assembly and speech are acceptable as long as they are not an effort to suppress views opposed by officials. Greater restrictions on protest assembly and speech have been placed on "new public spaces" such as shopping malls and sports arenas that are viewed as "limited public spaces." Even though sidewalks in front of abortion clinics are in the public forum, buffer zones of about 36 feet for demonstrations outside the entrance of abortion clinics were established by U.S. court decisions in 1994 (McCarthy and McPhail, 1998:88).

Since the 1960s when Lipsky outlined the dynamics of protest, a greater public commitment by authorities to First Amendment rights has arisen. This includes the commitment to the rights of citizen protest; commitment to content neutrality of speech; reasonable and narrowly drawn time, place, and manner restrictions; and advance permit requirements.

Litigation Relatively powerless groups can use legal leveraging to obtain recognition and to gain a place on the public agenda. Legal tactics can prove useful in forcing attention to the protest group's demands and to obtain settlements and policy concessions from state officials or other powerful groups (McCann, 1998:208–9). CARL sought injunctions to halt the proposed regional landfill. Residents of farm communities in Iowa sought to have Iowa, Minnesota, and other states participate in a moratorium on constructing factory-style hog production facilities. They sought a moratorium to cover all facilities that have permits but haven't been built.

McCann (1998:203–5) notes that litigation is critical during the earliest phases of organization and agenda formation. University faculty, for instance, analyzed their salary structure and concluded that they had grounds for a class action lawsuit because the salary structure appeared capricious and clearly discriminated against female faculty. A faculty group sought legal counsel before taking their case to the university administration and the faculty union. The administration and union made salary equity adjustments a feature of all contracts thereafter. American Indian groups have utilized judicial activism in the 1990s (Meranto, 1998).

By definition, relatively powerless groups are unable to directly retain legal resources that match those provided by the legal departments of major corporations and many other target groups. Some law firms that specialize in civil rights and property law may do *pro bono* work for relatively powerless groups. Some of these groups may have funds available to consult lawyers on a limited basis.

Target Groups

Protest activity is directed toward target groups. According to Lipsky (1968), the identifying characteristic of a target group is that it has the capacity to grant most or all of the protest group's demands. Target groups include numerous federal and state agencies, city governments, police departments, utility companies, school boards, local welfare offices, and university administrations. Lipsky argues that target groups usually are in a position to grant substantial concessions to protest groups, but he notes that target groups frequently claim to lack the authority or resources to meet protest groups' demands. This claim is one of several tactics calculated to thwart protest; if compelled to do so by third parties, target groups can usually grant substantial concessions to protest groups.

Access to Power Brokers In comparison with protest groups, target groups are likely to have far greater access to power brokers. Target groups often have institutionalized ties to power brokers. For instance, university presidents have institutionalized access to the business and civic leaders on the university's board of governors, while utility companies have institutionalized relationships with state legislatures and numerous large businesses. Target groups are also likely to enjoy less formal contacts with power brokers, including associations through business, community service organizations, country clubs, and churches. Target groups are, therefore, better able than protest groups to communicate their side of the dispute to powerful third parties.

Access to Media Target groups often enjoy institutionalized access to the media. These groups may have a communications staff and may hold regularly scheduled press conferences. Even at impromptu conferences, the communications staff can present well-designed and edited statements to reporters. Consequently, target groups usually have considerable opportunity and likelihood of getting their side of the story (spin) to the press. Target groups may also maintain informational websites and e-mail services that can provide current information.

Third Parties

Lipsky defines third parties as groups that can greatly influence the decisions of target groups with respect to protest. In protest, the main power linkage is between target groups and third parties, and a list of third parties would be nearly identical to a list of target groups. In practice, the difference between third parties and target groups is determined by the context of the conflict. For example, a school board might be a target group in one conflict and a third party in another.

Although target groups can essentially ignore protest groups, they cannot ignore the requests of third parties; often, this is because the third party stands in institutionalized relationship to the target group. If a city council is besieged by protest, the police department may function as a third party.

THE DYNAMICS OF PROTEST

For Lipsky, protest is the political resource of the powerless. Protest groups are severely limited in their capacity to bargain with or coerce target groups, which means that protest groups have no tangible resources to exchange for concessions from target groups. They cannot promise substantial numbers of votes or contributions, nor can they carry out successful strikes or boycotts.

The only immediate alternative open to protest groups is what Turner and Killian (1972:293) call persuasion—the use of symbolic manipulation without substantial rewards or punishments. Some types of persuasive protest tactics are designed to appeal to the good nature of target groups and third parties. These include the presentation of petitions, peaceful and orderly presence at meetings, and requests to third parties for assistance.

Other protest tactics, such as picketing, sit-ins, and the disruption of meetings, are designed to harass or embarrass a target group. These tactics usually call protest to the attention of third parties and the general public. It is the publicity and notoriety brought about by these tactics, and not the tactics themselves, that are most distressing to a target group.

By identifying protest as an activity of relativity powerless groups, Lipsky poses a fundamental distinction. Protest cannot be identified simply by actions such as picketing, sit-ins, or disrupting of public meetings; only when relatively powerless groups carry out these activities does protest occur. These tactics are the most important and perhaps the only way in which protest groups can influence target groups and third parties.

However, when the United Auto Workers picket an assembly plant, it is to maintain morale and discipline among the strikers. It is the activities at the bargaining table that are the most important influence on management. Behind the United Auto Workers' bargaining team stand thousands of dues-paying members, a staff of lawyers, testimony of economists, and a political organization. Picketing has little influence at the bargaining table. This is *power politics*.

In Lipsky's (1968) model of protest, the main power linkage is between the target group and third parties, and as we noted above, these two groups usually share both institutionalized and casual relationships with one another. In order for protest to succeed, protest groups must get third parties to urge concessions by target groups through these channels (see figure 14.1).

Third parties might urge target groups to make concessions for a number of reasons. Perhaps the most obvious reason is genuine sympathy for the protest group. Protest by handicapped or elderly groups is likely to generate considerable community support, for example. Third parties may also urge concessions in order to create difficulties for a target group. For instance, protest groups may be

FIGURE 14.1   *The Dynamics of Protest*

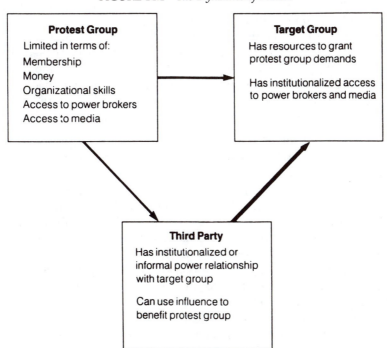

demanding the release of information concerning health hazards in a particular factory. Competitors may use their influence to obtain this information, knowing that it may prove damaging and will be difficult and costly to provide. Finally, third parties may urge concessions to gain material advantages for themselves. Builders' associations and labor councils urge city governments to undertake the remodeling of public housing in anticipation of contracts and jobs, for instance.

Why Protest Fails

As the political resource of the powerless, protest is not particularly valuable, because it often fails. According to Lipsky, protest seldom succeeds because many external constraints operate against those who attempt to lead protest. Further, target groups have an impressive arsenal of tactics to use against protest leaders and groups.

External Constraints on Leaders Those who organize and lead protest confront a number of external constraints that operate against the successful outcome of protest. The demands of family life and work limit the time leaders can devote to organizing protest, yet protest leaders must take the time to become familiar with the grievances of their followers. The meager resources of the constituency usually place severe limits on available protest tactics. Much of a leader's time and energy is spent in finding volunteers to perform essential tasks. Finally, protest leaders seldom have reliable access to the media. These constraints merit further discussion.

Strain of Competing Commitments Competing commitments posed by family and jobs are perhaps the most immediate constraint upon protest leaders. These commitments limit the time that leaders can devote to protest. Full-time jobs typically leave only nights and weekends free to organize protest, and part of this time is absorbed by commitments to family. Consequently, protest leaders seldom can devote full time to their protest efforts.

Indeed, much of the time used by protest must be "appropriated" from time usually devoted to family and job. Leaders shirk their share of household chores, miss family meals, and attend meetings that last into the early morning hours. Weekends are taken up by travel and more meetings, with little time left for family activities. At work, protest leaders may arrive late and leave early. It is not surprising that leading protest can precipitate problems at home and at work.

Familiarity with Constituency In the early 1960s, the Students for a Democratic Society (SDS) failed to organize protest among the urban poor near their campuses. The SDS was unsuccessful in part because, as affluent, upper-middle-class students, they did not correctly perceive the needs of those they were trying to help. The poor were interested in immediate problems, such as food, rent, and medical care, while the SDS was interested in more abstract objectives, such as building a nationwide political alliance between students and workers.

The poor were also familiar with the unpleasant outcomes of confrontations with authority, such as arrest, police harassment, and losing jobs and welfare benefits. The poor feared that they and not the students would bear the brunt of the consequences if protest led to trouble.

Not just anyone can lead and sustain protest. A leader must develop a clear understanding of the likes, dislikes, talents, and weaknesses of the constituency in order to plan protest strategy. Successful leaders have considerable firsthand experience with the problem they are protesting and may have a personal stake in the outcome. Thus, those who lead protest against racial discrimination have themselves experienced discrimination, and those whose neighborhoods have been contaminated by toxic wastes lead protests demanding cleanups and/or financial restitution.

Lack of Resources The lower the socioeconomic status (SES) of the constituency, the fewer resources there are available for travel, postage, telephones, and office space. Low-SES groups are also more subject than others to reprisals for protest activity. They have less job security and may be vulnerable to the loss of welfare benefits. Some constituencies may be hampered by the inability to speak English.

From the standpoint of leadership, the higher the socioeconomic status of the constituency, the greater the options for protest tactics. Having money to charter buses, trains and even airplanes gives leaders access to an increased number of demonstration sites. Middle- and upper-income groups have greater job security than low-income groups as well as more opportunities to take time off from work. These groups also have greater access to good typewriters, duplicating equipment, and sophisticated computers.

In general, the higher the SES of the constituency, the greater the resources available and the lower the vulnerability to reprisals. On the other hand, the higher the SES of the constituency, the lower the likelihood that they will need to resort to protest in order to make their needs and interests felt and heard.

Lack of Volunteers Protest leaders are dependent on the availability and goodwill of many volunteers. Volunteers provide secretarial services, canvass neighborhoods to distribute leaflets, solicit donations, and seek potential members. Leaders may also have to depend on others to volunteer the use of trucks, vans, automobiles, office space, and equipment.

Volunteers, however, are often unavailable when they are needed, and much of a protest leader's efforts are devoted to rounding up sufficient numbers of volunteers to carry out essential tasks. Protest leaders usually find it difficult to maintain a full-time, volunteer office staff. It is also difficult to carry out tasks requiring more or less continuous effort with volunteers, such as putting out newsletters on a fixed schedule.

Relatively powerless groups may have sufficient money available to hire full-time personnel. Doing so, however, may entail devoting additional resources to bookkeeping for tax withholding purposes and for following numerous employment practice requirements, and other laws (McCarthy and McPhail, 1998:100). If leaders are unfamiliar with these requirements, valuable organization time and energy may be directed away from protest actions.

Limited Access to Media As noted above, protest groups do not have institutionalized access to the media. Seldom can protest leaders devote full attention to the media, including the Internet, and they often use bizarre protest tactics to obtain attention. At times, protest leaders must make extreme statements, outlandish promises, and threats to the target group in order to maintain media coverage. In turn, this type of activity is often described in negative terms by the media (Blanchard, 1968).

Lack of Time Time also works against the protest effort. Groups may not have time to apply for nonprofit status. Often, protest fails to halt such target group projects as building hazardous waste dumps or reorganizing school districts. As these projects move to completion, protest is likely to be considered moot. Last minute agenda changes in meetings with target groups and third parties can work to the disadvantage of protest groups. Protest can become old news within weeks, and media coverage becomes increasingly tenuous. Further, as protest drags on, it is difficult to maintain the commitment and efforts of volunteers.

Target Group Tactics

Target groups are usually in a position to anticipate protest. This is particularly true when target groups attempt to construct nuclear power plants, dams, airports, highways, hazardous waste damps, or prisons. If protest is anticipated, the early work on these projects is likely to be done in secret. Land purchases, for example, are made as inconspicuously as possible. Only when the project is well underway do target groups go public and file for building permits and zoning changes or seek bond referendums.

Target groups may also seek to activate community support before protest develops. This includes making speeches to chambers of commerce and building trade councils that emphasize the sales revenues and jobs the project will generate. Finally, target groups may attempt to co-opt those in the community who might be likely to initiate protest.

If protest does develop, target groups have a number of effective tactics to use against protest. In general, these tactics are calculated to give the appearance of change and concern, while simply wasting time.

Granting Symbolic Satisfactions Target groups may grant symbolic satisfactions to protest groups in an effort to create an image of change and concern in the eyes of third parties. Such gestures include naming dams or airports after the heroes of protest groups. Pledges to carefully manage and monitor toxic waste dumps or to plant trees to improve the appearances of prisons may calm protest. Sometimes a target group may create its own commission to study the protest group's grievances. These symbolic satisfactions are granted using generous and tactful rhetoric, with full media coverage.

Claims of Constraint A target group may also claim that it lacks the money to meet the protest group's demands. This is a particularly persuasive tactic when budgets are notoriously tight. It is quite likely, however, that the target group's estimate of what it would cost to meet the demands is greatly exaggerated. Lipsky notes that if they are sufficiently pressed to do so, target groups can meet demands by restructuring their budget.

A target group may also claim that it lacks the authority to grant the protest group's demands. This is a particularly effective tactic if the protest group can be persuaded to take its grievances elsewhere. It is in the protest group's interest, however, to keep its efforts focused at the local level. When a group attempts to take its protest to the state legislature, for example, its effort will probably have much less impact than at the local level. This is because state legislative bodies routinely hear protest from all corners. A small protest group is likely to be ignored in the clamor for attention of the legislature. Also, it will be difficult for a protest group to carry on a lengthy protest if its members must commute great distances.

Response to the Worst A target group can disrupt protest by responding to the worst or most visible instance of the problem faced by the protest group. For example, if a group is protesting the poor condition of public housing, the housing agency might repair a few severely deteriorated apartments, using funds from the budget for routine maintenance. Of course, these projects would be given as much publicity as possible. Although a few apartments might be repaired, the overall condition of public housing would not be much improved.

Sometimes a target group may establish a "crisis program" to thwart protest. Crisis programs cover a wide range of grievances, and they include telephone "hotline" programs to report crimes or obtain psychological counseling, as well as rape counseling and drug rehabilitation programs. A crisis program gives the appearance of change and concern, but the intent is more to disrupt protest than to render a genuine service. Further, crisis programs are often funded by cutting the budget of less visible but more effective programs that benefit the protest group. Finally, crisis programs are far less expensive than comprehensive efforts to improve the quality of community life. Once they have created a crisis program, the target group can claim that the protest group is ungrateful or greedy if it asks for more.

Fear of Bad Precedents Target groups can often thwart protest by forcefully arguing that granting protest demands will set a bad precedent. Target groups argue that "if we give in to one protest group, we will have to give in to all of them." In general, this argument is well received by third parties. In practice, however, it is obvious that if a target group gives concessions to one protest group, it need *not* give concessions to other groups. The political process is not characterized by distributive fairness but by groups competing for scarce resources. When faced with this tactic, a protest group must be quick to counter with the argument that its demands are legitimate. What the target group does for other groups in the future is not the question.

The Search for Alternatives When a target group builds an airport or a hazardous waste dump or proposes to cut school budgets, it can disrupt protest by demanding that the protest group present an "alternative" to the target group's plan. This tactic immediately casts the protest group as a "bunch of complainers." At best, it can totally reorient the efforts of the protest group. Instead of maintaining pressure on the target group, protesters try to become amateur ecologists, engineers, city planners, and economists. While the protesters are trying to come up with an alternative plan, the target group's plan is moving forward. If the protest group actually succeeds in presenting an alternative plan, it can usually be dismissed as too costly, incomplete, or simply impractical.

An astute protest group can respond to this tactic by loudly noting that it is not its responsibility to come up with comprehensive plans. The group must point out that it is the target group's responsibility to come up with plans that are acceptable to concerned groups within the community.

Temporary Concessions A target group can often grant substantial portions of a protest group's demands and then phase the changes out once the protest group ceases to exist. During the 1960s, for example, protesting university students demanded a voice in such academic matters as course offerings and content, faculty retention, and grading policy. Students demanded to attend departmental faculty meetings to press these demands, and some departments allowed student representatives to do so. After several noisy meetings at which little real business was conducted, students failed to show up. In other departments, however, constitutions and official procedures were altered to include student representation on departmental committees. This represented an *institutionalization* of student demands. Today, in these departments, faculty members seek student votes on pending matters. Early in each academic year, the faculty urges students to elect their representatives so that departmental business can get underway.

Measures of Success

In the most obvious sense, protest is successful when the target group capitulates and grants most or all of the protest group's demands. In real life, this seldom occurs. Target groups have a wide range of tactics they can employ to waste time while projecting the appearance of change and concern. For protest groups, success often must be judged in terms other than immediate concessions from the target group.

Group Transformation For some protest groups, success is achieved by abandoning the arena of protest and transforming the protest group into a more powerful organization. Often this occurs when protest groups affiliate with larger, well-established organizations. For instance, after failing to achieve gains on their own, dissatisfied employees may join labor unions and work for change through the mechanism of collective bargaining. Groups protesting hazardous waste pollution in their community may affiliate with nationally organized environmental groups. When a protest group affiliates with an established organization, it may obtain resources such as financing, legal assistance, information, and the help of professional organizers. On the other hand, the protest group may lose a great deal of autonomy. The larger organization may insist that the protest group moderate its demands and alter its tactics. Further, the protest group must divert effort from its own concerns to the broader objectives of the larger group. Although substantial gains may be achieved through affiliation, the protest group, as such, ceases to exist.

Taking Credit for Changes Piven and Cloward (1979:36) argue that protest groups usually win only what "historical circumstance has already made ready to be conceded." In recent years, for example, utility companies across the United States have shelved plans to build nuclear-powered generating stations (Brewster, 1997). A number of nuclear power plants have been abandoned while under construction. It is difficult to attribute these developments solely to the "No Nukes" protests that plagued these projects, even though protest groups have taken or been given credit for this change in policy. Rather, it is quite clear that utility companies have found nuclear power plants to be more expensive to build, less reliable, and more expensive to maintain than was previously thought.

Target groups may cite protest as the reason for scrapping projects or policies they have already found to be unsound, too costly, or obsolete. Attributing change to protest is one way that target groups can eliminate the necessity of acknowledging their own mistakes. This stance can also foster the image that the target group is responsive and people oriented. The media may also identify protest as a major cause of change while ignoring underlying causes, and protest groups are usually willing to take credit for changes that would have occurred in the absence of protest. When protest challenges important policies and high-priority projects, it usually fails. When protest challenges policies or projects that target groups find burdensome, protest often succeeds.

Target Group Awareness At times, success must be defined simply in terms of compelling the target group to take the protest group into account. Protest may bring valid issues to the public eye that would have otherwise passed unnoticed. This does not mean that the protest group wins concessions; it may win little more than the target group's recognition that a problem actually exists. The target group may be able to explain its programs and objectives to the satisfaction of the protest group. In either event, the protest group has made an accounting of itself; it has not been ignored.

SUMMARY

In this chapter we have focused on protest—attempts by relatively powerless groups to influence the political process through pressure of petition, demonstrations, strikes, boycotts, and, occasionally, violence. Those who lead protest seldom are professional agitators or people skilled in the operation of politics.

The mass hysteria, emergent-norm, and value-added perspectives view protest as a manifestation of social unrest and as a phase in the life cycle of social movements. From the perspective of collective behavior, successful protest is highly dependent upon favorable public opinion, which is achieved by groups adhering to the pluralist rules of political moderation. Success is gained through petition, the formation of coalitions, and a willingness to compromise.

The collective action perspective takes a much more detailed and differentiated view of protest. Not only is protest a component of social movements, it is an important component of the political process. From the standpoint of the political process model of collective action, anger and indignation do not automatically translate into protest. Participants in protest must engage in reframing acts that focus attention on the conduct of authorities and identify their acts as a violation of the shared moral principles of the community. Protesters must also engage in divesting acts that declare them free to challenge and disobey authorities. Finally, participants must build loyalty to the protest group through shared acts of commitment, including protest humor.

Once initiated, protest may well fail to achieve the ends sought, because target groups and authorities have an impressive arsenal of tactics to use against protest. The findings of Gamson run counter to the assumptions about the dynamics of protest contained in general theories of collective behavior. Gamson finds little historical support for the assumption that moderate protest tactics are the most likely to bring success. Instead, those groups that used tactics of disruption and were willing to use violence if provoked were more likely than others to gain recognition as legitimate representatives of constituencies and to make tangible gains. This is not a call to violence but an acknowledgment that the pluralist tactics of moderation do not serve protest as well as is suggested by general theories of collective behavior.

McCarthy and McPhail (1998) discuss how protest has become institutionalized in the United States from the 1930s to the present. Legal reinterpretations of citizen protest rights have changed the ways in which police departments respond to protest. These changes have both made channels of protest more open to U.S. citizens and have greatly decreased violent police and civilian confrontations.

Lipsky discusses the constraints that operate against successful protest. In general, a lack of money and a lack of access to power brokers and the media hinder protest groups. Leading protest is often a thankless and exhausting task, and protest leaders are hindered by competing demands on their time and the availability of volunteers to assist them.

Target groups are in a much more enviable position. They can readily use tactics that waste time while giving the appearance of change and concern. Target groups often have considerable organizational and financial resources that they can use to thwart protest.

When protest groups do make tangible gains, it is often by way of group transformation. Through affiliation with national groups, local protest groups can acquire sufficient financial and organizational resources to enter the arena of "power politics." Sometimes protest groups succeed by taking credit for changes that were near at hand before their protest began. Finally, there is some merit to viewing success simply in terms of compelling the target group to take the protest group into account, even if gains are not realized.

In this chapter we have primarily discussed protest that revolves around localized concerns and grievances. Sometimes people use protest in an attempt to change conditions that are of much greater scope. This is when protest and social movements merge. In the next chapters we will examine the dynamics of social movements.

☙ CHAPTER 15 ☙

SOCIAL MOVEMENTS AS COLLECTIVE BEHAVIOR

> Not very often in history is a movement organization in the position to take office. The African National Congress (ANC)—a core organization of the South African antiapartheid movement—was. The unbanning of the ANC, along with other movement organizations such as the South African Communist Party and the Panafricanist Congress (PAC) in 1990, and the release of Nelson Mandela later that year marked the beginning of a process that reached a temporary culmination point with the inauguration of Nelson Mandela as president of South Africa and the establishment of a government of national unity. From an organization that had been banned and persecuted, the ANC moved to the center of the new power configuration. The movement literally took office. Thousands of former antiapartheid activists flocked into positions in the administration, not only at the national level but also at provincial and local levels. (Klandermans, Roefs, and Oliver, 1998:173)

The end of apartheid in South Africa and the orderly transition to a government of national unity was one of the major political events that occurred during the last two decades of the twentieth century. Another major event was the rapid disintegration of the Soviet Union, which happened officially on December 25, 1991, and the subsequent breakup of the Soviet bloc. The resulting political realignments included the emergence of democratic governments and market economies in countries such as Poland, the reunification of Germany, and the breakup of Yugoslavia with resulting ethnic conflict.

The dissolution of the Soviet Union and the end of apartheid were remarkable in many respects. The Soviet Union arose out of a massive, violent revolution and apartheid had a long, sad, and bloody history, yet the dissolution of the Soviet Union and the end of apartheid occurred short of open civil war. Each unfolded with great rapidity and surprised social scientists, political commentators, and public officials alike. President Bush aptly declared that these changes had created a "New World Order."

Both of these major events occurred by way of large-scale social movements. The African National Congress (ANC) was established in 1912 and was dedicated to achieving African unity and the vote through political means. In 1960 the South African government banned ANC after the government's massacre of peaceful protesters, and ANC thereafter advocated armed struggle. Strikes, boycotts, uprisings and armed violence occurred during the 1970s and 1980s. These involved a confusing pattern of both alliances and conflict among many groups. Violent conflict flared among ANC and other African groups as well as bandit organizations secretly supported by the government. African groups opposed the South African government's South African Defense Forces and secret police assassination squads. In spite of such open violence, mass demonstrations, strikes, and marches also occurred and the ANC was unbanned in February of 1990. For ANC, final victory came in 1994, as they became the majority party in the government of reconciliation.

The peaceful Solidarity Movement brought democratic institutions and a market economy to Poland in the 1990s. Solidarity began as a labor organization in the Gdansk shipyards and in 1991 became the majority party in the post-communist government.

ANC and Solidarity each had a charismatic leader who would ultimately be elected president of the nation. Nelson Rolihlahla Mandela was jailed in 1962 and sentenced to life imprisonment in 1967 for sabotage. It is significant that shortly after his release in 1990, Mandela and his delegation agreed to the suspension of armed struggle. He was inaugurated as State President of South Africa on May 10, 1994. Lech Walesa was a local union leader that encouraged workers at the Lenin Shipyard in Gdansk to go on strike in 1980. The strike quickly spread beyond the shipyards and culminated in the formation of the national Solidarity trade federation. In response, the Polish government imposed martial law, briefly imprisoned Walesa, and suspended Solidarity. In 1983 Walesa was awarded the Nobel Peace Prize. The mid-1980s witnessed many changes within the Soviet bloc, and in 1988 Solidarity again called nationwide strikes and was officially recognized by the Polish government. Early in 1989, the government and Solidarity entered round table negotiations for free elections. In 1990, Walesa was elected as the first president of Poland. In the 1995 presidential election, Aleksander Kwaniewski unseated him. (See chapter 16 for a more detailed discussion of the Solidarity movement.)

Social movements such as these are the most encompassing and largest-scale events included within the field of collective behavior and contain many other kinds of collective behavior, such as that of newly formed groups, crowd behavior, innovative behavior, protest, and collective violence. The term *social movement* has been applied to such large-scale events as the French, American, Mexican, and Russian revolutions (Wood and Jackson, 1982).

SOCIAL MOVEMENTS AND COLLECTIVE BEHAVIOR

In this chapter we will examine the mass hysteria, emergent-norm, and value-added perspectives of social movements. These traditional approaches focus on the issues of movement origins, movement character, and membership commitment and control. Although there are some fundamental differences among the perspectives in their approaches to these issues, there are also a number of important similarities.

Collective behavior perspectives characterize social movements as arising within groups facing some sort of social hardship, such as material deprivation, political oppression, and threats to ethnic survival. Social movements arise among groups that long for the renewal of cherished values; they seldom arise among contented or complacent groups.

Social movements are usually spoken of as pursuing goals, which broadly includes seeking or preventing change in society. Specifically, movement goals include reform and revolution, ethnic betterment or suppression, withdrawal from society, personal enrichment or transformation, and various forms of religious salvation. Movement ideology sets forth movement goals in dramatic terms and specifies broad strategies for attaining them.

Goals are pursued through uninstitutionalized and unconventional means. That is, much of the important work of social movements occurs outside established political parties and the legislative process, and social movements attempt to bring about change through such unconventional means as personal conversion, agitation, protest, force of example, force of numbers, and force of arms.

Established authorities oppose nearly all social movements at some point in their development. This opposition can take the form of attempts to co-opt or discredit leaders or their followers, subtle intimidation, and violent suppression. From the standpoint of the dominant society, social movements appear to be a source of unjustified and potentially dangerous disruption. Only occasionally do dominant groups welcome the changes promised or produced by a social movement (Wood and Jackson, 1982).

Finally, it is traditionally held that social movements seldom achieve their initial goals. Revolutionary groups usually fail; ironically, some reform movements, like Solidarity, attain state power, far exceeding the initially stated goals. During the course of a movement there may be changes in leadership personnel, and external conditions may bring about changes in movement membership and interests. The reactions of authorities may necessitate revisions of movement goals. If a movement is to make gains, goals must be altered and sometimes abandoned. In those instances where social movements are part of dramatic alterations in society, such as the Great Revolutions, actual changes may have little resemblance to the changes first sought by the movement.

MASS HYSTERIA THEORY

Blumer (1946) defines *social movements*, quite simply, as collective enterprises to establish a new order of life. He breaks them into the categories of general and specific movements. By general social movements, Blumer is referring to the gradual and pervasive changes in the values of people, such as those embodied in the labor movement, women's movement, and peace movement. General social movements have an unfocused character, with shifting leadership and informal membership. Their history is characterized by periods of intense activity and periods of relative calm or decline. A specific movement often arises out of a general social movement. A specific social movement has more clearly defined goals, definite leadership, and at times, formal membership. Reform and revolutionary movements typify the specific social movement.

Patterns of Social Unrest

Social movements and other forms of collective behavior arise out of conditions of *social unrest*—a generalized condition of aroused emotion and unease in society. During social unrest, people's behavior takes on a random or aimless character, and the source of this restlessness is only vaguely perceived. People experience excited feelings of apprehension, insecurity, and eagerness. During social unrest, people are easily irritated and more suggestible than usual; their attention spans are shortened, and they approach states of psychological instability.

Blumer identifies five types of social unrest. First, there is unrest characterized by *collective insecurity and wariness of the future.* This fear is unfocused, and people may simultaneously fear several threats to the future. Rapid social and technological change can foster this type of unrest. The year A.D. 2000 holds great significance in Western society. When Blumer presented his theory in the 1950s, few people were contemplating the approach of the millennium. In keeping with Blumer's discussion of social unrest, many events of the last decade of the twentieth century could be interpreted as "millennial social unrest." Regarding collective insecurity and wariness of the future, many interpretations of the Bible give great significance to the year A.D. 2000—the Second Coming of Christ, judgement day, or Armageddon. For believers and nonbelievers alike, the significance of the turn of a century gave reason for reflection. At the secular level, people were wary of the Y2K problem. For some, worries about the Y2K problem were groundless, and they believed that all computers would be up and running that first morning of the year 2000. For others, the Y2K effect promised to produce all sorts of technological disasters and breakdowns, leading to an end to civilization as we know it. For hundreds of armed militia groups, 2000 was the year they believed the United Nations would impose the New World Order—the year in which the U.N., aided by groups such as the Bureau of Alcohol, Tobacco and Firearms, would come for the guns of people like themselves throughout the world.

A second type of unrest is composed of *general feelings of frustration and protest over the present way of life.* Although the frustration is general, people share a willingness to violently attack prominent symbols of the displeasing way of life at the slightest provocation. Political oppression is likely to foster this type of unrest. Since the 1970s there has been a steady increase in the amount of political and social protest in the United States and other industrial democracies (Meyer and Tarrow, 1998). The next chapter will discuss the "institutionalization" of protest in the United States and other industrial democracies. Each year thousands of small, medium, and large protest demonstrations are carried out in Washington, DC. Very few of these demonstrations are carried out to celebrate people and events or support current social policies. The substantive focus of most of these demonstrations is to protest people, events, and social policy. Ironically, laws and police practices regarding protest have become less restrictive since 1970.

Social unrest may also take the form of *flight from the present life.* This type of unrest is marked by the rise of new philosophies and yearnings for utopian existence, and it is likely to occur when conventional philosophies no longer seem to speak to individual needs. Many New Age philosophies have developed cosmologies that portray life as existing on several parallel dimensions or planes. The Unification Church (chapter 4), Unarius (chapter 6), and other groups (the People's Temple of the Disciples of Jesus Christ, the Branch Davidians, Heaven's Gate, the Solar Temple, and Aum Shinri Kyo) to be discussed in this chapter all have subscribed to the "multiple planes of existence" view of reality. The People's Temple, the Branch Davidians, Heaven's Gate, and the Solar Temple have moved on to "higher planes" through mass suicide.

A fourth type of social unrest is characterized by those periods when *strong feelings of happy anticipation* and a desire to "do things" sweep across society. The early stages of economic recoveries and the first months of new political leadership may take on such characteristics. Early in 1998, the Dow Jones stock average passed the 9,000 mark for the first time in history. Some analysts stated that these stock prices were way beyond what was justified by earnings and general economic conditions. Federal Reserve Board Chairman Greenspan cautioned against such "euphoria." Stocks took a tumble to near 8,000 in midyear during the "Asian Crisis," but rebounded to over 9,600 in early January of 1999. This gave credence to the prediction by some analysts that the Dow would hit 10,000 by the millennium, as in fact it did on March 29, 1999.

Finally, there is the unrest of despair, which takes the form of *open and deep lamentation* or *fatalistic withdrawal from society*. National failures or severe economic deprivation may lead to such unrest. For the People's Temple, the Branch Davidians, Heaven's Gate, and the Solar Temple, the hope to transfer to another plane of being through suicide was coupled with a profound despair of the existing social order. Likewise, militia groups of the 1990s were based on the view that the present political, legal, economic, and social systems were completely and totally corrupt and unbearably repressive of human liberty. For these groups, the millennium would mark the start of their great battle against the New World Order.

The Life Cycle of Social Movements

Blumer suggests that there is a natural life cycle for social movements that is tied to the rise and decline of aroused emotion. Social movements have their beginnings in social unrest and collective excitement. Leaders channel this aroused emotion in the direction of institutional change. If movements are to succeed, aroused emotion must eventually be dampened and people's energies turned to the systematic pursuit of movement goals. Finally, enthusiasm for change must be transformed into discipline to maintain the gains of the movement.

The Preliminary Stage The preliminary stage of social movements is characterized by social unrest. The masses are restless and express vague feelings of uneasiness or unhappiness with existing social conditions. Agitators who instigate brief and localized outbursts of violence, revelry, or religious revival may heighten the general malaise. In the preliminary stage, movement organizations either have yet to form or consist of small, isolated groups of misfits.

The Popular Stage In the popular stage, social unrest is transformed into intense collective excitement, in part because people are increasingly certain about the cause of their discontent. Prophets play a central role in the development of this certainty. Prophets are intellectuals or others with a talent for creating a social myth to account for discontent. They develop ideas and images to account for present conditions and suggest ways to collectively establish a new way of life. The social myth may be simplistic and have no direct bearing on the actual causes of discontent, but due to heightened suggestibility, the social myth becomes the rallying cry and ideology of the movement.

Growth is rapid during the popular stage. Membership is drawn from idealists who are strongly committed to the movement's ideology, leadership, and goals. The intense personal devotion of their followers is a source of power for prophets and reformers who lead the movement. During the popular stage, formal structure is largely mitigated against by rapidly changing circumstances.

The Formal Organization Stage As movements develop, they may be hindered, challenged, or attacked by established authorities. Consequently, if it is to survive, the movement must be transformed into a disciplined organization capable of securing member commitment and pursuing effective strategies. Aroused emotion and ideological enthusiasm may actually hinder movement development at this stage. Aroused emotion weakens discipline, while zealous commitment to movement ideals precludes compromise. During the formal organization stage, idealists may well leave the movement. In any event, there is growth in the number of members who chiefly identify with the movement as an organization rather than as an ideology.

Strategists who have talents in the areas of long-range planning and compromise replace prophets and reformers as leaders. During this stage, the movement adopts a formal structure. The majority of the work is still done by volunteers, although critical positions are staffed by paid employees. Established authorities may recognize the movement as a potential ally in the pursuit of their particular aims. It is during the formal organization stage that movements make their greatest and most lasting gains.

The Institutional Stage The final stage of development begins when the movement becomes recognized as a more or less permanent and integral feature of society. In the case of reform movements, the central concern is to maintain hard-won gains. Now, administrators whose skills lie in institutionalizing the movement's day-to-day activities provide leadership. Membership views the movement as a means of livelihood or as an official agency that is especially considerate of their needs.

In the case of revolutionary movements, this stage begins shortly before the taking of power. No longer the enemy of the state, the movement now *is* the state. Even greater discipline is required of members, who must now guard against the undermining of their gains. The complete institutionalization of the movement may well mean the elimination of earlier institutions and, perhaps, the people in them. Ironically, the movement may have to purge itself of the idealists who have stuck with the movement from the beginning. These people are likely to be displeased with the compromises that have been made along the way to power, and their criticisms may be very sure sources of trouble as the movement consolidates its power. If they survive their purge, however, idealists may well furnish the active core for the next round of social movement activity.

Meaning-Seeking Movements: The Hippies

Not all movements that we normally think of as social movements follow the life cycle described by Blumer. Some movements seem to generate tremendous enthusiasm and depart from traditional lifestyles but do little else. The hippie movement of the late 1960s and early 1970s was such a movement. The hippies should not be confused with student radicals or motorcycle gangs. Nor should the hippie movement be confused with the student protest or antiwar movements. If there was any particular ideology of the movement, it could be summarized by the slogans of "dropping out" and "doing your own thing." Almost by definition, the hippie movement precluded institutionalization of these aims. There was very little formal organization within the movement. A few hippie communes assigned those present to tasks of cleaning and cooking but little else.

For a time, the most active center of hippiedom was the Haight-Ashbury district of San Francisco. Here, nearly continuous rock concerts, drug sales, and open street life gave the impression that one had truly escaped from the conventional world. To be considered a "true" hippie, one had to make at least one pilgrimage to "the Haight."

Hippies wore long hair and dressed in clothes of their own design. They often wore military clothing embroidered with flowers and peace emblems. The preferred mode of transportation was a van, equipped for camping and painted in psychedelic patterns. Otherwise, hippies hitchhiked. The lifestyle of hippies included free and open sex and the frequent use of drugs, principally marijuana and LSD. Hippies tended to shun hard liquor, drinking mostly beer and wine. It was considered improper for a hippie to refuse to share food with another hippie. They felt that sleep was a waste of time. Hippies would often go on sprees of drugs, sex, music, and carousing that would last for days; then, when total exhaustion set in, they would "crash," or sleep for a few days, "get their shit together," and start over again. Hippies often staged love-ins—open-air rock concerts with displays of affection, some nudity, the use of drugs, and general revelry. Hippies tried to live a life of nonviolence and love for humanity. They often attended antiwar rallies and honored labor boycotts, and they tried to ignore race as a social distinction.

The parents of hippies usually hated this lifestyle. Their children seemed to have no desire to achieve material success or settle down to any semblance of a conventional lifestyle. Parents worried for the safety of their children. Many stories circulated of hippies being killed while hitchhiking or making drug deals. Parents also worried that their children were scrambling their brains with too many drugs.

The hippie movement began to fade in the early 1970s. This decline was foreshadowed when many hippies "got clean for Gene" and worked for Senator Eugene McCarthy's bid for the Democratic presidential nomination in 1968. When Nixon was elected, hippies started to turn to other pursuits. Many became active in the ecology movement and attended the first Earth Day celebrations. Others "found Jesus" or joined the Moonies. Some, like Marshall Applewhite, built on New Age and junk cultural themes to create groups such as Heaven's Gate (see chapter 6). Many hippies finished college, married, and took jobs. A few of them established successful businesses that catered to their earlier lifestyle: organic foods, music, and clothing stores. However, a good number of hippies never found the bliss they sought. Perhaps the drugs could be blamed, but many have lived out disconnected, marginal and unhappy lives.

What types of social change did the hippie movement bring about? Some have argued that the change was decidedly negative, exemplified by the loosening of society's sexual mores. Still, as one commentator noted, as much as the hippies would like to think otherwise, they did *not* invent sex. Would drugs be a problem in society today if it had not been for the hippies? Certainly, the violence, death, and imprisonment that results from the crack trade today is far removed from the "peace-love" and "consciousness-expanding" drug use envisioned by the hippies. The hippies were the first to suggest the legalization of marijuana, although that seems as remote today as it did in 1970. Even the hippies' eccentric and casual style of dress soon gave way to the expensive chic of designer clothing and post-modern punk and grunge looks. If any social changes can be directly attributed to the hippies, they were inadvertent rather than planned.

Orrin E. Klapp (1972) identified the hippie movement as a movement oriented toward "meaning seeking." Such movements arise when people's social experiences generate intense boredom; they are a search for meaning as well as an emotional catharsis. According to Klapp, only modern and affluent societies are capable of generating such boredom. Boredom is increased in a society in which nearly everything is artificially packaged and prefabricated. Hippies preferred their communes to the "ticky-tacky" suburbs where all the houses and people were the same. Even in cities, hippies tried to grow some of their own food. Hippies often built their own houses, and they pioneered the construction of geodesic dome structures. Finally, boredom is increased in societies that are low in personal input and require little involvement. Perhaps the wildest political convention in our nation's history was the 1968 Democratic Convention in Chicago—the one the hippies crashed.

Features of meaning-seeking movements include the revelrous expansion of sensory horizons. Hippies did not use drugs for just another thrill; instead, they developed elaborate justifications for drug use, including the "expansion of consciousness" and "heightened creativity." Many terms used to describe drug-induced states, such as *spaced-out*, *freaking*, *bad trip*, and *psychedelic*, were coined or popularized by the hippies. Sock hops in the high school gym and jazz festivals gave way to the total sensory immersion of the rock concert-light shows of the Doors and the Grateful Dead.

Creativity is another characteristic of the meaning-seeking movement. The music, clothing, and art of the hippies clearly broke with tradition. Hippies enlivened the tradition of the street musician and personalized clothing design. Many elements of today's commercial art can be traced back to the psychedelic art of the hippies.

Finally, meaning-seeking movements are characterized by primitive romanticism, which includes freedom from external obligations. The philosophy of the hippies captured this ideal in two words: *dropping out*. Primitive romanticism includes roving and vagabondage, something the hippies developed to a science, and also includes a sense of wild naturalness, clearly signified by the hippies' long hair and beards. Finally, primitive romanticism is based on a life of immediate action. For the hippies, life was simply a matter of "doing your own thing."

In many respects, Klapp's description of meaning-seeking movements and how they arise seems more an attempt to account for the hippie movement than it is a general theory of social movements. Still, Klapp maintains that meaning seeking is found in nearly all social movements and is found in its purest form in movements such as the hippie movement. Meaning seeking is an important component in New Age religions. Groups such as the Branch Davidians, Heaven's Gate, and Solar Temple all sought meaning in what was for them a meaningless world. According to Klapp, these movements are collective attempts to escape the boredom of life in modern society. In this regard, the growth of militia movements in the 1990s could be viewed as a type of thrill seeking.

EMERGENT-NORM THEORY

Turner and Killian define a *social movement* as a collectivity acting with some continuity to promote or resist a change in the society or group of which it is a part. Social movement collectivities differ from formal organizations in that leadership is determined more by the informal response of members than by formal procedures for legitimizing authority. Further, social movement collectivities are more structured than *mass movements*, such as people caught up in clothing fads, and followings, such as those parents who raise their children according to the suggestions of Dr. Benjamin Spock.

Character and Process

For Turner and Killian, there are four important points regarding the character and process of social movements. First, unlike that of formal organizations, the character of movements changes from day to day. At one time, movement activities may center on clarifying and articulating objectives, while at another time, movement activities may center on recruiting new members. At still other times, movement activities may center on planning and carrying out demonstrations. Lofland (1979) noted that such shifts in focus might be planned by leaders to maintain a high level of member interest and involvement in the movement.

These observations might suggest that movements change through a life cycle process, as suggested by the mass hysteria approach. For Turner and Killian, however, the life cycle view better accounts for the way in which social movements like to portray their history rather than for the true sequence of events. Although social movements are continuously in flux, the nature of this change is such that no typical sequence is generally valid.

The second important point is that the course and character of social movements are shaped by the interplay between value, power, and participation orientations within the movement (see chapter 2). At times, movement activity is characterized by structuring beliefs, articulating grievances, and planning solutions to problems (value orientations). Such activities must at times compete with or be replaced by considerations for implementing solutions or reaching accommodations with groups and interests external to the movement (power orientations). Finally, at times, movements focus on meeting needs that rise because of participation in the movement. Members must obtain minimal levels of gratification in order to remain with the movement (participation orientations).

The third important point is that social movements are shaped by their relations with conventional groups. These relations include the ways in which external publics define movements and the kinds of support and opposition that movements encounter. These external relations can either strengthen or hinder and weaken social movements.

Every movement creates a public concern as to whether it is consistent with, irrelevant to, or contrary to existing values and power relationships within the society. Community reaction will in part determine a movement's access to legitimate means for promoting its goals. Such reaction can range from amusement and token support to informal hindrances and violent suppression. Turner and Killian emphasize that there is a reciprocal relationship between community reaction and movement strategy, goals, and structure.

The proliferation of religious cults in the United States illustrates this point. The emergence of Jesus movements in the late 1960s was seen by many commentators as a welcome departure from student activism and protest. Conservative spokespersons such as Paul Harvey and James Kilpatrick initially praised these movements as a voluntary repudiation of the moral permissiveness that characterized youth culture. Public approval turned to skepticism, however, as the number of Jesus groups increased and their religious practices become more unorthodox. Established churches began to include folk music and Bible study in efforts to compete with emerging sects.

By 1981 the new sects included variants of eastern religions such as the Krishna Consciousness, the Divine Light Mission, and the Rajneesh Neo-Sanyas International Commune. Within many sects, highly authoritarian structures and practices maintained strict control over members. Established churches now began to condemn the cults, and a general public concern emerged regarding the "brainwashing" techniques used by cults. Deprogramming groups were formed that actively opposed cults and, in some instances, technically kidnapped cult members in efforts to "save" them. Private investigation firms began to specialize in locating young people who had joined cults. The American Family Foundation Inc. was established in 1979 as a nonprofit organization to fund the study of cults and their psychological manipulation and abuse. AFF maintains a website and an active program of workshops and classes for clergy, educators and helping professionals.

Few new cults enjoy harmonious relationships with the communities in which they reside. The Rajneesh Neo-Sanyas International Commune for all practical purposes bought the town of Antelope, Oregon, after bitter and costly legal battles over zoning regulations and ordinances (Buckwalter and Legler, 1983). The Internal Revenue Service has challenged the tax-exempt status of many groups such as the Reverend Sun Myung Moon's Unification Church. Faced with such opposition, cults have taken on characteristics of conflict groups using the courts. In extreme instances, as with the People's Temple of the Disciples of Jesus Christ in the 1970s and the Branch Davidians in the 1990s, cults used armed conflict in dealing with those who opposed them.

Finally, social movements bring about normative transformations in society. They propose new views of the world and new social arrangements based on these views. Sometimes, as was the case with the hippies, the normative transformations that occur are not those originally envisioned or intended by the movement.

The Role of Emergent Norms

It is commonly thought that social movements arise among groups experiencing severe deprivation and that movement goals are generally aimed at removing the source of discontent. Turner and Killian (1972) take issue with these ideas. They note that it is not necessarily the most deprived groups or their most deprived members that form social movements. Further, movement goals do not necessarily correspond to the source of discontent. These anomalies can be explained in part by the *emergent norms* that guide social movements.

The Sense of Injustice For Turner and Killian, the common element in the norms of nearly all social movements is a sense of injustice—a clear conviction that existing conditions are wrong and must be changed. In the initial stages of the movement, this sense of injustice is expressed in the words of the agitator; later, it comes to be embodied in the jargon and songs of the movement. Satire of the values and behavior of groups that the movement opposes helps to express the sense of injustice. Finally, the sense of injustice may even be reflected in styles of dress adopted by the movement. In the 1960s, for example, radical college students pointedly abandoned Ivy League styles to wear the denims and boots of the working class. The jargon, songs, satire, and fashion of a movement all serve as a constant reminder that existing standards of what is necessary or desirable are in need of change.

For people in the movement and many outside the movement, the sense of what is just and unjust seems self-evident once it is established. Often, the most enduring product of a movement is the revised conception of justice, reflected in the powerful statements of leaders, in songs, and in styles of dress.

The sense of injustice is not an automatic outgrowth of deprivation. For a disadvantage to be considered an injustice, it must be shared by a group possessing its own internal communication network, sense of group identity, and subculture. These conditions are not met within many highly deprived groups: internal communication is sporadic or absent; the group is fragmented by divergent interests and needs; and its subculture is damaged or destroyed through contacts with dominant groups.

Charges of injustice are always based on unfavorable comparison with the wealth, freedom, or power possessed by another group. The sense of injustice is not likely to develop among groups with little knowledge of the lifestyles of others. People frequently counter charges of injustice by pointing out that others have a worse lot than that of the movement group. This tactic can be used to pit minority groups against one another. During the 1960s, for example, people who demonstrated against racism, poverty and the military draft were taunted by spectators and counterdemonstrators to "Go to Russia."

Like Blumer, Turner and Killian also note that intellectuals often play a central role in articulating the sense of injustice. For Turner and Killian, the strains of the intellectual role and the diversity of positions occupied by intellectuals ensure that they always will be concerned with uncovering social injustice. Rousseau, Adams, Jefferson, Marx, and Lenin were intellectuals who were very good at articulating and framing grievances and a sense of injustice that played a role in the French, American and Russian revolutions.

On the other hand, leaders such Jim Jones, David Koresh, and Marshall Applewhite were not intellectuals. They each had the ability to engage their sometimes captive following in long, exhausting, rambling harangues that conveyed more paranoia than social injustice.

Turner and Killian note that coming to view one's own lot as unjust requires some daring and confidence in being able to play a more important role than at present. Pariah groups and outcasts are slow to question their lot. People totally dependent on a dominant group are the least likely to challenge the propriety of their situation. In order to mobilize stigmatized groups, it is essential to arouse their sense of self-worth and confidence that they can better their lives.

Movement Goals Movement goals do not necessarily follow from the sense of injustice, nor do they always strike directly at the source of discontent. Causes of discontent are rarely so immediate and self-evident that collective discussion and definition is unnecessary. According to Turner and Killian (1972), people identify the source of their discontent on the basis of ideas presented to them with authority and clarity. Individuals' belief that they have correctly identified the cause of their discontent is based on their particular knowledge of external conditions, their views of human motivation, and social support for their emerging views.

Widely dissimilar goals can arise from nearly identical dissatisfying situations. Movement goals may take two general directions—societal manipulation and personal transformation. If changing society seems an appropriate response to the situation, movement goals may take the form of programs of reform, the elimination of "enemies" and their evil "conspiracies," or total revolution. If personal transformation seems an appropriate response, movement goals might be a particular type of personal religious conversion, the establishment of schools to teach language and job skills, or the establishment of separate communities.

For Turner and Killian, goals are the tangible accomplishments sought by the movement. They must be credible to the constituency; esoteric or idiosyncratic goals appeal to narrow audiences and serve to limit membership. Goals must unite rather than divide important constituencies within the movement. The movement must present a hierarchy of goals, including those that are immediately attainable. Achieving stated goals is one standard by which the movement's success or failure is judged.

Movement Ideology Movement norms are embodied in movement ideologies that offer simplifying perspectives through which people can make sense out of overwhelmingly complex events and find certainty in otherwise vague and ambiguous situations. Ideologies are normative worldviews that provide a simplified frame of reference for understanding events and people. Often, ideologies are portrayed as scientific views of the world. But such ideologies differ from scientific theories in that they are based on unfounded assumptions and use paranoid rather than scientific logic. These ideologies can attribute virtually any social ill to capitalism, imperialism, technology, communism, or the New World Order.

Ideologies place the movement and its goals in a moving time perspective. They detail past injustices and mistakes, present a simplified view of the present, and predict an inevitable future utopia. Ideologies closely identify the movement's goals and interests with the general welfare: ultimately, the movement represents what is best for society and the world. Quite often, movement ideology supports this view by laying claim to the virtues of the downtrodden, the patience and wisdom of the silent majority, or the superior contributions of a particular group.

Finally, ideologies create villains who conspire against the general good for their own sinister interests. For militia groups the villains are "the government"; the Bureau of Alcohol, Tobacco and Firearms; the United Nations; and the "New World Order." For the ecology movement, "greedy corporations" deplete resources, pollute and cause global warming. Fundamentalists see present-day moral decay as caused by "atheists and secular humanists." For Turner and Killian, villain ideology keeps people from acknowledging that the evil may have complex causes well outside the scope of movement understanding and goals.

Membership Commitment

> Good Lord! What possesses some people, to make them believe crackpot gurus so intensely that they're willing to kill rivals, strangers, their own children and themselves? This recurring pattern defies comprehension. . . . How can society be protected from potentially dangerous "fringies"—and what can be done to rescue the naive, vulnerable people who are drawn into such groups? The only method we can see is constant warnings. (Haught, 1995:14)

For many social movements, members need to be committed only to the extent that they are willing to attend meetings occasionally, sign petitions, and donate moderate amounts of money. Membership in a "respectable" social movement can be scheduled into a normal life pattern with little difficulty. For these movements, securing commitment from members centers on coordinating roles inside and outside the movement. For example, meetings are scheduled so that they do not conflict with work. Movements such as these frequently plan family-oriented activities such as picnics or carnivals. Some movements may provide such benefits as food co-ops or low-cost vacation plans for their members.

In other social movements, members must be committed to the extent that they will give nearly all their time and worldly goods to the movement, allow the movement to educate their children, and face physical dangers or even death. Rarely is membership commitment and control as total as that found within the People's Temple of the Disciples of Jesus Christ, led by Jim Jones. On Saturday, November 18, 1978, 913 members of this cult committed suicide at their jungle commune in Jonestown, Guyana. The suicides followed the murder of California Congressman Leo Ryan, members of his staff, and reporters who had visited the cult to investigate charges of mistreatment of cult members. Jim Jones had prepared his following for mass suicide for at least two years. They often practiced a communion-like ceremony in which members drank Kool-Aid. Jim Jones told his followers that someday the Kool-Aid would contain cyanide. Hours after he ordered the murders of the investigation team, Jones convened his "White Night," in which every member drank Kool-Aid laced with cyanide-based rat poison. Jones and over 900 people, including 300 children, died.

More "suicide cults" appeared in the 1990s. On April 19, 1993, for instance, CNN provided live coverage of the FBI's storming of the Branch Davidian compound near Waco, Texas. The Branch Davidians established their Mount Carmel Center in 1955 when they broke away from a splinter group of the Seventh-Day Adventists. The nearly forty-year history of the center was marred by leadership disputes, dissention, defection, violence, and murder. David Koresh joined the group in the late 1980s and quickly rose to the role of absolute leader. Koresh claimed to have received the revelation from God that he was the Antitypical Cyrus, an end-of-time prophet. As a prophet of God, Koresh established a style of leadership very similar to that used by Jim Jones. As part of the Davidians' "new light" doctrine, couples were separated and their marriages were dissolved; thereafter they were required to remain celibate. Koresh, on the other hand, took several "spiritual wives" within the group. This spiritual bond included sexual access, and Koresh claimed to have fathered at least twelve children. In addition to regular prayer, Koresh officiated over long and exhausting sessions of preaching, Bible study, and examinations of conscience. The Davidians grew their own food, and meals were eaten communally. They published their own magazine, and selected members were permitted to hold outside jobs but donated all proceeds to the organization. Koresh also hated and feared "the government," and consequently the group stockpiled explosives and large numbers of legal and illegal firearms.

Eventually, on February 28, 1993, Bureau of Alcohol, Firearms, and Tobacco agents raided the Mount Carmel Center in search of illegal weapons. The Davidians repulsed the raid with gunfire, killing four ATF agents. Six Mount Carmel Center members, including an infant, also died during the shootout. The FBI then besieged Mount Carmel and began negotiations for Koresh's peaceful surrender. Negotiations proved to be confusing and frustrating, and biblical scholars were consulted by the FBI in an effort to understand Koresh's demands. It finally appeared that Koresh was deliberately stalling for time to allow for defensive preparations such as booby traps.

On the morning of April 19, the FBI used tear gas in an attempt to clear the people out of the Mount Carmel Center. As the armored vehicles began to pump gas into the building, shots were fired at the FBI, and smoke and flames appeared at a window. The armored vehicles withdrew, but within moments the building complex was entirely aflame. Incendiary devices had been triggered throughout the building, killing nearly all of those inside, including Koresh. According to the FBI, 75 people died in the compound, including 20 from self-inflicted gunshots.

In the fall of 1994, over fifty people died as a result of a mass suicide and murder. All were adherents of the Order of the Solar Temple that came to the attention of the world when a number of chalets burned down in Switzerland and Canada within a period of a few weeks. Lead by Luc Jouret and Joseph Di Mambro, adults and children committed ritualistic suicide/murder in mirror-lined secret chapels, after which timed firebombs ignited the buildings. The Solar Temple members believed that they had been Knights Templar in a previous life. Death was a form of transit, and the cult members believed they were going to live on another star. Farewell letters said the believers were "leaving this earth" to escape "hypocrisies and oppression of this world." In Quebec, incendiaries ignited by a timer killed four people at a different branch of the Solar Temple. The Canadian group had been stockpiling weapons to prepare for the end of the world.

In April of 1997, the bodies of 21 women and 18 men were discovered in a rented mansion in Rancho Santa Fe, California. It was soon discovered that they all had been members of the Heaven's Gate cult and they had committed suicide in three groups on successive days (see chapter 6). They followed a religion that combined elements of Christianity and beliefs about the nature of UFOs. Heaven's Gate looked upon earth as being in the control of evil forces, and they perceived themselves as being among the elite who would attain heaven. They believed that the soul was a superior entity, which is housed temporarily in a body (the "container"). The final act of metamorphosis would be to disconnect or separate from the human physical container in order to migrate to the next level of existence. On May 6, 1997, two more members of Heaven's Gate decided to shed their containers and join their classmates and teachers. They had followed the separation ritual. The two men were found dressed in black, wearing black Nikes, and had small tote bags and purple shrouds next to them. One member was found dead with a plastic bag on his head. The other, who did not use the plastic bag, survived. Like their 39 "classmates" who went before them, they both ingested phenobarbital washed down with vodka.

While some leaders encouraged their followers to accompany them on life-ending journeys to another plane, others encouraged their followers to kill others. The Aum Shinri Kyo is a doomsday cult that gained its greatest notoriety for the March 20, 1995, sarin gas attack on the Tokyo subway that killed 12 and made thousands ill. *The New York Times* later claimed that the cult had also mounted at least nine earlier biological attacks that had gone unnoticed because the microbes and germ toxins that were released lacked sufficient virulence. The group was also linked to the murder of a lawyer who was preparing a case against the Aum Shinri Kyo. The wife and child of the lawyer were also murdered.

The group's name is a combination of *Aum*, which is a sacred Hindu syllable, and *Shinri Kyo*, which means "supreme truth." Aum Shinri Kyo was probably founded in 1987, and the group's belief frame combines elements of Buddhism and Christianity. Buddhist leaders in Japan have rejected Aum Shinri Kyo as a legitimate Buddhist faith group. Its leader, Shoko Asahara, is regarded as Christ by his followers. Using the book of Revelation from the Christian Scriptures and the writings of a sixteenth-century Christian astrologer, Nostradamus, he predicted major disasters to occur in the final years before the millennium. The group established a number of chemical factories and stockpiled various chemicals as preparation for this Armageddon.

Some people were drawn to the group because of a promise that they would develop supernatural powers; others were attracted by the group's rejection of the corruption and materialism that they saw throughout modern Japan. Many arbitrary, strict rules of behavior were enforced on the members. These rules were explained as being part of an ancient tradition. Asahara emphasized a siege mentality, holding that outside groups, including federal governments, were intent on destroying Aum Shinri Kyo.

What, if anything, can be said about the dynamics of cult-related mass suicide? Jack Douglas (1967) notes that there are several reasons why *individuals* may wish to commit suicide. Some people commit suicide for revenge—to embarrass or hurt those that they leave behind. Others commit suicide to change their identity in the eyes of others—to show that they are braver and better people than others realized. Some people commit suicide to gain the sympathy in death that was denied in life. Finally, some people may commit suicide to leave a troubled or meaningless life and find a better existence.

All these motives were made personally meaningful to the participants in the People's Temple, Branch Davidian, Heaven's Gate, and Solar Temple mass suicides. Leaders of these groups led frequent discussion of mass suicides in the months preceding the tragedies. These groups frequently discussed mass suicide and made preparations for suicide in the months preceding the actual suicides. After Congressman Ryan's death, for example, when the People's Temple group felt that they would soon be attacked by the Guyanese Army, the suicide ceremony began. Jones again reminded the members how their suicides would embarrass the United States in the eyes of the world. He said that everyone would come to realize that their group was composed of brave and principled people rather than social misfits. As they drank the poison, Jones assured members that they were "dying with dignity" and that others would soon feel sympathy and sadness for the cult. Finally, Jones assured the members that they were going on a final happy journey and would soon be reunited in "another life" (Cahill, 1979; Winfrey, 1979).

Leaders of these groups used tactics of persuasion that clearly spoke to common individual motives for suicide. By itself, however, such persuasion is not likely to produce the mass suicides witnessed in these instances. In addition, leaders created a communal environment in which they could exercise very tight control over the day-to-day activities of the group. The People's Temple group practiced the suicide ceremony almost daily. The other groups also developed and practiced a ritual through which they planned to end their lives. Poisons, weapons, and incendiaries were obtained beforehand and became familiar objects in the groups' physical environments. This context of social control was built up over months and perhaps years and greatly augmented the leaders' tactics of persuasion.

Turner and Killian note that membership in a "peculiar" or revolutionary movement requires that the member make a choice between the movement and a normal lifestyle. Securing commitment, in this instance, centers on encouraging a clear choice to join the movement and making that choice irrevocable. Soon after arriving in Jonestown, People's Temple members found that this decision was indeed irrevocable. Members who wanted to leave found that Jones was keeping their passports and money under lock and key. He also had an elite security guard that kept close watch over the commune. Dissatisfied members were publicly chastised for their lack of enthusiasm and adherence to temple principles. Simply running away was not an attractive alternative because of the dense and deadly jungle that surrounded the commune for miles. Finally, Guyanese authorities were likely to return to the commune any runaways who managed to escape through the jungle. The 54-day siege that preceded the assault on the Branch Davidian Center and the ensuing suicides effectively precluded individual defections. Some Heaven's Gate members had been with the group for over twenty years, and most had been with the group for at least five years. These people had retained few, if any, meaningful or regular contacts with family or friends outside the group.

Rarely is membership commitment and control as total as that found within the People's Temple, Branch Davidian, Heaven's Gate, and Aum Shinri Kyo groups. Still, there are groups that act on action frames that lead them to refuse to pay taxes and Social Security or to use credit cards, or to acquire illegal weapons. The "patriot movement" of the 1990s included militia, common law court, "sovereign citizens" or "freemen," tax protesters, and white supremacist groups. Violent incidents with the Republic of Texas, Aryan Nation, Montana Freemen, and the Branch Davidians have led to a suspected rise in membership and activity in these movements.

The Militia Watchdog, Klan Watch, and Watchman Fellowship's Index of Cults and Religions maintain websites that identify hundreds of groups that exercise tremendous control over their members. Leaders of such groups frame their control efforts in terms of religious, patriotic, or mystical themes. These action frames create extremely negative views of conventional society, utilizing what Turner and Killian (1972) refer to as *mystical symbols* that arouse uniform emotional responses among the audience. Mystical symbols include name-calling and inflammatory terms such as "jackbooted thugs" when referring to police, military or ATF personnel. The "New World Order" is a totally derogatory term in this frame, as are terms such as "plutocrats" and "international bankers." Some patriot movement groups refer to ordinary citizens as "frogs." The continuous use of such derogatory terms to refer to outsiders creates a sense of isolation that can be exploited by leaders. Ironically, scam artists can also exploit these movement views. Various scams claiming to help patriots conceal their incomes from the government have been carried out. Scams allowing patriots to "buy into" class action lawsuits against the government have also succeeded in divesting patriots of their money. The secretive sale of overpriced, old or obsolete gas masks, food rations, survival manuals, maps, compasses, communication equipment and illegal weapons has generated profits for those exploiting the patriot movement. An additional irony is that because patriot groups totally distrust "the government" and lawyers, they do not cooperate with law enforcement officials who are trying to apprehend or convict these swindlers.

Also within the action frames of these groups is a "siege" rhetoric that states that some tremendous catastrophe is at hand. In the 1970s "survivalists" framed their actions as a preparation for the imminent collapse of the government and a

Many patriotic militia groups frame their resistance to the imposition of the "New World Order," in which they envision the loss of their constitutional rights—primarily the right to bear arms.

rise in public disorder. Patriot groups, in contrast, have framed their actions as justifiable resistance to the imposition of the "New World Order" upon freedom-loving people.

Militia action frames include "The Minuteman Prayer":

> God grant me the serenity to accept the things I cannot change;
> the courage to change the things I can;
> and the superior firepower to make the difference.

A typical militia slogan is "I Love My Country . . . But I FEAR our Government." Militia action frames also include warnings such as:

> This NOTE is for all you FROGS out there. . . . The HEAT is being slowly increased. . . . YOU don't notice or care about the erosion of freedom and the heat being applied. Because it has not directly affected YOU as of yet. There will be a time in the NEAR FUTURE when OUR OWN U.S. MILITARY/BATF (jackbooted thugs) will come door to door for YOUR GUNS. To act then will be too late. . . . These elected BASTARDS must be made to understand THAT WE WILL NOT GIVE UP OUR RIGHT TO BEAR ARMS FOR ANY REASON! Finally, YOU are the reason AMERIKA is in the shape it is in by sitting there and letting other individuals carry the ball for you. The pot is beginning to

BOIL and you can't see it. . . . I submit . . . YOU ARE THE PROBLEM! GET
INVOLVED, and with GOD's help, we MAY be able to save FREEDOM in
AMERICA.

For Turner and Killian (1972), intense commitment to a movement is achieved
through (1) conversion, (2) esprit de corps, (3) rewards for participation, (4) personal identification with the movement, and (5) breaking ties to conventional life.
In the following section, we will discuss these elements of commitment separately. In practice, these elements often mesh with one another.

Conversion Saul's "seeing the light" on the road to Damascus and Muham-
mad's vision of the Archangel Gabriel on the Mountain of Light are accounts of
intense conversion experiences that occurred suddenly and forever changed the
life of the converts. Turner and Killian suggest that most cult members undergo
definite conversion experiences at some point early in their contact with the
group. Turner and Killian define *conversion* as a fundamental and wholehearted
reversal of former values, attitudes, and beliefs. Conversion is manifested in the
drastic repudiation of conventional patterns of speech, dress, living arrangements, and occupation. Those who have undergone conversions often refer to the
experience as "seeing the light," "getting the spirit," or "finding oneself," and
describe their conversions as short-lived, intense, and singular experiences that
occurred at important junctures in their lives.

Although conversion is usually described in highly personal terms, Turner and
Killian note that many social factors operate to bring about these experiences. They
draw heavily on Lofland's (1966) study of the Divine Precepts (a pseudonym for
Sun Myung Moon's Unification Church) in their characterization of conversion.
Converts to the Divine Precepts had usually reached a turning point in life when
their conversion experiences occurred. Turning points included divorce, a second
failure in college, failure in business, and a career disrupted by illness. People were
at a point in life when most major previous commitments had been fulfilled or abandoned. Conversion occurred when these people found companionship and social
support in a movement promoting interesting views. Many similar things can be
said of the converts to the People's Temple, Branch Davidians, and Heaven's Gate.

Esprit de Corps Esprit de corps, a sense of enthusiasm for and pride in the
movement, thrives on victory and often disappears quickly in the face of adver-
sity. Therefore, one ingredient in member commitment is movement success,
which is sometimes fabricated to create esprit de corps. Rallies are purposely
planned for small halls to ensure "capacity crowds," and attacks are made on
weak opponents to ensure victory.

Movements also maintain esprit de corps by establishing rigid standards for
membership, thereby creating clear in-group and out-group relationships. Members share a sense of belonging to a group that excludes those who are not "good
enough," "smart enough," or "strong enough" to belong. Movements in which
membership status is unclear or open to virtually anyone cannot establish such
sharp in-group/out-group distinctions.

Participation in rituals and ceremonies also creates esprit de corps. Turner and
Killian note, for example, how the mass rallies of the Nazi party generated movement spirit. The rallies brought together and offered something for every contingent of the movement, from the elite SS troops to the Hitler Youth groups. Songs
written especially for the movement were sung, honors were publicly bestowed,

and new plans and programs were unveiled. Major rallies were yearly affairs, and upon their completion the planning started for the following year's rally.

At Jonestown, the Mount Carmel Center, and the Heaven's Gate mansion, there were daily meetings, rallies, group prayers and songs, and chastisement sessions. Leaders used these opportunities to frame and maintain sharp in-group/out-group distinctions. Wayward members were publicly "corrected" and all members heard repeated, convoluted, and exhausting condemnation of the outside world in these sessions. While esprit de corps includes a positive group image, in these cases it also appears to include the hatred and fear of conventionality.

Rewards for Participation   Turner and Killian suggest that material rewards such as money and property seldom accrue to movement leaders or members in sufficient abundance to make participation lucrative. This applies to leaders such as Jim Jones, David Koresh, or Marshall Applewhite whom, as far as is known, did not acquire much personal wealth during their lives. On the other hand, Reverend Moon and the Rajneesh received much negative publicity regarding their Rolls Royce collections. Occasionally, movement leaders may also become public figures of sufficient stature that they are sought as highly paid lecturers. Some activists achieve enough notice that they are approached by established groups to serve as consultants or liaisons. However, nonmaterial rewards, such as status, companionship, and a sense of accomplishment, are usually more important than material rewards in maintaining movement commitment. The People's Temple and the Branch Davidians, for instance, were based on a hierarchical system of authority; members could advance into positions closer to Jim Jones or David Koresh.

Turner and Killian note that "license" may be a nonmaterial benefit of participation in some kinds of movements. For many people, a temporary escape from conventionality, boredom, and depression is a valuable commodity—a chance to create some memories to savor in later years. The wide-open lifestyle of the hippies of the 1960s is a case in point. Free sex, recreational drug use, frequent travel, and the general attitude of "doing your own thing" provided a very exciting episode in many people's lives. Adherence to the patriot community gives one an action frame in which ignoring taxes and possessing illegal explosives and firearms are identified as virtues.

Personal Identification with Movements   Loyalty to a movement is likely to be greatest among people who personally identify with the movement by thinking of themselves first and foremost as civil rights workers, eco-warriors, freemen, born-again Christians, feminists, and so on. Turner and Killian identify several ways in which such intense personal identification can be created. The most intense personal identification is probably created by movements and groups, such as Heaven's Gate, that demand that people adopt new names upon entering. Militant, separatist, or fiercely religious organizations utilize this form of commitment. In accepting new names, the members literally accept the identity that the movement has prepared for them.

Some movements foster commitment by refusing to acknowledge members' previous life experiences in the outside world. Thus people who have held high-status jobs before entering the movement will be ritualistically humiliated by being required to perform menial tasks. People possessing skills will be trained in new skills. In extreme instances, the movement will not even acknowledge marriages performed outside the movement. Some groups, such as the Unification Church, arrange marriages among the members. The Branch Davidians dissolved members' marriages.

Movements that demand extreme levels of personal commitment usually foster this by also demanding that members adhere to particular dietary rules, such as eating no pork, practicing vegetarianism, or only eating communally. Some movements enforce rules of dress that clearly set members apart from the rest of society.

Breaking Ties to Conventional Life Member commitment may be inadvertently strengthened by negative community responses to the movement. Even if negative reactions eventually destroy the movement, their immediate effect is to brand the members or make former membership a stigma. It then becomes difficult if not impossible for members ever to be fully reintegrated into the community.

Millennial movements usually demand a severance of ties to the outside world. This isolation seems quite reasonable in terms of the movement's ideology: the outside world will soon be destroyed or drastically altered. Maintaining interest in the outside world can only jeopardize one's future status in the new order.

Millennial and other social movements often demand that members turn over a large share of their income. In extreme cases, members may be required to turn over all their worldly goods, including land, businesses, houses, stocks and bonds, autos, Social Security checks, and credit cards. In return, the movement may provide them with food, shelter, and medical care. These practices create a strong incentive to stay with the movement: those who leave are virtually destitute.

Turner and Killian (1972) suggest that involvement in some social movements exposes people to intense and repeated damnation of conventional life. Jim Jones and David Koresh were noted for their long and exhausting tirades of condemnation of the outside world. These experiences can render people incapable of rejoining and performing competently in conventional society. Many recent efforts at deprogramming members of religious cults fail, in part because former members encounter intense difficulties in coping with family, neighbors, friends, and jobs.

Members of the People's Temple had limited ties to outside groups, and moving to Guyana usually severed any remaining outside ties. One indication of the limited ties to outside groups is that four months after the bodies had been returned to the United States, only about one-third of them had been claimed by family or friends (Winfrey, 1979). Seven of the 39 Heaven's Gate suicides remained unclaimed by families three weeks after their death.

Member Control

Committed members are not necessarily disciplined and obedient members. For many respectable movements, a highly disciplined constituency is not necessary or even desired. For peculiar or revolutionary movements, member control is of more vital concern. Overall movement success depends on maintaining strict control over members' actions. However, such strict control may make outside groups suspicious and even hostile to the movement. Unless member control can be maintained at such times, the movement may well collapse.

Much of what Turner and Killian say about maintaining membership control can be summarized as *intensive interaction*. Lofland (1966; 1977) also used this term to describe how the Divine Precepts group maintained control over its members. Almost constant, intensive interaction was found within the four suicide cults mentioned above. Members in these groups slept together in dormitories, ate together in communal dining halls, and worked together in fields, kitchens and laundries, or at their computers. There were almost daily meetings of the entire commune to pray, conduct business, engage in recreation or listen to the leader's preaching.

Movements foster intensive interaction in other ways. A meeting hall or headquarters can provide a place where members can gather for meetings or just "hang around." Weekends can be reserved for prayer meetings, picnics, or excursions for members. Movements typically create databases containing mailing lists, Internet addresses, and telephone numbers, and maintain Internet chat rooms for members to ensure frequent contact between the leaders and members.

Intensive interaction also means that movements try to promote a sense of urgency among the members. In many instances, the need for urgent action in pursuit of movement goals is fairly self-evident. At other times, movements become intensely involved in activities that seem only vaguely related to their stated goals. In either event, movements typically lose ground if they fail to keep their members busy.

For militant groups, intensive interaction centers on preparing for conflict. Day-to-day activity centers on learning how to use weapons and on martial arts drills. Members may practice mock attacks and stage war games. For millennial movements, intensive interaction centers on making preparations for the day of judgment. For nearly all social movements, intensive interaction develops around recruiting new members and planning demonstrations.

Lofland (1966; 1977) noted that Divine Precepts recruitment setbacks were immediately followed by periods of intense activity to achieve ends that usually had little relationship to movement goals. These activities included moving their headquarters or initiating remodeling projects. When these undertakings were completed, the movement turned again to recruiting new members. Although intensive interaction may involve the entire membership, it usually serves to maintain control over the central core of the movement.

Movement leaders can sometimes generate conformity among the members by threatening to leave the movement. Jim Jones frequently employed this tactic. Other leaders have impressed conformity on the movement by fasting or by doing some other penance for the errors of the followers. These tactics work only for leaders who enjoy nearly unanimous support within their movement. Without such support, these tactics can ruin a movement by destroying the leader's credibility or breaking the movement into factions.

Finally, movements maintain discipline by screening the membership. During the late 1950s, civil rights groups held workshops to train members in the tactics of nonviolence before they commenced lunch-counter and other sit-in demonstrations. People who planned to take part in the sit-ins were insulted, jeered, spat upon, slapped, punched, and kicked. Those who were unable to remain passive in the face of such abuse were not allowed to participate (Belfrage, 1965; Peck, 1962). Organizers of protest against the Vietnam War tried to exclude "crazies" from their demonstrations. Crazies often disrupted otherwise peaceful demonstrations by attacking police and spectators, damaging property, interrupting speeches, or acting bizarre in front of the television cameras. Attempts were made to exclude the crazies because they were unpredictable, and the antiwar movement was often judged on the basis of its most visible elements, such as the crazies. Finally, many felt that the crazies were actually police agents that were sent to incite violence and thereby discredit the antiwar movement (Marx, 1974).

Movement Decline

Turner and Killian note that both success and failure can lead to movement decline. Social reform groups, such as temperance leagues, suffered rapid decline after the Eighteenth Amendment made prohibition the law of the land in the 1920s. Likewise, the March of Dimes was established in 1938 as a nonprofit organization by President Roosevelt to raise money to fund research that would put an end to polio. The March ran annual fund-raising campaigns and became a large, popular, and high-profile organization. In April 1955, the Salk polio vaccine was announced to be "safe, potent and effective." One of the great medical victories of the twentieth century turned into a crisis for the March, which went into rapid decline after the vaccine virtually eliminated polio in the United States. The declining movement reorganized and started to raise money to support research that would put an end to "birth defects." Since there are thousands of types of mental and physical birth defects, no single discovery is likely to create another crisis for the organization. Likewise, doomsday prophecies that fail create similar crises for millennial movements.

Most movements, however, decline without obtaining clear success or having decisive failures. They just wither away. Many movements fail when major political parties adopt their rhetoric and, sometimes, their causes. The tax rebellion of the late 1970s consisted of numerous local movements to cut taxes. The rebellion floundered as tax cutting became a constant theme of the Republican and Democratic parties.

Movements that are clearly centered on a particular leader fail if the leader dies or is discredited. The Black Muslim movement fell into confusion and decline after the assassination of Malcolm X, and the anti-Communist movement of Senator Joseph McCarthy lost considerable headway following his congressional censure.

Finally, movements decline from what Turner and Killian (1972) describe as "combat fatigue." For many, intense involvement in a social movement places severe strain on their relationships with family, friends and neighbors, and on their careers. Movement activities are often emotionally and physically exhausting. People are drawn to social movements in part by the discovery of new, interesting, and rewarding interpersonal relationships. Over time, as with most social relationships, these ties lose some of their appeal. Indeed, although members may achieve considerable gratification while participating in social movements, for most people other stresses also accumulate as a result of participation, and the stresses eventually outweigh the gratification.

VALUE-ADDED THEORY

Neil J. Smelser (1962) distinguishes social movements from general movements. *General movements* are shifts in societal norms and values that occur sporadically and without unity or focus. These include the labor, peace, feminist, and environmental "movements." For Smelser, these movements are composed of many groups often working at cross purposes with one another and clearly lacking a sense of shared purpose. Periods of intense activity and periods of inaction characterize such movements. General movements represent a type of "cultural drift" and are not sufficiently crystallized to be considered collective episodes.

A social movement has a clear focus and a sense of direction and is likely to be composed of fewer groups than general movements. Participants in a social movement have a clear awareness of common identity, direction, and shared interests. Finally, a social movement is sufficiently coherent and concentrated in time and social strata that it constitutes a collective episode. For Smelser, there are two categories of social movements. Depending on their focus and the social conditions under which they develop, social movements are classified as either norm oriented or value oriented.

Norm-Oriented Social Movements

For Smelser (1962), a norm-oriented movement is a collective attempt to restore, protect, modify, or create norms in the name of a generalized belief. This definition means that participants in the movement are trying to change particular norms, or ways of doing things, in a society. The movement's focus is on the behavior of people either within the movement or outside the movement. Behavior may be changed directly, such as when a religious cult prescribes a certain lifestyle for its members, or indirectly, such as when a group works to get a particular law enacted. Any kind of norm—economic, political, educational, religious, or lifestyle—may become the focus of a movement. The result of a successful norm-oriented movement is usually a new lifestyle, custom, government agency, interest group, or political party.

The vanguard of a social movement is often a single group or organization. The Chicago Women's Club, for example, was the driving force behind the "child-saving" movement of the 1890s (Platt, 1969), which culminated in the establishment of the juvenile justice system in the United States. The Chicago Women's Club operated a coordinated campaign of public speaking and private lobbying that resulted in the Illinois Legislature passing, with little alteration, the club's plan for the treatment of young criminal offenders in the jails and courts. Within months, the Illinois plan had been adopted in five other states.

Sometimes the same norm-oriented movement works through one group and then another. Smelser notes that in the 1880s, grievances of Midwest farmers were first voiced through the Farmers' Alliance, an independent association. Grievances were later articulated through a rurally based political party, the People's Party. Finally, the Democratic party became the channel for the expression of grievances.

Occasionally, the norm-oriented movement will work through several groups simultaneously. The movement against the Vietnam War operated through numerous groups, ranging from newly emerged militant groups such as the Weathermen to long-established pacifist groups such as the American Friends Service Committee (Quakers).

The Value-Added Sequence of a Norm-Oriented Movement

In order to understand how the value-added process works to produce norm-oriented social movements, we must comment briefly on the nature of value-oriented social movements. As we shall see, norm-oriented and value-oriented social movements differ in scope. Norm-oriented movements seek to change a part of the society, while value-oriented movements frequently seek to change the entire society. The value-added process functions to keep a norm-oriented movement focused on a particular problem or issue.

Structural Conduciveness Norm-oriented movements are likely when social conditions encourage the expression of limited demands rather than demands for fundamental changes in society. Demands are more likely to remain narrowly focused in societies where there is a clear separation between political, military, economic, and religious authorities, as in many Western democracies. Also, demands are more likely to remain narrowly focused when no single ethnic group monopolizes a particular sphere of authority. Under these conditions, movement demands tend to be formulated more in terms of specific programs for normative regulation than in terms of sweeping changes.

In societies in which religious and political authorities are one and the same, demands for change inevitably tend to be defined as "crusades" or "heresies." In societies in which political and military authorities are closely tied, demands for change are likely to become defined as "subversion" or "treason." When a single ethnic group monopolizes political power, demands are couched in terms of the "moral rights" of the conflicting groups. Under such conditions, nearly any demand for change comes to be generalized into a conflict over fundamental values.

Norm-oriented movements are also encouraged by decentralized authority structures in which discontented groups can bypass the authorities and directly implement change. Thus, in the United States, newly formed religious groups are free to start their own private schools, segregationists are free to establish private playgrounds and pools, and natural food enthusiasts are free to start food cooperatives. Avenues for change, however, are never completely free of obstacles. If they were, change would occur without the need for joining together in a social movement.

Finally, norm-oriented movements are likely when there is a lack of opportunity for individual adaptive responses. Social movements among American farmers began to flourish in the 1880s because the frontier had disappeared, and farmers who experienced difficulties no longer had the option of moving westward and starting over.

Structural Strain According to Smelser (1962), collective behavior of any kind is an effort to reduce structural strain, which can arise in a number of ways. The most obvious and direct source of structural strain is a sudden decline in the availability of material rewards within a society. Economic recessions and depressions cause such declines. Lowered profits, unemployment, and inflation create conditions such that the people's earlier standards of consumption are no longer attainable. Marked shifts in the distribution of material rewards can also produce strain. Disasters, the relocation of factories and jobs, and the obsolescence of trades and skills can also produce strains in distribution.

Shifts in the definitions of major roles can produce conditions of strain. Changes in role definitions of women, for example, have brought about an awareness of the "glass ceiling" and collective demands by women for equal job opportunities and pay, daycare programs, and, recently, equal insurance and retirement benefits.

The rise of new values can create strain with respect to social conditions that were previously taken for granted. The rise of "quality of life" values led environmental groups to challenge longstanding industrial practices, such as the casual disposal of hazardous wastes. Campaigns to ban smoking in public places replaced ad campaigns to encourage smoking. Christian fundamentalists and others advocate banning pornography and gambling on the Internet.

For Smelser, all forms of collective behavior are an effort to reduce structural strain. To become a determinant of a norm-oriented social movement, structural strain must combine with conditions of structural conduciveness that narrow the focus of grievances.

Generalized Belief Generalized beliefs place blame on specific groups and their policies for the conditions of strain. For example, patriot groups blame the ATF, CIA, or FBI for their "loss of liberty." In the case of norm-oriented movements, generalized beliefs identify a rather clear and definite object of blame. More generalized objects of blame, such as the "multinational corporations," "the New World Order," or "the workings of Satan," are part of value-oriented movements.

Generalized beliefs go beyond merely casting blame. The generalized belief also offers a solution to the dissatisfying situation, such as passing a law, creating a regulatory agency, or scrapping an antiquated custom. Those committed to the belief feel strongly that adoption of the program will remove the source of the strain.

A generalized belief may be precipitated by the sudden symbolization of the conditions of strain. Such precipitating events include the arrest of a leader or a vicious act by a suspected agent. The clear refusal of authorities to take remedial action toward the dissatisfying conditions or the appointment of unpopular officials can also precipitate generalized beliefs. Finally, the threat of success by a countermovement can promote a generalized belief. Events such as these focus attention and beliefs on a particular person, agency, event, or situation. In addition, precipitating events create a sense of urgency.

Mobilization for Action Mobilization for norm-oriented movements occurs in three stages. First, there is the incipient phase of slow, searching activity. Typically, generalized beliefs have yet to become sharply focused, and a sense of urgency is absent. Movement followers are relatively few in number and are often people directly affected by the conditions of conduciveness and strain.

The real phase of mobilization occurs following sudden increases in conduciveness and strain and the full development of a generalized belief. Membership increases sharply among those experiencing strain. In the real phase of mobilization, the movement's program is discussed throughout the society, and speculation occurs as to the likelihood of movement success.

In the final, or derived, phase, members are attracted from more diverse groups than was initially the case. These new members often contribute to a widening or shift in movement aims. Once the movement's program has been implemented and its effects seen, changes in movement structure occur. Membership may be lost among initial followers because the program does not turn out to be as effective as envisioned in the generalized belief.

Changes in movement leadership usually occur during the derived phase. Leaders whose skills lie in the areas of stating grievances and developing campaign strategies are replaced by leaders with skills in seeking power and prestige for the movement. Leadership shifts during the derived phase contribute to changes in movement direction and membership.

Ironically, success can often lead to the disappearance of a movement because its reason for existence becomes moot. Failure leads either to the disappearance of the movement or to shifts in membership and goals. In the latter case, failed movements often leave behind small, highly cohesive interest groups.

Action of Social Control Authorities have the power to encourage, redirect, or suppress norm-oriented social movements. They may wish to encourage these movements in order to avoid the more sweeping challenges posed by value-oriented movements. For example, authorities may insist that movement expression remain within the bounds of law while also introducing bills requested by the movement. Further, authorities may give public hearing to complaints, even if there is no intention of acting on them.

Authorities may wish to redirect norm-oriented movements, again to avoid the more fundamental challenges posed by value-oriented movements. Authorities can redirect movements by encouraging particular kinds of programs or solutions and discouraging others. They can also redirect movements by co-opting the movement leadership through the manipulation of power and prestige rewards. Appointing leaders to commissions or agencies or granting them personal channels of communication with authorities can serve to redirect norm-oriented movements.

Authorities suppress norm-oriented movements in the hope that more general movements will not arise. Suppression may be blatant, as when authorities attempt to arrest or, in extreme instances, deport or kill movement followers. Under such conditions, a militant underground movement is usually created. Most suppression is less blatant.

Authorities who suppress norm-oriented movements may feel that they are being "quite reasonable" and may be unaware that they are encouraging less desirable collective expressions. This type of suppression includes the refusal to recognize the movement and its demands, as well as suggestions that the movement represents only a small and "noisy" or "uninformed" minority. Authorities can also suppress norm-oriented movements by taking sides with countermovement groups. Such acts arise from authorities' negative stereotypes of the movement and their sympathies for those who voice opposition to the movement. This lack of impartiality by authorities may channel norm-oriented movements into other types of collective behavior, such as hostile outbursts or value-oriented movements.

Value-Oriented Social Movements

A value-oriented social movement works toward a much larger and more general change in society than does a norm-oriented movement. Smelser (1962) defines the *value-oriented movement* as a collective attempt to restore, protect, modify, or create values in the name of a generalized belief. The generalized belief is often so elaborate that it takes the form of a complex worldview, or ideology. The belief sets forth new values or revives old values, and it views social relationships based on present values as evil, destructive, or in a state of decay. The rewards for complying with societal norms and conscientiously fulfilling statuses and roles are seen as worthless or unfair. In short, the generalized belief upon which a value-oriented movement is based portrays present social conditions as hopelessly beyond repair. Only a far-reaching and fundamental change can set things right.

For Smelser, in the most elementary form of the value-oriented movement, adherents see themselves not as agents of change but as beneficiaries of change. This is particularly true with *nativistic*, *messianic*, and *millennial* movements, which are dominated by mystical or religious beliefs. Nativistic movements occur among defeated and oppressed people who still retain remnants of their own culture. Although these people lack the means to overthrow their oppressor, they can envision a swift and imminent return to old and better ways. Smelser identifies the Ghost Dance movement among Native Americans as a nativistic movement.

The first Ghost Dance took place among the Paiute Indians on the Walker Lake, Nevada, Indian Reservation in January 1889. A Paiute shaman (medicine man) named Wovoka organized the Ghost Dance. In his early teens, Wovoka was orphaned and was cared for by a white family who named him Jack Wilson. When he was about thirty years old, Wovoka was struck down by a severe fever, during which he had mystical visions. Afterward, Wovoka claimed that he was Christ. He had been instructed by God to lead his people in the Ghost Dance in order to usher in a new era of peace and harmony between Indians and whites.

The Ghost Dance actually consisted of five all-night dances performed on consecutive evenings. A large dancing circle was prepared and temporary shelters built nearby. The Indians danced and sang both old songs and songs composed for the Ghost Dance. In some tribes, dancers often trembled violently and fainted. Among the Arapaho, some dancers would stand rigidly for hours in a trancelike state. During their faints or trances, dancers said they were transported to the Happy Hunting Ground, where they visited with their dead ancestors. Occasionally, those who fainted claimed to have been cured of diseases. On the morning of the fifth day, the dancing ended with a vigorous shaking of all the blankets brought to the dancing circle, a bath in nearby streams, and a feast. The series of five dances was then repeated at intervals.

Wovoka never left his reservation to spread the practice of the Ghost Dance. Arapaho and Cheyenne medicine men and chiefs visited Wovoka, who provided them with written instructions on how to perform the Ghost Dance. Mooney (1896) has preserved Wovoka's instructions to the Arapaho and Cheyenne:

> When you get home you must make a dance to continue five days. Dance four successive nights, and the last night keep up the dance until the morning of the fifth day, when all must bathe in the river and then disperse to their homes. You must all do this in the same way.
>
> I, Jack Wilson, love you all, and my heart is full of gladness for the gifts you have brought me. When you go home I shall give you a good rain which will make you feel good. I will give you a good spirit and give you all good paint. I want you to come again in three months, some from each tribe in Indian Territory.
>
> There will be a good deal of snow this year and some rain. In the fall there will be such rain, as I have never given you before.
>
> Grandfather says, when your friends die you must not cry. You must not hurt anybody or harm anyone. You must not fight. Do right always. It will give you satisfaction in life. The bearer of this letter has a good father and mother.
>
> Do not tell the whites about this. Jesus is now upon the earth. He appears like a cloud. The dead are all alive again. I do not know when they will be here; maybe this fall or in the spring. When the time comes there will be no more sickness and everyone will be young again.
>
> Do not refuse to work for the whites and do not make any trouble with them until you leave them. When the earth shakes do not be afraid. It will not hurt you.
>
> I want you to dance every six weeks. Make a feast at the dance and have food that everybody may eat. Then bathe in the water. That is all. You will receive good words again from me some time. Do not tell lies. (Mooney, 1896:23)

The Ghost Dance also spread by word of mouth from reservation to reservation. Within two years, the Ghost Dance spread among nearly all of the Indian tribes west of the Mississippi. The dance was modified in its transmission among the many tribes, but wherever it occurred, it was misunderstood and usually feared by whites (Mooney, 1896).

The Ghost Dance movement lasted less than three years. It occurred at a time when the policy of the United States government was to force the Plains Indians onto reservations. Even if they had been inclined to do so, it was difficult for the Indians to establish an emotional bond within the reservation. Federal administration of the reservations was notoriously corrupt and insensitive to Indian ways, and the reservations were often located in areas far from the Indians' traditional homes and hunting grounds. It was Army policy to move Indians during the winter months, when miserable weather made it difficult for Indians to flee in large numbers. When they arrived on the reservation, food rations and blankets were usually in short supply, shelter often consisted of drafty sheds with straw on the floor for bedding, and medical care and sanitation were minimal. Indians were often moved from one reservation to another with little forewarning or explanation (Brown, 1971).

By 1890 the power of the great Indian leaders was broken. Ironically, only a few of the chiefs had died in battle. Many had simply surrendered or had been arrested by the U.S. Army. Crazy Horse was assassinated after he surrendered to military authorities. Geronimo was sentenced to a long prison term and died in captivity, while some of the war chiefs, such as Satanata, killed themselves rather than submit to the indignity of prison (Brown, 1971). Chief Joseph (see chapter 8) was separated from the Nez Percé and exiled to Colville Reservation in Washington. Among the great leaders, only Red Cloud and Sitting Bull remained with their people, the Cheyenne and the Sioux.

Placing Indians on the reservations gave many whites their first close look at the remnants of Indian life. By the whites' standards, Indians seemed lazy, unclean, vicious, and superstitious. One goal of the Bureau of Indian Affairs was to "civilize" and Christianize the Indians. Consequently, when whites saw the Ghost Dance, they interpreted it as a threat. The Indians seemed to lose all interest in schools, church, and farming during the Ghost Dance, and in some instances outbreaks of violence occurred between Indians and whites during the dance. In fact, the reasons for these outbreaks had little to do with the Ghost Dance. Still, whites perceived the Ghost Dance as a preparation for war, failing to see that it was a blending of Indian and white cultures. The Ghost Dance was similar to many other Indian ceremonies and beliefs, but it also had its origins in the Christian beliefs that whites were imposing on the Indians. No agents from the Bureau of Indian Affairs ever questioned Wovoka about the Ghost Dance or the beliefs it embodied.

The Ghost Dance had perhaps its greatest impact among the Sioux. In 1890 the Sioux only recently had been driven onto reservations in the Dakota Territory (what is today North and South Dakota). The boundaries of these reservations were constantly renegotiated, and Indians lost more and more land to white settlers. Sitting Bull strongly advocated keeping Sioux land intact, and the renegotiations became increasingly bitter.

In the spring of 1890, the Ghost Dance was introduced by a Sioux medicine man, Kicking Bear, who had personally visited Wovoka. Kicking Bear considerably altered the Ghost Dance. He claimed that the ancestors visited during fainting and trances would soon return to the living world; further, the earth would be transformed—the buffalo would return and the whites would be swept away.

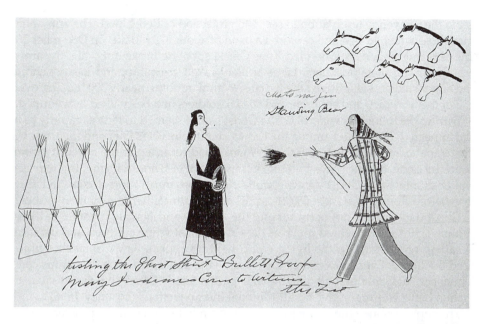

One of the beliefs in the Ghost Dance movement was that shirts and robes could be given the magical property of turning aside bullets. In this drawing made by Standing Bear, a Ghost Shirt is being tested. According to the artist, many witnessed this test. The Ghost Shirt became popular after the U.S. Army threatened the use of force to stop the Ghost Dance movement. (Photo courtesy of Milwaukee Public Museum.)

Still, Kicking Bear did not call for violence by the Indians—all they had to do was dance and sing. The coming messiah would take care of the whites. Among the first to perform the dance were the many Sioux women who had lost husbands in battles with the army; they eagerly awaited the return of their warrior husbands.

By fall, the Ghost Dance was disrupting reservation life. Many children stayed away from school, little work was being done on the farms, and trading post business had declined. The bureau and the army began to intimidate the Indians in an effort to halt the Ghost Dance. At this time Kicking Bear introduced the idea of the Ghost shirt, which had the magical property of stopping bullets. Indians wearing a Ghost shirt could continue the dance without fearing the soldiers. Almost immediately, the belief arose that a Ghost shirt would make a person invincible in battle. Whites sensed the potential for trouble in the Ghost shirt belief, and on November 20, the bureau issued the order to "stop the dancing."

Various forms of intimidation were used on the many reservations where Ghost dancing was occurring. Some reservation officials cut rations, while others promised more rations if Ghost dancing ceased. On the Sioux reservation, the Ghost Dance was being carried out during snowstorms and freezing weather. Although Sitting Bull probably viewed the Ghost Dance as a waste of time, it was decided that arresting Sitting Bull would halt the Ghost dancing among the Sioux. On December 15, 1890, an attempt to arrest Sitting Bull ended tragically. Sitting Bull and his son were killed, as were six of Sitting Bull's followers and six Indian policemen.

As word of Sitting Bull's death spread, hundreds of Sioux, including Kicking Bear, fled the reservation. Some rode into the Badlands to hide, while others tried to get to the Cheyenne reservation to seek the protection of Red Cloud. The army pursued those who had fled and captured a band of about 370 Indians on December 28. The next morning, near Wounded Knee Creek, shooting broke out while the army was disarming their prisoners. Light artillery raked the camp, and inexperienced and angry soldiers slaughtered the Indians. Within minutes, nearly 300 Indians, over half of them women and children, and 60 U.S. soldiers had been killed or wounded.

During the following year, 1891, the Ghost Dance seemed to fade as rapidly as it had appeared. It returned among the Kiowa about four years later and then among the Arapaho and Cheyenne. By then, Wovoka had returned to the obscurity from which he came, and he played no role in the revival of Ghost dancing. In their second encounter with Ghost dancing, authorities were much more accommodating than before. Today, the Ghost Dance is part of the cultural heritage of many tribes.

Ghost dancing did not occur among the Apache and Navaho people. In these cultures, ghosts were feared much as they are in most white cultures, and the idea of calling ghosts back to the living world held no appeal. Few Comanches practiced the dance. Even among the Sioux, where the dance had such disastrous consequences, only about half the Indians participated. Often the dance created friction between progressive and traditional Indian factions (Mooney, 1896).

The suppression of the dance by authorities probably led to more problems than the dance itself. Whites who had little understanding of the origins or nature of the dance concluded that it was "heathenistic" and fostered Indian violence. The violence, however, was largely a continuation of conflict patterns established well before the Ghost Dance era. Whites who feared the Ghost Dance failed to see the similarities between the dance and their own fundamentalist Christian revivals.

Messianic movements envision a similar transformation of the present order. The transformation is at the command of the savior or messiah, and followers of the messiah will be rewarded for their faith and loyalty by receiving preferred statuses in the new order. Perhaps the most successful messianic movement was the early Christian movement. Millennial movements are similar to messianic movements in that they envision the return of the savior on a day of judgment. The faithful will be rewarded and the unfaithful punished at the millennium.

Other value-oriented movements include sect formation. Sects are commonly defined as splinter groups from larger, established religions. The sect usually splits from the larger church because of differences over the interpretation of scripture or religious experiences. Thus, beliefs are the central focus of the sect at the time of its formation and departure from the parent church.

Utopian movements center on a unique lifestyle derived from the values of the group. Often, utopian movements rely on recruitment by example. The Utopian Socialists of the 1870s, for example, felt that their communes would be such models of order and prosperity that others would imitate them and voluntarily cast capitalism aside. Utopian movements, if they survive, usually evolve into small, exclusive, and self-contained groups with little interest in transforming the rest of society.

Finally, value-oriented movements include large-scale political revolutions that fundamentally transform or destroy the social institutions of the old order. The American Revolution overthrew the institutions of colonialism. The French Revolution ushered in a modern industrial order by demolishing the institutional base of the older agrarian society—the monarchy and the Church. The Russian Revolution swept away an unwieldy mixture of monarchy, feudalism, and capitalism to establish the basis of a socialist society.

The Value-Added Sequence of a Value-Oriented Movement

In the case of value-oriented movements, the value-added determinants function to keep the movement oriented toward producing a fundamental transformation of society.

Structural Conduciveness As noted earlier, value-oriented social movements are most likely in societies in which there is little if any separation between political, military, economic, and religious authorities. Under such conditions, any demand for normative change is likely to generalize immediately into value conflict.

Value-oriented movements, such as the Ghost Dance, are more likely than norm-oriented movements among groups with severely restricted access to legitimate channels for expressing grievances. Such groups include colonized peoples, slaves, native populations suppressed by foreigners, outcasts, and the extremely poor. Nativistic, messianic, and millennial movements are the most likely value-oriented movements to develop among these people.

Structural Strain Strain arises when people lack the knowledge and skills to cope successfully with problematic situations. When conditions producing strain are seemingly far beyond people's capacity to explain in ordinary terms, mystical explanations suggest themselves. Nativistic and millennial movements flourished during the plagues of the Middle Ages. Nativistic movements occur among colonial peoples who have not assimilated knowledge of the technology, economy, and customs of their masters.

Generalized Belief A value-oriented belief sets forth the role of the movement in the coming transformation of the social order. If members perceive that the means of bringing about change are closed to them, as is often the case among subjugated and demoralized people, then the movement is likely to assume a passive role in this transformation. The most passive form of a value-oriented movement is a collective retreat from everyday life into an intoxicating activity. Peyote cults among Indians of the Southwest exemplify this extreme form of a value-oriented movement. A less passive movement relies on the hope that rituals and supplication will bring forth the millennium of an avenging messiah or cultural hero. The Ghost Dance is an example of this form of movement.

Movements develop an activist orientation when members perceive the possibility of causing change themselves. The simplest form of activism is found in movements that try to achieve separation of the tormented from their tormentors. Such movements take the form of a migration in search of the "promised land" to establish a utopian community. A stronger activist orientation is found in evangelical movements, such as the born-again movement among fundamentalist Christians. Evangelism is partly based on the belief that mass conversions will change society in the desired ways. In extreme instances, conversion can be forced on others. The most developed sense of activism is found in movements that seek the outright destruction of the old order. Revolutionary movements such as the African National Congress and the antiapartheid movement fall within this category.

Mobilization for Action Charismatic leaders—people such as Wovoka—whose authority resides primarily in their personal manner, the force of their convictions, and their ability to convince others to follow them, almost always initiate value-oriented movements. Smelser notes that charismatic leadership is particularly valuable in the incipient phase of movement growth.

Value-oriented movements are more prone to the divisive effects of accommodation than are norm-oriented movements. Norm-oriented movements usually pursue definite and well-defined aims, and accommodations to achieve these aims can be readily evaluated in terms of their results. Value-oriented movements pursue much broader aims. After prolonged effort, idealists begin to feel that these aims cannot be realized, and they lose hope for the movement. Committed members begin to feel that practical compromises represent backsliding and degeneration of the movement. These concerns are likely to generate internal conflict that results in movement fragmentation or collapse.

Nearly all value-oriented movements fail to bring about the changes they envisioned. In the face of this failure, some movements fade away totally, though a few condense into closely-knit and exclusive groups. Some movements, such as the Communist party of the former Soviet Union, live on in institutionalized form to oversee the changes they produce.

Action of Social Control Smelser sets forth a model for peacefully containing value-oriented movements. First, authorities must clearly rule out the expression of hostility through violence by the movement. This is accomplished by the quick, decisive, and impartial use of force in response to the very first violent outbursts by the movement.

Second, authorities must rule out direct challenges to the legitimacy of the government. This is accomplished by clearly identifying those governmental activities that are not open to challenge. Any change in the scope of legitimacy must be clearly restricted and implemented by defined procedures, such as constitutional amendment.

Third, authorities must open manageable channels for peaceful agitation for change. They must permit a meaningful and public airing of grievances. They must at least accommodate and perhaps even encourage peaceful demonstration. The development of Public Forum Law will be discussed in the last chapter. This is the body of law that governs the expression of First Amendment rights and demonstrations in public places. Much of this law has developed since the 1970s and facilitates the peaceful expression of grievances.

Finally, authorities must make meaningful attempts to reduce the source of strain that initiated the movement. In fact, it may be difficult for authorities to take such a stance in those instances in which the strain derives from the status of colonial subject, slave, or outcast groups.

If authorities behave in this fashion, Smelser argues, then the value-oriented movement should make accommodations to the larger society or disappear altogether. In some instances, the value-oriented movement may be transformed into a less threatening, norm-oriented movement.

Summary

Social movements represent the most encompassing and largest-scale phenomena included in the field of collective behavior. In this chapter we have presented the traditional approaches to social movements embodied in the mass hysteria, emergent-norm, and value-added perspectives.

From the standpoint of mass hysteria theory, Blumer (1937:280) defines social movements as "collective enterprises to establish a new order of life." Social movements arise from a number of patterns of social unrest that make people psychologically receptive to movement ideologies that "explain" and offer "solutions" to their difficulties. A social movement follows a life cycle of increasing formalization until it comes to constitute a social institution. Klapp notes that some social movements lack the coherence of the life cycle suggested by Blumer. He refers to such movements as "meaning-seeking" movements, which arise from patterns of social unrest characterized by boredom with the established order. Klapp uses this line of analysis to explain the hippie movement of the 1960s.

From the standpoint of the emergent-norm approach to social movements, Turner and Killian define social movements as a collectivity acting with some continuity to promote or resist social change. They suggest that social movements develop through the interplay of value, power, and participation orientations rather than through a definite life cycle. Underlying nearly all social movements are norms that reflect a sense of injustice or the conviction that existing conditions are wrong and in need of change. Movement goals and ideology are not necessarily logically derived from the material conditions that give rise to the sense of injustice. Movement goals and ideology frequently take the form of scapegoating and simplified worldviews.

For Turner and Killian, the commitment of members to a social movement does not arise from their aroused emotion. Instead, membership commitment is maintained through processes of conversion, esprit de corps, rewards for participation, personal ties to the movement, and the breaking of ties with conventional life. Leaders of social movements maintain control over committed members by creating a siege atmosphere, or a constant fear of external attack, and maintaining what Lofland refers to as intensive interaction within the movement. Leaders may also exercise control by threatening to leave the movement and by excluding members who fail to live up to the standards of movement discipline. Finally, a social movement experiences decline when established groups adopt some of its rhetoric and causes, when movement leaders die or are discredited, and/or when members become exhausted and bored.

Smelser's value-added perspective defines social movements as uninstitutionalized efforts to alter the determinants of social action. Norm-oriented social movements are efforts to alter the normative structure of society and are characterized by reform movements. Norm-oriented movements are likely to arise in societies in which there is a clear separation between the economic, religious, and political spheres. Ample opportunities for the expression of dissent and the implementation of change without the approval of authorities also contribute to the formation of norm-oriented social movements. In the absence of such conditions, dissent is quickly labeled by authorities as heresy or treason. Under these conditions, social movements tend to pursue much larger social transformations. Smelser refers to these as value-oriented movements, which include nativistic, messianic, millennial, and revolutionary movements. These movements usually arise among the most severely oppressed people. Authorities are seldom able to make lasting, mutually agreeable accommodations with such movements.

⚞ CHAPTER 16 ⚟

SOCIAL MOVEMENTS AS COLLECTIVE ACTION

The collective behavior and collective action perspectives differ substantially in their characterizations and explanations of social movements. From the standpoint of collective behavior theories, social movements are sustained efforts to change the social structure through uninstitutionalized means. Social movements are also sporadic and transitory social phenomena. As discussed in the preceding chapter, the mass hysteria, emergent-norm, and value-added theories of collective behavior seek to explain the origins and life cycle of social movements.

These theories of collective behavior characterize social movements as arising from structural strains within society. Social movements develop by way of a natural "life cycle" beginning with a preliminary stage of mass excitement and social unrest and progressing to a popular stage of crowds and rapid growth. Mature social movements reach a formal stage during which issues are more clearly articulated and membership and leadership is stabilized. The final stage of the life cycle for social movements is institutionalization or decline. Some social movements acquire power positions in society so that they can implement their plans and goals. Short of this, movement goals and programs may be appropriated and enacted by established groups. Finally, because movement goals and programs have been appropriated by others, or because of a failure to make gains, some movements may lose membership and collapse (Turner and Killian, 1957:309–20).

Collective behavior theories acknowledge the diversity among social movements. The emergent-norm perspective differentiates between participation-, power-, and value-oriented social movements. Value-added theory distinguishes between the more focused, norm-oriented reform movements and broad, sweeping, value-oriented revolutionary movements. In addition, mass hysteria theory and emergent-norm theory each claim that certain kinds of people are drawn to social movements. It is the "true believers" (Hoffner, 1951) and "seekers" (Lofland, 1966), or the insecure, uneducated, young, misfits, riffraff, malcontents, and the gullible that are variously portrayed as the most likely adherents to social movements. From the standpoint of collective behavior theory, overall character and specific goals of social movements are determined by the kinds of people that are attracted to them.

In contrast to collective behavior theories of social movements, collective action theories note that movements use both institutionalized and uninstitutionalized means to pursue their aims, and that movements have become a more or less permanent feature of the political process of modern nations. For example, Tarrow (1994) argues that advanced industrial democracies such as the United States are in the process of institutionalizing the social movement form as a way of representing claims. Forms of social movement modes of action, such as "grassroots recruitment" and demonstrations, are now part of the conventional repertoire of political participation. In short, Western industrial democracies are becoming "social movement societies." Meyer and Tarrow define social movements as "collective challenges to existing arrangements of power and distribution by people with common purposes and solidarity, in sustained interaction with elites, opponents, and authorities" (Meyer and Tarrow, 1998:4).

From this standpoint, movements are perpetual features of present-day society and of democratic politics. Social movements represent such a vast diversity of claims that they cannot be accurately characterized by such simple labels as "norm-oriented" or "value-oriented" movements. Furthermore, all kinds of people use social movements to press their claims. Social movement planners now routinely utilize the services of media consultants, lawyers, and technicians. Businesses supply portable stages, outdoor sound systems, Jumbotrons, and even portable toilets for large demonstrations as well as for sporting events and rock, pop, and country music concerts. Printers can quickly supply signs, banners, shirts, caps, and buttons that are designed for specific demonstration events.

While once viewed as politically dangerous, demonstrations and other grassroots political activities such as petitions, boycotts, strikes, and sit-ins have come to be viewed as commonplace in the movement society and are accommodated, protected, and even promoted by authorities (Crozat, 1998). Petition drives to place referenda and initiatives on ballots for direct vote were once a rare occurrence but are now a common feature of state and local politics (cf. Babaszak, 1998). Initiatives supersede the traditional legislative process of passing bills through committees for floor votes by elected representatives. This has occurred for a number of controversial and far-reaching pieces of legislation such as California's Proposition 13 that greatly reduced California taxes and, consequently, school funding. Perhaps of even greater significance, in the social movement society, established groups have come to perceive an advantage in adopting or mimicking social movement strategies. Politicians scramble to lay claim to the titles of "political outsider," "independent," and "challenger " rather than "party loyalist" or "statesman."

The resource mobilization and political process approaches to social movements acknowledge the central role that social movement organizations (SMOs) play in collective challenges to existing arrangements of power and distribution by people with common purposes and solidarity; in sustained interaction with elites, opponents, and authorities. The resource mobilization perspective examines how organizations such as Greenpeace, Operation Rescue, the Christian Coalition, or the freeman militias mobilize or otherwise obtain resources to support their efforts. These resources include a sizable and active membership, well-attended demonstrations and rallies, and the ability to turn out campaign workers and votes for candidates and referenda. An important resource is money obtained from contributions from benefactors and members and money obtained by the fund-raising efforts of its members. Many organizations obtain funds through state and federal grants. Movement organizations such as the Promise Keepers seek corporate sponsorship for their rallies. Movements may seek resources in kind such as the donations of real estate, vehicles, and office equipment and supplies. Since the mid-1990s, movement organizations have also made extensive use of the Internet. The Move On group (www.moveon.org) that opposed the impeachment of President Clinton, for instance, later reported Internet contributions of nearly $14 million to support politicians who sought to focus on budget and social programs.

The political process model focuses on how movement organizations mobilize constituencies among aggrieved groups and how these people develop coherent plans for political action. Movement organizations must utilize the political opportunity structure available to them. This includes the use of existing legal channels to press their claims. Meyer and Tarrow (1998:4) note that social protest has become a perpetual element in modern life. Protest behavior is employed with greater frequency, by more diverse constituencies, and used to represent a wider range of claims than ever before. Professionalization and institutionalization has changed the social movement into an instrument of conventional politics.

Mass demonstrations such as the annual March for Life held in Washington, DC, or the 1997 campaign of mass rallies against the Italian government's latest finance bill (cf. Meyer and Tarrow, 1998) have become an established feature of the political process in Western industrial democracies. Improvisation and a sense that new and far-reaching social relationships were being forged characterized student demonstrations of the 1960s. Police, demonstrators and counterdemonstrators stood in uneasy relation to one another and fights, mass arrests, and the use of tear gas were common. In contrast, the demonstrations of the 1990s unfolded along much more predictable lines. Through the process of public order management systems (McCarthy and McPhail, 1998:91–92), starting times and routes of marches were decided upon well in advance by demonstration organizers and police; the marches were coordinated en route by trained parade marshals. These days marchers are more likely to have come to Washington, London, Paris, Rome, or Berlin by chartered coaches, trains, or airplanes than by hitchhiking or private vehicle.

The work of McPhail and McCarthy on the social organization of demonstrations and public order management systems offers us great insight into how demonstrations are presently organized and policed, and their impact on the political process. Public order management systems have been adopted by police in many of the world's great cities, such as London; New York; Rome; Washington, DC; and Chicago. Public order management systems are relatively permanent policies, technologies, and policing practices that have been adopted in these cities for the purposes of supervising access to, and demonstrations within, public spaces. Public order management systems include three important principles: negotiation between affected parties such as demonstrators, counterdemonstrators, residents, and police; advance planning by authorities; and the encouragement of planning by demonstrators. The aims of public order management systems is to "... achieve as much predictability about a protest event in advance of its occurrence as possible and to create effective lines of communication between affected parties that can be used by authorities if an event fails to follow its agreed-on course" (McCarthy and McPhail, 1998:92).

We will begin this chapter with the consideration of Poland's Solidarity Movement which, in the 1980s, utilized demonstrations, rallies, and strikes to press its demands upon the socialist government of Poland. Solidarity adopted a number of formal structures to take these actions. The movement's growing strength and increasing demands set a collision course with the government of Poland, and although government response shattered the formal structure of Solidarity in 1981, it still remains a force to be contended with in Polish society. In 1989–1990, Solidarity won major electoral victories throughout Poland, and Lech Walesa was elected president.

POLAND'S SOLIDARITY MOVEMENT

"Walesa is here! Walesa is here!" Cheers were raised as Lech Walesa, a short, stocky man with reddish-brown hair and a thick handlebar mustache, slipped over the fence and into the Lenin Shipyard at Gdansk, Poland. It was mid-August, 1980, and workers had called a peaceful strike to demand pay raises and improved working conditions. The strike looked as if it were about to collapse until Walesa made his appearance. The workers knew and respected Lech Walesa, the electrician who had been fired eight months earlier for trying to organize a trade union. He had also been one of the leaders during the violent Lenin Shipyard strike of 1970.

Immediately, Walesa and others set about organizing for a protracted strike. They set up the Inter-Plant Strike Committee to coordinate strikes in other areas of Poland and held meetings to clarify and agree upon worker demands. They also set up patrols to prevent the sabotage of shipyard equipment.

This was not the first time that Polish workers had tried to force concessions from their government. After World War II Poland was brought under Russian control, and in terms of its structure Poland's government was a carbon copy of the Soviet system. The Polish Communist Party was run by the Soviets, a Russian general acted as Polish minister of defense and commander-in-chief of the Polish Army, and Soviet officers held other high offices in Poland's armed forces and government.

In June of 1956, riots occurred in the western city of Poznan. Demands were made for better living conditions and increased economic and political freedoms. Rioting and strikes soon spread to other areas, and a new communist government was established in October. It was headed by Wladyslaw Gomulka, a Polish nationalist who had once been kicked out of the Communist Party and imprisoned for "right-wing" activities. Soviet officials were removed from their military and government posts and from Poland's Communist Party. Economic planning was decentralized, and workers' councils were established to increase productivity.

Although Russians were not returned to Polish offices, the economic reforms brought about by the Poznan rioting eroded quickly, in part because Polish industries and agriculture were in great need of modernization. Rioting broke out again in 1970, the most bitter at the Lenin Shipyard. Workers sabotaged machinery and destroyed the Communist Party headquarters, and many were killed as security police restored order. The Workers' Defense Committee was formed to obtain the release of those arrested. Gomulka resigned and was succeeded by Edward Gierek. Gierek established the modernization of the Polish economy as the government's first priority. Wages were raised, supplies of consumer goods were increased, and about $20 billion were borrowed from Western sources to finance the modernization of Poland's industry.

Poor planning and the oil crisis of the 1970s contributed to the failure of these efforts. The supply of consumer goods soon fell far short of demand, new factories were poorly designed and managed, and severe inflation and a thriving black market undermined economic reforms. Finally, on July 2, 1980, the announcement of price hikes of 60 percent for some cuts of meat touched off strikes and rioting (Schaufele, 1981).

Walesa presented the shipyard workers' demands to government negotiators in mid-August (see box, p. 422). During negotiations, nearly all forms of censorship were laid aside, foreign journalists operated freely, and strikers across Poland were able to use telephones and telexes. On August 31, the signing of the Gdansk Accords was televised throughout Poland.

The strikers won nearly all of their original demands. The accords assured government acceptance of free trade unions, independent of the Communist Party, as well as the right to strike. Other concessions included reduced censorship and union access to government broadcasting facilities. Gierek resigned as first secretary of Poland's Communist Party for health reasons, and Stanislaw Kania replaced him.

Within weeks nearly 10 million workers had joined numerous local unions under the popular title of Solidarity. During the same time, nearly a million people resigned from Poland's Communist Party. Economic conditions in Poland continued to deteriorate, while Solidarity pushed for more concessions. Walesa became a voice for moderation but still managed to win guarantees of a five-day work week on January 31, 1981. Nine days later, Kania was replaced by General Wojciech Jaruzelski.

Jaruzelski promised to honor the Gdansk Accords but requested that Solidarity, in turn, provide three months of labor peace to sort out the economy. Walesa also urged moderation, but wildcat strikes continued throughout the summer, and local unions began to demand the resignation of several communist officials. Walesa came under increasingly frequent attacks from other Solidarity leaders for being too moderate. Finally, on December 12, 1981, despite the efforts of Walesa, Solidarity called for both a national referendum on the future of the communist government and a re-examination of Poland's military alliance with the Soviet Union. To paraphrase one commentator, this would be nearly the same thing as the AFL-CIO closing most of our factories and refusing to call workers back to their jobs until the president and Congress resigned and the United States dropped out of NATO (Strybel, 1981). That evening, Jaruzelski declared martial law in Poland, set aside the Gdansk Accords, and outlawed Solidarity. Walesa and thousands of other Solidarity leaders and members were arrested within a few hours.

Walesa was released from prison in April 1983, whereupon he rejoined the Gdansk shipyard and continued to head the outlawed Solidarity Party. Later that year, Walesa was awarded the Nobel Peace Prize for his work to preserve freedom and protect human rights. Twice in 1988, Walesa led protests in the Gdansk Shipyard. These strikes marked the start of the transformation of Eastern Europe. Negotiations with the Polish government in early 1989 resulted in the lifting of the ban of Solidarity, and partially free elections were held in June. Solidarity candidates took all the seats they were allowed to contest. In 1990 Walesa was elected President of the Republic of Poland. He served as Poland's president until 1995, and by then Walesa and Solidarity had been witness to the dissolution of the Soviet Union.

The Demands of the Polish Workers

The Inter-Factory Strike Committee represents both work-teams and institutions whose functioning is socially indispensable. This committee's goal is the carrying-on of negotiations to fulfill the expectations of the striking work-teams.

One of the five conditions of beginning negotiations is the unblocking of all telephones.

The demands of the striking work-teams at workplaces and businesses represented by the Inter-Factory Strike Committee are as follows:

1. Acceptance of free trade unions independent of the party and employers in accordance with Convention No. 87 of the International Labor Organization ratified by the Polish People's Republic, concerning the freedom of the unions.

2. Guarantee of the right to strike and the security of the strikers and persons aiding them.

3. Compliance with the guarantee in the Constitution of the Polish People's Republic of freedom of speech, the press, and publication, and likewise the nonrepression of independent publishers, and the making available of the mass media to representatives of all faiths.

4. (a) A returning of their former rights to: people dismissed from work after the 1970 and 1976 strikes; students expelled from school for their convictions.

(b) The freeing of all political prisoners (among them, Edmund Zadrozynski, Jan Kozlowski, and Marek Kozlowski).

(c) An end to repression for one's convictions.

5. Making information available in the mass media about the formation of the Inter-Factory Strike Committee, and the publication of its demands.

6. The undertaking of actions aimed at bringing the country out of its crisis situation by the following means:

(a) The making public of complete information about the social-economic situation.

(b) Enabling all milieus and social classes to take part in discussions of the reform program.

7. All workers taking part in the strike are to be compensated for the period of the strike with rest leave paid for by the fund of the Central Council of Unions.

8. The base pay for each worker is to be raised by 2,000 zlotys/month as compensation for the recent rise in prices.

9. Automatic increase in pay is to be guaranteed, concomitant with the increase in prices and the fall in real income.

10. The internal market is to be fully supplied with food products, and only surpluses are to be exported.

11. "Commercial" prices are to be lowered, as is sale for hard currency in the so-called internal export.

12. The principle of the selection of management personnel on the basis of qualifications and not of party membership is to be introduced. Privileges of the SB (secret police), MO (regular police), and party apparatus are to be eliminated by equalizing family subsidies, abolishing special stores, etc.

13. Food coupons are to be introduced for meat and meat products (during the period of getting the market situation under control).

14. Retirement age for women is to be reduced to 50, and for men 55, or 30 years employment in the Polish People's Republic for women, and 35 for men, regardless of age.

15. Old-age pensions and annuities are to be brought into line with what has actually been paid in.

16. The working conditions of the health service are to be improved to insure full medical care for workers.

17. A reasonable number of places in day-care centers and kindergartens is to be assured for the children of working mothers.

18. Paid maternity leave for three years is to be introduced for the purpose of child-raising.

19. The period of waiting for apartments is to be shortened.

20. The commuters' allowance is to be raised from 40 to 100 zlotys, with a supplement benefit for separation.

21. All Saturdays are to be nonworkdays. Workers in the four-brigade system or round-the-clock jobs are to be compensated for the loss of free Saturdays with increased leave or with other paid time off work.

> Inter-Factory Strike Committee
> *Gdansk, August 22, 1980*
> *Free Printshop of the Gdynia Shipyards*

RESOURCE MOBILIZATION THEORY

We witnessed the rise of the Solidarity movement during times of economic hardship and political repression in Poland. Still, it is difficult to argue that these hardships were appreciably more severe that those experienced in Poland during the preceding two decades. Militia groups and religious movements flourished in the United States in the 1990s, during its longest sustained period of economic growth in the twentieth century. Theories of collective behavior all share a common assumption regarding social movements, namely, that they tend to occur during times of social stress. This long and widely held view has been referred to as the "breakdown" tradition of social movements (Tilly, 1975). Much discussion and research regarding social movements has sought to identify the stressful conditions in society that gave rise to the social movements of the 1960s. Empirical studies, such as those done by Gurr (1969) and Feierabend and colleagues (1969), examined relationships between measures of violent social movement activity and measures of system strain. These studies failed to show clear relationships between measures of social movement activity and measures of deteriorating social conditions (Snyder and Tilly, 1972).

Mayer Zald and Roberta Ash (1964) set forth the resource mobilization (RM) approach to social movements. Resource mobilization departs from the central concern of the collective behavior breakdown tradition, namely, identifying the kinds and levels of social strain that produce social movements. Instead, the central concern in the resource mobilization approach is gaining understanding of how social movements accumulate resources, how they acquire members, and how they maintain member commitment.

Resource Mobilization: Definitions

Resource mobilization (RM) theory defines a *social movement* as the opinions and beliefs that indicate preferences for changing statuses, roles, and relationships among groups within the society. Opinions and beliefs may also indicate preferences for changing the distribution of rewards within the society (McCarthy and Zald, 1977). A *countermovement* is the opinions and beliefs that arise in opposition to those of a social movement. Identified in this fashion, social movements and countermovements represent little more than noticeable shifts in people's views about their society.

Shifts of view, or social movements, become of consequence largely through social movement organizations. A *social movement organization* (SMO) is a complex and often formal organization that attempts to implement the goals of the social movement or countermovement. As such, the SMO represents the outward organizational manifestation of a social movement. An example of a social movement organization would be the Student Nonviolent Coordinating Committee (SNCC), which was organized in the 1960s to implement the goal of increased civil rights for African Americans. Contemporary SMOs include the Democratic Union and the Leningrad People's Front that promoted the democratic movement in Russia during the late 1980s (Zdravomslova, 1996:126–27). The pro-choice movement includes organizations such as the National Abortion Rights Action League (NARAL), the National Organization for Women (NOW), and the National Women's Health Network (NWHN) (Staggenborg, 1988:587–88).

The RM perspective considers groups to be SMOs when they have several levels of membership, lists of members, and a written document describing the structure of the organization (Zald and McCarthy, 1980; Gamson, 1975). A social movement organization is defined as an organized group that identifies its goals as changing some elements of the social structure and/or reward distribution of a society (Zald and McCarthy, 1980).

Some social movement organizations may be inclusive and require little more than a donation and pledge of general support from members. Many environmental action groups are of this sort. Inclusive SMOs require little further activity from their members once they join; members can openly belong to other organizations and groups; required meetings are rare, and members needn't adhere to any particular lifestyle.

Other social movement organizations are exclusive and may hold new recruits in a long "novitiate" period, requiring them to submit to organizational discipline and orders. The exclusive organization requires that a certain amount of energy and time be spent in movement affairs, and it may demand a particular lifestyle from its members. Religious cults such as the Moonies or Heaven's Gate fall within the exclusive organization category.

Some groups may well be active for extended periods while remaining comparatively undifferentiated (Staggenborg, 1988). This includes local grassroots groups that are sufficiently small and sufficiently like-minded that levels of membership, a list of members, and bylaws are not needed. Many of the small, rural black churches that offered support to or participated in civil rights marches would fall within this category. This would also describe the structure of "affinity groups" and "cells" within revolutionary groups such as the Weathermen during the 1960 and 1970s. Militia groups of the 1990s maintained web pages, but most neither maintained accurate membership lists nor created elaborate bylaws and levels of membership.

A social movement may foster a number of movement organizations that pursue nearly the same goals and use similar tactics. These groups compete for a limited amount of material resources and the same pool of potential members. In some instances, these SMOs may cooperate to mount large-scale demonstrations, boycotts, or lobbying campaigns. A cluster of similarly oriented and interrelated SMOs is referred to as a *social movement industry* (SMI). One example of an SMI consisted of the Southern Christian Leadership Conference, the Congress of Racial Equality, and the Student Nonviolent Coordinating Committee. These three civil rights organizations and their local chapters and affiliates pursued similar goals and employed similar tactics during the 1960s. Further, they competed for donations and membership among segments of the population sympathetic to the cause of civil rights. Today, we see similar SMIs in the areas of environmental concern, Christian religious fundamentalism, world health, and human rights.

The largest unit of analysis in the RM framework is the *social movement sector (SMS)*, which refers to the large conglomeration of all social movement organizations within the society. In the United States, this includes all the diverse groups promoting causes ranging from environmentalism to religious revival. It includes groups favoring or opposing abortion, gun control, legalized marijuana, school prayer, and nuclear arms control. According to the RM perspective, some societies can support larger social movement sectors than others. The size of the SMS is dependent on the amount of discretionary income and time available within the society. Societies in which people can contribute considerable money and time to their favorite causes will have larger social movement sectors than societies in which people have fewer of these resources.

Resource Mobilization: Basic Processes

Fundamental to the RM approach to social movements is the assumption that social movement organizations can be understood in terms of formal systems, or the institutionalization and goal displacement model of organizational transformation (Zald and Ash, 1964). What this means is that SMOs become increasingly formalized as they develop. The style of leadership, for example, comes to depend less on personal charisma and more on administrative skills. Social movement organization goals gradually shift from promoting social change to promoting the interests of the organization. In the end, fully developed SMOs function much like the formal organizations found in business and government.

Increased Formalization The formal systems approach stresses the importance of formalized, legal-rational structures of authority within bureaucratic organizations. Initially, most SMOs are based on informal, volunteer, charismatic leadership rather than professional staff and legal-rational authority. Typically, charismatic leaders create the rules under which they serve, and they have the power to alter these rules whenever they see fit. As an SMO continues to operate, the authority structure tends to evolve in a complex and formal way (Staggenborg, 1988). Rules that define the limits of authority proliferate and become more rational. Over time, then, systems of legal-rational authority emerge within SMOs, operating in much the same way as they do in bureaucracies. With professional staffing, leaders within the SMO become more or less interchangeable. Members of SMOs and bureaucracies see the authority structure as a way of "moving up" in the organization, thereby increasing member commitment.

As in bureaucracies, member commitment and productivity within an evolved SMO are maintained through the predictable reward structure of the organization. Some SMOs offer members salaries and room and board, while others may offer less tangible rewards, such as travel, achievement awards, and personal prestige. People take considerable time away from other concerns because the movement organization offers compensating material incentives.

Sources of Organization According to the RM perspective, SMOs develop formalized structures to facilitate the pursuit of goals. In the classic tradition of Weber, however, formalized structure emerges to achieve goals requiring large numbers of people and the performance of repetitive tasks or tasks requiring more or less continuous effort (Bendix, 1962:381–90). Because relatively small movement organizations seldom find it necessary to perform repetitive or contin- uous tasks, it would seem that pressures to formalize their structure must arise from other sources. For instance, groups may take on formalized structure because an outside authority requires that they do so. Some student groups, for example, develop constitutions and bylaws simply to meet university require- ments. Religious, environmental, and charitable organizations develop and expand structure to comply with federal rules for tax-exempt status. Unless these structures are monitored by outside agencies, they are often shams that are ignored in the day-to-day activity of these groups. At the very least, these struc- tures do not operate in the ways that they do in formal organizations that handle repetitive or continuous tasks.

Groups may also adopt formal organization of a bureaucracy for the sake of appearances and as a result of cultural expectations. In the United States, people impose formal structure on every conceivable voluntary association and special- interest group. These structures seem to arise without any apparent reason other than "that's the way things are done." For instance, parents in a small, poorly funded school system may elect a president, vice-president, treasurer, recording secretary, and publicity officer for their new band booster organization. They may also write and adopt standard operating procedures and bylaws. Creating and maintaining this structure may be an actual hindrance to effective fund raising and promotion of the band. In the end, such groups may have more officers than active members! Nonetheless, when people prepare to take collective action typi- fied by social movements, their first efforts tend to be organizational.

Leadership The RM perspective emphasizes how leadership evolves within movement organizations. As SMOs grow, leaders usually manage to get paid for their services; they may receive salaries and other perks or they may secretly or openly appropriate organizational resources. Leaders increasingly come to rely on professional support staff, such as telecommunication and data systems special- ists. Social movement industries may acquire a class of professional leaders. As in other areas of social and economic life, movement leaders may become inter- changeable. That is, they may move from one organization to another or hold interlocking offices. The RM perspective notes that it is possible for people to pur- sue careers within social movement industries and sectors. Social movement- related careers may closely resemble those in business and government; in fact, they may even lead to positions in business and government.

The RM perspective suggests that professionalized and bureaucratic styles of leadership are likely to produce gains for social movement organizations. Such groups are more likely, for instance, to engage in congressional lobbying through viable coalitions and to assume leadership roles within these coalitions (Staggen- borg, 1988). Groups employing informal, volunteer, and charismatic leadership are likely to be only minor participants in coalitions, be part of short-lived coalitions, or, like the Chicago Women's Liberation Union or the Reproductive Rights National Network, become inactive. Some informal organizations like Zero Population Growth transitioned to formal, professionalized groups (Staggenborg, 1988).

Forms of Organizational Administration From the standpoint of the RM perspective, the formal structure of movement organizations operates largely along the lines of bureaucratic administration. Central to the bureaucratic form of administration is the use of legal-rational authority that separates the office from the officeholder. Also central to the bureaucratic administration is formal training as a prerequisite of office and periodic review of performance. Though it is clear that many social movements utilize formal administration, the administration is often only a parody of, or bears no resemblance to, bureaucratic administration.

Administration within structured social movements often approximates what Weber termed *avocational* and *honorific administration* rather than the bureaucratic form. Both forms of administration operate in ways quite different from bureaucratic administration. In avocational administration, for instance, leadership and positions of influence fall to those who have the time and money to devote to these activities rather than to those who have had formal training or have talents in administrative skills. Many people in leadership and active core positions in social movements hold their positions by virtue of having the time (or having made the time) and the material resources that allow them to participate more intensely than the rank and file. Their positions depend not so much on training, leadership ability, or administrative skills as on their being able to devote more time to movement activity than others.

In honorific administration, position is bestowed on the basis of favor and personal loyalty to the leader rather than on formal training, administrative skills, or even job performance. Jim Jones of the People's Temple, David Koresh of the Branch Davidians, and Marshall Applewhite of Heaven's Gate used an honorific style of administration within their organizations. They handed out positions of authority to their favorites and demoted or punished those they found personally offensive or overly assertive. Jones kept incriminating statements and documents on all his lieutenants in order to assure their personal loyalty.

Avocational and honorific styles of administration are fundamentally different from bureaucratic administration. Neither style clearly differentiates between the office and the officeholder, as in the case of bureaucratic administration. In avocational and honorific administrations, the officeholders dictate the nature and powers of their office. In these forms of administration, there is seldom an orderly transfer of power. Transfer of power is characterized by conflict within the group, defections, factionalization, and purges. Often, charismatic leaders have no definite term of office—they are leaders for life—and the loss of a charismatic leader usually throws an organization into turmoil. In avocational administration, organizations often collapse because no one will assume the role of leader.

In avocational and honorific systems, there are few direct checks on the well-entrenched leader's power. Movement goals and tactical decisions for attaining them are likely to be set by the leader, however eccentric, rather than by the interplay of social movement industry forces and the needs of members, as suggested by the RM perspective.

In social movement organizations, power and influence go to those who can devote the most time and resources to movement activities. This is clearly the case in honorific and avocational style organizations. The leaders of the People's Temple, Branch Davidians, and Heaven's Gate developed an around-the-clock, seven-days-a-week style of leadership. They made captive audiences of their membership in closed meetings, often continuously lecturing and haranguing their members for hours to the point of exhaustion.

Organizational theory, which the RM perspective applies to social movements, has been developed largely with respect to bureaucratic forms of organization. Much organization that exists in social movements clearly operates along the lines of avocational and honorific administration. We know relatively little about these forms of administration. We should examine social movement organizations in order to better understand avocational and honorific forms of administration.

Member Commitment The RM perspective suggests that members remain committed to an SMO because they are rewarded for doing so. Rewards include *material incentives*, such as money and goods, *solidary incentives*, such as prestige, respect, and friendship, and *purposive incentives*, or the fulfillment of movement values. Some SMOs offer sufficient material and solidary incentives to maintain member commitment; in most SMOs, however, purposive incentives predominate. In practice, purposive incentives are usually manifested through achievements that give the appearance of furthering movement values and contributing to movement growth. These achievements include staging successful demonstrations, carrying out successful membership drives and effective fund raising. Thus the achievement of material rewards is essential for both member commitment and organizational success. As long as the movement can provide tangible benefits, members will remain enthusiastic.

A major task of movement leadership is to provide a structure of incentives that will attract and hold members. Some have argued that the RM perspective exaggerates the role of self-interest in social movement participation and ignores the role of interpersonal loyalties and obligations (Zurcher and Snow, 1981; Perrow, 1979). These relationships function more openly in avocational and honorific systems of administration than in bureaucratic systems. Further, it has been shown repeatedly that friends, family, acquaintances, and neighbors play an important role in involving people in collective behavior events of all kinds (cf. McPhail and Wohlstein, 1983). Many people become involved in social movements by way of shared activities with family members or friends. On the other hand, Lofland (1977) points out how some movement involvement is intensified by tactics that sever members' ties to their families and conventional groups. Finally, Jones, Koresh, and Applewhite maintained control over their groups through a combination of intense personal ties and interaction, misinformation, blackmail, threats, ritual chastisement, and isolation of group members from outside contacts.

In some instances, people flock to movement organizations to get information or to voice grievances. News events can result in a sudden surge in interest in particular social movement organizations. This was the case after the Three Mile Island nuclear accident (Barkan, 1979). People sought out antinuclear groups to get information about Three Mile Island and to voice their anger, fear and concern. Requests for information and applications for membership may quickly inundate SMOs that are accessible through the Internet. This sudden peaking in interest can create organizational dilemmas for these groups. People may temporarily utilize existing groups to express and resolve their grievances rather than to secure immediate tangible benefits.

Competition and Cooperation among Movement Organizations Within social movement industries and sectors, movement organizations operate in much the same way as private businesses, corporations, and government agencies do within their respective industries and sectors. Most often, SMOs compete for scarce resources, such as money and membership, although they occasionally cooperate to maintain mutually advantageous positions in these markets.

It would seem that organizations within a movement industry would cooperate with one another because they seek similar goals. But the RM perspective notes that a low level of cooperation between SMOs seems to be the rule. Nearly all social movements divide into "moderate" and "radical" factions at some point in their development (Haines, 1984). Consequently, even SMOs are in direct competition for the same resources of individual and institutional support. Individual support includes votes, contributions, dues, and donations of goods and services, while institutional support includes political favors and grants from government and private agencies. Movement organizers often rely on unemployment compensation for subsistence, and some student activists in the 1960s and 1970s received allowances from their parents (Zald and McCarthy, 1980). Under conditions of increased resource scarcity, fewer movements are likely to form, and conflict between existing movements is likely to occur.

Competition among inclusive organizations is likely to be civil and of low intensity. Because they require greater personal commitment from their members, competition among exclusive movement organizations is likely to be more intense and characterized by conflict, which can range from scathing public denunciations to sabotage and open violence. The RM approach was the first to emphasize that competition and conflict among social movement organizations can be more intense and consequential than the struggles of these organizations against organizations and agents of the established order. Perhaps internal dissension and group rivalry have destroyed more social movements than has oppression by authorities.

According to the RM perspective, cooperation can occur for various reasons. Cooperation is likely when external threats confront a number of SMOs in an industry. Government broadsides against "environmental fanatics" are likely to bring forth a united reply from environmental groups. Inclusive groups find it easier to take cooperative stances than exclusive groups. Cooperation is also likely when it is sure to produce immediate and tangible benefits. Movement organizations are likely to cooperate in order to press for passage of a mutually desired piece of legislation. In some instances, organizations may actually merge to win a coalition grant. Thus, small union locals merge to obtain greater financial and organizational support from national labor organizations. Finally, cooperation is likely among organizations that have overlapping membership and leadership. This type of cooperation was observed among the SNCC, CORE, and SCLC civil rights groups in the 1960s.

Political Process: The Merging of Social Movements and Conventional Politics

In the 1990s it became increasingly difficult to distinguish tactics used by social movement organizations such as Greenpeace, the Christian Coalition, the Libertarian Party, and state and local militias from those of long-standing organizations embedded in institutional politics. Indeed, since the 1970s both the Democratic and Republican parties have sought to accommodate and/or assimilate more marginal political groups from the Left and Right. Marginal groups have also sought to have their concerns addressed through the agendas of the two major political parties. In 1994, many disaffected groups entered electoral politics by way of H. Ross Perot's Reform Party of the United States of America. The end of the twentieth century saw the citizens of Minnesota so disaffected by traditional politicians that they elected Jesse ("The Body") Ventura, a former pro wrestler, as governor of their state on a third-party ticket. At one point in 1999, the names of real-estate magnate Donald Trump, actor Warren Beatty, and talk-show host Oprah Winfrey were bandied about by the media as potential presidential candidates.

The Democratic party has been influenced in its operation by minority groups, feminist groups, gay and lesbian groups, ecology groups, consumer groups and the poor. For the most part, these marginal groups operate from the view that government should act through legislative programs and regulatory practices to protect their rights. Fundamental Christian groups, from the Moral Majority of the 1980s to the Christian Coalition of the 1990s, and pro-life groups have almost all gravitated toward the Republican Party. These groups generally take anti-government stances such as term limits, no taxation, no regulations, and Freeman ideology. Some policies of the Reagan-Bush administration were framed in terms first used by militia, anti-abortion, and fundamentalist groups. Terms such as "confiscatory taxes," for instance, were used to refer to existing taxes in proposals to implement a flat tax. Republican Senator Arlan Spector referred to ATF and FBI officers as "jackbooted thugs" and their actions at Waco as "immoral." A second investigation of the Waco incident was opened in 1999 by Attorney General Janet Reno in response to new allegations that the FBI may have been responsible for the lethal Waco fire.

The Left Wing of the Democratic Party and the Right Wing of the Republican Party may push the parties away from traditional-style party politics to issue politics and unconventional tactics. During the 1990s social movement organizations brought a combination of tactics consisting of intense lobbying, grassroots campaigns, and demonstrations into the arena of conventional pluralist politics. These groups fully utilized the new media technology of the 1990s, including e-mail campaigns, the use of integrated cable television programs, and 800 and 900 telephone numbers or interactive websites where people could register their opinions on any topic imaginable. Numerous databases were integrated and then used for computerized mailings and telemarketing.

A clear example of the convergence of social movement and conventional political processes was the 1995 shutdown of the Federal Government by the Republican Party in their efforts to implement their *Contract with America* and the subsequent unsuccessful attempt to oust President Clinton. The new right wing of the Republican Party largely drove this agenda. The 1994 elections had brought the Republicans their most spectacular electoral gains since 1948, and they gained majority control of the House for the first time since 1952.

Merging with the Radical Right: *Contract with America*

The new majority in the 104th Congress announced a self-imposed deadline of 100 days in which to enact their large body of reform legislation, known as the *Contract with America*. The appropriation and budgeting process was to be held up until all the *Contract* items had been acted upon by Congress. The loud, "Our way or no way" approach to this legislation was a clear departure from the usual reliance on timetables, amendments and compromise that characterized traditional politics and was reminiscent of the politics of disruption advocated by protest groups in the 1960s. Congressional inaction with regard to the appropriations and budget process forced a brief shutdown of the Federal Government in 1995. The prominence of first-term members during the first 1000 days of the 104th Congress gave this crisis the appearance of "Amateur night at the Bijou." Polls showed that from January through April of 1995, approval ratings of the 104th Congress were at a tepid 35–40 percent and never exceeded the approval ratings of Clinton (Gimple, 1996:126–27).

The *Contract with America* did bring about a significant change in the agenda of American politics. Such agenda shifts are rare. In 1934, at a time when the country was ravaged by nearly 30 percent unemployment and a devastated world economy, the New Deal legislation was passed in a hundred days by a newly elected Congress. The New Deal was, in many ways, an emergency plan for economic rescue and recovery. It was also implemented by way of conventional politics.

Like the New Deal, the *Contract with America* came in with a new Congress and produced a new political agenda. On the other hand, the *Contract* reflected many ideological dissatisfactions with government policies and programs at a time when the economy was sound. The *Contract* contained ten bills and three resolutions dealing with a variety of issues. It included proposals for term limits, a simple flat tax, a balanced budget amendment and the prohibition of U.S. troops serving under the United Nations. The *Contract* had not been framed at a national convention or derived from congressional committees, nor had opinion polling been utilized to ascertain what items the American public would like to see in the *Contract* (Gimple, 1996:4–6). Instead, the *Contract* was entirely drafted early in 1994 by Newt Gingrich, then the Republican Minority Whip, and Richard K. Armey, Chair of the Republican Party, and their staffs. Moderate Republicans were, for the most part, excluded from this project (Gimple, 1996:15–21).

Many items contained in the *Contract* had, for years, been salient issues for Christian and marginal activist groups but had never before been given a hearing on the floor of Congress. During the 1980s, for instance, militia groups began to prepare for the day when the United States military would be placed under control of the United Nations as part of the "New World Order." The *Contract* was made Priority One by the Republican majority and resulted in a government shutdown when appropriations bills languished. Strident activist groups advocated the tactic of "shutting down the government" at anti-war rallies in the 1960s. It became a tactic of the majority party in Congress in 1995.

Merging with the Radical Right: Impeachment

After mid-year, attention shifted from the *Contract* and became increasingly focused on the ongoing investigations of Special Prosecutor Kenneth Starr. These investigations continued into 1996, and Republicans sought to make President Clinton's character the main issue in the presidential campaign. As a result, campaign rhetoric at the local, state, and national levels was dominated by personal attacks and counterattacks and contained much less discourse concerning political issues. If we could humorously characterize traditional campaign rhetoric as "promises, promises, and more promises," the campaign rhetoric of 1996 could well be characterized as "attacks, attacks and more attacks." Professional consultants and advertising agencies specializing in political campaigns produced most of these ads. The stridency, meanness, and sheer number of such ads were new to the arena of conventional politics. Soon, the term "attack ad" was coined to refer to this genre. A few of these ads were actually pulled early because they were seen as "going too far." Democrats also used attack ads, but Republicans were generally perceived as originating the strategy.

This strategy failed, with Clinton winning comfortably in the 1996 elections and Republicans making no substantial gains. During 1997 and 1998, strident attacks on the personal character of Clinton by the Republican right wing bore a strong resemblance to the attacks by right-wing Christian, Muslim, militia, and hate groups on the World Wide Web. The 1998 congressional campaign was well underway when Special Prosecutor Kenneth Starr finally submitted a report to Congress. The report contained four articles of impeachment.

With the president threatened with impeachment over a sex scandal, Newt Gingrich again identified the character of the president as the winning issue. The Republican campaigns were thus focused on the character of the president and, by implication, any Democratic candidate with close ties to the president. Attack ads from both Republican and Democratic sources exceeded those of the 1996 campaign. The 1998 November elections resulted in surprising losses for the Republican Party and the ouster of Newt Gingrich as Speaker of the House. Paradoxically, Clinton's job approval ratings began to climb immediately after the Republican *Contract with America* shutdown and continued to rise during the 1998 campaign. On February 12, 1999, a majority of the Senate voted to acquit the president and refused to vote a censure motion.

The attempt to impeach Richard M. Nixon was a much more bipartisan effort than the attempt to impeach William J. Clinton. Impeachment issues for Nixon focused on perjury and obstruction of justice with regard to a burglary of National Democratic Headquarters, a political crime. Impeachment issues for Clinton centered on perjury and obstruction of justice with regard to his sexual conduct. His conduct deeply offended and incensed fundamental Christians and other right-wing groups who openly demanded impeachment. For these groups, perjury and obstruction of justice seemed a peripheral and technical matter—they felt that Clinton was immoral and should be impeached for that reason alone. National opinion polls showed, however, that the general public saw this offensive behavior primarily as a private matter of concern to the Clinton family and not a national issue. Consequently, Clinton's job approval ratings climbed to record highs throughout the House impeachment hearings and Senate trial.

The rise in Clinton's job approval ratings to fantastic heights in the face of repeated charges of sexual misconduct defied conventional wisdom. It angered Clinton's enemies and befuddled political pundits. How could such discontinuity between political events and public perceptions develop? Perhaps this disassociation of Clinton's alleged sexual conduct from his presidential performance occurred because of fundamental changes occurring within the media. The number of cable and satellite television channels grew rapidly during Clinton's terms in office. Much of the expanded programming used to fill these channels consisted of investigative journalism shows, "reality-based" talk shows, and programs featuring paramedics, police, and the courts. Standards of journalistic excellence began to shift with the necessity of producing low-budget, weekly shows and reconciling conventional news coverage with information from the Internet.

As these trends developed, people began to perceive and speak of "news cycles." On a very predictable basis, every few weeks some item or event becomes "important news," generating focused and intense multimedia news coverage. This news might break on the Internet, be picked up on the cable news networks, move to the broadcast networks and interrupt other programming. The cycle would include numerous "special reports," "in-depth analysis by experts," and a great deal of repetition. "Further developments" could renew some cycles, but generally the cycle would last about a week. News cycles often focused on natural disasters, accidents, and crimes. While in progress, news cycles appeared to limit the coverage of other, unrelated or less tragic news. News cycles gave a subtle "manufactured" quality to the news. In many respects, the distinction between news programming and entertainment programming had become so indistinct as to trivialize real news. Some say the news media actually "construct" the reality of their viewing and reading audiences by their deliberate focus on some issues and lack of emphasis of others (Potter and Kappeler, 1998).

Before the Monica Lewinsky story broke in January of 1998, the public had endured nearly a year-long news cycle of the O.J. Simpson trial as well as several other prominent sexual/legal sideshows in the name of "journalism" and "real news." The public had by now also adapted to cable television channels and websites devoted to sex and pornography as well as channels and websites devoted to fundamentalist Christian programming. With the practice of "surfing" the channels and the World Wide Web, people became quite accustomed to moving from prurience to piety instantaneously. This immediate and continuous juxtaposition of the important and the trivial, of art and pornography, and of the real and the imaginary provides an undecipherable kaleidoscope of information. We are likely to witness further discontinuities between political events and public perceptions in the future.

From Grassroots to Astroturf Political Strategies

Another way in which social movement and conventional political tactics have merged is the use of "grassroots" support as a political resource. In July of 1984, United States Transportation Secretary Elizabeth Dole ordered automakers to equip at least 10 percent of 1987 cars with airbags or automatic seat belts. By 1990 all cars would have to be so equipped. Dole went on to add, however, that if a "sufficient number" of states passed mandatory seat belt use laws, the order would be eliminated. Auto manufacturers immediately launched a campaign to have mandatory seat belt laws passed in a "sufficient number of states" between 1984 and 1986. Their intense campaign was aimed at passing laws in the most populous states, including Illinois. Automakers acted through their usual lobbying networks and noted that they would not locate new automobile plants in states that did not have a mandatory seat belt use law. Automakers also utilized a type of *moral entrepreneurship* (Maguire, Hinderliter, and Faulkner, 1990), which included using entertainers to present the message that seat belts save lives and the "buckle-up-and-live" media campaign.

Finally, automakers heavily subsidized several groups nationwide that promoted the "morality" of seat belt legislation and presented themselves as "grassroots" organizations. In Illinois, the *Illinois Coalition for Safetybelt Use* distributed pamphlets proclaiming that seat belt use could reduce auto accident deaths by half in the United States. The *Coalition* clearly gave the outward appearance of "spontaneous, grassroots support" for seat belt laws at a time when letters to the governor were running 6–1 against the pending legislation. The Illinois house subcommittee had also received a petition with 11,000 signatures urging repeal of the law before it took effect on July 1, 1985 (Maguire, Hinderliter, and Faulkner, 1990:398–99). The repeal failed by three votes. Did the appearance of grassroots support for the bill make the difference?

The term "astroturf marketing" has come to be used to describe the creation of the *appearance* of grassroots support. Small, not-for-profit groups that may have only one major corporate donor act to show grassroots support for an issue in which the donor has a vested interest. Such groups may not be entirely bogus. Still, groups that utilize titles that begin with terms such as "Concerned Citizens for . . . ," "National Alliance of . . . ,""The Coalition to . . . ," "Committee for . . . ," "Volunteers to. . . ," "Parents Against . . . ," or "Council of . . . " may be considerably smaller than their imposing titles would indicate. They may contain directors and officers but few actual members. Hired help rather than volunteers do most of the day-to-day work. Groups utilize databases, telecommunication services, and media access provided by their chief supporter. Outside consultants have a major input in establishing the group's goals and strategies. Professional canvassers circulate their petitions and distribute their literature at parks, streets, malls and other public forums. Astroturf marketing creates the appearance of grassroots support for the general public, media, and lawmakers when none may exist.

Twentieth-Century Trends in the Political Process

During the twentieth century, trends in politics of advanced capitalist democracies leaned toward bringing social movements into institutional politics. The National Labor Relations Act (Wagner Act, 1935) brought protest and nonviolent strikes into the arena of legitimate political activity. The effect of the National Labor Relations Act was to greatly reduce labor violence. This legislation first guaranteed U.S. workers the right to organize and bargain collectively and eliminated previously legal prior restraints against protest and nonviolent strikes. Since the 1960s, classical forms of protest such as the sit-in, march, demonstration, vigil, occupation, and obstruction have been used to press a very wide range of causes outside the traditional labor and industrial relations arena. Many of these forms of protest are carried out by a cast of middle-class characters that decades earlier would have "written their congressman" in order to press their claims. Some protest events, like the annual March for Life demonstration, have become a regular feature of the Washington, DC, political scene.

It is increasingly difficult to distinguish between social movements and institutional politics. Movements like Greenpeace, the Christian Coalition, Operation Rescue, NOW, and Gay and Lesbian Americans use demonstrations, sit-ins and strikes to press their claims, but they also use the courts, lobbying, and the media. Many of these groups also maintain popular websites and operate major educational programs (Tarrow, 1998).

It's Called Astroturf Marketing, and It's a Billion-Dollar Industry

Never heard of it?

Well, if you haven't, it's probably because it relies entirely on deceit. You're not supposed to know what it is or how it works. Corporations are spending millions on public relations firms and false non-profit organizations to dupe you, the citizen.

Concerned? You probably should be.

Most of the bogus organizations in the astroturf arena focus on labor, environmental, and consumer issues. The groups have names like "Concerned Citizens for . . ." and "Coalition against . . ." and "Canadians (or Americans) working for (insert cause here)."

In at least one instance people have signed petitions for one group only to have their names transferred to another petition bearing the name of the real company or group behind the cause.

HERE'S HOW IT WORKS.

A telemarketing firm calls an unsuspecting consumer. The caller works for an automobile maker who opposes legislation calling for smaller, more environmentally friendly cars.

But the caller doesn't say, "I work for a disgustingly huge and powerful auto maker."

Instead, the caller says, "I'm calling for Friends of the Disabled, and we're hoping you'll support us in fighting this bill, which would force us to own smaller, less accessible cars."

It's meant to make the consumer feel like part of a local, grassroots effort to make the planet a better place to live. If it's successful, legislators are bombarded with complaints about the bill.

Astroturf: The best friend money can buy.

SOURCE: http://opera.cbc.ca/grass.html

Throughout the twentieth century, movements used activism at the federal, state and local levels. In the early part of the century, the National American Woman Suffrage Association and the National Woman's Party worked intermittently at state and national levels for the passage of an amendment to the U.S. Constitution granting suffrage to women. The Suffrage Amendment passed the U.S. Senate in 1917 and became the law of the land when Tennessee ratified the Nineteenth Amendment in August of 1918. Similarly, the Prohibition Party and other temperance groups, such as the Anti-Saloon League, worked at local, state and national levels to enact the Eighteenth Amendment prohibiting the manufacture and consumption of alcohol in the United States. Both the suffrage and temperance movements sustained their efforts over several decades and shifted among local, state and national strategies, employing a wide variety of tactics.

Likewise, the Christian Coalition was able to make gains at century's end by moving its focus from national to state levels and employing diverse tactics. In the 1980s, the Coalition utilized a media-based program of agitation in support of the candidacies of Ronald Reagan and Pat Robertson for the Republican presidential nomination. The Coalition decided it had gained very little from its focus on presidential politics. Consequently, in the early 1990s, under the direction of Ralph Reed, the Coalition utilized local church-based groups to gain seats at state Republican nominating conventions. The Coalition secured the nomination of sympathetic candidates in seventeen states, and the 1994 elections brought the Republicans major electoral gains and majority control of the House for the first time since 1952. The *Contract with America* advanced some, but not all of the Coalition's objectives.

Research on Demonstrations

Clark McPhail has studied demonstrations more extensively than any other sociologist; he is the great taxonomist of collective action. McPhail first trained teams of observers and began fieldwork in the 1960s observing strikes and demonstrations. In 1983, McPhail observed and analyzed 75 demonstration events in Washington, DC. It is from this work that McPhail provides us with the following description of how very large demonstrations are organized (McPhail, 1985).

Since 1992, McCarthy and McPhail have maintained the ongoing Collective Action Project. The Project is funded through National Science Foundation grants and is multifaceted. One objective of the Project is to create a database of descriptive information obtained by observing demonstrations. The Project trains teams of people to systematically observe and record the activities that occur during demonstrations in Washington, DC. The Annual March for Life and other very large demonstrations, such as the 1997 Promise Keepers Stand in the Gap Sacred Assembly of Men rally, have been observed.

Another major objective of the Project is to compare observational data with demonstration data drawn from archives such as newspaper accounts of demonstrations and television news coverage. Since the 1970s both U.S. and European scholars have overwhelmingly relied upon the archives of national daily newspapers to determine the issues, actors, and forms of collective action making up protest events, and to determine whether these events are orderly or disorderly. Cycles of protest events are also examined in relation to various archival measures of social, political and economic conditions as well as obstacles to or opportunities for collective action. In order to assess the accuracy of media portrayals of protest events and other archival data, the Project has coded all *Washington Post* and *New York Times* print stories about demonstrations in 1973, 1982 and 1991, as well as current demonstrations. The Project is also coding ABC, CBS and NBC evening telecasts of demonstrations. The comparison of this extensive database of media accounts of demonstrations against Project observations provides an empirical basis for assessing description bias in media accounts of demonstrations. McCarthy and McPhail have also participated with other international scholars who are examining the history of policing demonstrations in Western democracies.

Definitions McPhail has specified the common forms of gatherings, including the common forms of demonstration gatherings. He has also identified approximately forty elementary forms of collective action that commonly occur within demonstration gatherings. It is from these taxonomies that we are able to describe the social organization of demonstrations.

McPhail uses the term "gathering" rather than "crowd" when describing collective action. A *gathering* consists of two or more people occupying a common time/space frame. Thus defined, a gathering can consist of two people. The dyad is a fundamental unit of social interaction, and most people engage in dyadic interaction every day of their lives. Groupings of three, four, five and six people are also very common. These numbers accommodate many kinship, friendship or acquaintance clusters. Clusters or gatherings of seven or more people are increasingly rare, and we sometimes refer to these groupings as "small crowds."

When we go shopping or attend summer softball tournaments we encounter *prosaic gatherings*: public or semi-public gatherings that are casual and transitory, occasional and recurring. The numbers of shoppers and spectators may be small; on the other hand, the size of some prosaic gatherings may be intimidating. A *ceremonial gathering*, such as a funeral with full military honors at Arlington National Cemetery, is a solemn event that is carried out according to a complex and traditional protocol. The modal individual and collective action at a ceremonial gathering celebrates or mourns the status passage of some individual, group, or event. Ceremonial gatherings may be small and contain very little ritual or, like state funerals and celebrations of national independence, be carried out on a massive scale with large amounts of pomp and circumstance.

Demonstrations are gatherings within which the modal individual and collective behavior involves the protest or celebration of some principle, person, collectivity or condition. Washington, DC authorities issue permits for over 2,000 demonstrations each year. Demonstration gatherings may be as small as two people. Many demonstration gatherings in Washington, DC, contain fewer than a hundred people. Demonstration gatherings of a thousand or more are comparatively infrequent. Very large demonstrations contain hundreds of thousands of people and may occur no more than once or twice a decade. It is unlikely that a Washington, DC demonstration gathering has ever reached or surpassed a million persons. Ronald T. Wohlstein participated in the observation team at the Stand in the Gap rally. For Wohlstein, this was an opportunity to once again do fieldwork with friends and colleagues.

Very large demonstrations that contain hundreds of thousands of people occur no more than once or twice a decade. The 1995 "Million Man March" on Washington was one of the three largest demonstrations of the 1990s and was estimated to involve more than 800,000 participants. © Jacques M. Chenet/CORBIS.

The Politics of Counting the Crowd: Mann revisited

Twenty-five years ago, Leon Mann (1974) found a moderate relationship between the editorial position of newspapers regarding the merit of anti-war gatherings and the reported estimate of gathering size. Regarding the discrepancies in crowd counts between newspapers, Mann (1974:285) suggested, "Close agreement between newspapers might be the rule whenever a highly respected and authoritative source offers a size estimate of a gathering that is so obviously vast and impressive that there is little point in attempting to magnify or deflate it." Little, if any, attention has been directed toward this issue since that time. I assumed, and I suspect others made the same assumption, that since that time, progress in providing a reliable crowd estimate was well underway. Those of us interested in such matters followed the development of a fairly rigorous methodology by the government for making such estimates of gathering size in our nation's capital. I thought that by the mid-1990s the U.S. Park Police, the major police agency responsible for such estimates, had reached the status of "a highly respected and authoritative source." However, given the controversy surrounding the 1995 "Million Man March" in Washington and the continuing relationship between estimated size of political gatherings and public opinion about those gatherings, it seemed a worthwhile endeavor to revisit Mann's hypothesis.

The idea of re-examining Mann's work occurred to me after a trip to Washington, DC, to observe the Promise Keepers rally on October 4, 1997. It was a reunion of sorts. Clark McPhail and John McCarthy had been studying First Amendment demonstrations in Washington and had recruited and organized a team to systematically observe the demonstration rally. Since systematic observation requires many qualified volunteers, Clark thought I, along with David Miller and Chuck Tucker, might be interested in joining the observation team. We had worked with Clark in the late 1960s observing a number of demonstrations and a few riots. So when Clark called and asked if I would be interested in joining the team to systematically observe what would clearly be a very large mobilization, it felt like graduate school all over again. I mean the good part of graduate school—the excitement of sociological investigation in the field. For many of us, careers in teaching take us far afield from those kinds of experiences. Add to that the opportunity to be with colleagues I have worked with in the past—it took me back in time. The entire experience rejuvenated my enthusiasm for understanding the descriptive dimensions of collective behavior events.

After the return trip, I read a number of newspaper and magazine accounts of the Promise Keepers rally I had just observed. I was surprised by the references to the Million Man March, and I began to reflect on Mann's work. For example, the following appeared in the *Chicago Sun Times*, October 5, 1997 under Lynn Sweet's byline from the Sun Times Washington Bureau: "Promise Keepers organizers have a chance to equal or surpass the 837,000 men who filled much of the Mall for the October, 1995 Million Man March, organized by Nation of Islam Minister Louis Farrakhan exclusively for black men." So I asked myself, "What's going on here?" I was aware of the U.S. Park Police estimated size of the Farrakhan gathering at 400,000 and knew how they arrived at such estimates; but 837,000? I was baffled. I wanted to know what had happened; where the new estimate came from; how pervasive this was among newspapers; and, how newspapers decided on using this size estimate. Upon re-reading Leon Mann's work, the phrase that struck me was the suggestion that newspapers might agree on "the count" for gatherings if: (1) there was "a highly respected and authoritative source," and (2) the gathering was so "obviously vast and impressive that there is little point in attempting to magnify or deflate it." Since this did not mesh with my experiences, I thought there was not only an important personal question here, but one my peers might find sociologically significant as well.

To revisit Mann's hypothesis today required modifications in how the editorial position of a newspaper is determined. So I will briefly discuss how Mann conducted his original investigation, and then explain how things were modified to revisit the hypothesis using a contemporary demonstration—the Million Man March. However, it is important to discuss the issue of counting the crowd, as that provides the overall context for revisiting this hypothesis almost twenty-five years later.

I had a friend read an earlier draft of this paper. Next to this last quote was written her query: Does this mean, ultimately that the "million man" march really wasn't impressive and thus there was need to magnify it? Yes and no. From the organizers' perspective, the frame of a "million man" march required a larger turnout than the 400,000 estimated by the Park Police. Mobilizing 400,000 people is no small accomplishment and a truly impressive one. But when you compare it to the "frame" organizers want remembered when commemorating this event, that number fell short and became the point of contention.

In 1990, Congress requested that the Park Service develop a counting method that would be public, consistent, and as accurate as possible. Subsequently, the Park Service used a method of calculation based on (1) the known square footage of the National Mall, Ellipse, and the Washington Monument grounds; (2) the use of aerial photographs to ascertain the proportion of each area occupied by demonstrators and their belongings; and, (3) the estimated density of occupation of those areas. In all likelihood, these methods produced very accurate estimates of demonstration size. Park Service estimates, however, were often below those offered by demonstration organizers and supporters. These larger estimates employed the SWAG (Stupid Wild-Ass Guess) method of estimating crowd sizes. Contention over crowd size estimates became the focus of headlines and news stories. In the wake of the controversy regarding the Park Service's estimate of 400,000 as the size of the Million Man March, the Park Service is no longer providing estimates. People can come up with their own estimates!

Framing the size of demonstrations is of major consequence to one's political cause. The politics of counting the crowd seem to be headed toward asking those who would gain the most what they know the count to be! Newspaper reporters helped get themselves in this mess. It will be interesting to see them find their way out. Hopefully, we will not witness a move back toward SWAG to fill the gap created by the government's decision to no longer offer an official count.

—contributed by Ronald T. Wohlstein

Demonstrations typically follow the familiar form of the rally or march, or a combination of these. The most common demonstration event is the rally. A *rally* is a seated or standing gathering in which the majority of participants are located in arcs or rings around one or more speakers and perform speeches, songs, chants, and/or applause. The three largest demonstrations of the 1990s (the 1993 Gay Rights March on Washington, the Million Man March of 1995, and the 1997 Promise Keepers Stand in the Gap Sacred Assembly of Men) were primarily rally events. A *march* is the collective locomotion of rally participants to a park or other public forum area. Organizers and public officials have agreed upon the time and route of the march during the permitting process. Marchers generally proceed in a loose, rank-and-file fashion. Celebrities and organizers usually occupy the leading of the march. Those in the "celebrity ranks" of the march set the variable cadence of the procession. McPhail notes that the most common sequence of demonstration events is the rally-march-rally sequence. The 1963 March on the Pentagon took this form. An afternoon antiwar rally was held at the Lincoln Memorial, followed by a march to the Pentagon and an early evening rally at the Pentagon. This rally included civil disobedience, violence, and arrests. Other common sequences are the march-rally sequence and the rally-march sequence (McPhail, 1985).

Less common forms of demonstration events are the *picket*, *vigil*, and *civil disobedience*. When picketing, people walk single file or two or three abreast, carrying placards stating the focus of their protest or principle. While the permitting process in Washington, DC, places no restrictions on the substantive content of banners, placards or speeches of picketers, it can restrict the number of picketers, their location on sidewalks and their distances from building entrances. A vigil is a stationary line of people standing side by side and in a common direction, often carrying placards stating the focus of their protest or promotion. Pickets and vigils may be maintained for hours or days. For several years, anti-apartheid groups maintained a continuous, around-the-clock vigil outside the South African Embassy in London. The vigil ended when Nelson Mandela was released from prison. Both pickets and vigils may utilize portable sound equipment. Agreed-upon restrictions may be placed on the volume setting of this equipment.

Very few demonstrations involve civil disobedience and few acts of civil disobedience are disorderly or violent. During the 1960s civil disobedience included the open commission of illegal acts, primarily the burning of draft cards. Then, as now, civil disobedience also included sit-downs that blocked pedestrian or vehicular traffic, or otherwise obstructed routine movement in a thoroughfare, entryway, or place of business. In the 1960s civil disobedience often included the use of force by police in the course of halting the demonstration and making arrests. Protesters also often used force. The public order management system used by Washington, DC, and other large metropolitan police agencies today can better accommodate civil disobedience. Prior to the demonstration, authorities may have several meetings with protest organizers and other affected parties to negotiate the time, place, and manner of the demonstration, as well as march routes and rally sites. If authorities ascertain that civil disobedience is on the demonstration agenda, event planning may include disseminating forms soliciting prearrest information from those planning to be arrested, an outline of arrest procedures, and the rights of arrestees. Planning will also include provisions for the transportation of arrestees. Arrests will be made with the minimal use of force.

McPhail has identified approximately forty elementary forms of collective action that commonly occur within demonstration gatherings. These behaviors constitute an ever-changing "patchwork quilt" of activity. Collective action is seldom continuous or exhibited by all people in the gathering. Collective action includes facing in a convergent or common direction. People commonly face themselves in a convergent manner while conversing with their companions within the gathering. People typically arrange themselves in arcs and rings around a speaker. These facing arrangements change during the course of the gathering.

Moments of silence are not uncommon during rallies. More often, however, we hear intermittent voicing in common, such as cheering or singing. Such voicing in common takes the form of *vocalizing*, such as cheering, booing, laughing, hissing, or whistling; or *verbalizing*, such as chanting, singing, praying, or counting cadence. People intersperse voicing in common with conversations with companions and others in the gathering. During demonstrations, people move or position their bodies in a similar manner at the same time and direction. Collective locomotion takes the form of walking and, often, running, marching, sitting, standing and jumping. Kneeling, kowtowing and prostrating are often observed at religious demonstrations. During demonstrations people manipulate some portion of their bodies in common; this almost always takes the form of applause. People may also snap their fingers to show disregard, and gesture with fingers, fists, arms and hands. People collectively manipulate some other object, such as placards or banners. Police may hold batons or shields. Objects are thrown, including beach balls, water balloons, or rocks and teargas canisters. People may strike and break seats, fencing, or windows. People may embrace, carry, or strike another person. These elementary forms of collective action are described and illustrated with photographs in *The Collective Action Observation Primer* (McPhail, Schweingruber, and Berns, 1997).

The Social Organization of Demonstrations

In the parks, subways, and other public areas of large American cities, one can usually see a person who is carrying a placard or wearing a sandwich board displaying a message of protest, a warning, or a proclamation. These messages may be very bizarre or confusing, and the persons displaying them may seem quite eccentric. Occasionally, a few such people may carry out a demonstration; often they are largely ignored, and spectators may outnumber them. The Park Service police and the Metropolitan Police may issue on-the-spot demonstration permits to impromptu demonstrations. Many of the over 2,000 demonstrations held each year in Washington, DC, are small and probably include fewer than a hundred participants. Large demonstrations, of between a thousand and ten thousand participants, are comparatively rare. Very large demonstrations of more than 50,000 people comprise less than 1 percent of all demonstrations held in Washington, DC. Although they represent a very small percentage of all demonstrations, very large demonstrations are, nonetheless, perceived as important by the authorities, the media, and social movement organizations. Such demonstrations may be used to initiate or change national agendas and to press major political claims. To organize a demonstration by even a small, close-knit group takes some prior planning. To organize a very large demonstration, drawing together numerous groups requires an enormous amount of planning. The social organization of a very large demonstration is presented in figure 16.1.

The most elemental social grouping within large demonstrations is the social cluster of two to six people that constitute kin, friendship or acquaintance group. A large majority of people in demonstration gatherings are there with their kin, friends, or acquaintances (McPhail, 1997). People in these groups may have decided to come to the demonstration together, made travel and lodging arrangements, and traveled to Washington as a group. These people try to remain together during the demonstration, leave the demonstration together, and return home together.

Social clusters may, in turn, be part of larger delegations from neighborhoods, churches, schools or workplaces. Delegations are composed of members of unions, social movement organization chapters, and other special-interest groups. Delega-

FIGURE 16.1: Social Structure of a Large Demonstration

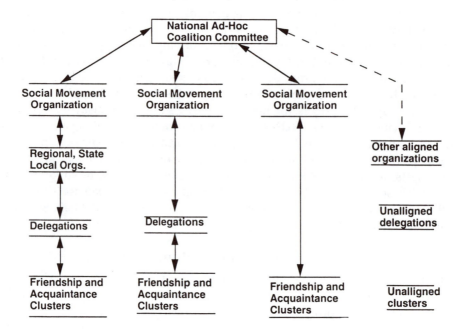

tions may identify themselves by dress, badges, placards, or banners. Large delegations may be assigned to satellite assembly sites distant from the main rally site and march to the rally site at times and by routes specified by the demonstration permit. In addition to activities planned for the demonstration, delegations may also follow additional agendas of meetings, rallies, memorials, worship services, and lobbying activities that have been scheduled before or after the demonstration. National, regional, or state social movement organizations, union organizations, and religious organizations recruit members to fill delegation quotas. The organizations may also arrange transportation, lodging, and meals for delegations.

Generally, it is a national coalition of groups that organize very large demonstrations rather than a single social movement organization. In the case of a demonstration such as the Promise Keepers Sacred Assembly of Men, the national Promise Keepers organization led a coalition of other religious groups who also supported and recruited delegations to attend the rally. A national coalition committee typically will have a coordinator, or chief of staff, and representatives from other member organizations. The national committee also consists of a support staff of technical specialists and clerical workers. The committee may include consultants who are veteran organizers, familiar with permitting procedures, and the public order maintenance system. Finally, the coalition may include celebrities who are associated with the cause and who are sought after by the media.

Organization and Planning Early in the planning, the national coordinator secures endorsements from the leadership of other issue-related national organizations. Endorsers usually include a wide range of churches and religious groups such as the American Women's Clergy Association, Sisters of Saint Joseph of Peace, or the Knights of Columbus. Unions and trade associations may endorse the demonstration. Professional and business associations and individual corporations may endorse the demonstration. McPhail notes that endorsers are expected to mobilize as many of their members as possible. Using the structure of existing churches, unions, and other social movement organizations to provide large delegations of participants for demonstrations is referred to as block recruiting. Other common ways of recruiting participants in demonstrations include the use of leaflets and media announcements. These methods are directed at individuals and probably are less effective than block recruiting. Finally, legislators, celebrities, and other individuals will be solicited for their endorsements.

Endorsers are also expected to contribute money and other services to the effort. Because they are contributing recruitment, money, and other services to the effort, endorsers expect a certain *quid pro quo* in return. Endorsers expect to have input in the formulating of the demonstration agenda and to receive a prominent place in the proceedings, including the opportunity to address the rally at length. Formulating the demonstration agenda includes determining the kind and sequence of demonstration events, for instance a rally, or a rally and a march, or whether civil disobedience will be used. The time and location of the rally and any march routes must be approved in the permit negotiation process with public officials. Setting the demonstration agenda also includes negotiating the order of marchers in the celebrity ranks and the selection and sequencing of rally speakers and performers. As the agenda is developed, printed materials such as programs, leaflets, banners, signs, badges, and t-shirts are designed.

Publicity An important element in the social organization of very large demonstrations is publicity. Coalition leaders determine the general outlines of a publicity campaign. Media specialists within the coalition committee staff create websites and contact wire services, newspapers, and talk shows. The media staff identifies sympathetic reporters and editors to receive background information on issues and prepared news releases. The media staff prepares coalition leaders for scheduled news conferences and other media events.

Logistics A very large demonstration is a logistical challenge and may come to utilize the talents of many specialists. Dozens of contracts must be negotiated prior to a very large demonstration. These include contracts for the printing of programs, leaflets, banners, signs, badges, and t-shirts. Thousands of buses may need to be chartered and arrangements made for their parking when not in use. For very large demonstrations, directions from public transportation terminals to satellite assembly sites and the routes of feeder marches to the primary assembly site must be provided to incoming delegations. Area churches and charitable organizations must be contacted to obtain temporary housing for disadvantaged or student participants.

Contracts for portable staging, sound and light systems, tents and toilets need to be obtained well in advance of the demonstration date. Medical aides, nurses, and emergency medics are recruited or volunteer to work at the demonstration site. Physicians are recruited to oversee the work of medical aides. Medical problems encountered at very large demonstrations include diabetic shock, heart attack, drug reactions, heat stroke, and sprains.

Liaison between coalition staff and police agencies may begin months in advance of the demonstration and may involve dozens of meetings at all organizational levels. The public order management system approach defines the role of police as protecting the demonstrators' First Amendment guarantees, and, if possible, to let demonstration organizers do the actual enforcement of the permit. Police are encouraged to engage in prior planning with demonstration organizers in order to facilitate the orderly exercise of the First Amendment. Police can provide a national coalition committee with useful advice regarding the management of very large numbers of demonstrators. Police are likely to be more aware of transportation and traffic problems associated with very large numbers, rally locations, and march routes than are demonstration organizers. Police will also try to ascertain in advance whether or not civil disobedience is planned. If civil disobedience is planned, police may familiarize organizers with arrest procedures, jail facilities, and bail and arraignment policies.

Public order management systems are based on the view that demonstration organizers, not the police, should take primary responsibility in controlling the demonstration events. Hundreds of demonstration marshals are needed to guide, direct, lead, and organize the individuals, clusters, and delegations which make up the demonstration. Consequently a major logistical challenge for national committee staff is the recruiting, training and coordinating of marshals. Veterans of previous demonstrations may be selected to serve as marshal supervisors. Generally, however, a substantial number of new marshals need to be recruited and trained. Some new marshals are trained by the Community Relations Service of the U.S. Department of Justice. Their training includes familiarization with the demonstration chain of command, and the agreed-upon agenda. Training also includes lessons from the *Rights, Rules and Responsibilities of Demonstrators and Marshals*, a document prepared by the National Organization for Women for demonstrations. Marshals may be trained specifically to work with buses, to work at rallies, or to accompany marches. Marshals must become familiar with the use of communication equipment and procedures. Finally, marshals must be prepared to handle medical problems and also violations of the demonstration permit, First Amendment rights, and any other laws during the demonstration.

Finally, the logistics for very large demonstrations includes the provision of legal assistance. Even if civil disobedience is not planned, legal observers are selected from lawyers, law students and paralegals. These people are trained to observe, and record in writing, any events that violate the permit, abridge First Amendment rights, or violate any other laws during demonstration. Legal observers prepare briefs and may testify as trained and impartial observers at later court proceedings, if any.

SUMMARY

In the early days of May, 1970, students at Kent State University held two peaceful antiwar rallies protesting the unannounced incursion of U.S. troops into Cambodia, an expansion of the Vietnam War. During the next 24 hours, attempts by police to break up gatherings of students resulted in violence, property damage and arrests. The mayor of Kent called the Governor of Ohio and requested that the National Guard be sent to Kent State. Kent State University administrators denounced the violence and banned further demonstrations. The Governor sent the Guard to Kent State with orders to break up any gathering on campus whether it was peaceful or violent. He authorized the use of every force of law and every possible weapon to make the county safe. In particular, the Governor denounced student demonstrators as ". . . the strongest, well trained militant group that has ever assembled in America" (Lewis, 1975). At noon on May 4, a company of National Guard opened fire on a gathering of students that were conducting an antiwar rally. Four students were killed, and nine were wounded.

In the six years preceding the deaths at Kent State, widespread and frequent violent disorders had become commonplace in the United States. Mississippi police had already killed two students at Jackson State University, and three students were killed and 27 wounded during a civil rights demonstration in Orangeburg, South Carolina. In some senses, college students fared comparatively well compared to the hundreds of people who had died in nationwide urban riots from 1965 through 1970. Virtually every city with a population of more than 100,000 had experienced violent disorder in this five-year period. The 1968 Democratic National Convention in Chicago was the scene of a week of disorder, violent confrontations between police and students, and mass arrests.

In the intervening three decades since Kent State, we have observed a dramatic change in the policing of demonstrations and other gatherings in the United States. In the 1960s, the prevailing "escalated force" strategy involved an initial show of force by the police, followed by a graduated escalation of force to control or disperse demonstrators (McPhail and McCarthy, 1998). Beginning in the 1970s the "negotiated management" style of policing demonstrations evolved in large U.S. cities, with a resulting decline in the frequency and intensity of violent disorder. Public order maintenance systems emphasize contact and interaction between police and demonstrators prior to and continuing through the demonstration itself.

Three presidential commissions of inquiry between 1968 and 1970 concluded that a nationwide change in policing methods was in order. Thus began an in-depth assessment of prevailing policing procedures. This assessment included an examination of the work of sociologists and other social scientists. Jerry Lewis' (1972) analysis of the tragic killings at Kent State, for instance, included the insight that the morning's events had closed all communication channels between students and the Guard, and that a few moments of negotiation could have prevented the killings. Terry Knoph (1969a; 1969b; 1975) identified "pro-social" forces in riots and the importance of maintaining communication between the police and community members. Authorities sought the views and recommendations of many sociologists, including McPhail.

Looking back, this author feels that sociologists have developed a great deal of knowledge regarding contentious politics, social movements, protest, and demonstrations since the 1960s. Furthermore, this knowledge has contributed to the well-being of our society. The knowledge and insight developed by sociologists and other social scientists has helped bring about a fundamental improvement in policing in the United States and other modern democracies. Once, our major cities endured rioting every summer; demonstrations often ended in violence, property damage, and mass arrests. Today, our cities are far calmer and demonstrations are an acceptable part of the political process.

We have discovered much about collective behavior and collective action in this past century. Much of this knowledge has been put to good use. Still, much is yet to be discovered. I hope many of you will join us on these new adventures.

Appendix
COLLECTIVE ACTION AND PERCEPTION CONTROL THEORY

Scattered throughout this text are several references to perception control theory, a perspective unfamiliar to most readers. Since my application of this perspective to collective action is one effort to address the shortcomings of both collective behavior and collective action explanations of collective phenomena, the author and editor have graciously invited me to offer the following synopsis.

The Decade of the Brain. About the same time that students of collective action were becoming disillusioned with the rational calculus model of purposive action, the U.S. Congress and President George Bush proclaimed the 1990s "the decade of the brain." While physical anthropologists tell us the structure of the human brain and the central nervous system have not changed over the past 30,000 years, more has been learned about the brain's structure and processes in the last two decades than in all previous history. The trillions of connections between the billions of neurons in our brain form a complex neural network. The neural net processes the primitive information received from our various sensory receptors (e.g., eyes, ears, nose, tongue, and skin). It makes possible both the storage of that processed information in and its retrieval from multiple memory sites distributed throughout the neural net. It conveys the electrical and chemical signals through the central nervous system and the spinal chord to the several hundred voluntary muscle control systems distributed throughout the body which are responsible for almost every verbal and nonverbal action in which we engage. Revolutionary new brain scanning and other research techniques document these general structures and processes. The scanning technologies provide dramatic representations of the brain areas where and while those processes take place. These also provide evidence for what I refer to as the images or "pictures in the mind's eye" of purposive actors.

Because human beings have always lived in constantly changing environments, their survival has depended on continuous interplay between the sensory receptors providing information about that environment, the brain that processes that information and the voluntary muscle systems that adjust the actions necessary to deal with those changes. This was no less true for our ancestors' survival in savannas filled with carnivorous wild beasts than it is for contemporary confrontations between public order police armed with shields and truncheons who face anarchist protesters armed with paving stones and Molotov cocktails. Every perception, thought, feeling, or recollection of any one of those individuals, every action they take or adjust, is a product of the connections and interactions, the "feed-forward" and feedback loops, in their respective neural nets.

Perception Control Theory. The theory I have found most useful for making sense of the ongoing relationships between sensory experiences, cognitive processing, and purposive adjustments of action in volatile environments is William T. Powers's (1973; 1998) perception control theory. There is considerable support for this theory in the contemporary neuroscience literature (e.g., the work of Antonio Damasio), as well as much compatibility with the earlier theoretical writings of John Dewey, G. H. Mead, and Erving Goffman, and the contemporary work of sociologists Peter Burke, Kent McClelland, and Charles Tilly.

The basic premise of perception control theory is that individuals act, or adjust their actions, in order to make their current perceptions correspond to or approximate their reference perceptions. By reference perceptions, I mean the image(s) or picture(s) "in the mind's eye" that the individual has retrieved from memory to serve as the goal, target or intended outcome to be accomplished by the adjustment of his or her actions.

Perception control is not about others controlling the perceptions of the individual by propaganda or "spin." Rather, it is about the individual adding layers of clothing in the wintertime and peeling them off in the summertime in order to keep his or her body temperature around 98.6 degrees. It is about adding just enough salt or pepper to one's food to make it taste just right according to the standard in the mind's "palette." It is about raising one's voice loud enough (in the mind's "ear") to be heard by oneself and one's companion over the ambient noise on the subway, at the concert, the rally, or the cocktail party. It is about organizing—about planning, preparing, and pulling off—the party, formal dinner, wedding, funeral, or protest event that corresponds to the picture in the organizer's head. While some reference perceptions are innate or hard wired (e.g., body temperature), most are acquired and modified in the course of the individual's interaction with others and his or her environment.

It is the disparity between the reference perception and one's current perception of the situation under consideration that ordinarily leads to immediate or eventual adjustments in actions. Those purposive adjustments almost always enter a dynamic environment containing random disturbances or deliberate obstacles. These bumps and blockades take their toll on the intended results of purposive actions. Consequently, the current perceptions of outcome frequently don't initially match the reference perceptions. Continuing disturbances yielding continuing disparities require continuing adjustments to realize and maintain the desired correspondence or approximation between current perception and reference perception. Any driver can appreciate the difficulty of maintaining the intended direction and path of his or her vehicle's movement on a bumpy or slippery roadway surface when there are strong and gusting crosswinds not to mention rain, sleet, or snowfall. Continuous vigilance and adjustment are essential to survival. The causal relationships between reference perception, purposive action, dynamic environment, and current perception are not linear, they are continuous and recursive. Thus, perception control theory is often labeled a "closed-loop, negative feedback" model of purposive action.

**A Single Closed-Loop, Negative Feedback, Control System
(After Powers, 1973)**

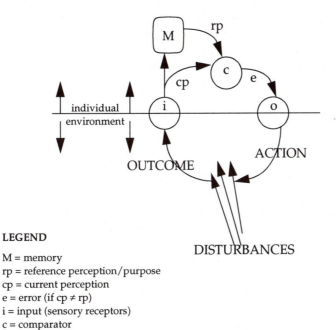

LEGEND

M = memory
rp = reference perception/purpose
cp = current perception
e = error (if cp ≠ rp)
i = input (sensory receptors)
c = comparator
o = output

Every individual brings to any point in space and time an accumulated and unique history of personal experiences stored in memories. Those memories provide the basis for the individual's definition or framing of new as well as familiar situations. Memories also constitute the repertoire from which the individual draws reference perceptions for purposive actions in the immediate or more distant future. The individual then adjusts his or her actions in order to reproduce or approximate once again what was recalled from his or her past experiences.

Alternating Individual and Collective Actions. Why must a theory of collective action in temporary gatherings include a theory of individual action? It is because the most characteristic feature of any temporary gathering is the ongoing alternation between individual and collective actions! Individuals interact with their companions and then act alone, they may then act collectively with a larger numbers of others in the gathering, then interact with their companions, and again act alone. An adequate theory of purposive action should explain both individual and collective action with the same set of principles.

Sources of Collective Action. How are two or more individuals, each with unique personal histories stored in memory, able to interact with one another let alone engage in more inclusive collective action? There are at least two compatible answers, although one is a bit more complicated. First, most all of us have had headaches and stomachaches. From experience we know that all the headaches are not alike, but they have sufficient similarities among them, and sufficient distinctions from stomachaches, that we place the former in a distinctive category labeled "headaches." We do the same with our experiences of stomachaches, toothaches, backaches, and even heartaches. While no one can experience another's aches, we can "share" the symbols or names given those different categories of experiences. Those symbols make up the language that makes communication possible about aches as well as assembling processes, actors, actions, and other objects and events.

Second, Charles Tilly has researched and written extensively about "repertoires" of political collective action, an idea similar to what some earlier scholars called "collective memory." Tilly compares repertoires of political collective action to the repertoires of melodies, chords, and keys familiar to jazz musicians. Musicians who are total strangers, but familiar with those repertoires, can "sit in" during jam sessions and make music together. The contemporary repertoire of political collective action includes vigils, picket lines, rallies, processions, and a slightly different form of "sit-in."

My extension of Powers's perception control theory of purposive individual action to purposive collective action turns on one fundamental assumption. For two or more individuals to engage in collective action—either parallel actions at the same time or different actions taken simultaneously or sequentially—they must adjust their respective individual actions to realize similar or related reference perceptions. There are three or more ways in which such similar or related reference perceptions can be established.

Independently. People who have interacted a great deal with one another, who are part of the same daily rounds, social networks, groups, and cultures, are more likely to have similar named categories of experiences stored in memory from which they can independently draw similar reference perceptions. For example, in many cultures applause is one appropriate way of showing approval or enjoyment of what one has seen or heard. In such cultures a gathering of individuals does not have to be asked or told, nor does anyone have to consult their neighbor about when to applaud when their team scores the game winning point, when a speaker finishes a compelling speech, or when a musician concludes a thrilling performance. Two or more members of a gathering can and do independently call up that reference perception as the appropriate outcome to achieve by slapping their open palms together and doing so at more or less the same time. Hence the collective action of applause.

Interdependently. We all have experienced something we did not initially understand clearly. We all have been confronted with a task we could not complete by our actions alone. Thus we frequently require the assistance or cooperation of one or more additional individuals. This problem can be as simple as not hearing or fully understanding what a speaker has just said to the gathering of which we are a part. Thus we may ask the person next to us to repeat what the speaker said or even what it meant. Or it could be the more complex problem of moving a sofa or other piece of large furniture up or down a stairwell or into an adjoining room. When one person requires the assistance of another, or when two or more people are confronted with a mutual problem to be solved, they can interact by signifying in words and gestures what needs to be done, and who will do what, when, where, and how. thereby they interdependently establish the similar or related reference perceptions in relation to which, simultaneously or sequentially, they will adjust their respective actions to solve the problem.

Adoption from a Third Party. The more complex the problem to be solved, and the more people required for that solution, the more important it becomes to have a single source of reference perceptions. I refer to that single source as a "third party," who addresses similar or different but related reference perceptions for adoption by two or more other individuals. The third party cannot stick those reference perceptions into the brains of the other individuals in question. They must adopt them as their own and then adjust their similar or different but related actions in order to realize the intended outcome established by the reference perceptions. Familiar examples of third parties include the principal organizer for large events (protests, weddings, funerals, reunions), the coach of an athletic team, the director of a church choir, the commanding officer of a military or police unit, the chief of a construction crew, etc.

It is often the case that the third party has devised a solution for a complex problem but requires the coordinated participation and cooperation of many others in order to realize that solution. When a large number of others are involved, all will not be able to see or hear the collective outcome of the individual actions they have contributed. Only the third party can perceive that outcome, compare it to the reference perception in his or her head, and then ask others to make the adjustments in their actions that will yield the collective outcome that approximates or corresponds to that reference perception. Whether the third party is an organizer, coach, choir director, commanding officer, or construction crew chief, his or her feedback and proposals to (and the adjustments by) the individual demonstrators, singers, rank and file officers, or construction workers, respectively, are essential to bring the envisioned collective outcome to fruition.

Third-party sources of reference perceptions are often necessarily supplemented by interaction between some individuals who do not hear or understand or perhaps are reluctant to do what the third party asks. And it is frequently the case that the actual implementation of what the third party asks other individuals to do assumes that they can and will independently draw upon their individual memories for additional bits and pieces of cultural knowledge to supplement what the third party has requested or proposed. Thus, the three sources of similar or related reference perceptions—independent, interdependent, or third party—can operate separately or in various combinations.

My application of Powers's perception control theory to individual and collective action is an unfinished work in progress, a product of the individual and collaborative contributions of my students, colleagues, and myself. Perhaps this synopsis will encourage others to undertake their own applications of perception control theory to the purposive individual and collective phenomena in which they are interested and to which David Miller's text provides an excellent introduction.

—*contributed by Clark McPhail*

BIBLIOGRAPHY

Abraham, Ken
  1997   *Who Are the Promise Keepers? Understanding the Christian Men's Movement.* New York: Doubleday.
Adams, David
  1996   The Weird Tale of the Goatsucker. *St. Petersburg Times,* March 21. Available: www.princeton.edu/~accion/chupa19.html
Adamski, George
  1955   *Inside the Spaceships.* Vista, CA: GAF International/Adamski Foundation, P.O. Originally published: London: Arco-Spearman.
Alinsky, Saul D.
  1972   *Rules for Radicals.* New York: Vintage Books.
Allport, Gordon W., and Leo J. Postman
  1965   *The Psychology of Rumor.* New York: Holt, Rinehart & Winston.
Angle, Paul M.
  1975   *Bloody Williamson.* New York: Alfred A. Knopf.
Arnold, Kenneth, and Ray Palmer
  1952   *The Coming of the Flying Saucers.* Amherst, WI: Amherst Press.
Aronson, Sidney
  1951   The Sociology of the Bicycle. *Social Forces* 30:305–312.
Asch, Solomon E.
  1958   Effects of Group Pressure upon the Modification and Direction of Judgments, in Eleanore E. Maccoby, Theodore Newcomb, and Eugene Hartly (eds.), *Readings in Social Psychology,* 3d ed. New York: Holt, Rinehart & Winston, pp. 174–183.
Astroturf: The Best Friend Money Can Buy. Available: http://opera.cbc.ca/grass.html
Atyeo, Don
  1979   *Blood and Guts: Violence in Sports.* New York: Paddington Press.
Aveni, Adrian
  1977   The Not-So-Lonely Crowd: Friendship Groups in Collective Behavior, *Sociometry* 40:96–99.
Babaszak, Lee Ann
  1998.   Use of the Initiative Process by Woman Suffrage Movements, in Costain, Anne N. and Andrew McFarland (eds.), *Social Movements and American Political Institutions.* Lanham, MD: Rowman & Littlefield, pp. 99–114.
Backman, Milton V., Jr.
  1980   *Joseph Smith's First Vision.* Salt Lake City, UT: Bookcraft.
BADIL
  1998   Badil Resource Center for Palestinian Residency and Refugee Rights. Available: www.badil.org

Bailey, Jane, and Clark McPhail
  1979   The Assembling Process: A Replication and Procedure for Further Study. Paper presented at the annual meeting of the Midwest Sociological Association, Minneapolis, Minnesota.
Barkan, Steven E.
  1979   Strategic, Tactical and Organizational Dilemmas of the Protest Movement against Nuclear Power, *Social Problems* 27 (1):19–37.
Bartholomew, R. E., K. Basterfield, and G. S. Howard
  1991   UFO Abductees and Contactees: Psychopathology or Fantasy Proneness? *Professional Psychology: Research and Practice* 22:215–222.
Barton, Allan H.
  1969   *Communities in Disaster: A Sociological Analysis of Collective Stress Situations.* Garden City, NY: Doubleday.
Beal, Merrill D.
  1963   *I Will Fight No More Forever: Chief Joseph and the Nez Percé War.* Seattle: University of Washington Press.
Belfrage, Sally
  1965   *Freedom Summer.* New York: Viking Press.
Bell, Daniel, and Virginia Held
  1969   The Community Revolution, *The Public Interest* 16 (Summer): 142–177.
Bendix, Rinehard
  1962   *Max Weber: An Intellectual Portrait.* New York: Doubleday.
Berk, Richard
  1974   A Gaming Approach to Crowd Behavior, *Sociological Review* 39:355–73.
Berk, Richard A., and Howard E. Aldrich
  1972   Patterns of Vandalism during Civil Disorders as an Indicator of Selection of Targets, *American Sociological Review* 37:535–547.
Bernhardt, Todd
  1997   Disaster Mythology: A Content Analysis from 1985 to 1995. Paper presented at the 1997 Midwest Sociological Society Meeting, Des Moines, Iowa.
Best, Richard L.
  1977   *Reconstruction of a Tragedy: The Beverly Hills Supper Club Fire.* Boston: National Fire Prevention and Control Administration, NFPA No. LS-2.
Black, Paul W.
  1912   Lynchings in Iowa, *Iowa Journal of History and Politics* 10:151–254.
Blanchard, Eric D.
  1968   The Poor People and the "White Press," *Columbia Journalism Review* 7:61–65.
Blumer, Herbert
  1937   Collective Behavior, in Robert Park (ed.), *Principles of Sociology.* New York: Barnes & Noble, pp. 219–288.
  1939   Collective Behavior, in Robert Park (ed.), *Principles of Sociology,* 2d ed. New York: Barnes & Noble, pp. 221–279.
  1946   Collective Behavior, in A. M. Lee (ed.), *New Outline of the Principles of Sociology.* New York: Barnes & Noble, pp. 170–222.
  1957   Collective Behavior, in J. B. Gittler (ed.), *Review of Sociology: Analysis of a Decade.* New York: Wiley, pp. 127–158.
  1969   Outline of Collective Behavior, in Robert R. Evans (ed.), *Readings in Collective Behavior.* Chicago: Rand McNally, pp. 65–88 (orig. pub. 1939).
  1972   Outline of Collective Behavior, in Robert R. Evans (ed.), *Readings in Collective Behavior,* 2d ed. Chicago: Rand McNally, pp. 22–45.
Boodman, Sandra G.
  1994   Mystery: Was It a Case of Mass Hysteria or Poisoning by a Toxic Chemical? *Washington Post,* September 13, WH, 10:3.

Brewster, Ethelyn O.
  1997   Three Mile Island: A Case Study for the 21st Century? Student paper, Department of Sociology and Anthropology, Western Illinois University.
Broom, Leonard, and Phillip Selznick
  1968   *Sociology: A Text with Adapted Readings*, 4th ed. New York: Harper & Row.
Brown, Dee
  1971   *Bury My Heart at Wounded Knee.* New York: Holt, Rinehart & Winston.
Brown, Earl
  1944   *Why Race Riots?* New York: AMS Press.
Brown, Roger W.
  1954   Mass Phenomena, in Gardner Lindzey (ed.), *Handbook of Social Psychology* (vol. 2). New York: Free Press, pp. 833–876.
Bruning, James L.
  1964   Leadership in Disaster, *Psychology* 1:19–23.
Brunvald, Jan Harold
  1993   *The Baby Train and Other Lusty Urban Legends.* New York: W.W. Norton.
Bruno, Jerry, and Jeff Greenfield
  1971   *The Advance Man.* New York: Bantam Books.
Bryan, John L.
  1983   *An Examination and Analysis of the Dynamics of the Human Behavior in the MGM Grand Hotel Fire.* (rev. ed.). Boston: National Fire Protection Association.
Buckner, H. Taylor
  1965   The Flying Saucerians: An Open Door Cult, in Marcello Truzzi (ed.), *Sociology and Everyday Life.* Englewood Cliffs, NJ: Prentice-Hall, pp. 223–230.
Buckwalter, Doyle W., and J. Ivan Legler
  1983   Antelope and Rajneeshpuram, Oregon—Clash of Cultures: A Case Study, *Urbanism Past and Present* 16 (8):1–13.
Bullock, Paul
  1969   *Watts: The Aftermath.* New York: Grove Press.
Burke, Peter
  1991   Identity Processes and Social Stress, *American Sociological Review* 56:836–849.
Burnette, Robert, and John Koster
  1974   *The Road to Wounded Knee.* New York: Bantam Books.
Bush, John C.
  1979   *Disaster Response: A Handbook for Church Action.* Scottsdale, PA: Herald Press.
Cahill, Tim
  1979   Into the Valley of the Shadow of Death, *Rolling Stone,* January 25.
California Governor's Commission on the Los Angeles Riots
  1965   *Violence in the City—An End or Beginning? A Report.* Los Angeles: City of Los Angeles.
Cantril, Hadley
  1940   *The Invasion from Mars.* New York: Harper & Row.
  1941   *The Psychology of Social Movements.* New York: John Wiley.
  1966   *The Invasion from Mars: A Study in the Psychology of Panic.* New York: Harper & Row.
Catton, William R., Jr.
  1957   What Kinds of People Does a Religious Cult Attract? *American Sociological Review* 22:563.
Chalker, Bill
  1996   *Australian Aboriginal Culture and Possible UFO Connections.* Available: www.ifog.org/project1947/forum/bcabor.htm
Clayman, Steven E.
  1993   The Anatomy of a Disaffiliative Response. *American Sociological Review* 56:110–123.

Clelland, Donald A., Thomas C. Hood, C. M. Lipskey, and Ronald Wimberley
  1974   In the Company of the Converted: Characteristics of a Billy Graham Crusade
          Audience, *Sociological Analysis* 35:45–56.
Cohen, Jerry, and William S. Murphy
  1966   *Burn, Baby, Burn! The Los Angeles Race Riots, August, 1965.* New York: Dutton.
Cohen, Warren
  1998   The Windy City's Tough Tack on Street Gangs. U.S. *News & World Report*, p. 30,
          December 14.
Coleman, James S., Elihu Katz, and Herbert Menzel
  1957   The Diffusion of an Innovation among Physicians, *Sociometry* 20 (December):
          253–270.
Coleman, Terry
  1972   *Going to America.* New York: Pantheon Books.
Conot, Robert
  1967   *Rivers of Blood, Years of Darkness.* New York: Bantam Books.
Cose, Ellis
  1997   …Promises. *Newsweek*, 130 (October 13):30–31.
Couch, Carl J.
  1968   Collective Behavior: An Examination of Some Stereotypes, *Social Problems*
          15:310–322.
  1970   Dimensions of Association in Collective Behavior Episodes, *Sociometry* 33:457–
          471.
Crozat, Matthew
  1998   "Are the Times A-Changin'?" Assessing the Acceptance of Protest in Western
          Democracies. In David S. Meyer and Sidney Tarrow (eds.), *The Social Movement
          Society: Contentious Politics for a New Century.* Lanham, MD: Rowman & Littlefield.
Cranshaw, Ralph
  1963   Reactions to Disaster, *Archives of General Psychiatry* 1:157–162.
Crop Circular, The
  1998   NBC's "Unmasked: The Secrets of Deception"—An Ugly Debrief. Available:
          www/nh/ultranet.com/~lovely/homepg.html
Curry, G. David, and Irving A. Spergel
  1990   *Differential Patterns of Gang Involvement among Hispanic and Black Adolescent
          Males: Promise for Prevention?* ERIC Accession Number: ED 320989.
Dacy, Douglas C., and Howard Kunreuther
  1969   *The Economics of Natural Disaster.* New York: Free Press.
Daily Telegraph
  1987   The *Poseidon* Disaster. Sunday *Telegraph*: 234, March 8.
Danzig, Elliott R., Paul W. Thayer, and Lila R. Galanter
  1958   *The Effects of a Threatening Rumor on a Disaster-Stricken Community.* Pub. no. 517.
          Washington, DC: National Academy of Sciences, National Research Council.
Davidson, J., and J. March
  1996   Traumatic Stress Disorders, in A. Tasman, J. Kay and J. Lieberman (eds.), *Psy-
          chiatry*, Vol. 2, pp. 1085–1098.
Davies, James C.
  1969   The J-curve of Rising and Declining Satisfaction as a Cause of Some Great Rev-
          olutions and a Contained Rebellion, in H. D. Graham and T. R. Gurr (eds.), *Vio-
          lence in America.* New York: Bantam Books, pp. 690–731.
Dean, Jodi
  1998   *Aliens in America: Conspiracy Cultures from Outerspace to Cyberspace.* Ithaca and
          London: Cornell Paperbacks.
Demerath, Nicholas J., and Anthony F. C. Wallace
  1957   Human Adaptation to Disaster, *Human Organization* 16:1–2.

Douglas, Jack D.
 1967   *The Social Meanings of Suicide.* Princeton, NJ: Princeton University Press.
Drabek, Thomas E.
 1969   Social Processes in Disaster: Family Evacuation, *Social Problems* 16:336–349.
Drabek, Thomas E., and J. Eugene Haas
 1969   How Police Confront Disaster, *Transaction* 6:33–38.
Drabek, Thomas E., and Enrico L. Quarantelli
 1967   Scapegoats, Villains, and Disasters, *Transaction* 4:12–17.
Duke, Kevin
 1997   January/February. The Second Opinion: Maybe It Was a Dream. *Camp Chase Gazette.* Marietta OH: Camp Chase Publishing Co.
Dunning, Eric, and Norbert Elias
 1972   Folk Football in Medieval and Early Modern Britain, in Eric Dunning (ed.), *Sport: Readings from a Sociological Perspective.* Toronto: University of Toronto Press.
Dunning, Eric, Patrick Murphy, and John Williams
 1986   Spectator Violence at Football Matches. *British Journal of Sociology* 37:221–224.
 1988   *The Roots of Football Hooliganism.* London: Routledge & Kegan Paul.
Dunning, Eric, and Kenneth Sheard
 1979   *Barbarians, Gentlemen and Players: A Sociological Study of the Development of Rugby Football.* Oxford: Martin Robertson.
Dynes, Russell R.
 1970   *Organized Behavior in Disaster.* Lexington, MA: Heath.
 1975   The Comparative Study of Disaster: A Social Organization Approach, *Mass Emergencies* 1:21–32.
 1978   Interorganizational Relations in Communities under Stress, in Enrico L. Quarantelli (ed.), *Disasters: Theory and Research.* Beverly Hills, CA: Sage, pp. 49–65.
Elias, Norbert, and Eric Dunning
 1986   *Quest for Excitement: Sport and Leisure in the Civilizing Process.* Oxford: Basil Blackwell Ltd.
Erickson, Kai T.
 1976   *Everything in Its Path: Destruction of Community in the Buffalo Creek Flood.* New York: Simon & Schuster.
Eszterhas, Joe, and Michael D. Roberts
 1970   *Thirteen Seconds: Confrontation at Kent State.* New York: Dodd, Mead.
Evans, Robert R., and Jerry L. L. Miller
 1975   Barely an End in Sight, in Robert R. Evans (ed.), *Readings in Collective Behavior,* 2d ed. Chicago: Rand McNally, pp. 401–415.
Fagan, Brian M.
 1976   Introduction, in Brian M. Fagan (ed.), *Avenues to Antiquity: Readings from Scientific American.* San Francisco: W. H. Freeman, pp. 1–8.
Federal Emergency Management Administration
 1998   A Letter from St. Croix. Available: www.FEMA.gov/
Feierabend, Ivo K., Rosalind L. Feierabend, and B. Nesvold
 1969   Social Change and Political Violence: Cross-National Patterns, in Hugh D. Graham and Ted R. Gurr (eds.), *Violence in America.* New York: Bantam Books, pp. 632–688.
Feinberg, William E., and Norris K. Johnson
 1988   Outside Agitators and Crowds: Results from a Computer Simulation Model. *Social Forces* 67:2:398–423.
 1990   Ambiguity and Crowds: Results from a Computer Simulation Model. *Research in Social Movements, Conflict and Change.* JAI Press, Inc.:12:35–66.
Fellows, William J.
 1985   "Play Up Pompey": A Critical Study of the Nature and Meaning of Football Singing. Monograph, Dept. of Sociology, University of Essex.

Figler, Stephen K.
    1981   *Sport and Play in American Life*. Philadelphia: Saunders College Publishing.
Fischer, Henry W., III
    1988   *Disastrous Fantasizing in the Print Media: Differences in How Natural versus Tech-*
            nological Disasters Are Portrayed over a Forty-Year Period. Alliance, OH: Social
            Research Center, Mount Union College.
    1994   *Response to Disaster: Fact versus Fiction and Its Perpetuation*. Lanham, MD: Uni-
            versity Press of America.
Form, William
    1958   *Community in Disaster*. New York: Harper & Row.
Franke, Richard H., and James D. Kaul
    1978   The Hawthorne Experiments: First Statistical Interpretation, *American Sociolog-*
            ical Review 43:623–643.
Freeman, J.
    1975   *The Politics of Women—Liberation*. New York: McKay.
Freud, Sigmund
    1945   *Group Psychology and the Analysis of the Ego*. London: Hogarth (orig. pub. 1921).
Fritz, Charles E.
    1961   Disaster, in Robert K. Merton and Robert A. Nisbet (eds.), *Contemporary Social*
            Problems. New York: Harcourt Brace Jovanovich, pp. 651–694.
Fritz, Charles E., and Eli S. Marks
    1954   The NORC Studies of Human Behavior in Disaster, *Journal of Social Issues* 10:26–41.
Fritz, Charles E., and J. H. Mathewson
    1957   *Convergence Behavior in Disasters*. National Research Council Disaster Study
            No. 9. Washington DC: National Academy of Sciences.
Fritz, Charles E., Jeanette F. Rayner, and Samuel L. Guskin
    1958   *Behavior in an Emergency Shelter: A Field Study of 800 Persons Stranded in a High-*
            way Restaurant during a Heavy Snowstorm. National Academy of Sciences,
            National Research Council. Washington, DC: National Academy of Sciences.
Fuller, John G.
    1966   *The Interrupted Journey*. New York: Dial Press.
Gales, Kathleen
    1966   A Campus Revolution, *British Journal of Sociology* 17:1–19.
Gallup Poll
    1973   The Gallup Poll: Public Opinion 1935–1971, Vols. 1 and 3. New York: Random
            House.
    1978   The Gallup Poll: Public Opinion 1972–1977, Vol. 1. Wilmington, Delaware: Schol-
            arly Resources.
    1979   The Gallup Poll: Public Opinion 1978. Wilmington, Delaware: Scholarly Resources.
    1988   The Gallup Poll: Public Opinion 1987. Wilmington, Delaware: Scholarly Resources.
    1991   The Gallup Poll: Public Opinion 1990. Wilmington, Delaware: Scholarly Resources.
    1997   The Gallup Poll: Public Opinion 1996. Wilmington, Delaware: Scholarly Resources.
    1998   The Gallup Poll: Public Opinion 1996. Wilmington, Delaware: Scholarly Resources.
Gambrell, Richard
    1980   Issue Dynamics in Student Movements, *Social Forces* (March): 187–202.
Gamson, William A.
    1974   Violence and Political Power: The Meek Don't Make It, *Psychology Today* (July):
            35ff.
    1975   *The Strategy of Social Protest*. Homewood, IL: Dorsey Press.
    1990   *The Strategy of Social Protest*, 2d ed. Belmont, CA: Wadsworth Publishing.
Gamson, William A., Bruce Fireman, and Stephen Rytina
    1982   *Encounters with Unjust Authority*. Homewood, IL: Dorsey Press.
Garrett, W. E.
    1980   Thailand: Refuge from Terror, *National Geographic* (May):633–642.

Gerlach, Luther P., and Virginia H. Hine
   1970   *People, Power, Change: Movements of Social Transformation.* Indianapolis, IN: Bobbs-Merrill.
Gies, Joseph, and Francis Gies
   1969   *Life in a Medieval City.* New York: Harper Perennial.
Gimple, James G.
   1996   *Fulfilling the Contract: The First 100 Days.* Boston: Allyn and Bacon.
Gleick, Elizabeth
   1997   The Marker We've Been Waiting For. *Time* (April 7).
Goffman, Erving
   1963   *Behavior in Public Places.* New York: Free Press.
   1974   *Frame Analysis.* Cambridge, MA: Harvard University Press.
Graebner, William
   1998   *The Age of Doubt: American Thought and Culture in the 1940s.* Prospect Heights, IL: Waveland Press.
Gregg, Richard B.
   1966   *The Power of Nonviolence.* New York: Schocken Books.
Grimshaw, Allan D.
   1960   Urban Racial Violence in the United States: Changing Ecological Considerations. *The American Journal of Sociology* (September): 109–119.
   1968   Three Views of Urban Violence: Civil Disturbance, Racial Revolt, Class Assault. *The American Behavioral Scientist* (March–April): 2–7.
Guillen, Abraham
   1973   *Philosophy of the Urban Guerrilla, The Revolutionary Writings of Abraham Guillen,* Donald C. Hodges (trans.). New York: William Morrow.
Gurr, Ted R.
   1969   A Comparative Study of Civil Strife. In H. D. Graham and T. R. Gurr (eds.), *Violence in America.* New York: Bantam Books, pp. 572–626.
Gutschenritter, Martin J.
   1977   Operation CB/ID: Crime Prevention's Answer to CB Radio Thefts. *Police Chief* (April):62.
Guttman, Alan
   1986   *Sports Spectators.* New York: Columbia University Press.
Haas, J. Eugene, and Thomas E. Drabek
   1973   *Complex Organizations: A Sociological Perspective.* New York: Macmillan.
Haines, Herbert
   1984   "Black Radicalization and the Funding of Civil Rights: 1957–1970." *Social Problems* 32:31–33.
Haught, James A.
   1995   And Now, the Solar Temple. *Free Inquiry* (Winter 1994/95).
Heirich, Max
   1971   *The Spiral of Conflict: Berkeley, 1964.* New York: Columbia University Press.
Herald-News
   1980   *Winds of Fury: The Will County Tornado of 1990.* Sun City West, AZ: C.F. Boone Publishing.
Hill, Kevin A., and John E. Hughes
   1998   *Cyberpolitics: Citizen Activisim in the Age of the Internet.* Lanham, MA: Rowman & Littlefield.
Hitler, Adolph
   1943   *Mein Kampf.* Boston: Houghton Mifflin.
Hobsbaum, Eric J.
   1959   *Social Bandits and Primitive Rebels.* New York: Free Press.

Hoffner, Eric
    1951   *The True Believer: Thoughts on the Nature of Mass Movements.* New York: Harper & Row.
Honduras Institute of Tourism
    1998   The Official Honduras Institute of Tourism Response to Hurricane Mitch. Available: www.hondurasinfo.hn
Hopkins, Bud
    1981   *Missing Time: A Documented Study of UFO Abductions.* New York: Richard Marek.
    1987   *Intruders: The Incredible Visitations at Copley Woods.* New York: Random House.
Houseman, John
    1948   The Men from Mars. *Harper's* (December): 74–82.
Howard, George Elliott
    1912   Social Psychology of the Spectator. *American Journal of Sociology* 18:36, 44.
Hundley, James R., Jr.
    1968   The Dynamics of Recent Ghetto Riots. *Detroit Journal of Urban Law* 45:627–639.
Hunter, Floyd
    1963   *Community Power Structure, A Study of Decision Makers.* Garden City, New York: Doubleday.
Hynek, James Allen
    1972   *The UFO Experience: A Scientific Enquiry.* New York: Ballantine Books.
Jacobs, David M.
    1975   *The UFO Controversy in America.* Bloomington: Indiana University Press.
    1980   The Debunkers. In Curtis G. Fuller (ed.), *Proceedings of the First International UFO Congress.* New York: Warner Books, pp. 123–138.
Jacobson, D. J.
    1948   *The Affairs of Dame Rumor.* New York: Holt, Rinehart & Winston.
Jahoda, Gloria
    1975   *The Trail of Tears.* New York: Holt, Rinehart & Winston.
Janowitz, Morris
    1968   *Social Control of Escalated Riots.* Chicago: University of Chicago Press.
Johnson, Donald M.
    1945   The Phantom Anesthetist of Mattoon: A Field Study of Mass Hysteria. *Journal of Abnormal and Social Psychology* 40:175–186.
Johnson, Norris R., William E. Feinberg, and Drue M. Johnston
    1994   Microstructure and Panic: The Impact of Social Bonds on Individual Action in Collective Flight from the Beverly Hills Supper Club Fire. In K. Tierney and R. Dynes (eds.), *Disaster, Collective Behavior and Social Organization.* Newark: Delaware University Press, pp. 168–189.
Jones, Rhys
    1971   The Demography of Hunters and Farmers in Tasmania. In Derek J. Mulvaney and Jack Golson (eds.), *Aboriginal Man and Environment in Australia.* Canberra: Australian National University Press.
Karter M. J., Jr.
    1996   *Fire Loss in the United States during 1995.* Quincy, MA: National Fire Protection Association, 1996.
Keerdoja, Eileen P., and Patricia J. Sethi
    1980   CB Couldn't Keep on Truckin'. *Newsweek* (July 21):12.
Kelner, Joseph, and James Munves
    1980   *The Kent State Coverup.* New York: Harper & Row.
Kemp, William
    1971   Energy Flow in a Hunting Society. *Scientific American* 225(3):104–115.
Kerckhoff, Alan C., and Kurt W. Back
    1968   *The June Bug: A Study of Hysterical Contagion.* New York: Appleton-Century-Crofts.

Kerckhoff, Alan C., Kurt W. Back, and Norman Miller
>   1965   Sociometric Patterns in Hysterical Contagion. *Sociometry* 28:2–15. Also in Robert R. Evans (ed.), *Readings in Collective Behavior,* 1975, 2d ed. Chicago: Rand McNally College Publishing.

Killian, Lewis M.
>   1952   The Significance of Multi-Group Membership in Disaster. *American Journal of Sociology* 57(4):309–314.
>   1954   Some Accomplishments and Some Needs in Disaster Study. *Journal of Social Issues* 10:66–72.

Kinston, Warren, and Rachel Rosser
>   1974   Disaster: Effects on Mental and Physical States. *Journal of Psychosomatic Research* 18(6):437–456.

Klandermans, Bert, Marlene Roefs, and Jophan Oliver
>   1998   A Movement Takes Office. In David S. Meyer and Sidney Tarrow (eds.), *The Social Movement Society.* Lanham, MD: Rowman and Littlefield.

Klapp, Orrin E.
>   1972   *Currents of Unrest: An Introduction to Collective Behavior.* New York: Holt, Rinehart & Winston.

Klein, Lloyd, and Joan Luxenburg-Ingle
>   1980a   Smokey and the Beaver: Police and Highway Rest Area Prostitutes. Paper presented at the 32d meeting of the American Society of Criminology, San Francisco.
>   1980b   Those CB Hookers are Giving Prostitution a Bad Name! Paper presented at the annual meeting of the Association for Humanist Sociology, Louisville, KY.

Kloehn, Steve
>   1997   As Promised, Rally Draws a Sea of Christian Males. *Chicago Tribune* (October 5), pp. 1, 17.

Knoph, Terry A.
>   1969a   Sniping—A New Pattern of Violence? *Transaction* 6:22–29.
>   1969b   *Youth Patrols: An Experiment in Community Participation.* Brandeis University: The Lemberg Center for the Study of Violence.
>   1975   "Rumor Controls: A Reappraisal." *Phylon* 36:23–31.

Kohl, Larry
>   1981   Encampments of the Dispossessed. *National Geographic* (June): 757–775.

Kurjack, Edward B.
>   1971   Prehistoric Lowland Mayan Community and Social Organization: A Case Study at Zibilchaltun, Yucatan, Mexico. Ph.D. diss., Ohio State University.

Ladner, R. A., B. J. Schwartz, S. J. Roker, and L. S. Titterud
>   1981   The Miami Riots of 1980: Antecedent Conditions, Community Responses, and Participant Characteristics. In L. Kriesberg (ed.), *Research in Social Movements, Conflict, and Change* (vol. 4), pp. 171–214.

Lang, Kurt, and Gladys E. Lang
>   1961   *Collective Dynamics.* New York: Thomas Y. Crowell.

LaPierre, Richard T., and Paul R. Farnsworth
>   1949   *Social Psychology.* New York: McGraw-Hill.

Lasdon, Naomi
>   1998   The Journey Home: A Local Woman Volunteers to Help Bosnian Refugees Return to Their Homes, Repairing the Physical—and Emotional—Wounds of War. *The Virgninan-Pilot and The Ledger-Star,* Final; Vol. 21, Issue 21, Daily Break Section.

Latané, Bib, and John Darley
>   1968   Group Inhibition of Bystander Intervention in Emergencies. *Journal of Personality ad Social Psychology* 8(4):377–383.

Lawrence, Paul R.
    1987   *Unsportsmanlike Conduct: The National Collegiate Athletic Association and the Busi-ness of College Football.* New York: Praeger
Lawson, Alvin H.
    1980   Hypnosis of Imaginary UFO "Abductees." In Curtis G. Fuller (ed.), *Proceedings of the First International UFO Congress.* New York: Warner Books, pp. 195–239.
LeBon, Gustave
    1960   *The Crowd.* New York: Viking Press. (Orig. pub. 1895).
Lee, Alfred M., and Norman D. Humphrey
    1968   *Race Riot (Detroit 1943).* New York: Octagon Books.
Leet, Duane A., George E. Rush, and Anthony M. Smith
    1997   *Gangs, Graffiti, and Violence: A Realistic Guide to the Scope and Nature of Gangs in America.* Incline Village, NV: Copperhouse Publishing.
Lenski, Gerhard, and Jean Lenski
    1978   *Human Societies: An Introduction to Macrosociology.* New York: McGraw-Hill.
Leslie, Desmond and George Adamski
    1953 *Flying Saucers Have Landed.* London: W. Laurie.
Levine, David Allan
    1976   *Internal Combustion: The Races in Detroit 1915–1926.* Westport, CT: Greenwood Press.
Levine, Gene N., and John Modell
    1965   American Public Opinion and the Fallout-Shelter Issue. *Public Opinion Quar-terly* 29:270–279.
Lewandowsky, Stephen
    1993   The Rewards and Hazards of Computer Simulations. *Psychological Science* 4:236–243.
Lewis, Jerry M.
    1972   A Study of the Kent State Incident Using Smelser's Theory of Collective Behav-ior. *Sociological Inquiry* 42:87–96.
    1982   Crowd Control at English Football Matches. *Sociological Focus* 15:417–423.
    1989   A Value-Added Analysis of the Heysel Stadium Soccer Riot. *Current Psychol-ogy,* Vol. 8, No. 1, Spring, pp. 15–29.
Lewis, Jerry M., and J. Michael Veneman
    1987   Crisis Resolution: The Bradford Fire and English Society. *Sociological Focus* 20(2) (April):155–168.
Lieberson, Stanley, and Arnold R. Silverman
    1965   The Precipitants and Underlying Conditions of Race Riots. *American Sociologi-cal Review* 30:887–898.
Lipsky, Michael
    1968   Protest as a Political Resource. *American Political Science Review* 62: 1144–1158.
Lofland, John
    1966   *Doomsday Cult: A Study of Convesion, Proselytization, and Maintenance of Faith.* Englewood Cliffs, NJ: Prentice-Hall.
    1977   *Doomsday Cult: A Study of Conversion, Proselytization, and Maintenance of Faith,* 2d ed. Englewood Cliffs, NJ: Prentice-Hall.
    1979   White-Hot Mobilization: Strategies of a Millenarian Movement, in Mayer N. Zald and John D. McCarthy (eds.), *The Dynamics of Social Movements: Resource Mobilization, Social Control, and Tactics.* Cambridge, MA: Winthrop, 221–228. Also in James L. Wood and Maurice Jackson (eds.), *Social Movements: Develop-ment, Participation, and Dynamics,* 1982. Belmont, CA: Wadsworth.
    1981   Collective Behavior: The Elementary Forms In Morris Rosenberg and Ralph H. Turner (eds.), *Social Psychology: Sociological Perspectives.* New York: Basic Books, pp. 441–446.

1995   White-Hot Mobilization, in John Lofland (ed.), *Protest: Studies of Collective Behavior and Social Movements*. New Brunswick, NJ: Transaction Books.

Lohman, Joseph D.
1947   *The Police and Minority Groups*. Chicago: Chicago Park District.

Mack, J.
1994   *Abduction: Human Encounters with Aliens*. New York: Simon and Schuster.

Mackay, Charles
1841   *Memoirs of Extraordinary Popular Delusions*. London: Richard Bently
1852   *Memoirs of Extraordinary Popular Delusions and the Madness of Crowds*. London: Office of the National Illustrated Library.
1932   *Memoirs of Extraordinary Popular Delusions and the Madness of Crowds*. Boston: L. C. Page.
1980   *Extraordinary Popular Delusions and the Madness of Crowds*. New York: Harmony Books.

Macy, Michael W.
1991   Chains of Cooperation: Threshold Effects in Collective Action. *American Sociological Review* 56:730–747.

Maddocks, Melvin
1978   *The Great Liners*. Alexandria, VA: Time-Life Books.

Maguire, Brendan, Rebecca Hinderliter, and William Faulkner
1990   The Illinois Seat Belt Law: A Sociology of Law Analysis. *Humanity and Society*, Vol. 14, No. 4:395–418.

Maguire, Brendan, and Polly F. Radosh
1999   *Criminology*. New York: Wadsworth.

Maguire, Brendan, and John F. Wozniak
1987   Racial and Ethnic Stereotypes in Professional Wrestling. *The Social Science Journal* 24(3):261–273.

Mann, Leon
1974   Counting the Crowd: Eeffects of Editorial Policy on Crowd Estimates. *Journalism Quarterly* 51:278–285.

March, J., J. Amaya-Jackson, and R. Pynoos
1996   Pediatric Post-traumatic Stress Disorder, in J. Weiner (ed.), *Textbook of Child and Adolescent Psychiatry*, 2d ed. Washington, DC: American Psychiatric Press.

Marighella, Carlos
1970   Minimanual of the Urban Guerrilla. *Tricontinental Bimonthly* (January–February): 16–56.

Marsh, Peter
1978   *Aggro: The Illusion of Violence*. London: J. M. Dent & Sons, Ltd.

Martin, Morgan
1964   The True Face of Disaster. *Medical Times* (February), Vol. 92, pp. 163–166.

Marx, Gary
1970   Issueless Riots, in M. Wolfgang and J. F. Short (eds.), *Collective Violence Annals of American Academy of Political and Social Science*. Philadelphia: American Academy of Political Science, pp. 21–33.
1974   Thoughts on a Neglected Category of Social Movement Participant: The Agent Provocateur and the Informant. *American Journal of Sociology* 80(2):402–442.
1980   Conceptual Problems in the Field of Collective Behavior, in Hubert M. Blalock, Jr. (ed.), *Sociological Theory and Research: A Critical Appraisal*. New York: Free Press.

Masotti, Louis A., and Jerome R. Corsi
1969   *Shootout in Cleveland*. New York: Bantam Books.

Mathisen, James A.
1992   Jocks for Jesus. *The Christian Century* (January 1): 11–15.

1997   Promise Keepers as Cheerleading Moral Crusaders: Bringing Muscular Christianity to Sports Stadiums in the 90s. Paper presented at the annual meeting of the Association of the Sociology of Religion, Toronto (August).

McAdam, Doug
1981   *Political Process and the Development of Black Insurgency, 1930–1970.* Chicago: University of Chicago Press.
1982   *Political Process and the Development of Black Insurgency.* Chicago: University of Chicago Press.

McAdam, Doug, John D. McCarthy, and Mayer N. Zald
1996   Introduction: Opportunities, Mobilizing Structures, and Framing Processes—Toward a Synthetic, Comparative Perspective on Social Movements, in Doug McAdam, John D. McCarthy, and Mayer N. Zald (eds.), *Comparative Perspectives on Social Movements.* Melbourne: Cambridge University Press, p. 6.

McCann, Michael
1998   Social Movements and the Mobilization of Law, in Anne N. Costain and Andrew S. McFarland (eds.), *Social Movements and American Political Institutions.* Lanham, MA: Rowman & Littlefield, pp. 201–215.

McCarthy, John D.
1996   Constraints and Opportunities in Adopting, Adapting, and Inventing, in Doug McAdam, John D. McCarthy, and Meyer N. Zald (eds.), *Comparative Perspectives on Social Movements: Political Opportunities, Mobilizing Structures, and Cultural Framings.* Melbourne, Australia: Cambridge University Press.

McCarthy, John D., and Clark McPhail
1998   The Institutionalization of Protest, in David S. Meyer and Sidney Tarrow (eds.), *The Social Movement Society: Contentious Politics for a New Century.* Lanham, MA: Rowman & Littlefield, pp. 83–110.

McCarthy, John D., Clark McPhail, and Jackie Smith
1996   Images of Protest: Dimensions of Selection Bias in Media Coverage of Washington Demonstrations, 1982 and 1991. *American Sociological Review* 61:478–499.

McCarthy, John D., and Mayer N. Zald
1973   *The Trend of Social Movements in America: Professionalism and Resource Mobilization.* Morristown, NJ: General Learning Press.
1977   "Resource Mobilization and Social Movements: A Partial Theory." *American Journal of Sociology* 82:1212–1241.

McClelland, Kent
1994   Perceptual Control and Social Power, *Sociological Perspectives* 37:461–496.

McFarland, Andrew S.
1998   Theories of American Politics, in Ann N. Costain and Andrew McFarland (eds.), *Social Movements and American Political Institutions.* Lanham, MD: Rowman & Littlefield.

McLuckie, Benjamin F.
1970   A Study of Functional Response to Stress in Three Societies. Ph.D. diss., Ohio State University.

McPhail, Clark
1971   Civil Disorder Participation: A Critical Examination of Recent Research. *American Sociological Review* 36:1058–1073.
1978   Toward a Theory of Collective Behavior. Paper presented at the Symposium on Symbolic Interaction, University of South Carolina at Columbia, March 17.
1983   On the Origins of Gatherings, Demonstrations, and Riots. Paper presented at the annual meeting of the Midwest Sociological Society, Kansas City, Missouri.
1985   The Social Organization of Demonstrations. Paper presented at the annual meeting of theAmerican Sociological Association, Washington, DC

1989   Blumer's Theory of Collective Behavior. *The Sociological Quarterly* 30:401–423.

1991   *Myth of the Madding Crowd.* New York: Aldine De Gruyter.

1994   The Dark Side of Purpose: Individual and Collective Violence in Riots. *The Sociological Quarterly,* 35:1–32.

1996   Acting Together: The Social Organization of Crowds. Invited keynote speaker, *Rediscovering the Crowd: An International Conference on Crowd Phenomena,* De Montfort University, Leicester, England, July 2–4, 1996.

1997   Stereotypes of Crowds and Collective Behavior: Looking Backward, Looking Forward, in Michael Katovich, Dan Miller and Stanley Saxton (eds.), *Constructing Complexity: Symbolic Interaction and Social Forms, a Festschrift for Carl J. Couch.* Greenwich, CT: JAI Press.

1999   Sport Gatherings, in *Beyond the Maddening Crowd.* Unpublished manuscript. Forthcoming. New York: Aldine De Gruyter.

2000   *Acting Together: The Social Organization of Crowds.* Hawthorne, NY: Aldine De Gruyter.

McPhail, Clark, and Jane Bailey

1979   The Assembling Process: A Procedure for and the Results of a Replication. Revision of a paper presented at the annual meeting of the Midwest Sociological Society, Minnespolis, MN.

McPhail, Clark, and Miller, David L.

1973   The Assembling Process: A Theoretical and Empirical Examination. *American Sociological Review* 38:721–735.

McPhail, Clark, William T. Powers and Charles W. Tucker

1992   Simulating Purposive Individual and Collective Action. *Social Science Computer Review* 10:1–28.

McPhail, Clark, and David Schweingruber

1997   A Method for the Analysis of Video Records of Collective Action. Paper presented at the annual meeting of the Midwest Sociological Society, Des Moines, Iowa.

McPhail, Clark, David Schweingruber, and Nancy Berns

1997   *The Collective Action Observation Primer,* 3d ed. Urbana: University of Illinois, Department of Sociology.

McPhail, Clark, David Schweingruber, and John McCarthy

1998   Policing Protest in the United States: 1960–1995, in Donatella della Porta and Herbert Reiter (eds.), *Policing Protest: The Control of Mass Demonstrations in Western Democracies.* Minneapolis: University of Minnesota Press, pp. 49–69.

McPhail, Clark, and Charles Tucker

1990   Purposive Collective Action. *American Behavioral Scientist* 34:81–84.

McPhail, Clark, and Ronald T. Wohlstein

1983   Individual and Collective Behaviors within Gatherings, Demonstrations, and Riots. *American Review of Sociology* 9:579–600.

1986   Collective Locomotion as Collective Behavior. *American Sociological Review,* 51 (August):447–463.

Mead, George H.

1938   *The Philosophy of the Act.* Chicago: University of Chicago Press.

Medalia, Nahum Z., and Larsen, Otto N.

1958   Diffusion and Belief in a Collective Delusion: The Seattle Windshield Pitting Epidemic. *American Sociological Review* 23:221–232.

Meehan, Joseph

1996   *Riverdance—The Show.* Available: http://faraday.ucd.ie/~joseph/riverdance/riverdance.html

Menzel, Donald H., and Lyle G. Boyd

1963   *The World of Flying Saucers: A Scientific Examination of a Major Myth of the Space Age.* New York: Doubleday.

Meranto, Oneida
  1998   Litigation as Rebellion, in David S. Meyer and Sidney Tarrow (eds.), *The Social Movement Society: Contentious Politics for a New Century.* Lanham, MA: Rowman & Littlefield.
Merton, Robert K.
  1960   The Ambivalences of LeBon's *The Crowd,* introduction to the Compass edition of *The Crowd.* New York: Viking Press.
Meyer, David S., and Sidney Tarrow
  1998   A Movement Society: Contentious Politics for a New Century, in David S. Meyer and Sidney Tarrow (eds.), *The Social Movement Society.* Lanham, MD: Rowman & Littlefield.
Meyersohn, Rolf, and Elihiu Katz
  1957   Notes on a Natural History of Fads. *American Journal of Sociology* 62:594–601.
Mileti, Dennis S., Thomas E. Drabek, and J. Eugene Haas
  1975   *Human Systems in Extreme Environments: A Sociological Perspective.* Monograph no. 21, Institute of Behavioral Science, The University of Colorado.
Milgram, Stanley, Leonard Bickman, and Lawrence Berkowitz
  1969   Note on the Drawing Power of Crowds of Different Size. *Journal of Personality and Social Psychology* 13:79–82.
Milgram, Stanley, and Hans Toch
  1969   Collective Behavior and Social Movements, in Gardner Lindzey and Elliot Aronson (eds.), *Handbook of Social Psychology* (vol. 4), 2d ed. Reading, MA: Addison-Wesley, pp. 507–579.
Miller, Dan E.
  1992   "Snakes in the Greens" and Rumor in the Innercity. *The Social Science Journal,* 4:381–393.
Miller, David L.
  1975   Class Attendance: An Empirical Examination of Periodic Assembling. Ph.D. diss., University of Illinois at Urbana-Champaign.
  1979   Assembling in the Company of Others. Paper presented at the annual meetings of the Midwest Sociological Society, Milwaukee, Wisconsin.
Miller, David L., Kenneth J. Mietus, and Richard A. Mathers
  1978   A Critical Examination of the Social Contagion Image of Collective Behavior: The Case of the Enfield Monster. *Sociological Quarterly* 19:129–140.
Mintz, Alexander
  1951   Nonadaptive Group Behavior. *The Journal of Abnormal and Social Psychology* 46:150–159.
Momboisse, Raymond M.
  1967   *Riots, Revolts and Insurrections.* Springfield, IL: Thomas.
Mooney, James
  1896   *The Ghost Dance Religion and the Sioux Outbreak of 1890.* Fourteenth Annual Report of the Bureau of Ethnography to the Secretary of the Smithsonian Institution, 1892–1893, J. W. Powell, Director. Washington, DC: Government Printing Office.
Morris, Aldon
  1981   Black Southern Sit-In Movement: An Analysis of Internal Organization. *American Sociological Review* 46:744–767.
Moss, Peter D., and Colin McEvedy
  1967   Mass Hysteria. *Scientific American* 216:58.
Mostert, Noel
  1974   *Supership.* New York: Knopf.
Murphy, Patrick, John Williams, and Eric Dunning
  1990   *Football on Trial.* London: Routledge & Kegan Paul, pp. 167–193.

Myers, Robert C.
   1948   Anti-Communist Mob Action: A Case Study. *Public Opinion Quarterly* 12:57–67.
Nash, Bruce, and Allan Zullo
   1986   *The Baseball Hall of Shame 2*. New York: Pocket Books.
National Advisory Commission on Civil Disorders
   1968   Report. Washington, DC: U.S. Government Printing Office.
National Institute for Standards and Technology
   1998   About HAZARD I, Fire Modeling and Applications Group. Available: http://
             fast.nist.gov/hazardi.html
National Opinion Research Center
   1954   *Human Relations in Disaster Situations*. Chicago: National Opinion Research
             Center.
New York Times, The
   1998   French Riot Police Try to Control British Hooligans. Associated Press. Tuesday,
             June 16. Available: www.nytimes.com
Nickell, J.
   1996   A Study of Fantasy Proneness in the Thirteen Cases of Alleged Encounters in
             John Mack's Abduction. *Skeptical Inquirer* 20, No. 3, 18.
Nieberg, H. L.
   1969   *Political Violence: The Behavioral Process*. New York: St. Martin's Press.
Nkrumah, Kwame
   1969   *Handbook of Revolutionary Warfare*. New York: International Publishers.
Norman, Ruth, and Charles Spaegel
   1987   *Preparation for the Landing*. El Cajon, CA: Unarius Publications.
Nye, Peter
   1988   *Hearts of Lions: The History of American Bicycle Racing*. New York: W. W. Norton.
Oberschall, Anthony
   1968   The Los Angeles Riot of August 1965. *Social Problems* 15:322–341.
Osborn, Adam, and John Dvorak
   1984   *Hypergrowth: The Rise and Fall of Osborne Computer Corporation*. Berkeley:
             Idthekkethan Publishing.
Palmer, Mark
   1998   You Could've Walked Away. *The Spectator*. ISSN: 0038-6952; Vol. 280, No. 9963,
             p. 14.
Park, Robert E. and Ernest W. Burgess
   1921   *Introduction to the Science of Sociology*. Chicago: University of Chicago Press.
Parsons, Talcott
   1951   *The Social System*. New York: Free Press.
Pauls, J. L.
   1977   Movement of People in Building Evacuations, in D. J. Conway (ed.), *Human
             Response to Tall Buildings*. Stroudsburg, PA: Dowden, Hutchinson and Ross, pp.
             281–292.
Pavord, Anna
   1999   *The Tulip*. New York: Bloomsbury.
Peck, James
   1962   *Freedom Ride*. New York: Simon & Schuster.
Penrose, L. S.
   1952   *On the Objective Study of Crowd Behavior*. London: H. K. Lewis.
Perrow, Charles
   1979   The Sixties Observed, in Mayer Zald and John D. McCarthy (eds.), *The Dynam-
             ics of Social Movements*. Cambridge, MA: Winthrop, pp. 192–211.
Perry, Joseph, and M. D. Pugh
   1978   *Collective Behavior: Response to Social Stress*. St. Paul, MN: West Publishing.

Perry, Ronald, and Michael K. Lindell
   1978   The Psychological Consequences of Natural Disaster: A Review of Research on
             American Communities. *Mass Emergencies* (September): 105–115.
Perry, S. E., Silbert, E., and D. A. Bloch
   1953   *The Child and His Family in Disasters.* Pub. No. 394. Washington, DC: National
             Academy of Sciences, National Research Council.
Peterson, Richard E., and John Bilorusky
   1971   *May 1970: The Aftermath of Cambodia and Kent State.* Berkeley, CA: The Carnegie
             Commission on Higher Education.
Piven, Frances F., and Richard A. Cloward
   1979   *Poor People's Movements: Why They Succeed, How They Fail.* New York: Vintage
             Books.
Platt, Anthony M.
   1969   *The Child Savers.* Chicago: University of Chicago Press.
Popplewell, Justice
   1985   Committee of Inquiry into Crowd Safety and Control at Sports Grounds. Lon-
             don: Her Majesty's Stationery Office.
Potter, Gary W., and Victor E. Kappeler (eds.)
   1998   *Constructing Crime: Perspectives on Making News and Social Problems.* Prospect
             Heights, IL: Waveland Press.
Powers, William
   1973   *Behavior: The Control of Perception.* Chicago: Aldine.
Promise Keepers
   1996   Official PK Website, *PK Times Front Page*, July 25. Available: http://
             www.promisekeepers.org/281e.htm
   1997a   Official PK Website, Fact Sheet (updated 1/6/97). Available: http://
             www.promisekeepers.org/21ca.htm
   1997b   Official PK Website, Questions. Available: http://www.promisekeep-
             ers.org.2de6.htm
Prince, Samuel Henry
   1920   *Catastrophe and Social Change.* New York: Columbia University.
Pruden, Durward
   1936   A Sociological Study of a Texas Lynching. *Studies in Sociology* 1(1):1–8. Also in
             Bobbs-Merrill *Reprint Series in the Social Sciences* S-479.
Quarantelli, Enrico L.
   1957   The Behavior of Panic Participants. *Sociology and Social Research* 41:187–194.
   1970   Emergency Accommodation Groups: Beyond Current Collective Behavior
             Typologies. In Tamotsu Shibutani (ed.), *Human Nature and Collective Behavior:
             Papers in Honor of Herbert Blumer.* Englewood Cliffs, NJ: Prentice-Hall, pp. 111–
             123.
Quarantelli, Enrico L., and Russell R. Dynes
   1968   Looting in Civil Disorders: An Index of Social Change. *American Behavioral Sci-
             entist* 5:7–10.
   1969   Dissensus and Consensus in Community Emergencies: Patterns of Looting and
             Property Norms. *Il Politico* 34:276–291.
Quarantelli, Enrico L., and James L. Hundley, Jr.
   1969   A Test of Some Propositions about Crowd Formation and Behavior, in Robert R.
             Evans (ed.), *Readings in Collective Behavior.* Chicago: Rand McNally, pp. 538–554.
   1975   A Test of Some Propositions about Crowd Formation and Behavior, in Robert
             R. Evans (ed.), *Readings in Collective Behavior*, 2d ed. Chicago: Rand McNally,
             pp. 370–387.
Rappaport, Roy A.
   1971   The Flow of Energy in an Agricultural Society. *Scientific American* 225(3):116–132.

Rogers, Everett M.
   1962   *Diffusion of Innovations*, 4th ed. New York: Free Press.
Rose, Jerry D.
   1982   *Outbreaks: The Sociology of Collective Behavior*. New York: Free Press.
Rosen, Richard D.
   1979   *Psychobabble*. New York: Avon Books.
Rosengren, Karl E., Peter Arvidson, and Dahn Sturesson
   1975   The Barsebak Panic: A Radio Program as a Negative Summary Event. *Acta Sociological* 57:309–314. Also in Meredith D. Pugh (ed.), *Collective Behavior: A Source Book*, 1980. St. Paul, MN: West Publishing.
Rosenthal, A. M.
   1964   *Thirty-Eight Witnesses*. New York: McGraw-Hill.
Rosnow, Ralph L., and Gary A. Fine
   1976   *Rumor and Gossip: The Social Psychology of Hearsay*. New York: Elsevier.
Ross, James L.
   1970   The Salvation Army: Emergency Operations. *American Behavioral Scientist* 13:404–414.
Roth, Robert
   1970   Cross-Cultural Perspectives on Disaster Response. *American Behavioral Scientist* 13:440–451.
Rudé, George
   1959   *The Crowd in the French Revolution*. Oxford, England: Clarendon Press.
   1964   *The Crowd in History, 1730–1848*. New York: John Wiley.
Sachs, Margaret
   1980   *The UFO Encyclopedia*. New York: G. P. Putnam's.
Sanders, William T., and Joseph Marino
   1970   *New World Prehistory: Archaeology of the American Indian*. Englewood Cliffs, NJ: Prentice-Hall.
Sann, Paul
   1967   *Fads, Follies, and Delusions of the American People*. New York: Crown.
Sapir, Edward
   1937   Fashion. In *Encyclopedia of the Social Sciences* (vol. 3). New York: Macmillan, pp. 139–144.
   1979   *Racial and Ethnic Groups*. Boston: Little, Brown.
   1983   *Sociology*. New York: McGraw-Hill.
Scanlon, Joeseph T.
   1977   Post Disaster Rumor Chains: A Case Study. *Mass Emergencies*, 2:121–126. Elsevier Scientific Publishing Company, Amsterdam. Printed in the Netherlands.
   1988   From the Titanic to the Stars: Canada's Pioneer in Collective Behavior—Samuel Henry Prince. Paper presented at the annual meeting of the American Sociological Association, Atlanta, Georgia. Emergency Communications Research Unit, Carlton University, Ottawa,Canada.
Schaefer, Richard T.
   1979   *Racial and Ethnic Groups*. Boston, Little, Brown.
   1983   *Sociology*. New York: McGraw-Hill.
Schaefer, Richard T., and David L. Miller
   1998   Race and the Promise Keepers: Stand in the Gap Rally, 1997. Paper presented at the meetings of the Midwest Sociological Society, 1998.
Schaufele, William E., Jr.
   1981   *Polish Paradox: Communism and National Renewal*. Headline Series 256. New York: Foreign Policy Association.
Schmitt, Raymond L.
   1991   Strikes, Frames, and Touchdowns: The Institutional Struggle for Meaning in

the 1987 National Football League Season. Paper presented at the 1991 Midwest Sociological Society meetings.

Schrier, Arnold
  1958   *Ireland and the American Emigration, 1850B1900*. Minneapolis: University of Minnesota Press.

Schweingruber, David
  1995   A Computer Simulation of a Sociological Experiment. *Social Science Computer Review* 13(3):351–359.

  2000   Mob Sociology and Escalated Force: Sociology's Contribution to Repressive Police Tactics, *Sociological Quarterly* 31(3): forthcoming.

Schweingruber, David, and Clark McPhail
  1995   A Methodology for Coding Videotape and Field Observations of Collective Action. Paper presented at the annual meeting of the American Sociological Association, Washington, DC, August 20, 1995.

Shadowlands Mysterious Creatures Page
  1988   Available: www.serve.com/shadows/creature.htm#loveland frog

Sharp, Lauriston
  1952   Steel Axes for Stone Age Australians, in Edward H. Spicer (ed.), *Human Problems in Technological Change*. New York: Russell Sage Foundation, pp. 69–90.

Shibutani, Tamotsu
  1966   *Improvised News: A Sociological Study of Rumor*. Indianapolis, IN: Bobbs-Merrill.

Silber, Earl, Stewart E. Perry, and Donald A. Bloch
  1957   Patterns of Parent-Child Interaction in Disaster. *Psychiatry* 21(2):159–167.

Simmel, George
  1904   Fashion. *International Quarterly* 10:541–558. Also in *American Journal of Sociology* 62, 1957.

Simon, H. A.
  1982   *Models of Bounded Rationality*. Cambridge, MA: MIT Press.

Singer, Benjamin, Richard W. Osborn, and James Geschwender
  1970   *Black Rioters*. Lexington, MA: D.C. Heath.

Small, Gary W., Michael W. Propper, Eugenia T. Randolph, and Spencer Eth
  1991   Mass Hysteria Among Student Performers: Social Relationship as a Symptom Predictor. *American Journal of Psychiatry*, 148:1200–1205.

Smelser, Neil
  1962   *Theory of Collective Behavior*. New York: Free Press.

Smith, Cecil W.
  1962   *The Great Hunger*. New York: Harper & Row.

Smith, Joseph
  1984   *The Personal Writings of Joseph Smith*, Dean C. Jessee (ed. and comp.). Salt Lake City, UT: Bookcraft.

Smith, Michael D.
  1983   *Violence and Sport*. Toronto: Butterworths.

Smith, Robert A.
  1971   *The Social History of the Bicycle, Its Early Life and Times in America*. New York: American Heritage Press.

Snow, David, Louis A. Zurcher, and Sheldon Eckland-Olson
  1980   Social Networks and Social Movements: A Microstructural Approach to Differential Recruitment, *American Sociological Review* 45:787–801.

Snyder, David
  1979   Collective Violence Processes: Implications for Disaggregated Theory and Research, in Louis Kriesberg (ed.), *Research in Social Movements, Conflicts and Change: A Research Annual* (vol. 2). Greenwich, CT: JAI Press, pp. 35–61.

Snyder, David, and Charles Tilly
  1972   Hardship and Collective Violence in France. *American Sociological Review* 37:520–532.
Spilerman, Seymour
  1970   The Causes of Racial Disturbances: A Comparison of Alternate Explanations. *American Sociological Review* 35 (August): 627–649.
  1971   The Causes of Racial Disturbances: Tests of an Explanation. *American Sociological Review* 36 (June):427–442.
  1976   Structural Characteristics of Cities and the Severity of Racial Disorders. *American Sociological Review* 41:771–793.
Squires, Chase, and Ralph Greer, Jr.
  1994   Frustration Mounts in Search. © 1994–95 *Herald-Journal* (Spartanburg, SC). October 30, 1994, p. 1, sec. 1.
Staggenborg, Suzanne
  1988   The Consequences of Professionalization and Formalization in the Pro-Choice Movement. *American Sociological review* 53:585–606.
Stalin, Joseph
  1953   *The Russian Social-Democratic Party and Its Immediate Tasks.* Moscow: Foreign Languages Publishing House.
Stewart, James R.
  1977   Cattle Mutilations: An Episode of Collective Delusion. *The Zetetic* 1:55–66.
  1980   Collective Delusion: A Comparison of Believers and Skeptics. Paper presented at the annual meeting of the Midwest Sociological Society, Milwaukee, Wisconsin.
  1984   On the Nature of Mass Hysteria. Paper presented at the annual meeting of the Midwest Sociological Society, Chicago.
Stewart, Robert L.
  1969   Toward a Behavioristic Behavioral Science. Department of Sociology, University of South Carolina (mimeographed).
Stone, Charles P.
  1969   The Lessons of Detroit, Summer 1967, in Robin Higham (ed.), *Bayonets in the Streets: The Use of Troops in Civil Disturbances.* Lawrence: University Press of Kansas, pp. 185–203.
Strasel, H. C., and Paul G. Larkin
  1968   *Rioters in Washington: A Study of People and Employment.* Falls Church, VA: Software Systems.
Strauss, Anselm L.
  1944   The Literature on Panic. *Journal of Abnormal and Social Psychology* 39:317–328.
Strieber, Whitley
  1987   *Communion: A True Story.* New York: William Morrow.
Strybel, Robert
  1981   Report from Warsaw. *PolAmerica Magazine* 4:8–27.
Tarde, Gabriel
  1903   *The Laws of Imitation.* New York: Holt, Rinehart & Winston.
Tarrow, Sidney
  1998   "The Very Excess of Democracy": State Building and Contentious Politics in America, in Anne N. Costain and Andrew McFarland (eds.), *Social Movements and the American Political Institutions,* pp. 20–38. Lanham, MD: Rowman-Littlefield.
Taylor, James B., Louis A. Zurcher, and William H. Key
  1970   *Tornado: A Community Response to Disaster.* Seattle: University of Washington Press.
Thomlinson, T. M.
  1968   The Development of a Riot Ideology among Urban Negroes. *American Behavioral Scientist* 2:27–31.

Tierney, Kathleen J.
    1994   Making Sense of Collective Preoccupations: Lessons from Research on the Iben Browning Earthquake Prediction, in Gerald M. Platt and Chad Gordon (eds.), *Self, Collective Behavior and Society: Essays Honoring the Contributions of Ralph H. Turner*, pp. 75–95. Greenwich, CT: Jai Press.
    1994   Property Damage and Violence: A Collective Behavior Analysis, in Mark Baldassare (ed.), *The Los Angeles Riots: Lessons for the Urban Future*, pp. 49–173. Boulder, CO: Westview Press.

Tilly, Charles
    1969   Collective Violence in European Perspective, in Hugh D. Graham and Ted R. Gurr (eds.), *The History of Violence in America: Historical and Comparative Perspectives*. New York: Praeger, pp. 4–44.
    1975   Revolutions and Collective Violence, in Fred Greenstein and Nelson Polsby (eds.), *Handbook of Political Science* (vol. 3). Reading, MA: Addison Wesley, pp. 483–555.
    1978   *From Mobilization to Revolution*. Reading, MA: Addison-Wesley.
    1993   Social Movements as Historically Specific Clusters of Political Performances, *Berkeley Journal of Sociology* 38:1–30.
    1995   *Popular Contention in Great Britain, 1758–1834*. Cambridge, MA: Harvard University Press.
    1996   The Invisible Elbow, *Sociological Forum* 11:589–601.

Time/CNN
    1997   *Poll: U.S. Hiding Knowledge of Aliens*. CNN Interactive. Available: 222/cnn.com/US/9706/15/ufo.poll/index.html

Times, The (London)
    1987a   Panic and Fighting would have Spread within Seconds. *Times* 3 (March 6), pp. 1–5.
    1987b   Survivors Relive the Terror and the Bravery. *Times* 3 (March 9), pp. 1–9.
    1987c   Nightmare that United Europe. *Spectrum* (March 9).

Timko, Nicole R.
    1998   Triumphs and Tribulations of the Federal Emergency Management Administration: A Sociological and Political History Analysis. Masters Thesis, Dept. of Sociology and Anthropology, Western Illinois University.

Tomlinson, Alan
    1986   Going Global: The FIFA Story, in A. Tomlinson (ed.), *Off The Ball: The Football World Cup*. London: The Pluto Press.

Traugott, Mark
    1978   Reconceiving Social Movements. *Social Problems* 26:38–49.

Tucker, Charles, David Schweingruber, and Clark McPhail
    1999   Simulating Arcs and Rings in Temporary Gatherings. *Journal of Human-Computer Studies* 50:581–588.

Tumin, Melvin M., and Arnold S. Feldman
    1955   The Miracle at Sabana Grande. *Public Opinion Quarterly* 19:124–139.

Turner, Ralph H., and Lewis M. Killian
    1957   *Collective Behavior*. Englewood Cliffs, NJ: Prentice-Hall.
    1972   *Collective Behavior*, 2d ed. Englewood Cliffs, NJ: Prentice-Hall.

Turner, Ralph H., and Samuel J. Surace
    1956   Zoot-Suiters and Mexicans: Symbols in Crowd Behavior. *American Journal of Sociology* 62:14–20.

Unarius
    1999   Unarius Academy of Science. Available: www.unarius.com

United Nations High Commissioner For Refugees (UNHCR)
    1998   *Refugees and Others of Concern to UNHCR 1997 Statistical Overview*. Statistical Unit, Geneva, July 1998. Available: www.unhcr.ch/

U.S. Committee for Refugees
   1997   1717 Massachusetts Ave., NW., Suite 701, Washington, DC 20036. Available: www.refugees.org/who/whomain.htm

U.S. Department of Energy
   1998   Internet Cookies. *Information Bulletin*, March 12. Available: http://www.vtr.net/cookies.html

Useem, Bert
   1997   The State and Collective Disorders: The Los Angeles Riot/Protest of April, 1992. *Social Forces* 7:357–377.

Vacca, Roberto
   1974   *The Coming Dark Age*. Garden City, NY: Anchor Press /Doubleday.

Vallee, Jacques
   1991   *Confrontations: A Scientist's Search for Alien Contact*. New York: Ballantine Books.

Vandenbussche, Fred
   1988   *Raise the Herald: The Battle after the Disaster*. Folkstone, Kent, U.K.: Bailey Brothers and Swinefen Ltd.

Veblen, Thorstein
   1912   *The Theory of the Leisure Class: An Economic Study of Institutions*. New York: Macmillan.

Velfort, Helene R., and George Lee
   1943   The Coconut Grove Fire: A Study of Scapegoating. *Journal of Abnormal and Social Psychology* 38:138–154.

Virginian Pilot and Ledger Star
   1998   The Journey Home: A Local Woman Volunteers to Help Bosnian Refugees Return to Their Homes, Vol. 21, Issue 21, Daily Break Section (1/17/98).

Walker, Henry Pickering
   1966   *The Wagonmasters: High Plains Freighting from the Earliest Days of the Santa Fe Trail to 1880*. Norman: University of Oklahoma Press.

Wallace, Anthony F. C.
   1957   Mazeway Disintegration: The Individual Perception of Sociocultural Disorganization. *Human Organization* 16:23–27.

Wallop, Malcolm
   1998   Unless Stopped, the Global Warming Movement Could Cause Economic Disaster. *World Oil*, 219:5.

Warheit, George J.
   1970   Fire Departments: Organizations during Major Community Emergencies. *American Behavioral Scientist* 13:362–368.

Wenger, Dennis E.
   1978   Community Response to Disaster: Functional and Structural Alterations, in Enrico L. Quarantelli (ed.), *Disaster: Theory and Research*. Beverly Hills, CA: Sage, pp. 17–49.

Westrum, Ron
   1978   Social Intelligence about Anomalies: The Case of Meteorites. *Social Studies of Science* 8:461–493.

Wheeler, Ladd, E. L. Deci, H. T. Reis, and M. Zuckerman
   1978   *Interpersonal Influence*, 2d ed. Boston: Allyn & Bacon.

Wheeler, Linda
   1997   Unofficial Estimates Point to Crowded Day on the Mall. *Washington Post* (October 5), p. A17.

Williams, Higbee
   1962   Mobs and Riots. *American Jurisprudence* 54:499–548.

Williams, John
   1985   Enter the Dragon. *Marxism Today* (May): 23.

1986   White Riots, in Alan Tomlinson (ed.), *Off The Ball: The Football World Cup.* London: Pluto Press.

Williams, John, Eric Dunning, and Patrick Murphy
1984   *Hooligans Abroad: The Behavior and Control of English Football Fans in Continental Europe.* London: Routledge & Kegan Paul.
1986   *The Luton Home Only Members Plan: A Preliminary Report.* Leicester: Sir Norman Chester Centre for Football Research. Available: 222.le.ac.uk.smccfr/fo.html

Winfrey, Carey
1979   Why 900 Died in Guyana. *New York Times Magazine,* February 25.

Woelfel, Joseph, John Woelfel, James Gillham, and Thomas McPhail
1974   Political Radicalization as a Communication Process. *Communications Research* 1:241–263.

Wohlstein, Ronald T.
1977   Filming Collective Behavior and the Problem of Foreshortened Perspective: A Corrective Method. *Studies in the Anthropology of Visual Communication* 4:81–85.
1982   Riot Participation: Some Proposals for Future Study. Paper presented at the Midwest Sociological Society, Kansas City, Missouri.
1992   Stereotypes of the Crowd and Collective Behavior in Introductory Sociology Textbooks. Paper presented at the annual meeting of the Midwest Sociological Society, Des Moines, Iowa.

Wood, James L., and Maurice Jackson
1982   *Social Movements: Development, Participation and Dynamics.* Belmont, CA: Wadsworth.

Wormington, H. M.
1957   *Ancient Man in North America,* 4th ed. Denver Museum of Natural History, Popular Series no. 4.

Wright, James D., Peter H. Rossi, Sonia R. Wright, and Eleanor Weber-Burdin
1979   *After the Clean-Up: Long Range Effects of Natural Disasters.* Beverly Hills, CA: Sage.

Zakon, Robert Hobbe
1997   Hobbe's Internet Timeline v3.0. Available:http://info.isoc.org/quest/zakon/internet/Historyu/HIT.html

Zald, Mayer N., and Roberta Ash
1964   Social Movement Organization: Growth, Decay, and Change. *Social Forces* 44:327–341.

Zald, Mayer, and John D. McCarthy
1980   Social Movement Industries: Competition and Cooperation among Movement Organizations, in Lewis Kriesberg (ed.), *Research in Social Movements, Conflicts and Change* (vol. 3). Greenwich, CT: JAI Press, pp. 1–20.

Zdravomslova, Elena
1996   Opportunities and Framing in the Transition to Democracy: The Case of Russia, in Doug McAdam, John D. McCarthy, and Meyer N. Zald (eds.), *Comparative Perspectives on Social Movements: Political Opportunities, Mobilizing Structures, and Cultural Framings.* Melbourne, Australia: Cambridge University Press.

Zinn, Howard
1964   *SNCC: The New Abolitionists.* Boston: Beacon Press.

Zurcher, Louis A.
1968   Social-Psychological Functions of Ephemeral Roles: A Disaster Work Crew. *Human Organization* 27:281–297. Also in Meredith Pugh (ed.), *Collective Behavior: A Source Book,* 1980. St. Paul, MN: West Publishing.

Zurcher, Louis A., and David Snow
1981   Collective Behavior: Social Movements, in Ralph Turner and Morris Rosenberg (eds.), *Social Psychology.* New York: Basic Books, pp. 450–482.

Name Index

Subject Index